LIVING WITH
ANTISEMITISM

THE TAUBER INSTITUTE FOR THE STUDY OF EUROPEAN JEWRY SERIES

Jehuda Reinharz, General Editor

1

GERHARD L. WEINBERG, 1981
World in the Balance:
Behind the Scenes of World War II

2

RICHARD COBB, 1983
French and Germans, Germans and French:
A Personal Interpretation of France under
Two Occupations, 1914–1918/1940–1944

3

EBERHARD JÄCKEL, 1984
Hitler in History

4

Edited by FRANCES MALINO
and BERNARD WASSERSTEIN, 1985
The Jews in Modern France

5

JACOB KATZ, 1986
The Darker Side of Genius:
Richard Wagner's Anti-Semitism

6

Edited by JEHUDA REINHARZ, 1987
Living with Antisemitism:
Modern Jewish Responses

Edited by Jehuda Reinharz

LIVING WITH
ANTISEMITISM

Modern Jewish Responses

 Published for Brandeis University Press by
University Press of New England
Hanover and London, 1987

University Press of New England

© 1987 by Trustees of Brandeis University

Printed in the United States of America

LIBRARY OF CONGRESS CATALOGING-IN-PUBLICATION DATA

Living with antisemitism.

(The Tauber Institute for the Study of European
Jewry series ; 6)
"Based on . . . lectures given at the Tauber Institute
for the Study of European Jewry between 1984–1986 . . . as
well as on papers invited by the editor"—
   Includes index.
   1. Antisemitism. 2. Jews—Politics and government.
3. Jews—History—1789–1945. 4. Holocaust, Jewish
(1939–1945) 5. World War, 1939–1945—Underground
movements, Jewish. I. Reinharz, Jehuda. II. Series:
Tauber Institute series ; no. 6.
DS145.L628   1987   305.8'924   86–40388
ISBN 0–87451–388–X
ISBN 0–87451–412–6 (pbk)

Contents

Preface

This volume examines the Jewish response to antisemitism in the modern period in various parts of the world. The term "Jewish response" refers to the multitude of individual and community reactions that have differed widely according to local conditions. Much has been written on the phenomenon of antisemitism. The scholarly literature has tended to concentrate on its history and evolution over the past centuries or on its physical, economic, cultural, and political impacts. The reaction of Jews and the organized Jewish community to antisemitism, however, has been a relatively neglected subject. It is my hope that this book will serve as a stimulus to further serious discussion of Jewish reactions to antisemitism in both its historical and contemporary contexts.

The twenty-two essays in this volume deal with the variety of responses and use different approaches to understand their subject matter. Some focus on key personalities or thinkers, some on court cases; others deal with organizations or family histories; and still others deal with a larger movement or questions of a general theoretical nature. The essays are organized by region and/or subject matter. Within each part they are presented chronologically to the extent possible. The majority of the essays are revised versions of lectures given at the Tauber Institute for the Study of European Jewry at Brandeis University during 1984–86. The remainder have been commissioned specifically for inclusion in this book. None of the essays has been published previously.

Throughout the planning and preparation of the book I benefited from the advice of my friend, Professor Ben Halpern. Dr. Ann Hofstra Grogg, who has worked with me as copyeditor on previous volumes, has proven, once again, to be an indispensable collaborator. She has also prepared the index. Sylvia Fuks Fried has played an important role in the final stages of this manuscript. I also wish to acknowledge the goodwill and cooperation of the editors and staff of the University Press of New England, whose encouragement and faith in the Tauber Institute have made possible the publication of the entire series.

Waltham, Massachusetts   J.R.
June 1986

INTRODUCTION

Ben Halpern

Reactions to Antisemitism in Modern Jewish History

To understand Jewish responses to antisemitism, one must first understand that which occasions them. Antisemitism is a phenomenon of tremendous historical weight and proportions but of rather indeterminate, protean nature. Its description varies in bewildering ways; arguments about its prevalence and effects are beset by verbal disputes over slippery connotations. A definition of antisemitism is therefore vital for clarity, if nothing more.

A least-common-denominator definition drawn from current usage may be phrased as follows: Antisemitism is a hostile attitude toward the Jews that has become institutional and traditional.[1] This implies, first, that antisemitism is a group prejudice taught in certain societies and not merely an aversion traceable to particular experiences; second, that it does not necessarily, and always, end in eliminating the Jews but may become a persisting condition of their lives. Jews, in fact, have lived for many centuries dispersed among societies with traditions of antisemitism. Since they were generally outnumbered, and outmatched in physical power, by those hostile to them, antisemitism was obviously counterbalanced by an adequate degree of tolerance among the non-Jews in societies where Jews survived as a recognizable group.

Antisemitism and tolerance alike are, then, universal conditions of life for Jews as a group traditionally significant for Gentiles. By definition, the two attitudes vary inversely in relation to each other, in intensity and extent. An equilibrium in their relative proportion, acceptable to both Gentiles and Jews, is a necessary condition for Jews'

1. See Ben Halpern, "What Is Antisemitism?" *Modern Judaism* 1 (1981): 251–62.

continuing as a recognizable group in Gentile societies, since (as the long history of expulsions, massacres, and migrations of Jews graphically demonstrates) excessive antisemitism may effectively liquidate their community.

What is an acceptable equilibrium point in the tolerance-antisemitism ratio also varies among different historical periods and different societies in the same period. In order to place the issue properly in the perspective of modern Jewish history, we must sketch a contrasting model of the institutional (that is, jointly acceptable) equilibrium between tolerance and antisemitism in what we may call the premodern period. This refers, in the Jewish historiographic convention, to the time and places when the Jewish position in society (and, to an extent, that of others as well) was defined and justified on sacral rather than secular grounds—certainly so in formal, conscious terms, whatever the other operative considerations. The substitution of secular categories by the eighteenth-century Enlightenment, followed by the emancipation of the Jews in the West, upset the premodern equilibrium previously found acceptable and required that a new equilibrium be defined and defended.

It should be noted that to describe historical conditions—which by their very nature are events in process—in terms of an equilibrium point is to apply an abstraction to history.[2] Jewish responses to antisemitism, if taken as involving such an equilibrium, are conceived as responses mediated by an abstract, general presupposition—sacral, religious, for the premodern Jewries; secular, civil, for modern Jewries.

The presuppositions underlying the Jewish position in premodern societies were shared (ambivalently) by Jews and Gentiles, especially Christians, in the most characteristic cases of interest to us. The Jews, both sides agreed, were consigned to Exile to do penance: as God's Chosen People, for their own and the world's Redemption,

2. This implies an approach to historical analysis set forth by Max Weber in his concept of "ideal types," together with what Karl Popper calls "the logic of situations" in his *Poverty of Historicism* (Boston, 1957), pp. 147–49. The universal incidence in Jewish history of antisemitism and tolerance, in inverse proportion to each other, is taken as a situation that objectively requires random responses to tend toward an equilibrium. Rational analysis of the situation and of the required responses yields ideal types of response that should be able to interpret actual events and historical actions with high (or at least significant) probability. In the discussion that follows there is, however, no attempt to derive a logically exhaustive set of responses meeting the situational requirement. Responses discussed are those derived intuitively from the record of actual events.

Jews said; in sign of their rejection by God, and as witness to the
Revelation of Gospel, Christians held. Both sides were also agreed
that the exiled Jews must suffer subjugation to Gentile rule and a
regime of segregation: in order to protect their sanctities (and themselves), Jews said; to guard Christians from religious infection (and
Jews from assault), according to Christian views. Under these terms
of understanding, an equilibrium between Gentile tolerance and
hostility could be not only tolerable for Jews; it could also be rationalized by beliefs shared with Christians but held by Jews in their
own version, one sharply opposed to the common contempt in which
others held them.

What was peculiar to the premodern Jews (especially in the classic
Eastern European case), and conditioned their typical responses to
surges of antisemitism, was their immunity to shame reactions that
a modern Jew might think inescapable in such a social position as
they accepted. They were detached from the values of the Gentile
society about them so fully that outer humiliations could not easily
penetrate the defenses of their culture and touch them inwardly.
They spoke enough Polish to deal with their Gentile clientele in business matters, but little more. Among themselves they spoke Yiddish;
they prayed and kept records and documents in Hebrew and Ara-
maic. They lived by and under Gentile law in pertinent respects but
maintained their own inner laws (with or without official sanction)
in matters between Jew and Jew. What counted most was a good
name in their own community, even for credit outside. Their standards of pride and shame, esteem and contempt, were their own,
able to turn not only aside, but inside out, contemptuous stereotypes
and stigmas applied to them collectively by outsiders.[3]

The religious mythos of Exile and Redemption, in its Jewish version, gave the restrictions, subjugation, and stigmas—the institutionalized antisemitism of their premodern status—a sublimated
significance that made them inwardly innocuous, if not benign, and
not merely outwardly acceptable. At this equilibrium point of tolerance-antisemitism, hostility seemed to require a response only when

3. As with other ideal types, some cases (Ashkenazim) exemplify this response to the
premodern situation better than others (Sephardim), to whom it applies only subject
to important modifications. Influences retained in Poland by Ashkenazim expelled
from Germany (Yiddish, the Magdeburg municipal code) cannot be compared with the
ties to Iberian culture that Sephardim brought with them to Holland. See Daniel Swe-
tschinski, "The Portuguese Merchants of 17th Century Amsterdam: A Social Profile"
(Ph.D. diss., Brandeis University, 1980).

it deviated from the institutional and traditional norm; the remedy sought then was (mainly by appeals to authority on the outside) to restore the norm. Expulsions, massacres, and forced conversions were calamities that destroyed the equilibrium and required a different response, but this, too, was traditional in form. Appeals to Gentile overlords against mob action were supplemented by institutions of Jewish mutual aid, traditionally available to ransom captives, help those in flight, and succor widows and orphans. Even the response to those who persecuted them was cast by Jews in a traditional, abstract, and typological mold. The concrete oppressor, whose image certainly evoked natural reactions of fear and rage, fell into ready patterns for imagining the villains of Jewish history. Every generation, as the Passover Haggadah said, had its Haman; the features of the contemporary enemy receded into the traditional image and became blurred. All Israel's foes, indeed, were merely instruments of God's will—a conception that could only dilute the animus specifically attaching to them. Whatever remained to be done to blur the concreteness of immediate pain was accomplished by rituals of grief, which sublimated Jewish catastrophes by incorporating them in the liturgy of mourning for the national Exile.

In these ways the traditional Jewish community was given its relatively high degree of immunity from reactions of shame when others sought to humiliate or degrade it. It is the most general sign that a Jewish community has become modern that it reacts with shame to insults and aspersions, as well as acts of overbearing oppression, addressed to it by outsiders. The response of a Jew who can be shamed by Gentiles is characteristically different from the response of one who cannot.

Jew-hatred, the usual term for antisemitism in the premodern Jewish lexicon, did not call for a direct, face-to-face response, apart from prudent measures of propitiation or avoidance. When the counterpart whom Jews saw themselves as confronting in their afflictions was not the Gentile, a mere tool of God's wrath, but God Himself, accommodation to Gentile standards was a matter of superficial significance. At times, as in challenges to theological debate by churchmen or litterateurs, a more substantive, direct response was required; the risks of these (usually coerced) confrontations made the powerless Jews prefer to avoid them. But such a disputation was hardly likely to make either side more open to the values held by the other; rather, it would probably harden the initial position of each.

The modern Jew cannot deal with antisemitism in the same way; his most significant relations with Gentiles—those that confirm him as "modern"—cannot present them as stock characters in the traditional drama of Exile and Redemption. The French Revolution and its legacy of emancipation not merely broke down ghetto walls; it offered Jews a new identity, as nationals of the country of which they became citizens. The identification required went far deeper than the attachment of a premodern Jew to the locality whose lord or municipal council granted him the privilege of residence. It entailed a direct, rather than mythically mediated, relation with his Gentile fellow citizen, whom he experienced as a concrete entity, not as a typical representation of legendary avatars. A Jew could now be a "Frenchman of the Mosaic persuasion," as they liked to say, and if he encountered antisemitism in acting out this role, it was a rude challenge (rather than a standard confirmation) involving his very identity. Such a challenge was shame inducing—and it was very often unexpected. The shame became palpable at the very inception of the emancipation that produced the new Jewish identity; the shock of antisemitism—unforeseen—came later.

The critique of all positive religions by deism and the Enlightenment began to neutralize conventional sacral discriminations upon which the premodern Jewish status was based, and the emancipation at the end of the eighteenth century replaced them with universal principles of human rights and the secular institution of citizenship. These revolutions in culture and the civil polity, steadily eliminating old disabilities of the Jewish condition, also undermined traditional institutions developed by Jews to adjust to life in Exile. A new equality and full participation in the secular life of their country—now presented as the sovereign patrimony of the nation to which they could belong as citizens—were apparently offered Jews, in the most consistent reading of the new order that was proposed. But its most radical and consistent advocates were also rigorous in their demands that Jews scrap old ways considered tainted with an offensive past. Jews could not open up to the promise of a better future without also responding to the judgments upon their tradition, voiced by many of their emancipators in hostile terms, in which old themes of the antisemitic tradition were restated in modern versions. The chief target of liberal objections was the Ashkenazi Jews, the most isolated from influences of their Gentile environment in the past; and the Talmud, which was considered the ultimate source of the objectionable economic and social behavior of this tradition-bound community, was the chief butt of hostile cultural criticism by liberal Gentiles. A new breed of liberal Jews could not respond to these challenges with indifference.[4]

Jews who shared in the new humanist culture of the Enlightenment, abandoning the shelter of relative cultural isolation, were now obliged to defend themselves in renewed disputations with Gentile critics of Jews and Judaism—under conditions far different, of course, from the medieval encounters. Moses Mendelssohn popularized terms later generally accepted for this argument by reducing the dogmatic content of Judaism to the universal rationalist truths accessible to reason and defining the particular revelations specific to Jews alone as a body of divine legislation for the moral education and government of the community of the Chosen People. He held these divinely instituted laws to bind Jews in an eternal covenant, and this was his answer to those who challenged his right to remain a Jew while otherwise fully committed to the enlightened culture of contemporary, advanced Christian thinkers. It was not an answer that served many of the Jewish writers who had to face the same challenge, now flung at them (in transformations of the traditional view of the Jews as rejected by God) by post-Christians or freethinkers who held Judaism to be an irrelevant encumbrance in modern history and questioned the right of modern men to remain apart from Gentiles as Jews. Much of modern Jewish intellectual history, of an academic kind, has been involved in the effort to answer such cultural antisemitism.[5]

The same attack had to be dealt with in a more consequential form in seeking a new antisemitism-tolerance equilibrium in the social and political spheres. So outspoken an advocate of Jewish emancipation as Christian Wilhelm von Dohm nevertheless felt that Jews had to be barred from public office until a more liberal treatment had sufficiently "ameliorated" their social and economic habits and cultural traits. This assumption—that the traditions, characteristic of Ashkenazi Jews particularly, were an impediment that had to be overcome by reform before Jews could be granted full equality—

4. These themes have been thoroughly explored in Jewish historiography. For a compact survey, see Shmuel Ettinger, "The Modern Period," in *A History of the Jewish People*, ed. H. H. Ben-Sasson (Cambridge, Mass., 1976), pp. 741–63.

5. See Alexander Altmann, introd. to Moses Mendelssohn, *Jerusalem* (Hanover, N.H., 1983). Nathan Rotenstreich has summed up his long preoccupation with the problem of the encounter of Judaism with history in his *Tradition and Reality* (New York, 1972).

persisted after the emancipation Dohm advocated was legally enacted. Napoleon ordered a Sanhedrin convened to answer questions
brusquely put on this score, and, in spite of satisfactory answers
from the Jewish notables and rabbis, he placed Alsatian Jewry under
special disabilities for a ten-year probationary period until they
could demonstrate effective "amelioration" and reform.

Outside pressure of this sort, blatant in this well-known case and
persistent in less formal ways, may have been less effective in undermining Jewish tradition than the shame reactions of Jews themselves, many of whom accepted the negative appraisals of Jews and
Judaism implicit in the Gentile culture they absorbed.[6] The changes
in Jewish habits of worship, to achieve a decorum conforming to the
style of churches in their respective countries, reflected the sensitivity of Jews to outside pressures perhaps less than their internalized
local standards. Both factors combined in producing the efforts of
French Jews to "regenerate" their community by vocational training
for "productive" occupations, or the efforts to suppress "white slave"
traffickers and gangsters in the New York slums. Ills and evils, universally recognized and odious in the Jews' sanctified tradition, became more salient and urgently in need of remedy when they drew
the attention of outsiders and excited latent antisemitism.

A more specific impact of this kind may be noted in certain other
well-known changes in traditional Jewish social and political attitudes. The most self-conscious reform of those in the throes of emancipation was directed at the basic national myth of Exile and Redemption, upon which traditional Jews formed their self-image. To
accede to a new national identity, as Frenchmen, Germans, or British of Mosaic persuasion, made it hard to believe oneself in exile;
and praying for a Redemption that would restore a Jewish monarchy
in Palestine seemed to newly modern Jews to support the antisemites in their accusations of disloyalty to the state. Revisions in
the ritual and creed of Reform Judaism were specifically intended to
meet both needs: to overcome the "cognitive dissonance" between
identifying beliefs of traditional and modern Jews and to forestall
antisemitic charges of "dual loyalties."

Less deliberate but equally self-conscious were some adjustments
made in traditional modes of Jewish political action. The traditional

6. See, e.g., Jay R. Berkovitz, "French Jewry and the Ideology of Regeneration to
1848" (Ph. D. diss., Brandeis University, 1982).

status of Jews entailed a far-reaching detachment and quietism in political matters, considered the sphere of Gentiles. But when the conventional status of tolerated Jews was severely threatened, then (and only then, as a community) they reacted with efforts to secure their collective interests and reclaim the privileges of residence. Among the newly emancipated Jews, the right to take part in their country's public affairs and politics was a cardinal test of their emancipation. This, however, was conceived as a strictly individual right; any political activity of Jews as a separate collective body was renounced as unbefitting a religious association and belying the equality and integration of Jews with their Gentile fellow citizens. For Jews to act as a body politically in their own interest, instead of individually (if not indistinguishably from Gentiles) in the general interest, would give support to the antisemites' charges that Jews were an alien entity in the state.

What has been described hitherto are reactions characteristic of insecure liberal Jews, common in initial responses to an emancipation instituted but not yet fulfilled entirely. Jews won over to liberal and Enlightenment ideas under these conditions felt obliged to suppress features of their traditional position highlighted by hostile critics: the ethnic quality of their religion, their constricted and disreputable economic functions. They took refuge, for the Jewish identity they retained, in an abstracted ethical monotheism distilled from the whole flow of Jewish history and answering to the enlightened, rational universalism they shared with liberal Gentiles. In all this, together with inner needs, there was felt the pressure to convince others—outsiders—that Jews deserved, or would soon deserve, their emancipation.

Insecurity was sustained among Jewish liberals by the long delay of political emancipation in many modernizing nation-states—and also by the unforeseen limits of social integration flowing from emancipation, once achieved. If Jewishness were to be confined to the synagogue and private worship, liberal Jews who accepted such "terms of emancipation" expected to be equal and integrated, free from discrimination, in all else. They found that the effective line of demarcation for Jewishness was somewhat different: not between secular and sacred but between public and the wide range of private affairs, even among consistent liberals and, in the last analysis, in their own inner needs. Privileged Gentile economic positions and social status were private assets not surrendered or indiscriminately shared under the terms of emancipation; emancipated Jews, for their part, achieved upward mobility chiefly in pursuits closely tied to the traditional Jewish occupations or easily accessible from the old vantage points. All this left the emancipated Jewish community much less than fully integrated. Jews felt obliged to respond as to an antisemitic threat when Gentile discrimination closed certain private (not to speak of public) channels of advancement to them. Gentile antisemitism was aroused by the advances of Jews in the private (not to speak of public) spheres most accessible to them—the press, commerce and finance, and the domains of culture open to free lances.

Such disharmonious results—disharmonious in their own ways for both Jews and Gentiles—were generally dealt with by tacit accommodations, but there were some who sought a theoretical justification for them. The expedient adopted by Jews and Gentiles alike—each in their own sense—was the doctrine of race, made popular especially by the social theorists of Darwinist biological determinism.

For Jews the concept of a legacy of racial traits was useful in solving certain problems in the ideology of a reformed, liberal Judaism. Reform had abandoned most of the ceremonial laws and practices that most visibly distinguished traditional Jews from Gentiles; and if only an ethical, universalistic, rational monotheism remained of the traditional faith, it became hard to explain why Jews needed to continue apart from other universalistic, unitarian monotheists who were Gentiles. The contention that only Jews held to a truly rational, unalloyed monotheism was less than cogent in regard to such Christians. If one had to insist nevertheless on a divinely imposed mission for the Chosen People, justifying their continued separation from such Christians, the idea that Jews had a special racial gift for religious and ethical insight offered a rationalization based on currently fashionable assumptions.

For Gentiles the notion of racial flaws in Jewish character had often been adopted as a defense against the unwelcome side effects of too great success in mass conversion—as now of emancipation—of Jews. Both Muslims in North Africa and Christians in the Iberian Peninsula, after forced mass conversions of Jews, balked at their social integration and avoided this consequence by making purity of blood a criterion for acceptance among the truly faithful and for discrimination against the new converts. This, of course, was an attitude that left no way out for Jews unable to bear the burden of their identity; Richard Wagner offered only death as the road to transfiguration for the wandering Jew. There were Jews, convinced of the antisemitic racist diagnosis of their case, who chose this way out for themselves even before the Hitler regime left no other choice but the form of their death for all those caught in the inferno of the Third Reich.[7]

Apart from such expressions of insecurity, there were other responses to antisemitism among Jews secure in their liberal or Jewish identity, or in both. Typical of such responses was the assumption that, contrary to the precepts of insecure leaders, Jews must act politically in defense of their collective interests; that they should appear in such causes, by preference, openly, in their own person; that they should respond with pride to whoever sought to shame them. This attitude was fundamental to the activity of such Jews, secure in their liberalism, as Gabriel Riesser and Adolphe Crémieux. It was expressed also, implicitly or explicitly, in the activities of such bodies as the Alliance Israélite Universelle or the Centralverein deutscher Staatsbürger jüdischen Glaubens. The international activities of the Alliance (which, to be sure, fell in with the interests of French foreign policy and enjoyed official favor) were no less committed to the collective welfare of the Jews as a people than to the values of the Enlightenment and emancipation that they proposed to extend worldwide. The Centralverein, at its inception, was for its members an expression of Jewish pride (of the same vintage as that of their contemporary, Theodor Herzl) no less than of demonstrative security in their identity as German liberals. For such liberals the proper response to antisemites was a direct answer (in the most effective way, public or private); as for Jewish failings, they should be remedied in the Jews' own interest, not as a prerequisite for claiming Jewish rights.[8]

Still another reaction arose in Russia late in the nineteenth century—a nationalist Jewish response to antisemitism. There emancipation was not only interminably delayed (as also in Rumania), but to many it seemed definitively aborted. The reluctance of Russian progressive revolutionaries to condemn the pogroms of the 1880s, and especially the open approval of such mob action by some of

7. See Felix A. Theilhaber, *Judenschicksal* (Tel Aviv, n.d.).
8. See Jehuda Reinharz, *Fatherland or Promised Land: The Dilemma of the German Jew, 1893–1914* (Ann Arbor, 1975).

them, turned many Jewish liberal and radical enthusiasts back to a Jewish, rather than Russian, national self-image. The same primary orientation was shared in later years by the Jewish socialists who formed the Bund as a national proletarian union for the (economic and political) defense of Jewish interests. They fought as proletarians in the general Russian interest on the assumption that the empire (as well as the Russian Social Democratic party) should be reconstituted as a federation of its component nationalities—including the Jews—at least for cultural matters. Bundists argued that, unless Jews organized politically to fight in the ranks of the proletariat specifically in their own national interest, they could not hope for true equality of rights even after a successful social revolution. But this conclusion, while certainly arising from experiences of antisemitism among Gentile workers, was not argued from that base; rather it tended to be put as a case of the general Marxian proposition that only those proletarians who fought for their freedom would achieve it—or deserved to. Zionists, however, generally more secure in their Jewish identification, based their parallel doctrine of autoemancipation squarely on an analysis of the nature of antisemitism.[9]

The Zionists (dialectically resuming a position similar to that of tradition) assumed that antisemitism was not an accident but an essential condition attendant on the exiled survival of the Jews. They theorized that it was a necessary hostility arising from the universal antipathy to the stranger, or a form of ghost fear induced among Gentiles by the preternatural, millennia-long survival of the Jewish people without a homeland and the political sovereignty required for the survival of others. This analysis entailed a program to cope with the menace of antisemitism quite different from that natural to other views.

The liberal view of antisemitism was based on the optimistic assumption that it was an irrational relic of the past and the further progress of mankind would altogether abolish it. That left the generation which still faced remaining traces of antisemitism the task of removing them by the standard methods of enlightenment and the enhancement of social welfare. This entailed also directing efforts at those lagging elements in society still bogged down in igno-

9. See Jonathan Frankel, *Prophecy and Politics: Socialism, Nationalism and the Russian Jews, 1862–1917* (Cambridge, 1981); Henry J. Tobias, *The Jewish Bund in Russia from Its Origin to 1905* (Stanford, 1972).

rance and irrational resentments; and given the shame reactions of liberal Jews still insecure in their emancipation, Jews themselves could often be those "targeted," as we now say, for improvement. More securely liberated Jews, especially after greater experience with the antisemitism of enlightened and free peoples, reacted with shame to the insult of antisemitism and replied with demonstrations of pride. Nevertheless the response to antisemitism in such cases was a measure of social control, of policing; progress, in its irresistible march, remained the cure that would ultimately eliminate the disease.

On the Zionist view—that antisemitism was a permanent condition of the Jewish dispersion and homelessness was thus its specific cause—there was also a specific cure, which depended on action by the Jews themselves. Their return to their ancestral home, as a sovereign nation, would undercut antisemitism at its roots, and to achieve this, they must first of all will to do it. Such an attitude implied a sharp opposition to the currently accepted Jewish tactics for dealing with antisemitism. The Zionists tended to consider efforts to counteract antisemitic propaganda as at best ineffective palliatives, while methods of evading hostile notice by "improving" Jews for the sake of a better public image appeared shameful and without honor. Some Zionists of an optimistic liberal and rational bent believed that, since the removal of Jews to their own old home would relieve antisemites of their presence, they could hope for an agreement by which both sides would gain; reasonable antisemites might exert their political power to help Jews gain a homeland of their own. Other Zionists were less sanguine about the prospect of a surgical solution of the Jewish Problem and about the total excision of antisemitism by such a rationally engineered mass migration. They expected Diaspora Jewish communities to persist, at least for the foreseeable future, and to face continuing antisemitism. The community growing up in freedom in the homeland would supply a model, and an authentic revival of Jewish values, that would stiffen the pride of Diaspora communities.

The rise of the State of Israel in 1948 was an event not realistically expected by the generation who experienced it in the decades of laborious effort before. The most optimistic dared hope only for something less far reaching and prayed for a longer period of grace before facing the crucial decisions it required. But neither did the most pessimistic among Zionists anticipate anything like the Holocaust.

This was an expression of antisemitism that broke any possible human understanding, let alone one that a Jew, however piously submissive, could tolerate. Not only Zionists but all Jews had to reconsider their condition of life in the past generation.

For Zionists, the creation of Israel demonstrated, among other unforeseen results, that antisemitism was perhaps even more permanent than they had imagined. Jews returned to their homeland in massive numbers—many Diaspora communities were effectively liquidated in the exodus—and they achieved independent sovereignty there. But antisemitism, supposedly cut off at the roots, did not die out. Instead Israel became its prime target in the new era. The liberal approach suffered no less severe an assault. Hitler's reign in Germany shattered beyond repair confidence in the march of progress as the cure of antisemitism. More permanent causes than the mere backwardness of marginal social groups, and more radical cures than previously applied, had to be found. The attempt to eradicate antisemitism by ecumenical, theological reforms is one such approach.

Thus, the problem of establishing a new equilibrium point for the antisemitism-tolerance ratio is reopened. In the new situation Zionists must somehow avoid treating normal national enmities as basic antisemitism; liberals must learn how to cope with basic antisemiism other than as normal social friction; and both, to put up with less than total success.

WESTERN EUROPE

Michael Burns

Emancipation and Reaction

The Rural Exodus of Alsatian Jews, 1791–1848

In the months following July 1789, leaders of the French Revolution struggled with conflicting interpretations of the Rights of Man and debated the public worthiness of actors, executioners, Protestants, and, near the end of the agenda, Jews. New men had moved to the center of power to shape a new nation and extend the frontiers of citizenship. In political clubs and assembly halls in Paris and Versailles they addressed, among other issues, the question of whether members of the nation of Israel could ever, or should ever, become members of the nation of France. Speaking for others in the National Assembly, the Abbé Henri Baptiste Grégoire, opponent of slavery in the colonies and advocate of Jewish assimilation at home, agreed that it would be difficult but not impossible to incorporate Jews into "universal society." Another observer noted that as long as they were "denied everything as a nation, but granted everything as individuals" they could and "must be citizens."[1]

Emancipation came, but in stages. In January 1790 the National Assembly extended the "rights of active citizens" to Avignonese Jews and to the Sephardim of Spanish and Portuguese origin who were

---

1. Patrick Girard, *Les Juifs de France de 1789 à 1860: De l'émancipation à l'égalité* (Paris, 1976), pp. 38–39, 50, and passim; François Delpech, "La Révolution et l'Empire," in *Histoire des Juifs en France*, ed. Bernhard Blumenkranz (Toulouse, 1972), p. 280; Eugen Weber, "Reflections on the Jews in France," in *The Jews in Modern France*, ed. Frances Malino and Bernard Wasserstein (Hanover, N.H., 1985), p. 16. For more on the background to emancipation, see Arthur Hertzberg, *The French Enlightenment and the Jews* (New York, 1968); and for the Abbé Grégoire and others (the observer quoted is Count Stanislas de Clermont-Tonnerre), see the excerpt from the French National Assembly's debate on the eligibility of Jews for citizenship in *The Jew in the Modern World: A Documentary History*, ed. Paul R. Mendes-Flohr and Jehuda Reinharz (New York, 1980), pp. 103–7.

concentrated, for the most part, in the port cities of Bordeaux and Bayonne. Vital to the economy of Southwest France since the sixteenth century, Sephardi Jews had long enjoyed special privileges granted by the Old Regime, and now, in the second year of revolution, the new assembly continued the tradition.

It took more debate and frequent protest, however, to grant those rights to the Ashkenazim of Central and Eastern European origin, most of whom lived in poor communities within scores of villages and small towns along the Rhine Valley in the provinces of Upper and Lower Alsace. For a millennium, a blend of regional culture and Jewish historical experience had shaped those communities, making them, by the late eighteenth century, a "veritable human and spiritual reservoir of French Judaism."[2] Nearly twenty-five thousand Jews, or more than half the French-Jewish population, lived in Alsace, and not a few revolutionary officials, looking east, suspected their allegiance to the laws and customs of the "nation of Israel" and their dangerous proximity to Germanic states across the Rhine. In addition, traditions of "rapacious" usury and commercial competition worried officials unwilling to face the chaos and consequences of popular anti-Jewish rebellion. It had a long and violent history in Alsace.[3]

For these reasons and others, debates over the public worthiness of the "generally despised" Jews of Alsace and neighboring Lorraine stretched on for months.[4] Citizenship did not come until nearly two years after it had been granted to the urban and highly assimilated Sephardim. But come it did. Jewish notables joined revolutionary leaders to announce their hope that enlightenment and emancipation would forge a new patriotism and that modern progress would end centuries of suffering, "bondage and abasement."[5] Absolute legal equality would not be secured until a half century later when the July Monarchy abolished a special oath (*more Judaico*) required in legal proceedings. But after September 1791, all French Jews were

2. Girard, *Les Juifs de France*, p. 110.

3. For population statistics and more, see the excellent study of the region by Paul Leuilliot, *L'Alsace au début du XIXeme siècle: Essais d'histoire politique, économique et religieuse, 1815–1830* (Paris, 1959), 3:233–34. See also Girard, *Les Juifs de France*, p. 22; and Delpech, "La Révolution," p. 281.

4. Frances Malino, *The Sephardic Jews of Bordeaux: Assimilation and Emancipation in Revolutionary and Napoleonic France* (University, Ala., 1978), p. 56.

5. See Berr Isaac Berr, "Lettre d'un Citoyen," in *Jew in the Modern World*, pp. 107–10.

freed from Old Regime restrictions on landholding, marriage, migration, and more, and all were promised the basic rights of active citizens.

In the Alsatian countryside, however, Jews were not liberated from suspicion, threats, and sporadic popular rebellion. The ancient problem of concentrations of Jewish communities still brought forth concentrations of violence, despite the legal and theoretical advances of the Revolution; enlightened edicts, designed in Paris, could not sweep away benighted habits of prejudice entrenched in the eastern provinces. Through the Revolution and the first half of the nineteenth century, anti-Jewish uprisings became part of the modern dilemma faced by a central state in search of national order and unity, and by newly emancipated citizens in search of justice.

Depending on cycles of economic and political crisis, Jews and Gentiles within Alsatian communities lived in a "situation of stable accommodation"[6] or clashed in open and bloody rebellion. Conflict resurfaced when the secular passion of nationalism, born of revolution, joined the economic and religious prejudices that had turned country people against Jewish moneylenders and "Christ killers" for centuries. Of course, Christian usurers throughout France also felt the resentment of their peasant debtors—Alsatian Jews were not the only targets of rural anger—but the sins of Gentile moneylenders could be absolved with the lowering of interest rates or the canceling of loans, while Jewish sins were not so easily forgiven. Christian usurers had not been persecuted as deicides for centuries; nor had they been the victims of countless massacres, at least in the post-Roman world. Jews "attacked for their religious beliefs," writes historian Robert Anchel, "were simultaneously harassed because of their commercial activities" and, during the Reign of Terror, because of their suspect patriotism.[7] Like their German co-religionists would learn in 1848 in the neighboring Black Forest region, Alsatian Jews found that revolution and liberation could provide a catalyst for resentment and a stage for renewed persecution.[8]

6. Frances Henry uses this description for relations between Jews and Gentiles in the Rhine Valley in the twentieth century; it applies to communities in French Alsace in the nineteenth. See her *Victims and Neighbors: A Small Town in Nazi Germany Remembered* (South Hadley, Mass., 1984).

7. Robert Anchel, *Napoléon et les Juifs* (Paris, 1928), p. 21.

8. Jehuda Reinharz, *Fatherland or Promised Land: The Dilemma of the German Jew, 1893–1914* (Ann Arbor, 1975), p. 2.

Shock troops of the Terror in the eastern provinces vandalized synagogues and Jewish cemeteries along with Christian churches and monuments. Invoking modern, "patriotic sentiments" but using ancient methods of persecution,[9] provincial Jacobins swept through Jewish communities, where the "obstinate attachment" of the Ashkenazim to strange religious rituals exasperated Jacobins as much as did Catholic practices; for Jacobins, Jews and Jewish customs were doubly foreign. One official in the region demanded an "*auto-dafé* in the name of Truth of all Hebrew books," and another insisted that Jews, steeped in superstition, will never "open their eyes to reason." Still another asked if they should not be treated to the "regeneration of the guillotine."[10] More important, fierce popular action often accompanied the inflammatory rhetoric of the Terror. In communities along the eastern border of France, hostility and fear marked the early epoch of emancipation.

Yet the epoch brought unprecedented opportunities as well. Since the Middle Ages, Alsatian Jews had been confined to the countryside and prohibited from residing in most cities. Forced to pay a humiliating "Jewish tax" (*Judenzoll* or *péage corporel*) upon entering towns, they could transact business during daylight hours but were chased through city gates at sundown.[11] Now, with the right of geographic mobility shared by all French citizens, they could move to Strasbourg, Colmar, Mulhouse, or on to Paris; later, with the corporate restrictions of the Old Regime abolished and the economic dislocations of the Napoleonic Wars subsiding, they could enter the burgeoning industries and related trades of urban France and, above all, urban Alsace. In increasing numbers through the early decades of the nineteenth century, Jewish peddlers and merchants moved with their families from the hinterlands to the cities, a feature of their modern history that fits the broad-gauge patterns of a changing industrial world. Motives behind the exodus of Alsatian Jews did

9. Revolutionary violence in Alsace is outlined in Georges Weill, *L'Alsace française de 1789 à 1870* (Paris, 1916), pp. 14–15; François-Georges Dreyfus, *Histoire de l'Alsace* (Paris, 1979), pp. 186–96; and Anchel, *Napoléon*, pp. 14–25. See also Moses Ginsburger and Ernest Ginsburger, "Contributions à l'histoire des juifs d'Alsace pendant la Terreur," *Revue des Etudes Juives* 47 (1903): 283–99.

10. Quotations from Delpech, "La Révolution," p. 284; and Anchel, *Napoléon*, p. 18.

11. For specific examples, see Franklin L. Ford, *Strasbourg in Transition: 1648–1789* (Cambridge, Mass., 1958), pp. 17–18; and Ernest Meininger, *Histoire de Mulhouse* (Mulhouse, 1923), p. 95. See also Paul Lévy, *Les Noms des Israélites en France: Histoire et dictionnaire* (Paris, 1960), p. 61; Robert Anchel, *Les Juifs de France* (Paris, 1946), pp. 236–37; and Anchel, *Napoléon*, p. 38.

not, however, always fit the patterns of their Christian neighbors.[12]

Conventional wisdom has it that in the decades between the fall of Napoleon and the rise of *fin-de-siècle* antisemitism Jews enjoyed a "period of tranquillity exceptional in their history,"[13] interrupted only momentarily by rebellion in Alsace in 1848. But conflict, not calm, marked rural Jewish communities in the second and third decades of the century, when country people threatened moneylenders, demanded an end to their debts, and, not infrequently, turned to violence. At the same time the parallel growth and concentration of Alsatian industry during these years provided new opportunities, and the rights of citizenship permitted Jewish migration to urban centers. This conjuncture radically transformed the lives of many, perhaps most, Alsatian Jews and was no less significant than the critical period following 1870, when thousands of Jews in the region "opted" for France.[14] In the early stage of migration, notes Patrick Girard, Jews who left their native villages lost their "rural character" as they moved into an "urban milieu" and a setting "favorable to acculturation."[15] For them, rural exodus was both a choice and a necessity—a chance to seize new opportunities and escape old prejudices rekindled.

In southern Alsace, in the department of the Haut-Rhin—the administrative unit shaped from the Old Regime province of Upper Alsace—many Jewish families migrated only a short distance, to Mulhouse, then still officially called Mülhausen, a textile city and a principal urban center of the region. There, in "la ville la plus française de l'Alsace,"[16] they began the process that Michael R. Marrus has defined as assimilation—"the process by which individuals of Jewish background assumed an *identity* which is essentially French."[17] The "universal society" hoped for by the Abbé Grégoire in 1790 took time and travel.

---

12. Details of Jewish migration will be discussed below. For general patterns in France, see Abel Chatelain, *Les Migrants temporaires en France de 1800 à 1914* (Paris, n.d.); and Eugen Weber, *Peasants into Frenchmen: The Modernization of Rural France, 1870–1914* (Stanford, 1976), pp. 278–91.

13. See, for example, François Delpech, "De 1815 à 1894," in *Histoire des Juifs*, p. 305.

14. On exodus after 1871, see Dreyfus, *Histoire de l'Alsace*, pp. 251–61; Meininger, *Histoire de Mulhouse*, p. 122; and Michael R. Marrus, *The Politics of Assimilation: A Study of the French Jewish Community at the Time of the Dreyfus Affair* (Oxford, 1971), p. 33.

15. Girard, *Les Juifs de France*, p. 114.

16. Frédéric Hoffet, *Psychanalyse de l'Alsace* (Paris, 1951), pp. 73–74. For clarity and consistency I shall use the more familiar name, Mulhouse.

17. Marrus, *Politics of Assimilation*, p. 2, his italics.

I

Napoleon had been in power for five years and on the imperial throne for one when debates concerning Alsatians of Jewish background resurfaced, and the threat of social upheaval along the eastern border attracted the emperor's attention. Reports had it that the emancipated Ashkenazim of Alsace had not ended their "shameful" practices of usury, nor had they abandoned their "fanatical" adherence to the Talmud. As one critic put it, they had not "replaced cupidity with love of country nor ridiculous superstitions with reason."[18] In close-knit communities they maintained particularistic "Mosaic" systems of charity and communal life, as well as religious rituals and forms of dress that, to outsiders, still suggested a dark and mysterious Orientalism or, worse in this age of European conflict, Germanic influence. Even their daily speech—Judeo-Alsatian dialect, a variant of Yiddish—served as a linguistic sign of their marginality and intransigence; and they used Hebrew, local authorities had reported a few years earlier, "to correspond with foreigners and to spy."[19]

Vital signs of cultural distinction—including regional language and dress, fervent religious belief, and distrust of the central state and of Paris—could be found among Bretons, Basques, Flemings, and Occitanians; and Eugen Weber is right to suggest that the intransigence of the Jews was less threatening to national unity than the cultural barricades built by massive numbers of provincials throughout France.[20] Nonetheless, Alsatian Jews had been awarded

18. See the long report from Wintzenheim in the Archives départementales du Haut-Rhin, Colmar (hereafter ADHR), V 611, and the comments of the subprefect of Altkirch, June 7, 1806, ibid. See also Anchel, *Napoléon*, p. 24; and Delpech, "La Révolution," p. 284.

19. For the report on Hebrew and espionage, see Anchel, *Napoléon*, p. 23; see also Girard, *Les Juifs de France*, p. 63. The most thorough overview of Alsatian Jewish culture is Freddy Raphael and Robert Weyl, *Juifs en Alsace: Culture, société, histoire* (Toulouse, 1977). Also useful are Daniel Stauben, *Scènes de la vie juive en Alsace* (Paris, 1860); Michel Lévy, *Coup d'oeil historique sur l'état des Israélites en France et particulièrement en Alsace* (Strasbourg, 1836); and the numerous general histories of the region cited above. Well into the nineteenth century, Alsatian Jews "apparaissent comme le groupe le plus déshérité et le plus retardaire." Raphael and Weyl, *Juifs en Alsace*, p. 369.

20. On entrenched regional particularisms, see Weber, *Peasants into Frenchmen*, passim; Weber, "Reflections on Jews," p. 16; Girard, *Les Juifs de France*, p. 33; and Michael Burns, *Rural Society and French Politics: Boulangism and the Dreyfus Affair, 1886–1900* (Princeton, 1984), pt. 1. In 1848 the mayor of Strasbourg said, with some irony, that "Alsace is just as much French as Brittany, Flanders and the country of the Basques,

special dispensation when revolutionary leaders, after agonizing debate, granted them the rights of active citizens. They, in turn, had a special duty to fulfill the obligation of assimilation, even if they were "never quite told what . . . to prove."[21]

Napoleon would help them decide. Responding to new outbreaks of anti-Jewish violence in the eastern provinces in 1805 and 1806 and to rumors, unfounded but believed, that usurers were charging annual interest rates of 75 percent, the emperor considered restrictions on moneylending and revised methods of Jewish assimilation.[22] He would not allow "a debased, degraded nation, capable of every vileness, to take possession of the two beautiful departments of Alsace," the Haut-Rhin and the Bas-Rhin. Always keen on border security and military strategy, he warned that "it would be dangerous to let the keys to France . . . [fall] into the hands of a population of spies who are not attached to the country."[23] At the time of Napoleon's statement, 1806, Alsatian Jews had been French citizens for fifteen years.

Contrary to popular legend and imperial opinion, usury had been a largely Christian practice in France, despite restrictions and threats of excommunication. Even in Alsace, with its large number of Jewish lenders, non-Jewish innkeepers, merchants, and others lent at exorbitant rates, leading one official to report that Christian usurers "inspired such terror in their victims that debtors dare not lodge complaints." Villages throughout Alsace were full of Christians who were as "Jewish as the Jews." Following ancient habit, most observers naturally defined non-Jewish moneylenders as "Christian Jews";[24] after all, usury was considered the "habitual occupation" of the nation of Israel.[25] The Old Testament had instructed that "to a foreigner you may lend upon interest, but to your brother you shall

---

and so she will remain"—which is to say, not very French at all. See Daniel Blumenthal, *Alsace-Lorraine* (New York, 1917), pp. 26–27.

21. Arthur Hertzberg, quoted in Robert Alter, "Emancipation, Enlightenment and All That," *Commentary*, February 1972, p. 67.

22. The main study of this period is Anchel's *Napoléon;* see also his *Les Juifs,* pp. 240–57.

23. Quoted in Girard, *Les Juifs de France,* p. 75.

24. Reports from communes of Guebwiller, Giromagny, and Belfort, ADHR, V 611. For more on usury in Alsace, see Leuilliot, *L'Alsace au début,* 2:189; Anchel, *Les Juifs,* pp. 13ff.; Raphael and Weyl, *Juifs en Alsace,* pp. 370–71; Girard, *Les Juifs de France,* p. 73; Roland Marx, "Les Juifs et l'usure en Alsace," *Saisons d'Alsace,* nos. 55–56 (1975); and Burns, *Rural Society,* pp. 127–28, 169.

25. Report to prefect, September 9, 1823, ADHR, V 611; see also Anchel, *Les Juifs,* p. 13, where usury is described as the "innate vocation" of the Jews.

not," and for centuries Jews had done just that—by necessity and often under pressure. Excluded from most artisanal trades and guilds under the Old Regime, forbidden from owning land and forced to pay popes, princes, feudal lords, and kings for their protection, Jews, be they prosperous court subjects or the poor peddlers of Alsace, had little choice but to continue the tradition that had helped them survive.[26]

During the Revolution one sensible observer had explained that "men who possess nothing but money cannot live but by making that money valuable," and most Jews have been "prevented . . . from possessing anything else."[27] Furthermore, country people often profited from Jewish moneylending; in Alsace significant numbers of farmers and others purchased *biens nationaux* thanks to loans from local Jews.[28] Of course, like their Christian counterparts, some operated as rapacious speculators, but the majority of Jews in villages and small towns throughout Alsace were as poverty striken (and as law abiding) as their country neighbors. Most Jews who did lend money provided an essential service in a rural world where modern, institutional sources of credit had not yet penetrated.

But the historical details of Jewish usury interested Napoleon less than stability along the eastern frontier and the unification of France. During every wave of social and economic crisis in Alsace, Jews served as immediate, customary targets of peasant discontent; for country people they assumed the dual historical role of unrepentant slayers of Christ and harsh masters of rural credit. The emperor, faced with new crises, aimed to stem that social disorder and secure, at last, the dissolution of traditional Jewish communities and their assimilation into the French fatherland.

"If I ruled the Jewish people," Napoleon once said, "I would reestablish Solomon's Temple."[29] In that spirit, after convening an Assembly of Jewish Notables to examine critical questions of law and custom, the emperor established in 1807 a Grand Sanhedrin of seventy-one prominent Jews based on the political and religious

26. Deut. 15:1–11. On the changing history of protection and punishment, see George LaPiana, "The Church and the Jews," *Historia Judaica* 11 (1949):117–44.

27. Clermont-Tonnerre in the French National Assembly's debate, *The Jew in the Modern World*, p. 104.

28. Leuilliot, *L'Alsace au début*, 2:176. Peasants in the Haut-Rhin bought *biens nationaux* "grace aux emprunts consentis par les juifs et qu'ils avaient eu ensuite 'la barbare ingratitude' de les dénoncer pour faire prendre par l'Empereur les fameux decrées de 1808." Ibid., 3:237. See also Anchel, *Napoléon*, p. 34 n. 2.

29. Quoted in Girard, *Les Juifs de France*, p. 71.

institution of ancient Israel. Both assemblies submitted reports clarifying misunderstandings of Jewish customs, including money-ending, which, they explained, is permitted only in commercial speculation and never at "usurious" rates. They reconfirmed the integrity of the religious community within the national community and stressed the patriotic devotion of French Jews.[30]

Perhaps satisfied that he had sufficiently evoked from Jews "spontaneous feelings of gratitude,"[31] Napoleon dissolved the Grand Sanhedrin only a few weeks later and, with his Council of State, drafted a series of three special decrees designed to settle the Jewish Question in France. Issued in early 1808, the first two dealt with the reorganization of consistories and concerned all French Jews. The third, however, later known as the Infamous Decree, was designed for the problematic Jews of the eastern provinces. All debts owed to Jewish moneylenders were annulled or reduced, and a special annual license ensured that Jews involved in commerce (potential usurers) would be monitored. No new Jewish residences could be established in the two departments of Alsace, and migration to the interior required special permission. Finally, French Jews, unlike French Christians, could not arrange for military replacements; they had to serve.[32]

Provincial officials applauded their emperor's severe controls, if not his desire to achieve the assimilation of Jews. They had languished too long in a "state of abasement," officials confirmed; their "shameful" speculation must cease and they must be taught the lessons of "civil morality."[33] The content and tone of local reports suggest that most provincial observers were less sanguine about the acculturation of Jews than were Parisian policy makers. Local observers were, among other things, products of provincial culture and regional prejudice. Still, both factions agreed on firm controls.

Nearly two decades after emancipation, the Jews of Alsace and Lorraine had been singled out for discriminatory measures and a

---

30. On the Assembly of Jewish Notables and the Grand Sanhedrin, see the selections in *The Jew in the Modern World*, pp. 112–24; Girard, *Les Juifs de France*, pp. 76–86; and Anchel, *Napoléon*.

31. *The Jew in the Modern World*, p. 123 n. 2.

32. The decrees are reproduced in Girard, *Les Juifs de France*, app.3. Malino does a splendid job of summarizing their content and impact in *Sephardic Jews of Bordeaux*, pp. 108–11. See also Weill, *L'Alsace française*, pp. 48–49; and Delpech, "La Révolution," pp. 296–97.

33. For responses to the early decrees in the Haut-Rhin, see *enquêtes* through May and June 1806, ADHR, V 611.

special economic regime that would last ten years. With one "sweep of the despot's pen," a local committee of Jewish notables later reported, Napoleon had taken away the rights of citizens.[34] It would not be the last broken promise of the Revolution.

At first the decrees may have helped control outbreaks of popular violence in the Alsatian countryside. But the ravages and distractions of war and enemy occupation during these years did as much as official monitoring of moneylending to reduce the number of rebellions, if not the pervasiveness of anti-Jewish sentiment. As in previous centuries, Alsace served as a "shock line" of European conflict,[35] with Austrian, Russian, and other troops seizing, losing, then seizing again villages and towns along the Rhine Valley. With other opportunists of war, some Jews made a profit speculating in grain and livestock, and, typically, the entire community was accused of traitorous allegiance to enemy troops.[36]

But it was not until the collapse of Napoleon's empire in 1815, and the expiration of his decrees three years later, that anxious officials noted a "reprise" of Jewish usury and rumors of new and widespread popular discontent.[37] Economic crisis fueled by nearly two decades of war sent desperate peasants in search of credit. The newly formed Bank of France had no intention of serving peasant debtors in distant provinces; country people would have to wait for the emperor's nephew, Napoleon III, for institutions of rural credit. With no alternative, they turned to local lenders, including Jews now free from the constraints of imperial edicts. In the five years following 1818 in the Altkirch region of the Haut-Rhin, Jewish loans nearly doubled, and those included only reported mortgages. Alsatian officials warned that without swift renewal of the 1808 decrees the region would fall "in servitude to the Jews," the "political lepers" of France.[38]

Fears of renewed violence were well founded. In September 1819, in the hinterlands of Mulhouse and north in the wine-growing bourg

34. See the long manifesto from Alsatian Jewish notables to the minister of the interior, 1823, ibid.

35. Hoffet, *Psychanalyse de l'Alsace*, p. 27.

36. Altkirch official to prefect, September 9, 1823, ADHR, V 611. For the impact of the occupation in southern Alsace, see Meininger, *Histoire de Mulhouse*, p. 98; and P. R. Zuber, *Rixheim* (Mulhouse, 1947), on file in ADHR.

37. Leuilliot, *L'Alsace au début*, 2:192. See also the police reports dating from 1819 in ADHR, 4 M 44.

38. Haut-Rhin official, quoted in Leuilliot, *L'Alsace au début*, 2:182. Between 1818 and 1823 *créances hypothécaires* increased from 4.7 to 7 million francs. Ibid., p. 191.

of Ribeauvillé, police reported that Jews had sought protection after attacks by gangs shouting "Hep, Hep!"—an anti-Jewish chant imported from across the Rhine. The murder of a German poet and playwright sympathetic to the Jews sparked riots among students in the town of Würzburg; while pillaging Jewish homes and shops, they shouted the medieval marching chant of the Crusaders. Southwest of Würzburg in the rural areas of Baden, peasants took up the chant and, with their own grievances, turned on local Jews. A short time later the slogan and the violence reached the countryside of French Alsace.[39] One enlightened official, the minister of the interior, ordered that Jews seeking refuge should not be refused the "hospitality and protection that France extends to all foreigners." With striking efficiency, the minister's message to the prefect of the Haut-Rhin reached the mayor and the police of Ribeauvillé, and, for the moment, the Jews of that locality were protected.[40]

But the occasional tolerance of French bureaucrats had little impact on long traditions of rural prejudice. In the aftermath of the Hep-Hep riots came more reports of peasant discontent and Jewish fears. Rumor had it that during the decade of the Napoleonic decrees Jews had perfected "clandestine" usurious practices.[41] Now, with the end of restrictions, moneylending was more difficult than ever to monitor, and more dangerous. By 1822, according to the prefect, the situation had become intolerable. The following year an ominous report announced that peasants throughout the southern Haut-Rhin were in the mood for a "Saint Bartholomew's Day for the Jews."[42]

Paris officials ordered a new and thorough inquiry into Jewish moneylending in the eastern provinces. In the Haut-Rhin a few localities had been fortunate, as one witness said, to have escaped the "Judaic leprosy" of moneylending.[43] But others lodged complaints

39. Police report on the environs of Mulhouse, September 30, 1819, and *juge de paix* report on Ribeauvillé, September 27, 1819, ADHR, 4 M 44. For the background of the riots, see Eleonore O. Sterling, "Anti-Jewish Riots in Germany in 1819: A Displacement of Social Protest," *Historia Judaica* 12 (1950): 105–42. For more on events in Ribeauvillé, see Moses Ginsburger, "Juifs et Chrétiens à Ribeauvillé en 1819," *Bulletin de la société historique et archéologique de Ribeauvillé* (Colmar) 7 (1937): 65–66; and Leuilliot, *L'Alsace au début*, 3:243.

40. Minister's report, October 18, 1819, ADHR, 4 M 44; Ginsburger, "Juifs et Chrétiens," pp. 65–66.

41. See the assessments of the previous years in reports dated August 22, and 25, 1823, and October 26, 1829, ADHR, V 611.

42. On the situation in 1822, see the note from the subprefect of Altkirch, January 1823, ibid. For the peasant protest in 1823, see Leuilliot, *L'Alsace au début*, 3:244 n. 7.

43. Quoted in Leuilliot, *L'Alsace au début*, 2:189.

along with their lists of usurers and questioned the worthiness of Jews. "We now see the mistake" of granting them the rights of citizens; "the law of the state is merely a means for them to secure domination. . . . should we continue to extend that law to those who do not fulfill the duties that it imposes?"[44] Among those duties, it seemed, was that all lenders should concede to conditions demanded by their debtors and that all Jews should suffer punishment for the crimes of a few.

In response to accusations of avarice and ingratitude and to threats of new limitations on their civil liberties, a group of Jewish notables, speaking for "ten thousand French citizens" in their area of Alsace, confirmed that a new persecution was under way: "again there is talk of punishing the entire [Jewish] nation." If there remain "misery and vice" among some Jews, they concluded, it is because of unjust laws like the decrees of 1808.[45]

As in the past, the conflict moved beyond the heated words of government officials and Jewish notables. Popular actions that followed the economic crisis of 1816–17 and the expiration of the Napoleonic decrees continued through the 1820s and beyond. In Durmenach, south of Mulhouse near the Swiss border, peasants "inflamed by wine" on a "jour de fête" marched to homes of their Jewish lenders. They pushed through doorways, demanded an end to their debts, and announced that they would "exterminate them all."[46] Perhaps these were the fierce words of relatively harmless drunks in search of adventure—sad examples of rural hooligans on festival day. Their immediate intentions, however, are less important than their habitual choice of victims and the fear that their threats must have engendered among the Jews of Durmenach and scores of other communities. In Zillisheim, close by Mulhouse, gangs attacked the synagogue and threw Jews in the river.[47]

In 1829 local enemies of the unpopular French monarch, Charles X, used the issue of moneylending to stir up trouble in the region and accused the royal government of protecting the Jewish population more than its victims. Jews knew the limits to that protection, but on the eve of the Revolution of 1830 it mattered more to local insurgents that anti-Jewish rhetoric worked to attract popular polit-

44. Report from an official in Wintzenheim, n.d. [1823?], ADHR, V 611.
45. Manifesto of Alsatian Jewish notables, 1823, ibid.
46. The local witness is quoted in Leuilliot, L'Alsace au début, 2:184.
47. Ibid., 3:245.

ical support.[48] The following year, when a new tax was levied on livestock, Jews involved in horse and cattle trading became the targets of local riots, and during wine harvests in Wintzenheim and Ribeauvillé, police prepared for attacks on Jewish moneylenders, customary rituals of violence in those areas made worse by the conjuncture of national revolution. Long before Karl Marx elaborated on the connection, Alsatian country people equated Jews with commerce, capitalism, and abuses of state power and blamed them for troubles whether caused by Parisian policies, enemy troops, or acts of God.[49] Finally, in 1832, an official in Colmar summarized the prevailing view: "the Israelites of the Haut-Rhin are a veritable plague on Alsace."[50]

In the years between the end of the Napoleonic era and the early 1830s, at least three waves of anti-Jewish uprisings of varying intensity swept through Alsace, particularly in the rural regions south of Colmar toward Mulhouse. Incidents of brutal physical persecution may have been more common in previous centuries when Crusaders supported by rebellious peasants forced the Christian baptism of Jewish children and massacred their parents; not until the twentieth century would the scope and methods of medieval cruelty be matched, then surpassed. But it is significant that in rural Alsace during the early decades of the nineteenth century memories of past persecution (including recent memories of the Great Fear and Terror) were vivid and that new threats, sparked by periodic crises, created an oppressive climate of hostility and fear.

Anti-Jewish conflict would continue in the countryside in the years to come, most notably during the Revolutions of 1848, when peasants blamed moneylenders for the economic crisis that devastated much of French agriculture between 1846 and 1852.[51] But by then many Alsatian Jews had left the countryside for the industrial cities of the region. Still others had moved beyond the borders of Alsace,

48. Reports to the prefect through 1829, ADHR, V 611.

49. On the 1831 riots, see Zosa Szajkowski, *Poverty and Social Welfare among French Jews, 1800–1880* (New York, 1954), p. 8; for Marx and Jews, see *Karl Marx: Early Writings*, trans. and ed. T. B. Bottomore (New York, 1964), pp. 1–40.

50. Report from Colmar, August 8, 1832, ADHR, V 611. On violence in Ribeauvillé and elsewhere in the early 1830s, see police report June 18, 1832, ibid., 4 M 44; Moses Ginsburger, "Les Juifs à Ribeauvillé et à Bergheim," *Bulletin de la société historique et archéologique de Ribeauvillé* (Colmar) 8 (1938): 25; and Szajkowski, *Poverty and Social Welfare*, p. 23.

51. Dreyfus, *Histoire de l'Alsace*, pp. 230–32; Meininger, *Histoire de Mulhouse*, p. 106; Weber, *Peasants into Frenchmen*, p. 39.

especially to Paris, though the critical moment of that exodus would come later. Between 1784 and 1866 the Jewish population of Alsace increased from twenty thousand to thirty-five thousand. Despite some emigration out of the area during the early decades of the nineteenth century, most Jews remained within the eastern provinces. They migrated, however. They left bourgs and villages like Rixheim, Ribeauvillé, Botwiller, and others, and their numbers helped create, or recreate, the great Jewish quarters of Alsatian cities.[52]

Again, the exodus of rural Jews reflected the general, nationwide pattern of migration. The concentration of textile and other industries, along with the related deindustrialization of the countryside, led cottage workers, artisans, day laborers, rural merchants, and others to abandon their native villages in search of new opportunities in the urban world. This left, as one historian describes it, a "traditional" countryside dominated by peasants working their fields.[53] Prohibited from owning land for centuries and rarely turning to agriculture after emancipation, Jews were among the first to join that vast exodus out of the Alsatian countryside to the region's cities and industrial centers.

Migration came earlier in the eastern provinces than in many other parts of France. Traditional cotton and cloth mills survived in the Vosges region and along the Rhine Valley, but beginning in the late eighteenth century, textile industries mechanized and expanded. Then, after the economic and political dislocations of war and the return to relative stability, they centralized and attracted more and more country people from the hinterlands. The celebrated "dynamic" entrepreneurs of Alsace had infused massive amounts of capital into chemical works, textile factories, and other industries from Belfort in the south to Strasbourg in the Bas-Rhin department to the north. Some of those industries suffered a crisis of overproduction in the late 1820s, but after 1830 expansion continued with renewed vigor. Beyond doubt, a key moment of industrial growth in Alsace came during the generation following 1818.[54]

---

52. On population statistics, see *recensements*, ADHR, 6 M 6–9; and Szajkowski's figures in *Poverty and Social Welfare*, p. 8. For personal reminiscences of migration, see Stauben's account of Botwiller in *Scènes de la vie juive*.
53. Charles Tilly, "Did the Cake of Custom Break?" in *Consciousness and Class Experience in Nineteenth Century Europe*, ed. John Merriman (New York, 1979), p. 37. See also Burns, *Rural Society*, pt. 1.
54. Henry Laufenburger, *Cours d'économie alsacienne* (Paris, 1930), 1:83, 124; 2:10, 62, 76–78, 379ff.; *Centenaire de la société industrielle de Mulhouse* (Mulhouse, 1926), p.

In the countryside that same period was marked by an escalation of anti-Jewish violence. To a great extent conflict had been sparked by economic crisis, the expiration of measures controlling money-lending, and the decline of rural industries. Village trade, including Jewish trade, suffered. Now, thanks to emancipation, many peddlers and merchants who served as intermediaries between country and town prepared to leave villages and settle in the cities of Alsace. The modern expansion and concentration of large-scale industry after the Napoleonic Wars provided a motivation for Jewish exodus, while renewed outbreaks of anti-Jewish violence provided the occasion. Turning to the promise of urban civilization and industrial progress, most Jewish families in the Bas-Rhin department moved from communities in the hinterlands of Strasbourg to the city. South, in the Haut-Rhin, they migrated to the administrative capital, Colmar, or to the leading textile center, Mulhouse, formerly an independent republic affiliated with Swiss cantons but attached to France since 1798.[55] In Mulhouse, Jewish migrants found not only economic opportunities but a new environment of tolerance.

II

One village mayor speaking for others in the southern Haut-Rhin reported that population decline in the countryside was due to the fact that "many families have left for . . . Mulhouse, America and Africa."[56] Distant journeys to other continents, though not uncommon by the first half of the nineteenth century, were beyond the means of most Alsatian country folk. Above all, the rural migrants who remained in southern Alsace set off for the cities of the region. Barely six thousand people lived in Mulhouse at the time of its union with France, but by the 1820s that number had more than doubled, and shortly after midcentury it approached fifty thousand.[57]

Located on the southern plain of Alsace, north of Switzerland and

---

17 and passim; *Histoire documentaire de l'industrie de Mulhouse au XIXeme siècle* (Mulhouse, 1902), 1:220–22; Dreyfus, *Histoire de l'Alsace*, pp. 223–24.

55. Anchel, *Napoléon*, pp. 29, 38–39; Girard, *Les Juifs de France*, pp. 11, 116; Delpech, "La Révolution," p. 282; Marrus, *Politics of Assimilation*, p. 32. On Mulhouse and Switzerland, see Meininger, *Histoire de Mulhouse*, p. 91 and passim.

56. Mayor's note, August 25, 1846, ADHR, 6 M 83. See also the *listes nominatives* for Haut-Rhin communes in ibid., ser. 6 M.

57. Laufenburger, *Cours d'économie*, 2:240; *recensements*, ADHR, 6 M 4–9; *Histoire documentaire de l'industrie*, 1:32.

the Jura mountain range and a scant fifteen kilometers west of the Rhine River and the German border, Mulhouse had long been favored by its geography, climate, and natural resources. The river Ill, a tributary of the Rhine, flowed through the city dividing into canals that, for generations, propelled the water mills of small industries. Companies dealing in printed calico since the eighteenth century became major concerns in the first half of the nineteenth century, making Mulhouse, like Rouen to the east and Lille to the north, a thriving textile center. Large, mechanized cloth and cotton mills with branches for spinning, blanching, and printing dominated the city economy. Unlike many other textile centers, however, Mulhouse remained competitive by specializing in quality goods for affluent customers. Paint factories experimented with chemical techniques to achieve new colors for printed fabrics, and much of the lush trimming found in the overdraped, overstuffed interiors of nineteenth-century bourgeois homes came from the factories of Mulhouse.[58]

For the Jews of the region, the city had a checkered past of prejudice and exclusion alternating with periods of tolerance and accommodation. Permitted to live there in the early Middle Ages and allowed to construct a small synagogue, Jews were persecuted in the thirteenth and fourteenth centuries and expelled in the fifteenth century when Swiss troops seized their property and destroyed their homes. The history of the Jews in Mulhouse is a microcosm of their plight throughout Western Europe. Depending largely on the benevolence or maliciousness of popes, princes, or occupying soldiers, Jews may have been protected (for a price) or punished for the moneylending services they had been forced to provide.[59]

Another feature of the city's history, however, less typical of urban centers in the region, also had an important impact on the Jewish population. Since the sixteenth century, Mulhouse had been a powerful center of Protestantism in the midst of an overwhelmingly Catholic Alsace. In 1575, when the city sent troops to aid victims of the Saint Bartholomew's Day Massacre, most Protestants still followed the teachings of Ulrich Zwingli, not surprising in an area long influenced by its proximity to Switzerland.[60] To the north, Luther-

58. Emile Cacheux, *Etude de moyens pratiques de détruire la misère . . . suivie de l'histoire d'une ville industrielle* [Mulhouse] (Paris, 1876), pp. 30–31; Laufenburger, *Cours d'économie*, 1:131; 2:7; *Histoire documentaire de l'industrie*, 1:261ff.

59. Meininger, *Histoire de Mulhouse*, pp. 20, 25, 46.

60. Laufenburger, *Cours d'économie*, 2:221–23; Meininger, *Histoire de Mulhouse*, pp. 52–56.

anism gained modest support in a few localities, and Lutherans followed their leader in showing little sympathy for the Jews ("our plague, our pestilence"). But by the seventeenth century the Calvinism that "profoundly marked" the ascendant bourgeoisie of Mulhouse included more tolerance for the Jews, as well as that spirit of work, austerity, and investment that was a very real (if frequently stereotypical) feature of the "Protestant ethic."[61] In the nineteenth century Mulhouse continued to be an almost exclusively Protestant city, with religious life "impregnating civic life." In 1836 nearly half the deacons and other lay members of the Protestant consistory were "captains of industry," while not a single Catholic owned a significant enterprise in the city throughout the nineteenth century.[62]

Jews, on the other hand, would launch a number of formidable enterprises. There is little doubt that the Protestants and Jews of Mulhouse, unlike their co-religionists in most Germanic states or northern Alsatian communities, shared a climate of tolerance and industry that had been shaped by their common historical experience as victims and survivors in Catholic Alsace. That union would continue through the late nineteenth century throughout France when antisemites attacked the marginal trinity of Protestants, Jews, and Freemasons, and into the twentieth century when Protestants sheltered French and foreign Jews escaping Nazi and Vichy tyranny. If there was an Alsatian city in which Jews might feel welcome during the critical period following the Napoleonic era, Mulhouse was that city.[63]

Still, a generation earlier, on the eve of the Revolution, officials continued to bar permanent Jewish residents. Peddlers could transact business if they paid a special "Jewish tax" and left by nightfall, but they had to live beyond the city gates in villages and towns through the Rhine Valley and Vosges Mountains. When riots erupted in those rural communities during the Great Fear—above all, when

61. Philippe Dollinger, "Bourgeoisies d'Alsace," in *La Bourgeoisie alsacienne: Etudes d'histoire sociale*, ed. Jean Schlumberger et al. (Strasbourg, 1954), p. 488; Schlumberger, introd., ibid., p. 12; Dreyfus, *Histoire de l'Alsace*, p. 227. On Luther and the Jews, see Luther, "On the Jews and Their Lies" (1543), trans. Martin H. Bertram, in *Luther's Works*, vol. 47, ed. Franklin Sherman (Philadelphia, 1971), pp. 121–306.

62. Laufenburger, *Cours d'économie*, 2:226–30; Dreyfus, *Histoire de l'Alsace*, p. 227.

63. Dreyfus discusses the closeness of Protestants and Jews in Mulhouse in the nineteenth century in *Histoire de l'Alsace*, pp. 227ff. For Protestants and Jews in the late nineteenth century, see Stephen Wilson, *Ideology and Experience: Antisemitism in France at the Time of the Dreyfus Affair* (Rutherford, N.J., 1982), pp. 704–5; and for the twentieth century, see Philip Hallie, *Lest Innocent Blood Be Shed* (New York, 1979).

peasants in the Sundgau region of southern Alsace turned on local Jews—officials in Mulhouse dropped restrictions and passed a series of measures permitting Jews to take refuge in the city. In appreciation, those who had been sheltered composed a prayer to thank the magistrates and town councilors for their "hospitality." This modern image of Mulhouse as a tolerant city of refuge and opportunity would help attract Jewish migrants over the coming years.[64]

When the six-hundred-year-old republic ceased to exist and Mulhouse became part of French Alsace, city leaders could no longer determine when, how, and how many Jews would be permitted to enter. Having the rights of active citizens—at least the new right to migrate and settle in urban centers—Alsatian Jews were now free to make those decisions for themselves.

At first, few did. War, enemy occupation, and cycles of economic crisis delayed migration from villages and small towns, largely because those events momentarily retarded the growth of industry in the area. Only four hundred Jews had moved to Mulhouse by 1822, the year the new synagogue was inaugurated. Barely a decade later, however, the Jewish population had tripled and, as another symbol of changing customs, Jews could now be buried in city cemeteries. At midcentury the Jewish population approached two thousand, or nearly 7 percent of the city's residents at a time when the Jewish population of Paris stood at less than one-half of 1 percent.[65]

Settling in modest quarters in neighborhoods near the rue de la Synagogue, the new Jewish residents of the city rarely continued the practice of moneylending. Separation from peasant borrowers and urban alternatives to traditions of rural credit led almost all the Jews of Mulhouse toward new and various "affaires commerciales," however modest.[66] In the cities of Alsace in the early nineteenth century, the son of a rural scrap-iron dealer "could become a hardware merchant, the son of a livestock broker could become a tanner, the son of a peddler could open a fabric shop" or, eventually, a textile factory.[67] In Mulhouse a number of Jews did just that.

---

64. *Histoire documentaire de l'industrie*, 1:117–18; Meininger, *Histoire de Mulhouse*, p. 88; Anchel, *Napoléon*, p. 10 n. 1.

65. *Recensements*, ADHR, 6 M 9; Leuilliot, *L'Alsace au début*, 3:234; Meininger, *Histoire de Mulhouse*, pp. 100–103; Szajkowski, *Poverty and Social Welfare*, p. 71 n. 161; Marrus, *Politics of Assimilation*, p. 30.

66. Leuilliot, *L'Alsace au début*, 2:191.

67. For this description of urban social mobility, see Raphael and Weyl, *Juifs en Alsace*, p. 381; see also Szajkowski, *Poverty and Social Welfare*, p. 74.

The experience of one family migrating from the hinterlands in the 1830s was typical of others and illustrates problems and promises common to many Alsatian Jews in the first half of the century. In the village of Rixheim east of Mulhouse, Jacob Dreÿfuss worked as a *revendeur*, an all-purpose profession of retail trade that, throughout Alsace, included the peddling of old clothes, secondhand objects, religious books, engravings, and trinkets. Each Sunday, Jewish peddlers set out from Rixheim and other villages to sell their wares in the countryside. Sometimes they dodged stones thrown by village hooligans or, as on Good Friday and Holy Saturday in the area around Rixheim, passed bonfires set by Christian children shouting "Sticks, sticks to burn the Wandering Jew!" Before sundown on Friday, Jacob Dreÿfuss and his comrades returned to their communities to spend the Sabbath with their families.[68]

With his son, Raphael, born in 1818,[69] Jacob might have traveled to nearby Mulhouse to deliver the few products still crafted by Rixheim cottage workers. But the long tradition of rural peddlers acting as vital intermediaries between country and town was moribund. When Jacob and Raphael returned from trips to the city they brought stories of new, steam-powered textile factories and, it seemed, limitless opportunities for merchants with a knowledge of retail trade, for country peddlers like Jacob Dreÿfuss. Perhaps other family members and friends had prospered in Mulhouse and encouraged Jacob to migrate with his wife, Rachel, and their son. In the early 1830s, with Rixheim's economy in transition and with Mulhouse growing rapidly, the family considered leaving the Alsatian village of their ancestors.[70]

In the years leading to that time of decision, anti-Jewish rebellions erupted in the Altkirch region where the Dreÿfuss family lived. To supplement his peddling and retail trade, Jacob had lent money at interest to villagers desperate to purchase land and deprived of any other access to credit. His recorded loans ranged from 140 francs to

---

68. For information on the Dreÿfuss family in Rixheim, see Landser notary, ADHR, 4 E; birth records, ibid., 5 E 416; and *cadastres*, ibid., 3 P 1434. On peddlers and customs, see Raphael and Weyl, *Juifs en Alsace*, pp. 317, 362–63. Dreÿfuss is sometimes given as "Dreyfus" by French officials. Following the family's custom of spelling the name "Dreÿfuss" until the mid-nineteenth century in Mulhouse, I have kept that form in this essay.

69. Birth records, May 12, 1818, ADHR, 5 E 416.

70. On Rixheim's economy during these years, see Laufenburger, *Cours d'économie*, 2:77; and Zuber, *Rixheim*, pp. 11ff.

a day laborer, to 2,300 francs to a village widow, and reflected the regional average. Far better off than many local Jews, Jacob was hardly exceptional. At times of rural crisis, however, Alsatian country people considered most Jewish moneylenders exceptionally appropriate targets, and during the popular uprisings of 1832 men like Jacob Dreÿfuss became the victims of new threats.[71]

With only one son and no need to provide for a daughter's dowry, and with money saved from peddling, moneylending, and rent on small parcels of land in Rixheim, Jacob could now move to the city with his family. Along with hundreds, then thousands of his coreligionists throughout the Alsatian countryside, they left a rural world where Jews had lived and worked for more than a millennium, never to return.

Jacob Dreÿfuss died shortly after settling with his wife and son in Mulhouse.[72] A few years later Raphael married Jeannette Libmann, a seamstress recently arrived in the city from Ribeauvillé.[73] Using lessons learned from his father in the countryside, Raphael opened a small *maison de commission* and worked as an intermediary between textile producers and buyers, a profession not uncommon to the Jews of Mulhouse. By the 1850s Jeannette had left her job and Raphael had saved enough to launch his own cotton mill on the rue Lavoisier near newly constructed *cités ouvrières*.

The family prospered in many ways. Jeannette had nine children, seven of whom survived—four sons and three daughters. If reproductive patterns suggest social mobility, the large family in Mulhouse had improved its lot since previous generations when the poverty and hardships of rural life limited Dreÿfuss families to one or two children. By the end of the century, three sons managed their father's business—Raphael Dreyfus et Cie (the family had dropped the umlaut and second Germanic "s" from the name a few years before)—and made that textile company a major enterprise in Alsace.[74]

Only the youngest son did not pursue his father's trade. After the

---

71. "Inscriptions de créances prises par les juifs . . . 1813–23," ADHR, V 612–13; for Rixheim and "Jacques Dreyfus," see ibid., V 613.

72. *État civil* Mulhouse, May 27, 1838, ibid., 5 E 337.

73. Marriage records, April 18, 1841, ibid.

74. For the family in Mulhouse, see *recensements*, ADHR, 6 M 142, 170, 202; on the *maison de commission*, see *Histoire documentaire de l'industrie*, pp. 951ff.; and on the Dreyfus industry, see Mulhouse civil engineer's report, ADHR, 5 M 78, and *Histoire documentaire de l'industrie*, 1:498.

Franco-Prussian War he moved with his oldest sister to her husband's home in Carpentras, a southern French town with a large and ancient Jewish community, and then on to Paris. There, in 1878, he entered the Ecole Polytechnique and the officer corps of the French army. Grandson of Jacob and Rachel, Alfred Dreyfus aimed to fulfill his obligations to the Revolution and emancipation.[75]

III

At the time of Captain Dreyfus's arrest in 1894, the Jewish population of Paris approached fifty thousand, more than half the Jews of France and one hundred times the number that had resided in the capital on the eve of the Revolution. Across the nineteenth century most had migrated from Alsace. In his masterful study of the politics of assimilation, Michael R. Marrus confirms that "the Alsatian element of the Paris Jewish population was clearly predominant" by the end of the century.[76] Overwhelmingly rural two generations before, the majority had lived in small communities in the eastern provinces in an environment that Claude Vigée later described as doubly marginal: "To be born both Jewish and Alsatian," he wrote, "is to feel oneself doubly Jewish"[77]—twice removed from the dominant Christian and Paris-centered culture of France. Migration from Alsace to the interior, to Paris and beyond, was a crucial stage in the process of assimilation. But no less important was the first migration of Jews from the countryside to the cities within their native region, from villages like Rixheim to provincial centers like Mulhouse.

Emancipation decrees struck down Old Regime restrictions on mobility, landowning, and more, and prepared the way for exodus. But the abstractions of citizenship and equality, the political and legal victories of emancipation, did not lead to concrete benefits for most Jews until urbanization and the growth and concentration of industry provided new opportunities in the decades following the Napoleonic Wars. "Triumph over degrading misery," write two historians of Alsace, was achieved when Jews exercised the rights of-

75. For information on Alfred Dreyfus before the Affair, see H. Villemar, *Dreyfus Intime* (Paris, 1898), pp. 7–16; Jean Denis Bredin, *L'Affaire* (Paris, 1983), pp. 19–46; and my forthcoming history of five generations of the Dreyfus family.

76. Marrus, *Politics of Assimilation*, p. 2; on the Paris Jewish population, see p. 31.

77. Quoted in Raphael and Weyl, *Juifs en Alsace*, p. 424.

fered by emancipation and left the countryside for the city.[78] Like
their Christian countrymen, they left declining rural trades in search
of new jobs and a better life. Unlike Gentiles in Alsace, however, Jews
confronted other immediate issues that figured in their strategies of
escape.

When Napoleon attempted to secure stability in the eastern provinces and finalize the assimilation of Alsatian Jews into the French
nation, he issued edicts that institutionalized the separation of those
Jews for a decade and gave state support to provincial traditions of
prejudice. Local observers and officials in Alsace, products of their
provincial culture, supported the emperor's restrictions on Jewish
commerce and mobility while questioning the wisdom of Parisian
edicts that aimed to make Frenchmen of Jews. Many of those observers shared the popular belief that Jews still existed as a nation
within a nation, a community apart, and that their assimilation
would be not only difficult but dangerous. For decades following
emancipation, Parisian policies could not eradicate provincial habits of intolerance shaped over centuries by religious fervor and secular customs of distrust.[79]

To escape the consequences of those customs, many Jews in southern Alsace chose the cities of the region as havens of opportunity and
protection. In the sixteenth century one of those cities, Mulhouse,
had supported Protestant victims of the Saint Bartholomew's Day
Massacre; in the nineteenth century it accepted migrants from the
hinterlands where country people were reportedly in the mood for a
modern "Saint Bartholomew's Day," this time "for the Jews." Mulhouse offered economic opportunity and a tradition of tolerance at a
time when Alsatian Jews needed both.

Across centuries of Jewish historical experience hostile environments had encouraged the separation and isolation of Jewish communities. Survival depended on their cohesion and unity. This is not
to say that Jewish communities within villages and towns were
"mere creations of antisemitism";[80] self-definition was more complex

---

78. Ibid., p. 417.
79. For comments by observers in Alsace, see mayor's report, June 2, 1806, ADHR,
V 593; report dated May 30, 1806, ibid., V 611; and the undated report [1823?] in which
one official questions whether "on doit inconsidérément leur [Jews] conserver le droit
de citoyen qui leur a été inconsidérément accordé par suite d'une effervescence funeste
et d'une belle théorie politique soi-disant philanthropique." Ibid.
80. See Hannah Arendt's comments on this question, and her response to Jean-Paul
Sartre, in her *The Origins of Totalitarianism*, new ed. with added prefaces (New York,

than that. But those localities did serve as rural areas of refuge for thousands of Jews escaping persecution throughout Europe since the Middle Ages, and to a great extent they remained unchanged until the early nineteenth century. Then, decades after emancipation, renewed violence hastened the dissolution of ancient Jewish traditions by encouraging migration out of ancestral villages to cities and industrial centers. Hostilities that in the past had solidified communities now led to their dispersion and assimilation. It was not the only paradox of the postemancipation era in France.

The sacred story of an earlier exodus describes a dramatic flight from bondage toward freedom. Similarly, accounts of Jewish exodus in modern France describe the bondage of the Old Regime and the freedom of 1791. When, on the centennial of the Revolution, a French rabbi called it "our flight from Egypt . . . our modern Passover,"[81] he captured both the sincere homage that Jews paid to the epoch of emancipation and the collective amnesia with which they suppressed memories of those troubled, often terrifying years. Over generations, the half-life of collective memory preserved the promise, and erased the punishment, that followed emancipation.

1973), p. xv. See also Rabbi Zadoc Kahn's remarks on communities of suffering in Marrus, *Politics of Assimilation*, p. 28.
    81. Quoted in Marrus, *Politics of Assimilation*, p. 91; and on p. 96 see Theodore Reinach's remark, "Every Jew today having heart and memory . . . is a son of the France of 1791." For more on recent interpretations of emancipation and its impact, see *Jews in Modern France*, p. 5.

Jonathan Frankel

Crisis as a Factor in
Modern Jewish Politics, 1840 and 1881–82

The crises created by acts of Judeophobic, antisemitic aggression played a crucial role in the history of the Jewish people during the nineteenth century. A direct challenge to the security of the Jews in one country or another could not go unanswered, especially when, as was so often the case, it came in times of peace and relative tranquillity. The Jews had to respond in some way. But how to interpret the challenge, how best to react, were questions of the highest complexity; and the answers varied radically according to time and place.

After all, so long as they lived their lives in the Diaspora, scattered and essentially landless minorities, the Jews as a collectivity did not have to face the tests regularly imposed on sovereign nations by war or revolution. Of course, such all-engulfing eruptions caught up Jews and Jewish communities, often with far-reaching results, but only as parts within a greater whole. In contrast, events such as the Damascus blood libel of 1840, the Mortara case of 1858, the recurring anti-Jewish excesses in Rumania during the 1870s, the pogroms of 1881–82, the expulsion from Moscow ten years later, and the Dreyfus Affair involved the Jews, first and foremost, precisely as Jews, as a collective entity. It is this fact that lends these episodes their unique importance for the historian of modern Jewry. In studying them, he may hope to find his way to realities, forces, that in normal times remained hidden far beneath the surface of everyday existence. In this sense these crises in Jewish life were the nearest equivalent to war and revolution in the history of a state, a sovereign society. At such a juncture, every assumption, however time honored, may be called into question, and ideas, normally too utopian to voice, can enter the discourse of the everyday. This is the extraordinary moment in the onward flow of time.

Crisis brought a number of interconnected issues into play. To what extent did the Jews act in accord with a sense of solidarity? How far did this impulse embrace Jewry across international frontiers—across Europe? throughout the world? Had not acculturation, assimilation, allegiance to the host society, nation, nationalism undermined, in part or *in toto*, supraterritorial loyalties? With Judaism and Jewry under the most intense scrutiny, what positions were adopted by the public at large, by the various strata that in every country made up the majority society? And how, in turn, did these reactions influence the response of the Jews? Above all, was that response effective? And did it bring with it any lasting change in attitudes or institutions?

I

Of all such episodes in the nineteenth century, by far the most significant was surely that involving the pogroms and the reaction to them in the years 1881–82. There are strong grounds for seeing here a decisive turning point. From then on can be dated the gradual but unbroken emergence of the new movements that, in constant rivalry and interaction, would transform the structure and content of Jewish politics—Jewish (Yiddish-speaking) socialism and populism, proto-Zionism (Hibbat Zion), and territorialism. On one side of the divide, according to this historiographical perception, was the era in which the Jews of Europe expected emancipation and worked for integration into the host societies; while, on the other stretched the era in which the goal was increasingly proclaimed to be auto-emancipation, collective liberation, national self-determination.

Given that this thesis, however schematic and one-dimensional, is essentially correct (and there seems to be no adequate reason to doubt that it is), there still remain a number of related and fundamental questions facing the historian. In particular, it has to be asked in what relationship Jewish nationalism and socialism, increasingly important after 1881–82, stood to the politics that had previously predominated—to the "emancipationist" system on the one hand, and to the "traditional" on the other.[1]

1. For some recent essays on Jewish political traditions, see Daniel Elazar, ed., *Kinship and Consent: The Jewish Political Tradition and Its Contemporary Uses* (Washington,

II

There are, of course, highly complex and emotive issues involved here. Indeed, to take just one important example, a reader turning for enlightenment on this subject to such a *locus classicus* as the essays (*Be-mifneh ha-dorot*) by the late Ben Zion Dinur will find it difficult, although perhaps not impossible, to reconcile the various strands of thought to be found there. Dinur saw the primary theme in modern Jewish history as the constant struggle within the collective organism between integrative and disintegrative, centripetal and centrifugal forces. Very much in the manner of Perez Smolenskin and Ahad Ha-Am, he described Westernization in Jewish life, the Berlin Haskalah, and the process of integration into the host societies during the nineteenth century in terms of self-denigration and, indeed, self-destruction.[2]

In the context of this struggle, Dinur discerned a number of disparate forces that nonetheless supplied Jewry with the vitality to survive. Most notably, he traced a new determination to resettle the Holy Land back to the late seventeenth century and saw there the beginnings of an unbroken process that would culminate eventually in Hibbat Zion and Herzlian Zionism. He dated the start of the modern period in Jewish history not from Baruch Spinoza or the Haskalah or the French Revolution but from about 1700, particularly from the *aliyah* in that year of Yehuda He-Hasid and his followers. Dinur discovered the modernity in this group of ultraobservant and, to all appearances, highly traditional Jews in their readiness to undertake the large-scale move to the Holy Land even before the coming of the Messiah.[3] In sum, he stressed the high degree of continuity that in his view fused the nationalism of post–1881–82 with the rabbinic, self-enclosed but nonetheless (as he saw it) modern world of piety.

To round out the picture, Dinur could simply have emphasized those facts that illustrated the ever-growing inroads made by assimilation and disintegration in Western Jewry. But he was far too sensitive a historian to do that. And he duly noted the Jewish solidarity

D.C., 1983). I am grateful to Eli Lederhendler, who has allowed me to read his work in progress: "From Autonomy to Autoemancipation: Russian Jewish Political Development in the 19th Century and Its Roots in the Public Life of Traditional Communities," a Ph.D. dissertation to be submitted to the Jewish Theological Seminary of America.

2. Ben Zion Dinur, *Be-mifneh ha-dorot: Mehkarim ve-iyunim be-reshitam shel ha-zmanim he-hadashim be-toldot Israel* (Jerusalem, 1972), pp. 9–18.

3. Ibid., pp. 26–29.

that manifested itself in such affairs as the Damascus case, the proliferation of the new and extensive Jewish press, and the establishment of such organizations as the Alliance Israélite Universelle.[4] What remains unclarified is how these examples of communal vitality in the West could be explained. Were they merely the exception that proves the rule, or perhaps a reassertion of the collective subconscious still fed subterraneously from the sources of age-old tradition, or, again, a premonition of later nationalism? Had Dinur pursued this line of questioning further he might have modified his tendency to describe modernization and Haskalah as simply standing in direct negation to the forces of collective survival, to the continuum made up of traditional Judaism and Jewish nationalism.

As against Dinur's approach, it will be argued here that, in fact, the historian is best served by first conceptualizing the three categories under discussion—the traditional, the liberal or emancipationist, the postliberal or autoemancipationist—as strictly separate categories. Once they are initially held separate, as it were, the attempt can be made to trace the ways in which they interacted. Rather than Dinur's dichotomous analysis, the basic framework, then, becomes triadic, and the primary process, rather than linear, becomes dialectic—with a thesis (the traditional), an antithesis (emancipationism), and a synthesis (autoemancipationism).

But that can only be a beginning. To go a step further with Hegelian terminology, one stage is not only negated by the next but is also subsumed within it. A discontinuity, however sharp, can still encompass a high degree of continuity. Moreover, beyond this, it has to be remembered that the Jewish people during the nineteenth century increasingly took on the forms of voluntary association as the communities lost much of their autonomous (state-backed) power. Emergent movements, however popular or confident, did not have the means to crush or eliminate preexisting institutions and ways of thought. The old continued to exist side by side with the intermediate and the new. Internal revolution within the Jewish collectivity involved no bloodshed, no expropriation, not even in most cases any clear transfer of power, but rather the proliferation of rival power centers, movements, and ideologies. Such revolution is, indeed, very much more a historiographical construct than a clearly defined historical event.

4. Ibid., pp. 36–46.

III

Crises such as those of 1881–82 and 1840 indeed cannot be fully understood except in terms of constant interaction among the highly disparate, often hostile, forces at work within, and on the periphery of, the Jewish world. True, in the period from April 1881 until the summer of 1882, the most conspicuous development was the emergence, almost overnight, of a politics radical in thought and action, in content and style, within the Russian-Jewish world. A new phenomenon with the most far-reaching consequences, autoemancipationism has naturally riveted attention on itself.[5] The emigrationist ideas, whether centered on a territory in North America or on Palestine, were, of course, not entirely new; but the widespread support now given them, in the wake of the pogroms, undoubtedly was. So, too, was the startling analysis of M. L. Lilienblum in his article of October 1881 in *Razsvet* (Dawn), where he argued that the high point of European liberalism had been passed and that the rising waves of extreme nationalism were bound, eventually, to make life simply untenable for an awkward minority such as the Jews.[6]

In the name of *Palestinstvo* (a proto-Zionism) and *Amerikanstvo* (a proto-territorialism), the intelligentsia challenged the political leadership of the St. Petersburg oligarchy (the Gintsburgs, the Poliakovs) and the spiritual leadership of the inward-looking rabbinical circles. It sought to assume these roles for itself.[7] To mobilize public opinion, poets, writers, journalists, and students made remarkably effective, unprecedented use of the Jewish press, both in Hebrew and in Russian, as well as of mass petitions and synagogue demonstrations.[8]

The founding of the agricultural colonization parties or youth

5. On the crisis of 1881–82, see, for example, Samuel Leib Zitron, *Toldot Hibat Zion*, vol. 1: *Me-reshit yeme ha-tnuah ad she-nitasher vaad Hoveve-Zion be-Odesah* (Odessa, 1914); Yisrael Klausner, *Be-hitorer am: Ha-aliyah ha-rishonah me-Rusyah* (Jerusalem, 1962); David Vital, *The Origins of Zionism* (Oxford, 1975); Shmuel Yavnieli, ed., *Sefer ha-Zionut*, vol. 2: *Tkufat Hibat Zion* (Tel Aviv, 1942).

6. M. L. Lilienblum, "Obshcheevreiskii vopros i Palestina," *Razsvet*, nos. 41–42 (October 1881): 1598–1600, 1638–41.

7. For a broader survey of this development, see Jonathan Frankel, *Prophecy and Politics: Socialism, Nationalism and the Russian Jews, 1862–1917* (Cambridge, 1981), pp. 57–64, 74–90.

8. See, e.g., Yehuda Slutsky, *Ha-itonut ha-yehudit-rusit ba-meah ha-tsha-esreh* (Jerusalem, 1970), pp. 121–41; M. Ben Hillel Ha-Cohen, *Olami*, vol. 1 (Jerusalem, 1927), pp. 164–66.

movements—Am Olam and the Bilu[9]—did more than anything else to demonstrate the intense atmosphere of the times and the depth of the commitment. The dramatic departure of many hundreds of young men and women determined to lay the foundations of a Jewish territory in the American West or in Palestine made a deep impression on Russian Jewry. Although the emigrants' grandiose schemes soon shattered on the rocks of harsh reality, the change in the nature of Russian-Jewish politics was to prove both permanent and profound.[10]

What took place in 1881–82, however, cannot be adequately described in these terms alone, even though the radically innovative developments surely represent the most important theme. The truth is that strands drawn from the traditional, premodern strata of Russian Jewry were thickly interwoven into the fabric of events at this juncture. The most obvious example, perhaps, is the fact that the great majority of the Jews who went to settle the land in Palestine in the early 1880s were fully observant Jews, many from Rumania, eager to maintain the ordinances as laid down by rabbinic law and, it would seem, moved to become colonists as the result of religious impulse. Of course, this does not mean that they would have contemplated so drastic and dangerous a move if the Jewish people in Eastern Europe had not been put into a state of extreme turmoil by the emigration debate. They were moved by the great expectations then current, but how far their motives were political rather than religious, even perhaps messianically inspired, remains very much an open question. Of all the many colonies then founded, only Gederah and, to some extent, Rishon le-Zion were recognizably the work of the radical intelligentsia.[11]

Hardly less striking was the role played in key political ventures and innovations by a number of famous rabbis. The Hasidic move-

9. On Am Olam, see Avrom Menes, "The Am Oylom Movement," *YIVO Annual of Jewish Social Science* 4 (1949): 9–33; and Hasiyah Turtel, "Tnuat 'Am Olam,'" *Heavar* 10 (1963): 124–43. On the Bilu, see Shulamit Laskov, *Ha-Biluim* (Tel Aviv, 1979).

10. For an analysis of the part played by members (later ex-members) of the Am Olam in America, see Ezra Mendelsohn, "The Russian Roots of the American Jewish Labor Movement," *YIVO Annual of Jewish Social Science* 16 (1976): 150–77.

11. On the development of the First Aliyah, see Mordechai Eliav and Yemima Rosenthal, *Sefer ha-aliyah ha-rishonah* (Jerusalem, 1981); and Yehoshua Kaniel, *Hemshekh u-tmurah: Ha-yishuv ha-yashan ve-ha-yishuv he-hadash bi-tkufat ha-aliyah ha-rishonah ve-ha-shniyah* (Jerusalem, 1981).

ment, it is true, remained aloof, seeking to preserve its own way of life untouched by anything that smacked of secularism or modernization. (Only with the establishment of Agudat Israel in 1912 did the Hasidim adopt modern organizational means to attain that same ultraconservative end.) But among the Lithuanian Mitnagdim, the situation was different. There, cooperation with nonobservant or radical or even anticlerical Jews was not always automatically excluded. Thus, Rabbi Yitzhak Elkhanan Spektor of Kovno, aided by his assistant Yaakov Halevi Lifshits, worked together with such prominent *maskilim* as the poet Yehuda Leb Levin to ensure that detailed reports of the pogroms reached the Jews in the West. The two highly influential articles published on the subject in the *Times* of London in January 1882 were based on material smuggled out of Russia disguised as a rabbinical legal opinion printed in Hebrew.[12]

During the 1880s Spektor was among those rabbis who identified themselves with the emergent Hibbat Zion movement even though its most prominent leaders, such as Lilienblum and Lev Pinsker, were *maskilim* by origin and still, in large degree, by outlook. Numered among these rabbis, too, were Naftali Zvi Berlin (head of the Volozhin Yeshivah), Mordekhay Eliasberg, and, of course, Shmuel Mohilever, who played a central role in the movement.

The nationalist intelligentsia and the more open strata within the traditional world strongly influenced each other.[13] The enormous stir caused by the youth triggered off highly emotional reactions in wide circles where the Exodus from Egypt, the River Sambation, the Ten Lost Tribes, and the Mountains of Darkness were very much part of a real world still saturated with messianic expectations.[14] A mass following—a *narod*—was thus there ready at hand for the new claimants to leadership. But there was a price to be paid. Many of the *maskilim*, now full-fledged nationalists, had come out initially in favor of a territory in the New World where the Jews, in their view, would best be able to build a modern and liberal society free from theocratic or theological aspirations and clerical interference. But men such as Yehuda Leb Levin, Lev Levanda, Ludwig Zamenhof,

12. On this episode, see Yaakov Halevi Lifshits, *Zikhron Yaakov* (Frankfurt a.M., 1924), 3:20–89.

13. For a valuable insight into this interaction, see the massive correspondence reproduced in A. A. Drouyanov, ed., *Ktavim le-toldot Hibat Zion ve-yishuv Eretz Israel* (Odessa, 1919; Tel Aviv, 1932).

14. See, e.g., Shmarya Levin, *Youth in Revolt* (London, 1939), pp. 30–35.

and Lev Pinsker soon went over to the pro-Palestine camp, yielding to the power of a popular sentiment.

However, a three-dimensional analysis of 1881–82 cannot ignore the decisive impact made likewise by the intervention and the image of Western Jewry. The great debate on organized emigration—its necessity, advisability, and destination—was sparked off in large part in the summer of 1881 by rumors of a decision supposedly taken by the Alliance Israélite Universelle to pay the passage of Russian Jews to America. This rumor contained only a small kernel of truth; the Alliance was thinking in terms of a strictly limited project.[15] Yet so great was the belief in the almost unlimited influence and power of the Jewish plutocracy in the West that the realities of the situation made little difference. The Russian-Jewish intelligentsia and, even more perhaps, the masses were convinced that, in the last resort, they could count on Western Jewry to underwrite their plans and projects.

Furthermore, in this relationship, too, the actions of each group fed those of the other. The Alliance was, in fact, stampeded by the massive flow of refugees across the frontier into paying for far more Jews to cross the Atlantic than it had planned. This action served to fuel the expectations of Russian Jewry still more. And hope was further stimulated, later in 1881, by the news that the Hebrew Emigrant Aid Society had been founded in New York and that Baron Maurice de Hirsch had apparently offered a million francs to advance Jewish agricultural settlement overseas.[16]

In turn, the reports smuggled out by Rabbi Yitzhak Elkhanan Spektor and his group, once published in the *Times,* helped produce a major movement of public protest in England early in 1882. Its high point was the meeting at the Mansion House, presided over by the Lord Mayor of London and addressed by, *inter alia,* Cardinal Henry Edward Manning and the earl of Shaftesbury, that resulted in the collection of large sums of money for aid to Russian Jewry.[17] Thus the pattern of 1881 was largely repeated in the spring of 1882. Once again, hopes of a grandiose emigration scheme soared; new

15. On the initial plans of the Alliance in the summer of 1881, see Alliance Israélite Universelle, *Bulletin mensuel,* no. 10 (October 1881): 161; *American Hebrew,* September 8, 1881, p. 33; *Jewish Chronicle,* October 7, 1881, p. 7.

16. *Jewish Chronicle,* October 7, 1881, p. 7.

17. "The Mansion House Meeting," *Jewish Chronicle,* February 3, 1882, pp. 1–4, and February 17, 1882, p. 3.

parties and movements were founded; and the representatives of Anglo-Jewry found themselves arranging the transport and passage of thousands of Russian Jews, including the main Am Olam groups, to the United States.

Amid all this unprecedented flurry of activity, one episode perhaps stands out as exceptionally revealing. Among the emissaries chosen by the chief rabbi, Samuel Montagu, and other members of the Mansion House Committee, was Laurence Oliphant, an English gentleman and eccentric who, like so many Victorian men of letters, was chronically attracted to bizarre social experiments in utopian living, communalism, and free love. Oliphant came from an intensely evangelical family, and in 1880 he had published a detailed book that laid forth plans for the restoration of the Jews to Palestine.[18] His presence in Brody as an emissary of the Mansion House Committee, and later in Constantinople, was followed with intense interest by the Jews in Russia. It was confidently predicted that he would gain the Holy Land for the Jews by diplomatic means or even by personal purchase. Messianic longings were drawn to him as though to a magnet, and his mere presence at the center of the stage helped sustain the confidence of the Bilu and other such groups into the summer of 1882.

Myths, focused primarily on Western Jewry—but also as in this case on Christians—played a crucial role in the formation of the new Jewish politics. Yet, like prophecies, myths are often self-fulfilling. A number of the leading Jewish bankers were now inspired to devote large sums to Jewish colonization and agrarian efforts. Jacob Schiff financed settlements in America on a modest scale; Maurice de Hirsch would soon undertake his massive colonization effort in South America; Baron Edmund de Rothschild was induced, following meetings with Rabbi Shmuel Mohilever and with Yosef Feinberg from Rishon le-Zion, to underwrite the new colonies in Palestine. Without his support, they would have collapsed.[19] Thus, the nationalist movement was sustained not only by the radically new but, in essential ways, by forces drawn from both the traditional and the Western subworlds within Jewry.

18. Laurence Oliphant, *Land of Gilead, With Excursions in the Lebanon* (Edinburgh, 1880).

19. See, for example, Dan Giladi, "Ha-baron, ha-pkidut ve-ha-moshavot ha-rishonot be-Eretz Israel: Haarakhah me-hadash," *Cathedra* 2 (1976): 59–68; and Simon Schama, *Two Rothschilds and the Land of Israel* (New York, 1978).

IV

While the crisis of 1881–82 has been the subject of intense historiographical interest almost throughout the twentieth century,[20] the
Damascus case has attracted comparatively little close attention.
The one overall account that goes into considerable detail remains
Heinrich Graetz's very impressive chapter in his *History of the Jews*
written more than one hundred years ago, although it should, perhaps, be added that J. M. Jost also gave considerable attention to the
case.[21] A number of specialized articles illuminate limited aspects of
the affair without making any attempt to discuss its overall significance;[22] and it is not assigned much space in the general histories.

Up to a point, this neglect by historians is justified. The Damascus
case was surely more a landmark than a crossroads; it cannot compare in importance with the crisis in Russia some forty years later.
Yet, when all is said and done, the events of 1840 absorbed the attention of world Jewry and riveted non-Jewish interest upon the Jews in
ways probably without example between 1815 and the 1870s or
1880s. The space assigned to the case by Graetz and Jost reflected
contemporary opinion. And the subsequent decline in interest has,
surely, to be explained in part by the fact that modern Jewish history
has increasingly been written in the twentieth century from the nationalist vantage point.

The degree of solidarity displayed by the organized Jewish communities in France, England, the United States, and, in more passive

20. Suffice it to mention Drouyanov, Zitron, Yavnieli, Breiman, and Klausner. See,
in addition to the works listed in nn. 5 and 13, Shlomo Breiman, "Ha-mifneh ba-
mahshavah ha-ziburit ha-yehudit be-reshit shnot ha-shmonim," *Shivat Zion* 2–3 (1951–
52): 83–227.

21. Heinrich Graetz, *Geschichte der Juden*, vol. 11 (Leipzig, 1900), pp. 464–500, published in English as *History of the Jews* (Philadelphia, 1895; reprint, 1956) 6:632–66;
J. M. Jost, *Neuere Geschichte der Israeliten von 1815 bis 1845*, vol. 2 (Berlin, 1847), pp.
345–84, vol. 10, pt. 2 of Jost's *Geschichte der Israeliten seit der Zeit der Maccabäer bis
auf unsere Tage*.

22. Albert M. Hyamson, "The Damascus Affair, 1840," *Transactions of the Jewish Historical Society of England* 16 (1952): 47–71; N. M. Gelber, "Österreich und die Damas-
kusaffaire im Jahre 1840," *Jahrbuch der Jüdisch-Literarischen Gesellschaft* 18 (1927):
217–64; S. W. Baron, "Abraham Benisch's Project for Jewish Colonization in Palestine
(1842)," in *Jewish Studies in Memory of George A. Kohut*, ed. S. W. Baron and Alexander
Marx (New York, 1935), pp. 72–85. See also three new studies: U. R. Q. Henriques,
"Who Killed Father Thomas?" in *Sir Moses Montefiore: A Symposium*, ed. V. D. Lipman
(Oxford, 1982), pp. 50–75; Tudor Parfitt, "'The Year of the Pride of Israel': Montefiore
and the Blood Libel of 1840," in *The Century of Moses Montefiore*, ed. S. L. and V. D.
Lipman (Oxford, 1985), pp. 131–48; Jane S. Gerber, "The Damascus Blood Libel—Jew-

ways, in Germany, and the forces that they mobilized on behalf of
their brethren in Damascus and Rhodes do not easily fit into accounts that (like Dinur's) place the greatest emphasis on the assimilation and communal decline of Western Jewry. Thus an untypical
statement by Abraham Geiger has received inordinate attention. In
a private letter not published until 1896, Geiger declared that "for
me it is more important that Jews be able to work in Prussia as
pharmacists or lawyers than that the entire Jewish population of
Asia and Africa be saved, although as a human being I sympathize
with them."[23] There is a tendency to portray the action of the Jews
in 1840 either as a throwback to traditional norms (Moses Montefiore, for example, being described as the last in the line of *shtadlanim*)[24] or else as a reaction against the prevailing norm. As S. M.
Dubnov put it, the case brought with it a reassertion of

> Jewish self-consciousness at a time when West European Jewry had
> yielded to the charms of assimilation and disintegrated and split up into
> groups of Frenchmen, Englishmen, Germans of the Mosaic faith. . . . [It]
> was the beginning of later attempts to consolidate Jewry at first for phil-
> anthropical, cultural and political mutual aid, and later for a national
> ideal.[25]

But here, again, it is surely preferable not to merge the like with
the unlike. The Damascus Affair offered the Jews of the West the
opportunity, in coming to the aid of two distant communities in dire
distress, to march under the standard of a liberalism triumphant.
They were acting, as they saw it, in accord with, not in contradiction
to, the spirit of the times. Even if Judaism were to be defined strictly
in religious terms, stripped of national connotations—and very
many Jews were in fact reluctant to make so clear a distinction—its
adherents could still recognize a duty to assist their "co-religionists"
endangered by arbitrary tyranny and barbarism. Indeed, the Damascus case is precisely of interest as the first full-scale example
within the Jewish world of the emancipationist style of politics.

---

ish Perceptions and Responses," in *Proceedings of the Eighth World Congress of Jewish
Studies (Division B)* (Jerusalem, 1982), pp. 105–10.

23. "Abraham Geigers Briefe an J. Derenbourg [November 22, 1840]," *Allgemeine
Zeitung des Judenthums* 60, no. 24 (June 12, 1896): 284.

24. See, e.g., Howard Sachar, *The Course of Modern Jewish History* (New York, 1958),
pp. 133–36.

25. S. M. Dubnov, *Noveishaia istoriia evreiskogo naroda ot frantsuzskoi revoliutsii do
nashikh dnei*, vol. 2 (Riga, 1938), p. 241, published in English as *The History of the Jews*,
vol. 5 (London, 1973), p. 250.

In the campaign, which was launched soon after the news of the blood libels, tortures, and terror in Damascus and Rhodes reached Europe in April 1840, the arguments and the means employed had very little in common with those traditionally associated with the *shtadlan*. Adolphe Crémieux, Moses Montefiore, and the many other Jewish spokesmen chose to take their stand as members of European civilization, equally entitled with all other citizens (even if not fully emancipated in England) to appeal to the rights of man. They chose their methods accordingly. In large part, they acted out in the open, determined, as it was so often put at the time, to win their case before "the court of public opinion." A flow of letters to the editor was maintained. As documents came in from the Middle East, they were translated, distributed to the press, and published. Politicians and ministers were lobbied officially in London, Paris, Washington, and these efforts, too, were made public. It was arranged for questions to be asked in Parliament and in the Chambers of Deputies and Peers; the subsequent exchanges, too, were reported and became cause for comment in the press. On July 3, 1840, a protest meeting was held in the Mansion House, and the Lord Mayor followed it up by sending appeals to the various governments of Europe; again the correspondence was published.[26] Public subscriptions were launched to help finance the mission of Montefiore and Crémieux to the Middle East, and this undertaking in turn was given maximal publicity.[27]

The results of that expedition were also carefully packaged with an eye to effect. In its own terms, it was actually a failure in that it had gone out with the express purpose of arranging a full inquiry and fair trial, which it was unable to do. But Montefiore and Crémieux, making the best use of the firmans issued by Mehemet Ali and the sultan, did all they could—and quite effectively—to present the expedition as a triumphant success.

Of course, it was easier to conduct such a campaign in England, where the government, and especially Lord Palmerston, the foreign secretary, supported the Jewish cause, than in France, where the gov-

26. "Persecution of the Jews in Damascus: Great Meeting at the Mansion House," *Times* (London), July 4, 1840; "The Jews in the East," ibid., July 24, 1840.
27. On the mission, see *Diaries of Sir Moses and Lady Montefiore*, ed. Louis Loewe (London, 1890); and *The Damascus Affair: Diary of Louis Loewe, July–November, 1840* (Ramsgate, 1940).

ernment of Adolphe Thiers, hostile and embarrassed by the case, sought to keep it out of the public eye.[28] That Crémieux, with the backing of the Consistoire Central, was ready to persist in the cause, even in defiance of his own government, demonstrates how little there was here of traditional *shtadlanut*. Crémieux—a brilliant advocate, vice-president of the Consistoire, well known for his persistent opposition to the use of the *more Judaico* (Jewish oath), a dedicated liberal who was named minister of justice after the February Revolution—was ready to defy Thiers in the name of French values, as he understood them.[29] Rather like Gabriel Riesser, who a few years before had brought out his journal *Der Jude* as a blow on behalf of a liberal Germany, Crémieux saw Jewish solidarity in the right cause as the highest expression of French patriotism.[30]

This argument is by no means meant to imply that the Western Jewish leaders were acting solely out of motives of abstract ideology or pure altruism. On the contrary, they themselves were often ready to admit that the accusations leveled against the Jewish communities of Damascus and Rhodes, if only because they were so widely credited in Europe, constituted a direct threat to their own interests and security.[31] As they saw it, the struggle of enlightened reason against medieval reaction and Judeophobia, which they tended, overschematically, to identify in large measure with forces within the Roman Catholic church, was one and indivisible.

Still, the story of the Jews in 1840, like that of 1881–82, incorporated not only a major but also minor themes. The principal actors may not have acted as *shtadlanim*, but it is well to remember how close many in that generation of Western Jewry were to a traditional way of life. A decisive role in the Damascus Affair was played by the Rothschild family, whose connections with the European governments in London, Paris, Naples, and, above all perhaps, Vienna were invaluable. Without its moral and financial backing, provided largely but not always behind the scenes, the campaign could never

---

28. See the official statements by Adolphe Thiers, "Chambre des Deputés," *Journal des Debats*, June 3, 1840, and "Chambre des Pairs," ibid., July 11, 1840.

29. See Solomon Posener, *Adolphe Crémieux: A Biography* (Philadelphia, 1940).

30. See, for example, Moshe Rinott, "Gabriel Riesser: Fighter for Jewish Emancipation," *Leo Baeck Institute Year Book* 7 (1962): 11–38.

31. See, e.g., the speech of Bernard Van Oven at the meeting in the Great Synagogue on June 23, 1840: "We must put an end to the persecution in Asia, and if possible punish the persecutors, lest their success should encourage similar attempts nearer home, where there is enough, and more than enough, to stimulate bigotry and to tempt avarice." *Morning Herald* (London), June 25, 1840.

have won such broad support or achieved such success. Indeed, the fact that Montefiore was a close relative made it something of a family affair.

But at that time the Rothschilds almost literally were still only one step out of the ghetto. Anselm, of course, was still in the family home in the Jewish quarter of Frankfurt am Main and strictly observant. Solomon, in Vienna, although enjoying the title of baron, usually lived in a hotel because Jews were denied the right of permanent residence within the city. James, in Paris, disowned his niece in London when in 1840 she entered into the first mixed marriage in family history. Much of the correspondence, including that of its younger members, was still conducted in Yiddish, replete with Hebraisms.[32] It is thus hardly surprising that their almost instinctive reaction to the Damascus Affair was little different from that which would have been expected of such Jews so exalted by wealth throughout the centuries. And, indeed, the same can be said of the community leaders in Constantinople and Alexandria, who responded at once to the calls for help and were able to achieve much for the hapless victims in Damascus and Rhodes long before intervention from Europe could make itself felt.

Again, in 1840 as in 1881–82, messianic expectations and impulses of the most varied kind came into play. First, there was the fact—pure coincidence, it would seem—that 5600 in the Jewish calendar (corresponding to 1839–40) had been awaited for decades by many rabbinic and kabbalistic authorities as the year of the messianic coming. Were the tragic events in Damascus and Rhodes, then, a sign of the times, or birthpangs?[33]

What the Jews, especially the most orthodox and observant, did and thought was, in turn, closely followed by the English Christian missionaries, particularly by the London Society for the Promotion of Christianity among the Jews, which had dozens of posts scattered across Europe and the Middle East. In these circles, too, millenarian

32. Two recent additions to the large number of historical works on the Rothschild family are Anka Muhlstein, *Baron James: The Rise of the French Rothschilds* (New York, 1982); and R. W. Davis, *The English Rothschilds* (Chapel Hill, N.C., 1983). I wish to take this opportunity to thank N. M. Rothschild and Sons, London, for kindly permitting me to consult the archive of the bank, and Mrs. Yvonne Moss, the archivist, for her great help in locating much relevant material.

33. On the year 5600 as a messianic year, see A. G. Duker, "The Tarniks," in *The Joshua Starr Memorial Volume* (New York, 1953), pp. 191–202; and Aryeh Morgenshtern, *Meshihiyut ve-yishuv Eretz Israel ba-mahazit ha-rishonah shel ha-meah ha-19* (Jerusalem, 1985).

hopes flourished and the restoration of the Jews to Palestine was often seen as the necessary prelude to the second advent of Christ. It was hoped that when the Jewish Messiah failed to come in 1840, conversions to Christianity would greatly increase. In March of that year one of the missionaries in Jerusalem, G. W. Pieritz, a convert from Judaism, went specially to Damascus to seek ways of aiding the Jews there, and his written reports published in Europe exerted great influence precisely because he was considered an unbiased source.[34]

Intervention by millenarian societies and leaders in London with the British government followed two directions. They called for the defense of the Jews in Damascus and Rhodes, here working along the same lines as the Anglo-Jewish community. But they also took the opportunity provided by the Jewish plight and the impending war against Egypt for the control of greater Syria (including Palestine) to urge restorationist policies on the British government. As Anthony Ashley Cooper, soon to become the seventh earl of Shaftesbury, was not only the most prominent evangelical advocate of the Jewish restoration to Palestine but also Palmerston's stepson-in-law, such proposals were not dismissed out of hand.[35] On the contrary, in a well-known dispatch of August 1840 to the British ambassador to the Porte, Palmerston suggested that the Turkish government should be encouraged to promote large-scale Jewish settlement in Palestine.

> There exists at present among the Jews dispersed over Europe a strong notion that the Time is approaching when their nation is to return to Palestine; and . . . their thoughts have been bent more upon the means of realizing that wish. . . . It would be of manifest importance to the Sultan to encourage the Jews to return to, and to settle in, Palestine: because the wealth which they would bring with them would increase the resources of the Sultan's Dominions.[36]

Given the fact that the vast majority of European Jews were then living either closed within the premodern world of Eastern Europe or had set their sights firmly on equal citizenship and integration,

---

34. See "Extract of Letters from Mr. Pieritz, a Christian Missionary Living at Jerusalem, to the Jews at Alexandria," *Times* (London), July 6, 1840, supp.; and a further report from Pieritz, ibid., August 13, 1840.

35. See Edwin Hodder, *The Life and Work of the Seventh Earl of Shaftesbury, K.G.* (London, 1887); and the diary of Lord Ashley deposited at the Royal Commission on Historical Manuscripts, Chancery Lane, London.

36. Quoted in Albert M. Hyamson, *The British Consulate in Jerusalem in Relation to the Jews of Palestine, 1838–1914*, vol. 1 (London, 1939), pp. 33–34.

they could hardly be expected, in the main, to welcome the many projects of this nature then being mooted and publicized in England.[37] Most Jews simply ignored them. Some rejected them in anger, as did Ludwig Philippson, for example.[38] But there were also those who welcomed them with great excitement. A man like Yehuda Alkalai, still thinking largely in kabbalistic terms, saw in them a sign of the oncoming messianic age.[39]

More remarkable was the reaction of significant groups within the younger generation of German and Austrian Jewry, particularly the students. Frustrated by the lack of progress toward emancipation, shocked to the marrow by the widespread abuse heaped on the Jews in the German press during the Damascus case, they saw in the Palestine projects a welcome ray of light. It was at this point that Moses Hess wrote his article on the return of the Jews to Palestine, which he then put aside for more than twenty years, only to publish it finally as part of *Rome and Jerusalem*.[40]

The group led by Abraham Benisch, Moritz Steinschneider, and Albert Löwy was, of course, far more determined and resolute. Following meetings with Crémieux and Montefiore, they managed to have a detailed memorandum submitted to the Foreign Office in London through the good offices of W. T. Young, the British vice-consul in Jerusalem.[41] What is more, one of the German-Jewish periodicals, *Der Orient*, edited by Dr. Julius Fürst, published their ideas frequently and at length. Of course nothing concrete could come of such projects at that time; they were clearly premature. Nonethe-

---

37. Two recent books on the nature of Anglo-Jewish society and politics are Todd M. Endelman, *The Jews of Georgian England, 1714–1830: Tradition and Change in a Liberal Society* (Philadelphia, 1979); and M. C. N. Salbstein, *The Emancipation of the Jews in Britain: The Question of the Admission of the Jews to Parliament, 1828–1860* (Rutherford, N.J., 1982).

38. [Ludwig Philippson], "Tages-Controle," *Allgemeine Zeitung des Judenthums* 4, no. 37 (September 12, 1840): 544. Philippson wrote of proto-Zionist plans: "And what would a pitiful [Jewish] Free State be able to create in an empty corner except a trivial questionable existence amidst Muslims and Egyptians? What would a colony of homeless Jews be able to do? It would exist only by the grace of distant Powers . . . without purpose or direction."

39. E.g., Jacob Katz, "The Jewish National Movement: A Sociological Analysis," in his *Emancipation and Assimilation Studies in Modern Jewish History* (Farnborough, England, 1972), pp. 129–45, esp. pp. 133–34.

40. See Moses Hess, *Rom und Jerusalem: Die letzte Nationalitätsfrage* (Leipzig, 1862), pp. 26–28.

41. Baron, "Abraham Benisch's Project," pp. 77–82; Hyamson, *British Consulate in Jerusalem*, 1:41.

less, it is certainly significant that what can only be categorized as autoemancipationist themes were taken up so readily among the German-Jewish intelligentsia of the 1840s—a startling reminder of how often radical ideas that first caught on in the Germany of pre-1848 were to emerge again in the Russia of post-1881.

The Damascus case was by no means the high point of the emancipationist model of Jewish politics. Following the Mortara case of 1858, those politics took on permanent, institutional form with the establishment of the Alliance Israélite Universelle in 1860. Affiliated organizations, the Allianz in Berlin and in Vienna and the Anglo-Jewish Association in London were set up in the following years. As Michael Graetz has demonstrated so convincingly, the Alliance was initially the work of a group of men who had been influenced by theories of radical change and perceived Judaism as essentially a universalist system of social ethics.[42] It was natural enough that Crémieux should have become its president and, likewise, that its differences with the Consistoire and the Rothschilds should have been quickly reconciled. Over the next two decades the Alliance was active in the establishment of modern Jewish schools in the Middle East, a project launched by Crémieux in Egypt in 1840; in diplomacy, particularly its action on behalf of Rumanian Jewry culminating in the settlement at the Congress of Berlin;[43] in Palestine, with the foundation of the Mikveh Israel agricultural school; and in the Russian Empire, with the aid for selected emigrants to the United States in 1869–70.

All these projects were seen as an expression of the liberal, the emancipationist creed of Western Jewry. When 1881–82 came, the leaders of the new Jewish nationalism in Russia turned to the West with quite other expectations. They were to be sorely disappointed—but not entirely.

42. Michael Graetz, *Ha-periferyah haytah le-merkaz: Prakim be-toldot yahadut Zarfat ba-meah ha-19* (Jerusalem, 1982).

43. See, e.g., L. P. Gartner, "Roumania, America and World Jewry: Consul Peixotta in Bucharest 1870–1876," *American Jewish Historical Quarterly* 58 (1968–69): 25–117; and F. R. Stern, *Gold and Iron: Bismarck, Bleichröder and the Building of the German Empire* (New York, 1977).

Todd M. Endelman

Conversion as a Response to Antisemitism in Modern Jewish History

Since the early 1970s the question of Jewish responses to antisemitism has become a central issue in the study of modern Jewish history. As a subject for research and reflection, it has joined that small group of topics that dominate the agenda of Jewish historiography of the modern period—emancipation, Haskalah, religious reform, Zionism, and antisemitism itself. To date, virtually all the work on this topic has centered on organizational, or communal, responses to antisemitism, in particular on the creation of defense agencies such as the American Jewish Committee and the Centralverein deutscher Staatsbürger jüdischen Glaubens and their efforts to combat bigotry and discrimination. By contrast, historians have shown little interest in the impact of antisemitism on ordinary Jews who were not communal leaders. Their reactions, as individuals, have been ignored, or at best tacitly subsumed under their membership in a larger community.[1] Historians have simply assumed that the

I wish to express my gratitude to the National Endowment for the Humanities, the Memorial Foundation for Jewish Culture, the American Jewish Archives, and the Office for Research and Graduate Development, Indiana University, for providing funds that allowed me to undertake this work. I am also grateful to Jack Rakove, Alvin Rosenfeld, and Steven Zipperstein for kindly agreeing to read an earlier draft of this essay and offering me their comments and suggestions.

1. Scholarly neglect of the impact of antisemitism on personal behavior and character is a relatively recent phenomenon. In the 1930s and 1940s there was considerably more interest in the psychological dimension of the Jewish response to antisemitism than in recent decades. See, for example, Theodor Lessing, *Der jüdische Selbsthass* (Berlin, 1930); and Kurt Lewin, "Bringing Up the Jewish Child" and "Self-Hatred among Jews," in *Resolving Social Conflicts: Selected Papers on Group Dynamics*, ed. Gertrud Weiss Lewin (New York, 1948), pp. 169–200. Their work has had little, if any, influence on contemporary historians working on Jewish reactions to antisemitism.

the defense organizations represented their views and acted on their behalf.

This emphasis on Jewish responses at the communal level has not been fortuitous. It is far easier to construct the views and activities of organizations that sought to influence public opinion than to evoke the private concerns of individuals who took no part in communal affairs and preferred to devise their own personal solutions to antisemitism. The former inevitably leave printed and archival records of their work; the latter only infrequently set down in writing their reactions to contemporary events. Historians generally know where to find the records of communal agencies and leaders (assuming they have survived the hazards of war, revolution, and neglect), but they encounter serious obstacles when they seek to discover the sentiments of Jews who shunned involvement in communal matters.

There is, however, a more profound reason for the current preoccupation with communal, rather than personal, responses. Over the past quarter century, controversies surrounding the behavior of Jews during the Holocaust have commanded a central place in Jewish intellectual life. In the wake of the accusation by Hannah Arendt and others that the Jews of Europe cooperated in their own destruction—and the related charge that Western European Jewry responded timidly to the rise of political antisemitism in the half century before Hitler—some historians naturally sought to demonstrate the contrary: that is, that the acculturated Jews of the West acted wisely and honorably when their enemies rose up against them. Where Hannah Arendt saw only the bankruptcy of Diaspora Jewry's political behavior, historians like Ismar Schorsch, Marjorie Lamberti, and Naomi Cohen have found a strong measure of sagacity, courage, and dignity.[2]

One notable exception to the generalization about the present-day lack of interest in the impact of antisemitism on individual character is Peter Gay's "Hermann Levi: A Study in Service and Self-Hatred," which first appeared in the *Times Literary Supplement*, no. 3814 (April 11, 1975): 402–4, and is reprinted in his *Freud, Jews and Other Germans: Masters and Victims in Modernist Culture* (New York, 1978), pp. 189–230.

2. The following are representative of this current in recent Jewish historiography: Ismar Schorsch, *Jewish Reactions to German Anti-Semitism, 1870–1914* (New York, 1972); Schorsch, *On the History of the Political Judgment of the Jew*, Leo Baeck Memorial Lecture 20 (New York, 1977); Marjorie Lamberti, *Jewish Activism in Imperial Germany: The Struggle for Civil Equality* (New Haven, 1978); Lamberti, "Liberals, Socialists and the Defense against Antisemitism in the Wilhelminian Period," *Leo Baeck Institute Year Book* (hereafter *LBIYB*) 25 (1980): 147–62; Naomi W. Cohen, *Not Free to Desist: A History of the American Jewish Committee, 1906–1966* (Philadelphia, 1972).

This reevaluation of Jewish political behavior, however, has had an unfortunate, although unintended, consequence for understanding Jewish responses to antisemitism. By focusing attention on the activism of communal agencies, whose work can be interpreted in a heroic light, it has blunted interest in reactions outside the political arena. It has led historians to ignore the ways in which antisemitism unsettled the lives of ordinary Jews—disrupting their careers, wounding their pride, shattering their dreams—and how they responded to this agitation and discrimination at the personal level. Some of these responses were not heroic, for many Jews chose to flee from their Jewishness when antisemitism threatened to frustrate their careers or undermine their social standing. One of the most radical responses was to abandon the Jewish community altogether and convert to Christianity. Between the French Revolution and World War II, hundreds of thousands of Jews chose to solve the Jewish Question for themselves in this way.[3] They sought to overcome anti-Jewish hostility by ceasing to be Jewish, by embracing the majority faith in the hope of merging with the surrounding population. Indeed, apostasy may have been a more popular response than political activism, at least in Germany and Austria, where the number of converts appears to have been exceptionally large.

Since the mid-eighteenth century apostasy has been a marked feature of Jewish life everywhere in the West, but not equally so at all times and in all places. The flight from Jewishness became more

---

3. It is impossible to be any more precise about the number of Jews in Europe and America who converted to Christianity in the modern period. For Great Britain, France, and the United States, where membership in a religious body was voluntary and an individual's religious affiliation a matter of indifference to the state, there are no statistics on Jewish conversions. Missionary organizations in these countries published figures on the number of souls they had saved, but these statistics are unreliable for two reasons. First, the conversionist societies tended to inflate the number of converts they made, many of whom returned to Judaism once they had received the material benefits offered to them at the time of their baptism. Second, these conversionist groups worked only among the Jewish poor. Thus, the figures they reported do not include cases of apostasy at more respectable levels of Jewish society—which, in fact, were probably more numerous than those at the bottom of the social ladder. In Central Europe, where religious affiliation and civil status were linked, state bureaucracies generally monitored movement from one religion to another. Even in these states, however, there are no complete series of statistics for the period 1815–1939, and, when available, the figures are often defective. For example, in imperial Germany, Jewish children under the age of fourteen who were baptized by their parents were not considered by the state as converts to Christianity. For a brief survey of the quantitative dimensions of apostasy in Central Europe, see Arthur Ruppin, *Ha-sozyologyah shel ha-yehudim*, 2d ed. (Tel Aviv, 1933–35), vol. 1, pt. 2, chap. 17.

intense in certain contexts than in others, to the extent that it is appropriate to speak of waves of apostasy sweeping over the Jews of a particular locale. Most of these surges of apostasy were linked to the rise of political antisemitism in Central Europe after 1870 and to its exploitation by the Right in the years between the two world wars, although, as we shall see, the relationship between persecution and apostasy is not always so straightforward as it might at first appear to be.

The most widely documented renewal of antisemitism in the modern period was that in the newly created German Empire during the final quarter of the nineteenth century. There the character of Jewish integration into state and society was called into question with unprecedented vehemence. Hostility to Jews blocked occupational and social mobility. Criticism of Jews and Judaism was deemed respectable in cultural and political circles, as well as in the university. With the full-blown emergence of the Jewish Question, the temptation to abandon Judaism increased and the number of converts mounted dramatically. In Prussia in the mid-1870s, about fifty Jews converted to Christianity each year; by the late 1880s, more than three hundred did so annually; in 1902, the number of converts topped four hundred. In Germany as a whole, for which no statistics are available for the period before 1880, the rise was equally dramatic: in the early 1880s, there were at least two hundred conversions a year; twenty years later, more than five hundred a year. In relative terms, this means that in the 1880s there was one conversion a year for every 2,200 Jews in Germany; in the early 1900s, one for every 1,100 Jews. More significant, in Berlin, where the center of gravity of German Jewry lay, the ratios were much lower: about one for every 600–650 Jews in the period 1882–1908. (In reality, the number of Jews leaving Judaism was much greater, since these figures do not include converts to Catholicism and children baptized by their parents. Felix A. Theilhaber estimated that at the turn of the century German Jewry was losing at least one thousand persons a year.)[4] On the eve of World War I, alongside Germany's Jewish population of

4. Nathan Samter, *Judentaufen im neunzehnten Jahrhundert* (Berlin, 1906), pp. 145–46; Jacob Lestchinsky, "Ha-shmad be-arazot shonot," *Haolam* 5, no. 8 (1911): 5–6, and no. 10 (1911): 6; Felix A. Theilhaber, *Der Untergang der deutschen Juden: Eine volkswirtschaftliche Studie*, 2d ed. (Berlin, 1921), p. 117. The figures in both Samter and Lestchinsky include only conversions to the Evangelical church, whereas Theilhaber included in his estimate both converts to Catholicism and children under the age of fourteen.

620,000, there may have been as many as 100,000 converts and children and grandchildren of converts.[5]

One sign of the ubiquity of apostasy in German Jewry was the vehemence with which communal leaders denounced it. The Centralverein deutscher Staatsbürger jüdischen Glaubens, the chief defense organization and most representative body of liberal assimilationist opinion, mounted a scathing polemic against the *Taufjuden*, who were, in its eyes, traitorous cowards, "renegades who sacrifice their honor and conviction to win recognition." Committed to fostering pride and self-respect among acculturated middle-class Jews, the Centralverein denounced apostates as the most dangerous enemies of Jewish survival in Germany, not only because they depleted the ranks of the community but also because they substantiated the antisemitic canard that Jews were unscrupulous opportunists. Moreover, the Centralverein leadership believed that the willingness of some Jews to convert in order to find posts in the public sector delayed the attainment of full emancipation, since the government could claim that Jews were not being denied access to government employment at all. To counter the rising tide of baptisms, the Centralverein emphasized in its publications the positive values of Judaism and the importance of the Jews as its bearers, and, simultaneously, how little Jews would gain by converting. In 1910 the organization became so alarmed that it even began sponsoring mass meetings to denounce conversion, one of which attracted several thousand persons.[6]

In *fin-de-siècle* Vienna, where antisemitism was at least as virulent and pervasive as in Berlin, conversion to Christianity was even more common, continually increasing at a faster pace than the Jewish population as a whole. In the period 1868–79 there was one convert for every 1,200 Jews; in the 1880s, one for every 420 Jews; in the first decade of this century, one for every 230 Jews.[7] (By comparison, in

5. Gershom Scholem, "On the Social Psychology of the Jews in Germany, 1900–1933," in *Jews and Germans from 1860 to 1933: The Problematic Symbiosis*, ed. David Bronsen (Heidelberg, 1979), p. 11. Donald L. Niewyk estimates that there were as many as sixty thousand baptized Jews and children of baptized Jews in the Weimar period. Since he does not include the grandchildren of converts in his estimate, he and Scholem are in approximate agreement about the general dimensions of this group. *The Jews in Weimar Germany* (Baton Rouge, 1980), pp. 98–99.

6. Schorsch, *Jewish Reactions to German Anti-Semitism*, pp. 139–42; Jehuda Reinharz, *Fatherland or Promised Land: The Dilemma of the German Jew, 1893–1914* (Ann Arbor, 1975), p. 83.

7. Lestchinsky, "Ha-shmad be-arazot shonot," *Haolam* 5, no. 1 (1911): 15.

Berlin, the ratio between converts and the community as a whole changed very little between 1882 and 1908, ranging between 600 and 650 per annum. The more explosive increase in Vienna was undoubtedly due to the ban in Austria on marriages between Jews and Christians. For a mixed couple to marry, one of them had to convert to the religion of the other—which was not the case in Germany.) So common was apostasy in Vienna that, according to the admittedly biased nationalist newspaper *Jüdisches Volksblatt*, there was "hardly one [well-to-do] family that has not given thought to conversion."[8]

The most dramatic instance of large numbers of Jews seeking refuge from antisemitism in the church occurred in Hungary immediately after the end of the First World War. In the decades before the war the number of converts was not high, in either relative or absolute terms. In Budapest, the second largest Jewish community in Europe, there were only 135 conversions per annum in the period 1896–98, 170 in the period 1899–1901, 208 in the period 1902–1904. Although baptism was necessary to obtain certain government posts and to gain entry into elite social circles, the regime was sufficiently liberal to instill confidence in the Jewish population and thereby forestall the emergence of conversion as a common response to antisemitism. After the collapse of the Habsburg Empire, however, the number of conversions shot up dramatically. The four-and-a-half-month communist regime of Béla Kun, a Jew, in 1919 elicited a virulently antisemitic counterrevolution—the White Terror. As in postwar Germany, Jews were blamed for all of Hungary's ills. Riots and acts of violence against Jews in the early months of the new regime, in addition to the general instability of the period, spread panic and fear among Jews. Beginning in August 1919, thousands streamed into church offices, particularly in Budapest, seeking conversion as quickly as possible. In the last five months of 1919 alone there were 7,146 baptisms; the following year, 1,757; in 1921, when the political situation stabilized, only 584. (By contrast, in the mid-1920s, the number of conversions per annum fell to less than 200.)[9]

8. *Jüdisches Volksblatt*, October 24, 1902, quoted in Marsha L. Rozenblit, *The Jews of Vienna, 1867–1914: Assimilation and Identity* (Albany, 1983), p. 135.

9. Lestchinsky, "Ha-shmad be-arazot shonot," *Haolam* 5, no. 6 (1911): 6; Yehuda Don and George Magos, "The Demographic Development of Hungarian Jewry," *Jewish Social Studies* 45 (1983): 193–94, 212; Zeev Rotics, "Be-shulei ha-netunim ha-statistiyim al hamarot ha-dat be-kerev yehudei Hungaryah, 1900–1941," *Studies on the Holocaust Period* 1 (Tel Aviv, 1978): 223–24. Rotics believes that the actual number of conversions in the years 1919–21 may be closer to fifteen thousand, since, in the chaotic conditions at the time, not all conversions were properly arranged and recorded.

In the liberal states of the West, on the other hand, where the Jewish Question was far less acute than in Central Europe and where very different social and political circumstances generally prevailed, apostasy never grew significantly. Rabbis and lay leaders in France, Great Britain, and the United States decried declining synagogue attendance, the decay of religious traditions, and at times the danger of intermarriage, but they consistently failed to mention apostasy as a threat to the well-being of their communities. When interviewed in 1897 for Charles Booth's survey, *Life and Labour of the People in London*, Chief Rabbi Hermann Adler discussed the character and extent of intermarriage but said not a word about conversion, an issue he surely would have raised if it had been a real concern. Lewis S. Benjamin, writing in the *Nineteenth Century* in 1912, flatly stated that "the number of converts [in England] is so small as to be immaterial."[10] Similarly, in reviewing the state of French Jewry in 1891 for the readers of the *Jewish Quarterly Review,* Simon Debré declared that apostasy from Judaism to Christianity was "absolutely unknown," even in instances of mixed marriage. Since France was a land of unbounded liberty, he explained, Jews there had no reason to convert.[11]

In the United States as well apostasy, while perhaps more common than in France and England, never took on epidemic proportions. It remained an infrequent response even in the interwar years, when antisemitism impinged on the lives of American Jews more directly than either before or after the world wars and when, in the words of one observer, Judaism was still "a great inconvenience, an obstacle in the path of one's ambition to succeed in the world." The great

10. Interview with Hermann Adler, Charles Booth Collection, Manuscript Room, British Library of Political and Economic Science, London School of Economics, London, file B197, p. 17; Lewis S. Benjamin, "The Passing of the English Jew," *Nineteenth Century* 72 (1912): 502.

11. Simon Debré, "The Jews of France," *Jewish Quarterly Review* 3 (1891): 393. Recent research supports Debré's observation. See Michael R. Marrus, *The Politics of Assimilation: A Study of the French Jewish Community at the Time of the Dreyfus Affair* (Oxford, 1971), pp. 60–61; Stephen Wilson, *Ideology and Experience: Antisemitism in France at the Time of the Dreyfus Affair* (Rutherford, N.J., 1982), p. 516; Patrick Girard, *Les Juifs de France de 1789 à 1860: De l'émancipation à l'égalité* (Paris, 1976), pp. 156–59; François Delpech, "La seconde communauté juive de Lyon (1775–1870)," *Cahiers d'histoire* 13 (1968): 64; Paula Hyman, *From Dreyfus to Vichy: The Remaking of French Jewry, 1906–1939* (New York, 1979), p. 137. Hyman notes that only 769 Jews converted to Catholicism in Paris between 1915 and 1934, of whom 43 percent were immigrants— that is, very likely from the lowest economic stratum in the community. Material benefits offered by missionary groups, rather than career enchancement, undoubtedly motivated them to embrace Christianity.

mass of American Jews, descendants of recent immigrants from Eastern Europe or immigrants themselves, lived in self-segregated urban neighborhoods and had few social contacts with non-Jews. As Herbert Gans noted thirty years ago, while many intellectuals tried to escape Judaism, the bulk of American Jewry never even considered the possibility. They assimilated culturally to the majority but continued to live among Jews "without questioning their own Jewishness or its ineluctability."[12]

In those countries in which apostasy was a frequent response to antisemitism, there is strong evidence to suggest that those who converted were not representative (in a sociological and demographic sense) of the Jewish community as a whole but were drawn, rather, from those who were most exposed to discrimination and exclusion. Everywhere intellectuals and professionals constituted a disproportionate percentage of those who formally abandoned Judaism, since they, more than businessmen, clerical and manual workers, and petty merchants, faced obstacles to their social and economic advancement by reason of their Jewishness. In a sample of 370 male converts in Vienna in the period 1870–1910, civil servants, professionals, and students (who were probably preparing for careers as professionals and civil servants) represented slightly more than half of the total number of apostates.[13] Similarly, in a sample of 262 men who withdrew from the Prague community in the period 1868–1917, 44 percent were professionals, public servants, or students, while hardly any were self-employed businessmen.[14] In Berlin in the period 1873–1906 university students constituted 36 percent of converts of known occupation.[15] Indeed, in some Jewish families in imperial Germany, the son interested in a career in the university or the civil service converted while the son entering the family business or industry remained Jewish.[16]

12. Samuel N. Deinard, *Jews and Christian Science* (Minneapolis, 1919), p. 61; Deborah Dash Moore, *At Home in America: Second Generation New York Jews* (New York, 1981), pp. 30, 85–86; Herbert Gans, "American Jewry: Present and Future," *Commentary*, May 1956, p. 426.

13. Rozenblit, *Jews of Vienna*, p. 137.

14. Michael Anthony Riff, "Assimilation and Conversion in Bohemia: Secession from the Jewish Community in Prague, 1868–1917," *LBIYB* 26 (1981): 83–84.

15. Arthur Ruppin, *The Jews of Today*, trans. Margery Bentwich (London, 1913), p. 194.

16. Abraham A. Fraenkel, *Lebenskreise: Aus den Erinnerungen eines jüdischen Mathematikers* (Stuttgart, 1967), p. 97; Leonard Baker, *Days of Sorrow and Pain: Leo Baeck and the Berlin Jews* (New York, 1978), p. 96.

Jews who received a university education were prime candidates for apostasy not only by reason of the obstacles they faced in their careers. The university experience in itself acted as a dissolvent of ethnic loyalties. The worlds of science and literature that students encountered there were dazzling, opening up before them broader horizons than they thought they could ever find within the narrow limits of Jewry. Mostly ignorant of Jewish tradition and psychologically ill prepared—by virtue of their assimilationist upbringing—to withstand the antisemitism that flourished in the universities, they gave up an allegiance that had become an intolerable burden while allying themselves unambiguously with the seductive worlds of *Wissenschaft* and *Kultur*. The Nobel laureate chemist Fritz Haber, who converted to Christianity as a student even before he had decided on an academic career, recalled that he and his friends considered themselves to be thoroughly German, philosophy and science having eroded any ties they had felt to Judaism. For him, conversion to Christianity was not a religious decision but a demonstration of allegiance to a cultural community.[17]

Even in the liberal states of the West, where conversion was usually unnecessary for career advancement, university life worked to loosen ties of communal solidarity among young Jews by exposing them to social and cultural concerns broader than those they had encountered previously. Simeon Singer, rabbi of the New West End Synagogue in London, recognized this danger when he told a group of Jewish students at Cambridge in 1893 that they were constantly being made aware "how learning and culture and many of the highest gifts of the intellect and the spirit are to be met with outside the limits of Judaism."[18] In France, England, and America, however, students were not so much likely to convert as to give up Jewish prac-

17. Rudolf A. Stern, "Fritz Haber: Personal Recollections," *LBIYB* 8 (1963): 88. Maximilian Harden (b. Felix Ernst Witkowski) also claimed that he had adopted Christianity because it had seemed to him "the way of life corresponding to the higher culture." Harry F. Young, *Maximilian Harden: Censor Germaniae* (The Hague, 1959), p. 12. It is difficult to know how to evaluate claims like Haber's and Harden's. On the one hand, while there is no *prima facie* reason to doubt their sincerity, it is true, nonetheless, that such views made conversion more palatable by defining it as an act of cultural allegiance rather than simple opportunism.

18. Simeon Singer, *The Literary Remains of the Rev. Simeon Singer*, ed. Israel Abrahams (London, 1908), 1:156. For a number of examples of Anglo-Jewish youth whose university experience led them away from Judaism, see Todd M. Endelman, "Communal Solidarity among the Jewish Elite of Victorian London," *Victorian Studies* 28 (1985): 491–526.

tices, sever their links with Jewish groups, and, in many cases, enter into mixed marriages.

When young men deserted Judaism, they often did so before encountering specific obstacles to their advancement. They acted instead on the reasonable expectation that whatever career path they chose they would find greater success and perhaps greater happiness as Christians than as Jews. Richard Lichtheim, a prominent figure in the Zionist movement in the first part of this century, recalled in his memoirs that his father, a prosperous Berlin grain broker, asked him one day—he was fourteen at the time—if he wanted to convert. Most of his father's relatives had become Christians—some had been Christians for two generations—but his father had himself rejected conversion as undignified. By the turn of the century, however, when he was less sanguine about the future than he had once been, his diminishing sense of security led him to propose baptism to his son, who, after all, might want to become a lawyer or a doctor rather than a grain merchant.[19]

In many instances parents who remained Jewish baptized their children at an early age in order to spare them any unnecessary unpleasantness later in life, regardless of their future prospects. When Theodor Herzl proposed mass baptism as a solution to the Jewish Question in 1893—before arriving at his Zionist solution—he was particularly concerned about the future of his son Hans. He admitted in a letter to the industrialist Baron Friedrich Leitenberger that he would not himself abandon Judaism, but would consider it for his son.

> When I think of his future, I am ready to admit that the pressure of his Jewishness will teach him much concerning humanity. But I ask myself whether I have the right to make life so superfluously difficult for him as it has become for me and will become in increasing measure. . . . That is why we must baptize Jewish children while they are still incapable of giving themselves an accounting, and while they can still feel nothing either for it or against it.[20]

Parents sought to spare their children—boys and girls alike—humiliation and insult as they grew up. In Heinrich Graetz's "Correspondence of an English Lady on Judaism and Semitism" (1883), a Jewish mother who urges Jews to baptize their children asks in anguish:

19. Richard Lichtheim, *She'ar yashuv: Zikhronot ziyoni mi-Germanyah* (Jerusalem, 1953), p. 19.
20. Theodor Herzl to Friedrich Leitenberger, quoted in Alex Bein, *Theodore Herzl: A Biography*, trans. Maurice Samuel (Philadelphia, 1943), pp. 90–91.

Should we expose them to the ridicule of their classmates and to the spiteful allusions of teachers who fancy themselves comic with their Jewish intonation? Should our sons be barked at in the army by some coarse sergeant or some insolent boor of a second lieutenant simply because they are Jews? Should they fulfill their military service conscientiously only to be discriminated against? Should our daughters who attend a public ball, even if graced with physical and spiritual charm and impeccably and modestly dressed, be scorned by geese with crosses on their breasts, avoided by the men and forced into a gloomy corner?[21]

In some instances Jews already in the midst of their careers were required to convert in order to obtain posts that would otherwise have remained closed to them. In perhaps the most famous instance of this kind of bargain, Gustav Mahler accepted Catholicism in Hamburg in 1897 in order to become director of the Vienna Court Opera. Jewish doctors in Berlin, Vienna, and other large cities converted in order to gain promotions in hospitals and municipal medical services.[22] Careerist conversions were especially commonplace in academic life, where the number of Jewish candidates for advancement was greatly disproportionate to the number of Jews in the population at large. Government and university officials made it quite clear to Jewish *Privatdozenten* that promotion without baptism was nearly impossible. The philosopher Franz Brentano at the German University of Prague urged that his Jewish students who intended to pursue academic careers be baptized, not out of concern for their souls but rather for their future success. For him conversion to Christianity was merely a matter of form, a question of putting on the correct dress for an academic career. (He encouraged his Jewish students to join the Protestant church, which he referred to as "the religion for those lacking religion.") When *Privatdozent* Harry Bresslau, a medieval historian, complained to Leopold Ranke that his religion was hindering his career, Ranke flatly advised him to become a Christian. Bresslau rejected the advice but succeeded, nevertheless, in eventually obtaining a professorship in 1890—not at an old German university, however, but at the University of Strasbourg, which was professionally and geographically on the periphery of German aca-

21. Heinrich Graetz, "The Correspondence of an English Lady on Judaism and Semitism," in his *The Structure of Jewish History and Other Essays*, trans. and ed. Ismar Schorsch (New York, 1975), p. 192.

22. See, for example, the case of Dr. Ludwig Klaar (1849–1922), a distinguished diagnostician in Vienna who was repeatedly passed over for promotion because he refused to convert (although sorely tempted to). George Clare, *Last Waltz in Vienna: The Rise and Destruction of a Family, 1842–1942* (New York, 1982), pp. 21–23.

demic life. Like the other unconverted Jewish professors at the university, Bresslau baptized his children (one of whom later married Albert Schweitzer) in the hope of sparing them the anguish he had faced.[23] Many more Jews who hoped to climb the academic ladder converted at the outset of their careers. For example, in 1909–10, when almost 12 percent of the *Privatdozenten* at German universities were Jews, another 7 percent were converts. At the full professorial level, less than 3 percent were Jews, while another 4 percent were converts.[24]

In those Jewries with high rates of conversion, the majority of converts were men, since they were far more likely than women to have careers and thus run head on into discrimination. On the other hand, most women, at least before the First World War, remained enclosed in a private network of family and friends, cut off from the social and occupational temptations that led to conversion. There were some groups of Jewish women, however, whose lives took them beyond these confines and who chose to leave Judaism in response to the hostility they encountered in the larger society. Women in the lower middle class increasingly entered into paid employment in the late nineteenth and early twentieth centuries—as clerks, teachers, domestics, dressmakers, and so forth—and frequently they found that conversion aided them in finding a position. Thus, in Berlin, for example, the share of women in the total number of conversions rose considerably during this period. In the decade 1873–82, women accounted for only 7 percent of those converting; by 1908, 37 percent; and by 1912, 40 percent.[25]

23. Samuel Hugo Bergmann, "Emil Utitz: Darko ha-tragit shel melumad yehudi," *Molad* 15 (1957): 626; Friedrich Meinecke, *Strassburg, Freiburg, Berlin, 1901–1919* (Stuttgart, 1949), p. 27; James Brabazon, *Alfred Schweitzer: A Biography* (New York, 1975), p. 153, where it is reported that a granddaughter of Bresslau believed that Bresslau might have become a Christian, but "his pride and dignity would never let him take a step which might seem to have been motivated by expediency."

24. Fritz K. Ringer, *The Decline of the German Mandarins: The German Academic Community, 1890–1933* (Cambridge, Mass., 1969), p. 136.

25. Lestchinsky, "Ha-shmad be-arazot shonot," *Haolam* 5, no. 11 (1911): 6; Marion A. Kaplan, "Tradition and Transition: The Acculturation, Assimilation, and Integration of Jews in Imperial Germany—A Gender Analysis," *LBIYB* 27 (1982): 18. Since 84 percent of female converts in Berlin in the period 1873–1906 were from the lowest income groups, the increase in the share of women in the total number of conversions is clearly due to greater numbers of women from the lower middle class abandoning Judaism. In Vienna 53.3 percent of the converts in Rozenblit's sample were male, 46.7 percent female. Most of these female converts, however, were not becoming Christians in order to find employment but rather because they were marrying Gentiles and Austrian law prohibited intermarriage. Rozenblit, *Jews of Vienna*, pp. 136–39.

At the other extreme of the social hierarchy, among the banking and industrial elites of Central European Jewry, women were also likely to be tempted to convert by Gentile hostility. Here, at the apex of Jewish society, the yearning for social advancement sometimes led wealthy parents, whose control over marital arrangements lasted until after World War I, to marry their daughters to Christian noblemen.[26] These nuptials, the English novelist Cecily Sidgwick remarked, "are just as businesslike as if the *Schadchan* had arranged them and received his commission. The Graf or the Major gets the gold he lacks, and the rich Jewess gets social prestige or the nearest approach to it possible in a Jew-baiting land."[27] (Mixed marriages such as these, however, were not so frequent as cartoons and anecdotes would lead one to believe.)[28] When such matches occurred, the Jewish partner inevitably converted, for aristocratic society in imperial Germany and the Habsburg Empire was too intolerant to permit the wife to retain even a nominal Jewish affiliation. (In England and France, in contrast, the daughters of the Rothschilds and other wealthy Jewish banking families married into titled families without converting.) Parents who arranged matches such as these were convinced that they could do little to improve their own social standing, given their Jewish background and their roots in commerce and finance. Instead they hoped to enhance their daughters' chances for success by acquiring for them high-ranking husbands of the Christian faith.

Whether male or female, wealthy or poor, converts were overwhelmingly young persons, individuals about to embark on a career or a marriage who, we can assume, were pessimistic about their future if they remained Jews. In a sample of 1,037 Viennese Jews who left Judaism between 1870 and 1910, 40 percent of the men and 48 percent of the women were in their twenties, and 28.5 percent of the men and 27 percent of the women in their thirties.[29] In Berlin in the period 1873–1906, 42 percent of all converts (excluding those under

26. For some examples of such marriages, see Lamar Cecil, "Jew and Junker in Imperial Berlin," *LBIYB* 20 (1975): 49, and the sources cited there. For parental control of marriage arrangements in general, see Marion A. Kaplan, "For Love or Money: The Marriage Strategies of Jews in Imperial Germany," ibid., 28 (1983): 263–300.

27. Cecily Sidgwick, *Home Life in Germany* (London, 1908), p. 80. Sidgwick was the daughter of a German Jew who settled in England in 1848, married a Christian, and raised his children in the Church of England.

28. Kaplan, "Tradition and Transition," p. 16.

29. Rozenblit, *Jews of Vienna*, p. 137.

age fourteen, whose conversions were not registered) were in their teens or twenties, 31 percent in their thirties.[30] In a sample of Prague Jews who resigned from the community in the period 1868–1917, the majority of the men were between eighteen and thirty years old.[31] In most cities converts over the age of forty were usually persons about to marry for a second time or whose parents had died and who now felt free to change their religion.

In general, there were many Jews who were tempted to convert but chose not to do so because they felt constrained by other considerations. More religiously indifferent Jews would have become Christians had they not felt that baptism was, in the words of Gershom Scholem's father, "an unprincipled and servile act" at a time when antisemitism was on the rise. Walther Rathenau, who was consumed by loathing for his origins and officially withdrew from the organized Jewish community in 1895, nevertheless refrained from embracing Christianity, since as a nonbeliever he saw conversion for opportunistic reasons as a degrading act. As the sociologist Arthur Ruppin noted at the turn of the century, "If numbers of men and women cannot decide to be baptised, it is not so much because of their love of Judaism as of their unwillingness to face the reproach of cowardice and treachery by deserting a minority which is in danger, and is being attacked on all sides."[32] In some instances potential apostates refrained from cutting their ties to Judaism out of respect for—or fear of—their parents. Oskar Ehrenberg, the pampered son of a wealthy cartridge manufacturer in Arthur Schnitzler's novel of fin-de-siècle Vienna, Der Weg ins Freie (1908), is prevented from converting by the knowledge that his father would disinherit him were he to do so.[33] In a few cases social pressures, such as the disapproval of friends or the gossip that would ensue, worked to restrain assimilated Jews from taking the final step. The late Joseph Wechsberg recalled that in the Moravian town in which he grew up in the 1910s and 1920s "the small-town atmosphere prevented many an assimilant from 'going too far,' converting to Catholicism and changing his

30. Lestchinsky, "Ha-shmad be-arazot shonot," *Haolam* 5, no. 11 (1911): 7.
31. Riff, "Assimilation and Conversion in Bohemia," p. 85.
32. Gershom Scholem, *From Berlin to Jerusalem*, trans. Harry Zohn (New York, 1980), p. 11; Schorsch, *Jewish Reactions to German Anti-Semitism*, pp. 145–46; Ruppin, *Jews of Today*, p. 194.
33. Arthur Schnitzler, *The Road to the Open*, trans. Horace Samuel (New York, 1923), p. 10.

name, if it sounded 'too Jewish.'" When a classmate named Kohn
appeared in *Gymnasium* one day and announced that his new name
was Kresta, everyone was shocked. In the end, Wechsberg added, it
did not help him: when he became involved in arguments on the
soccer field, he remained Kohn.[34]

Although the great waves of conversion in the modern period can
be linked to currents of antisemitism, it would not be correct to infer
from this relationship that rates of apostasy were always directly
proportional to levels of antisemitism. The relationship between intolerance and persecution, on the one hand, and the flight from Jewishness, on the other, is not so straightforward. In many areas where
antisemitism truly embittered the lives of Jews, apostasy was, in
fact, less common than in communities where, by comparison, discrimination was mild. In the Russian Empire, for example, where
Jews suffered more grievously from antisemitism than elsewhere in
Europe, where public policy was openly antisemitic, conversion
made far fewer inroads than in Western and Central Europe. True, it
was not uncommon in certain circles, such as those embracing university students, St. Petersburg bankers and industrialists, and Russified intellectuals,[35] but among the great mass of Jews—those who
suffered most, at least materially, from the welter of tsarist restrictions—apostasy was not a frequent response to the burden of being
Jewish. During the years 1880–1905, according to reports of the Holy
Synod, less than five hundred Jews a year joined the Orthodox
church—at a time when the Jewish population was more than five
million.[36]

The reasons for this are not difficult to fathom. As long as the Jewish masses were impoverished, attached to Jewish tradition, inward
looking, and culturally distinct from the surrounding peoples, con-

34. Joseph Wechsberg, *The Vienna I Knew: Memories of a European Childhood* (Garden City, N.Y., 1979), p. 83. See also Riff, "Assimilation and Conversion in Bohemia," p.
73.

35. Biographical sketches of several dozen Russian converts, many of them *maskilim*
and Russified intellectuals, can be found in Samuel Leib Zitron, *Me-ahorei ha-pargod:
mumarim, bogdim, mitkahashim* (Vilna, 1923–25).

36. Robert F. Byrnes, *Pobedonostsev: His Life and Thought* (Bloomington, Ind., 1968),
p. 207. The figures cited in the article on conversion to Christianity in the *Evreiskaia
Entsiklopediia*, vol. 11, col. 894, are higher: 689 a year during the period 1881–90 and
1,020 a year during the period 1891–97. Even the higher numbers are relatively insignificant, however, given the total Jewish population. (Neither set of statistics includes
conversions to Protestantism or Catholicism.)

version was not an option or strategy that would have readily come to mind.[37] The Jewish population of the Russian Empire, even as late as the eve of the Revolution, was still overwhelmingly traditional in its outlook, despite the inroads made by secular ideologies. Most of the tsar's Jews, unlike their counterparts further west, never saw themselves as Russians or Poles or Lithuanians. The idea of ending their isolation from Gentile society through conversion to the majority faith would have seemed absurd to them. They were simply too distant from the non-Jewish world—too immersed in traditional ways of thinking—for the idea of complete assimilation through conversion to take root. In addition the contempt Jews felt for the Orthodox church in particular made conversion an even more remote possibility. Regardless of their attitude to enlightenment, Jews associated the established faith of the tsarist empire with political repression and intellectual obscurantism. In their eyes, its representatives were boorish and unlettered, like the primitive peasants whom they traded with and looked down upon.

In Central Europe, on the other hand, considerable estrangement from Judaism preceded the rise in antisemitism at the end of the last century. By the 1870s and 1880s large numbers of Jews, particularly those who had become comfortably bourgeois, had ceased to feel pride in their Jewish identity or find meaning in Jewish worship or ceremonies.[38] Exposure to secular intellectual currents had undercut traditional religious commitments, while pressure to conform to the cultural and social norms of the majority, which was constantly being fueled by virulent antisemitism, corroded the bonds of communal solidarity. Consequently Jewish attachments and concerns assumed a secondary importance among large sections of the Ger-

37. This is not to say, of course, that the Jewish poor in the Russian Empire never converted. There, as elsewhere, dire poverty led small numbers to seek to improve their lot by embracing Christianity. See Michael Stanislawski, "Jewish Apostasy in Russia: A Tentative Typology," in *Jewish Apostasy in the Modern World: Converts and Missionaries in Historical Perspective*, ed. Todd M. Endelman (New York, forthcoming).

38. There are no social histories of Jewish practice and belief in nineteenth- or early twentieth-century Germany—or, for that matter, in any other community—and thus these generalizations are, quite frankly, impressionistic. Nevertheless, from my reading of memoirs of the period and the little secondary literature that touches on the subject, I believe the picture I have drawn here to be reasonably accurate. See, for example, Gershom Scholem's description of the religious attitudes of his parents' generation in turn-of-the-century Berlin in *From Berlin to Jerusalem*, pp. 9–12; or Michael Hamburger's memories of growing up in an upper-middle-class Berlin Jewish home in the 1920s and 1930s, *A Mug's Game: Intermittent Memoirs, 1924–1954* (Cheadle, Cheshire, 1973), p. 21.

man-Jewish middle class. Many who attended services on the High Holidays or who celebrated Passover seders in their homes did so only out of a feeling of family obligation or social propriety. In Arthur Schnitzler's family in Vienna in the 1860s and 1870s, only his maternal grandmother observed Jewish rituals in any way, and she limited her observance to fasting on Yom Kippur, spending the day in synagogue, and eating *matzot* on Passover:

> Her children and grandchildren, as long as they continued to celebrate the Day of Atonement, did so mainly for her sake, and after her death solely out of a feeling of reverence for her. . . . The generation which followed, in spite of all stubborn emphasis on racial solidarity, tended to display indifference to the spirit of Jewish religion, and opposition, sometimes even a sarcastic attitude, to its formalities.[39]

When Jews such as these converted to escape the disabilities of Jewishness, they did not experience a radical break with the past, since previous estrangement from their ancestral faith had prepared the ground for the rupture. A nominal Christianity replaced a nominal Judaism. (There were, to be sure, conversions of conviction now and then, but they were numerically insignificant in comparison to those for pragmatic reasons.)[40]

Beyond the question of the relationship between antisemitism and conversion there remains the further matter of the efficacy of baptism as a strategy for circumventing discrimination and prejudice. Were converts able to leave the taint of Jewishness behind them? How successfully could they bury their origins and merge into the mainstream? In short, did apostasy work?

If we consider only the careers of the best-known apostates—Ra-

39. Arthur Schnitzler, *My Youth in Vienna*, trans. Catherine Hutter (New York, 1970), p. 13.

40. There is no comparative study of Jews who became Christians out of sincere conviction, although there is abundant material for such a study, given the prominence of many of these former Jews in literature, politics, and religion. Among those who come to mind immediately are Friedrich Julius Stahl, August Neander, Paulus Cassel, and Karl Stern in Germany; Alphonse and Théodore Ratisbonne, Francois Libermann, David Drach, Jean de Menasce, Maurice Sachs, and Simone Weil in France; Boris Pasternak in Russia; Abraham Capadose in Holland; and Michael Solomon Alexander, Moses Margoliouth, Christian David Ginsburg, Hugh Montefiore, and Victor Gollancz in England. At the same time it should be recognized, however, that converts like these were a tiny minority of the total number. As Fritz Mauthner noted in 1912: "It is indeed not impossible that an adult and educated Jew would become a Christian out of conviction. It is only that in my life I have not seen such a case. In the vast majority of cases the adult convert is brought to profess a creed in which he does not believe out of higher or lower reasons of expedience." *Judentaufen*, ed. A. Landsberger (Munich, 1912), p. 76, quoted in Schorsch, *Jewish Reactions to German Anti-Semitism*, p. 139.

hel Varnhagen, Heinrich Heine, Karl Marx, Benjamin Disraeli, Bernard Berenson, Gustav Mahler, for example—it is clear that conversion failed to obscure their origins. All of these individuals were regarded by their contemporaries as Jews, even when, like Marx and Disraeli, they had been baptized as children. As Heine remarked in a letter to Moses Moser in 1826, "Isn't it ridiculous that I am no sooner baptized than I am upbraided as a Jew?" Disraeli, who lived in a more tolerant society than Heine, nonetheless experienced considerable hostility on account of his Jewish origins when he launched his political career in the 1830s. On one occasion, when he faced the voters of Maidstone, he was greeted with cries of "Shylock!" and "Old Clothes!" Throughout his life the British public viewed him as a Jew, although it is also true that he himself cultivated his Jewish image from the mid-1840s on, having learned that efforts to obscure his origins were futile. Mahler, too, found that his baptism did very little to placate those who were hostile to him on account of his Jewish birth. According to Alma Mahler, "he was not a man who ever deceived himself, and he knew that people would not forget he was a Jew just because he was sceptical of the Jewish religion and baptized a Christian."[41]

The inability of baptism to obliterate the Jewishness of public figures like Mahler is not surprising. Long before the language of pseudoscientific racial antisemitism became widely known, popular opinion in many countries accepted the notion of the immutability of Jewishness in one sense or another. In Central Europe especially, Jewish character was considered inflexible and thus impervious to baptism. In 1791, in a pamphlet protesting the entry of Jews into Berlin society, Karl Wilhelm Friedrich Grattenauer held that baptizing Jews was akin to "trying to wash a blackamoor white," while in a more vicious vein Johann Gottlieb Fichte declared in 1793 that the only way to give Jews citizenship was "to cut off their heads on the same night in order to replace them with those containing no Jewish ideas." Seventy years later Moses Hess, in his *Rome and Jerusalem*, observed that baptism was unable to save Jews from the hatred of the German people. "The Germans hate the religion of the Jews less

41. Heinrich Heine to Moses Moser, January 9, 1826, in *Heinrich Heine: A Biographical Anthology*, ed. Hugo Bieber, trans. Moses Hadas (Philadelphia, 1956), p. 205; Todd M. Endelman, "Disraeli's Jewishness Reconsidered," *Modern Judaism* 5 (1985): 109–123; Alma Mahler, *Gustav Mahler: Memories and Letters*, ed. Donald Mitchell, trans. Basil Creighton, 3d ed. (Seattle, 1975), p. 101.

than they hate their race," he remarked, "they hate the peculiar faith of the Jews less than their peculiar noses." Baptism could not reshape Jewish noses, he added, or turn black frizzy hair blond. The journalist Otto Glagau articulated popular feeling in the mid-1870s when he declared that Jews constituted a united chain "from the baptized minister to the last Polish schnorrer." At times Germans even detected the taint of Jewishness in children born to former Jews years after the parents' baptism. Georg Simmel, for example, was unable to obtain a full professorship in a German university for more than thirty years because he was seen by many as an essentially Jewish personality—despite the fact that his parents were baptized several years before his birth, that he himself had been baptized and was completely estranged from Jewish matters, and that his wife was Christian.[42]

In Central Europe less prominent converts from Judaism also found that baptism did not secure their unqualified admission into Gentile society. A baptized Jew could become an officer in a smart cavalry regiment in *fin-de-siècle* Austria, but he could not avoid conflicts with his comrades on account of his former religion—so a lieutenant of Jewish birth with a long, blood red saber scar on his forehead told Arthur Schnitzler. In a memoir of interwar Vienna, Joseph Wechsberg recalled a socially ambitious aunt who found a brokendown minor aristocrat to marry her beautiful daughter and, in preparation for their union, had the daughter baptized. The church authorities, however, would not allow the wedding to be celebrated in one of Vienna's old distinguished churches, such as the Augustinerkirche or St. Stephen's, since the daughter had been baptized only a short time before the ceremony. Civil servants of Jewish origin in imperial Germany found that their origins, even after baptism, could still obstruct promotion into the upper ranks of the state bureaucracy. Karl Julius von Bitter, once an official in the Ministry of the Interior and then *Regierungspräsident* in Silesia, was rejected as minister of the interior in 1895 due to what a contemporary diarist called "his still somewhat Semitic tendencies." The following year,

42. Karl Wilhelm Friedrich Grattenauer, Johann Gottlieb Fichte, and Otto Glagau, quoted in Jacob Katz, *From Prejudice to Destruction: Anti-Semitism, 1700–1933* (Cambridge, Mass., 1980), pp. 56–57, 269; Moses Hess, *Rom und Jerusalem: Die letzte Nationalitätsfrage* (Leipzig, 1862), p. 14; Gay, *Freud, Jews and Other Germans*, pp. 98, 121–22. Gershom Scholem remarked in his memoirs that Georg Simmel was widely regarded "as the very quintessence of a Talmudist." *From Berlin to Jerusalem*, p. 67.

when most ministers and Wilhelm II were willing to accept him as minister of trade, Prince Clodwig zu Hohenlohe-Schillingsfürst, the chancellor, prevented the appointment because he thought Bitter was "an ambitious Jew."[43]

In general, Christians of Jewish origin who attempted to move into Gentile spheres in Central Europe encountered some degree of hostility (with the possible exception of bohemian literary and artistic circles). Resentment and fear of Jews were too deeply embedded in popular consciousness for it to be otherwise. In addition, those who converted were suspected by Gentile colleagues and acquaintances—quite correctly, in most cases—of having done so for base motives. Thus the very act of conversion, which was meant to free Jews from the opprobrium attached to their origins, inadvertently worked to reinforce stereotypes about Jewish opportunism. Indeed, Peter Gay maintains, these converted Jews were "if anything, more conspicuous than those who held, no matter how tepidly, to their ancient label, for they labored under the added reproach of cowardice, social climbing, secret service in a world-wide conspiracy—in a word, self-seeking mimicry."[44]

The ability of converts in Central Europe to secure acceptance into Gentile society was also undermined by their concentration in large cities and their overrepresentation in certain professions, since these tendencies undoubtedly made their numbers seem larger than they actually were and therefore exaggerated the threat they represented. Thus the very success of anti-Jewish forces in pressuring Jews into becoming Christians created an unforeseen obstacle to these new Christians' integration: the number of converts was simply too great to be absorbed into the Gentile mainstream, or at least so many thought. Consequently, like their counterparts in late medieval Spain, Jewish converts in Berlin, Vienna, Budapest, and other large cities came to constitute a society of their own or continued to maintain social contacts with their former co-religionists. In either case

43. Schnitzler, *My Youth in Vienna*, p. 211; Wechsberg, *Vienna I Knew*, pp. 137, 181; J. C. G. Rohl, "Higher Civil Servants in Germany, 1890–1900," in *Education and Social Structure in the Twentieth Century*, ed. Walter Laqueur and George L. Mosse, Harper Torch Book ed. (New York, 1967), p. 112. In tsarist Russia, too, converts faced widespread hostility and bureaucratic discrimination. See Michael Stanislawski, *Tsar Nicholas I and the Jews: The Transformation of Jewish Society in Russia, 1823–1855* (Philadelphia, 1983), p. 148; Zitron, *Me-ahorei ha-pargod*, pp. 191–204; Hans Rogger, "The Jewish Policy of Late Tsarism: A Reappraisal," *Wiener Library Bulletin* 25, nos. 1–2 (1971): 48–49.

44. Gay, *Freud, Jews and Other Germans*, p. 174.

they remained unassimilated into the host society. The converted Jew in Weimar Germany, Hannah Arendt recalled, "only rarely left his family and even more rarely left his Jewish surroundings altogether." Conversion did not usually bring in its wake a radical separation from friends, family, and community, as it had in earlier periods, largely because religion, with its strictures about associating with apostates, had ceased to be an important influence in the lives of most Jews. In fact there were quite a number of families in Germany that had been nominally Christian for several generations yet remained ethnically Jewish, since their children found their mates among families of similar origin or married Jews who had not formally abandoned Judaism. Many marriages recorded as intermarriages were really unions between converted Jews, or their children, and Jews who still belonged officially to the Jewish community.[45]

If baptism did not purchase acceptance into Gentile society, at least in Central Europe, and most converts there remained unassimilated, still constituting a distinct group on the periphery, why did Jews continue to leave Judaism?

The answer is, of course, that while conversion did not usually bring in its wake integration into non-Jewish society and protection from antisemitism, it still offered concrete rewards. After all, baptism allowed Disraeli to enter Parliament, Marx's father to retain his legal practice in Trier after the withdrawal of the French, Mahler to become director of the Vienna Court Opera, and thousands of other Jews to obtain posts that otherwise would have been closed to them. Those who became Christians probably believed that, in the final analysis, a converted Jew was indeed in a better position to get ahead than an unconverted one, no matter how imperfectly baptism worked as a shield against antisemitism. Moreover, while those who converted may not have been able to enjoy fully the fruits of their baptism, under some circumstances their children and grandchildren were able to. If the descendants of converts married into Christian families of non-Jewish origin and if this multigenerational process of integration began before the end of the nineteenth century, when the number of converts multiplied and antisemitism became more intense, then they were usually able to bury their Jewish past and blend unobtrusively into the surrounding society. As Alexander Hohenlohe observed in his memoirs:

45. Hannah Arendt, *The Origins of Totalitarianism*, new ed. (New York, 1966), p. 64.

If the father or grandfather had allowed himself to be baptised . . . and
if the son had refurbished the tarnished glory of some noble family with
his inherited wealth by marrying one of the daughters, then people were
prepared to disregard his race so long as this was not all-too-obvious in
his facial features.[46]

It is instructive to compare the relative inefficacy of apostasy in
Central Europe in the late nineteenth and early twentieth centuries
with the more immediate and substantial rewards that it brought in
France, England, and the United States, where antisemitism was
weaker and conversion less common. Here the motives for embracing Christianity were somewhat different. Generally Jews in these
countries did not need to become Christians in order to advance
their careers. More frequently they became Christians in order to
complete their integration into Gentile circles. For them baptism
came as a final step in a process of assimilation that was already
well advanced, immersion in Gentile society preceding their baptism, rather than the reverse.

A good illustration of the rapidity with which former Jews could
move into the American mainstream may be seen in the family history of C. Douglas Dillon, ambassador to France in the Eisenhower
years, secretary of the treasury in the Kennedy administration, president of the Metropolitan Museum of Art. Dillon's paternal grandfather, Sam Lapowski, was an immigrant from Poland who set up as
a shopkeeper in West Texas. He prospered sufficiently that he sent
his son Clarence away to Worcester Academy and then to Harvard
(class of 1905), where social antisemitism in those years excluded
Jews from club life and branded them as outsiders. At Harvard, Clarence changed his name to Dillon and cut his ties to Judaism. Three
years after graduation, he married Anne McElden Douglas, daughter
of a wealthy Presbyterian coal dealer in Milwaukee and sister of a
Harvard College roommate. When he had made enough of a success
in business to be listed in *Who's Who*—he eventually built Dillon,
Read & Co. into one of the nation's largest investment firms—he
gave his father's name as Dillon in his biography. His son C. Douglas
went to Groton and completed the process of assimilation into the
nation's old elite by abandoning his mother's Presbyterianism for the
school's Episcopalian faith.[47]

46. Quoted in Rohl, "Higher Civil Servants in Germany," p. 111.
47. Leon Harris, *Merchant Princes: An Intimate History of Jewish Families Who Built
Great Department Stores* (New York, 1979), p. 67; *El Paso Herald Post*, January 9, 1961.

In many instances American Jews who were distant from Jewish concerns and already socially integrated into the larger community married Gentiles but did not themselves convert at the time. These persons, however, almost inevitably raised their children within the majority faith. Bernhard Schlesinger, father of the Harvard historian Arthur Schlesinger, Sr., emigrated to America as a youngster from East Prussia and settled in a small Midwestern town (Xenia, Ohio) just after the Civil War, as did thousands of other German-Jewish immigrants. There he operated a number of small businesses, none too successfully, and eventually married, in 1873, a Christian woman in a ceremony performed by the pastor of the German Reformed church. Although his wife was not a regular churchgoer and he himself an agnostic, their children were raised as members of the German Reformed church, since his wife felt that in so devout a community as Xenia her children should do as their playmates did.[48] This pattern was repeated in thousands of instances in nineteenth-century America. Jews well integrated into the larger communities in which they were living chose Gentile wives and thereby quietly dropped the Jewish affiliations of their youth. The Christian upbringing that they gave their children only confirmed the distance they had already traveled from their origins.

In England, too, the number of converts was small enough and the host society sufficiently tolerant that baptism worked remarkably well in bringing former Jews into the mainstream of national life.[49] In the first half of the nineteenth century several dozen Sephardim from prosperous, highly acculturated families embraced Christianity and subsequently merged into the upper or upper-middle classes. The most famous individual from this group was, of course, Benja-

---

A daughter-in-law of Nathan Lapowski, one of Sam's brothers, claimed that Sam's wife's maiden name was Dillon and that she was of French descent. Eleanor K. Lapowski to Jacob R. Marcus, March 3, 1975, Lapowski Family, Miscellaneous File, American Jewish Archives, Cincinnati. However, according to *The National Cyclopedia of American Biography*, 62:243–44, Clarence's mother's maiden name was Sternbach. Despite his father's efforts to bury his Jewish roots, C. Douglas Dillon found that even in the United States the ethnic origins of the fathers can come to haunt the sons: Dillon spent years on the waiting list of Washington's exclusive Chevy Chase Club and was admitted only when he assured club traditionalists that he was no more than 25 percent Jewish! *New York Times*, January 16, 1962.

48. Arthur M. Schlesinger, *In Retrospect: The History of a Historian* (New York, 1963), pp. 6–9, 12.

49. On apostasy among the Jews of Britain, see Todd M. Endelman, *Radical Assimilation in Anglo-Jewish History: Conversion and Intermarriage from the Resettlement to World War II*, forthcoming.

min Disraeli. Although his political enemies made the most of his Jewish ancestry (and his extravagant Jewish chauvinism), he succeeded nonetheless in penetrating into aristocratic social circles and eventually in dominating the Tory party. No baptized Jew, no matter how talented, could have risen to similar heights in Germany or Austria. Other converts of Sephardi origin seem to have encountered even fewer obstacles than he. Disraeli's uncle Joshua Basevi, a Lloyds underwriter, who withdrew from the Jewish community about the same time as Isaac D'Israeli, also followed his brother-in-law in baptizing his children. His son George became one of the most prominent architects of the early Victorian period, his best-known buildings being the Fitzwilliam Museum at Cambridge, the Conservative Club in St. James's, and the main part of Belgrave Square. Manasseh Masseh Lopes and his father, a wealthy West Indian merchant who settled in England in the mid-eighteenth century and set himself up as a country gentleman at Clapham, both converted in 1802, just prior to the former's election to Parliament that year. He held his seat in the House of Commons until 1829, with the exception of two years that he spent in prison for electioneering bribery and corruption. Other converted Sephardim also made their way into Parliament before mid-century. David Ricardo, who left Judaism in 1793 when he married the daughter of a Quaker physician, sat for the rotten borough of Portarlington from 1819 until his death four years later. Ralph Bernal, whose father broke with the Sephardi community in the late 1780s and raised his children as Christians, was in Parliament from 1818 until 1852; for twenty years he served as chairman of committees of the House of Commons.

During the Victorian period, to cite another instance of the efficacy of baptism, hundreds of German-Jewish immigrants in the Midlands and the North, mostly textile merchants engaged in overseas commerce, joined Unitarian chapels and merged into the mercantile elites that dominated public life there. In Nottingham, for example, the lace merchant Lewis Heymann was a prominent figure both in the High Pavement Chapel and in city government, serving as alderman and mayor, while his fellow Unitarian, the silk merchant and brewer Edward Goldschmidt, served as alderman for almost twenty years. These German Jews, like most Jews in Britain who formally abandoned their religion, encountered little difficulty in completing their assimilation. True, their former identity might be thrown in their face if they became embroiled in a public controversy, but there is no evidence that they or other converts were excluded from Gentile circles or denied access to offices and posts on account of their ancestry.

The efficacy of conversion in the liberal states of the West contrasts sharply with its more limited usefulness in escaping the "misfortune" of Jewish birth in Central Europe. There, as we have seen, while baptism opened up new areas of employment for former Jews, it could not save them from social discrimination and popular contempt. Thus, ironically, in those countries where Jews most needed a strategy to save them from mounting antisemitism, the flight from Judaism proved to be far less effectual, at least in the short run, than in those places where Jews were more secure and less in need of a means of escape. That this should have been so was no accident, for the circumstances that made apostasy uncommon in France or Britain also assured the final assimilation of the few who did take that radical step. Whether with the passage of several generations, families of Jewish descent in Berlin and Vienna could have blended into their surroundings with the same success as their counterparts in London and New York much earlier, we can never know, since the Nazi years cut short this attempt at radical assimilation. In the end, baptism was no more successful than other strategies, short of emigration, in shielding Jews from disaster.

Stuart A. Cohen

Anglo-Jewish Responses to Antisemitism
Suggestions for a Framework of Analysis

The history of modern Anglo-Jewish reactions to antisemitism presents two problems of a methodological nature. The first, and most obvious, is the comparative mildness of the phenomenon under discussion. Jews in Britain suffered very few of the trials, tribulations— and sheer horrors—inflicted on their co-religionists on the European mainland. To say that is not to deny the notorious medieval legacy of English antisemitism, whose residual traces permeated later British culture.[1] Neither can the darker aspects of the post-Cromwellian narrative be ignored. It is not often recognized, for instance, that Anglo-Jewry's attainment of full legal emancipation in 1860 was a tardy process; the measure was passed some eighty years after Jews had been accorded equal legal status in New York and sixty years after similar legislation had first been enacted in revolutionary Europe.[2] What is more, subsequent progress—although steady—was

1. The most striking incidences of medieval English antisemitism were the Norwich blood libel of 1140, the York massacre of 1190, and the expulsion of 1290. On these see, respectively, J. R. Marcus, *The Jew in the Medieval World* (Cincinnati, 1938), pp. 121–26, 131–36; and S. A. Singer, "The Expulsion of the Jews from England in 1290," *Jewish Quarterly Review* 4 (1964): 117–36. More interesting, from a cultural viewpoint, is the fact that, even before their readmission to England in 1656, Jews continued to be targets of literary prejudice and religious zeal. This is amply demonstrated in Bernard Glassman, *Anti-Semitic Stereotypes without Jews: Images of the Jews in England, 1290–1700* (Detroit, 1975); and Harold Fisch, *The Dual Image* (New York, 1971). On the concurrent, and not entirely contradictory, trend of philosemitism, see David Katz, *Philosemitism and the Readmission of the Jews to England, 1603–1655* (Oxford, 1982).

2. The most recent, and most detailed, chronology of the process is M. C. N. Salbstein, *The Emancipation of the Jews in Britain: The Question of the Admission of the Jews to Parliament, 1828–1860* (London, 1982). Still valuable, however (and certainly from the viewpoint of the present essay), is Israel Finestein, "Anglo-Jewish Opinion during the Struggle for Emancipation (1828–1858)," *Transactions of the Jewish Historical Society of England* 20 (1964): 113–43. On the Georgian prelude, the authoritative work is Todd M. Endelman, *The Jews of Georgian England, 1714–1830: Tradition and Change in a Liberal Society* (Philadelphia, 1979), esp. pp. 272–88.

uneven. Modern British history is punctuated with occasional anti-Jewish riots; it is more often characterized by social antisemitism—sometimes explicit, sometimes thinly disguised under the euphemism of "antialienism." Nevertheless, even when all this is said—as it must be—it still remains true that modern Britain witnessed no dramatic blood libel, no Dreyfus Affair, no Beilis case, not even a Leo Frank case; there was no official *numerus clausus* and, of course, no such savagery as was evident in Nazi Europe. In short, British history provides none of the watersheds that have supplied historians of other communities with the frameworks of reference against which Jewish reactions to antisemitism can be measured and analyzed.

The second methodological difficulty is of a different sort, and indeed in some ways contradicts the first. It can perhaps best be portrayed by reference to the absence of a definite article in the title of this paper. The subject of discussion is not *the* Anglo-Jewish response to antisemitism but various Anglo-Jewish responses. In part, of course, the use of the plural is attributable to historical convention—the tendency of historians to hedge their bets. But it is also—indeed, in this case, primarily—dictated by the nature of the topic. Baldly put, the topic simply does not allow of a mono-factor analysis. Even the most cursory survey of Anglo-Jewish history reveals the impossibility of identifying any single, or even perennially dominant, Anglo-Jewish response to antisemitism. On the contrary, what has to be noted immediately is the wide spectrum of such responses. At one end of the scale there existed a tendency to ignore or excuse antisemitic phenomena in British life. Characteristic proponents of this attitude either ascribed individual instances to a temporary aberration of the British way of life or adopted the warped apologetic stance of somehow making the victims responsible for their own misfortune. At the other end of the scale are to be found the advocates of a blatant and robust Jewish reaction to each and every perceived manifestation of prejudice, whatever its source. It was the proponents of this viewpoint who, in their more violent moods, advocated mass defiance of the law (the platform of the National Union for Jewish Rights during the conscription controversy of 1916–17) or physical defense (the policy of the Jewish People's Council during the mid-1930s).

What is more, to these two poles of response must be added an entire range of other intermediate alternatives. During the nineteenth and twentieth centuries some Jews in Britain proposed that antisemitism be "solved" by assimilation, others that it be uprooted by total revolution—whether it be of Gentile society in its entirety (the panacea of the communists) or of the Jewish world (the Zionist solution). Still other circles described themselves as middle-of-the-road pragmatists, neither denying the existence of antisemitism in Britain nor despairing of its local solution. Rather, they proposed treating each incident individually, and by a process of pressure: in some cases this might involve public meetings or, as was the case in Manchester in 1908, the organization of an ostensibly Jewish "vote" at elections; in others it might take the more discreet form of a private meeting with influential personalities in British public life.[3]

Those, it must be stressed, were not exclusive responses; they were articulated concurrently. What is more, they were recurring and can be identified in almost every one of the modern community's generations. In outline, many of those positions were articulated within the small coterie of the Anglo-Jewish elite that lobbied on behalf of the Jewish Naturalization Bill of 1753. They were clarified during the communal debates on emancipation between 1828 and the 1850s and seem to have become crystallized by the turn of the twentieth century in the wake of the massive influx into the community of large numbers of Eastern European Jews. Further developments of the principal themes, but not their radical reformulations, were prompted by subsequent events: the conscription controversies of World War I and the Bolshevik outcry immediately thereafter, the agitations engendered by Oswald Mosley during the 1930s, Britain's mandatory policy in Palestine (particularly during its last two most violent years), the Suez Crisis, Colin Jordan's para-fascist activities during the 1960s, and, most recently, the communal attempt to define the degree and nature of the threat posed by the National Front.[4]

Needless to say, this is a very summary sketch of the range and variety of Anglo-Jewish responses to antisemitism in modern British

3. For a comparatively early (and remarkably incisive) diagnosis of the two poles here presented as well as the intermediate positions, see the report of the discussion following Rev. Morris Joseph's address to the West London Synagogue Association on "Anti-Semitic Trends in England," *Jewish Chronicle*, July 4, 1913, pp. 17–19.

4. Those and other milestones are touched upon in V. D. Lipman, *Social History of the Jews in England, 1850–1950* (London, 1954); and Lipman, ed., *Three Centuries of Anglo-Jewish History* (London, 1961). The most recent events are sketched in Sidney Levenberg, "The Development of Anglo-Jewry, 1962–1967," in *Jewish Life in Britain, 1962–1977*, ed. S. L. Lipman and V. D. Lipman (New York, 1981), pp. 175–80.

history. But, even as it stands, it does serve to illustrate the nature of the methodological difficulties already referred to. On the one hand, antisemitism, although perennial, was in Britain certainly of a lower intensity than in the majority of other European countries (the most important exception, perhaps, being Holland); it would thus appear to have called for a rather limited range of responses. On the other hand, the evidence indicates that, in fact, those responses repeatedly covered a broad spectrum—as broad, in fact, as any to be found in the larger Jewish communities that labored under the burden of far greater misfortunes.

Perhaps it is this methodological dilemma that accounts for a curious bibliographical gap. We do possess studies that plot, often in detail, the incidence of antisemitic phenomena in modern Britain.[5] Some of these works, together with other monographs, also specifically address particular features of the Anglo-Jewish response.[6] But, despite the plethora of individual studies, we do not (to the best of my knowledge) possess a synoptic analysis, one that might correlate Anglo-Jewish perceptions of the incidence of antisemitism (both at home and abroad) with the Jewish reactions and thereby produce a typology of political action that would reflect on the ambience, mores, and structure of the community over a lengthy period of time. Thus, notwithstanding the notable revival that is presently taking place in Anglo-Jewish history, here is one field in which students of the community are at a disadvantage. They possess nothing to compare, for example, to the studies of French Jewry in the nineteenth and twentieth centuries compiled by Michael R. Marrus,

5. Notably, Colin Holmes, *Anti-Semitism in British Society, 1876–1939* (London, 1979); G. C. Lebzelter, *Political Anti-Semitism in England, 1918–1939* (London, 1978); and W. F. Mandle, *Anti-Semitism and the British Union of Fascists* (London, 1968). For earlier incidents, see T. W. Perry, *Public Opinion, Propaganda, and Politics in Eighteenth Century England: A Study of the Jew Bill of 1753* (Cambridge, Mass., 1968); Bernard Gainer, *The Alien Invasion: The Origins of the Aliens Act of 1905* (London, 1972); J. A. Garrard, *The English and Immigration, 1880–1910* (London, 1971); and Aaron Goldman, "The Resurgence of Anti-Semitism in Britain during World War II," *Jewish Social Studies* 46 (1984): 37–50. Some contemporary surveys of the post–World War II phenomenon are in C. C. Aronsfeld, "Anti-Jewish Outbreaks in Modern Britain," *Gates of Zion* 6, no. 4 (1952): 15–18.

6. E.g., Geoffrey Alderman, "The Anti-Jewish Riots of August 1911 in South Wales," *Welsh History Review* 6 (1972): 140–200; Steven Bayme, "Jewish Leadership and Anti-Semitism in Britain, 1898–1918" (Ph.D. diss., Columbia University, 1977); Max Beloff, "Lucien Wolf and the Anglo-Russian Entente, 1907–1914," in his *The Intellectual in Politics and Other Essays* (London, 1970), pp. 111–42; and Meir Simpolinsky, "Hamemshalah ha-britit ve-ha-shoah" (Ph.D. diss., Bar-Ilan University, 1977), chaps. 2, 11, 13, 15.

Paula Hyman, and Phyllis Albert; or to the monographs on the German community by Ismar Schorsch and Jehuda Reinharz; or to Nathaniel Katzburg's pieces on Hungary; or to the various accounts of Jewish defense activities in the United States and in pre- and post-revolutionary Russia.

This is not the occasion to attempt a full-scale rectification of that situation. The purpose of the present paper is more limited; it aims to propose an analytical framework that might facilitate an examination of Anglo-Jewish responses to antisemitism and take specific account of the peculiarities of the case. That objective might best be attained through the identification and examination of three primary issues: (1) the various perceived environments in which different responses were articulated; (2) the various types of antisemitic phenomena to which reactions were formulated; and (3) the various sections of the community that advocated the differing responses. The remainder of this paper will be devoted to a brief discussion and illustration of each of these three issues.

I

Any attempt to reconstruct the images that, at various times, members of the Anglo-Jewish community had of their Gentile environment must begin with a truism: for the vast majority of the Jews of Britain throughout the modern period the point of departure was a prevailing atmosphere of trust rather than of terror. For them the norm was tolerance, a tolerance that seemed, moreover, to have been neither imposed on British society by a foreign power nor mandated to the great British public by the idiosyncratic interests of a ruling clique. It was, rather, a norm that had about it the aura of an organic growth. Tolerance, so Jews came to understand, had been implanted in British society by the philosemitism of Puritan divines.[7] It seemed to have been nurtured by the eighteenth-century British Enlightenment and become enshrined in the philosophical tradition of liberal utilitarianism that was England's, and Scotland's, most noteworthy contribution to contemporary political theory and practice.

As we have already had occasion to note, this ambience was never so persuasive or pervasive that it could altogether foreclose debate

---

7. As David Katz has now shown, this was an unabashedly egocentric form of philosemitism, but philosemitism nevertheless. See his *Philosemitism*.

on the manner in which the community might best respond to perceived deviations from the norm. On the contrary, it can be argued—not entirely paradoxically—that it was the very prevalence of a norm of tolerance that presented some Jews with their greatest conceptual difficulties. It enabled them to approach the phenomenon of antisemitism in two very different ways. One, and certainly the more optimistic, was to regard antisemitism as a momentary phase of European culture that was neither inevitable nor ineradicable. As much, indeed, was proven by the British experience itself. As a domestic phenomenon, it could be argued, antisemitism had declined concomitantly with the permeation of the British national character by a spirit of enlightenment. Its occasional resurgence was thus an aberration.[8] At one level outbursts of antisemitism could be attributed to the "foreign" behavior of some Jews (particularly the immigrants) rather than to the intrinsically evil nature of its perpetrators.[9] Less distastefully, they could be ascribed to extraneous pressures on the country's cultural equilibrium: momentary waves of economic dislocation (whether during the early industrial revolution or the 1930s); temporary national xenophobia (as during the Eastern Crisis of 1877, the Boer War, or World War I); or excessive party rivalry (which was one Jewish reaction to the Indian Silver and Marconi scandals prior to World War I).

Whichever the case, those outbursts of antisemitism were perceived as deviations from the norms of tolerant liberalism that seemed to be the dominant characteristic of modern British society. That, indeed, was the perspective which infused the writings of, for instance, Lucien Wolf and Claude Montefiore, two of the most articulate and influential exponents of the "optimistic" school of Anglo-Jewish thought during its Edwardian era. As these men repeatedly

8. E.g., "There is no Jewish problem in England, I say. There is only an artificial problem created deliberately by Nazi ideologists." Neville Laski, *Jewish Rights and Jewish Wrongs* (London, 1939), p. 124.

9. Manifestations of this approach were numerous at the turn of the century, particularly in the pages of the *Jewish Chronicle*. See Stanley Kaplan, "The Anglicanization of the East European Jewish Immigrant as Seen by the London *Jewish Chronicle*, 1870–1897," *YIVO Annual of Jewish Social Science* 10 (1955): 267–78. They were still present during the 1930s. One example is provided by a pamphlet issued in 1938 by the Board of Deputies of British Jews entitled, *While You Are in England: Helpful Information and Guidance for Every Refugee*. It contained a somewhat smug summary of English manners as well as information about the country. For more sympathetic views of the immigrants during these periods, see W. J. Fishman, *East End Jewish Radicals, 1875–1914* (London, 1975); L. P. Gartner, *The Jewish Immigrant in England, 1870–1914*, 2d ed. (London, 1973); and A. J. Sherman, *Island Refuge* (London, 1973).

explained, it was the point of departure which principally distinguished the British Jew from, for example, the Russian *maskil* of the early nineteenth century. The latter, too, could argue that, theoretically speaking, antisemitism was ultimately eradicable, even in the tsar's domains. But for the Russian *maskil* to take that position, and thence to posit that protest and debate were viable responses, demanded a leap of imagination. He had to go beyond his existing environment and relate to abstracts: the first principles of humanism or the translation of natural rights into law. In Britain, Jews could talk of concretes, a fact that made such responses seem far more rational.[10]

But there was quite another, pessimistic, way of looking at matters. Britain's tolerance toward the Jews could be considered in some way temporary, restricted to a small liberal group, and, even then, protected by a very thin crust. Scratch it anywhere in British society, and one would discover a far less comforting state of affairs. As much was self-evident to Haham Moses Gaster, an immigrant from Rumania, a Zionist, and one of Wolf's and Montefiore's principal communal antagonists. Notwithstanding his acknowledgment of the benefits of Jewish emancipation, and of the history of that process, at root Gaster remained suspicious of the entire world of the Gentiles. They could never really be trusted to overcome their hereditary burden of medieval Christian prejudice, far less to accept Jews as truly equal citizens. Even in England, Gaster argued—and argued in print—the Jew would always be regarded as an alien. "The claim to be Englishmen of the Jewish persuasion—that is English by nationality and Jewish by faith—is an absolute self-delusion."[11]

In that particular exchange, Montefiore was not lost for a reply: "That . . . book," he responded, "is *too* bad—the Zionists want to make all gentiles anti-Semites."[12] But Gaster's case could still carry conviction. After all he, and like-minded members of the community, could point to a very wide range of domestic sources from which

10. See, e.g., Claude Montefiore, "Assimilation: Good and Bad," *Papers for the Jewish People* 9 (London, 1909); Montefiore, "What Would You Have Us Do?" ibid., 11 (London, 1913); and Lucien Wolf, "Anti-Semitism," *Encyclopaedia Britannica*, 11th ed. (1911), 2:134–46.

11. Moses Gaster, "Judaism: A National Religion," *Zionism and the Jewish Future*, ed. Harry Sacher (London, 1916), pp. 87–98.

12. Montefiore to Wolf, July 11, 1916, Records of the Board of Deputies of British Jews, London, General Correspondence, file c 11/2/3/9; and "Zionism," by "An Englishman of the Jewish Faith" [Montefiore], *Fortnightly Review*, November 1916, pp. 819–26.

antisemitic actions and utterances seemed to emanate. They came from the Left as well as the Right of the British political spectrum (from J. A. Hobson, Henry Hyndman, and Beatrice Potter as well as Arnold White, William Evans-Gordon, and the *Morning Post*) and to give rise to the foundation of political organizations as well as to generate sporadic outbreaks (the British Brothers' League and the British Union of Fascists were outgrowths of several other organizations, and perhaps therefore symptomatic of a wider malaise). Antisemitism was evident among both upper and lower classes;[13] it affected small Jewish communities as well as the larger concentrations (witness the Limerick incidents of the 1890s, the South Wales riots of 1911, and the northeastern disturbances of 1946, as well as the Battle of Cable Street). Worst of all, these might be reflections as much of official attitudes as of popular prejudice. Restrictions on alien immigration (in 1905, 1911, and the 1930s) might provide one example of legislation that could not be averted or rescinded simply by apologetics. But what lesson about the ambience of British society was to be drawn, for instance, from Britain's mandatory policy in Palestine or, to take an earlier example, from the very publication of the Balfour Declaration? Did that act signify philosemitism, or was it fundamentally and insidiously antisemitic? The question, as is well known, seriously troubled Edwin Montagu, at the time secretary of state for India, so much so that he was prepared to compose what must surely be one of the most rebarbative memorandums ever placed on the cabinet table, which he entitled "The Anti-Semitism of the Present Government."[14]

The British government's support for political Zionism—the target of Montagu's extraordinary outburst—was, even by his own standards, a very peculiar form of antisemitism. And yet the terms in

---

13. On the post–World War II situation in Bethnal Green, see the sociological study by J. H. Robb, *Working-Class Anti-Semite* (London, 1954). A more recent and more comprehensive study of an earlier period in Yorkshire history is J. B. Buckman, *Immigrants and the Class Struggle: The Jewish Immigrant in Leeds, 1880–1914* (Manchester, 1983).

14. Dated August 23, 1917, the paper by Edwin S. Montagu has been published in *Edwin S. Montagu and the Balfour Declaration* (New York, 1973), pp. 123–27. Among other things, it argued: "More and more we are educated in public schools and at the Universities, and take our part in politics, in the Army, in the Civil Service of our country. And I am glad to think that the prejudices against inter-marriage are breaking down. But when the Jews have a national home, surely it follows that the impetus to deprive us of rights of citizenship must be enormously increased. . . . I would ask of a British Government sufficient tolerance to refuse to endorse a conclusion which makes aliens and foreigners by implication, if not at once by law, of all their Jewish fellow-citizens."

which even that episode was considered and debated by Jews in England does illustrate the range of perspectives about the Gentile environment that have to be considered in all discussions of the subject. The communal debate, at this level, was not about tactics but about environmental strategy. Optimists as well as pessimists agreed that British society contained both philosemites and antisemites or (in the terms used by Jacob Katz) that there existed both tolerance and exclusiveness. Where they differed was in their estimation of which was the more fundamentally prevalent. This was a difference that could cut across otherwise clearly demarcated Anglo-Jewish alignments and must therefore constitute the first issue to be considered in any analysis of the subject.

II

The need for clarification becomes even more evident once attention is turned toward another feature of the topic: the various types of antisemitism to which Anglo-Jewry felt it necessary to respond. Here, too, the problem is not to accumulate examples but to assess and catalog the evidence. The challenge, therefore, is to construct a framework of analysis that might facilitate an understanding of the range of Anglo-Jewish responses to antisemitism by accommodating both the various expressions of the phenomenon itself and the different social and temporal contexts of its individual manifestations.

Of the several organizational devices that might help solve the problem, two seem to be particularly popular. One is the conventional chronological approach, which relates each incident of antisemitism in turn, seeking for prior antecedents and later echoes. Although this method does certainly retain our awareness of the constantly ticking clock, it seems to misplace certain emphases. Even in its most sophisticated versions (a category that certainly includes Colin Holmes's *Anti-Semitism in British Society*), it tends to depict antisemitism as an unfolding occurrence, whereas (as Holmes's book itself demonstrates) in Britain that was not the case. Here antisemitism experienced retreats as well as advances, repetitions as well as innovations. An alternative method might be to catalog antisemitic incidents by their degree of violence; to construct, as it were, a scale at one end of which would be the riot and at the other the offensive cartoon or the discriminatory notice. This appears to be a more promising approach, not least because Jewish respondents to antisemitism themselves often thought in such terms. One example is provided by the work of the Board of Deputies of British Jews during the 1930s. Injuries to Jewish life or damage to Jewish property were dealt with by the board's Defence Committee (called the Co-ordinating Committee between July 1936 and November 1938), which then organized a petition, a meeting of protest, or, in the extreme cases of overseas antisemitism, could attempt to work through the Joint Foreign Committee and consider a boycott of German goods. Infringements of the law in matters of housing or trading licenses were, on the other hand, dealt with by the Law and Parliamentary Committee, which usually approached the relevant department of government or individual MPs. Anti-Jewish publications or speeches, to take a third case, could be answered in kind by the Publications Committee, whose secretariat helped to prepare a *Jewish Defence Campaign Speaker's Handbook* in 1937 and distributed Neville Laski's *Jewish Rights and Jewish Wrongs* in 1939. All very neat; but perhaps rather too much so. The deficiency in this method of analysis (and indeed, if the board's critics are to be believed, the deficiency in the responses to which it gave rise) lay in that it tended to avoid, and sometimes to ignore, the question of the precise motive of the individual antisemitic incident and the nature of the pattern of which it formed a part. Intellectual analysis was, in this case, subordinated to bureaucratic convenience.[15]

Any attempt to rectify this situation by the imposition of a different set of categories is bound to appear somewhat artificial. No single, synoptic classification of antisemitism can ever be entirely satisfactory. Nevertheless, it is significant that during the nineteenth and twentieth centuries several Jews in Britain did attempt a methodological typology. What has to be noted, moreover, is that their principal interest was in antisemitic motives and intent. In this respect, the community's apologetic literature—notwithstanding dif-

15. The activities of the Board of Deputies of British Jews and the conflicts between it and the Jewish People's Council are described in Lebzelter, *Political Anti-Semitism in England*, pp. 136–54. See also reports of debates at the board in the *Jewish Chronicle*, July 24, 1936, p. 20, and October 23, 1936, p. 13, and of the Jewish People's Council Conference in ibid., November 20, 1936, p. 20. The extent to which primary materials exist for an extensive study at Anglo-Jewish institutional responses to antisemitism is demonstrated by the "Report on the Records of the Board of Deputies of British Jews," compiled by Roberta Routledge in 1978, available at Board of Deputies headquarters in London.

ferences in tone and nuance—reveals a distinct sense of unity. From the methodological viewpoint, a clear line might be drawn between the pamphlet literature of the 1830s, the benchmark article on Jewish citizenship written by Rabbi (later Chief Rabbi) Hermann Adler for the *Nineteenth Century* in July 1878, Wolf's piece in the 1911 edition of the *Encyclopaedia Britannica*, and Laski's *Jewish Rights and Jewish Wrongs*. All portrayed antisemitism as a composite phenomenon, necessitating atomistic categorization in terms of purposes rather than manifestations. It was this approach that seems to have influenced the range of Anglo-Jewry's responses (certainly at the organizational level) to individual instances of antisemitism. It is this approach, too, that, with the aid of more recent psychological and sociological studies, might profitably be employed by modern historians. With its help, the latter might grope toward a typology of antisemitic phenomena in British life. In turn, this might contribute to an understanding, not of the phenomena themselves (which is not really the subject of the present paper) but of Jewish responses to them.

Tentatively, I would suggest that such a typology might consist of a matrix consisting of three tiers. These might here be labeled categorical, *ad hoc*, and ambivalent. By the first, categorical, I refer to an ideologically grounded rascist antisemitism, one that expressed a genetically based hostility toward all Jews, who were regarded as a totally alien element in society and thought to exercise a dangerous influence on the non-Jewish environment. As Léon Poliakov's exhaustive survey has shown, antisemitism of a categorical variety was also not cut of one cloth.[16] But what was common to all its variants was that this version was all-embracing; it viewed all Jews, and all forms of Judaism, as culturally antagonistic. It was not dependent on the specifics of Jewish behavior.

This type of antisemitism, in its modern form, was of course far more prevalent in Europe than in Britain.[17] But British Jews could never be totally insular. For one thing, categorical antisemitism did have its occasional British versions, some of which were echoes of European doctrines. As much is evident from the romantic Catholic conservatism propagated by Hilaire Belloc and G. K. Chesterton, the

16. Léon Poliakov, *The History of Anti-Semitism* (London, 1965–75).
17. Indeed the latest authoritative study—Jacob Katz, *From Prejudice to Destruction: Anti-Semitism, 1700–1933* (Cambridge, Mass., 1980)—contains not a single reference to Britain after the eighteenth century.

notion of Jewish Bolshevism popularized in the *Morning Post,* and the *Stürmer*-like rehashes of the *Protocols of the Elders of Zion* (in England, *The Jewish Peril*) favored by some members of the British Union of Fascists. In all of these cases the Jews had become a metaphor for all that was obnoxiously conspiratorial and for all that had supposedly caused matters in Britain to go wrong.[18] As such, the community's room for maneuver, collective and individual, was severely restricted. Protest and the publication of counterarguments were, of course, tried; recourse was occasionally had to the courts (as in the case of the successful injunction against the publication in 1908 of Sir Richard Burton's *Human Sacrifice against the Sephardim or Eastern Jews).*[19] But the trust placed in these measures was by and large restricted to those who had a basically optimistic view of the staying power of British tolerance. Even then it was sometimes halfhearted. Others placed their trust elsewhere: in Zionism, in communism or, of course, in God.

Overseas manifestations of categorical antisemitism could be otherwise treated. Accordingly, in these cases Anglo-Jewish responses were more edifying, and more consistently forthright. It was here that the weapons of mass public protest, political and economic pressure, and diplomatic initiatives were most often employed, notwithstanding the awareness on the part of those who engineered such measures that their actions exposed them to the very charge of a Jewish international conspiracy which often generated the original outbreak.[20] The record of such Anglo-Jewish actions is both long and distinguished. It stretches from Sir Moses Montefiore's intervention

18. See the analysis in Robert Skidelsky, *Oswald Mosley* (London, 1975).

19. Minutes of Board of Deputies meetings, April 17 and May 15, 1898 and October 25, 1908, in Board of Deputies Records, B3. See also Holmes, *Anti-Semitism in British Society,* pp. 137–38.

20. Particularly was this so in the case of Lucien Wolf, who, as secretary of the Conjoint Foreign Committee of the Board of Deputies and the Anglo-Jewish Association (after 1917 known as the Joint Foreign Committee), was quite properly regarded as the communal equivalent of a "foreign secretary." Wolf's diplomatic initiatives on behalf of Jews in Central and Eastern Europe (before, during, and after World War I), his public exposure of the *Protocols,* and his prolific journalistic activity (notably the publication of *In Darkest Russia*) all warrant detailed attention. Even a limited survey would seem to excuse Wolf, at least, from most of Hannah Arendt's well-known strictures on the chronic submissiveness of Jewish communal leaders. See Bayme, "Jewish Leadership," pp. 256–64; and Hannah Arendt, *The Origins of Totalitarianism,* 2d ed. (New York, 1958), pp. 23–25, 54. An indication of the materials that exist for a study of Anglo-Jewish responses to antisemitism through the life and work of Lucien Wolf is provided by the catalog of his papers at the YIVO Institute in New York, published by Zosa Szajkowski in *YIVO Bleter* 43 (1966): 283–96. See also Board of Deputies Records, files c 11/5 and c 11/12.

in the Damascus blood libel of 1840 through the lobbies organized at the Congress of Berlin in 1878 and the Versailles Peace Conference in 1919. It also includes public and private responses to the Kishinev pogrom of 1903, to Nazi outrages during the 1930s and 1940s, and to the plight of Soviet Jewry during our own day. An initial survey of these incidents indicates that, throughout, it is possible to discern a feeling (albeit often unspoken) that it was the categorical nature of those particular manifestations of antisemitism that necessitated an unequivocally categorical response.[21]

Ad hoc antisemitism, the second tier of the proposed matrix, was perceived as a different matter. Primarily this was because it was directed not against the Jews as a corporate entity and in all cases but against individual Jews in specific and one-to-one situations. In many cases—perhaps most, for all we know—*ad hoc* antisemitism might have been a subconscious or residual derivation of the categorical variety. But certain distinctions between them must still be drawn, certainly from the viewpoint of the Jewish response. For one thing, *ad hoc* antisemitism was not as sophisticated, laying no claims to philosophical underpinnings. For another it was, in the British case certainly, more pervasive. Its manifestations were not restricted to areas of Jewish concentration and of social unrest (Bethnal Green or the Leylands) but also occurred in scattered settlements and in relatively quiescent and supposedly cultured circles, a category that includes All Souls College, Oxford, early in the twentieth century.[22]

In this category, too, no absolutely uniform response is discernible. Jewish reactions to *ad hoc* antisemitism in Britain (as well as to the categorical variety) seem often to have been determined by the wider view that the victim had of the essential ambience of British society

21. There still exists no full-length study of Anglo-Jewish diplomacy. Probably the nearest we have is Lucien Wolf's own *Notes on the Diplomatic History of the Jewish Question* (London, 1919). The above comment is, therefore, based solely on preliminary readings. One other example (the reaction to Kishinev) is discussed in Stuart A. Cohen, *English Zionists and British Jews: The Communal Politics of Anglo-Jewry, 1895–1920* (Princeton, 1982), pp. 71–76.

22. Note, e.g., A. F. Pollard's description of the college election meeting that discussed Lewis Namier's candidacy in 1911: "The meeting on Friday morning for the election of Fellows was lively and I was told the debate was the best on record. . . . The lawyers could not conscientiously run a law candidate, so we had two for history. The best man by far in sheer intellect was a Balliol man of Polish-Jewish origin and I did my best for him, but the Warden and majority of Fellows shied at his race, and eventually we elected the next two best." Julia Namier, *Lewis Namier: A Biography* (London, 1971), p. 101.

(much also depended on the personality and position of the Jew concerned, but that is a matter which must be deferred for the moment). Those with a fundamentally optimistic view did have recourse to the existing law.[23] Another option was to organize a parliamentary lobby in order to deal with individual cases, such as the Sunday Trading Laws. Where these means were inappropriate, Jews affected by *ad hoc* antisemitism could press on regardless, believing—as many did—that in the long run the British people would never allow prejudice to cloud their respect for excellence. This belief permeated the world of sport, as well as that of the professions, business, and entertainment; it seems certainly to have been the philosophy of Harold Abrahams. But a fundamentally pessimistic view of the resilience of British tolerance could produce the contrary response of individual flight. Most obviously is this illustrated by the cases of those Jews who attempted to deny their attested Jewish origins (as did G. J. Goschen, chancellor of the exchequer, 1887–92) or to come to a curious alliance with their antisemitic challengers (as did, to quote another sporting example, Kid Lewis, the boxer, who was an early member of the British Union of Fascists). Most dramatically, however, was this reaction manifest in the actions of those who physically departed from Britain. Perhaps the notable instance of this category of behavior was provided by Sir Edgar Speyer, who, after immigrating to London from Germany in 1887 and becoming naturalized in 1892, had involved himself in the world of philanthropy, music, and Liberal politics, and in 1909 had been created a privy councilor. In 1915, when anti-German (and specifically anti-German-Jewish) feelings ran high, his origins were recalled. Others in the same position wrote "loyalty letters" to the *Times*, but Speyer refused to do so. Although the courts justified his position on the Privy Council (his foreign birth notwithstanding), Speyer packed in all his British affairs and went to New York. His action was frowned upon by some members of the community, but it was not necessarily unique.[24]

Between the poles of categorical antisemitism (which was atypi-

---

23. In these legal actions they could be helped by several Jewish legal experts. H. S. Q. Henriques was one. As vice-president of the Board of Deputies (and chairman of its Law and Parliamentary Committee), he took a personal interest in numerous Jewish cases. He also wrote a massive tome, entitled *The Jews and the English Law* (Oxford, 1908), specifically for the purpose of encouraging his co-religionists to overcome discriminatory practices.

24. See Holmes, *Anti-Semitism in British Society*, pp. 131–32.

cal) and *ad hoc* antisemitism (which was common) there lay a third tier, which I have here labeled ambivalent. This was the form of hostility evinced not toward Jews as a totality, nor toward particular Jews as individuals, but toward groups of Jews: poor immigrants, rich financiers, social revolutionaries, politicians, and the like. Its ambivalence lay in that while, on the one hand, it denied antisemitic premises with regard to Jews as a whole, it justified antisemitism with regard to certain sections of Jewry. It distinguished, as it were, between some Jews and others, between those who could be tolerated and those who had to be excluded. This was the view taken, for instance, by Arnold White when advocating restrictions on Jewish immigration at the turn of the twentieth century; by Leo Maxe, who castigated the "loud, sophisticated, byzantine" entourage surrounding Edward VII; and by Arnold Leese, who founded the Imperial Fascist League in the 1920s in order to combat the baneful influence on Britain's imperial policy said to be highlighted by the appointment of Lord Reading as viceroy of India.[25]

In a way, as the sociologists tell us, this behavior can be seen as a variant of the ingroup-outgroup phenomenon. Parallels can be found in the animosity expressed in Britain toward Chinese laundrymen, Italian restauranteurs, German clerks, gypsy entertainers, West Indian bus drivers, and Pakistani grocers.[26] But it did have a particular Jewish aspect. Most of those other groups possessed what has been termed a "licensed preserve"; they kept, by and large, to specific areas of activity. The Jews, for all their preferences for some occupations, attempted to penetrate all areas of society, and to bunch together while doing so.

This peculiarity was recognized by British Jews themselves. Perhaps it helps to explain yet another Jewish response—that of dispersion and the low profile. In the apologetic literature this was expressed in the warning that, when protesting against antisemitism, Jews should be careful "in the first place, not to put purely Jewish interests before those of the State of which we are citizens."[27] That sentiment was not as innocent as it sounds. What underlay it was a feeling that, in some way, the ambivalent form of antisemitism was

25. Geoffrey Alderman, *The Jewish Community in British Politics* (Oxford, 1983), pp. 86–87.
26. See Ernest Krausz, *Ethnic Minorities in Britain* (London, 1971).
27. Laski, *Jewish Rights and Jewish Wrongs*, p. 131.

justified and that neither counterargument nor active defense was really appropriate. The Jews themselves, natives as well as immigrants, had somehow to become less visible. One way, the most drastic, was simply not to come to Britain in the first place, which was why the Jewish Board of Guardians, for instance, at one time adopted a policy of financing the return passage of immigrant Jews to Eastern Europe. Similarly, during World War I, even several Zionists could support the government's threat that those Russian Jews who did not enlist in the British army would be returned to the care of the tsar.[28] But there were also other, less draconian, instances of a similar process of thought. In political life this attitude expressed itself in the persistent refusal of Jewish MPs to form their own lobby and in the loud communal protestations against the creation of a Jewish vote.[29] In the professional field it took the form of attempting to avoid Jewish occupational "bunching" by launching various programs of diversified education (and opposing, at one stage, the foundation of Carmel College).[30] In the demographic sphere there were attempts to disperse the community by constructing 4 percent dwellings or by establishing a provincial congregations fund. Whether or not one sympathizes with these responses is not, of course, the point. What is at issue is that they have to be distinguished from other responses and might perhaps be so distinguished by identifying the form of antisemitism that they were designed to combat.

III

There remains, finally, the third of the coordinates—that of the identity of those Jews who viewed British society in different ways and who responded variously to the different forms of antisemitism. Enough, surely, has already been said to demonstrate that modern Anglo-Jewry, although a highly organized community, has never

---

28. See, respectively, V. D. Lipman, *A Century of Social Service, 1859–1959: The Jewish Board of Guardians* (London, 1959), pp. 89–96; and David Yisraeli, "The Struggle for Zionist Military Involvement in the First World War, 1914–1917," in *Bar-Ilan Studies in History*, ed. Pinchas Artzi (Ramat Gan, 1978), pp. 197–213.

29. See Alderman, *Jewish Community*, who concludes that these protests were more often unavailing than is usually thought.

30. David Stamler, "Kopul at Carmel," in *Memories of Kopul Rosen*, ed. Cyril Domb (Wallingford, 1970), pp. 99–101.

been uniform. Despite the plethora of communal bodies, unanimity could not be imposed, and was never attained. Camps and parties can be discerned within synagogal groupings, within cultural and political institutions (the English Zionist Federation and the Inter-University Jewish Federation, the Friendly Societies), and even within bodies like the Board of Deputies and the Anglo-Jewish Association, which were supposed somehow to embrace all others. Cutting across all functional divisions were differences of personal experience, class, domicile (provincial communities had a life quite different from that of London), religious observance, political affiliation (as regards Zionism, not British political parties), and, perhaps most important of all, land of origin.[31]

Many of these differences were reflected during the sporadic discussions of possible Anglo-Jewish responses to antisemitism that were occasionally held at the Board of Deputies. Consequently it would be patently incorrect to divide this third coordinate along an axis whose principal division was between "official" and "unofficial" Anglo-Jewry and to take all that was said at the board (or was printed in the Jewish Chronicle) as "representative" and regard as "unrepresentative" all that was printed in the immigrant Yiddish press or pronounced at other forums. The two sources often reflected each other.[32]

For the purposes of analyzing Anglo-Jewish responses to antisemitism, the community might instead be dissected along a different axis, one that aims to reflect the degree to which individual Jews perceived their own primary identities. At one end of the scale could be placed those for whom their Jewishness was central to their existence and aspirations. Thus it was ideologically for the Zionists, professionally for the lay and clerical Jewish civil servants (native and immigrant), socially for those who mixed predominantly with other Jews (at both work and leisure), and emotionally, culturally,

31. A discussion of the institutional implications is included in Stuart A. Cohen, "Communal Change and Institutional Resilience," in Public Life in Israel and the Diaspora, ed. S. N. Lehman-Wilzig and Bernard Susser (Ramat Gan, 1981), pp. 64–90.
32. This was certainly so in the case of the Kishinev episode referred to above. Discussions at the Board of Deputies and even in the Conjoint Foreign Committee reflect an awareness of what was being proposed at such immigrant forums as the Kishinev Atrocities Relief Committee, whose members, in turn, seem to be cognizant of discussion at the Conjoint Foreign Committee. In some cases Moses Gaster appears to have deliberately acted as go-between. See the correspondence for May and June 1903 in the Moses Gaster Papers, Mocatta Library, London.

and religiously for those who, even though they mixed freely with non-Jews in their professional and social lives, made no bones about where their primary loyalties lay.[33]

At the other end of the scale would stand those Jews who felt their Jewishness to be peripheral to their existence and aspirations, an accident of birth that certainly influenced their lives (not least when they were confronted with antisemitism) but which did not give their lives focus. Such was the case not only with the much-maligned assimilationists among Jewry's upper classes (the court Jews or the Cousinhood), nor only with the Jewish socialists and anarchists of the late nineteenth century (Aaron Lieberman's early disciples) and Communists of the mid-twentieth century (those who returned Phil Piratin to Parliament as Communist MP for Mile End in 1945). Both of these groups clearly aspired to assimilation into a wider Gentile framework: British in the first case and the universal proletariat in the second. It was also true of the apparently larger number who, even if they did not avoid other Jews (nor even the synagogue), sought social and professional satisfaction primarily elsewhere and therefore neither accepted public Jewish office nor lived in the larger Jewish concentrations of settlement.

Were a statistical analysis possible of the community throughout the period (and it is not), we would probably find that the majority of Anglo-Jewry stood at neither pole but were somewhere in between. But this situation, although eminently reasonable, was not necessarily comfortable. On the contrary, the very existence of the two extreme poles (minority though they were) might have induced a feeling among the majority of marginality, a sense not that they had a foot firmly planted in each of two worlds (to use the title of one of David Daiches's books) but that they really stood somewhere on the fringes of both. Specifics are, of course, hard to come by. But the literature of the period does leave an impression that the masses of the community—the rank-and-file members of synagogues and the contributors to major Jewish philanthropies—felt neither completely integrated nor totally segregated. Their sense of marginality

33. The most prominent example to come to mind is that of Samuel Montagu (after 1911 Lord Swaythling), whose will gave rise to legal proceedings because it specified that his children would receive bequests only provided "they were professing the Jewish religion and not married to a person who did not profess the Jewish religion." See Holmes, *Anti-Semitism in British Society*, p. 256; and L. H. Montagu, *Samuel Montagu First Baron Swaythling* (London, 1913).

was sometimes articulated, most prominently by such figures as Col. Albert Edward Goldsmid and Claude Montefiore, men who would otherwise be considered atypical members of Jewry's upper class, and by Abraham Bezalel and Joseph Dywien, working-class leaders of the same period. All moved restlessly between the spheres of intensive Jewish communal activity and devotion to causes that were of predominantly Gentile concern. And yet, at the end of the day, they could feel curiously alien to both.[34]

Such a classification of the Anglo-Jewish community might, perhaps, further refine our understanding of two facets of our case: first, the variety of the community's responses to antisemitism (after all, the people who proposed those responses spoke from different positions); and, second, the vacillation that accompanied individual decisions on strategy. The latter, which was frequent, was not simply the result of some disrespectful sense of timidity but of a more finely tuned sense of marginality. It was this sense that, especially at moments of high tensions and passions, brought to bear on the issue of antisemitism perceptions which ranged far beyond the issues immediately at hand.

If, then, I might be permitted to summarize my argument, it is for a multifaceted examination of Anglo-Jewish responses to antisemitism and, more specifically, for one that establishes a conceptual framework within which the subject might be profitably analyzed. I have here outlined three issues that I consider to be the most relevant, each containing subcategories, and what I would stress is that no single one of them can be studied in isolation. They have to be employed in tandem, through the medium of a series of specific case studies, each of which might identify the precise location of the source of the response within the cube and might also measure the different weights of the different axes at various points. Such a study would doubtless reveal that there are occasions when the order of the questions might be rearranged, when it would be more profitable to begin an inquiry by asking how individual Jewish

34. Thus, e.g., Claude Montefiore: "Sometimes I get so sick . . . that I feel tempted to chuck all Jewish work and retire . . . and live exclusively as an ordinary Englishman among my *English* neighbours, my own *people* as I call them." Montefiore to Sheldon Blank, April 15, 1917, Sheldon Blank Papers, American-Jewish Archives, Cincinnati, box 625.

respondents related to the degree of their own Jewish identity before examining their perspectives on exclusiveness and tolerance in British society, or the type of antisemitic phenomenon being studied. But, whichever the case, all three issues deserve to be addressed.

Arnold Paucker

The Jewish Defense against Antisemitism in Germany, 1893–1933

Say not the struggle nought availeth

—Arthur Hugh Clough

The main subject of this essay, the Centralverein deutscher Staatsbürger jüdischen Glaubens (CV), was founded more than ninety
years ago.[1] What is known as its "defense struggle" lasted forty years
until its apparent end, almost unmarked, at the hands of the Nazis
in 1933. Jewish defense work, as understood here—primarily legal
activity carried out in public, though also covertly pursued in the
last stages of the Weimar Republic—did not and could not exist for
the Jewish community once the National Socialist dictatorship was
established.[2]

In the Germany of fifty years ago, changes in the Jewish self-image
were rife. Thereafter came a temporary rejection of liberalism born

1. This essay is based to a large extent on my book *Der jüdische Abwehrkampf gegen
Antisemitismus und Nationalsozialismus in den letzten Jahren der Weimarer Republik*,
Hamburger Beiträge zur Zeitgeschichte 6, 2d ed. (Hamburg, 1969); and my study "Zur
Problematik einer jüdischen Abwehrstrategie in der deutschen Gesellschaft," in *Juden
im Wilhelminischen Deutschland, 1890–1914*, ed. Werner E. Mosse and Arnold Paucker,
Schriftenreihe wissenschaftlicher Abhandlungen des Leo Baeck Instituts 33 (Tübingen,
1976). The reader is referred to these two publications for further details. Some other
contributions of mine to the topic are mentioned in the notes. The present paper follows (though it has been expanded) a German version, "Die Abwehr des Antisemitismus in den Jahren 1893–1933," in *Antisemitismus: Von der Judenfeindschaft zum Holocaust*, ed. Herbert A. Strauss and Norbert Kampe, Schriftenreihe der Bundeszentrale
für politische Bildung 213 (Bonn, 1984), which also contains a critical bibliography of
all the English and German literature on the Jewish defense in Germany published
since 1945. The bibliography has been omitted in the present essay. A number of the
more recent studies, however, some findings of which have been incorporated here, are
cited in the notes.
2. This generalization needs to be qualified. With the enemy controlling a repressive
government, anti-Nazi activities by Jewish bodies had to cease. Yet certain defense

of disappointment; naïve trust in mankind's progress was lost, together with the certainty of a pluralistic society. Some Jews even drew an inner satisfaction from this situation, and no one would later more deeply regret that response than Robert Weltsch, the brilliant editor of the *Jüdische Rundschau*, as he recollected his leading articles.[3] But why should only German Jews be blamed for this rejection of liberalism? We need but to recall the note of resignation sounded by the well-known British historian H. A. L. Fisher in the last chapter of his great European history of the failed liberal experiment, the chapter in which he pondered upon the forces of intolerance.[4] Belief that the Jews would be integrated into Germany, that they would be able to defend their rights in a society of which they, too, were part, was shattered throughout the Jewish community, and especially among younger Jews. It will be seen later that this fact was to take on immense significance for German-Jewish historiography. Jews today worldwide, beset by self-criticism, wonder which political groups they should join, what policies they should follow, in order to ensure the continuance of the Jewish people. Anyone who maintains a constant awareness of the theme "defense against antisemitism" can see the threads that connect our present situation and the past.

I

In 1895, two years after its foundation, the Centralverein deutscher Staatsbürger jüdischen Glaubens presented its monthly journal to the public for the first time. It spoke then—surely with calculated exaggeration—of the war in which German Jews found themselves engaged and that threatened to become another Thirty Years' War.[5] The "Thirty Years' War" was to become a war of forty years, and German Jews were to be the vanquished.

---

stances could be maintained, often bravely, in a transitory period. I deal with those in my paper "Jewish Self-Defence," in *Die Juden im Nationalsozialistischen Deutschland/ The Jews in Nazi Germany, 1933–1943*, ed. H. Arnold Paucker, Schriftenreihe wissenschaftlicher Abhandlungen des Leo Baeck Instituts 45 (Tübingen, 1986), pp. 55–65.
    3. Robert Weltsch in his postwar correspondence and in many conversations with the author in the London Leo Baeck Institute.
    4. "The Hitler revolution is a sufficient guarantee that Russian Communism will not spread westward . . . there may be secrets in Fascism or Hitlerism which the democracies will desire, without abandoning their fundamental character, to adopt." H. A. L. Fisher, *A History of Europe* (London, 1935), 3:1209.
    5. *Im deutschen Reich* 1, no. 1 (July 1895): 2.

History, we know, deals harshly with the losers: compassion and generosity play little part in scholarship. Accordingly the Jewish Centralverein and the Jewish defense as a whole were quickly heaped with abuse and irony. Moreover, since wisdom comes cheap after the event, a whole array of "what-should-have-been-dones" was soon marshaled. Accordingly, one of the reproaches made against the officials of the Jewish defense organization grew out of the argument that, since irrational attitudes are immune to factual information and sane discussion, the only recourse against racial prejudice is to dispense with efforts at rational counterarguments from the very outset. Again commentators point to gross errors of analysis and find it regrettable that the Jewish defense was at the time quite unfamiliar with today's current theories on the function of outgroups in a frustrated society.

The decisive factor, however, in the unfavorable verdict on the Jewish defense has been that the failure of German-Jewish symbiosis led to a distancing from traditional defense. Evaluation of defense has been increasingly influenced by the intellectual makeup of a younger generation that flatly refused—sometimes even with anger—to have anything to do with it. Members of that generation either took the Jewish nationalist position and from that standpoint often treated the "assimilatory" endeavors of their fathers (self-identified as Germans) with undisguised mockery, or, with increasingly socialistic leanings, they showed an outright scorn of the "bourgeois" limits that Jewish defense activity set for itself, supplementing their censure with instructions on how to build a better world. And here I must disclose an interest, for I, too, have come from the socialist Zionist youth movement. Its influence on its members' consciousness cannot be ignored, since our group has produced many historians who after the Second World War turned first and foremost to Jewish historiography. We dismissed the CV and the Jewish defense as hopelessly mismanaged: once and for all, we thought, they had disappeared as subjects for research.

Painstaking historical analysis into this chapter of the German-Jewish past was initiated only at the beginning of the 1960s. I am told that I myself set the first stone of the avalanche in motion and thereby achieved the uneasy position of a "patriarch of defense scholarship." One cannot but rejoice that in the past twenty years intensive research in this field has developed so far, bringing considerable insights into German-Jewish conduct and Jewish endeavors to counter organized antisemitism in the imperial epoch and in the Weimar Republic. The initial investigations into the Jewish defense in Weimar Germany undertaken by my colleagues and myself formed part of the research program organized by the London Leo Baeck Institute, whose founding generation—both Zionists and "Centralvereinlers"—had for the most part buried their thirty-year-old differences. While our work was at first limited to the later period, these researches were soon extended by American historians back to the Wilhelminian Reich. Indispensable for an understanding of the earlier period are, above all, the works of Ismar Schorsch,[6] Marjorie Lamberti,[7] and Jehuda Reinharz.[8] The impartiality and objectivity of their studies are outstanding.

Alongside all the widely diverse and highly critical viewpoints, past disdain for the German-Jewish will to resist has frequently mellowed into a eulogy. In the main I ally myself with these positive conclusions of younger American scholars. Furthermore, more recent works by West German historians have now appeared: Barbara Suchy has written of the progressive-based Verein zur Abwehr des Antisemitismus (Abwehrverein),[9] a non-Jewish organization, though in part supported by Jews, and Ulrich Dunker on the Reichsbund jüdischer Frontsoldaten.[10] These represent important treatments by German scholars of this subject, no longer the sole province of Jew-

---

6. Ismar Schorsch, *Jewish Reactions to German Anti-Semitism, 1870–1914* (New York, 1972). Schorsch dwells in particular on the raising of Jewish consciousness that resulted from the defense work of the CV.

7. Marjorie Lamberti, *Jewish Activism in Imperial Germany: The Struggle for Civil Equality* (New Haven, 1978); and her essays listed in the bibliography in Paucker, "Die Abwehr des Antisemitismus." Lamberti's work is most valuable on the Jewish fight for civil rights, though her analysis of the Zionist-CV conflict remains controversial.

8. Jehuda Reinharz, *Fatherland or Promised Land: The Dilemma of the German Jew, 1893–1914* (Ann Arbor, 1975); and his essays listed in the bibliography in Paucker, "Die Abwehr des Antisemitismus." Reinharz's studies form the most exhaustive treatment on the differing attitudes of the German Zionists and the CV vis-à-vis the danger of antisemitism. See also Reinharz, "The Zionist Response to Antisemitism in Germany," *Leo Baeck Institute Year Book* (hereafter *LBIYB*) 30 (1985): 105–40.

9. Barbara Suchy, "The Verein zur Abwehr des Antisemitismus (I): From Its Beginnings to the First World War," *LBIYB* 28 (1983): 205–39; Suchy, "The Verein zur Abwehr des Antisemitismus (II): From the First World War to Its Dissolution in 1933," ibid., 30 (1985): 67–103. Suchy marshals much evidence of goodwill, but also of inherent weaknesses, on the part of the liberal allies of the Jews.

10. Ulrich Dunker, *Der Reichsbund jüdischer Frontsoldaten, 1919–1938: Geschichte eines jüdischen Abwehrvereins* (Düsseldorf, 1977). This is the only detailed, and most instructive, survey of the specific fight waged by Jewish World War I veterans against antisemitism in Weimar Germany; the only problem here is that the leadership of a soldiers' organization, to which almost all Jewish war veterans automatically belonged, was certainly to the right of the general Jewish political outlook.

ish writers on history. Again, the American historian Donald L. Niewyk, in his first history of Jews in the Weimar Republic, deals with Jewish defense activity.[11] For the period of the First World War and the early years of Weimar, too, the gaps are slowly closing.[12] Publications on Wilhelminian Germany bulk large.[13] These works of research are impressive. In addition, there are many articles and books on ideological changes in German Jewry.

As to the political defense against antisemitism and Nazism, it is today both interesting and informative to observe that it is precisely the CV which has been affected by the broadening of research and the reversal of judgment. I should like to put forward three points that in my opinion have markedly, perhaps decisively, caused a shift in Jewish defense historiography. First, the question ever more penetratingly raised by Jews after the catastrophe: Was everything really done to counter the looming menace of National Socialism? Imagine the position of a Zionist grandfather cross-examined by his grandson: "And what did you do against fascism before 1933?" The grandfather might reply that he collected money for Palestine and prepared within himself for emigration. But this scarcely constitutes a satisfactory answer.[14] Second, it is beyond question that in modern Western countries the vast majority of Jews have opted for integration within their pluralist societies, setting aside all the significance that Israel obviously holds for them. Within those societies they still defend themselves by methods, allegedly improved and sophisticated, yet not so unlike those of the "old-fashioned" CV in Germany. Third, minority research has increasingly advanced. The Jewish minority before 1933 was defending itself in a relatively free Germany and making use of a most forceful and complex defense apparatus. It is that very experience which is significant for other minorities

11. Donald L. Niewyk, *The Jews in Weimar Germany* (Baton Rouge, 1980).
12. David Joshua Engel, "Organized Jewish Responses to German Antisemitism during the First World War" (Ph.D. diss., University of California, Los Angeles, 1979); and his most recent "Patriotism as a Shield: The Liberal Jewish Defence against Antisemitism in Germany during the First World War," *LBIYB* 31 (1986): 147–71, which constitutes a critique of CV policy during the war years.
13. It is not possible to list all the essential reading here, and the reader should consult the bibliography in Paucker, "Die Abwehr des Antisemitismus." One important recent essay should, however, be mentioned: Evyatar Friesel, "The Political and Ideological Development of the Centralverein before 1914," *LBIYB* 31 (1986): 121–46, which provides an interesting reassessment of CV ideology during the first two decades of the organization's existence.
14. The problem of the Zionist directive to stay out of German politics will be dealt with below.

covering some of the same ground as their predecessors in seeking self-preservation. All this has brought about a situation in which, among Jews themselves, inveterate enemies of the "assimilationists" are today paying tribute, even though grudgingly, to the CV. Only the great Jewish scholar Gershom Scholem could not to the end of his days refrain from elegant, witty, biting attacks on the CV. Speaking in public in West Germany and the United States, he gave vent to an animosity stemming from the era of Wilhelminian Germany.[15] To say that he was wrong on this point is not to detract from the fame of his learning. In this respect, he was the odd man out.

II

A date still historic in the annals of German Jewry is March 26, 1893, when the CV was founded in Berlin. All historians agree that this day marks a turning point in Jewish self-perception. The establishment of the organization at that precise point in time was determined by various factors that had sometimes accelerated, sometimes delayed, its development.[16]

A series of events taking place immediately before the establishment of the CV or just at the time it was being founded must rank as external impulses.[17] In 1891 a ritual murder accusation at Xanten in western Germany had sharply stimulated antisemitic agitation. On December 2, 1892, the program of a major political party—the Tivoli Program of the Deutschkonservative Partei—for the first time called for restraints on "Jewish influence." In Prussia electoral alliances were made between antisemites, conservatives, and members of the Nationalliberale Partei. The Deutsche Freisinnige Partei—the political home of German Jews since 1884—had split into the Freisinnige Volkspartei and the Freisinnige Vereinigung. In the Reich-

---

15. For instance, Gershom Scholem, "On the Social Psychology of the Jews in Germany, 1900–1933," in *Jews and Germans from 1860 to 1933: The Problematic Symbiosis*, ed. David Bronsen (Heidelberg, 1979), p. 18.

16. On the prehistory of the CV, see the still-useful Paul Rieger, *Ein Vierteljahrhundert im Kampf um das Recht und die Zukunft der deutschen Juden* (Berlin, 1918), pp. 7–13; Schorsch, *Jewish Reactions to German Anti-Semitism*, pp. 23–107; and Reinharz, *Fatherland or Promised Land*, pp. 1–36.

17. In the following concise survey on the CV in Wilhelminian Germany I follow essentially my study "Zur Problematik einer jüdischen Abwehrstrategie," and detailed source references are generally dispensed with. The reader should consult this essay in German and then above all Schorsch, *Jewish Reactions to German Anti-Semitism;* Reinharz, *Fatherland or Promised Land;* and Lamberti, *Jewish Activism in Imperial Germany.*

stag elections of 1893 the two groups had lost almost half their former votes; in contrast, the antisemites could chalk up impressive electoral successes. It was impossible to ignore the heightened menace to *de jure* emancipation so far as it had already been achieved by the Jews in Germany.

Two factors in the Jewish and philosemitic camps had eased the way for the establishment of a Jewish defense organization. The first was the precedent provided by Jewish students who, ever since 1880, had closed their ranks against the antisemitic student movement in German universities. The militant reaction in one sector of Jewish academics was a prerequisite for the process of foundation. These self-confident Jews formed the leadership cadre for a broadly based Jewish self-defense organization. The second factor arose in January 1891 with the creation of the non-Jewish Verein zur Abwehr des Antisemitismus[18] under the leadership of German liberal politicians. Outside help provided a valuable initiative, yet it was two edged. Many Jews welcomed the opportunity to operate in this field as "Germans"; most were merely prepared to show goodwill toward the Abwehrverein, to give financial support, but nothing more. The Abwehrverein itself grew increasingly insistent that Jews should commit themselves in their own cause. Its own philosophy, moreover, was scarcely pluralistic, and its demand that Jews should "assimilate" often went far beyond the concessions that Jews were ready to make, since they had no wish to abandon their identity. The step from the first setting up of a large non-Jewish defense organization, therefore, to a second, Jewish, structure seemed almost inevitable.

During more than twenty years of antisemitic hostility, there had certainly been no lack of indignant voices and discussions. Nevertheless Jews had not produced any long-term effective organization. The fact that in 1893 the Jewish community considered sending a delegation to the Kaiser "to beg the monarch for a shield and protection against antisemitism"[19] was singularly indicative of Jewish thinking. Militant defense was not for them. The Jewish elites rejected all contact with independent activity, especially if it seemed to be directed against the state. Out of fear, a policy of their own that would bring

---

18. See Suchy, "Verein zur Abwehr des Antisemitismus (I)"; Schorsch, *Jewish Reactions to German Anti-Semitism*, pp. 80–101; and Reinharz, *Fatherland or Promised Land*, pp. 35–36.

19. [Raphael Löwenfeld], *Schutzjuden oder Staatsbürger? Von einem jüdischen Staatsbürger* (Berlin, 1893), p. 6.

Jews into prominence was avoided. The majority undoubtedly argued that one should not take offense too easily or make too much fuss: hostility to Jews would soon die down again. Moreover, to found a nationwide defense organization supported by Germany's Jewish population would amount to a public admission that integration at the social level had in some degree failed and that emancipation had not been carried through successfully or adequately. It took two waves of antisemitism and two decades of internal change before a comprehensive defense movement could assert itself. The very process of founding was continually hampered by weighty opposition. One might be tempted to say that in its early stages the movement had more difficulty with co-religionists than with the enemies of Judaism.

The standard bearers for the process of establishment came from a section of Jewish intellectual society whose assimilation into the German environment had progressed the furthest and who therefore felt themselves most deeply wounded by the evidences of ill will. It was precisely these people who would become the vanguard of conscious Jewishness, since one result of antisemitism was that many who had become deeply alienated from Judaism now found their way back by the path of self-defense. The first stage in the CV's historic function was the conversion of "fringe Jews" into "defiant Jews."

Its ever-broadening organization, the CV asserted, finally made it a truly representative agency mirroring the members of the Jewish religious community. Its social and political structure, however, together with a localized concentration of power, demonstrates that this claim, though in large measure borne out, was not altogether valid. Some parts of the Jewish population were unequally represented in proportion to their numbers: the capital Berlin, for example, was and always remained overrepresented, while the lower social classes were inadequately represented. In fact, Jewish workers and lower-paid employees, who after 1900 strengthened their support for the Sozialdemokratische Partei Deutschlands (SPD, the Social Democrats), already regarded that party as speaking also for their "Jewish" interests. In the last phase of the empire, moreover, the movement of a "disappointed" younger generation toward socialism and Zionism was already clearly marked, though its main impetus was to come in the Weimar period. The further extremes of Jewish Orthodoxy were unequivocally hostile to the CV: in general they shunned the fight against antisemitism, regarding antisemitism as the scourge of God, a righteous judgment.[20] While now and again Zionists did belong to the CV, they can only be seen as hopelessly underrepresented, even in proportion to their small numbers at that time. The foregoing by no means exhausts the number of groups unrepresented or inadequately represented by the CV (the resident Eastern Jews, for example, might also be mentioned),[21] yet all of them were minorities. The predominant majority of the Jewish community—liberal in religion, assimilated, German in feeling, middle class—regarded the CV as an appropriate spokesman on their behalf.

Questions of Jewish self-defense are closely linked to the political alignment of Jews. The position of the CV in German politics can be understood only against the background of a lasting political change within German Jewry, namely, that bourgeois Jews did not share in the reactionary shift taking place in German liberalism from the late 1870s onwards. Jewish emancipation, despite formal legal guarantees, was in reality still far from achievement; the natural political home of bourgeois Jews was still in the ranks of the opposition, and they continued to belong to the left wing of bourgeois liberalism.

Taking Jews as a whole, this meant that since the foundation of the Second Reich their prevailing political position had steadfastly remained left of center.[22] Their link with the progressives continued as a characteristic throughout the whole Wilhelminian period. The Jews became a "loyal opposition"; the social structure of the majority precluded any more markedly leftward orientation. Only a minority of Jews had not shared in the withdrawal from national liberalism following its move to the right. Jewish conservative voters were so insignificant in number that one cannot speak of a "conservative constituency," however small. However, the trend toward the SPD was ever more pronounced and after 1900 increased sharply among German Jewry.

20. On the attitude of Jewish Orthodoxy in detail, see Sanford Ragins, *Jewish Responses to Anti-Semitism in Germany, 1870–1914* (Cincinnati, 1980). The book is of value in this particular respect; in other matters it is based on a dissertation completed in 1972, and the author has not taken note of later research.
21. Most of these recent immigrants from Eastern Europe, however, had not obtained German citizenship.
22. For Jewish political allegiances in Wilhelminian Germany still basic are Ernest Hamburger, *Juden im öffentlichen Leben Deutschlands: Regierungsmitglieder, Beamte und Parlamentarier in der monarchischen Zeit, 1848–1918* (Tübingen, 1968); and Jacob Toury, *Die politischen Orientierungen der Juden in Deutschland Von Jena bis Weimar*, Schriftenreihe wissenschaftlicher Abhandlungen des Leo Baeck Instituts 19, 15 (Tübingen, 1966).

The search for a foothold in German politics to enable the promotion of Jewish interests meant, at parliamentary level, first and foremost preventing the election of antisemitic deputies. The CV endeavored to ensure the defeat of antisemitic candidates by providing campaign backing to philosemite politicians, in the expectation that the candidates so assisted would broach the question of Jewish rights in the Reichstag and *Länder* parliaments. Officially the CV held a position of neutrality between the parties. When it came to practical application, however, the carefully formulated principle of neutrality remained mostly theoretical. After all, it was precisely because the political world had now formally split into antisemites and philosemites that the organization had become indispensable. Antisemites, overt or covert, were proliferating, and, as a basic principle, anyone to the right of the Nationalliberale Partei was excluded from the system of neutrality. While the CV was reproached for giving little support to the "parties of government," it had to be admitted that despite their loyal patriotism, Jews were obliged to belong to the opposition parties: it was impossible for them to back a system that, in practice, left the Emancipation Laws of 1869 largely unfulfilled.

However, since all parties without exception did relatively little or nothing to enforce equal Jewish rights, in this respect a certain neutrality did hold sway. Early on it had been noted—and the observation was repeated time and again—that no single party forcefully championed a policy that would end discrimination. Analysis of CV publications during the Second Reich leads to the unavoidable conclusion that only very rarely and sporadically did Jews make any pact with groups other than left-wing liberals. Left-wing liberalism was their political home, while candidates standing somewhere between conservatives and progressives had always to be carefully scrutinized, no matter whether they had previously proffered political support or the Jews had independently decided to give them their support. In general, only socialists and left-wing liberals could be reckoned as philosemitic—or, more truthfully, not antisemitic. Given the Jewish social structure, this automatically led to the alliance of the CV with *Freisinn* and *Fortschritt*.

In fact, the left-wing liberals frequently showed themselves true to their principles as conscientious spokesmen for equal Jewish rights. Notwithstanding occasional discontent and disillusionment, neither Jews as a group nor the CV had any valid reason for outright alienation. Left-wing liberalism may in many ways have proved inadequate as the effective representative of Jewish interests; nevertheless, the CV always stressed that Jewish interests were linked with liberal policies. Quite apart from the fact that Social Democracy was not compatible with Jewish class structure, most Jews looked down on the socialists as antipatriotic and subversive, a situation that the CV had to take into account, especially in its first ten years. It goes without saying that its bourgeois leaders and Jewish dignitaries did not desire a closer relationship with the socialists. All the same, a number of Social Democrats did belong to the CV throughout the Wilhelminian period.

A slow change in the attitude of the CV may cautiously be said to date from the Reichstag elections of 1903. Social Democracy became respectable and revisionist; its liberal reliability began to be more widely recognized. We may discern more wholehearted praise for Social Democracy as an electoral alternative. "Misguided" coreligionists, who might on grounds of class have preferred an antisemitic candidate to a socialist, were rapped on the knuckles. At the same time, a firm connection with the SPD remained out of the question for a bourgeois Jewish organization, and no belated wishful thinking can be allowed to obscure the fact that such an alignment would have meant that both groups would have been fatally compromised by any official mutual contact. In any event, twenty years of experience had undoubtedly taught the Jewish defense that even so-called philosemitic parties were not prepared to go to the lengths necessary in promoting Jewish demands. At heart, the defense of Jewish rights was for them a side issue.

III

The CV's defense activity rested on the twin pillars of Germanness—Deutschtum, as it was called then—and Jewishness. Unquestionably, toward the end of the Wilhelminian era most German Jews had no difficulty in subjectively perceiving their own "Germanness," while among the emancipated and assimilated Jews of the CV the question of Jewish values became ever more acute. Some Jews quit their religious communities, yet continued their "Jewish" fight against antisemitism from within the CV, so that the organization—however circuitously—reinforced Jewish consciousness. But equally it cannot be doubted that the CV and bourgeois Jewry in general shared many of the axioms of an arrogant German nationalism. And indeed, seeing that the primary object of the German Jews was to make their way into German society, how could they have remained unaffected by the monstrous growth of a nationalism totally characteristic of the whole epoch?

Yet it may be noted that the CV in no way advocated unlimited chauvinism, and its resistance to that unnatural growth often provided a weapon for antisemites. It opposed military adventurism, warmongering, and all imperialist power politics,[23] since its leaders saw clearly that war and chaos would damage a minority such as the Jews. From the distance of today, carefully considered political stances evolved in different conditions must be distinguished from "nationalist" effusions. Over the previous two decades, the CV had developed in all its utterances a "house style" that perpetually veered between an obligatory professional pessimism—Germany is threatened by anarchy—to ritual exhortation of the faithful—the victory of reason is at hand. We must, as it were, subtract a few percent to arrive at the CV's true assessment of the situation. Similarly, in the "unswerving maintenance of German sentiments" there sometimes appeared gross exaggeration; a more pronounced caution would often have been preferable. Under hostile provocation, attempts were again and again made to prove the genuine depth of Jewish love for Germany, to show that apart from a religious particularity, a Jew was every bit as German as the next man. While it was originally legitimate for the CV to adopt the description *deutsch-national* in juxtaposition to *jüdisch-national*, it bordered on stupidity to continue its use long after the antisemitic Deutschnationaler Handlungsgehilfenverband had arisen and when an antisemitic Deutschnationale Volkspartei (DNVP, the German National People's party) was about to be established. In this way the strategy of defense was flawed. If some historians today classify the CV as conservative and moderately reactionary, it must be admitted that the organization itself is not free of all responsibility for such confusion. Even in Wilhelminian Germany, moreover, the Jewish defense sometimes showed more coolness than necessary towards the Left. As a result many Jewish intellectuals were driven leftward, and even be-

23. There is indeed a fair amount of evidence for this in the Jewish press, which is quite remarkable considering the general political climate. See *Im deutschen Reich* 17, no. 10 (October 1911): 553–56, and no. 12 (December 1911): 676; ibid., 18, no. 11 (November 1912): 395–96, and no. 12 (December 1912): 552.

fore 1914 nationalist protestations by the CV had scared away some of the younger people.

To what extent, by this time, was a Jewish organization such as the CV identified with the imperial German establishment and class structure? Assuredly it posed no clear opposition to the existing social order—that could not have been expected. Because it was fighting for recognition of the rights of a disadvantaged minority, however, its attitude was that of a critical, though loyal, opposition. As a body of liberal-minded citizens and as representative of a population group denied full civic rights by the prevailing social order, the CV assumed an additional role, furthering the cause of progressive development and working for liberalization of the ruling establishment. In this way its own distinctive point of view became sharply defined, and some marked features peculiar to a Jewish defense organization are plainly discernible in retrospect.

The CV's anti-antisemitic counterpropaganda has always been summed up in the useful overall concept "apologetics." For Jews, apologetics was a time-honored undertaking—forced upon them by their enemies—but the CV used it systematically and achieved a measure of mass circulation for its printed publications. Compared with previous attempts, this methodical refutation of antisemitism was a decided improvement, though technically very inept beside what was to follow in the Weimar period. The boldly conceived apologetics built up by the CV in the twenty or so years from 1893 to 1914 presented more problems than all its other activities, for the subject has always been controversial for Jews. The organization believed that the public was amenable to education, while Zionists rejected that idea.

Refutation, generally dictated by enemy attack, is indeed a ticklish affair. In 1893 the CV had not set its sights very high, and eventually it found itself forced to counter any number of allegations against Jews, ranging from usury to ritual murder, from the teachings of the Talmud to military unfitness. All had to be tackled manfully, occasionally with a flight into the grotesque, as in 1909 when the CV sought the advice of an orthopedic surgeon in the hope of putting an end to the notion that flat feet were a distinctly Jewish racial feature.[24]

24. For this purpose, the CV conscripted a noted specialist, one Dr. Muskat, who expatiated on the topic at length in *Im deutschen Reich* 15, no. 6 (June 1909): 354ff.

The difficulty of reasoned refutation was that, short of preaching entirely to the converted, argument could really only be directed to the thin stratum of people willing enough to show goodwill but not yet "converted." They alone were responsive to rebuttal of antisemitic allegations. There were certainly more such people in the German Empire than in post-1918 Germany. When, decades later, apologetics had at last been refined and perfected, the stratum of goodwill among its counterdisputants had already melted away. The fact that apologetics did not seize the mass imagination, however, in no way justifies the conclusion that it would have been better to discontinue it. Representative leaders of the Jewish community at the time saw it as their duty and obligation to take a stand against antisemitic lies.

In the main, while modern observers of the CV pay high tribute to its extended practical activity, nearly all stress the theoretical limitations in its analyses of antisemitism. Its understanding of the sociological functions of antisemitism, of the deeper religious and psychological roots, was inadequate. In the course of events, the outcome was bound to diminish later assessments of the organization's effectiveness. Yet in one respect the CV should certainly not be blamed: after all, before 1914, it could scarcely put into practice ideas that were not to be substantiated by research until a much later date. The notion that the CV was mistaken in every way is quite incorrect: it is unreasonable to demand of Jewish functionaries in the days of the Second Reich that they should comprehend social and psychological concepts that, in many cases, social scientists would not arrive at until the middle of the twentieth century. Before 1914 the state of knowledge concerning antisemitism and the means of combatting it were indeed insufficient, but, considering the period and the character of the Jewish group, what was done was by no means inappropriate.

In one respect the CV can be "reproached" in this context: it never ceased to believe in "a remedy," in the sense that antisemitism could be controlled, that it was "a phenomenon linked with the dark past," that its impact could be reduced, scaled down, even utterly eliminated. The intervening years have rendered it impossible for us to share the naïve nineteenth-century belief in "progress": not only have we witnessed the destruction of European Jewry, but we can see in our own day how minorities continue to be disadvantaged and persecuted.

IV

By taking a leap forward to Jewish defense activity in the critical
years from 1928 to 1932[25] and briefly sketching its development,
such important aspects as the struggle within the legal arena must
necessarily be excluded.[26] The fierce clashes within Jewry itself—
controversies on defense attitudes, problems of continually changing
tactics and strategy—can receive only a bare mention here.

The creed of Germanness and CV patriotism have already been
discussed. They are important in considering the Jewish defense attitude in the Weimar Republic, since, notwithstanding all the rigid-
ity and extravagance accompanying an often overstated patriotism,
the people involved were in no way at all "German nationalists" in a
politically partisan sense, though this is sometimes maintained due
to an ignorant confusion of terminology.[27] Leaving aside these misunderstandings, however, there still remain doubtful points and
problems that cannot be set out in detail here. Defense activity was
carried on by non-Zionists and anti-Zionists; even faced with Nazi
hostility, it was still marked by steadfast patriotism. It is not possible to deal here with Zionist criticism of this feeling of Germanness, but it can be said that the Zionist analysis of the German situation undoubtedly had surer and deeper foundations. Most Jews did
not realize that the German people were making ready to exile their
Jews. With all respect for the Zionist "critique of Germanism" and
the radical, Zionist solution of projecting wholesale emigration, total abstention from German politics was no answer to the specific
German situation; even at the time it was open to question and to-

25. In this brief account of the Jewish defense in the last five years of the Weimar
Republic, I largely follow my book, *Der jüdische Abwehrkampf*, and other essays, giving
only some additional source references. The period before 1928 would seem to be still
insufficiently explored. It took longer for the younger functionaries in the CV to reas-
sert themselves, and the reason for this may have to be sought in CV policy in World
War I.
    26. For legal defense consult Ambrose Doskow and Sidney B. Jacoby, "Antisemitism
and the Law in Pre-Nazi Germany," *Contemporary Jewish Record* 3, no. 5 (1940): 498–
509; Donald L. Niewyk, "Jews and the Courts in Weimar Germany," *Jewish Social Studies* 37 (1975): 99–113; Arnold Paucker, *Der jüdische Abwehrkampf*, pp. 74–85, 263–65.
    27. I have already discussed this above and in greater detail in "Zur Problematik
einer jüdischen Abwehrstrategie." I have also dealt with defense verbiage and some
linguistic curiosities in this context in ibid., pp. 525–26, and in "Jewish Defence
against Nazism in the Weimar Republic," *Wiener Library Bulletin* 26, nos. 1–2 (1972):
21.

day still has to be rejected.[28] As early as 1930, however, abstention was giving way to a united Jewish effort against fascism. On the German political spectrum, between 1928 and 1933 the Jewish defense remained bourgeois Left or shifted to the Social Democratic Right. There was a small Jewish right wing in the Weimar Republic that decried defense activity as "snooping after Nazis and antisemites" and whose real preference would have been for the glorious National Revolution.[29] Even we had our three-quarter fascists; but, with a forbearing glance at those poor distracted souls who would later suffer so much punishment, incarceration, and murder, let us continue with our theme.

For forty years the Jewish defense had occupied itself with refutation of antisemitism, but after 1928 it switched to anti-Nazi propaganda. Traditional anti-antisemitic argumentation to some extent joined and blended with modern mass propaganda. Though often sure aimed and polished, every so often it would show itself as bungling and vulnerable. Still, it was continually revised and reworked with Teutonic thoroughness. And indeed, the Jewish defense in the Weimar Republic can be perceived as an early voice of warning against National Socialism within German society. The merit of this service to German democracy is in no way diminished by the fact that Jews in the weak republic were in any case the most endangered group, or because Jewish defense officials (who even in 1928 had noted a recrudescence of the Nazi movement) were professional anti-antisemites; it may also be that they were inclined to professional pessimism by many years of dealing with antisemites and right-wing extremism. What is unfortunately true is that their observations were not taken seriously, even among their own Jewish ranks, and were initially branded as alarmist. Nevertheless, from mid-1928 onward, the CV registered with growing anxiety and concentration the forward march of the National Socialist movement, its spread in town and country, its build up of cells in institutions ranging from

28. There can be little controversy on this untenable position today. Yet again further research establishes that Zionist attitudes were by no means clear cut. There were segments within the German Zionist movement that advocated anti-Nazi activity and collaboration with the CV in the fight against antisemitism. We are indebted for a much more differentiated picture to Reinharz, "Zionist Response."
29. The best accounts of these Jewish groupings are by Carl J. Rheins, "The Verband nationaldeutscher Juden, 1921–1933," *LBIYB* 25 (1980): 243–68; and "Deutscher Vortrupp, Gefolgschaft deutscher Juden," ibid., 26 (1981): 207–29.

the civil service to industrial concerns, its penetration of the army, police, and local government. And the CV insistently set these facts before their co-religionists and the German public.[30]

Mere recording of the Nazi advance in no way satisfied the Jewish defense, which, as early as 1929, mounted a comprehensive campaign against the party. Available sources show that Social Democratic party leaders, for example, took hardly any notice of these warnings and defense struggles until late in 1930; in their opinion, the whole affair was an exaggerated concentration on an unimportant extreme right-wing association. Even up to the election of September 1930, efforts to convince Reich ministers of an ever-increasing danger for the most part failed. Many examples could be given to show how these representations were politely but firmly set aside as symptoms of a Jewish anxiety, understandable indeed, but verging on the neurotic. However that might be, the Jewish defense, together with non-Jewish militant opponents of Nazism, for nearly two years desperately and often vainly endeavored to awaken the leaders of the Republic from what they could see was a fatal torpor.[31]

The CV was able to play its part in this way because, in the years before the establishment of the Nazi dictatorship, Jewish defense activity was increasingly directed to one paramount aim, that is, safeguarding both equal Jewish rights before the law and also the German Republic that guaranteed them, together with thwarting the take-over of government by a powerful nationalist party. Recourse to law had been the least controversial activity of the Jewish defense. But reactionary judges, derisory sentences, and, eventually, Nazi defendants' domination of proceedings caused this legal means of defense to backfire.[32] Well before the disintegration of the Republic and the collapse of protective law, there thus came about a radical alteration in the work of defense itself and in the dimensions of its field of action in a way undreamed of by the prominent personages and Jewish notables who had set up Jewish self-defense in Wilhelminian Germany. The attempt to influence German politics had always been attended by controversy; now it became the major preoccupation.

30. See Paucker, *Der jüdische Abwehrkampf*, pp. 15–25, 241–44.
31. Ibid., pp. 85–86, 265–66.
32. See the sources cited in n. 26, above.

V

Closely bound up with the task of the Jewish defense against anti-semitism and National Socialism was, of course, the question of allies, united fronts and popular fronts against fascism, and these presented serious difficulties to the middle-class Jewish community of the Weimar Republic. Jewish behavior patterns later gave rise to many misunderstandings, so that a few words on the political alliances and orientations of the German Jews are not out of place here. Unfortunately, a school of political mythology has recently arisen (particularly in the Federal Republic of Germany) that categorizes the Jewish population in the pre-Nazi epoch as predominantly reactionary and German-nationalistic, while the Jewish defense organizations are regarded as fiendish agents for the narrow class interests of the property-owning Jewish bourgeoisie. Such interpretations bear little relationship to the real situation of the Jews in the Weimar Republic; they are usually presented, moreover, with deadly seriousness and without any charity or understanding for the tragic dilemma of German Jewry.[33]

The political attitude of the German-Jewish majority may, of course, be varyingly assessed. To some extent this is a question of applying different ideologies or terminologies. In one sense only can the body of German Jewry be understood as a conservative community directed at safeguarding the status quo: as a group, it overwhelmingly rejected the idea of a revolutionary transformation of capitalist society and the concept of a violent upheaval. It constituted a loyal left-liberal opposition of second-class citizens in Wilhelminian Germany and thereafter, eventually, committed supporters of the Weimar Republic, in which Jews now enjoyed complete equality in practice as well as in theory. Certainly the life-styles and ideals of German Jews were more conservative than their political allegiances, but their party-political commitments and voting patterns have been reliably established by students of German-Jewish

33. Some such strictures are merely vituperative and the commentators singularly ill informed. For more weighty Marxist criticism, consult the literature listed in the bibliography in Paucker, "Die Abwehr des Antisemitismus." Deserving of special mention is a work by a collective of Marxist historians, Klaus Drobisch, Rudi Goguel, and Werner Müller, *Juden unterm Hakenkreuz: Verfolgung und Ausrottung der deutschen Juden, 1933–1945* (Berlin, 1973), published in the German Democratic Republic, since it presents in its first part a fairly balanced view of the Jewish defense efforts.

political history: by far the greater part of bourgeois German Jews remained consistently left of center, as outlined above in the discussion of Wilhelminian Germany. The disjunction from their German class counterparts widened still more in the Weimar Republic as middle-class Germany became a willing tool of fascism, so that a voting pattern arose that did not fully conform to Jewish interests at the general social level. The reasons for this "Jewish class anomaly"[34] are rooted in a hundred years of German history. German nationalism and the German Right were overwhelmingly antisemitic, and long before the rise of National Socialism German Jews were excluded from a political position and a political community perhaps better suited to their class structure. Their path diverged from that of the German bourgeoisie; whatever the reason, only a misguided economic determinism can in retrospect invent for the Jewish community—admittedly bourgeois rather than proletarian—a reactionary stance in party politics.

While the German Jews can to some degree be placed on the political Left, this can in no way be taken to mean the radical Left. Disregarding insignificant groups of the moderate Right or a pathological fringe of enthusiasts for right-wing extremism, and similarly leaving aside the small, though slowly growing, band of communist sympathizers, it may be said of the great mass of German Jews that they originally stood to the left of center and gradually shifted further left. Their major linking with the left wing of the Deutsche Demokratische Partei (DDP, the German Democratic party) dissolved as soon as the Nationalsozialistische Deutsche Arbeiterpartei (NSDAP) grew to a mass movement and a large-scale drift to the SPD began.[35] In broad outline, the facts are beyond question. Those who reject them, who deny the unambiguously progressive character of the German-Jewish community, who maintain that German

34. This felicitous expression is borrowed from Eva G. Reichmann, whose works, above all *Hostages of Civilisation: The Social Sources of National Socialist Anti-Semitism* (London, 1950), are essential background reading for any student of Jewish self-defense in Germany.

35. This development cannot here be traced in detail: exhaustive treatises on the period 1870–1933 already exist, and my own researches have shown that in 1932 some 70 percent of German Jews must have voted for the working-class parties. Paucker, "Jewish Defence against Nazism," p. 27. The very high figure computed here for the Jewish left-wing vote is possibly more representative of the large urban centers. For a cautious and judicious approach envisaging a somewhat lower percentage, see now Ernest Hamburger and Peter Pulzer, "Jews as Voters in the Weimar Republic," *LBIYB* 30 (1985): esp. 55–59. The estimates are the result of Pulzer's research into Jewish electoral behavior.

Jews were inherently unable to fight fascism since they did not condemn it in principle but merely opposed its antisemitic content—these people are quite simply guilty of distorting history.

Parallel with the rather progressive alignment of German Jews, explained by the history of antisemitism, alliances were made for practical reasons with groups whose rejection of antisemitism was not altogether to be trusted. In all probability the extent of Jewish participation in German politics has been underestimated, for even in Wilhelminian Germany Jewish pressure groups were fairly active, as Marjorie Lamberti has pointed out.[36] With the continual growth of National Socialism, moreover, Jews greatly intensified attempts to influence political parties within the Republic. Collaboration with the antireligious Left was, naturally, out of the question for any body representing the interests of the Jewish religious community. The brusque refusal by the CV and other Jewish organizations to have anything *officially* to do with the Kommunistische Partei Deutschlands (KPD, the Communist party of Germany), whose party line was rarely unequivocal, and their rejection of joint defense efforts with the Communists in a popular front against National Socialism, merit at least a particular mention here. I stress "officially," since exchanges of propaganda material and anti-Nazi information between the CV and the KPD did occasionally occur. In the last few months before the Nazi seizure of power, in some German towns, troops of billposters were seen, drawn jointly from the Reichsbund jüdischer Frontsoldaten and the Rotfrontkämpferbund—but this was something of an exception.[37]

After all the intervening years, the Jewish defense still comes under fire from extreme left-wing critics for not making such a pact with the Communists. In point of fact, the Jewish defense collaborated right across the political spectrum (the DNVP and NSDAP excepted): from the forces of arch-conservatism, by no means wholeheartedly in favor of the Weimar Republic, to left-wing socialists. As German democracy entered its final phase, the *democratic* socialists were to prove the best allies for the Jews in the struggle against Nazism. Nevertheless, the CV's original watchword of political neutrality, dating from Wilhelminian Germany, was still maintained: there should be neither a firm commitment nor a preference for

---

36. Lamberti, *Jewish Activism in Imperial Germany*.
37. Dr. Alfred Laurence, Isle of Wight, interview with author, London, August 1978.

any one party, and, similarly, "There is no German-Jewish party." Whether this was always the best course must remain in doubt. Even while the Republic lay in its death agony, the Jewish defense was still unshakably convinced that the very structure of the Jewish population, coupled with its continual position of peril, should preclude an alliance with any particular political party.

Collaboration with German democrats did not mean open, demonstrative support—that was not what the Jews had in mind and would in any case prove dangerous for the democratic parties—it took the form of financial donations. Although theory and practice rapidly split asunder, widely varying parties received funds till the bitter end. The aid given to quite distinct political parties, so long as they were fairly reliable on the Jewish Question and even though among themselves they were often at loggerheads, was attacked at the time and later, mainly by socialists. In practical terms the Jewish defense found that neutrality was not always advantageous and sometimes proved a clumsy strategy. The CV itself was split on this question. The younger generation leaned toward the socialists, while older people complained that the resources available were increasingly allocated to the Social Democrats. A defense organization representing a bourgeois and politically disunited Jewish community could not, however, propose an open and exclusive alliance with the Social Democrats. Nor did the SPD desire such an alliance, no doubt believing that it would be an act of political suicide. A tacit understanding was the shrewdest tactic.

The temptation over the years to minimize or overstate these financial gifts must be resisted. Friend and foe alike held vastly exaggerated notions of the wealth controlled by the Jewish organization. In particular, the *völkisch* press became very excited about the "fortunes" dangled by the Jews before their "hirelings" and traitors to the fatherland who perfunctorily attacked antisemitism and received their due remuneration. In point of fact, defense activities were neither so primitive nor so lavish. It is only to be regretted that the means available were not more abundant and that the help given, direct or indirect, was not funded to anything like the same extent as the millions put at the disposal of the seditious National Socialist movement by powerful figures of German finance. As regards direct donations, undoubtedly it was the SPD that received the lion's share in the last phases of the Weimar Republic. In 1931 the suggestion was even made that the CV might provide workers with weapons to oppose an expected Nazi *Putsch*. The eccentric who put this fantastic idea forward was soon disillusioned.[38] Given the power relationships existing immediately before 1933, the Jewish defense was quite unable to supply firearms to defend the Republic as well as fulfilling its other tasks.

VI

Returning to a more realistic footing, the CV's achievement as the central defense organization of German Jewry is still impressive. In the critical years 1928–33 there appears in the foreground close collaboration with those forces within German Social Democracy, who from the outset had promoted a most active struggle against Nazism and had shown themselves as doughty and resolute fighters against the Nazis. In this respect the far-reaching cooperation with the Reichsbanner Schwarz-Rot-Gold must be particularly emphasized: this was a nonparty defense formation in which, because of the other parties' lukewarm attitude, the SPD played the leading part. To the best of its ability, the Jewish defense supported the Reichsbanner, whose activists had recognized the National Socialist threat almost as early as the Jewish officials and had committed themselves untiringly to anti-Nazi agitation. Despite its socialistic orientation, the Reichsbanner did not formally declare itself as belonging to any particular political party, a neutrality that allowed the Jewish organization to join it in anti-Nazi propaganda. Thus were created the changes marking the last phase of Jewish defense activity in a Germany that was still free: first, alliances with democratic agencies of the socialist working class, and, second, widely effective mass propaganda.

The new line was supported mainly by the younger officials of the CV; it was never a monolithic institution, and clashes over the feasibility of its methods were no rarity. Central to the basic discussion on strategy was the question whether to throw the weight of activity behind mass propaganda or to win over Germany's intellectual, social, and political elites, with all their influence. Older board members, grown gray in defense action under the law, continued to believe that a better course would be to use the limited Jewish resources for long-term educational work rather than squander them

---

38. Hans Reichmann, interviews with author, London, 1962–63.

on ephemeral electoral propaganda. The proponents of the "elite approach" were typically professional men and upper-middle-class Jews incapable of coming to terms with the age of mass propaganda. For a generation reared in imperial Germany, effective adaptation to a revolutionary situation was quite simply impossible. On the other hand, younger officials were turning ever more sharply away from the long-practiced method of simply parrying enemy attack. They recognized as early as 1929 that, against the continual advance of National Socialism and its rabble-rousing propaganda, the use of civilized means must fail; the only way to confront Nazism was by a massive militant Jewish counterattack aided by republican organizations. To concentrate on mass propaganda, to carry the fight into the streets, had now become an inexorable necessity.

The statutes of the CV and the ideas of most members envisaged a Jewish defense limited to opposing antisemitism; but this strategy was rejected by younger officials, and the organization's new tactics were in line with their position. Older members passionately disapproved of an exclusive preoccupation with the struggle against the NSDAP; younger people ever more urgently pressed home their conviction that antisemitism in particular should not be regarded in isolation from other threats to the Jewish minority, that the task of the Jewish community was to combat National Socialism as an *integral whole*. Total defense against Nazism was a theme signifying a revolutionary change of direction for the representatives of a bourgeois Jewish self-defense organization. In retrospect, the good sense of this change in direction can only be confirmed; for the Jewish group the only question can and must be that of total defense against fascism: this is our bitter lesson drawn from a terrible past.

The outcome of the fresh strategy was a massive propaganda campaign against the Nazis beginning as early as 1929. However, that this initiative came from the Jewish side, originating mainly in the CV, remained virtually unknown until the 1960s. The facts, already published in detail, may be taken as read.[39] Here, in my opinion, a considerable and by no means ineffectual defense achieved by the Jewish community against German fascism bears witness to the German-Jewish will to self-preservation.

Such activities had to be screened from the official Jewish defense, not merely because Jewish organizations still felt total defense

39. See Paucker, *Der jüdische Abwehrkampf*, pp. 110–28, 275–81.

against National Socialism to be controversial, but also because tactical considerations demanded that this work must be camouflaged. Earlier, it is true, anonymous and politically neutral anti-Nazi propaganda had been disseminated by the CV; however, as National Socialism grew to a major political force, it became quite impossible to sail openly under Jewish colors. The point had been reached at which the Jews of Germany weakened the force of their arguments simply because it was they who were pleading their own cause. Mass agitation against fascism under recognizably Jewish auspices would have been rendered suspect to large groups of the population and to that extent would have failed in its effect. Indeed it was feared at the time that it would be inadvisable to mention the Jewish origin of this propaganda—even to socialist workers. And the Jewish defense was probably correct in its assessment of the tragic contemporary situation.

The covert propaganda office set up in 1929—twelve months before the NSDAP's electoral triumph of September 1930—is known to history as the "Büro Wilhelmstrasse."[40] Following the Nazi victory at the polls, the office was no longer ignored by the republican parties; it supplied their propaganda apparatus with counterpropaganda and information on the NSDAP. It can be said without exaggeration that a very considerable proportion of the election propaganda and antifascist material identified as republican originated from the Büro Wilhelmstrasse or at the very least was based on its preliminary work.

Documentation of this propaganda effort is still extant and available for researchers in German and Jewish archives. Apart from a few ill-conceived ideas—a sticker proclaiming "The Nazis are our misfortune," for example, inadvertently betrayed its Jewish authorship by imitating the notorious Nazi slogan "The Jews are our misfortune"[41]—the propaganda usually hit the mark. In my view, it may be described without qualification as skillful, based on firstclass investigative groundwork, technically well produced, and soundly argued. Such camouflaged propaganda was, of course, di-

40. For a detailed account, see ibid. Much of this information was disclosed to the author by surviving functionaries of the CV. A detailed exposition was furnished by Walter Gyssling, "Propaganda gegen die NSDAP in den Jahren 1929–1933," deposited in the London Archives of the Leo Baeck Institute for use for a contemplated history of the CV.

41. For a reproduction of this very rare sticker, see the illustrations between p. 84 and p. 85 of Suchy, "Verein zur Abwehr des Antisemitismus (II)."

rected at the "intelligent" person and the "enlightened" workers. While it pointed up the contradictions of Nazi promises, the mass audience for those promises was no longer susceptible to that kind of reasoned explanation. In the end, almost at the eleventh hour, new methods of propaganda were used in an attempt to adapt to the changed situation.

In 1932 the biologist Serge Chakotin recommended that the SPD should revolutionize its previous combat procedures by the use of "senso-propaganda," an emotional appeal that might awaken the fighting instinct of the masses against Nazism. He emphasized that, if freedom were to be maintained, Hitler's own weapons must be turned against him. Meanwhile, within the Jewish defense, once so obsessed with "enlightenment," younger officials had reached very similar conclusions. At this point, crucially, the representatives of what was primarily a defense organization were ready to make common cause with militant socialist agitators. Typically, however, the official SPD was unable to summon up enthusiasm for these novel methods. Yet in regions where such a system was applied, backed up by the Jewish defense, it was not without success. In certain districts the new electoral strategy, cheerfully mocking Nazis with satirical verses, symbolic colors, music, and so on, did lead to a distinct fall in NSDAP votes. All these new propaganda techniques—the adoption by the republican, antifascist Iron Front of the effective "Three Arrows" symbol as a counter to the swastika and the use of the "Freedom Salute" as counter to the Nazi "Heil Hitler"—manifest a brief resurgence of the fighting spirit of the socialist working class and of a defiant republicanism—a last flare of the lamp.[42]

The initiators of both the traditional and the new types of mass propaganda later looked carefully at the problems relating to their activities. The propaganda of rationality scored but modest success with an overwrought public whipped up by agitators. It was produced by a neutral organization unable and unwilling to exercise any control over the policies of parties using the material emanating from the Jews. We can never know whether the new kind of symbolic propaganda, based on what nowadays seem really rather primitive theories of mass psychology,[43] would have turned the tables. The Jew-

---

42. The CV collaborated closely in these efforts with men like Julius Leber, Carlo Mierendorff, and Kurt Schumacher, who later played such a distinguished part in the German resistance.

43. Serge Chakotin, *The Rape of the Masses* (London, 1940), however, still merits the attention of the student of the period.

ish contribution was not inconsiderable, but the Jewish defense was never more than an auxiliary. This was essentially intrinsic in all Jewish defense activity: it could provide only the response to another's propaganda.

It should also be pointed out that occasionally, particularly in the 1932 transition phase of the National Socialist take-over, the Jewish defense maintained relations with rightist circles. This is, of course, an extremely "distasteful" topic. While the Nazi party was still insignificant, the Jewish defense directed its fire mainly at enemies of the Republic and the antisemites constituting the conservative and nationalist groups, so that, disregarding the *völkisch* splinter groups, the primary target was the German National People's party. Feelers were put out to the reactionary elements at that time considered "more respectable"—toward people, for example, who disliked the antisemitism of an organization that in other respects they supported. Attempts to gain influence within certain contemporary rightist circles, even at the eleventh hour, included contacts with non-Nazi soldiers' associations, talks with captains of industry to warn them of the NSDAP's "dangerous" plans for the economy, as well as other approaches for which these two examples must suffice.[44] Many of these dubious attempts at rescue stemmed from a panicky fear for the safety of the Jewish population, and they were inspired in no small degree by what happened on July 20, 1932, when the democratic forces in Prussia abandoned their position of authority without a struggle, leaving an appalling impression on the Jewish defense.

In addition, there was no lack of attempts to exploit the continual backbiting and quarrels within the Nazi party. With an optimism matched to its aims, however, the CV saw a process of disintegration where there were at most traces of disruption, and it was somewhat naïve in its overestimation of the NSDAP's perpetual palace revolutions. For this reason it sought to forge links with the National Socialist renegades, including the Strasser wing. At one time there was even a harebrained scheme to buy Hitler out. Any activity that promised a split in the NSDAP was regarded as helpful and sometimes even funded, surely a case of throwing good money after bad.

It may not appear necessary to discuss such defense ideas as the

44. In my paper on "Jewish Self-Defense" I deal briefly with these controversial approaches in the light of later German developments leading to the events of July 20, 1944.

airy dream of independent quasi-military Jewish action, but retrospective advice even of this nature has been given to the Jews. It is, of course, true that Germany then was an unrivaled paradise for paramilitary formations. We have already noted how the CV (together with the Reichsbund jüdischer Frontsoldaten) collaborated with the Reichsbanner Schwarz-Rot-Gold, the most important republican defense organization. Had, for example, civil war broken out in 1932, one consequence would have been an attack by right-wing extremists on the Jewish population and able-bodied male Jews would have been drawn willy-nilly into the armed struggle. In such a situation, tens of thousands of German Jews would quite unquestionably have joined the ranks of the republican militias and defense formations to fight for the protection of democracy in Germany. I would not here expand on this theme were it not that the world has latterly been treated to fanciful notions about the possibility of independent action by armed German Jews organized in their own self-defense corps. Such ideas, of course, lack any comprehension of the structure of Germany in those days. Autonomous armed resistance was quite unthinkable for the Jewish community.

VII

German Jewry's defense against antisemitism was a battle fought on the retreat, one in which the small German-Jewish population was largely isolated. Only modest successes were possible, for the Jews as a bourgeois community without backing from broad masses of the electorate were exposed to attack from an antisemitic mass party. In the last phase of the Weimar Republic the majority of the population segment most resembling the Jews in social makeup was already longing for a fascist dictatorship. The Republic could no longer command a broad consensus that might have overcome the attraction of National Socialism. Retrospective blame cast upon the small Jewish minority, the idea that their activities should have been primarily constructive or that in some way it was they who had to heal the deep malaise of German society, are utterly mistaken. Such criticism grotesquely raises to the status of historical fact the Nazi propaganda theme of "Jewish power." With limited resources and few alternatives, though helped by large sections of the Jewish population, Jewish organizations did their best to prevent abrogation of their rights. But substantial support from the German people was not forthcoming. And finally: Ought the Jews to have renounced defense and preempted the advancing tangible threat by an immediate exodus? No minority cleaving to self-respect and dignity can voluntarily give up its rights of citizenship.

All such conclusions, reached for example by those whose research centered round the London Leo Baeck Institute, have not been uncritically accepted. Left-wing social theoreticians have continued to sneer at the bourgeois Jewish defense struggle and to maintain that the "German-nationalist attitudes" of the Jewish Centralverein are paraded by us and glorified as resistance to fascism.

Yet despite fierce and not unfounded criticism of the Jewish defense against antisemitism and National Socialism, no one—not even with the advantage of hindsight—has indicated a better path it could have taken. It may well be true that German Jews, just because of their social origins, were ill prepared in the extreme for revolutionary mass politics and that only very slowly could they adapt themselves to unconditional war against fascism. Possibly the alliance with the socialist working class should have been closer; it may indeed be that the Jewish community's strategy in this crisis of German society should have raised up more positive aims, in the sense of a much stronger and more practical affirmation of the libertarian ideals of the Republic. For antisemitism cannot be fought in isolation. Jewish self-defense is bound up with the fight for free institutions and for their improvement; nor can it sever itself from the struggle of other oppressed minorities for their rights. On this point many sins of omission may be noted; nevertheless, the Jewish defense in the latter years of the Weimar Republic succeeded in adapting itself to the new situation, freeing itself from time-honored traditional methods of combatting antisemitism in order to develop a more direct antifascist strategy.

The question may be raised whether at that time the Jewish defense was sufficiently antifascist, hampered as it was both by its patriotic and nationalistic pronouncements about the blessings and splendors of its ardently loved German fatherland and also by Jewish conservative and financial interests, to whom the ever-increasing collaboration of Jewish officials with the German working class was an abomination. Yet in those days, who indeed was antifascist enough? Perfect antifascism did not exist in the Weimar Republic. The Communists were more occupied with decrying the Social Democrats as "Social Fascists" and from time to time struck pacts with the Nazis. Prussian Social Democrats had allowed themselves to be driven from office in July 1932. Evidence exists to show that at the time officials of the bourgeois Jewish defense were advising the SPD government to an armed resistance.[45] Liberals had dwindled pathetically out of fear for their private fortunes, which a more strongly authoritarian, if necessary even a fascist, state seemed likely to defend better than a "Left" administration. In this overall picture of faintheartedness and vacillation before the onward rush of Nazism, of a Republic lacking its due quota of democrats, of republicans struck blind, in a country with no broad antifascist trend and certainly few *Edelantifaschisten,* the Jewish defense appears to have acquitted itself reasonably well.

The fact that many Jews in this desperate plight did their best to stand up to the Nazi danger is seen from the attempts to mobilize democratic Germany against Nazism as soon as the menace loomed up. Evidence for these endeavors, of course foredoomed to failure, is to be found in existing documents.[46] Characteristic of the last despairing phase of defense is the massive propaganda campaign against the Nazis—fed with material from Jewish sources—that could boast some measure of success wherever it was consistently carried through with support from democratic forces. Had democracy been saved then, the Jewish defense would assuredly have had to be regarded as a major factor in its preservation.

The collapse of the Weimar Republic led to a worldwide catastrophe and the greatest tragedy in the history of the Jewish people. It is fifty years and more from the day when the majority of Germans set out to expel us from our homeland. No democrat, no socialist, no Christian, and certainly none of us survivors of the Nazi terror can deny recognition to those Jewish men and women who year in, year out, did their utmost to prevent the victory of fascist barbarism in Germany.

45. Hans Reichmann, interviews with author, London, 1962–63; corroborated by Alfred Hirschberg, interview with author, London, July 1963; and Alfred Wiener, interview with author, London, August 1963.
46. Apart from all the evidence in Paucker, *Der jüdische Abwehrkampf,* see also Arnold Paucker, "Documents on the Fight of Jewish Organizations against Right-Wing Extremism (1923–1932)," *Michael* 2 (Tel Aviv, 1973): 216–46.

Paul Mendes-Flohr

Martin Buber and the
Metaphysicians of Contempt

... being perceived wrongly is no less painful than
being treated wrongly.

— Franz Rosenzweig, "Apologetic Thinking," 1923

The philosopher of dialogue, Martin Buber (1878–1965) was singularly devoted to the politics of reconciliation. His concept of dialogue was to become one of the distinctive code words of our century,
and it served to foster a new, dynamic conception of tolerance as a
creative process of mutual accommodation and trust. In varied and
often painfully complex situations, he would amplify and add nuance to the notion of dialogue as both an interpersonal and an intercommunal ethic of tolerance promising a fuller and more humane
existence. In the imagination of the twentieth century—an age engulfed by the flames of hatred and fanatic strife—Buber has thus
often been associated with such apostles of peace as the Mahatma
Gandhi and Bertrand Russell, who consistently raised a prophetic
voice urging moral resistance to enmity and needless conflict.

Indeed, Buber cast a noble, conciliatory figure—but some would
also say benighted. It is claimed that Buber underestimated the
power of evil and its insidious, persistent nature. In particular, his
irenic commitments are said to have rendered him indifferent to the
pernicious reality of antisemitism. Yet a careful reading of his writings will show that the issue of antisemitism loomed large for him.
Especially when read palimpsestically, his writings betray a hidden
text that constitutes a sustained critique of what the philosopher

133

Ernst Bloch (1885–1977) was to call "metaphysical antisemitism,"[1] namely, the tendency to repudiate Judaism as a spiritually and culturally jejune religion "essentially" alien to the Christian and European sensibility.

Expressed with the inflections of learned discourse, metaphysical antisemitism provided contempt of the Jew and Judaism with a devious respectability. As Buber embarked on his literary career, this type of antisemitism gained renewed momentum with the publication of such "scholarly" works as Adolf von Harnack's *Wesen des Christentums* (1900) and Werner Sombart's *Die Juden und das Wirtschaftsleben* (1911). While focusing on the "essential" and perduring ethical dimension of Christianity, Harnack (1851–1930) in his immensely popular study argued that the religion of Jesus was the authentic spiritual heir to the biblical faith of Israel and that Judaism survives only as a sterile and spiritually unedifying "legalism." Moreover, Harnack averred, although the Jews' "stubborn" survival had perhaps once been justified by virtue of their millennial anguish, bearing as it did witness to the manifest truth of Christianity, this justification had been decisively eliminated with their emancipation. Hence, contemporary Judaism is utterly bereft of any compelling *raison d'être*. Harnack, who regarded himself as a liberal and an opponent of political antisemitism, even suggested that the continued and obstinate survival of the Jews in the modern liberal state, which had offered them equal rights and the opportunity to integrate into the life of the dominant Christian society, was an expression of arrant ingratitude.[2]

Originally delivered as a series of lectures at the University of Berlin during the winter semester of 1899–1900, Harnack's volume underwent fourteen printings by 1927 and was translated into fourteen languages.[3] Sombart's study was considerably less popular, but

1. Ernst Bloch, *Geist der Utopie*, 2d ed. (Berlin, 1923), p. 330. Bloch specifically refers to views of Judaism inspired by—or exhibiting an affinity with—the teachings of the Christian gnostic Marcion that will be discussed in section III of this essay. For a systematic historical and philosophical analysis of this species of antisemitism, see Nathan Rotenstreich, *Jews and German Philosophy: The Polemics of Emancipation* (New York, 1984).

2. Uriel Tal, "The Controversy about 'The Essence of Judaism' according to Jewish and Christian Sources of the Early Twentieth Century," in *Perspectives of German-Jewish History in the 19th and 20th Century*, Publication of the Leo Baeck Institute, Jerusalem (Jerusalem, 1971), p. 63.

3. Rudolf Bultmann, introd. to Adolf Harnack, *What Is Christianity?* trans. T. B. Saunders (New York, 1957), p. vii; Uriel Tal, *Christians and Jews in Germany: Religion,*

it, too, had a great impact on the educated public. Ostensibly offering a revision of Max Weber's famous thesis on Protestantism and
the origins of capitalism, Sombart (1863–1941) contended that the
Jews were both the purveyors of capitalism and the source of its
distinctive ethos. According to this distinguished economic historian, Jewish values and ingrained sensibilities—arid intellectualism,
a calculating intelligence, insatiable desire, a double ethic—display
a peculiar affinity to the ethical codes and attitudes required by capitalism, and, indeed, it is thus not surprising, in his judgment, that
all the major economic developments and instruments of capitalism
could be traced to the Jews. Unlike Weber, Sombart regarded capitalism as an odious and pernicious development that was fundamentally alien to Christian and German ("Aryan") civilization; his
ascription of the "original sin" of capitalism to Jewry then had an
unambiguous message, one that he preferred to leave implicit in his
"scholarly" account.[4]

Buber's response to these professorial calumnies and their like was
twofold: he would challenge the slanderous accusations by addressing educated non-Jews and, *pari passu*, his fellow Jews of Western
culture. The latter clearly concerned him more. As votaries of Western culture, Buber's fellow Jews were not only exposed to the evil
opinions of them sponsored by the metaphysicans of contempt, but
they had also with varying measure internalized and come to share
these opinons. The more deracinated and assimilated, the greater
the tendency to accept the regnant image of Judaism in Western culture. Bereft of an alternative image, the Jew beheld the reigning neg-

Politics, and Ideology in the Second Reich, 1870–1914, trans. N. J. Jacobs (Ithaca, N.Y.,
1975), p. 205. On Harnack's influence on "the masses of educated people at the turn of
the century," see Paul Tillich's recollection: "Harnack himself once told me that in the
year 1900 the main railway station in the city of Leipzig, one of the largest in Central
Europe, was blocked by freight cars in which his book *What Is Christianity?* was being
sent all over the world. He also told us that this book was being translated into more
languages than any other book except the Bible. This means that this book, which was
the religious witness of one of the greatest scholars of the century, had great significance to the educated people prior to the First World War." Paul Tillich, *Perspectives on
19th and 20th Century Protestant Theology*, ed. C. E. Braaten (New York, 1967), p. 222.
It is not surprising that Harnack's comments about the "essence of Judaism" evoked
vigorous and ramified Jewish responses, as witnessed by the multitude of essays,
monographs, lectures, and even sermons by Jews devoted to Harnack's book. See Tal,
"Controversy about 'The Essence of Judaism,'" pp. 62–87.
    4. See Paul Mendes-Flohr, "Werner Sombart's *The Jews and Modern Capitalism:* An
Analysis of Its Ideological Premises," *Leo Baeck Institute Year Book* (hereafter *LBIYB*)
21 (1976): 87–107.

ative image as his self-image.[5] Thus was born the tragic perversity of Jewish antisemitism, or what Theodor Lessing "diagnosed" in pathological terms as "Jewish self-hatred."[6]

In the throes of assimilation the Western Jew became estranged from himself and his ancestral religion and perceived Judaism through the distorting and hostile prism of the educated European. Hence, as Buber observed in an essay on Henri Bergson and Simone Weil—French Jews, who *mutatis mutandis* in affirming Christian spirituality, repudiated the religion of their birth in terms familiar to contemporary educated discourse—the spiritual reality of Judaism was no longer even known to the Jews themselves. Both Bergson and Weil, Buber noted, "turned away from a Judaism they did not know; in actual fact, they turned aside from a conventional conception of Judaism created by Christianity."[7] With the contemptuous opinions of metaphysical antisemitism in mind, Buber would indefatigably seek to retrieve for the educated Jew—and non-Jew—of the West the spiritual reality of Judaism.

I

Lord, Lord, shake my people,
Strike it, bless it, furiously, gently,
Make it burn, make it free,
Heal your child.

God give the lost glow,
Back to my people.

—Martin Buber, "Prayer," 1899

Buber's *apologia contra judeophobiam* was confounded by the fact that he himself was beholden in part to the negative image of Judaism, both the metaphysical variety and the more popular perceptions of allegedly typical "Jewish" behavior. Ahron Eliasberg (1879–1937), who befriended Buber while they were both students at the University of Leipzig during the academic year 1897–98, recalled that Buber was then given to the "usual Jewish antisemitism"—

---

5. Sander L. Gilman, *Jewish Self-Hatred: Anti-Semitism and the Hidden Language of the Jews* (Baltimore, 1985).

6. Theodor Lessing, *Der jüdischer Selbsthass* (Berlin, 1930).

7. Martin Buber, "The Silent Question" (1952), in his *On Judaism*, ed. N. N. Glatzer, trans. Eva Jospe et al. (New York, 1967), p. 209.

"really Jewish" (*echt jüdisch*) was a scornful reproach often voiced by the young Buber.[8] For Jews of Buber's class in Central Europe, however, such an attitude was not uncommon. As Buber's contemporary and disciple, Robert Weltsch (1891–1982) of Prague noted, in the bourgeois circles of his youth, it was deemed tactless, or rather outright hostile, "for anyone to say he was a 'Jew,' and naturally every Jew of good bourgeois standing avoided doing so." This studious reticence regarding one's Jewish provenance, Weltsch emphasized, "was not simply opportunism. It also stemmed from a genuine embarrassment, engendered by an unclarity about what Judaism really meant. As the word 'Jew,' emptied of all positive content, had shriveled up into a mere name of derision, it seemed only proper not to use it."[9]

For many Western Jews, particularly of the educated bourgeoisie, Zionism provided a framework that allowed them for the first time to declare themselves to be "Jews," unself-consciously and without shame. Indicative of this rehabilitation of the term was the proposal for a Zionist journal that Buber—who joined the Zionist movement when he and Eliasberg founded in the winter of 1898 the first chapter of the movement in the city of Leipzig[10]—developed together with Chaim Weizmann (1874–1952). The contemplated journal was to be named *Der Jude* (The Jew). Buber and Weizmann set forth their proposal in a flier they distributed toward the end of 1903. The journal was envisioned as a monthly—eventually, perhaps, a weekly— that would assume the form of a "European review" designed to stimulate a free, unbiased discussion of the ramified problems of contemporary Jewish life and existence. The journal, moreover, would be unencumbered by the tendentiousness of the party politics that Buber and Weizmann felt befuddled the nascent Zionist movement. The overarching objective of the journal was, however, to promote the "Jewish renaissance"—the renewal of Judaism as a dynamic creative culture. *Der Jude*, Buber and Weizmann exuberantly exclaimed, would seek "to enflame the [Jewish people's] will for a future." This objective, they continued, is "best captured by the name *'der Jude'*"—an assertion that, although stated without explanation,

8. Ahron Eliasberg, "Aus Martin Bubers Jugendzeit: Errinerungen," *Blätter des Heine-Bundes: Eine jüdische Buchgemeinde* (Berlin) 1, no. 1 (1 April 1928): 4.
9. Robert Weltsch, introd. to Martin Buber, *Der Jude und sein Judentum: Gesammelte Aufsätze und Reden* (Cologne, 1963), p. xv.
10. Eliasberg, "Aus Martin Bubers Jugendzeit," p. 5.

implied in the context of the proposal a proud individual, confidently rooted in his primordial identity and culture.[11]

The name of the proposed journal harkens back, apparently consciously, to the journal of the same name founded and edited by Gabriel Riesser (1806–63) from 1832 to 1833. This great defender of Jewish emancipation in Germany also called his journal *Der Jude* precisely because the term had become one of abuse and degradation.[12] Riesser's journal sought to enhance the dignity and rights of the Jew as an individual. Buber and Weizmann understood their journal as contributing to the vindication of the Jew as a proud member of a living people. As Buber later explained, their gallant forerunner, "Riesser had intended his periodical for the individual Jew for whom he sought equal status before the law. . . . We give our organ the same name, but we are not concerned with the individual, but with the Jew as the bearer and beginning of nationhood."[13]

These lines are cited from the inaugural editorial of *Der Jude*, whose actual publication was deferred until 1916. Buber, now acting alone without Weizmann, published the journal in response to the antisemitism that emerged during the First World War and had brought to the fore with heightened urgency the Jewish Question, especially as focused in the ever-worsening plight of Eastern European Jewry. The name on the masthead of Buber's journal, *Der Jude*, no longer simply designated the individual Jew and his rightful demands as a citizen, but also the representative Jew who unabashedly asserts his identity and demands, as Buber put it in his inaugural editorial, "of liberty and freedom of life and work for a hitherto suppressed national community." Through *Der Jude*, Buber concluded, "we want to realize the Jew whose exalted image we bear in memory and in hope."[14]

Under Buber's deft stewardship, *Der Jude* became not only the most sophisticated journal within the Jewish community but one of the most intellectually engaging periodicals in the Weimar Repub-

11. This flier is reproduced in Hans Kohn, *Martin Buber: Sein Werk und seine Zeit*, 2d ed. (Cologne, 1961), pp. 296–300. For a discussion of the collaboration between Weizmann and Buber on this project, see Jehuda Reinharz, *Chaim Weizmann: The Making of a Zionist Leader* (New York, 1985), pp. 134–36.

12. Moshe Rinott, "Gabriel Riesser: Fighter for Jewish Emancipation," *LBIYB* 7 (1962): 11–38.

13. Martin Buber, "Die Losung," *Der Jude* 1, no. 8 (April 1916): 3.

14. Ibid.

lic.[15] Buber rendered *Der Jude* a forum in which the finest minds of Europe, Jewish and non-Jewish, Zionist and non-Zionist, liberal and Orthodox, would discuss in an informed and probing manner issues of Jewish life and letters. Unflinchingly, *Der Jude* dealt with the most painful and complex problems facing Jewry. Special issues, for instance, were devoted to *Antisemitismus und Volkstum, Judentum und Deutschtum,* and *Judentum und Christentum.* In these hefty volumes, Jews and non-Jews of diverse opinions—indeed, from Buber's point of view, often rather reprehensible opinions—were to participate.[16] Buber's journal thus subtly provided Zionism—whose sponsorship of the journal remained unobtrusive and discreet yet undisguised— with legitimacy in circles that otherwise held it in contempt. Representing a proud and nationally conscious Jewishness, Zionism became a genuine partner in dialogue with other perspectives on Judaism and Jews.[17] Furthermore, in a period of mounting antisemitism, as one of Buber's early associates in the journal, Viktor Jacobson (1869–1934), wrote to him, *Der Jude* seemed to be a most effective response. Shortly after the publication of the first issue of *Der Jude,* Jacobson wrote Buber an exuberant letter.

> Yesterday I read a review of *Der Jude* in the Berlin Catholic daily, *Germania,* and I hasten to tell you that the review has strengthened my conviction that *Der Jude* constitutes first-class, great *political action.* Just now, when we hear from all sides how the flood of attacks and defamations on the Jewish name rises ever higher it is an absolute necessity that we, too, say our mind in an honorable, forceful fashion.

"In this sense," Jacobson exclaimed, "*Der Jude* is, indeed, the only proper form of defense against antisemitism." Jacobson concluded by observing that the Zionist leader Vladimir Jabotinsky (1880– 1940) "once put it quite beautifully: 'Zionism is really a revolution of Jewish pride.' In this very sense, *Der Jude* should also have its effect."[18]

15. Arthur A. Cohen, ed., introd. to *The Jew: Essays from Martin Buber's Journal, Der Jude, 1916–1928* (University, Ala., 1980), pp. 9–14. Franz Rosenzweig referred to *Der Jude* as "the one organ of German Jewry that can be taken seriously." Rosenzweig to his parents, October 10, 1916, in his *Briefe,* ed. Edith Rosenzweig (Berlin, 1935), p. 125.
16. The symposia sponsored by *Der Jude* are discussed *in extenso* in my "Ambivalent Dialogue: Jewish-Christian Theological Encounter in the Weimar Period," in *Judaism and Christianity under the Impact of National Socialism, 1919–1945,* ed. Otto Dov Kulka and Paul Mendes-Flohr (Hanover, N.H., 1987).
17. See my "Martin Bubers' Rezeption im Judentum," *Martin Bubers Erbe an unsere Zeit,* ed. Werner Licharz and Heinz Schmidt (Offenbach, 1987), forthcoming.
18. Viktor Jacobson to Martin Buber, May 25, 1916, Buber, *Briefwechsel aus sieben Jahrzehnten,* ed. Grete Schaeder (Heidelberg, 1972), 1:438.

II

"This much is certain: play-actor or genuine
human being; capable of beauty, yet ugly;
lascivious as well as ascetic; charlatan or player-
at-dice; fanatic or cowardly slave—the Jew is all
of that." Jakob Wassermann once summed up in
these words what I consider to be the basic
problem of Jewry, the enigmatic, awesome, and
creative contradiction of its existence.

—Martin Buber, "Judaism and Mankind," 1910

Der Jude would not, however, confine itself to promoting Jewish
pride and cultural renewal. It would also, Buber insisted, direct critical attention "to all that is pernicious in Jewish society, to all the
shortcomings of the Jewish community and its institutions, and to
all that is sick and degenerate in the Jewish people [*Volksorganis-
mus*]."[19] This focus on the "pernicious," "sick and degenerate" aspects
of Jewish life typified much of Buber's writings from his earliest essays on Jewish affairs. Indeed, in his very first effort at Zionist prose,
"Jüdische Renaissance," published in *Ost und West* in January 1901,
he decried the Jews as a people whose "feeling for life has been dis-
located," as a people marked by "an unfree spirituality and the compulsion of a tradition divorced from [the life of] the sense." The Jews,
alas, are a spiritually torpid people "enslaved to an uncreative
money economy."[20]

Elsewhere Buber made biting reference to the "enigmatic, awesome contradictions" of the Jews: "No other people has begotten
such base adventurers and betrayers, no other people such exalted
prophets and redeemers."[21] Similarly, he bemoaned the "pure ritualism" of the rabbis, which has "deprived the Jews of all religiosity
and spiritual inwardness" and continues to exercise its baleful influence on the attitudes of the secular Jews of modernity, especially
manifest in their "barren intellectualism" and unbridled mercantile
values. Hence, Buber contended, the Jews often associate themselves
with "capitalism's most degenerate forms," and with this reprehen-

19. Buber, "Die Losung," p.2.
20. Martin Buber, "Jüdische Renaissance," *Ost und West* 1, no. 1 (January 1901), cols.
7–10, reprinted in Buber, *Die Jüdische Bewegung: Gesammelte Aufsätze und Ansprachen,
Erste Folge: 1900–1914* (Berlin, 1916), p. 12.
21. Martin Buber, "Judaism and Mankind" (1910), in his *On Judaism*, p. 24.

sible alliance "modern Judaism has reached its lowest point." "To me," Buber opined, "the most repulsive of men is the oily war profiteer, who does not cheat any God, for he knows none. And the Jewish profiteer is more repugnant than the non-Jewish, for he has fallen lower." But, Buber testified, "My deepest revulsion is incited by still another man, the man who cheats the God he knows, the man who discusses his business prospects while wearing *tephillin* [the phylacteries donned by Orthodox Jews during the weekday morning prayer]." As an explanation for this arrant behavior, Buber sarcastically suggested that the "motley rabble" who ran along as the Children of Israel came out of Egypt (Exod. 20:32), intermingling with them, have gone amok, threatening to dominate contemporary Jewry.[22]

The egregious features of Jewish life that Buber enumerated with caustic detail correspond to what non-Jewish authors often venomously criticized about the Jews and Judaism. In contrast to the antisemites, however, Buber claimed that the lamentable aspects of Jewish life are not essential and inevitable manifestations of Judaism, but are rather remediable consequences of Israel's unfortunate fate as an exile people. Zionism taught Buber that Exile—*galut*, in Hebrew—is the source of Jewry's endemic maladies, political and spiritual. *Galut* is fundamentally a perversion, a tragically abnormal and anomalous existence that has distorted and perverted the Jewish spirit and ethos.[23] As Buber put it in his essay "Jüdische Renaissance," *galut* is a "torture screw" (*das Exil wirkt wie eine Folterschraube*).[24] Paradoxically, the Zionist conception of *galut* as an analytical category with which to explain the woes of Jewish life in the Diaspora seems to have allowed many Jews to give uninhibited vent to their negative views of existing Jewish life—views apparently imbibed unwittingly from Gentile traducers of Jews and Judaism. As the late Israeli historian Yehezkel Kaufmann (1889–1962) sought to demonstrate, such an internalization of antisemitism was a central dynamic in the shaping of the Zionist imagination. Zionism, he averred, "actually based the national movement on a rationale of charges that it took over from the antisemites, and attempted to find a core of justice in the hatred of the Jews. . . . Jews of the

22. Martin Buber, "The Holy Way" (1918), in ibid., pp. 129–32, 147–48.
23. For a brief but penetrating analysis of the Zionist conception of *galut*, see Ben Halpern, *The Idea of the Jewish State* (Cambridge, Mass., 1961), pp. 95–104.
24. Buber, "Jüdische Renaissance," p. 14.

galut . . . really deserve to be hated; their customs, tendencies, businesses, attitudes to their environment etc., are the source of the hatred, the justifiable hatred. Therefore, they must leave the *galut*."[25] Although perhaps somewhat overstated, Kaufmann's thesis is well documented. It would suffice here to illustrate it with a citation from one of the most "saintly" figures of the Zionist movement, Aaron David Gordon (1865–1922). With reference to the *galut* Jew, this spiritual leader of Zionist settlement in Palestine exclaimed, "Here, before us today, life has revealed the disease of parasitism in all its ugliness and rot. All our strength devoted to healing the nation must be centered in this labor of cure, of surgery."[26]

But as a vision of a new and dignified future for the Jewish people, as suggested in the citation from A. D. Gordon, Zionism effected, if one may employ a Hegelian term, a "sublation" (*Aufhebung*)—a psychical and ideational transposition—of the perceptions of Jewish life borrowed from the antisemites, transforming them into a demand for the healing and liberation of the Jewish people from the scourge of *galut*.[27] In fact Buber expressly regarded Zionism as a dialectical response to *galut*. Zionism, he held, was an inexorable outcome of a historical process engendered by Israel's exile and the insinuation of lowly, alien forces into the lives and souls of the Jews. In the modern period this process has intensified and, having reached its grotesque limits, propels ever-increasing numbers of Jews, especially among the youth, to resolve "to drive the moneylenders of out of [his or her] temple" and to reject "a common bond with the nay-minded, the play actors, the lustful, the dice players, the abject slaves" among their fellow Jews of the *galut*.[28]

Zionism, then, was for Buber only superficially a matter of adopting a particular ideology. "It means," he contended, "a confrontation between men who make choices and men of complacent *laissez-faire*, . . . between elemental Jews [*Urjuden*] and *galut* Jews."[29] Accordingly,

---

25. Yehezkel Kaufmann, "Anti-Semitic Stereotypes in Zionism: The Nationalist Rejection of Diaspora Jewry," *Commentary*, March 1949, p. 241.

26. A. D. Gordon, "The Nation and Labor," in his *Collected Writings*, ed. Shlomo Zemach (Jerusalem, 1952), p. 282.

27. It is, of course, only within the perspective of this dialectic that the Zionist critique of the "*galut* Jew" is to be fully appreciated. In his eagerness to betray the "antisemitism" of his fellow Zionists, Kaufmann overlooked this dialectic, a fact that perhaps recommended his essay's inclusion in the volume of anti-Zionist reflections edited by Michael Selzer: *Zionism Reconsidered: The Rejection of Jewish Normalcy* (New York, 1970), pp. 117–30.

28. Buber, "Judaism and Mankind," p. 31.

29. Ibid.

Buber understood Zionism as a necessary dialectical movement within Jewish history in which the excrescences of *galut* Judaism are expunged. This expurgatory process is initially led by a relatively select few—the *halutzim*, the pioneers—who will return to Zion and *Urjudentum*, a primal, authentic Judaism. Hence it is of utmost importance that the "motley rabble" of *galut* Jewry be kept at bay and not be allowed to spoil the work of redemption: "We know the 'motley rabble' only too well, compulsive compromisers who are hostile to the work of [Zionism] and who violate all pure becoming in Judaism. We do not know how far we shall succeed in keeping them out of the land where they probably will smell an opportunity for exploitation and profit."[30]

In this peroration to an address of 1918 to Zionist youth, Buber conjoined derogatory stereotypes of the *galut* Jew—the "motley rabble"—with an endorsement of Zionist elitism, the then-governing policy of upbuilding the Jewish community of Palestine through select immigration of youthful *halutzim* dedicated to the lofty goals of the movement, thus assuring that Zion would indeed witness the social, moral, and spiritual renewal of the Jew. Buber's support of Zionist elitism conflicted with his genuine concern and oft-expressed solidarity with the Jewish masses—a conflict that recurrently presented him with a dilemma as the Zionist movement was faced with the exigent demand for mass *aliyah* or immigration to Palestine of Jewish refugees (as opposed to idealistic pioneers) from Polish antisemitism in 1920s, from Nazi Germany in 1930s, and later from the death camps of a ravaged Europe.[31] Although he acknowledged with sincere commiseration the need of these masses to find a refuge in Zion, Buber would not allow himself to abandon the elitist view of Zionist priorities, and thus he never adequately resolved his dilemma.[32]

The one particular "perversion" attendant to Israel's tragic sojourn in Exile that exercised Buber most was the triumph of rabbinic ritualism and legalism which, in his judgment, "emasculated" Jewish life and spirituality.[33] Alas, he bewailed, "Rabbinism" had become

---

30. Buber, "Holy Way," pp. 147–48.
31. Martin Buber, *A Land of Two Peoples*, ed. Paul Mendes-Flohr (New York, 1983), pp. 151–54, 157–59, 164–68.
32. Ibid. See also Dina Porat, "Martin Buber and Palestine during the Holocaust, 1942–44," *Yad Vashem Studies*, forthcoming.
33. On Buber's view of Jewish religious practice, see my "Secular Religiosity: Reflections on Post-Traditional Jewish Spirituality and Community," in *Approaches to*

the "official" Judaism of the *galut*. But, in contrast to Harnack and other Gentile critics of "the religion of the Pharisees," Buber contended that there was another, to be sure "unofficial" but nonetheless authentic, form of Judaism that exists "underground," persevering in the unfavorable conditions of *galut*, the "primal" Jewish sensibility. This primal Judaism (*Urjudentum*)—grounded in an unquenchable quest for an "intimate" relationship with God, "spontaneous" spirituality, "passion," "ecstatic phantasy," "inwardness"—endured in the myth and mysticism that the Jewish people continued to cherish despite the imperious rule of rabbinic Judaism.[34] Buber would dedicate prodigious efforts to disclosing for both the Jewish and the Gentile public this "hidden" dimension of Jewish religiosity, myth, and mysticism.

This emphasis on myth and mysticism was not at all arbitrary. At the turn of the century there was a sudden and ramified interest in the mythic imagination and ecstatic spirituality. This "return" to a pre-Enlightenment wisdom—said to be best represented by medieval and Oriental spirituality—was an integral aspect of a quest to overcome what was increasingly perceived as the spiritual desert created by the arid rationalism and soulless practicality of bourgeois, enlightened civilization.[35] Buber himself was to play an active and seminal role in this quest, publishing in the decade prior to the First World War important and exquisitely produced editions of, *inter alia*, Celtic, Chinese, Finnish, Flemish, and Jewish myths and legends as well as writing extensively on Christian and Oriental mysticism.[36]

From the very start of his engagement in this literature, Buber was distressed by the then fashionable tendency to contrast the "Pharisaic legalism" of the Jews with the mystical piety and spiritual inwardness of other traditions. The publisher and Maecenas of the mystical revival, Eugen Diederichs (1867–1930), for instance, pontificated that "the Jews lived according to a sterile law from which they

---

Modern Judaism, ed. Marc Lee Raphael, Brown Judaic Studies 49 (Chico, Calif., 1983), pp. 19–30.

34. Martin Buber, "Jewish Religiosity" (1916), in his *On Judaism*, pp. 83, 79–94.

35. See my "*Fin-de-Siècle* Orientalism, the Ostjuden and the Aesthetics of Jewish Self-Affirmation," *Studies in Contemporary Jewry*, Published by the Institute of Contemporary Jewry, the Hebrew University of Jerusalem, vol. 1 (Bloomington, Ind., 1984), pp. 96–139.

36. See my introd. to Martin Buber, *Ecstatic Confessions*, trans. Esther Cameron (San Francisco, 1985), pp. xiii–xvii.

intellectualized and suffocated all inner spirituality."[37] Buber, who befriended Diederichs and published with him his highly acclaimed collection of *Ecstatic Confessions* (1909)—which brought together mystical testimonies from various Oriental and Occidental traditions—recalled a conversation he had with the great publisher who adamantly refused to believe that the Jews had any capacity for mysticism and myth. Upon completing his first book on Hasidism, *Die Geschichten des Rabbi Nachman* (The Tales of Rabbi Nachman, 1906), which contained a long introduction on the Jewish mystical tradition, Buber promptly dispatched a copy to Diederichs with a note reminding him of their conversation several years earlier.[38]

Buber had the occasion to develop his views on the subterranean survival of an authentic, primal Judaism in his famous addresses on Judaism delivered between 1909 and 1911 to the Bar Kochba Jewish students' association of Prague.[39] His notes for these addresses, preserved in the Martin Buber Archive at the Jewish National and University Library, Jerusalem, contain several folio sheets with citations in three parallel columns from Werner Sombart, Otto Weininger (1880–1903), and Houston Stewart Chamberlain (1855–1927), each asserting that Judaism is utterly bereft of any competence for mysticism and religious mystery.[40]

From Sombart, *Die Juden und das Wirtschaftsleben*, Buber jotted down the following extracts: "The Jewish religion knows no mystery"; "The Jewish religion does not know the condition of ecstasy in which the believer is united with the Godhead."[41] Among the passages Buber transcribed from the writings of Otto Weininger, a Viennese Jewish author whose contempt for Judaism surpassed that of most Gentile antisemites, are "Among the Jews there is no genuine mysticism"; "To be sure, there are no Jewish murderers, but surely

---

37. As paraphrased by George Mosse, *The Crisis of German Ideology: Intellectual Origins of the Third Reich* (New York, 1964), p. 57.

38. Martin Buber, *The Tales of Rabbi Nachman*, trans. Maurice Friedman (Bloomington, Ind., 1956); Buber to Eugen Diederichs, January 21, 1907, Buber, *Briefwechsel*, 1:253.

39. Martin Buber, *Drei Reden über das Judentum* (Frankfurt a.M., 1911). These addresses are translated in *On Judaism*, pp. 11–55.

40. Martin Buber Archive, Jewish National and University Library, Jerusalem, varia 350, fol. *heh* 22.

41. Buber lists these citations without giving their source, but he does note the pagination, thus enabling the quotations to be traced to Werner Sombart's *Die Juden und das Wirtschaftsleben* (Munich, 1911), p. 237.

there are also no Jewish saints."⁴² The political philosopher and unabashed racist Chamberlain, who regarded the Jew and Arab as one in their incorrigible Semitism, is cited by Buber as claiming that "for no human being is mysticism so inaccessible [as it is for the Arab]"; "The Semite bans from religion all wonder and creative phantasy."⁴³

It is not surprising that Buber's Prague addresses on Judaism contain polemical allusions to these remarks. Buber made them while establishing the existence of an ongoing Jewish mystical tradition. He also availed himself of the opportunity to challenge other defamations of Jewish character. With elliptical reference to Sombart, he accepted the thesis that the Jew is "spurred on" by an "urge for acquisition." This urge, however, Buber noted, need not lead necessarily to capitalism, for

> this urge . . . is directed not toward [the Jew's] personal comfort but toward the happiness of the next generation. The next generation . . . is in turn charged with the task of taking care of still another generation, so that all reality is dissolved in the care for the future. . . . This tendency awakens Messianism in the Jew, the idea of an absolute future that transcends all reality of past and present as the true and perfect life.

Messianism, Buber underscored, "is Judaism's most profoundly original idea"—an idea that decisively shaped the moral and spiritual imagination and texture of Western civilization.⁴⁴ Again referring indirectly to Sombart and other learned students of "the psychology of Judaism," Buber questioned the contention that Jews were and have essentially remained a "nomadic people," deducing "from this all sorts of Jewish character traits, real and alleged."⁴⁵ Buber undoubtedly had in mind such statements by Sombart as the following:

> Throughout the centuries . . . Israel had remained a desert and nomadic people. . . . Yes, they became town-dwellers. . . . Now, the modern city is nothing but a great desert, as far removed from the warm earth as the desert is, and like it forcing its inhabitants to become nomads. . . . A determination to reach some goal is a nomadic virtue, and the Jews' thousand years' wandering only developed this nomadic virtue in them. The promised land throughout their journeyings was always before them; it was always something to be reached, something to be

42. Weininger, *Geschlecht und Charakter* (Vienna, 1903), pp. 467–68, 421.
43. For these citations Buber provides neither the source nor the pagination. We may surmise, however, that they are from Chamberlain's *magnum opus, Die Grundlagen des neunzehnten Jahrhunderts* (Munich, 1901).
44. Martin Buber, "Renewal of Judaism" (1911), in his *On Judaism*, p. 50.
45. Martin Buber, "The Spirit of the Orient and Judaism" (1915), in ibid., p. 71.

achieved. . . . The importance attached by the Jews to results of action may have been the cause and effect at once of their capitalistic undertakings.[46]

Countering such askewed and invidious arguments, Buber marshaled biblical and cognate evidence indicating that the Jews in their formative period were basically an agrarian people.

All of the Palestinian period attests to so great a love of the soil and the exaltation of its cultivation as is found but in a few other nations. . . . Seldom has there been another people so self-contained and so glorying in its rootedness. . . . The whole spiritual and religious life of ancient Judaism was closely bound up with the life of the soil, the life of the familiar earth.

The fact is, Buber pointedly noted, it was only with their Exile that "the Jews indeed became a nomadic people." Although "robbed of its natural context," Buber declared, reiterating his central thesis, the primary reality of Judaism "lived on [among] its heretics" and "in the Messianic movements, which arose in the swirling flames of its ecstatic faith . . . , and in the world of Jewish mysticism which, subterraneously tended the sacred fire of the ancient bond with God." Moreover, Buber emphasized in his rebuttal of Sombart and others that the primal Jewish reality, potentially, lives on in the soul of every Jew: "One can detect all this [even] in the most assimilated Jew, if one *knows* how to gain access to his soul." These traits of an enduring, albeit suppressed primal Judaism, Buber contended, are more readily discernible among the Jewish masses of Eastern Europe, who, to be sure, "are poor in the skills of civilization." Yet "despite the encroachments of corruption and corrosion," these denizens of "the Ghetto" are "rich in the power of an original ethos and spirit of immediacy [with the divine]." Here, Buber defiantly explained, among the simple Jews, especially the Hasidim, "stunted and distorted yet unmistakable, is Oriental strength and Oriental inwardness."[47]

The response of non-Jewish reviewers of Buber's earliest writings on Judaism confirmed for him that his form of *apologia* was effective. Typical was a 1906 review of *Die Geschichten des Rabbi Nachman* by an Austrian critic who observed that "even for Schopenhauer, the

---

46. Werner Sombart, *The Jews and Modern Capitalism*, trans. M. Epstein (New York, 1951), pp. 303, 308, 314.

47. Buber, "Spirit of the Orient and Judaism," pp. 72, 73, 74–75, 76, italics in original. The original text has "Asiatic" instead of "Oriental." The two terms were interchangeable for Buber, indeed for his generation in general.

most bitter opponent of Jewish-Protestant rationalism," Buber's book would have been a veritable "revelation" (Enthüllung). "He would have ceased to generalize so thoroughly his deep antipathy for the Jews. . . . I, too, have never come across a book that could convince the enemies of modern, half-enlightened, semiassimilated Jewry of the deep [spiritual] forces that had stirred so powerfully in this people."[48] There were, however, reviewers who begrudged the Jews the very spirituality identified by Buber as primal Judaism. A reviewer writing in 1908 in the prestigious Neue Metaphysische Rundschau suggested that the "hostile" reception accorded the Baal Shem Tov, the founding personality of Hasidism, was yet another example of how the Jews rejected a noble teacher.

> If I am not mistaken, [Buber's Legends of the Baal Shem] will find more Christian adherents [Freunde] than it will among the Jews themselves. Speaking through the Baal Shem is a great, holy wisdom, an ancient theosophical teaching whose protective vessel was to be Judaism. . . . [But] the wisdom of this teaching has been adopted by other peoples, and the Jewish people continue to err as it has since the time of the patriarchs.[49]

Such scornful reviews were, however, few. Most reviews were in varying measure sympathetic to the image of the Jew portrayed in Buber's Hasidic tales and other writings on Judaism. Indeed, the Hasidic expression of Jewish spirituality—as rendered by Buber— quickly became part of the esthetic universe of the educated European.[50] To be sure, this esthetic appreciation of Buber's Hasidism did not necessarily entail a fundamental revision of one's views of Judaism and Jews. Buber, of course, knew this. But he had also assumed that the refined liberal discourse and prevailing commitment to humanistic values that still largely characterized the cultural life in Wilhelmine Germany would in time allow for the recognition of the "primal Jewish spiritual reality," especially as embodied in Hasidism, as a "primal human reality."[51] As much as one recognizes, Buber held, the teachings of the Zen masters or the legends of the pre-Christian Celts and Finns as essential human truths, so one may recognize in the mystical lore of the despised Jews a fount of universal

48. Unsigned review in Österreichische Rundschau, January 1, 1907, p. 7.
49. Unsigned review in Neue Metaphysische Rundschau 12, no. 2 (November-December 1908): 115–16.
50. For a comprehensive survey of the reviews of Buber's early Hasidic writings, see my "Fin-de-Siècle Orientalism," pp. 116–20.
51. Buber, "Judaism and Mankind," pp. 23–25.

wisdom. Such recognition, he hoped, would lead to a sense of shared humanity with the Jews.

While Buber was working on his second volume of Hasidic writings, *The Legends of the Baal Shem* (1908), a vicious pogrom was perpetrated against the Jewish community of Bialystok in Russian Poland. This well-orchestrated assault of the mobs against the Jews lasted for three full days, leaving seventy dead and ninety gravely injured. In a letter to a friend, Buber expressed his deep anguish over these events and revealed that *his* answer to the outrage of antisemitism was his work on Hasidism.

> I am now working on a story which is my answer to Bialystok. It is called *Adonai* [God, i.e., the spiritual reality of the Jew]. . . . I am now in the midst of the first real work period of my life. You are my friend and will understand me: I have a new answer to give everything. Only now have I found the form for my answer.[52]

Buber was, however, eventually to realize the limitations of this "answer."

In the wake of the First World War, Europe witnessed a radical eclipse of liberal optimism and was gripped by a miasmic sense of cultural crisis—and by a concomitant intensification of metaphysical as well as vulgar antisemitism. Buber now felt increasingly obliged to reassess the liberal presuppositions of his *apologia contra judeophobiam*. His strategy of seeking to rehabilitate the image of Judaism and the Jew before the forum of educated European opinion would undergo considerable revision.

III

Test yourself on humanity. It makes the doubter
doubt, the man of belief believe.
—Franz Kafka, *Das Schloss*, 1926

The convulsive, brutal reality of the Great War left deep wounds and profound confusion. Out of the vortex of a protracted and tragically senseless war, accompanying revolutions, and economic and social dislocations emerged a bewildered Europe. For many the war put the lie to the liberal, humanistic presuppositions of the nineteenth century. Virtually every sphere of intellectual and imaginative life was affected by a sense of despair. In the realm of theological

---

52. Buber, letter of December 1906, quoted in Kohn, *Martin Buber*, p. 310.

reflection, especially within German-Protestant circles, this despair was marked by a shift from Kantian-inspired moral theology—which placed emphasis on the Christian's moral responsibility for the social realm—to a reaffirmation of the soteriological vision of the New Testament and the promise of individual salvation through Christ. In contrast to its previous focus on the ethical teachings of Jesus, Christian theology was now recast in more distinctively Pauline tones, highlighting man's fallen state and utter dependence on God's grace and deliverance. The efficacy of the moral deed and the meaningfulness of history, accordingly, were increasingly called into question. The emerging religious mood thus suggested that human initiative was of little avail; man's only hope was divine salvation.

The Protestant theologian Karl Barth (1886–1968) was the first to give this position a sustained articulation. His *Epistle to the Romans* (1919; 2d rev. ed., 1921) contains a devastating critique of liberal theology, which he charged had obfuscated man's dependence on divine grace and thereby encouraged human hubris. Barth insisted that not only human will but also reason were vitiated by the Fall. A sinful, finite man stands in need before a transcendent, otherworldly God.

This dramatic departure from the worldliness and optimism of moral theology can also be discerned in the post–World War I work of Adolf von Harnack, arguably the greatest representative of Protestant liberalism. In 1921 Harnack published his magisterial study on Marcion, the second-century Christian heretic: *Marcion: Das Evangelium von dem fremden Gott*.[53] Regarding himself a disciple of Paul, Marcion elaborated the apostle's distinction between law and grace with a far-reaching gnostic twist: the God of the Old Testament—the God of Creation—is not identical with the true God, who is essentially alien to this fallen world and is manifest only in the person of Jesus the Christ. The God of the Old Testament—"the God of Israel"—Marcion emphasized, is the God of law and (an ultimately illusory) justice; the God of the New Testament is the God of love and salvation. Marcion urged Christianity to dissociate itself from the Old Testament and the delusive concept of Creation and to cling to the only true God and hope, Jesus the Christ. In his scholarly

---

53. Harnack's interest in Marcion goes back to his first scholarly, but unpublished, essay for which the University of Dorpat had given him a gold medal. William Pauck, *Harnack and Troeltsch: Two Historical Theologians* (New York, 1968), p. 9.

analysis of the sources and message of Marcion, Harnack did not hesitate to endorse the heretic's theology.

> In the second century, the rejection of the Old Testament would have been a mistake and the Great Church rightly refused to make this mistake; its rejection in the sixteenth century was due to the power of a fateful heritage from which the reformation was not yet able to withdraw; but its conservation as a canonical book in modern Protestantism is the result of a paralysis of religion and the church.[54]

In a letter he wrote to a friend discussing his book on Marcion, Harnack restated this thesis in more explicit and decisive terms.

> Is it not so that the Ancient Church was not aware of the fact that truth too develops? . . . I did not find it difficult to cause my children to accept the teaching that the Old Testament is now antiquated and only in certain parts still appealing and valuable. It is the law and history of the Jews; *our* book is the New Testament.[55]

Franz Rosenzweig (1886–1929) was quick to detect in Harnack's fascination with Marcion an ominous development. He read Harnack's monograph not simply as a scholarly treatise but as indicative of a profound crisis in Christianity and an incipient gnostic mood encouraging not only a rejection of the Old Testament and the God of Creation but also a hatred of the people to whom this God first revealed Himself. In a letter of July 29, 1925, to Buber, with whom he was then working on their translation of the Hebrew Scripture into German, he wrote:

> It should be quite clear to you that the situation for which the neo-Marcionites [e.g., Harnack] have striven to achieve on the theoretical plane in actuality has already been obtained. . . . When the Christian speaks of the Bible, he means only the New Testament, perhaps together with the Psalms, which then he mostly believes already belong to the New Testament. Thus in our new translation of the Hebrew Bible we are becoming missionaries.[56]

The Buber-Rosenzweig translation of the Hebrew Bible was not simply another translation but rather an attempt to capture in German the unique cadences, inflections, and texture of the Hebrew and thus quicken anew for both Jew and Gentile the power of the Word

---

54. Adolf von Harnack, *Marcion: Das Evangelium vom fremden Gott*, 2d ed. (Leipzig, 1924), p. 127.
55. Harnack to Karl Holl, quoted in Pauck, *Harnack and Troeltsch*, pp. 38–39 n. 62, italics in original.
56. Franz Rosenzweig to Buber, July 25, 1925, *Briefe und Tagebücher*, ed. Rachel Rosenzweig and Edith Rosenzweig-Scheinmann (The Hague, 1979), 2:1055–56.

spoken by God to Israel. Accordingly, through this what Buber called a "colometric" translation, the abiding speech and *ergo* Presence of God—and his ever-renewed relation with the world of His creation—become manifest to all mankind.[57] For Rosenzweig and Buber, the God present in the Hebrew Scripture is not merely the God of the Jews; He is indeed the God of Creation, and thus of the shared destiny of *all* the world. In retaining the "Old Testament" despite Marcion's exhortations, Rosenzweig and Buber observed, Christianity in effect acknowledged that salvation as a universal reality must be grounded in Creation. In a now-famous theological exchange in 1916 with Eugen Rosenstock-Huessy (1888–1973), a Christian (of Jewish origin), Rosenzweig noted that the church, following a period of "gnostic naïveté," came under the sapient tutelage of Augustine and realized that without the concept of Creation the universality of the promise of salvation and thus of the church and its power over history are deprived of their ontological basis and compelling authority.

Paul's theory concerning the relation of the Gospels to the Law could have remained a "personal opinion"; the Hellenizing "spiritual" Church (of John's Gospel) of the first century, in the marvelous naïveté of her "spiritual believers," had scarcely worried about it. Then came gnosticism, which laid its finger on Paul and sought to weed out the personal element from his theory and to develop its objective aspects in distinction from the personal in it. (Paul said: "The Jews are spurned, but Christ came from them." Marcion said: "Therefore the Jews belong to the devil, Christ to God.") Then the Church, which hitherto had been quite naïve in its own gnosticism . . . , suddenly seeing this, pushed the spirit to one side in favor of tradition, and through a great *ritornar al segno* fixed this tradition by returning to this cardinal point, to its founder Paul; that is, she deliberately established as dogma what previously had been considered Paul's personal opinion. The Church established the identity of the Creator (and the God revealed at Sinai) with the Father of Jesus Christ on the one hand, and the perfect manhood of Christ on the other hand, as a definite, correlated Shibboleth against all heresy—and thereby the Church established herself as a power in human history. . . . Thus, in the firm establishment of the Old Testament in the Canon, and in the building of the Church on this double scripture (Old and New Testament) the stubbornness of the Jews is in fact brought out as the other half of the Christian dogma [that is], its formal consciousness of itself.

57. "Our translation [of the Hebrew Bible] is the first *colometric* one, that is, the first that gives to the text its natural articulation, regulated by the laws of human breath and of human speech, each one of which represents a rhythmic unit." Quoted in Maurice Friedman, *Martin Buber's Life and Work: The Middle Years, 1923–1945* (New York, 1983), pp. 59–60.

The Old Testament and thus also the Jews remain essential to the church's understanding of itself. To be sure, as Rosenzweig ironically put it, the Jews have remained part of Christian consciousness in a most ambivalent manner: Christian affection for the Jews as the custodians of the Old Testament has been catechized as the dogma of "Israel's stubbornness." But this "dogmatic" ambivalence, as Rosenzweig urged his epistolary adversary to admit, was no mere theological exercise, for it cannot but have engendered contempt of the Jews. "In actual practice . . . the theological idea of the stubbornness of the Jews works itself out [as] *hatred of the Jews.*"[58]

Rosenzweig regarded this ambivalence as inherent in the church's historical and theological relation to Judaism. But actual contempt, he intimated, could be restrained, if not totally overcome, if the church would acknowledge that it needs "the synagogue" in fulfilling God's work of reconciling divine creation, which is intrinsically good (see Gen. 1:31), and human history. In this work—and in the fact that both trace their dispensation to divine revelation—Judaism and Christianity share something in common "against paganism and 'natural religion.'"

> Behind the images of these coins [Judaism and Christianity] is hidden the same metal. The forms of holiness themselves are different, but the final root in the soul [is common]. . . . This common religion, quite real, is the human aspect of the common objective origin of revelation, also quite real, just as the complementary contrast between their saints is the human aspect of the objective oneness of the two faiths, a oneness determined by their common goal. Hence the common distinction of this religious life from all that stands outside revelation (or puts itself outside). . . . [a pagan][59] doesn't know, and cannot know, the quite otherworldly attitude of the soul that yet breathes the world with every breath, an attitude that is peculiar to religion within revelation (because only revelation means that overshadowing of the world by another world, which is the objective presupposition of that attitude of the soul). *How* that breathing of the world happens is the great contrast between Jew and Christian, but *that* it happens is their common ground.[60]

In *The Star of Redemption* (1921) Rosenzweig would elaborate this complementarity of the synagogue and the church in his theory of

58. Franz Rosenzweig to Eugen Rosenstock-Huessy, October 1916, *Judaism despite Christianity: The "Letters on Christianity and Judaism" between Eugen Rosenstock-Huessy and Franz Rosenzweig,* ed. Eugen Rosenstock-Huessy (New York, 1971), pp. 110, 112, italics in original.

59. The text actually reads "Islam," which Rosenzweig regarded as a "primitive" form of monotheism, and thus virtually pagan.

60. Rosenzweig to Rosenstock-Huessy, pp.164, 165–66.

two, coeval covenants, each requiring one the other according to God's *Heilsplan*.[61] It was therefore of utmost importance that Christianity resist the attempts of the neo-Marcionites to renounce the Old Testament. Rosenzweig was undoubtedly particularly distressed by the fact that this neo-Marcionism was sponsored by both liberals such as Harnack, who regarded the Old Testament as an encumbrance to the continued spiritual and moral refinement of Christianity, and *Deutsche Christen*, who emerged most forcefully from the embers of the First World War seeking to free Christianity from "alien, Semitic" sensibilities and to render the Christian *kerygma* compatible with the German, "Aryan" soul.[62]

The project to re-Hebraize the Bible was thus, according to Rosenzweig, in the forefront of the struggle against metaphysical antisemitism and "the neo-Marcion aspiration to drive the Bible from German culture."[63] In a letter to a friend, Rosenzweig conceded the enormity of the task to preserve the Old Testament as part of the Christian sensibility and took solace in the prospect that "quite possibly after seventy years a new return [to the Old Testament] will follow this *golus bovel* [the Babylonian exile, which lasted seventy years]." "In any case," he bravely concluded, "it is only the beginning of the task and not the final outcome that is in our province."[64] Alas, Rosenzweig and Buber did not have seventy years to check the spread of neo-Marcionism. As Buber later noted, "Three years after the death of Harnack in 1930, his idea, the idea of Marcion, was put into action; not however by spiritual means but by means of violence and terror." Buber is elliptically referring to the infamous "Aryan paragraph" by which the Nazi state, in Buber's words, "placed before the Church one of two alternatives: either to exclude Judaism and the spirit of Israel entirely from its midst . . . , or else to be overthrown together with Judaism. The gift of Marcion had passed from Hadrian into other hands."[65]

61. Franz Rosenzweig, *The Star of Redemption*, trans. William Hallo (New York, 1970), pt. 3.

62. On Rosenzweig's understanding of the *Deutsche Christen* as neo-Marcion, see Martin Buber, "Die Schrift und ihre Verdeutschung," in his *Werke: Schriften zur Bibel*, vol. 2 (Kösel, 1964), p. 1182. On the *Deutsche Christen*, see Klaus Scholder, *Die Kirchen und das Dritte Reich* (Frankfurt a.M., 1972), 1:93–109, 239–76.

63. Quoted in Buber, "Die Schrift und ihre Verdeutschung," pp. 1181–82.

64. Rosenzweig to Eugen Mayer, December 30, 1925, quoted in ibid., p. 1182.

65. Martin Buber, "The Spirit of Israel and the World Today," in his *Israel and the World: Essays in a Time of Crisis*, trans. J. M. Lask, 2d ed. (New York, 1963), p. 192.

Buber accepted Rosenzweig's conception of their Bible translation as a "mission" to Christianity. "Although I am a radical opponent of all missionary work," he wrote, "I allowed myself to accept the mission, for it appertains neither to Judaism *per se* nor to Christianity *per se*, but rather to their shared primal truth [*Urwahrheit*], on whose rehabilitation the future of both depends."[66] The neo-Marcion attempt to discredit the Old Testament and the God of Creation, Buber averred, strikes at the very core of Western civilization and its humanistic foundations, namely the fundamental assumption that history and morality are ontologically and existentially meaningful processes. The nullification of this assumption breaks open the floodgates of cynicism and nihilism, attitudes that gain expression in the gnostic and Marcion disdain for the mundane order celebrated by the Hebrew Scripture as Creation. Indeed, Buber maintained, Western humanism is ultimately rooted not in Greek *sophia* but in the biblical concept of Creation. Hence the struggle against neo-Marcionism—which Rosenzweig and Buber regarded as the most pernicious form of metaphysical antisemitism—is eminently more than a question of securing the dignity and honor of Judaism; it is rather a struggle on behalf of Western civilization, on behalf of giving shape to a more just and compassionate human order. Biblical humanism, as Buber explained in 1934 to an audience of German Jews still smarting from the wounds of the initial Nazi assault on their humanity, affirms that "the world is a creation, not a reflection, not semblance, not play. The world is not something which must be overcome. It is a created reality." It is a reality, however, whose realization requires human partnership in God's work. It is a reality, Buber emphasized, that is "created to be hallowed. Everything created has a need to be hallowed. . . . Hallowing enables the [world] to fulfil the meaning for which it was created. The meaning with which Creation informed man, informed the world, is fulfilled through hallowing." In contrast to gnosticism and Pauline Christianity—which Buber viewed as a dialectical adumbration of Marcionism and its "gnostic" desanctification of the world—Judaism seeks neither to transfigure the world into something "wholly spiritual" nor to "overcome" it by spirit. "The spirit does not embrace a holy world, rejoicing in its holiness, nor does it float above an unholy world, clutching

66. Buber, "Die Schrift und ihre Verdeutschung," p. 1182.

all holiness to itself: it produces holiness, and the world is made holy."[67]

The mission to fend off the threat of neo-Marcionism was now to guide Buber's conception of the struggle against metaphysical anti-semitism. After Rosenzweig's death in December 1929, he carried on alone the translation of the Hebrew Bible into German, a task that the tragic events of the 1930s obliged him to complete, paradoxi-cally, in a land where Hebrew was the mother tongue and only after the forces of nihilism made their frantic onslaught on the Jews and Western civilization.[68] Not insignificantly, perhaps, before leaving Germany in March 1938 for Palestine—a step he repeatedly post-poned in order to help fortify his fellow Jews in their "spiritual re-sistance" to the Nazi regime[69]—Buber made several anguished and to him unsatisfactory attempts to translate the Book of Job.[70] Years later he would refer to Job as "my father." Incessantly abused and disgraced, Job did not succumb to despair but persisted in his faith: "My father Job (no Israelite, it seems, and yet my father) protests and trusts in one; we come to feel that he loves God, whom he charges with injustice, but that to love his own fate remains alien to him to the end, and God encourages him to not to love it."[71]

Even prior to the ascension of Adolf Hitler to power, as already noted, Buber engaged Christian adversaries in theological debate.[72] In the course of these encounters he defended the integrity of Juda-ism and refined his own understanding of his ancestral faith, partic-ularly his appraisal of the Pharisees. Debating the opponents of Jewry, he realized that the anti-Pharisaism that pervaded modern attitudes toward Judaism was not only a distortion but animated virtually every species of metaphysical antisemitism.[73] Thus, in re-

67. Buber, "The Power of the Spirit" (1934), in his *Israel and the World*, pp. 180, 181.
68. Buber, "Die Schrift und ihre Verdeutschung," pp. 1175–82.
69. Ernst A. Simon, "Jewish Adult Education in Nazi Germany as Spiritual Resist-ance," *LBIYB* 1 (1956): 68–104 passim.
70. "In den letzten Jahren meines Aufenthalts in Deutschland hatte ich mich Mal um Mal an der Übersetzung des Buches Hiob versucht, stiess aber immer wieder auf Schwierigkeiten, derengleichen mir bei der bisherigen Arbeit nicht begegnet waren." Buber, "Die Schrift und ihre Verdeutschung," p. 1180. The Martin Buber Archive pos-sesses three different, almost complete translations of the Book of Job, each of which Buber regarded as unsatisfactory.
71. Buber, quoted in *Philosophical Interrogations*, ed. Sydney Rome and Beatrice Rome (New York, 1970), p. 92. Cf. "I stand over against God because I have been set by him in my own being in the most real sense, that is, I have been 'created.'" Ibid.
72. For a full account of these encounters, see my "Ambivalent Dialogue."
73. G. F. Moore, "Christian Writers on Judaism," *Harvard Theological Review* 14, no. 3 (July 1921): 197–254.

viewing the various Christian contributions to a special issue (*Sonderheft*) of *Der Jude*, published in 1927, devoted to Jewish-Christian relations, Buber observed that "throughout the articles of this issue . . . I found repeatedly the words 'Pharisee,' 'Pharisaic,' 'Pharisaism.' They refer both to a historical category and to one (not *the*, to be sure, but *one*) essential feature of Jews and Judaism." Unfortunately, Buber emphasized, the authors' understanding of this aspect of Judaism reflects such gross misconceptions that they in effect "have joined the ranks formed by the evangelists [*Evangelisten*, i.e., proselytizers] which, in their procession through the ages, are more of an issue to the Jews than the whole phalanx of the 'antisemites.'" Buber laconically adds, "but not merely to the Jews."[74]

Contrary to prevailing prejudice (to which, as noted earlier, he himself was beholden), Buber maintained, the Pharisees were not advocates of "the rigid Law." In fact the Pharisees seem to have been confused with the Sadducees, who indeed "tore the Law dwelling in sacred history and in the sacred Book from the living moment and thereby removed the Law from the path of men." The Pharisees, on the other hand, "saw in the written Torah only the kernel of a living tradition," to be interpreted and constantly adapted to the flow of life. Far from being votaries of a rigid legalism, Buber argued, the Pharisees sought to serve God, "who does not wish to have His manifestation encapsulated, but who, like the work of His creation, 'daily renews' His revelation."[75]

For Buber the Pharisees were now no longer the representatives of a spiritually desiccated expression of Judaism that falsified the primal spirit of Israel. In fact, he now argued, the Pharisees assured that this primal spirit would remain a living tradition bound to the real, unfolding life of the Jews. In this crucial respect, according to Buber, Jesus' position on the Law was typically Pharisaic. For like the Pharisees, Jesus rejected "the Sadducaean dichotomy between Then and Here, between Revelation at Mount Sinai and the living moment." The difference between Jesus and the Pharisees is not with regard to the understanding of the Law but rather how to quicken the relation with God promoted by the Law. Toward this end, however, Jesus

does not, like the Pharisees, in order to find a unification of both [the Revelation and the living moment] enter into the situation of Now. In-

74. Buber, "Pharisaism," in *The Jew*, p. 225.
75. Ibid., p. 226.

stead, he wishes to enter the cloud over the mountain, the cloud from which the voice resounds. He wants to penetrate to the ultimate intention of God, the ultimate absoluteness of the Law. . . . He wants to "fulfil" the Law, that is to say, to invoke its original fulness and make it real.

But in his manifest passion to fulfill the Law, Buber opined, Jesus lacked the sober spiritual realism of the Pharisees. Jesus failed to consider "the fact that the people will not be able to breathe within the original purity [of the Law] any better now than then. As a matter of fact, Buber insisted, the Pharisees were no less passionate in fulfilling the true spirit of the Law than Jesus. Being the realists that they were, they simply wanted "reality—not just any reality, but the reality from the Word. They [wanted] life—not just any life, but life in the Presence. And thus . . . they [had] to content themselves with staying here below, beneath the cloud." Bound to the terrestrial, the Pharisees affirmed the world; they were individuals "who, not merely with some, but with all manifestations of [their] life actively affirmed the world as God's world." In a word, Buber held that in accepting the yoke of the Law, the Pharisees gave living testimony to their belief in the God of Creation.[76]

In the course of his theological encounters with Christians, Buber was chagrined to learn that most of his opponents were not prepared to transcend a polemical mode of discourse. On one occasion he exasperatedly declared: "I have once again . . . noted that there is a boundary beyond which the possibility of encounter [Entgegen] ceases and only the reporting of factual information remains. I cannot fight against an opponent who is thoroughly opposed to me, nor can I fight against an opponent who stands on a different plane than I."[77] This comment was prompted by a German Christian of decidedly conservative loyalties. Buber was also to learn that there were limitations to the possibilities of a genuine dialogue even with liberal Christians. On the eve of Hitler's appointment as chancellor, Buber engaged the liberal theologian Karl Ludwig Schmidt (1891–1956) in a public debate on the "Church, State, Nation, Jewry."[78] Schmidt was no timid liberal. The journal he had edited since 1922,

76. Ibid., pp. 228–30. Because of its affirmation of Creation, the Talmud "makes taboo any reaching beyond the Messianic into the eschatological, beyond the salvation of mankind into the transformation of the world." Ibid., p. 230.
77. Martin Buber, "Bericht und Berichtigung," Der Jude, Sonderheft, Judentum und Deutschtum (1926), p. 87.
78. Karl Ludwig Schmidt and Martin Buber, "Kirche, Staat, Volk, Judentum: Zwiegespräch im jüdischen Lehrhaus in Stuttgart am. 14. Januar 1933," Theologische Blätter 12, no. 9 (September 1933): 257–74.

Theologische Blätter, had become the forum of the most forward-looking Protestants, as is evidenced by the frequent appearance on its pages of Karl Barth and religious socialists such as Paul Tillich. Moreover, Schmidt's journal was in the forefront of the struggle against the *Deutsche Christen* and, later, against Hitler's attempt to "Aryanize" the Evangelical church.[79] Schmidt also recurrently and vigorously denounced political and racial antisemitism. Yet, as it became evident in his exchange with Buber, theologically he could not free himself from the classical Christian perception of Judaism as an anachronistic, spiritually moribund religion. Further, Schmidt insisted, the Christian is obliged to remind the Jew that *extra ecclesiam nulla salus* and, accordingly, concluded his remarks with a non-conciliatory proclamation.

> Were the Church more Christian than it is, the conflict [*Auseinendersetzung*] with Judaism would be sharper than it now is. From the very beginning of Christianity, this sharp conflict has existed. . . . We Christians must never tire of keeping this one conflict alive.[80]

Buber, to say the least, was piqued that in "the atmosphere of impending crisis" a leading voice of liberal Christianity found it impossible to accept his plea to establish a radically new approach to Jewish-Christian encounter.[81]

How Buber envisioned this new type of encounter was already adumbrated in the discussions that preceded the debate with Schmidt. The agreed-upon guidelines specified that the speakers would address the subject "neither polemically nor apologetically," but objectively and forthrightly.[82] Buber also sought to stipulate that his Christian partner in the debate, Schmidt, should bracket his theological "preconceptions" and allow Judaism to speak for itself. This demand was implicit in Buber's objection to Schmidt's suggestion that the title of the debate make reference to the "synagogue" as the theological counterpoint to the "church."[83] Although the term "synagogue" might very well be a meaningful category for Christian theological self-understanding, Buber contended, it is not at all in accord

79. Oscar Cullman, "Karl Ludwig Schmidt, 1891–1956," *Theologische Zeitschrift* 12, no. 1 (January-February 1956): 1–9.

80. Schmidt, "Kirche, Staat, Volk, Judentum," pp. 258, 272–73.

81. Buber to Maurice Friedman, n.d., quoted in Friedman's introd. to his translation of Buber's response to Schmidt: Buber, "Church, State, Nation, Jewry," in *Christianity: Some Non-Christian Appraisals*, ed. David W. McKain (New York, 1964), pp. 176–88.

82. Schmidt, "Kirche, Staat, Volk, Judentum," p. 259.

83. Buber, "Church, State, Nation, Jewry," pp. 176–77.

with the Jewish people's self-understanding. The Jews, Buber insisted, experience themselves as a living reality and faith, and not just as a theological abstraction or as an ecclesiastical order as is implied by the term "synagogue." To underscore the experienced reality of the Jews, Buber would have thus preferred the term "Israel." Schmidt was only willing to compromise on the term *Judentum*, which denotes both Judaism and Jewry, his debate with Buber being finally billed, as noted, "Church, State, Nation, Jewry" (*Kirche, Staat, Volk, Judentum*). For Buber the acknowledgment of the Jewish people as a living historical—and *ergo* spiritual—reality was a crucial element in the struggle not only against theological prejudice but also in the perhaps more urgent task to undermine the cognate calumnies of metaphysical antisemitism. Herein he gave determined expression to his Zionist conviction that antisemitism could ultimately only be countered by the Jews' self-assertion as a living, proud people.

For Buber, however, Zionism was eminently more than a means to neutralize the antisemitic argument. The return to Zion, Buber held, would allow the Jews to reassume their primal religious task of affirming in the concrete reality of their collective life the world as Creation, thereby effectively challenging those who claim that the world is bereft of meaning and purpose. In this respect, Zionism would counter the deeper forces feeding antisemitism. Significantly, one of the first public lectures Buber gave after his immigration to Palestine in the late winter of 1938 was addressed to the question of antisemitism and the neo-gnostic forces that counsel despair and moral cynicism.

Presented in December 1939 in Rehavia, a neighborhood in Jerusalem then inhabited predominantly by recent immigrants from Central Europe, Buber's lecture was entitled "The Spirit of Israel and the Present Reality."[84] Buber opened with a question that un-

---

84. Martin Buber, "Ruah Israel bi-fnei ha-metziut ha-nokhahit," *Haaretz*, December 30, 1938, p. 2. The original handwritten version of the lecture is found in the Martin Buber Archive, varia 350, fol. *heh* 24a. There are, however, only minor differences of style between the two versions. The lecture in *Haaretz* included some significant omissions from the Hebrew collection of Buber's writings, *Teudah veyeud*, 2d ed. (Jerusalem, 1984), pp. 101–11. In 1946 Buber delivered the same lecture in London in English, but with substantial revisions: "The Spirit of Israel and the World Today." Details regarding the location and impact of the original Hebrew lecture were provided by Nathan Rotenstreich, emeritus professor of philosophy at the Hebrew University, Jerusalem, interview with author, August 1985. In a recently published letter to Buber, December 27, 1938, the novelist S. Y. Agnon makes enthusiastic reference to a recent lecture by

doubtedly burdened everyone in the tightly packed audience: "For many years now, Jews all over the world have been asking one another: 'How is it all going to end? Are we completely in the hands of evil?'"[85] Buber ascribed the "momentary" triumph of "the reign of evil" to the insecurity, loss of confidence in humanity, and, correspondingly, loss of faith in a "truth that transcends the opposition of sects and nations—a loss of faith in the possibility of a life of justice and righteousness, of a life of [human] unity and peace."[86]

But Israel—the Jewish people—is not to succumb to despair; nor is she to yield to the current moral cynicism that claims "that the period of humanism is past."[87] In Jobian defiance of despair and cynicism, Buber averred, Israel is to persevere in giving witness that there is a purpose to Creation, and that as a partner in Creation man is to perfect the portion of the universe allotted to his care. At this juncture in history, however, it is manifestly evident that the Reign of Evil cannot be opposed by words and pious affirmations. "For in this hour even the most elevated speech is deprived of the power to sustain and arouse hope in the face of the prevailing despair. Speech has no power against the aggression of those who are nurtured by despair."[88]

Addressing an audience of Jewish immigrants who had come to Palestine to rebuild their lives in the ancient homeland, Buber contended that the only effective answer to the counsel of despair—and thus antisemitism as well—would be to assure that the concrete social and political reality of the new community unfolding in Zion would reflect the pristine spirit of Israel: "the spirit of fulfillment of the single truth, that man has been created for a purpose."[89]

Israel's singular association with the idea of Creation, Buber con-

---

the philosopher, apparently "The Spirit of Israel and the Present Reality": "Sir and Esteemed Friend. I shall do something which is not my wont to do, but my heart tells me to do so and I shall heed it. These past two days I am reflecting on your lecture about the Spirit of Israel. I will not be exaggerating if I should say that I have not—nor has all of Jerusalem—heard such a lecture in years. I wanted to tell you this immediately after the lecture, but I noted you were tired. . . . It would be most worthwhile and only proper if you would have your lecture printed and distributed in thousands of copies for the sake of those who could not come to hear you." "S. Y. Agnon Writes to Martin Buber," *Haaretz*, September 15, 1985, p. 18.

85. Buber, "Spirit of Israel and the World Today," p. 183. When it does not deviate from the original Hebrew version of Buber's lecture, the English translation will be cited.

86. Buber, "Ruah Israel," p. 105.

87. Buber, "Spirit of Israel and the World Today," p. 189.

88. Buber, "Ruah Israel," p. 105.

89. Buber, "Spirit of Israel and the World Today," p. 185.

tinued to explain, is "one deep and unconscious reason [for anti-semitism] that is true for all periods of the exile" among the Christian nations. All other "reasons for antisemitism advanced by the Christian nations . . . are superficial and transitory." Dispersed among the Christian nations, the Jews embodied "a charge from heaven," a demand recorded "in a book which became sacred for them too when they became Christians."

> It is unique in human history, strange and awesome, that heaven should make a specific demand in reference to human behavior, and that the demand should be recorded in a book, and that the book should be the heritage of a people which is dispersed among all the nations with this, its holy book, which is holy for all the nations as well. The demand stands above and remote from the nations . . . ; it hovers high over them as the demand which their God makes of them.

This demand, which the ubiquitous presence of the Jews did not permit the Christian nations to forget, was indeed onerous and, Buber reasoned, of necessity engendered a profound resentment to the Jews. There "stood that unfortunate Jewish people, bearing the book which was its own book and at the same time part of the holy book of the nations. That is the real reason for their hatred. . . . That is the perennial source of antisemitism."[90]

This resentment of the Jews, according to Buber, naturally enough led Christians periodically to wish to distance themselves from the Jews and "their" book. This tendency is already discernible with Paul, the apostle to the Gentiles, who taught that Jesus fulfilled the Torah and, as Buber put it, "demanded nothing of his true believers save faith." But resentment of the Jews and the Torah, Buber held, leads dialectically from Paul, who nonetheless maintained the unity of the Hebrew Scripture and the Gospel, to Marcion. This gnostic seer sought to do what Paul—and most Christians since Paul—could not do: to sever the Hebrew Bible from the Christian Testament and to distinguish the God of Israel—the creator of the *imperfect* world—and the unknown God of salvation, the God of Jesus Christ.[91]

The church did not follow Marcion, Buber observed, but his teachings remained a compelling alternative, albeit denied and repressed. Hidden within the breast of the Christian, Marcionism persisted there as a constant tension, a tension that burst the bounds of Christian conscience and led to the renewed interest in Marcion and his

90. Ibid., p. 189.
91. Ibid., p. 190.

gnostic doctrine, even among such reputable theologians as Adolf von Harnack who, Buber emphasized, "was not in the least an anti-semite and represented a broad liberalism." But, every Christian should know, Buber cautioned with prophetic intonation, that "the extrusion of Judaism from Christianity means an extrusion of the divine demand and concrete messianism; its separation from the divine truth calling for fulfillment."[92]

Why the contemporary world is particularly prone to a renewal of Marcionism, Buber did not explain. In a book written just after the Second World War, *Two Types of Faith*, he would proffer an explanation. (Indeed, this book seems to have been prompted by the question of what in the nature or structure of Christian faith renders it, in Buber's view, vulnerable to gnostic-Marcion temptations.) With the advent of the modern world, Buber noted, there has been an incipient sense of alienation and cultural despair. Since the First World War in particular, this mood had deepened. Increasingly Christians have given expression to these "dark feelings" by turning to Paul, who was acutely aware of the horror and wrath of this, our unredeemed world. Thus, "the strength of the Pauline tendencies in present day Christian theology is to be explained by the character-istic stamp of the times. . . . Those periods are Pauline in which the contradictions of human life, especially of man's social life so mount up that they increasingly assume in man's consciousness of existence the character of fate." To be sure, the Pauline Christian maintains a commitment to the struggle for a more just world, but, cowering before "the threatening clouds," he places his faith and hope in Jesus the Savior. Soteriological hope replaced concrete messianism. Not-withstanding his quest for otherworldly salvation, Paul himself bravely opposed "the ever approaching Marcionite danger," for he realized that a victory for Marcion—and the sundering of the Crea-tor and the Savior—would spell the destruction of Christianity. Yet, in Buber's judgment, "Marcion is not to be overcome by Paul"—"this seems to me to be more strongly recognized again in Christendom of today."[93]

Numbed by the "impenetrable darkness" of existence, Paul no longer trusted the world and history. His emphasis on the salvation of the soul, Buber held, placed a severe, perhaps intolerable strain

92. Ibid., pp. 192, 193.
93. Martin Buber, *Two Types of Faith: A Study of the Interpretation of Judaism and Christianity*, trans. N. P. Goldhawk (New York, 1961), pp. 162–63, 166, 167.

on the Christian's dedication to a concrete—that is, social and historical—messianic vision. In contrast to the Pauline Christian, Buber insisted, the Jew tenaciously retains trust in the Creator God and *ergo* the prophetic promise of a this-worldly redemption. This is not to suggest that the Jew does not know the wrath and pain of existence. For, indeed, the Jew seems destined to suffer "every misery."[94]

In fact, according to Buber, it is no fortuity that the Pauline mood of the present era was most poignantly expressed by a Jew, Franz Kafka (1883–1924). For Buber, the author of *The Trial* and especially *The Castle* was the archetypal Jew of the era, an unprecedentedly tormented time in which Kafka (the Jew) was "its most exposed son." Kafka finds himself in a world governed by capricious, cruel forces; in the "thick vapors of a mist of absurdity" that envelop this world of these troubled times God Himself is "removed into impenetrable darkness," but for Kafka there is no savior. Yet Kafka is not shorn of hope, or trust, in the world. "For the Jew, in so far as he is not detached from the origin, even the most exposed Jew like Kafka, is safe. All things happen to him but they cannot affect him."[95]

"In spite of all" his woe, Kafka—the Jew—resolutely refuses the Pauline promise of personal salvation. He refuses not because of a spiritual obduracy, Buber insisted, but because his abiding trust in the God of Creation does not allow him to relinquish the conviction in the ultimate victory of justice as a blessing for *all* the denizens of the created universe. Buber cited Kafka as testifying that "we were created to live in Paradise, Paradise was appointed to serve us. Our destiny has been changed; that this also happened with the appointment of Paradise is *not* said." Gently and shyly, Buber commented, Kafka affirms that the horror and absurdity of our existence *need not be.* "Without disowning reality," Kafka—the Jew—perseveres in his trust in the God of Israel—the God of Creation and Justice. Hence, Kafka "describes, from innermost awareness, the actual course of the world, he describes most exactly the rule of the foul devilry which fills the foreground: and on the edge of the description he scratches the sentence: 'Test yourself on humanity. It makes the doubter doubt, the man of belief believe.'"[96]

94. Ibid., p. 169.
95. Ibid., pp. 168, 166, 168.
96. Ibid., p. 168.

CENTRAL AND
EASTERN EUROPE

Jacob Toury

Defense Activities
of the Österreichisch-Israelitische Union
before 1914

The Emergence of a Defense Bureau

The Österreichisch-Israelitische Union (Austro-Israelite Union, or ÖIU) was founded in Vienna on April 26, 1886. At first it was but one of several local organizations established by Viennese Jews as a reaction against growing antisemitism. The Union's first statutes promised to strengthen Jewish cultural ties and to establish Jewish institutions of learning. This meant, among other things, that quite a number of the founding members were intent upon shaking up the somnolent oligarchic board of the Jewish community, the Israelitische Kultusgemeinde (IKG), in order to reactivate Jewish life in Austria's capital. Moreover, some even hoped to turn the Union into something of a political lobby that might enable them to dabble in general municipal politics or even to influence the choice of candidates for statewide elections.[1]

While the activists in the Union achieved their first aim—the takeover of the IKG—with surprising ease and dexterity[2] and became after 1888–89 and for years to come its leading faction, success eluded them in their wider aim of influencing general elections and general politics. The onset of their activities coincided with an al-

1. On the founding of the Österreichisch-Israelitische Union and its first statutes, see Jacob Toury, "Troubled Beginnings: The Emergence of the Oesterreichisch-Israelitische Union," *Leo Baeck Institute Year Book* (hereafter *LBIYB*) 30 (1985): 457–75.
2. Union activists achieved their victory in part by forming a coalition with the elders of the *minyanim* (*Bethaus*) outside the Inner City. See Jacob Toury, "Years of Strife: The Oesterreichisch-Israelitische Union's Contest for Leadership of Austrian Jewry," ibid., 33 (1988): forthcoming.

most permanent crisis of Austrian parliamentary government that
was fueled by the emerging forces of nationalism among the various
peoples under the Habsburg rule.

One feature of the clash of nationalities in the face of an unstable
central administration was the appearance of a violent antisemitism
in each and every national camp, be it Polish, Czech, or German,
which could draw strength from deep-rooted, ever-present religious
Jew-hatred.[3] The politically ambitious members of the Österreichisch-Israelitische Union very quickly became aware that their
personal political chances against Christlichsozial (Christian-Social)
and pan-German antisemitic candidates were slim indeed and that
even their traditional liberal allies of the once-progressive Constitutional party had given in to anti-Jewish attitudes or, at least, were
not averse to certain electioneering agreements with antisemitic
candidates—even in Vienna, where Jewish electoral influence was
not wholly negligible.

The Jewish inhabitants of greater Vienna accounted for about 5
percent of the total population, and their percentage was especially
high in the two inner precincts of Kaiviertel and Leopoldstadt. This
concentration provided considerable competition for Vienna's lower
middle classes and hence stimulated violent anti-Jewish agitation.
On the crest of an antisemitic wave, the Christian-Social leader Karl
Lueger was duly elected mayor of the imperial city, even against the
express wish of the emperor, and finally installed in his office in
1897.[4]

In such a situation, the whole of Jewish existence in Vienna, which
for some decades had seemed secure under successive, moderately
liberal governments, suffered a severe shock. Jews were forced to
readjust to surroundings suddenly quite inimical, and many of them
in the Austrian capital now began to realize that defense had to be
the order of the day.

In response to this challenge, the Österreichisch-Israelitische
Union, in March 1895, finally decided to set up a Rechtsschutz Comité, (Legal Defense Committee), which had to cope with an ever-

3. Jew-hatred in Austria was mainly Roman Catholic in character. See Peter G. J.
Pulzer, *The Rise of Political Anti-Semitism in Germany and Austria* (New York, 1964);
I. A. Hellwing, *Der Konfessionelle Antisemitismus im 19. Jahrhundert in Österreich* (Vienna, 1972); and Werner J. Cahnman, "Adolf Fischhof and His Jewish Followers,"
LBIYB 4 (1959): 111–39.
4. Karl Lueger was installed only after his third election and after a face-saving
delay of his confirmation by Emperor Franz Joseph.

increasing number of appeals for help. Consequently, on December 15, 1897, the Rechtsschutz Comité was turned into a full-fledged Rechtsschutz und Abwehr-Büro (Legal Aid and Defense Bureau),[5] headed by an able secretary—Siegfried Fleischer—and staffed by a small but efficient office force. At its service stood a not quite regularly appearing bulletin—the *Mitteilungen der Österreichisch-Israelitischen Union*, founded in 1889. Later, under Fleischer's editorship, starting on January 1, 1901, the bulletin became the *Monatsschrift der Österreichisch-Israelitischen Union*.

The chronology of these events makes it obvious that the German-Jewish defense organization, the Centralverein deutscher Staatsbürger jüdischen Glaubens (CV), founded in 1893, had already overtaken the older Union of Vienna and taught it a lesson or two in practical apologetics. One of the first expedients was the establishment of a Rechtsschutz Commission in Berlin, which in 1896 strengthened its position and enlarged its scope by becoming the central Rechtsschutzstelle of all the local branches of the CV, and hence of German Jewry as a whole.[6] But, as specific data on the activities of the CV's Rechtsstelle are lacking, a detailed comparison between Vienna and Berlin is, unfortunately, impossible. At any rate the new Rechtsschutz und Abwehr-Büro in Vienna quickly established itself as an integral part of the Österreichisch-Israelitische Union and soon came to be regarded as the most essential contribution of its parent organization to Jewish existence in the whole of Cisleithanian Austria.

Only scant records remain of the earlier Rechtsschutz Comité and its activities from March 1895 to December 1897. In any case during the tumultuous years of Lueger's ascent to power in Vienna (1895–97) the Österreichisch-Israelitische Union busied itself almost exclu-

5. *Mitteilungen der Österreichisch-Israelitischen Union* (hereafter *Mitteilungen*), no. 69 (March 1895): 2, includes an advertisement announcing the founding of a Rechtsschutz Comité. The establishment of the Rechtsschutz und Abwehr-Büro on December 15, 1897, is mentioned in ibid., no. 105 (May 1898): 4.

6. For the establishment of the Centralverein deutscher Staatsbürger jüdischen Glaubens, see Ismar Schorsch, *Jewish Reactions to German Anti-Semitism, 1870–1914* (New York, 1972), chaps. 4, 5; and Sanford Ragins, *Jewish Responses to Anti-Semitism in Germany, 1870–1914* (Cincinnati, 1980), Chap. 3. For the dates of the Berlin Rechtsschutz Commission and Rechtsschutzstelle, see Arnold Paucker, "Zur Problematik einer jüdischen Abwehrstrategie in der deutschen Gesellschaft," in *Juden im Wilhelminischen Deutschland, 1890–1914*, ed. Werner E. Mosse and Arnold Paucker, Schriftenreihe wissenschaftlicher Abhandlungen des Leo Baeck Instituts 33 (Tübingen, 1976), p. 509. On the CV's political outlook, see Jehuda Reinharz, *Fatherland or Promised Land: The Dilemma of the German Jew, 1893–1914* (Ann Arbor, 1975), pp. 37–89.

sively with party politics and electioneering. Thus from April 1896 to March 1897 the Rechtsschutz Comité met only seven times, and it cannot be said that legal work was regarded as of equal importance with general politics.

Nevertheless even at this early stage it became clear that the fight for right and justice could not be waged in Vienna alone, for anti-semitism was physically more dangerous to provincial Jewry than to the Jews of the imperial city, where even under Lueger a sem-blance of law and order prevailed, occasional Jew-baiting notwith-standing. Consequently the committee started to establish contacts in the provinces, and in March 1897 it proudly announced that com-petent trustees in sixty-two Cisleithanian towns had been recruited.

Yet the account of legal battles waged was less impressive. Of twenty-one cases that had been brought to the attention of the com-mittee, only sixteen had been pursued until legal action could be taken. As all the committee's proceedings were *in camera*, no partic-ulars of the cases and their outcomes were recorded.[7] But it soon became clear that "in the rather tight framework of mere juridical defense [*Rechtsschutz*], the vast majority of torts and offenses per-petrated by our adversaries . . . cannot satisfactorily be repulsed." Attacks on "Jewry as a whole" were especially difficult for a small committee without official legal standing to handle.[8] Thus the board of the ÖIU decided to enlarge the defense organization into a semi-autonomous body, whose task should be "to provide unfailing [doc-umentary] evidence, to keep track of and to repulse all attacks, lies and calumnies." Soon, a generally usable formula defining the func-tion of the Rechtsschutz und Abwehr-Büro was developed: its task was to supply "legal aid without cost in all cases where the consti-tutional rights of the Jews as such are discriminated against."[9]

The activities of the Rechtsschutz und Abwehr-Büro are well doc-umented from its founding (December 15, 1897) to the twenty-fifth anniversary of the Österreichisch-Israelitische Union in April 1910.[10] On the strength of such records it becomes possible to measure suc-

---

7. Annual report of Secretary Josef Fuchs to the General Assembly of the Österreich-isch-Israelitische Union, April 29, 1897, *Mitteilungen*, no. 96 (May 1897): 8.
8. Ibid., no. 105 (May 1898): 4.
9. Ibid., and no. 107 (October 1898): 2.
10. The main source is the comprehensive survey in honor of the Union's twenty-fifth anniversary, "25 Jahre Österreichisch-Israelitische Union," in *Monatsschrift der Österreichisch-Israelitischen Union* (hereafter *Monatsschrift*), April 17, 1910, no. 4, pp. 32–55.

cess and failure of its organized legal defense. Moreover, certain general implications for defense work against antisemitism might be culled from the reported successes and failures of this early defense organization.

The First Attempts at Defense Work

Siegfried Fleischer, who from the outset acted as head of the Defense Bureau (and from 1899 also as secretary of the Union as a whole),[11] claimed in 1910 that during slightly more than twelve years of existence his office had successfully concluded more than five thousand cases, restoring justice and honor to an even greater number of oppressed or innocently accused co-religionists.[12] If correct, this would mean an average of more than four hundred cases a year.

From certain indications it seems quite possible that about four hundred files—at first rather less, but later even more—landed on the desk of the Defense Bureau. But the successful conclusion of so many cases must be regarded rather as a mode of expression in keeping with the anniversary spirit in which the statement was made. In any case, the sources by no means testify to such overwhelming accomplishments.

For instance, a report prepared by the Union's first secretary, Josef Fuchs, specifies the files handled by the bureau from December 1897 to April 1899, that is, during its first sixteen months of activity. Of a total of 426 files, only 313 were classified as "cases" (Fälle); the others seem to have been treated as information for further reference or were not found deserving "a more intensive treatment."[13] And even of the 313 case files, only 150, or not quite one-half, demanded or were accorded legal aid or politico-legal intercession with legislative or executive instances. The measures taken by the bureau during that phase are summarized in table 1.

11. Ibid., p. 23. Fleischer followed Josef Fuchs, the first secretary of the Union and editor of the *Mitteilungen*, and he was later editor of the reorganized *Monatsschrift*. The dates of Fleischer's respective incumbencies (the Defense Bureau from 1897, the Union itself from 1899, the editorship of the *Monatsschrift* from 1901) are not above doubt, because for a short interval Sigmund Mayer is mentioned as head of the Defense Bureau. See *Mitteilungen*, no. 114 (November 1899).

12. *Monatsschrift*, April 17, 1910, no. 4, p. 20.

13. Report of Secretary Fuchs to the General Assembly, April 22, 1899, *Mitteilungen*, no. 114 (November 1899): 3–6.

Table 1. Measures Taken by the Defense Bureau, December 1897–March 1899

Kind of Action Taken	December 1897–March 1898		April 1898–March 1899		Total	
	Number	Percentage	Number	Percentage	Number	Percentage
Enforcement of press corrections (retractions, apologies, factual *démentis*)	23	56%	54	47%	77	50%
Legal aid in court cases	12	29%	33	29%	45	29%
Political or constitutional steps (intercession with government offices, audiences, interpellations, petitions)	6	15%	27	24%	33	21%
Total	41	100%	114	100%	155	100%

SOURCE: Report of Secretary Josef Fuchs to the General Assembly of the Österreichisch-Israelitische Union, April 22, 1899, *Mitteilungen der Österreichisch-Israelitischen Union*, no. 114 (November 1899): 3–6; and eighty-two cases specified in ibid., no. 105 (May 1898): 5–6.

The first eighty-two cases handled by the Defense Bureau from December 15, 1897, to March 31, 1898, are, by a happy coincidence, even more specifically itemized.[14] From this itemization, however, it becomes clear that the bureau defined "success" as meaning rather less than a full victory in legal proceedings, with punishment meted out to the culprits or a stern government measure launched to rectify infringements of constitutional rights. Sometimes "success" lay in the mere fact that members of the bureau were received by a high government official, even if decisive steps, in accordance with the Union's requests, were forthcoming only in extreme circumstances. Moreover, from subsequent figures it appears that almost any action taken by the bureau came to be regarded as a success in itself, for out of eighty-two files, only forty-one were found fit to be included in the summary given in table 1. What happened then to the other cases? Table 2 aims at answering this question.

The political steps, as well as the last three items in table 2, throw light on a most problematical side of all defense activities because they point to the limits of juridical and constitutional action. Jewish complainants were sometimes ready to report antisemitic imputations to the Defense Bureau, but, for commercial or personal reasons, they abstained from authorizing the lawyers of the Union to take legal action. The Defense Bureau, left to its own devices, often did not find a lever for pursuing a case in court. According to Austrian law, "a Jewish individual, a Jewish association, nay even the IKG itself, had no right to appear as suitors in cases of offense against Jewry as a whole [Gesamtjudenschaft]."[15] In such cases it was necessary to compel the Staatsanwalt (public prosecutor) to institute proceedings on his own initiative. But this happened only on rare occasions and generally after due preparation, for example, through an audience with the minister of justice.

And even the highest executive office was powerless when the tort was perpetrated by a member of the legislature (the Reichsrat or the Niederösterreichischer Landtag—the Lower Austrian Diet) and during its sessions. Consequently, certain antisemitic legislators—at first Ernst Schneider and later Gregorig and others—availed themselves of the fact that the dissemination of proposed legislation, together with its exposition, even if not treated in plenary session, was

14. Report to the General Assembly, April 23, 1898, ibid., no. 105 (May 1898): 5–6.
15. This is the explanation given by Hof- und Gerichtsadvocat Dr. Julius Kann at a meeting of the Union in 1892, reported in Mitteilungen, no. 40 (April 1892): 12.

Table 2. The Defense Bureau's First Eighty-Two Cases, December 1897–March 1898

Kind of Action Taken	Number	Percentage
Enforcements of press corrections	23	28.1%
Legal aid in court cases	12	14.6%
Political or constitutional steps	6	7.3%
2 Interpellations of ministers		
2 Interpellations of Parliament		
1 Petition to Lower Austrian Diet		50%
1 Manifest in the liberal press		
Cases filed for information purposes only	17	20.9%
Cases discussed in the Jewish press only*	2	2.4%
Complaints not authorized by persons affected	4	4.8%
Actions not possible owing to lack of power of attorney or legal standing	7	8.5%
Specific accusations based (partly) on fact	11	13.4%
		50%

SOURCE: Report to the General Assembly, April 23, 1898, *Mitteilungen der Österreichisch-Israelitischen Union*, no. 105 (May 1898): 5–6.

*The chief Jewish paper in Vienna was then Dr. Joseph S. Bloch's *Österreichische Wochenschrift*, which was in itself very active in anti-antisemitic polemics. See Jacob Toury, *Die Jüdische Presse im Österreichischen Kaiserreich, 1802–1918* (Tübingen, 1983), chap. 13.

quite unimpeachable. Thus they could even use their own news-paper to print their anti-Jewish proposals, accompanied by hateful commentaries, without fear that their sheets might be confiscated; for such was the scope of parliamentary immunity.[16]

Therefore, one of the first steps of the Defense Bureau was aimed at denouncing antisemitic activities in the Reichsrat, and especially in the Lower Austrian Diet. The petition cited in table 2 relates to that step. The antisemitic deputy Gregorig referred in one of his speeches to certain allegations against Jewish entrepreneurs as em-ployers of Christian girls and women, giving as the factual base for his *Pauschalverleumdung* (collective calumniation) a report of the Ethical Society in Berlin, where entrepreneurs in general, but by no means specifically Jewish businessmen, were indicted. The Defense Bureau, after having received a communication in this vein from the Berlin society, prevailed upon a liberal deputy in the Lower Austrian Diet to petition its president, Baron Gudenus, to correct the facts and bring the full text of the petition to the attention of the Diet. The text voiced, among other things, the painful impression caused in Jewish circles by the fact that President Gudenus had not imme-diately called Gregorig to order for his highly offensive remarks.

Yet this first Jewish attempt at defense on a parliamentary level quickly came to naught. The Christian-Social majority of the Diet simply voted against the reading of the ÖIU's protest in the plenary session of February 3, 1898, and the full text thus remained among the printed papers of the House and was not even reported in most of the Austrian press.[17] This means that the calumniation of Jewish businessmen went without censure and without correction in public, and the problem of parliamentary defense procedure did not find a viable solution.

When in 1910 the Defense Bureau reviewed its successes, it omit-ted all references to the hapless Gregorig Affair. And, in fact, of the eighty-two cases summed up in table 2, only three were found wor-thy for inclusion in the twenty-fifth anniversary survey of the

16. Ibid. The whole passage refers to Ernst Schneider's nefarious activities as a member of the Lower Austrian Diet before the establishment of the Defense Bureau.
17. The whole episode is reported here according to an account in *Österreichische Wochenschrift*, 1898, no. 6, pp. 101–2. The *Mitteilungen*, owing to infrequent appear-ance, contains only relatively short and rather noncommittal references to the case. *Mitteilungen*, no. 105 (May 1898): 6ff.

Rechtsschutzarbeit;[18] even so, only with a fair amount of goodwill might one find a modicum of success in these cases.

One reason for such a disproportionate rate of failure was inherent in the character of defense activities in general: the Defense Bureau initiated its actions only *after* an antisemitic attack had occurred. And if the first event that triggered a series of energetic protest actions by the Viennese Union, December 1897 to February 1898, was a wave of Jew-baiting and pillaging of Jewish property in Prague and other Czech towns (not unconnected with general political unrest against the government of Graf Casimir Badeni and its proposed legislation in the question of national languages), it was not even a matter of purely Jewish implications that caused the unrest. Consequently, when Siegfried Fleischer, after a visit to Prague, prepared a memorandum on the Czech excesses and when the prime minister, Baron Paul von Gautsch, accepted it in an audience granted to the heads of the Union,[19] these actions did not alleviate the plight of the victims. Even the fact that Gautsch acted upon the information contained in the memorandum and on February 7, 1898, ordered the dissolution of the Czech antisemitic association Národní Obrana in Prague and its branches in seven other towns as instigators of the riots—even this was a formal success only. Other associations sprang up almost immediately, and antisemitism was not at all weakened by the Defense Bureau's action.

A similar combination of formal success and factual impasse was the result of a third case handled by the Defense Bureau before April 1898. This time the democratic MP for the First District of Vienna (Kaiviertel), Dr. Ferdinand Kronawetter, agreed to intervene with the minister of commerce in the case of a Jewish master carpenter of Cracow, whose acceptance by the local carpenters' society had been postponed for almost ten years and who was thus handicapped in the pursuance of his calling. Although the minister promised administrative steps to enforce the carpenter's rights, the Cracow corporation continued to disregard the government's rescripts. When the officials at the Ministry of Commerce changed, the case simply

18. "25 Jahre," pp. 32–55; and for the first short period, *Mitteilungen*, no. 105 (May 1898): 6ff. The semester April-September 1898 is broadly treated in *Mitteilungen*, no. 108 (November 1898): 3–19.

19. The audience took place on January 6, 1898, during Gautsch's first, short-lived ministry, immediately following that of Graf Casimir Badeni (November 1897–March 1898). See "25 Jahre," p. 32.

vanished from the agenda, of both the ministry and the Defense Bureau.[20]

Apart from these three cases—the Gregorig petition, the Czech excesses, and the Cracow carpenter's plight—that brought the Österreichisch-Israelitische Union two formal victories and one painful rebuff, the Defense Bureau also, according to tables 1 and 2, engaged in a conspicuous number of skirmishes with the editors of anti-Jewish newspapers and pamphlets. And thus did Sigmund Mayer, the vice-president (later president) of the ÖIU describe the practice of his Defense Bureau with regard to libel and calumniation, not only in Vienna, but also in the provinces: "Day by day our secretary minutely scrutinized the antisemitic papers, visited the slandered persons, collected the facts, asked for power of attorney, and finally took legal action. And in most cases we got gratifying results."[21] The offending papers were forced to retract or even to print a "humble apology,"[22] fines were imposed, and, explained Mayer, after "three years of uninterrupted legal battles the calumniations against the 'little Jew' were discontinued," not only in Vienna, but "in the whole of Cisleithania."[23]

That was a gratifying result—as far as it went. But from then on the calumniators, instead of spelling out names of persons or places, generally went over to using initials only: for example, "The Jewish peddler A—in N—. . . ." This method enabled the papers to rehash defamatory reports on past and forgotten incidents, thereby implicating people long dead, and even to invent accusations, without fear of prosecution.

In a similar vein antisemitic boycott propaganda was reshaped. The papers, by suppressing specific names and addresses of Jewish firms, were able to evade costly suits of damages. Yet, certain general slogans, such as "Christians, buy only from Christian shops!" did reappear regularly, especially before Christmas, and became a fixture of anti-Jewish boycott tactics.

20. Ibid.; and "Affäre Kleinberger," *Mitteilungen*, no. 108 (November 1898): 8–10. The *Mitteilungen* also reported that Jewish shoemakers were not accepted into the association and were fined by the municipality because they had to be members in order to ply their trade. Nonmembers were not allowed to keep apprentices or to bid on contracts for public works.

21. Sigmund Mayer, *Ein jüdischer Kaufmann, 1831–1911* (Leipzig, 1911), p. 314.

22. See, e.g., the apology of Ernst Vergani, as reported in "25 Jahre," p. 33.

23. Mayer, *Ein jüdischer Kaufmann*, p. 314.

Nevertheless, in curbing the activities of the antisemitic press, the Defense Bureau's labors achieved a certain undeniable success. For even if a total victory in the legal fight against slander and boycott was out of the question, it seems certain that without the bureau's constant vigilance against libelous and damaging propaganda, attempts at poisoning the public mind might have multiplied manifold. Similar conclusions may also be drawn from the other activities of the Defense Bureau during the first period of its existence, and perhaps even from all its Jewish defense activities.

The Main Areas of the Defense Bureau's Activities

Five areas of the Defense Bureau's defense work remain to be considered: electioneering, that is, taking political steps with a view to strengthening the forces of law and order in the self-governing assemblies, from village council to Reichsrat, and responding to organized (or semiorganized) pogroms, to accusations of ritual murder and other kinds of blood libel, to manifestations of antisemitism in government institutions and among local and central civil servants, and to the particularly Galician scourge of kidnapping children and baptizing them by force in certain monasteries.

Political campaigning was not the business of the Defense Bureau and has to be disregarded in our present context,[24] whereas pogroms, blood libels, and kidnapping constituted perhaps the most desperate and troubling assignments for the bureau from April 1898 onward.

Riots

The six months between April and October 1898 were darkened by widespread pogroms in Western and Central Galicia.[25] Although perpetrated by different groups of the population, mainly during the months of May and June 1898, they may possibly "have been instigated by a common center of agitation," claimed the *Mitteilungen*,[26] and been connected with the impending regional elections. Informed

24. Political campaigning is treated prominently in Toury, "Years of Strife."
25. This period is summed up in *Mitteilungen*, no. 108 (November 1898): 3–19.
26. ". . . welche alle auf einen gemeinsamen Agitationsherd hinweisen." Ibid., p. 4. The places, regions, and groups of population specifically mentioned (ibid., pp. 3–6) were: Kalwaria, Catholic pilgrims; Tluste (region of Zaleshchiki), Masovian laborers; in the regions of Jaslo, Rzeszow, Sanok, Przemysl, and, lastly and most beastly, at Nowy Sacz and Stary Sacz (Neu- and Alt-Sandec), the outrages and lootings were perpetrated by local peasants.

circles laid the blame for the antisemitic outbreaks, especially the thirty in the Sanok region, on the unscrupulous electioneering campaign of Father Stojalowski, the Jesuit candidate for that constituency.[27]

What could the Defense Bureau do to stem the flood of pogroms in Galicia? First, it alerted the Jewish members of the Reichsrat from Galicia, who all belonged to the Polish faction[28] and who immediately contacted the Polish governor of Galicia and their non-Jewish parliamentary colleagues from the affected regions. But, except for a sympathetic communique from the latter, no practical aim was served. Meanwhile, two ÖIU board members were received in audience on June 10, 1898, by Prime Minister Graf Leo Thun, with whom they pleaded for energetic measures in Galicia. Ten days later Fleischer, the secretary of the Defense Bureau, traveled to Galicia to collect exact information on the cause and the scope of the outrages. He arrived during the pillaging of the Jews of Nowy Sacz. When their cries for help arrived by telegraph in Vienna, the president of the ÖIU, Kaiserlicher Rat Wilhelm Anninger, donned his tails and top hat[29] and petitioned Graf Thun outright for dispatch of military reinforcements and for the proclamation of martial law in the affected areas. The next day, the prime minister did as he had been asked, and soon the riots subsided.

The ÖIU had risen to the dangerous situation, and its intervention had brought an—albeit belated—success. On the strength of it the Defense Bureau instituted an inquiry into the socioeconomic background of the riots, and the heads of the Union then tried to institute constructive measures to improve conditions in Galicia. The Jews, they urged, should establish an umbrella organization, and, indeed, a first *Gemeindetag* was convened during December 1898. Education should be advanced, and in the economic field the Union even tried to promote small industrial enterprises, to be financed in cooperation with the Parisian Jewish Colonization Association and other Jewish organizations.

27. Simon Dubnov, *Weltgeschichte des Jüdischen Volkes*, vol. 10 (Berlin, 1929), pp. 94–95.

28. See *Mitteilungen*, no. 108 (November 1898): 3–19. The Polish faction was the Koło Polski or Polenklub. The one and only Jew of somewhat independent leanings, Dr. Joseph S. Bloch, had in 1895 been deprived of his seat by the Polish faction on a technicality.

29. This donning of ceremonial dress was often mentioned in a disparaging manner, especially by Zionist detractors of Jewish notables and their method of personal intercession with personages in high places.

But very little came of it.[30] No major funds for the industrialization of Galician Jewry were raised; no major educational reforms were achieved; and not even the *Gemeindetag* developed into a continuous organizational platform for Galicia. Moreover, in spite of all measures, excesses in Galicia were repeated, although on a smaller scale, and there were also outbreaks in Bohemia and Moravia at the turn of the century.[31] In short, the Defense Bureau's measures may possibly have alleviated a desperate situation, but they fell short of curing it.

Pogrom propaganda in Galicia reached a new peak during 1903, probably in the wake of the slaughter in Kishinev, and again the Defense Bureau found itself compelled to appeal to the prime minister, then Ernest von Koerber. This time more than fifty rioters from Uhnow and Zablotov were apprehended and rather severely punished.[32] But again in 1906 Galician Jews were in jeopardy, and again the pogrom propaganda was influenced by events in Russia. But this time the quick oppression of unrest was in the interest of the government, and the agitation subsided very soon.[33]

Generally speaking, the Defense Bureau and the Union succeeded in Galicia only as far as the central government was ready to lend decisive help for maintaining a semblance of order. But on the other hand, the ÖIU's endeavors to mobilize Jewish investments, or Jewish and non-Jewish legislators and the general press, for a major program of ameliorations in Jewish Galicia remained of no avail.

In other words, the Austrian political scene was not sufficiently democratized for the utilization of public opinion as a means for influencing government attitudes. In any case the heads of the Union continued to adhere to the time-hallowed belief that defense against anti-Jewish attacks was still best served by direct intercession with the powers that be—and in the highest places possible.

Blood Allegations

Soon after the semiorganized riots came one of the ever-recurring accusations of ritual murder. The first accusation was made in January 1899 in Nowy Sacz, one of the centers of the previous atrocities, and it renewed the tension in that stricken community. Again the

---

30. For particulars, see Mayer, *Ein jüdischer Kaufmann*, pp. 326–33.
31. Ibid., p. 334.
32. "25 Jahre," pp. 43–44.
33. Mayer, *Ein jüdischer Kaufmann*, p. 346.

Defense Bureau sent a delegate to the scene in order to ascertain the facts and oversee the correctness of the investigation. And again an audience with the minister of justice, on January 27, 1899, was necessary to ensure a proper investigation of the case, in which murder had indeed been perpetrated, but neither Jew nor Jewish ritual was involved.[34]

But the blood libel went unchecked. Even in the university town of Innsbruck, schoolchildren were required to use a primer containing passages on ritual murder. The Defense Bureau tendered a formal protest at the Ministry of Education, but without tangible results.[35] Small wonder that in the big cities, Vienna or Prague, antisemitic papers could openly accuse Jews of extracting blood from the veins of Christian housemaids and selling it to their coreligionists! The Defense Bureau again petitioned Prime Minister Graf Thun, who caused a Prague evening paper to publish a "definite *démenti*" of that story.[36]

Despite of the immediate response of the ÖIU to every blood accusation, the atmosphere was well prepared for the biggest libel since Tisza-Eszlar in April 1882, that of Polná in Bohemia. In 1899 a destitute cobbler, Leopold Hilsner, was made the scapegoat for the murder of a young seamstress, and after protracted legal proceedings he was sentenced for life in 1901. The whole sorry story has been repeatedly told.[37] Here only the part played by the ÖIU is relevant.

1. The Defense Bureau engaged counsel for the defendant.

2. In a memorandum to the minister of justice, the Defense Bureau protested against the allegations of ritual murder in the antisemitic papers.

3. The Defense Bureau also repeatedly complained, from May 1899 to August 1900, about the exhibition and sale of pictures of alleged victims of ritual slaughter.

4. Concurrently with Hilsner's trial, the Defense Bureau investigated and uncovered a murder, a suicide, and a disappearance (two

34. "25 Jahre," pp. 32–33.
35. Ibid. The protest was dated December 15, 1898. Another accusation of ritual murder was made in Slovakia. It was investigated by the Defense Bureau on May 25, 1898, and found utterly without factual base. Ibid.
36. Ibid. The petition was dated June 10, 1898, and fully reported in *Mitteilungen*, no. 107 (November 1898): 11–13.
37. See especially the early reaction of Tomáš Masaryk, *Die Notwendigkeit der Revision des Polnaer Prozesses* (Vienna, 1899), and later the research sponsored by the ÖIU: Arthur Nussbaum, *Der Polnaer Ritualmordprozess* (Berlin, 1906).

in Bohemia, one in Moravia), all three of which had at first been reported as ritual murder, apart from similar, but minor, allegations in Slovakia and Galicia.

5. The Defense Bureau also prompted the public prosecutor to confiscate a Czech booklet on ritual murder in Brno.

6. The Defense Bureau printed and distributed five thousand copies of a booklet entitled *Bullen der Päpste und Stimmen christlicher Zeitgenossen gegen den Ritualmord.*[38]

All these steps were taken *before* the final sentence was pronounced against Hilsner. Later the ÖIU renewed its endeavors to reopen the trial after sponsoring a thorough review of the case.[39] In 1907 it even offered a substantial reward for any information that might lead to a reconsideration of the verdict and/or the establishment of Hilsner's innocence.[40]

At a first glimpse all these activities seem to have been of little avail. Blood allegations reappeared almost every year, all over the realm, generally in springtime on the eve of Passover. And—as if to give proof of the futility of rational arguments against them—tales of ritual murder recurred in one place alone, the ill-fated small town of Nowy Sacz, on no less than three occasions (1899, 1903, 1908) during the period under review.[41]

To sum up, in the years between 1898 and 1910, the Defense Bureau had to initiate at least thirty-five actions involving blood allegations, twenty-two of them in connection with disappearances or death by violence and thirteen on the occasion of propaganda in pictures, pamphlets, or newspapers.[42] The geographical distribution of these blood allegations is given in table 3a. The picture presented in the table suggests that blood allegations occurred in the rural Slavic parts of Cisleithania, while the centers of propaganda were in the large cities.

The frequency distribution according to years, as presented in table 3b, also shows an interesting pattern. The first period includes the protracted unrest caused by the trial of Hilsner, but it probably

38. "25 Jahre," pp. 34–37.
39. This review was Nussbaum's *Der Polnaer Ritualmordprozess.*
40. The offer of the reward was dated July 10 and reprinted in *Monatsschrift,* August 1907, no. 8, p. 1.
41. "25 Jahre," p. 34ff., under the respective years.
42. Ibid. As the survey contains only the most notable cases handled by the Defense Bureau, it is probable that the actual allegations treated were far more numerous. The statistics in tables 3a and 3b are based only on the cases quoted in the report.

Table 3a. Regional Pattern of Blood Allegations, 1898–1910

Region	Number	Character
Galicia (mostly in the western regions)	8	3 of them in Nowy Sacz alone, generating danger of pogroms
Bohemia (5 of them in Prague)	11	the 5 in Prague in print
Moravia (3 of them in Brno)	6	the 3 in Brno in print
Slovakia	3	
Austria (6 of them in Vienna)	7	all 7 in print
Total	35	

SOURCE: "25 Jahre Österreichisch-Israelitische Union," *Monatsschrift*, April 17, 1910, no. 4, pp. 32–55.

Table 3b. Chronological Pattern of Blood Allegations, 1898–1910

Years	Number
1898–1901	16
1902–1905	14
1906–1909	5
1910	0
Total	35

SOURCE: "25 Jahre."

also contains echoes of the Konitz Affair in Germany and of a blood allegation in Vilna, both in 1900.

After Hilsner's trial the Defense Bureau stepped up its activities against the blood libel, and results improved. In 1903 some people who had been attacked in antisemitic papers as accessories to the Polná murder sued their detractors with the help of the ÖIU. The detractors were fined. After that, the number of sentences against the disseminators of blood allegations rose steadily. Whereas the rate of convictions before 1902 was insignificant, in the final period, 1906–09, it reached almost 100 percent of all the cases tried. The next year was startling: from April 1909 to March 1910 no case of blood allegation came to the attention of the Defense Bureau. But a marked increase was again recorded in the Jewish papers after 1911, in the wake of the case of Menahem Mendel Beilis in Russia.

In short, even fines did not deter antisemitic propagandists from rehashing their age-old allegations, if and when circumstances were favorable. Of what avail, then, was even the temporary remission achieved by the Defense Bureau? Here again one ought to bear in mind what all the Jewish defense organizations have reiterated from their beginnings to the present day: "Perhaps more important" than the actual "steps taken by us," explained the *Monatsschrift* of the ÖIU, are all the untold woes "that we have averted by our mere existence" as an organized and active body.[43]

The importance of averting attacks before they developed can be seen specifically in the other areas of defense work the Defense Bureau undertook: combatting antisemitism in government bodies, both central and local, and forestalling the results of the repeated attempts at kidnapping and baptizing Jewish children in Galicia.

Antisemitism in Government Agencies

Protests against antisemitic utterances and practices in higher and lower echelons of the civil service were on the agenda of the Defense Bureau literally from the outset of its activities. Among the first cases was that of a junior high school teacher in Vienna who in an election speech on June 20, 1898, had advocated solving the Jewish Question by "simply shooting the Jews." Yet it soon became obvious that not only "could the authentic text not be ascertained," but it was even questionable whether the ÖIU or the IKG were, from a judicial point of view, "legitimized to prefer charges" in a case against "the K. K. Professor." In order to avoid raising that moot question, the two Jewish bodies decided to protest, each in a separate memorandum: the Defense Bureau before the minister of the interior, the IKG to the minister of education. No response to these memorandums was ever received.[44]

The IKG and the Defense Bureau were far more successful in another case, one concerning Jewish pupils in Viennese elementary schools.[45] The Jews of Vienna were proud that they had been admitted to general schools since Emperor Joseph II's Edict of Toleration of 1782, and they had for scores of years repulsed attempts at establishing separate Jewish schools in the Austrian capital.[46] The

---

43. *Monatsschrift*, April 17, 1910, no. 4, p. 20.
44. The case is not mentioned in "25 Jahre" but is reported in *Mitteilungen*, no. 108 (November 1898): 15–16.
45. Again this case was not reported in "25 Jahre," but is reviewed in ibid., pp. 17–18.
46. See Zvi Reinman, "An Attempted Establishment of a Jewish Elementary School in Vienna (1854–1863)," *Michael* 2 (Tel Aviv, 1973): 108–20.

reason they decided against segregated education was that they felt children should learn brotherhood and loyalty to a common fatherland as early as possible, and, moreover, segregation was a flagrant violation of the constitution.

Now, with the official installation of the head of the Christian-Social party, Karl Lueger, as mayor of Vienna, the attempt at segregating Jewish pupils was renewed by the municipal school board in an administrative ruling of September 1899 that in the future pupils were to be enrolled in strict accordance with denominational characteristics. While the IKG petitioned the Ministry of Education, asking that the rescript be countermanded, the Defense Bureau mobilized its trustees in the various Viennese districts against the school board and also persuaded some twenty parents to take specific steps by empowering the IKG "to pursue the case in court, and, if necessary up to the Highest Administrative Instance." Moreover the ÖIU called a large protest meeting against the intended segregation and empowered Jewish members of the Lower Austrian Diet and of the Reichsrat to intervene with the Ministry of Education against the school board. Consequently the ministry not only inhibited the implementation of the edict but also sent one of its officials to a Christian-Social meeting called to demonstrate full popular approval of segregation. The ministerial representative, by his prerogative power, precluded the assembly from voting on the issue by dissolving it.[47] Afterward the minister himself publicly reiterated the principle that denominational segregation was contrary "to the laws in force and to all general directions based upon them."[48]

A similar victory was won by a combined Jewish intervention ten years later, when a Christian-Social member of the Reichsrat, a teacher named Schmid, tried to enact, through the Budget Committee's antisemitic majority, a *numerus clausus* for Jewish pupils in secondary schools. Although two-thirds of the committee consented to Schmid's motion, it was thrown out by the House, not least because of a public protest meeting on March 13, 1908, organized by the ÖIU and its Defense Committee. In its strong protests against this "first attempt to abrogate full Jewish citizen's rights by parlia-

47. This case was not mentioned in "25 Jahre," but is reviewed in *Mitteilungen*, no. 108 (November 1898): 18.
48. See a delayed report in ibid., no. 114 (November 1899): 5.

mentary legislation," the meeting was supported by about one hundred Jewish communities throughout Cisleithania.[49] Yet, impressive as the meeting was, the main reason Schmid's motion was thwarted was the unequivocal stand taken by the Jewish members of the Reichsrat on all sides of the House who followed the lead of the four members of the National Jewish Club.[50] The speeches of two of them—Adolf Stand and Arthur Mahler—were cited by the *Monatsschrift* for treating Schmid's motion as an episode in the struggle for Jewish rights. They did

> far, far more than simply correct a single wrong [*weit, weit mehr als die Abwehr eines vereinzelten Unrechts*]. They established the right of the Jewish people in Austria to a life of full equality with all the other nations of this realm, by proudly and confidently stressing the equal worth [*Gleichwertigkeit*] of the Jewish people on a cultural, moral and intellectual level.[51]

Such high praise in the pages of the ÖIU's official organ, which generally and on principle fought Zionism and national Jewish politics, contains perhaps also a grain of self-criticism: the basis of the bureau's whole strategy of defense was rather small, as was the whole political outlook of the ÖIU. During its prolonged existence until 1938, it never succeeded in breaking out of the narrow confines of Austro-German liberalism. Sometimes certain members seem to have chafed against such narrowness, but they did not ever really break those ideological fetters.

At any rate, when constitutional principles of citizens' rights were involved, the Defense Bureau could muster the broadest support from all parts of the Jewish public. And perhaps—not least in consequence of such a general consent—government agencies upheld Jewish equality against major antisemitic attacks, as, for example, the attempt of Lueger's Christian-Social municipality to prohibit kosher butchering in the Austrian capital in 1906.[52]

This does not mean, however, that Jewish complaints against government agencies or officials were always successful. On the contrary, the number of certain kinds of complaints, such as the one against the teacher who had advocated "simply shooting" the Jews,

---

49. *Monatsschrift*, April 1908, no. 4, pp. 2–7.
50. Ibid., June/July 1908, nos. 6/7, p. 1. The motion was defeated in plenary session, 205 to 162.
51. Ibid., pp. 4–5.
52. Ibid., May 1906, no. 5, p. 7.

did not succeed and had to be dropped, often on account of bureaucratic stubbornness and governmental inertia. But there were cases in which a formal success was achieved while in fact no practical redress could be effected. For example the Defense Bureau issued several complaints against governmental and municipal tenders for administrative posts or public works in which only Christian firms were invited to compete or a certificate of baptism was one of the requirements stipulated. Although nearly all complaints of that sort were set right by repeating the tender without the unconstitutional conditions, the damage was already done, and Jews had been warned off.

While even a formal success—for instance, a reprimand for an antisemitic clerk—made the statistics look good, it scarcely retarded the spread of antisemitism. Moreover, with regard to actions against government agencies and officials, the Defense Bureau's statistical summary appears to have been heavily doctored by the omission of a large proportion of unsuccessful actions.[53] Thus if one considers only the cases mentioned in the ÖIU's publications, the rate of formal success is as high as 60 percent and more. But the number of cases treated by the Defense Bureau was, as already indicated, far in excess of those reflected in this essay, and thus one cannot assume that the rate of formal success exceeded the 50-percent mark. In general it appears that the higher the instance with which the complaint was made, the higher the rate of success, although even ministerial intervention often fell short of tangible results and achieved primarily *formal* redress. Yet this record does not detract from the importance of the Defense Bureau's efforts to protect Jewish constitutional rights in the face of antisemitic attempts to abrogate them one by one. Table 4 summarizes the Defense Bureau's efforts against official discrimination.

It has already been mentioned that successful protests against discriminatory tenders (for contracts and so forth) constituted formal victories only. This and the rather remarkably low rate of success of complaints against antisemitic clerks and officials seem to stem from bureaucratic solidarity, which sheltered the colleagues against disciplinary action. Even the cases involving officials of the courts of law barely reached an average rate of success.

53. See, for example, the cases cited in nn. 44 and 45 above.

Table 4. Complaints against Government Agencies, 1897–1910

	Outcome			
Instance	Unknown or Indifferent	Negative	Positive	Percentage Positive
Parliamentary bodies	—	2	1	33%
Military personnel	1	—	1	50%
Teachers	1	1	1	33%
Schools	1	—	2	67%
Clerks and officials	3	2	2	28.5%
Law clerks	—	2	3	60%
Tenders and situations vacant	—	—	6	100%
Others (kosher slaughtering)	—	—	1	100%
Totals	6	7	17	57%

Kidnapping and Forced Baptism

A possible motive for the recalcitrant behavior of some of the law clerks is suggested by the religious character of the final, and perhaps most painful, group of cases undertaken by the Defense Bureau.

The practice of kidnapping Jewish children, mostly girls, in order to have them baptized in a Catholic monastery, was almost endemic in Galicia.[54] It often involved complaints against court personnel or policemen who countenanced such occurrences. Thus the results of Jewish intercession seem to have depended upon quickness of action, for once a child was baptized, by the technicalities of Austrian law the case had to be adjudged with regard to age of consent (fourteen) and only secondary importance was allotted to the parents' right to bring up their children in accordance with their religious traditions. One case based on both the parental right and the age of consent was successfully concluded by the Defense Bureau in 1902–03. The ÖIU represented a father whose divorced wife had had her children baptized while they were more than seven but less than fourteen, which was the age during which Austrian law recognized the paternal right of decision. Consequently the baptisms were annulled, and the children were returned to their father.

In another case involving a girl just over the age of fourteen, a Cracow court validated the declaration of the girl—drawn up within

54. See *Österreichische Wochenschrift*, 1900, no. 8, pp. 137–39, where four cases between 1880 and 1890 are mentioned.

the nunnery and in the presence of the prioress—that she had freely decided to convert and to stay in the convent.[55] It is probable that the convent was the nunnery of the Felician Sisters, which was most frequently involved in these kinds of kidnapping cases. The girl in question seems to have been Michalina Araten of Cracow, kidnapped in January 1900. Hers was the last case on record in which the kidnapped child was not returned to his or her parents. Yet this turning point in the Galician practice was reached only after the Defense Bureau had activated public opinion, the courts of law, and the minister of justice and other ministries; moreover, it had succeeded in arousing the interest of the Emperor Franz Joseph, who granted a personal audience to the frantic father of the girl.[56] But even this unprecedented intervention was to no avail. Probably the naïve utterance of one of the ministers that "secular power stops at the walls of a monastery"[57] aptly summed up the attitude then prevailing in Catholic Austria.

But at last, at the threshold of the twentieth century, something did give. The unhappy end of the Araten story was almost the last instance of religious intransigence in kidnapping cases. Only one later occurrence, whose outcome remained obscure, is on file.[58] All the other sixteen cases reported ended with the return of the children to their parents and to Judaism.[59] Some of the kidnappers were even sentenced to terms of imprisonment.

Thus one can safely conclude that in this delicate field of activity the Defense Bureau reaped its most impressive successes—more than 88 percent. Yet religious anti-Judaism, although a constant irritant, was no longer the main source of Jewish apprehension.

Cases of economic boycott and racial discrimination increased in number, especially after 1905, and the rate of success in these instances was far below average: satisfactory results could be observed in only 15 percent of all boycott cases tackled by the Defense Bureau. But even when boycott notices were confiscated and penalized by

---

55. Mayer, *Ein jüdischer Kaufmann*, p. 338. See also n. 58 below.

56. Seventy liberal papers reported sympathetically and in detail on the affair. "25 Jahre," pp. 34–35.

57. *Österreichische Wochenschrift*, 1900, no. 8, p. 137.

58. "25 Jahre," p. 45. The kidnappers were prosecuted, but the return of the girl is not reported. It is even possible that Mayer, *Ein jüdischer Kaufmann* (see n. 55 above) referred to this or a similar additional case.

59. All are mentioned in "25 Jahre."

Table 5. Cases of Appeal to a Ministry

Resort	1897–1904	1905–1910	Total
Prime Minister	12	2	14
Ministry of Justice	11	25	36
Ministry of Education	6	2	8
Others	10	12	22
Total	39	41	80

fines or had to be retracted, the main damage had already been done by the initial publication, while the deterrent effect of the penalizing measures was almost negligible.

Statistical Summary

If the methods of the Österreichisch-Israelitische Union and its Rechtschutz und Abwehr-Büro differed from those of the German Centralverein deutscher Staatsbürger jüdischen Glaubens, it was mainly in the direct intervention with government offices and ministers. In Germany an appeal to the highest echelons was regarded as an extraordinary step of unproven merit, while in Austria, out of a total of 175 cases included in this review, no less than 80, or 45.7 percent were proffered to one of the ministries for redress (see table 5).

The decline in the number of appeals to the prime minister's office after the demission of Ernest von Koerber is probably due to a change in character of cases handled. Fewer pogroms and blood allegations, but more boycott cases and racial antisemitic press campaigns came to the Defense Bureau's attention and had to be taken up with the Ministry of Justice. Intercessions on ministerial level were successful in 50 percent of the cases, while 27.5 percent ended in clear failure. Of the twenty-one cases that were brought to courts of law by the Defense Bureau, or were supported by it in court, exactly two-thirds ended favorably for the Jewish side. A short balance sheet of failures and successes pertaining to the various kinds of defense activities undertaken by the Defense Bureau, is presented in table 6.

Yet the gravest responsibilities of the Österreichisch-Israelitische Union—defense against the ever-present threat of anti-Jewish riots

Table 6. The Defense Bureau's Rate of Success

Kind of Action Taken	Total Number of Cases	Outcome					
		Indifferent Results	Negative Results	Percentage Negative	Positive Results	Percentage Positive
Combatting forced baptism	18	—	2	11.0%	16	89.0%
Legal aid in general court cases	21	5	2	9.5%	14	66.0%
Special cases:						
Blood allegations	8	—	1 (Polná)		7	
Abductions	6	—	1 (Araten)		5	
Total court cases	35	5	4	11.5%	26	74.3%
Complaints against government agencies and officials	30	6	7	23.0%	17	57.0%
Enforcement of press corrections (retractions, apologies, factual *démentis*)	47	10	12	26.0%	25	53.0%
Intercession with the highest legislative and executive branches	80	22	20	25.0%	38	47.5%
Action against boycotts	40	34	6	85.0%	6	15.0%

NOTE: Several cases are listed under more than one heading. Hence the total is far in excess of the actual cases and has not been summarized.

in town and country and the recurrent blood accusations throughout the realm—are insufficiently represented in this summary, for they appear only insofar as they came to court. But although the rate of convictions against the perpetrators of blood accusations was impressive, even one case that miscarried—like the murder trial of Leopold Hilsner—strengthened antisemitism more than could be compensated by all the Jewish victories in court. Moreover, one ought to keep in mind that the actions listed in table 6 are only a small percentage of the approximately five thousand files opened by the Defense Bureau. The character of most of the others probably did not lend them to public discussion or to much rejoicing over satisfactory outcome. For instance, if a summary of all the boycott cases handled by the Defense Bureau shows a rate of effectiveness of only 15 percent, that probably reflects the extent of the Defense Bureau's achievements in combatting antisemitism more realistically than the additional figures in table 6.

On the other hand, the statistics in table 6 do not at all testify to the restraining influence of a defensive body, whose watchful presence and "mere existence," said the *Monatsschrift*, served as a "prohibitive" influence against the intrusion of antisemitic principles and tendencies "into the administration, into civic society and into day-to-day business affairs."[60]

In fact, this deterrent factor seems to have been of at least equal value with the active defense measures the Österreichisch-Israelitische Union took in courts and government offices, in newspapers and public meetings. But perhaps still more than all of these, the fighting spirit of the ÖIU's Defense Bureau succeeded in rallying a frightened and incoherent mass of Jews into the semblance of a common front against antisemitism.

60. *Monatsschrift*, April 17, 1910, no. 4, p. 20.

Robert S. Wistrich

Social Democracy, the Jews, and Antisemitism in *Fin-de-Siècle* Vienna

The response of Jewish communities in various European states to the rise of the organized antisemitic movement that emerged in the early 1880s is a complex subject, one that deserves more attention in depth than it has hitherto received from historians. Jews in Central and Western Europe, once they had overcome the initial shock of seeing their civil equality challenged by the antisemites within less than a decade of their emancipation, generally sought to wage a juridical and political battle for public opinion; their hope was to strengthen those forces within Gentile society that opposed antisemitism. At the same time Jewish defense organizations such as the Österreichisch-Israelitische Union in Austria and the German Centralverein deutscher Staatsbürger jüdischen Glaubens were founded in the decade after 1885; their objectives focused around the need to refute the arguments of the antisemites and strengthen Jewish consciousness in the face of the new threat. Nevertheless, at the ideological level, even the Jewish defense organizations never abandoned the optimistic and self-confident faith of an earlier generation in the liberal credo of emancipation. While emphasizing to a greater degree than their predecessors the need to instill Jewish values and pride in their communities, the defense organizations ultimately believed that antisemitism was a transient sickness—a revival of medieval prejudices encouraged by reactionary forces—that would be overcome by the fuller integration of Jews in Gentile society.

This optimistic view was especially prevalent in Central Europe and remained an article of faith for the Jewish establishment before 1914 in spite of the fierce challenge provided by the Zionist analysis of the Jewish Question. It was held with particular tenacity by the

Jewish leadership in Austria-Hungary, in spite of the fact that it was in Vienna—capital of the multinational empire of Franz Joseph—that antisemitism achieved unparalleled electoral successes at the turn of the century. It would appear that for liberal Viennese Jewry, the impact of Catholic and German nationalist antisemitism was largely offset by the illusion of security they felt as loyal citizens of the ruling House of Habsburg, whose head was known for his sharp disapproval of the plebeian revolt embodied in local anti-Jewish agitation. Moreover, in contrast to the Second Reich or even the Third French Republic, with their insistence on full *national* integration, the Habsburg rulers demanded only the more traditional form of loyalty to the emperor and economic assimilation to the needs of the supranational dynastic state.

In this essay I shall not be dealing with the totality of Jewish reactions in Vienna after 1880 to the new hostility engendered by antisemitism but rather with one specific and neglected feature which may help to illuminate that response—namely the attitude of the Jewish leadership of the Österreichische Sozialdemokratie (Austrian Social Democratic party). This party, whose establishment in 1889 was largely the work of the Jewish-born physician Victor Adler, was not, of course, a "Jewish" movement, and many Gentiles were prominent in its leadership. From the standpoint of Jewish history, its Jewish intellectual elite might even seem to constitute a marginal phenomenon of no interest or importance to specifically Jewish interests or concerns. Yet this impression would be misleading, for the involvement of Jews in European socialism was an important and significant trend in the history of Jewish assimilation in the nineteenth and twentieth centuries. The reaction of Jewish socialist intellectuals to antisemitism, especially in Vienna where they held such an influential position in the labor movement, is therefore an illuminating indicator concerning the problem that antisemitism posed to assimilated Jews in general.

In some respects the socialist position was a continuation of established liberal theories of human equality and the desirability of full Jewish integration into the national body politic that dated back to the French Revolution of 1789. On the other hand, from the beginning of its history socialism had an emphasis with respect to Jewish social and economic activity that was different from its liberal predecessors. Since the first half of the nineteenth century, Jews had been identified on the Left with petty huckstering and the allegedly "parasitic" middleman occupations. Karl Marx had made it clear in his *Zur Judenfrage* (1844) that "Emancipation from *haggling* and *money*, from practical, real Judaism would be the self-emancipation of our time."[1] Marx's anti-Jewish stereotypes had a powerful influence on the Jewish (and non-Jewish) leaders of the Österreichische Sozialdemokratie, and they were reinforced by the prevalence in the border regions of the Habsburg Monarchy of masses of *Ostjuden*. For the Austrian Marxists the economic role of Galician Jews seemed a microcosm of everything that was "parasitical" in a decomposing feudal society gradually being infiltrated by capitalism.

Moreover, Galicia, the home of two-thirds of Austrian Jewry in the nineteenth century, was perceived by most socialists (as indeed by the liberal Gentile "enlighteners," the Josephinian bureaucrats, and the Jewish *maskilim* before them) as the realm of *Halb-Asien*. In other words the Austro-Polish province was seen as everything that was antithetical to the progress, culture, and humanity symbolized by Europe. *Halb-Asien*[2] was a realm of darkness, sordid barbarism, clerical fanaticism, and violent hatreds. The Jewish ghettos reflected this backwardness with their obscurantist superstitions, their clinging to obsolete customs and to the Yiddish language (invariably considered by liberal and socialist "enlighteners" as a corrupt and vulgar jargon), and their incorrigible ethnic particularism. Above all Jewish Galicia with its myriad *Luftmenschen* appeared to the socialists as the living incarnation of Marx's haggling, usurious, and nonproductive Jew. Thus socialist reactions to Austrian antisemitism, like those of the assimilated Jewish bourgeoisie of Vienna, were from the outset colored and complicated by this background. The fact is that, to a remarkable degree, the Jews in the German-Austrian socialist leadership internalized the commonplace anti-Jewish stereotypes of their Gentile environment concerning the ghetto Jews and traditional Judaism. Precisely because they considered themselves to be in the vanguard of "progress," leaders like Victor and Friedrich Adler, Otto Bauer, Friedrich Austerlitz, and Wilhelm Ellenbogen, who were already thoroughly Germanized in culture, shared the re-

1. Karl Marx, "On the Jewish Question" (1844), in his *Early Writings*, introd. Lucio Colletti (London, 1975), p. 236.
2. The term *Halb-Asien* (Half-Asia) was coined by the Austrian writer, Karl-Emil Franzos (1848–1904). His tales and sketches, entitled *Aus Halb-Asien*, were first collected in two volumes in 1876. Franzos understood by *Halb-Asien* not only a geographical area (including Rumania and southern Russia as well as Galicia and Bukovina) but a condition in which European culture and Eastern *Unkultur* coexisted.

vulsion of most Gentile Austrians against the shabby outward appearance, stubborn orthodoxy, insular customs, and national separatism of traditional Jewry.

Though Austrian socialists of Jewish origin were by no means blind to the real perniciousness of modern antisemitism, their opposition to anti-Jewish agitation was in some respects paralyzed by their own hostility to the *Ostjuden* and the unconscious self-hatred it engendered. It must not be forgotten, moreover, that Jewish socialist intellectuals, in Austria as elsewhere, had often arrived at their socialism through a critique of "Judaism" that later turned into a radical critique of bourgeois society. In this respect they were the true heirs of the great German-Jewish iconoclasts of the first half of the nineteenth century—Karl Ludwig Börne, Heinrich Heine, Karl Marx, and Ferdinand Lassalle. Like their forerunners (with the exception of the repentant Heine) they regarded "Judaism" in the socioeconomic sense as a symbol of alienation and the antithesis of the universal dialectic of human emancipation. Jewry was perceived as the embodiment of greed, egoism, and the capitalist ethic as well as one of the pillars of European feudal reaction. In their hostility to the Rothschilds and the Jewish *Finanzaristokratie*, for example, there was little to distinguish the Viennese socialists from the Austrian antisemitic parties. Much the same could be said of the near-consensus existing between socialists (both Jew and Gentile) and the Viennese antisemites on the subject of the *Ostjuden*.

In a famous passage on the Galician *Ostjuden* who settled in Vienna's Second District, the Leopoldstadt, during and after the First World War, the novelist Joseph Roth observed: "It is terribly difficult to be an East European Jew; there is no harder fate than to be an East European Jewish alien in Vienna. . . . For the Christian-Social party, they are Jews. For German Nationalists, they are Semites. For Social Democrats, they are unproductive elements." Both the Christlichsoziale Partei and the Deutschnationale Partei, as Roth pointed out, "include antisemitism as an important point in their programs." The Sozialdemokraten, on the other hand, "fear being labeled as a 'Jewish party.'"[3] This perceptive summing up of the situation in the 1920s is no less valid for the late Habsburg period, as I have endeavored to show in a number of articles and in my recent book dealing

3. Joseph Roth, *Juden auf Wanderschaft* (Berlin, 1927), quoted in his *Romane-Erzählungen-Aufsätze* (Cologne, 1964), pp. 559ff.

with socialism and the Jewish Question in Germany and Austria-Hungary before 1914.[4] The Social Democrats in Habsburg Austria, influenced as they were by classic leftist prejudices against both Jews and Judaism and entangled in a defensive and largely futile war to prove that they were not a *Judenschutztruppe* (Jewish protective guard), could scarcely wage an effective battle against militant political antisemitism. The fact that the Austrian Social Democrats did eventually take a stand against the Catholic and pan-German varieties of antisemitism that exercised such an influence in nineteenth- and twentieth-century Austria should not obscure the extent to which the party leadership itself flirted with and even contributed to the growth of the phenomenon.

The discussion of socialist and Marxist attitudes to antisemitism (whether in Austria or elsewhere) has often been confused by the erroneous and illogical assumption that left-wing parties are immunized against racial, religious, or ethnic prejudice.[5] The theory and above all the *praxis* of the Austrian workers' movement are a good illustration of how unfounded this assumption is when examined in the light of concrete historical situations. Not only was the labor movement far from immune to the cultural and political antisemitism that began to pervade broad strata of German-Austrian society from the early 1880s onward, but it was from the outset permeated with prejudices against Jews.[6] This was true at the mass level, as it was in the upper reaches of the Austrian party. The major difference was that in contrast to the German Nationalists or the Christian Socials, this "socialist" antisemitism was never really activated or used as a major strategic weapon in politics. It did not feature in official party platforms, nor was there any intention of deliberately and actively discriminating against Austrian Jews, though calls to limit their presence and influence within the Socialist party were

4. Robert S. Wistrich, *Socialism and the Jews: The Dilemmas of Assimilation in Germany and Austria-Hungary* (London, 1982).

5. Paul Massing, *Rehearsal for Destruction: A Study of Political Antisemitism in Imperial Germany* (New York, 1949), p. 151. See also, for examples of this viewpoint, Peter Pulzer, *The Rise of Political Anti-Semitism in Germany and Austria* (London, 1964), p. 259; and, more recently, Reinhard Rürup, "Sozialismus und Antisemitismus in Deutschland vor 1914," in *Juden und Jüdische Aspekte in der Deutschen Arbeiterbewegung, 1848–1918*, ed. Walter Grab (Tel Aviv, 1976), pp. 203–27.

6. See Avram Barkai, "The Austrian Social Democrats and the Jews," *Wiener Library Bulletin* 24, nos. 1, 2 (1970): 32–40, 16–22. For a more detailed analysis, see Robert S. Wistrich, "Austrian Social Democracy and Antisemitism, 1890–1914," *Jewish Social Studies* 38 (1975): 323–33.

heard on several occasions.[7] The main expression of socialist antisemitism lay, however, in the highly ambivalent stance adopted toward the rise of a populist and remarkably successful *Antisemiten-
bewegung* in Vienna after 1890. The seeds of the failure adequately to
resist and combat the propaganda of this movement are already apparent in a letter of Karl Kautsky from Vienna in 1884 in which he
complains: "We are having trouble preventing our own people from
fraternizing with the antisemites. The antisemites are now our most
dangerous opponents, because their appearance is oppositional and
democratic, thus appealing to the workers' instincts."[8]

Kautsky as a Marxist naturally attributed the impact of these
early antisemitic appeals of Georg von Schönerer's Deutschnationale
directed at the Austrian workers to the *kleinbürgerlich* character of
the Viennese population.[9] His Austro-Marxist pupils, like socialist
theoreticians in other European countries, continually sought to explain antisemitism at this time in purely socioeconomic terms as a
reaction of *déclassé* petit bourgeois strata to the impact of large-scale
capitalist methods of production.[10] This explanation admittedly has
a certain validity for Vienna, where the artisanal character of local
industry and the crisis of the craftsmen were indeed central to the
origins of the antisemitic movement in the 1880s. It is also true,
moreover, that at least in the early phases of industrialization in
Austria there was less of a clear dividing line between the lower
Bürgertum and the proletariat, so that typical antisemitic stereotypes might in the early 1880s more easily have infiltrated the nascent working class.[11] Nevertheless the classic Marxist schema, according to which antisemitism (to quote Friedrich Engels's letter of
1890 to an Austrian correspondent) is exclusively a reaction of
"medieval, declining strata against modern society,"[12] is only par-

7. See, for example, *Verhandlungen des sechsten österreichischen Sozialdemokrati-
schen Parteitages* (Vienna, 1897), pp. 91–92; and the discussion in Wistrich, *Socialism
and the Jews*, pp. 265–68.
8. Karl Kautsky to Friedrich Engels, June 23, 1884, *Friedrich Engels Briefwechsel mit
Karl Kautsky*, ed. Benedikt Kautsky (Vienna, 1955), p. 125.
9. Kautsky to Engels, December 22, 1884, ibid., p. 159.
10. Wilhelm Ellenbogen, "Der Wiener Antisemitismus," *Sozialistische Monatshefte*,
September 1899, pp. 418–25.
11. On this point, see Gerhard Botz, Gerfried Brandstetter, and Michael Pollak, *Im
Schatten der Arbeiterbewegung: Zur Geschichte des Anarchismus in Österreich und
Deutschland* (Vienna, 1977).
12. For the full text of Engels's letter of March 21, 1890, written to Isidor Ehren-
freund, a Jewish bank employee in Vienna, see *Arbeiterzeitung* (Vienna), May 9, 1890;
and *Marx-Engels Werke* (East Berlin, 1963), 22:570.

tially applicable to Austria or to other European societies in the late nineteenth century. Furthermore, as the record of the Austrian socialists was to show, such views, while ostensibly intended to demonstrate and warn against the "reactionary" character of antisemitism, proved quite insufficient to guarantee the immunization of the labor movement against ethnic prejudices.[13] The Marxist assumption that modern capitalism must inexorably lead to the disappearance of the premodern, preindustrial lower middle strata in the population and thereby to the collapse of the antisemitic movement was also to prove illusory, especially in the Central European context. This was, moreover, a decidedly flimsy basis on which to wage a successful resistance to antisemitic demagogy. Its only practical result was the propagation of a new Marxist dogma in the 1890s to the effect that historical development would inevitably drive the antisemitic *Kleinbürgertum* into the arms of the only truly consistent anticapitalist party—the Social Democrats.[14]

In their reliance on this rather mechanistic and fatalistic concept of historical development, the Austro-Marxist theoreticians were not essentially different from their colleagues in most other European social democratic parties. The social, economic, and political context in which they operated, however, *was* substantially different, and it is this which perhaps explains why the concessions they made to antisemitic terminology and attitudes appear to be greater than one would have a right to expect. In the first place the Jewish Problem in Vienna had become more acute by the 1890s than elsewhere in Western or Central Europe, though parallel developments did occur all over the Continent. Between 1869 and 1880 the Jewish population had risen from 40,227 (6.10 percent of the total population) to 72,588 (10.06 percent). By 1910 there were 175,818 Jews in Vienna (8.63 percent of the city's population), where fifty years earlier there had been only 6,217 (2.16 percent)—a stupendous rate of growth that, when related to the occupational structure of Viennese Jewry and the historic traditions of Judeophobia in Catholic Austria, makes the rise of political antisemitism seem less than surprising. From the socialist standpoint, moreover, the economic structure of Viennese

13. For a diametrically opposed view on the question of "immunization," see John Bunzl, "Arbeiterbewegung, 'Judenfrage' und Antisemitismus: Am Beispiel des Wiener Bezirks Leopoldstadt," in *Bewegung und Klasse: Studien zur österreichischen Arbeitergeschichte*, ed. Gerhard Botz, Hans Hautmann, Helmut Konrad, and Josef Weidenholzer (Vienna, 1978), p. 760.

14. Wistrich, *Socialism and the Jews*, pp. 250–56.

Jewry, and in particular its crucial role in banking, industrial capitalism, commerce, department stores, the liberal press, and the free professions, did not make the Jewish community appear as the natural ally of a proletarian movement.[15]

Even among the poorer Jews of the Leopoldstadt, who had immigrated after 1860 from Hungary, Galicia, or Moravia, there were serious social and cultural obstacles to participation in the labor movement. Most of the immigrant Jews of lower status were not genuine proletarians, and very few were factory workers.[16] They did not live in the typical proletarian quarters of Ottakring, Hernals, or Favoriten, and a far greater proportion of Jews than Gentiles, even at the lowest levels of society, were *selbstständig*.[17] Even more significant, the poorer Jews were far from assimilated, retaining in many cases their distinctive language (Yiddish), their dress, mannerisms, mores, and exotic religious customs. At the turn of the century, with the increased immigration to Vienna of the more traditionalist and orthodox *Ostjuden* from Galicia, the cultural gap between this Jewish sector and modern Social Democracy appeared almost unbridgeable.[18] The rise of Jewish nationalism in *fin-de-siècle* Vienna was a further factor alienating an important section of the Jewish population from the Austrian Social Democrats; the latter were totally unsympathetic either to Zionism or to the more modest claims for Jewish cultural-national autonomy in Galicia and Bukovina.[19]

On the other hand, by the end of the nineteenth century there were also the first clear signs of active Jewish participation in the Austrian labor movement. The most striking feature of this new trend was the role played by a growing section of the Jewish intelligentsia in the

15. For an elaboration of this point, see Robert S. Wistrich, "Victor Adler: A Viennese Socialist against Philosemitism," *Wiener Library Bulletin* 27, n.s. no. 32 (1974): 26–33.

16. On the occupational structure of the Jewish and Gentile population in the Leopoldstadt, see Bunzl, "Arbeiterbewegung," pp. 743–750.

17. For further details, see the illuminating demographic study by Marsha L. Rozenblit, *The Jews of Vienna, 1867–1914: Assimilation and Identity* (Albany, 1983), pp. 78–79, who argues convincingly that Jewish residential distribution in Vienna did not depend on class: "Poor Jews shunned residence in the lower-class outer districts in order to live side by side, if not with wealthy Jews, certainly with middle-class Jews in the Leopoldstadt (II) and the Alsergrund (IX)."

18. Ibid., p. 43. Rozenblit emphasizes that the Galician Jews were not only the most recent and the most religious of the Jewish immigrants to Vienna around 1890 but also had a keen sense of themselves as a distinct group—"an East European outpost in a sea of Central European Jews."

19. Wistrich, *Socialism and the Jews*, pp. 309–43. See also Robert S. Wistrich, "Austrian Social Democracy and the Problem of Galician Jewry, 1880–1914," *Leo Baeck Institute Year Book* (hereafter *LBIYB*) 26 (1981): 89–124.

leadership of the Social Democratic party, in the party press, and in its myriad cultural, youth, and sport organizations. This intelligentsia was already thoroughly Germanized and identified itself with the zeal of neophytes with both the national and the social objectives of the pan-Austrian labor movement.[20] Along with this assimilated stratum of middle-class intellectual Jews, there was also a palpable drift toward Social Democracy among the new class of *Handelsangestellten*, who constituted a significant proportion of Vienna Jews by the turn of the century.[21] A small nationally minded sector among these commercial employees became attracted to labor Zionism after 1900, though not to an independent "Bundist" Jewish workers' movement that had no cultural or socioeconomic base under Viennese conditions. The Poalei Zion organizations in Austria before 1914, it should be noted, recommended voting for the Social Democrats wherever Jewish national candidates were not available.[22] After the First World War the drift of Vienna Jews toward the Social Democrats, which had occurred before 1914 largely among the educated bourgeois and intellectual strata of Jewry, became a flood, and, as a result, the image of "Red Vienna" literally fused in antisemitic circles with that of "Jewish" subversion.[23] Both Jews and Marxists were allegedly bent on the systematic destruction of traditional Catholic society and culture.

The seeds of this postwar clerical and fascist propaganda against Red Vienna can be found, however, in the late Habsburg period. It was no accident, for example, that the young Adolf Hitler explicitly related his hatred of Jews and Social Democrats to his experiences in turn-of-the-century Vienna. The fear and anxiety induced by the *Judensozi* (the so-called Jewish Social Democrats) were rooted in the class distinctions that continued to pervade Gentile Austrian society and were exacerbated by the impact of the Christian-Social agitation after 1900. Having finally conquered the city of Vienna in 1897, that Catholic populist party under the leadership of Karl Lueger turned

20. Wistrich, *Socialism and the Jews*, pp. 332–34.
21. Bunzl, "Arbeiterbewegung," pp. 746–50; and Rozenblit, *Jews of Vienna*, pp. 48–70, who points out that Viennese Gentile *Angestellte* generally worked for the imperial and municipal civil service, while Jewish employees worked as clerks, salesmen, or managers in the business world.
22. For further details, see Ber Borochov, *Ktavim* (Tel Aviv, 1955–66), 3:496–500, 534, 536.
23. On the massive electoral swing toward the Social Democrats among Viennese Jews during the First Austrian Republic, see Walter B. Simon, "The Jewish Vote in Austria," *LBIYB* 16 (1971): 97–123.

the burden of its propaganda against its newest and most dangerous rival, the rising Social Democratic party. Christian Socialism sought at the turn of the century to become *the* party of the Viennese German bourgeoisie and the supreme defender of *Mittelstand* interests against the "Red Menace." Karl Lueger, who in the 1890s had so successfully united the middle and lower *Bürgertum* against the decaying liberal order in the name of traditional ideals of Austrian *Bürger* culture, now found a new rallying cry in the crusade against Social Democracy.[24]

The Red Menace and the Jewish Question merged in the propaganda of Lueger's movement from the moment it had achieved office. Anti-intellectualism, *Mittelstand* phobias concerning proletarianization, anxiety over socialist atheism, and petit bourgeois fears of Jewish competition were cleverly exploited by the Christian Socials to mobilize their bourgeois clientele. It was from this agitation, which was the first systematically to synthesize hatred of socialists and Jews, that Hitler picked up his hysterical anti-intellectualism as well as his fateful identification of Marxism with Jewry.[25] Furthermore, it was in Vienna that Hitler "discovered" the decisive role that Jewish intellectuals played in the Marxist parties and the roots of what he subsequently convinced himself was a satanic conspiracy against the German *Volk*. "The names of the Austerlitzes, Davids, Adlers, Ellenbogens, etc.," he histrionically recalled in *Mein Kampf*, "will remain forever engraven in my memory."[26]

Hitler's assumptions, which ultimately led to the mass murder of European Jewry, were of course utterly remote from the actual theories of Austro-Marxism and from the *praxis* of the Social Democratic movement in Austria-Hungary. Not only did Hitler completely ignore the pronounced German character of the Austrian Social Democratic party (and its strong emotional attachment to the idea of *Anschluss*), but he clearly knew nothing whatsoever about the outlook and attitudes of the Jewish intellectuals prominent in the labor movement.[27]

24. John W. Boyer, *Political Radicalism in Late Imperial Vienna: Origins of the Christian Social Movement, 1848–1897* (Chicago, 1981).

25. See John W. Boyer, "Karl Lueger and the Viennese Jews," *LBIYB* 26 (1981): 139–40; and Robert S. Wistrich, "Karl Lueger and the Ambiguities of Viennese Antisemitism," *Jewish Social Studies* 45 (1983): 251–62.

26. Adolf Hitler, *Mein Kampf*, trans. Ralph Manheim (Boston, 1942), p. 61.

27. For Hitler's encounter with the Austrian Social Democrats in Vienna, see the interesting, if impressionistic, book by J. Sydney Jones, *Hitler in Vienna, 1907–1913:*

Far from favoring "Jewish" interests or identifying with other Jews—whether in ethnic, religious, or class terms—the so-called Jewish leadership of the Austrian Social Democracy bent over backwards to *dissociate* themselves from their former co-religionists. In order, perhaps, to refute the antisemitic attacks on their leadership, they indulged in strategies either of avoidance, trivialization of antisemitism, or even sophisticated justifications that only revealed the extent of their alienation from Jewry. The founder and leader of the Social Democratic party in the Habsburg Empire, Victor Adler, son of a wealthy Jewish family from Prague, a fervent German nationalist in his younger days and a convert (to Protestantism) at the age of twenty-six, set the tone on this as on other major issues. Adler resolved his own personal Jewish Question by adopting an official policy of neutrality on all problems involving conflicts between philo- and antisemites. In practice, under Viennese conditions of the 1880s and 1890s, this meant favoring the antisemites as against their liberal "philosemitic" opponents. Otto Bauer, who belonged to the younger generation of Austro-Marxists, later continued this policy, writing in 1910 that "Marx's essay on the Jewish question [of 1844] already differentiated us sharply from liberal philosemitism."[28]

The reluctance of the Viennese Social Democrats to recognize the specificity of the Jewish Question, especially in its national dimension, reflected two distinct traditions—that of the liberal assimilationist Jewish bourgeoisie and that of Marxist ideology—which came together in a common antipathy to feudal-clerical antisemitism, to the *Ostjuden*, and to Zionism. At the 1897 party congress, delegates found themselves dragged, as a result of Lueger's triumph in Vienna, into an unexpectedly frank discussion of both anti- and philosemitism: it was interestingly enough a rank-and-file socialist Jew from Moravia—Jakob Brod—who challenged Victor Adler's policy of indifference to antisemitism as being one of the causes of the Social Democrats' defeats in the recent Reichsrat elections.

The party's strategy, thus far, has been to remove at all cost any suspicion that it is Judaized. We simply wished to demonstrate that we are not slaves of the Jews. But I say to you that even if we live a hundred years, we will never convince the petite bourgeoisie. What have the comrades from the party leadership done to persuade the unenlightened ele-

---

Clues to the Future (New York, 1983); and Robert S. Wistrich, *Hitler's Apocalypse: Jews and the Nazi Legacy* (Lòndon, 1985), chap. 1.

28. Otto Bauer, "Sozialismus und Antisemitismus," *Der Kampf* 4 (1910–11): 9.

ments that there is a Jewish proletariat alongside the Jewish bourgeoi-sie? In Vienna, "Jew" and capitalist are synonymous terms. I have never known it mentioned in the *Arbeiterzeitung* or at any meeting (shout: Oho!) that the Jewish proletariat is the most oppressed, miserable, and backward of all (Shout: but yes!). I mean, it has not been discussed enough.[29]

Brod's criticisms, angrily rebuffed at the congress, pointed to one of the fundamental weaknesses in Viennese socialist efforts to coun-ter antisemitic demagogy. Instead of emphasizing the class differ-entiation within Austrian Jewry, the socialists frequently equated capitalism and Jewry, along the familiar lines of Christian-Social ideology. Since the *Judengeist* according to Marx, as well as Baron Karl von Vogelsang (Lueger's spiritual godfather), was identical with the "spirit of capitalism," it followed that a consistent antisemite should ultimately wish to join the only party that was determined in both theory *and* practice to eliminate capitalism as a whole and with it the basis for the separate economic existence of Jewry. In this way the Austrian Social Democrats both implicitly and explicitly could try to appeal to an antisemitic mass constituency, seeking to present themselves as the most rigorous adversaries of "Jewish" (and Gentile) capital.

This indirect use of antisemitic rhetoric under a Marxist veil to undermine the Christian-Social adversaries of the labor movement was a dangerous game to play. It immediately differentiated the So-cial Democratic party from the liberals, who, in spite of their own equivocacy on the Jewish Question, never adopted such dubious tac-tics. It should be remembered, moreover, that until the crushing lib-eral defeat in Vienna in 1897 the Social Democrats had concentrated most of their fire against the liberals as the "class enemy" and even expressed open sympathy with Lueger's successful crusade against Austro-liberalism.[30] The Social Democrats had frequently de-nounced the Viennese *Judenpresse* (itself a classic antisemitic expres-sion) as the bastion of liberal capitalist opinion and above all for opposing the demands of the workers for universal suffrage. In the eyes of Victor Adler and his colleagues the *Neue Freie Presse* and the capitalist Jewry it represented were and remained a more dangerous enemy of the labor movement than the rowdy antisemitic *Kleinbür-*

29. *Verhandlungen*, p. 87.
30. See, for example, Friedrich Austerlitz, "Karl Lueger," *Die Neue Zeit* 2 (1900–1901): 36–45.

gertum of Vienna.[31] Hence the Marxist insistence on equating the so-called dangers of philosemitism (i.e., the defense of "capitalist" Jewry) with those of antisemitism and the actual Social Democratic practice of striking harder at the former. As Jakob Brod put it at the 1897 party congress: "If here and there he (Comrade Dr. Adler) dealt the antisemites a blow, he made quite certain that the liberals came in for similar treatment (Cries of: Quite right!)"[32] The party leadership, including Adler, Engelbert Pernerstorfer, and Franz Schuhmeier, rejected this critique even though politically the liberals were, by 1897, clearly a spent force; they initially refused to see that the real obstacle and danger to the workers' movement came from Lueger's cohorts.

Thus Franz Schuhmeier characteristically declared: "Indeed, the liberals are simply waiting for the moment, when we make the antisemites the sole object of our attack, to rehabilitate themselves." Adler himself reaffirmed that: "We have always said: Let the Christian-Socials work, for they are working for us in the last analysis. I still think so, even today." With regard to the Jews, Adler sarcastically asserted: "The special feature of the Jewish question as it exists here in Vienna, is that the capitalist bourgeoisie has a Jewish complexion. That the Jews must suffer this burden is sad. But we are also tired of always finding Jews in our soup."[33]

Adler's strategy cannot, however, be explained away as a *natural* reaction to the predominantly bourgeois ethos of Viennese Jewry (somewhat exaggerated by the Social Democrats) or to its socio-economic influence. From a Marxist viewpoint it would indeed have been more logical for the labor movement to favor an alliance with progressive Austro-liberal elements (among whom the Jews were well represented) against the feudal-aristocratic ruling classes of Austria-Hungary. But the Social Democrats preferred to exploit the profound unpopularity of the liberals for their own purposes, and they obviously calculated that defense of the Jews was not a vote-catching cause in Vienna. Moreover, if the Marxist assumption was correct that Austrian antisemitism was no more than a temporary phenomenon of *Mittelstand* protest doomed to disappear, there was indeed reason to welcome the Christian-Social victory over liberal-

31. "Die Neue Freie Presse," *Arbeiterzeitung* (Vienna), June 30, 1893.
32. *Verhandlungen*, p. 87.
33. Ibid., pp. 92, 101, 103.

ism; why not wait patiently to inherit the Promised Land once the *Kleinbürger* awoke from his illusions and turned to the only party that was truly anticapitalist?

The positive fruits of this strategy would become apparent after the First World War once a truly democratic suffrage permitted the working masses to assert their full voting power in Vienna. In the meantime, during the Lueger era (1897–1910) the Social Democrats, as the leading opposition to the ruling Christian-Social administration of Vienna, continued to demonstrate their ambiguity on the Jewish Question. The main thrust of their policy and propaganda on this issue was to paint Lueger and his colleagues as hypocritical *Judenknechte* who did business with rich Jews and cynically hoodwinked the "fools of Vienna"—the petit bourgeois masses who had put them in power.[34] Lueger was pictured as the Roman Catholic protector of the Rothschilds and Gutmann brothers, the Jewish barons of high finance and industry. Not the Social Democrats but the Christian Socials were the real *Judenschutztruppe*. As for the Jews of Vienna, they still controlled the metropolitan liberal press, the banks, big industry, the universities, the arts and sciences, if one were to believe the Viennese *Arbeiterzeitung*.[35] The socialist central organ outdid itself in turning antisemitic demagogy on its head: "If there is anyone to whom one can apply the word 'Judaized,' it is to the Viennese mayor."[36] The point that its editor, Friedrich Austerlitz (himself a Moravian Jew), wished to make with this kind of witticism was that never had Jewish millionaires prospered as much as under Lueger's rule—a classic example of what Hitler later also condemned as Christian-Social *Scheinantisemitismus* in his *Mein Kampf*.

Socialist use or misuse of this type of rhetoric was doubtlessly intended dialectically to unmask Christian hypocrisy by the inversion or mimicry of familiar antisemitic terminology—thereby exposing the gap between words and deeds, theory and practice that typified Christian-Social rule. Unfortunately, the result was that antisemitic stereotypes of radical provenance which equated "capitalist" and "Jew" received a new kind of respectability and legitimacy precisely because they were used by those who claimed that they were actually fighting against antisemitism. In the context of *fin-de-siècle* Vienna, far from immunizing the workers against Judeo-

---

34. "Christlich-sozialer Schwindel," *Volkstribune*, February 21, 1906, p. 2.
35. Friedrich Austerlitz, "Luegers Tod," *Arbeiterzeitung* (Vienna), March 11, 1910.
36. *Arbeiterzeitung* (Vienna), April 6, 1900.

phobic prejudices, the Social Democrats tended, in my opinion, to reinforce their potency in the belief that such equivocation and ridicule would ultimately work to their advantage.

The socialist policy toward antisemitism, as I suggested in my introductory remarks, was to a large extent the expression of a dilemma inherent in the modalities of Jewish assimilation in its socialist form. The road to socialism for many Jewish intellectuals had indeed been opened as a result of the *failure* of alternative routes to integrate themselves in European society. Socialism, however, demanded the radical casting off of Jewish particularism and the rejection of the Jewish commercial world and of ethnic and family backgrounds. Already alienated from Judaism and Jewry, radical Jews felt obliged to seek a revolutionary "solution" to the Jewish Question. As I have indicated, their critique of modern "Judaized" society could at times merge with Christian-Social and racialist attacks against liberal capitalism and Jewry. Nevertheless there were also important differences. Radical Jews, unlike the Catholic antisemites, did not desire the restoration of the Christian society or state. Nor, in contrast to the German Nationalists, did they visualize a drastic solution to the Jewish Question on the lines of imposing racial homogeneity by discriminatory legislation. The socialist response to antisemitism was "Jewish" precisely in its *universalism* and supranationalism—epitomized by the attempt to resolve the economic critique of Judaism into the broader framework of the overthrow of capitalism. The socialist vision incorporated elements of antisemitism while claiming to "transcend" its partiality through the utopia of a classless society in which traditional Jewish and Christian identities would automatically dissolve. Thus the antisemitic implication of the assault on Jewish egoism, materialism, and insularity was partly neutralized by a secular Marxist messianism that owed not a little to Jewish inspiration.

Moreover, the socialist condemnation of money as a *universal* form of alienation, affecting both Christian and Jew, did undermine at least one of the central premises of antisemitism—namely its insistence on singling out "Jewish" materialism as a *unique* and eternal characteristic of a specific race. Socialist Jews in Austria, as elsewhere, had to negate this premise of racial antisemitism if they were not to cut out the ground from under their own feet. They could always point to their own socialist commitment as the living proof that the curse of Jewish "materialism" could be exorcised and purged, that Jews could selflessly devote themselves to a universal ideal and to egalitarian values. In this they followed the methodology of Börne and Marx, who had first linked de-Judaization (or the purging of Jewish characteristics) with the general cause of human liberation. In *fin-de-siècle* Vienna, this self-cleansing and radical negation of "Judaism" invariably meant a dual assault on the economic "domination" of liberal Jewry *and* on the reactionary obscurantism of ghetto Jewry.

This is what linked the Jewish socialist intellectuals with the relentless guerrilla war waged against the *Neue Freie Presse* and the *Ostjuden* (not to mention the Zionist movement) by Karl Kraus, Vienna's foremost satirist and a thoroughly Germanized Jew, though by no means left-wing in outlook. What was striking in the socialist case was that such self-negation and internalization of the antisemitic incubus could coincide with openly paraded universalist pretensions. Nothing testifies more to the personal and social pressure exercised by an antisemitic Gentile environment than such contradictions. The "Jewish" leaders of Austrian Social Democracy had eradicated the Jewishness from their identity and replaced it with the quasi-messianic identification with the proletariat as the chosen instrument of world history, postulated by Marx. Yet this act of self-negation did not and could not resolve their Jewish Problem in the context of antisemitic Vienna. Their origins not only placed them in a precarious position of perpetual self-examination and ultimately of self-denial, but, by virtue of the exploitation of the issue by their political adversaries (first and foremost by Lueger's Christian-Social movement), pushed them on the defensive. Their vulnerability was a revealing barometer of the dilemma inherent in assimilation in the Central European context and the excruciating responses to antisemitism that it could sometimes engender.

It is this sociopsychological problem that has to be borne in mind when examining the ambiguities of the Austro-Marxist position on the Jewish Question. There were, to be sure, sound sociological reasons for this ambiguity. In Vienna, bourgeois society did indeed appear to be more specifically "Jewish" than elsewhere in Central or Western Europe (with the possible exception of Budapest); in Vienna, too, there was a growing *Ostjuden* problem that complicated the general Jewish response to antisemitism. Finally, in the Habsburg capital antisemitism was a popular cause for social, economic, and ideological reasons that had no parallel in Europe at the time. These were mitigating circumstances that help one to understand why the Austrian socialists were so hesitant in engaging in a head-on confrontation with antisemitism. But in the final analysis it is the Jewish origins of the socialist leadership that best explain the riddle of its ambivalent and convoluted stand on the Jewish Question.

Hillel J. Kieval

Nationalism and Antisemitism
The Czech-Jewish Response

Introduction

The seven decades from the Revolutions of 1848 to the end of
World War I brought major economic, political, and cultural changes
to the Czech lands of Bohemia, Moravia, and Upper Silesia. Bohemia
underwent large-scale industrialization during the 1850s and 1860s
and quickly became the economically most advanced region in the
Habsburg Monarchy after Vienna.[1] The constitutional reforms of the
early 1860s were accompanied by measures that allowed for administrative and cultural autonomy at the local level. At the end of the
decade Vienna provided for the separation of church and state in
public education and established a network of state-run primary and
secondary schools that were to be administered by local and provincial governments. Such developments bestowed on both the German
and the Czech national movements a favorable cultural and political
environment. The new school system, moreover, helped to win over
the very population pools on which nationalists would draw for
years to come: the educated children of wealthy peasants, teachers,
salaried professionals, and skilled artisans.[2]

At the same time the two national movements broke away from

I would like to dedicate this essay to Franklin L. Ford, on the occasion of his sixty-fifth
birthday.

1. On the economic modernization of Bohemia, see Jaroslav Purš, "The Industrial
Revolution in the Czech Lands," *Historica* 2 (1960): 183–272; Nachum Gross, "The In-
dustrial Revolution in the Habsburg Monarchy, 1800–1914," in *The Fontana Economic
History of Europe*, ed. Carlo Cipolla, vol. 4, pt. 1 (London, 1973), pp. 228–78; and John
Komlos, ed., *Economic Development in the Habsburg Monarchy in the Nineteenth Cen-
tury* (Boulder, Colo., 1983).

2. On the political liberalizations of the 1860s, see C. A. Macartney, *The Habsburg
Empire, 1790–1918* (New York, 1969), pp. 495–568; and Bruce M. Garver, *The Young*

the narrow control of landed, provincial elites and established themselves as mass movements. The Universal education and scientific training in the mother tongue (a hallmark of Habsburg multiethnic toleration) coincided with the drive for social mobility to produce a new political force aimed at securing occupational opportunity as well as cultural autonomy in the industrial, social order.[3] Party politics and parliamentary life provided the major vehicles for the articulation of national claims on the central government. The political parties, however, were forced to adapt to a series of electoral reforms and expansions of the franchise culminating in universal male suffrage in 1907.[4] Yet none of the transformations in Austrian and Bohemian life were sufficient to tear apart the fabric of the state. Only with the advent of the First World War and the defeat of the Central Powers did the monarchy collapse and make way for smaller states based on the principle of national self-determination.

Jewish-Gentile relations in Bohemia and in the capital city of Prague were molded to a certain extent by changes that were taking place in society at large. Factors such as the demographic revolution in the countryside and migration to industrial centers touched both Jews and non-Jews, though not always to the same degree or with the same results. Thus while the Jewish population of Bohemia rose by almost 26 percent over the second half of the nineteenth century, the general Bohemian population increased by slightly less than one-third.[5]

Meanwhile tens of thousands of rural Czechs poured into Prague between 1870 and 1900, pushing the population of the city from

Czech Party, 1874–1901, and the Emergence of a Multi-Party System (New Haven, 1978), pp. 29–59, 88–98. On educational reform and national education, see Jan Šafránek, *Školy české: Obraz jejich vývoje a osudů*, vol. 2 (Prague, 1918); Jaroslav Kopáč, *Dějiny české školy a pedagogiky v letech 1867–1914* (Brno, 1968); and Karel Adámek, *Z naší doby*, vol. 2 (Velké Meziříčí, 1887), pp. 1–153.

3. See, generally, the several works by Anthony D. Smith devoted to the theme of nationalism and social and cultural change: *Theories of Nationalism* (London, 1971); "Ethnocentrism, Nationalism, and Social Change," *International Journal of Comparative Sociology* 13 (1972): 1–20; and *The Ethnic Revival* (Cambridge, 1981).

4. Stanley B. Winters, "Kramář, Kaizl, and the Hegemony of the Young Czech Party," in *The Czech Renascence of the Nineteenth Century*, ed. Peter Brock and H. Gordon Skilling (Toronto, 1970), pp. 282–314; Garver, *Young Czech Party*, pp. 121–308 passim.

5. There were approximately 75,500 Jews living in Bohemia in 1850—representing 1.72 percent of the total population; in 1890 the number of Jews reached its peak of 94,500, but the ratio of Jews to the total population had fallen slightly, to 1.62 percent. Jan Heřman, "The Evolution of the Jewish Population in Bohemia and Moravia, 1754–1953," in *Papers in Jewish Demography, 1973*, ed. U. O. Schmelz, P. Glikson, and S. Della Pergola (Jerusalem, 1977), p. 259.

198,600 to more than 382,000. The Jews, however, underwent urban-ization at a faster pace than non-Jews. The mainly Czech-speaking Jews who settled in the capital during the same period overwhelmed the older German-Jewish strata and, for a few decades at least, ac-tually increased the ratio of Jews to non-Jews in the city. The Jewish population of Prague stood at 15,214 in 1869; by 1900 it exceeded 27,000, virtually the entire increase resulting from in-migration. In 1869 Jews constituted 6.3 percent of the population of Prague; they were 7.5 percent in 1880 and 7.9 percent in 1900.[6] Jewish population growth peaked in 1890. Thereafter the absolute number of Jews throughout the province declined. And even though a greater and greater percentage of Czech Jews chose over the decades to live in the capital city, this number could not keep up with the parallel movement of non-Jewish Czechs. By 1921, for example, 40 percent of all Bohemian Jews lived in Prague, but these 32,000 individuals con-stituted only 4.7 percent of the city's total population, which had grown to well over 675,000.[7]

Numerous other factors conditioned the Czech-Jewish relationship in the last half of the nineteenth century. The final removal of all restrictions on Jewish occupational choice, accomplished in 1859, and the concurrent occupational restructuring of the non-Jewish population led to competition between the two groups in the areas of educational opportunity and economic mobility, particularly in the provincial towns.[8] On the other hand, the Bohemian tradition of religious dissent and anti-Catholic sentiment and the rapid pace of secularization in the Czech lands helped to ensure that popular at-titudes toward Jews, if not necessarily friendly, were nonetheless a

6. Jan Havránek, "Demografický vývoj Prahy v druhé polovině 19. století," *Pražský sborník historický* (Prague, 1969–70), p. 73; Jan Heřman, "The Evolution of the Jewish Population in Prague, 1869–1939," in *Papers in Jewish Demography, 1977*, ed. U. O. Schmelz, P. Glikson, and S. Della Pergola (Jerusalem, 1980), pp. 53–67.

7. Heřman, "Evolution of the Jewish Population in Prague," p. 54. A more thorough discussion of the effects of demographic change on the Jews of Bohemia can be found in Hillel J. Kieval, *The Making of Czech Jewry: National Conflict and Jewish Society in Bohemia, 1870–1918* (New York, 1987), chap. 1.

8. On the gradual emancipation of Bohemian Jewry, see Wolfdieter Bihl, "Die Ju-den," in *Die Habsburgermonarchie, 1848–1918*, ed. Adam Wandruszka and Peter Urban-itsch, vol. 3 (Vienna, 1980), pp. 890–96; and Wolfgang Häusler, "Toleranz, Emanzipa-tion und Antisemitismus: Das Österreichische Judentum des bürgerlichen Zeitalters (1782–1918)," in *Das Österreichische Judentum* (Vienna, 1974), pp. 89–108. On the eco-nomic factors behind Jewish-Gentile conflict in the Czech lands, see Häusler, "Toler-anz, Emanzipation und Antisemitismus," pp. 103–22; and Christoph Stölzl, "Zur Ge-schichte der böhmischen Juden in der Epoche des modernen Nationalismus," pt. 2, *Bohemia* 15 (1974): 129–57.

great deal more tolerant than what was to be found in the Polish territories, Russia, and Rumania.

Of all of the ingredients that went in to constructing the Jewish-Gentile relationship in the Czech lands, however, one stands out as the overriding factor. This was the force of the Czech national movement after 1870 and, in particular, the pressures that it placed on the Jewish population. The struggle for power on the basis of national culture was not unique to the Czech lands, but it achieved—for a variety of reasons—a level of intensity and degree of pervasiveness not duplicated in other parts of the Habsburg Monarchy. The Czech-German national conflict affected all areas of social, cultural, and political life and transformed otherwise universal social processes into specifically Bohemian phenomena.[9]

The relentlessness with which the Czech national movement pursued its goal of self-rule inevitably would have affected the structure and content of Jewish life in the region. The Jews, however, were particularly vulnerable to nationalist conflict. The long process of emancipation—set in motion by the modernizing reforms of Joseph II in the 1780s but not realized on the political plane until 1867—had established an alliance between the Jews of the monarchy and German culture. The state-supervised system of Jewish primary education operated in the German language, even in the fully Czech-speaking countryside; communal institutions and private businesses were required to keep their records in German; Jewish names were Germanized; upwardly mobile Jewish children competed for places in elite German secondary schools and universities; and, indeed, the final surge toward the political integration of Jews into the monarchy occurred under the auspices of Austrian-German liberalism, the main beneficiary of the constitutional reforms of the 1860s.[10]

In Prague the German-Jewish alliance was more pronounced than

9. Jiří Kořalka, "Das Nationalitätenproblem in den böhmischen Ländern, 1848–1918," Österreichische Osthefte 5 (1963): 1–12; S. Harrison Thomson, "The Czechs as Integrating and Disintegrating Factors in the Habsburg Empire," Austrian History Yearbook 3, pt. 2 (1967): 203–22; and Jan Havránek, "The Development of Czech Nationalism," ibid., pp. 223–60.

10. Hillel J. Kieval, "Caution's Progress: The Modernization of Jewish Life in Prague, 1780–1830," in Toward Modernity: The European Jewish Model, ed. Jacob Katz (New Brunswick, N.J., 1986); Ruth Kestenberg-Gladstein, Neuere Geschichte der Juden in den böhmischen Ländern, pt. 1: Das Zeitalter der Aufklärung, 1780–1830 (Tübingen, 1969); Ludvík Singer, "Zur Geschichte der Toleranzpatente in den Sudetenländern," Jahrbuch der Gesellschaft für Geschichte der Juden in der Cechoslovakischen Republik 5 (1933): 231–311; and Christoph Stölzl, "Zur Geschichte der böhmischen Juden in der Epoche des modernen Nationalismus," pt. 1, Bohemia 14 (1973): 179–221.

elsewhere. As residence, occupational, and educational restrictions eased, Jews effectively integrated with urban, middle-class Germans, swelling the ranks of their schools and supporting their theaters and civic groups. At the end of the century Jews made up nearly half of the German-language community in the city. They clearly were vital to any enterprise that sought to promote and defend the interests of the ethnic German population in Prague and, as a result, experienced relatively little social discrimination on the part of Prague Germans. The antisemitism of the pan-Germans did not make inroads in the capital city until the 1890s.[11]

It was the Czech-Jewish masses that largely transformed the character of Jewish Prague at the end of the nineteenth century. Rural in origin, and as much at home in Czech as in German culture, they represented in many respects the Jewish counterpart to the Czech migration. The major difference was that the rural Jews had lived for nearly a century with the German institutions of the Josephine era. They certainly did not view these agencies with malevolence and for the most part were prepared to integrate into the German-Jewish strata of Prague.[12] Nevertheless the Czech-Jewish migration did bring in its wake a small, self-conscious movement dedicated to Czech-Jewish integration and acculturation. Middle-class professionals, shopkeepers, and literati—often recent arrivals to the city—created institutions in the 1870s, 1880s, and 1890s, such as the Spolek Českých Akademiků-židů (Association of Czech Academic Jews), the Or-Tomid Society for the reform of public worship and ritual, and the Národní Jednota Českožidovská (Czech-Jewish National Union), that aimed at reducing the level of German influence in Bohemian-Jewish life and effecting a Czech-Jewish political rapprochement.[13]

The original political allies of the Czech-Jewish movement, the Young Czech, or National Liberal, party, placed constant pressure on Czech Jews to wean their co-religionists away from German culture. Some, such as the journalist Josef Kořán, did so in sympathetic but

11. Gary B. Cohen, "Jews in German Society: Prague, 1860–1914," *Central European History* 10 (1977): 28–54. See also Cohen, *The Politics of Ethnic Survival: Germans in Prague, 1861–1914* (Princeton, 1981), passim.
12. This issue is discussed at greater length in Kieval, *Making of Czech Jewry*, chaps. 1, 2.
13. *Dějiny českožidovského hnutí* (Prague, 1932); Vlastimila Hamáčková, "Débuts du mouvement assimilateur tchéco-juif," *Judaica Bohemiae* 14 (1978): 15–23; Josef Vyskočil, "Die Tschechisch-Jüdische Bewegung," ibid., 3 (1967): 36–55.

direct appeals. Others, like the economist Karel Adámek, issued ominously threatening anti-Jewish diatribes, which accused Bohemian Jews of running a rearguard action in defense of Austrian-German supremacy.[14]

Easily the most sensitive subject in Jewish relations with Czech nationalists at this time was education. Liberal Czech nationalists correctly viewed universal education in their own language as a principal guarantor of ethnic Czech mobility and power. The schools not only were receptacles for the growing surplus of children born to Czech parents but also prepared the sons of migrating peasants and petty merchants for careers in industry, the bureaucracy, and the professions. It was important to Czech nationalists that the schools not serve an assimilatory or denationalizing function (as they once had) and that they not be used to create a "German presence" in regions which otherwise would have possessed no ethnic German element. From this perspective the network of Jewish primary schools that dotted the Czech countryside stood out as an anomaly. Tied to the Germanizing, centralist policies of enlightened absolutism, those schools perpetuated an unnatural German-Jewish alliance, prevented Jewish children from developing a proper Czech national sentiment, and enticed the hundreds of non-Jewish children also enrolled in them away from the Czech camp.[15]

In the minds of both Jewish and Gentile Czech nationalists, the schools had to go. The Czech-Jewish National Union embarked on a determined campaign during the last decade of the nineteenth century to close these vestiges of German-Jewish culture in the Czech countryside. Aided by the progress that Czech national sentiment had already made within the Bohemian-Jewish population and prodded by the radicalization of political life throughout Bohemia after 1896, the National Union achieved what it certainly viewed as

14. Josef Kořán's appeals appeared in the *Czech-Jewish Almanach* in 1886 and again a decade later. See Josef J. Kořán, "Židovské školy v Čechách," *Kalendář česko-židovský* 6 (1886–87): 97–102; and "Židovské školy v Čechách roku 1894–95," ibid., 16 (1896–97): 152–57. Karel Adámek sprinkled complaints and threats against the Jews of Bohemia throughout his four-volume opus on Czech political economy and culture, *Z naší doby* (Velké Meziříčí, 1886–90).

15. Adámek remarked in 1887: "The Jews in both Bohemia and Moravia are—alongside the bureaucracy—certainly the most powerful German factor in Slavic circles; and the Jewish confessional schools, like the [German] Schulverein schools, are a dangerous lever in the Germanization of Czech cities and communities." *Z naší doby*, 2:20. The problem of the German-Jewish schools and the Czech national movement is discussed in detail in Kieval, *Making of Czech Jewry*, chap. 2.

a stunning success. Of the 114 German-Jewish schools that existed in Bohemia in 1885, fewer than 30 remained in 1900. By 1910 the number had fallen to 5, and, for all intents and purposes, the traditional German-Jewish alliance in the Czech countryside was dead.[16]

The Radicalization of Czech Politics: The 1890s

The Czech nationalist politicians of the late nineteenth century were both products and promoters of the economic transformation of the Czech countryside. They fostered economic modernization as a vehicle of Czech cultural and political autonomy. And, as the growing provincial middle class ran into competition from older economic strata—represented largely by ethnic Germans and Jews—they employed nationalist ideology in an effort to overtake them. Thus Czech politicians launched an economic campaign in the early 1890s against Jewish merchants and shopkeepers that went by the passwords Svůj k Svému (each to his own). The Svůj k Svému program held that the nation had to protect its economic base, promote its own productive forces, and keep out foreign competition and exploitation. To many Czech nationalists, Jewish businesses—like the Jewish schools—represented Austrian-German intrusion into Czech affairs, not to mention German economic domination, and were thus not welcome. Many Jewish establishments were ruined as a result, particularly those that had operated in small towns and villages and were totally dependent on Czech patronage for their survival.[17]

The first half of the 1890s also produced generalized industrial unrest, popular violence, and mass demonstrations in favor of universal suffrage. Much hostility, born of social frustration and psychological insecurity, eventually deflected to Jews on account of their nationally ambiguous and hence controversial status. Accusations of ritual murder and ensuing riots against Jews erupted in a number of

16. The figures derive from Kořán, "Židovské školy v Čechách," Kalendář česko-židovský 6 (1886–87): 97–102; Die Juden in Österreich (Berlin, 1908), pp. 83, 84, 87; and Statistická příručka Království českého (Prague, 1913), p. 131.
17. Michael A. Riff, "Czech Antisemitism and the Jewish Response before 1914," Wiener Library Bulletin 29, no. 39–40 (1976): 8–9. See J. Svozil, "Několik slov o heslé Svůj k svému," Naše Doba 8 (1900–1901): 641–46, for a moderate Czech view on the use of economic boycott as a weapon in the national controversy; and Českožidovské listy, March 1, 1898, pp. 1–2, for a Czech-Jewish view.

small towns and villages.[18] The revival of the blood libel in post-industrial Bohemian society shielded people from the need to face certain realities, such as suicide among young, single, and often pregnant females. The rationalizations of some public officials in the wake of anti-Jewish accusations testify to similar distortions of painful facts. One Czech weekly reported that the Jews had brought the rioting on themselves through their economic behavior and their support of the German cause. A medical officer who examined the body of a dead servant girl discovered in Kolín actually concluded that the root of the problem lay in the maintenance of a German-Jewish primary school in that town.[19]

For all of the unpleasantness of the early 1890s, the last half decade of the century witnessed even greater social and political radicalization. Faced with a greatly expanded franchise in the 1897 Reichsrat elections, the Young Czech party organization in Prague nominated a vocal antisemite, Václav Březnovský, to run in the city's new fifth curia.[20] When the Jews of Prague swung their support to the Social Democratic candidate, who ultimately lost the election to Březnovský, segments of the nationalist press lashed out at them with vengeance. The National Liberals Karel Adámek and Jaroslava Procházková published works that denounced the Jews for their exploitative economic and political behavior.[21] The clerical Rudolf Vrba helped to popularize the views of the French antisemite Édouard Drumont with his scatological attacks in *Národní sebeochrana* (National Self-Protection). By the end of this long volume, Vrba had called for a great many curative measures. These included, among others, state control of the stock market and the banks; a ban on Jewish immigration and new Jewish settlement; removal of Jewish students from public schools; exclusion of Christian servant girls from Jewish households; institution of the death penalty for international white slavery; the banning of Jews from public office; the

18. Allegations of ritual murder and anti-Jewish disturbances occurred in the town of Mladá Boleslav in 1892 and in Kolín, Kutná Hora, and Kladno in 1893. Riff, "Czech Antisemitism," pp. 9–10.

19. Both incidents are reported in ibid., p. 10.

20. The franchise for the 1897 elections was expanded to include all males over age twenty-four in a new, fifth curia. Garver, *Young Czech Party*, pp. 231–37. On Václav Březnovský, see Christoph Stölzl, *Kafkas Böses Böhmen: Zur Sozialgeschichte eines Prager Juden* (Munich, 1975), pp. 61–62.

21. Karel Adámek, *Slovo o židech* (Chrudim, 1899); Jaroslava Procházková, *Český lid a český žid: Časové úvahy* (Prague, 1897).

restriction of Jewish doctors to Jewish patients and Jewish lawyers to Jewish clients; and a general review of the Talmud and the Shulhan Arukh.[22]

Jewish security in life and property, as well as the position of Jews in the Czech national movement, shifted dramatically during the last days of November 1897. Following the elections to the Reichsrat, the Austrian prime minister, Casimir Badeni, had issued a pair of language ordinances that sought to meet many of the demands of the Czech nationalists while ensuring that the Czech lands remained an integral part of the monarchy. The proposed legislation provoked much controversy among Austrian-Germans, however, mainly because of a provision that would have required that all civil servants in Bohemia and Moravia—after a short period of time—show proficiency in both German and Czech or face dismissal.[23]

German deputies in the Reichsrat resorted to filibuster and other obstructionist tactics in an effort to thwart the new legislation and bring down the Badeni government. Mass demonstrations and popular violence erupted in the streets of Vienna and Graz, as well as in the German towns of northern and western Bohemia, where the targets of unrest were not only Czech student groups but also Jews. At the end of November, Badeni resigned. This act set in motion a new series of violent demonstrations, this time in Prague and the Czech countryside.[24]

For three days following Badeni's resignation, the streets of Prague served as a battleground for rival armies of urban agitators. German university students taunted Czech crowds with boisterous renditions of patriotic songs, such as the "Wacht am Rhein," and open air marches to their civic center, the German Casino. Czech-speaking mobs marched in retaliation to the New German Theater and bombarded it with stones; violence broke out in residential neighborhoods; eventually the army had to be called up to restore order.[25]

22. Rudolf Vrba, *Národní sebeochrana: Úvahy o hmotném a mrávním úpadku národa českého* (Prague, 1898), esp. pp. 396–98. For a close examination of this volume and the works by Adámek and Procházková, see Kieval, *Making of Czech Jewry*, chap. 3.

23. Berthold Sutter, *Die Badenischen Sprachverordnungen von 1897: Ihre Genesis und ihre Auswirkungen vornehmlich auf die innerösterreichischen Alpenländer* (Graz, 1960–65), vol. 1; Winters, "Kramář, Kaizl, and the Young Czech Party," p. 304.

24. See Sutter, *Die Badenischen Sprachverordnungen*, vol. 2; and Riff, "Czech Antisemitism," pp. 11–12.

25. This description relies heavily on the discussion of the Prague disturbances in Kieval, *Making of Czech Jewry*, chap. 3. Its sources are Sutter, *Die Badenischen Sprachverordnungen*, 2:231–32; and Riff, "Czech Antisemitism," pp. 11–12.

More violence erupted the second day. Masses of people attacked German-owned stores, coffee houses, and private homes near the fashionable Příkopy (Graben) and Wenceslaus Square. The crowds destroyed every plate of glass on the New German Theater, attacked the German Schulverein school in the Královské Vinohrady district, and smashed the windows of synagogues in both there and in Žižkov. Vienna now increased the military presence in Prague from two to four battalions of sharpshooters and two battalions of infantrymen.[26]

After the third day of rioting the government declared a state of martial law, but not before the synagogue in Smíchov and many other private homes and institutions had succumbed to the popular fury. Miraculously, no one had been killed. Nevertheless the riots were traumatic for those active in the Czech-Jewish movement, to say nothing of the rest of the Bohemian-Jewish community. The carefully constructed plans and cherished hopes of countless Czech-speaking Jews lay strewn along the sidewalks of Prague and dozens of smaller communities together with the shards of glass and broken furniture from Jewish homes and shops.

The liberal Czech press did nothing to soften the blow of what became known as the December Storm. *Národní listy* (National Press), closely associated with Young Czech policies, reported that the Prague disturbances had been precipitated by German and Jewish provocations, that the coffee houses from which German students had taunted the Czech population were frequented mainly by Jews, and that "Semitic" faces could be seen outlining the doors of the cafés.[27] Among Jewish observers even the most charitable had to conclude that the Czech national establishment had abandoned the Jews in their hour of need. The less sanguine began to fear that something much worse was happening.

Czech Jews barely had a chance to recover from the shocks of 1897 when a new calamity struck. On April 1, 1899, in the eastern Bohemian town of Polná, a nineteen-year-old dressmaker named Anežka Hrůzová was found murdered in a quarter of the town inhabited by poor Jews. Leopold Hilsner, a Jewish vagabond of apparently unsa-

26. Riff, "Czech Antisemitism," p. 12; Sutter, *Die Badenischen Sprachverordnungen*, 2:231.
27. "Bouřlivý den v Praze," *Národní listy*, November 30, 1897; "Drůhý den po německé provokáci," ibid., December 1, 1897, both cited in Riff, "Czech Antisemitism," pp. 11–12.

vory character, was arrested and charged with the crime. The prosecutor, in determining the probable motive for the killing, emphasized the fact that the girl's body—which obviously had been stabbed or punctured—lay, as the indictment read, in "an insignificant pool of blood, no bigger than a hand."[28] He did not entertain the possibility that the small amount of blood found with the corpse indicated that the woman had been killed somewhere else and her body later moved.

During the ensuing trial both the Catholic and the liberal newspapers of Bohemia charged that Hilsner had killed a young Christian woman to use her blood for ritual purposes. And, as the body was discovered in early April, generally the season in which Passover falls, they presumed that the blood was used in the preparation of Passover *matzot*. To exacerbate matters, the opportunistic Young Czech politician Karel Baxa—who years later became mayor of Prague—volunteered to represent the dead girl's mother at the trial. He more than anyone contributed to the sensationalism of the proceedings, introducing the blood libel whenever possible. In his charge to the jury Baxa urged that the "motive" behind the murder be carefully considered. "The murderers [it was assumed that two other, unknown, assailants were involved] were not concerned simply with her life; everything depends on the method of the murder, which is still unknown to us." The perpetrators, he concluded, had "murdered a Christian person, an innocent girl, in order to obtain her blood."[29]

Although the court in Kutná Hora found Hilsner guilty of murder and sentenced him to hang, this was not to be the end of the matter. Hilsner found his Émile Zola in the person of Tomáš Masaryk, professor of philosophy at the Czech University in Prague and the leader of a breakaway progressivist faction within the Czech national movement known as the Realist party. Masaryk placed his career in jeopardy when he published and had circulated a pamphlet that ridiculed the blood libel and called for a new trial.[30] Indeed a new trial was ordered to take place in Písek in October 1900. But the same

28. Quoted in František Červinka, "The Hilsner Affair," *Leo Baeck Institute Year Book* 13 (1968): 145.
29. Quoted in ibid., p. 147.
30. Tomáš G. Masaryk, *Nutnost revidovati proces polenský* (Prague, 1899). On Masaryk's role in the defense of Hilsner against the blood libel, see Ernst Rychnovsky, "Im Kampf gegen den Ritualmordaberglauben," in *Masaryk und das Judentum*, ed. Ernst Rychnovsky (Prague, 1931), pp. 166–273.

personnel appeared to try the case, and no new evidence was introduced. Once again Hilsner received a guilty verdict, though this time
the emperor commuted his sentence to life imprisonment.[31]

Redefining the Czech-Jewish Relationship

Had the outpouring of popular antisemitism in 1897 and 1899
been confined to the fringes of respectability, leaders of the Czech-
Jewish movement would have greeted it with stoicism. They might
have agitated for a speedier implementation of school closings and a
more thorough bilingualism in the public life of the Jewish community, but they would not have doubted for a moment the correctness
of their overall cultural and political strategy. It was clear, however,
that *Národní listy* and part of the leadership of the Young Czech party
had colluded in the attacks against the Jews. This realization
stripped the Czech-Jewish movement of its confidence. How was it
to answer the charges of opponents that Czech liberalism had abandoned the Jews of the Czech lands? Indeed, what could the Czech-
Jewish National Union or the Association of Czech Academic Jews
offer their own members by way of consolation?

Given the depth of their commitment to Czech national culture,
most Czech-Jewish leaders showed remarkable independence and
courage in reacting to the crisis of the late-1890s. When the Svůj k
Svému operation achieved its full force under the direction of Národní Obrana (National Defense), leaders of the Czech-Jewish movement rose one by one to denounce it. Many admitted that they had
been prepared to weather the storm in the name of national economic development and full autonomy had the boycott been applied
strictly on an individual basis against German nationals or clear
supporters of the German national camp. But the tactic had been
applied indiscriminately to Jews as a whole, ruining the livelihood
of thousands in the process. Thus Czech Jews publicly withheld support for the economic program of the national movement.[32]

Eduard Lederer (1859–1941), the Prague- and Vienna-educated
lawyer who was to assume a leading position in the Czech-Jewish

31. Leopold Hilsner finally received a pardon in 1918. He died, a poor peddler who
went by the new name of Heller, in 1928. Červinka, "Hilsner Affair," p. 149.
32. Numerous articles appeared on this theme in the Czech-Jewish press between
1897 and 1900. In particular I would point to the lead article, "Svůj k svému," in *Českožidovské listy*, March 1, 1898, which appeared under the by-line "L."

movement after the turn of the century, began openly to question the basis of the Jewish–Young Czech alliance shortly after the elections of 1897.[33] The National Liberals, he acknowledged, spoke for the majority of the Czech nation, and, until recent weeks, Jews had found in them a natural ally. However, memories of Březnovský's nomination and election and the provocative behavior of *Národní listy* hovered over the heads of Czech Jews like a cloud. The "liberal" parties in the Czech lands were abandoning liberalism. Worse yet, they ignored or belittled the accomplishments of the Czech-Jewish movement. The Social Democrats, in Lederer's view, were not much better. They considered the nationalist activity of the Czech Jews to be antiquated and a barrier to modern development. Only the left wing of the liberal camp, made up of the Realists and the Progressives, offered some cause for optimism. The *Rozhledy* and *Samostatnost* circles may not have jumped and cheered for Czech Jews, but they did at least write respectfully about Lederer's movement and considered it a legitimate political force.[34]

In the immediate aftermath of the December Storm, Lederer lashed out at the Young Czechs, laying the blame for the violence in no uncertain terms at their feet.[35] Subsequently Maxim Reiner, leader of the Czech-Jewish Political Union, publicly denounced the Young Czech party for having flirted with Vienna's racial antisemitism in collusion with the Christian-Social movement. He expressed dismay that the mouthpiece of Czech liberalism, *Národní listy*, had gloated over the two convictions of Capt. Alfred Dreyfus in France and had accused Dreyfus's supporters of having perpetrated a Jewish cabal. In a revealing moment of self-criticism, Reiner admitted that the Czech-Jewish establishment had seriously underestimated the effects of radical groups such as Národní Obrana, whose agitation throughout Prague and the Czech countryside helped to make way for the December Storm. Yet the Czech political press was

---

33. Eduard Lederer, in "Lueger triumfans," *Českožidovské listy*, April 15, 1897, reported on a recent meeting in Prague of the supporters of the antisemitic mayor of Vienna, Karl Lueger. Lederer listed the names of several Czech political leaders who were in attendance, among them Březnovský, Father Šimon of the Christian-Social party, and Karel Baxa. See also Lederer, "Politické strany české a hnutí českožidovské," *Českožidovské listy*, September 15, 1897.

34. Lederer, "Politické strany české a hnutí českožidovské." *Samostatnost* (Independence) was a "radical progressive" journal founded by Antonín Hajn in 1897. *Rozhledy* (Perspectives) was edited by progressive, reformist intellectuals from 1892 to 1901.

35. Eduard Lederer, "Pražská tragedie židovská," *Českožidovské listy*, December 15, 1897.

no less myopic. A considerable portion of it had been content to pay lip service to the official program of the Young Czechs, which abjured antisemitism while it encouraged the actions of the antisemitic movement.[36]

Reiner's analysis of the political relations of the Czech-Jewish movement followed a pattern that was characteristic of the difficult time in which he was living. He began with a litany of charges and accusations against the Czech nationalist establishment but ended with the counterbalancing argument that invariably started with the word "nevertheless." Reiner proclaimed that his movement would hold fast to this long-standing position of working, as Czechs, for Czech national rights. But at the same time it would insist that Jews achieve full equality and freedom within Czech society.

> We wish to be equals among equals in both rights and duties. We shall gladly lend our strength to the service of the nation. We want to fulfill this obligation and shall do so, conscientiously and resolutely as in the past. On the other hand we do demand that we and our actions—our persons and our deeds—be judged according to truth and justice, not with vision clouded by hatred.[37]

In the aftermath of the shock of 1897, the major Czech-Jewish organizations determined not to be taken by surprise should another outburst of anti-Jewish agitation occur. Thus when the Hilsner murder trial began in 1899, they were prepared to respond with a coordinated publicity campaign of their own. The Czech-Jewish National Union published and distributed more than seven thousand copies of a Czech translation of the Berlin theologian Hermann Strack's pamphlet, *Against the Ritual Murder Superstition*. The National Union attached to Strack's work excerpts from Anatole Leroy-Beaulieu's *Israel among the Nations* as well as a communication from Masaryk that had appeared in the *Neue Freie Presse* of Vienna.[38] The industrialist Bohumil Bondy, the Pardubice physician Viktor Vohryzek (1864–1918), and others distributed pamphlets of their own and occasionally placed articles in Czech newspapers, such as *Hlas národa* (Voice of the Nation), the organ of the Old Czech party. The

---

36. Maxim Reiner, "O nynějších poměrech hnutí českožidovského," speech delivered to the general meeting of the Czech-Jewish Political Union, June 10, 1899, published in *Českožidovské listy*, June 15, 1899.

37. Ibid., p. 4.

38. See "Národní jednota českožidovská," *Kalendář česko-židovský* 21 (1901–02): 146. Anatole Leroy-Beaulieu, a Catholic, defended the Jews against antisemitism during the Dreyfus Affair.

movement also received help from the Faculty of Medicine at the Czech University, which publicly debunked the supposedly "scientific" bases of the ritual murder allegations.[39]

But most impressive in the eyes of the Czech-Jewish masses—as well as their leaders—was the powerful stance that Masaryk himself had taken. His petition for a new trial had so outraged nationalist students at the university that they physically prevented him from lecturing and forced him to take a temporary leave of absence from teaching. The Czech-Jewish National Union singled Masaryk out for having displayed "manly courage." "Professor Masaryk ... stepped into the confusion of battle for truth and justice, unafraid of the abuse that he had to suffer. For that he has our fervent, genuine thanks."[40]

That their movement was facing an important crossroad was clear to all the participants in Czech-Jewish politics on the eve of the new century. The younger generation of Czech-Jewish intellectuals, represented by Eduard Lederer and Viktor Vohryzek, realized that the marriage to the Czech National Liberals had soured irretrievably. But they were reluctant to sue for formal divorce. Instead the preferred tactic during the initial regrouping of the Czech-Jewish movement was to cajole and admonish. Lederer caused a small furor in 1898 when he published an exposé in the pages of *Českožidovské listy* (Czech-Jewish Press) on the Jews and Social Democracy. Still, he did not go so far as to advocate a formal split with the Young Czechs. He was content up to this point to urge Czech Jews to question political orthodoxies and show greater sympathy for the just causes of the Czech working class.[41]

It was only in 1900, when Viktor Vohryzek used the pages of *Českožidovské listy* to publish a long and influential piece entitled "Epištoly k českým židům" (Letters to Czech Jews), that a new foundation was laid for the Czech-Jewish relationship. Vohryzek departed radically from the position of most Czech-Jewish leaders of his day when he argued that, ultimately, the causes of Jewish suffering and persecution in all countries lay not in some misdirected historical

---

39. "Národní jednota českožidovská," p. 146.
40. Quoted in ibid., pp. 146–47. See also the general discussion in Červinka, "Hilsner Affair."
41. Lederer, "Židé a sociální demokracie," *Českožidovské listy*, June 15, 1898, pp. 2–4. The paper's editors, aware of the volatile nature of the piece, placed the word "uvažuje" (contemplates) in front of the author's name rather than the usual "napsal" (written by).

evolution, poorly conceived government policies, or the stubborn refusal of Jews to assimilate. The basic factors lay in human nature itself. Antisemitism was in the end a psychological and a moral problem. Like other forms of hatred and intolerance, it arose from atavistic instincts in man, from some inborn defiance of his other, humanistic, nature.

> Just as the child, who has hardly learned to move about, breaks and destroys everything that comes into his hands; just as the hunter chases down and destroys game, not out of need, but for amusement based on destructive instincts; so, too, does the person who possesses power destroy those who are weak—as a pastime, for his own whim and amusement.[42]

Hatred, no less than love, was a basic human instinct.

By arguing that the chief causes of antisemitism lay within human nature and did not derive from any particular behavior on the part of Jews, Vohryzek conveyed two key messages to his readers. The first was that neither recent history nor patterns of cultural allegiance—whether alone or in tandem—could account for the manifestation of anti-Jewish behavior. The Jews of Bohemia and Moravia had done nothing to warrant or "deserve" the violence that had been directed at them, a notion that many Czechs, Jews included, had been willing to entertain. The second message, perhaps more important, was that antisemitism ultimately was a Czech and not a Jewish problem. It reflected a moral defect in the character of the Czech people, one that was being exploited by nationalist politicians for selfish and shortsighted purposes. In the last analysis, the Czech soul, not the Jewish soul, suffered from antisemitism's poison.[43]

By way of conclusion, Vohryzek advised Czech Jewry to do two things. First, it ought to wait out the decline of the National Liberal party.

> If the Czech nation were once again to return to Hussite liberalism, I would not hesitate to proclaim that we would soon succeed in reaching that point in which all Czech Jews would be in the Czech camp as loyal sons; but it would have to be sincere liberalism, not the comical pre-elections kind in which Jews cannot and do not believe.

No one expected a return to the ideals of the Czech past to be accomplished soon. In the meantime Jews were to prepare an "antidote" to

42. Viktor Vohryzek, "Epištoly k českým židům," *Českožidovské listy*, March 15, 1900, reprinted in Vohryzek, *K židovské otázce: Vybrané úvahy a články* (Prague, 1923), pp. 15–16.
43. Ibid., pp. 26–31, 35.

the poison that had infected the Czech nation. "Our antidote is the strengthening of all progressive influences . . . the battle against hypernationalism and clericalism. The antidote is the struggle against the dark."[44]

Vohryzek called upon Czech Jews to learn how to defend themselves—to straighten their backs, as he put it—and not to "fall down in the dust before every journalistic bandit." They had to act with dignity and pride in order that basic human consideration dictate the conduct of others toward them. This is not to say that there was not a great deal wrong with the nature of Jewish cultural and economic life in the Czech lands. Vohryzek felt that it was just as incumbent upon Jews to examine their faults as to defend their rights. Jews still pursued dangerous and unsavory economic occupations such as moneylending and the production and distribution of liquor. Jewish life required a thorough, ongoing reform—a renewal, based on the spiritual purposefulness, the social ethics, and progressive outlook of the prophets of the Old Testament. But the issue of internal reform and redirection, Vohrysek warned, was for Jews to face on their own. Society at large was in no position to pass judgment.[45]

A formal opposition within the Czech-Jewish movement crystallized around Lederer, Vohryzek, and Bohdan Klineberger (1859–1928) between the years 1900 and 1904.[46] The Czech-Jewish youth organization in Pardubice, where Vohryzek lived and worked, provided the institutional setting. In 1903 this group changed its name from Veselost (Mirth) to the more sober sounding Rozvoj (Development) and began to address what it considered the pressing cultural, religious, and economic matters of the day. Rozvoj set for itself three main objectives: to deepen the sense of Czech national identity among the Jews, to reorient and modernize Czech Jewry socially and economically, and lastly to transform Judaism itself, to teach Jews the difference, as the group put it, between religion and piety.[47]

Rozvoj inaugurated an educational program for adults that featured lectures on science, economics, business, and contemporary Jewish issues by some of its own members as well as distinguished speakers from Prague and the countryside. In April 1904 the Pardu-

44. Ibid., pp. 33–34.
45. Ibid., p. 34.
46. *Dějiny českožidovského hnutí*, pp. 9–11. See also Kieval, *Making of Czech Jewry*, chap. 3.
47. "Zpráva o činnosti spolku 'Rozvoj,'" *Kalendář česko-židovský* 25 (1905–06): 178–79.

bice organization oversaw the first meeting of Pokrokové Židovstvo (Progressive Jewry), which, it hoped, would serve as the nucleus for the Czech-Jewish movement of the future.[48]

Vohryzek, the main intellectual inspiration of Rozvoj, was also the driving force behind a new and independent newspaper of the same name. Between 1904 and 1907 he financed, edited, and did much of the writing for the progressive and antiestablishment fortnightly. By 1907 Rozvoj had replaced Českožidovské listy as the paper of choice among Czech-national Jews. Českožidovské listy ceased publication; Rozvoj changed to a weekly format, moved its editorial offices to Prague, and went on to publish the single most influential journal of Czech-Jewish opinion down to the Nazi occupation.[49] When Vohryzek established the Svaz Českých Pokrokových Židů (Association of Progressive Czech Jews), the Rozvoj "Putsch" of 1907 was complete. Designed to serve as an alternative to the Czech-Jewish Political Union, which coordinated Jewish support for the Young Czech party, Vohryzek's progressive association consisted primarily of Jewish supporters of Masaryk's Realist party and encouraged Czech Jews to support socially "progressive" political causes.[50]

Rozvoj invited Czech-Jewish intellectuals to redefine the goals of the assimilationist movement, to address issues that the older Czech-Jewish movement—in its haste to achieve specific social and political objectives—had failed to resolve. Masaryk, for example, had long challenged Czech Jews to define precisely what type of assimilation they envisaged. How far was the merger of Czech and Jewish culture to go? The editors of Rozvoj felt it was time that a concrete response be forthcoming, one that took into account such questions as the future of Judaism itself as well as the ethical basis of the Czech-Jewish relationship.[51]

From the start Rozvoj marked a departure from the staid and cau-

---

48. Ibid., pp. 177–81.
49. Oskar Donath, Židé a židovství v české literatuře 19. and 20. století, vol. 2 (Brno, 1930), pp. 186–94. The first number of the Prague-based Rozvoj was issued on July 5, 1907.
50. Dějiny českožidovského hnutí, pp. 10–11.
51. See Vohryzek's inaugural column in Rozvoj, "Několik slov úvodem," reprinted in Vohryzek, K židovské otázce, pp. 41–47. Vohryzek's overriding fear was that, with the loss of purpose and direction, the Czech-Jewish movement would eventually lose whatever influence it once had on Bohemian Jewry. "Our intellectual fund has not sufficed," he complained, "has not been equal to the difficulties of our tasks. If our defense is to be successful, it will be necessary to advance further toward the revision of our program." Ibid., p. 42.

tious journalism of the recent past. It was introspective but persistently eschewed apologetics, positivist in tone yet highly sensitive to religion and ethics. *Rozvoj* offered no excuses for the relative lateness of the emergence of a self-consciously Czech-Jewish movement. Nor did it provide comfort to Czech nationalists who continued to mistrust it. Vohryzek reminded his readers that the task of de-Germanizing the Jewish population of Bohemia had been enormous. Have no illusions on this score was the oft-repeated, if implicit, message. Bohemian Jewry had been a thoroughly Germanized population; even the Yiddish that Jews spoke was a version of German. And yet, whatever obstacles the structural conditions of Jewish life had placed before the Czech-Jewish movement, the Czech people themselves had exacerbated. Their finest literary figures had rejected Jewish overtures in the 1840s, and their urban masses had rioted against the Jews in 1848, forcing many to flee. The collective Jewish psyche found it difficult to forget such outbursts of hostility.[52]

An interesting by-product of the *Rozvoj* circle's rejection of Czech liberalism and simultaneous discovery of Masaryk was the priority that it now gave to questions of religion and ethics. Vohryzek, in his inaugural column in *Rozvoj*, went so far as to suggest that the failure to investigate the religious underpinnings of modern culture had been the greatest mistake of the Czech-Jewish movement to date.[53] Czech Jews, he argued, had overestimated the power of secular, liberal nationalism to effect a successful integration of Jews into Czech society. In addition they had seriously underestimated the residual strength of traditional antisemitic attitudes within the overall Czech population. Nationalism devoid of a religious foundation operated outside the bounds of morality and ethical purpose, for it was religion that both transmitted and made manifest the ethical component in culture; religion defined the ultimate ideals of national activity.[54]

The Czech-national Jews of 1904 found much inspiration in Masa-

---

52. Ibid., pp. 43–44.

53. Ibid., p. 43. This discussion is based in part on my article, "In the Image of Hus: Refashioning Czech Judaism in Post-Emancipatory Prague," *Modern Judaism* 5 (1985): 141–57.

54. Vohryzek wrote in "K myšlenkové krisi našich dnů": "What we long for is not the philosophical transformation of religion, but the religious transformation of philosophy; we do not want religion to become popular philosophy, but rather philosophy [i.e., moral philosophy] to be our faith." *Rozvoj*, 1904, reprinted in Vohryzek, *K židovské otázce*, p. 106.

ryk's oft-expressed call for a return to the spiritual values of the Czech Reformation.[55] Lederer's *Žid v dnešní společnosti* (The Jew in Contemporary Society) had argued along similar lines: all of society required a radical redirection; the principle of nationality had to be tempered by that of social justice, as expressed in the Gospels.[56] Both the *Rozvoj* and the Masaryk circles, in fact, wrote of the need for national renewal based on moral regeneration. Thus Masaryk urged in 1910: "The leaders of our reformation have but one message for us all, repeated and reechoed over our land: regenerate, reform the individual, regenerate, reform the whole people."[57]

When *Rozvoj* dedicated many of its early numbers to discussion of the moral transformation of Czech society, it did so not only out of devotion to Masaryk but also because of its conviction that Jews had a special contribution to make in this area. Czech Jews, Vohryzek argued, were in a position to draw upon the resources of rabbinic and biblical Judaism to aid in the creation of a new religious and philosophical consensus, which was to "unite us in a single cultural whole."[58]

Pessimism concerning the present state of Czech-Jewish relations was combined in the writings of Lederer and Vohryzek with hope for a future reconciliation. The Czech-Jewish relationship could still be salvaged; with renewed effort from both sides, a future based on autonomy and freedom, cultural symbiosis and ethical perfection, could still be reached. "The Czech nation may have spurned us for the moment," Vohryzek mused, "but it needs us urgently; and the day will come when it will acknowledge that."[59] In the closing pages of *Žid v dnešní společnosti*, Lederer was possessed of a similar vision. The Czech-Jewish experiment could be saved, he asserted, if it were mounted on a new ethical foundation, modeled on the teachings of Hillel, Jeremiah, and Jesus of Nazareth.

55. See Tomáš Masaryk, *Česká otázka: Snahy a tužby národního obrození* (Prague, 1895); and *Naše nynější krise* (Prague, 1895). Perhaps the clearest statement of Masaryk's views on Jan Hus, the Czech Reformation, and contemporary Czech nationalism can be found in a speech that he delivered several years later, in 1910, "Master Jan Hus and the Czech Reformation." It has been reprinted as "Jan Hus and the Czech Reformation" in T. G. Masaryk, *The Meaning of Czech History*, trans. Peter Kussi (Chapel Hill, N.C., 1974), pp. 3–14.

56. Eduard Lederer, *Žid v dnešní společnosti* (Prague, 1902), p. 152.

57. Masaryk, "Hus and the Czech Reformation," p. 14.

58. Vohryzek, "Národohospodářské úvahy," *Rozvoj*, 1904, reprinted in Vohryzek, *K židovské otázce*, p. 127.

59. Vohryzek, "Několik slov úvodem," p. 46.

The demagoguery of our day, countenanced from above and below, eventually will peter out. It is a fever which does not consume society, an illness, out of which the people will emerge healthier than before. . . . A wave will once again roll, which will lead society out of the depths of today's decay to a level of higher consciousness [*nazírání*]. Likewise, antisemitism—one of the manifestations of this demagogic fever—will pass simultaneously with it; and of its effects only a few fires on the field of culture will remain, nothing more.[60]

Long-Term Implications

There is little doubt that the tremors of the late 1890s placed a psychological strain on the Czech-Jewish relationship. The specter of popular violence countenanced by political opportunism menaced the collective consciousness of the Jewish population. Even so, popular violence rarely materialized, and when it did occur, as in the late fall of 1918, it was in the context of anti-German, anti-Austrian agitation.[61]

Did the tensions and antagonisms of the turn of the century discourage Czech-Jewish acculturation and social integration? On one level, yes. An undetermined number of Czech-Jewish intellectuals defected from the movement and cultivated a Jewish national identity.[62] In fact Zionism was most active in Bohemia in the 1890s in the largely Czech-speaking cities and towns. It began as a protest movement of merchants and small shopkeepers, threatened by the economic antisemitism of Czech nationalists. Only later did the largely German-speaking university students of Prague join the ranks of the

60. Lederer, *Žid v dnešní společnosti*, p. 111.

61. On the antisemitic riots in Prague during the formative weeks of the new Republic, see Christoph Stölzl, "Die 'Burg' und die Juden," in *Die "Burg": Einflussreiche politische Kräfte um Masaryk und Benes*, ed. Karl Bosl, vol. 2 (Munich, 1974), pp. 79–110.

62. Alfred Loewy, one of the founders and the first president of Bar Kochba, the Prague student Zionist organization, grew up in Domažlice in Western Bohemia. He had attended a Czech *Gymnasium* and was graduated from the Czech Medical Faculty in Prague. It was Loewy, Samo Grün (son of the Prague rabbi, Nathan Grün), and a handful of Czech-speaking university students in Prague who helped to transform the Verein der jüdischen Hochschüler into an explicitly nationalist organization. Another important defector from the Czech-Jewish movement was Ludvík Singer (1876–1931), a native of Kolín and graduate of the Law Faculty of the Czech University in Prague. Singer joined the Zionist movement in 1907 and from 1910 served as chairman of the Zionist District Committee of Bohemia. He cofounded the Jewish National Council in October 1918 and headed the Jewish party in the Czechoslovak Republic. On the "Czech" origins of Prague Zionism, see Ruth Kestenberg-Gladstein, "Athalot Bar Kochba," in *Prag vi-Yerushalayim: Sefer le-zekher Leo Herrmann* (Jerusalem, 1954), pp. 86–110; Arthur Bergman, "Zikhronot mi-tekufat Bar Kochba," in ibid., pp. 111–19; and Kieval, *Making of Czech Jewry*, chap. 4.

Zionists and eventually move into the intellectual elite of the world-wide movement.[63]

If the fortunes of Jewish nationalism were enhanced by the intolerance of Czech Gentiles, the same cannot be said for German national culture. In part this was because radical German politics in Austria, particularly in the Bohemian provinces, harbored even stronger anti-Jewish attitudes than its Czech counterpart.[64] But more important is the fact that the Jewish population of Bohemia had been involved in a process of secondary acculturation—adapting to the linguistic, cultural, and social realities of an industrialized, Czech-dominated setting—long before the anti-Jewish wave set in. In this context the psychological strain of Czech-Jewish conflict had the effect of speeding up the process, of completing the de-Germanization of Bohemian Jewry ahead of schedule.

Evidence for the increase in the pace of secondary acculturation can be found, for example, in the school-closing statistics. The steepest decline in the number of German-Jewish schools occurred between 1895 and 1900, when sixty-two schools were closed, nearly 70 percent of the total.[65] Similarly, the 1900 state census recorded an apparent about-face in the linguistic loyalties of Bohemian Jewry. For the first time the majority of Jews in Bohemia (55 percent) indicated Czech as their daily language.[66] Some Jews would return to listing German as their principal language in 1910, after political tempers had cooled. But neither the German language nor German nationality would ever again regain its premier position among Bohemian-Jewish loyalties. One could conclude, then, that the rate of Czech-Jewish acculturation shot up in the short term, thereafter becoming more gradual. It never leveled off.

---

63. Two rural Czech Jews, Filip Lebenhart and Karl Rezek, founded the first overtly Zionist organization in Bohemia, the Jüdischer Volksverein "Zion," in 1899. Comprised primarily of small merchants, office workers, and shopkeepers, the organization enjoyed immediate popularity among provincial Jewry. In 1900 it set in motion the first Jewish response to the Svůj k Svému campaign: a popular savings bank, which dispensed emergency funds to merchants who were in danger of financial collapse. See Kieval, *Making of Czech Jewry*, chap. 4.

64. On German antisemitism in Austria, see Peter G. J. Pulzer, *The Rise of Political Anti-Semitism in Germany and Austria* (New York, 1964), pp. 127–88; and Andrew G. Whiteside, *Austrian National Socialism before 1918* (The Hague, 1962), pp. 51–87.

65. J. J. Kořán, "Židovské školy v Čechách roku 1894–95," *Kalendář česko-židovský* 16 (1896–97): 152–57; *Die Juden in Österreich*, pp. 83, 84, 87.

66. *Die Juden in Österreich*, p. 109; Gary B. Cohen, "Ethnicity and Urban Population Growth: The Decline of the Prague Germans, 1880–1918," in *Studies in East European Social History*, ed. Keith Hitchins,vol. 2 (Leiden, 1981), p. 14.

Turn-of-the-century antisemitism also produced long-term political implications for Czech Jews. To begin with, it forced the builders of the Czech-Jewish alliance to give up their plans of barely a quarter of a century and literally to chart a new course. This time around they could not be content merely to find a willing host to Jewish aspirations. They had to demand sympathy and understanding in return. Indeed the Czech-Jewish intellectuals around the *Rozvoj* circle expected that their future partners in the national cause would submit—as they themselves had—to a spiritual revolution on the personal plane and a strict test of ends and means on the political. Purity of motive and the justifiability of action were the new watchwords.

By becoming more selective and demanding in its political relationships, the Czech-Jewish movement severely reduced the field of potential allies. This fact was to be of enormous consequence in the decades to come. Rightly or wrongly, the only groups with which Czech-national Jews could comfortably work after 1897 were the Realists and the Czech Social Democrats. The former were always a small, relatively insignificant party, suspect in the eyes of the general population because of their intellectualism. The Social Democrats, on the other hand, had not supported the radical, State Right program of the Young Czechs and the National Socialists and toiled under the unwanted label of national capitulators.[67]

For two brief decades the political gamble of the Czech-national Jews paid off royally. Masaryk, living in exile in the United States, found himself in the perfect position to direct the postwar fortunes of the future Czechoslovak state. Both the Czech- and the German-speaking Jews of Bohemia and Moravia lined up eagerly behind him in October 1918. The Jews may have been the only ethnic group in interwar Czechoslovakia to accept the new political order wholeheartedly.[68]

At the end of the Second World War, Jews who had been active in socialist and communist politics, together with their non-Jewish comrades, willingly accepted the opportunity to govern. These were the heirs of the Jewish-socialist alliance of the turn of the century.

67. Hans Mommsen, *Die Sozialdemokratie und die Nationalitätenfrage im habsburgischen Vielvölkerstaat* (Vienna, 1963); Ruth Roebke-Behrens, "The Austrian Social Democratic Party, Nationalism, and the Nationality Crisis of the Habsburg Empire, 1897–1914," *Canadian Review of Studies in Nationalism* 8 (1981): 343–63.

68. Stölzl, "Die 'Burg' und die Juden," passim.

Even after the Communist party coup of 1948, a number of Jews remained in positions of power. Only with the Slánský trials of the 1950s did active Jewish participation in Czechoslovak politics come to an end.[69] It was at this point also that the Czech-Jewish experiment had run its course.

69. Rudolf Slánský (1901–52) had been secretary general of the Czechoslovak Communist party. Of the fourteen leading party members who were put on trial in the early 1950s for conspiracy against the state, eleven were Jews. Eight, including Slánský, were executed; three were sentenced to life imprisonment.

David Vital

Nationalism, Political Action, and the Hostile Environment

A large part of the history of the Jews is the history of the effects
upon them of the hostile environment in which it has been their lot
to live—an environment, be it said, which they had long tended to
take as a matter of course and the origins and deeper causes of which
they did not much question. They were very far from being "God's
pampered people," as John Dryden called them; nor were they quite
the "headstrong, moody, murmuring race" he thought them to be. Or
rather, if matters are now different, if Dryden's description fits them
a little better, why that is one of the surer pointers to the great transformation of Jewry that has occurred in our own times.

It will be said, rightly, that not all of the Jewish past was an unhappy product of external pressures, perhaps (but that is clearly a
subject for separate analysis and debate) not even the greater part.
Yet it can hardly be denied that through the life of the Jews there
has run a continuous thread of crippling and ultimately catastrophic
hostility. What their history might have been and how their culture
and religion might have developed had they been free to evolve socially in unconstrained circumstances we do not and cannot know.
Nor can we assess the degree to which exogenous influences were
consequences, however indirect or remote, of essentially endogenous
developments. We can only compare greater and less constraints,
greater or less hostility, more or less freedom, at different times and
in different places. And we can add the thought that at its points of
departure and change the history of the Jews, like that of other
peoples, was always subject to, as one might say, both "pull" and
"push." There was response to pressure, chiefly hostile pressure:

push. There was action, movement, change, rethinking that were functions of some sort of attraction to, and a striving after, alternative modes and models and goals: *pull.* And clearly there is little in their history in its life-enhancing, as opposed to purely catastrophic, aspects, particularly in their modern history, that can be explained except in terms of the *combined* effects of push and pull. For typically, push alone led to assimilation, apostasy, a falling apart, entropy; whereas it is precisely one of the distinguishing features of the modern national tendency in Jewry—even in its early and very tentative forms—that to the hostile push there was added a crucial pull to a positive, attractive, if still very imperfectly conceived alternative condition. But that said, it must be stressed that what, in due course, made of this tendency a force—a force for actual change in Jewry—was an additional ingredient: political action. And it was the establishment of institutions through which the nationalist tendency would be articulated and action channeled and brought to bear on specific targets that consolidated this force in Jewish public life.

I

Even a cursory examination of the *nation* as a social and political structure and of *nationalism* as a social and political dynamic suggests that these are rarely, if at all, entirely natural (as opposed to invented and artificial) phenomena. In an important sense and to an important degree they are, in a word, man-made, at least partly products of design—such that if they are to occur, and *a fortiori* if they are to succeed, there must be more or less deliberate encouragement and nurturing by interested parties. The rise and fall of nations and the waxing and waning of nationalist tendencies, moods, and movements, far from being part of some primordial human order on a par with the family or clan or tribe, are likely to be at least part-products of special and explicit thought, purposeful social action, and organized, institutional arrangements.

It is evident, and the literature on the subject is more than abundant, that such key and familiar national indicators as language, culture, compact settlement, common history (true, or mythic, or invented, but at all events accepted) neither suffice to make a nation (in the sense of it being a going social and political concern) nor need all be present and at full strength at one's creation. A great deal has been written in recent years of "nation building," much of it fanciful. But as the American experience illustrates famously and the experience of some of the new Middle Eastern and Southeast Asian states seems at least tentatively to suggest, statehood—which must, of course, be man-made and by design—may both precede the nation in time and be the central engine of its rise and development. Even where the group in question does possess the features that we tend to associate with the "nation," and all the more so where it does not—or does not possess them at full strength, or possesses other countervailing characteristics—political will, leadership, organization, and action are all indispensable to the transition from the potential to the actual, to its entry with full force into the arena of history.

It is thus well in accord with the general pattern that the distinctive, and in many ways crucial, component of modern Jewish nationalism has been the *political*. Insignificant, virtually invisible, in the early period of the modern era (say, the first decades of the nineteenth century), it took on ever more formidable proportions as the modern national tendency gathered force. So much so, indeed, was this the case that it is not too much to argue that modern Jewish nationalism at its most powerful, most characteristic, and most important as regards its role in Jewish society and its cumulative impact on the history of the Jews, was and is political before all else. Equally, it is by the assimilation of political categories into its thinking and the adoption of political modes in its action—and all for the attainment of explicitly political purposes—that modern Jewish nationalism has been rendered unmistakably *modern* and a fresh stage in Jewish history for which no precedents or analogues can be discerned, at any rate since the onset of the Exile, was ushered in.

The terms "political" and "national" are, of course, notoriously loose. But it is plain that in the present context, namely that of Jewish public life, they point to a distinction that may properly be drawn between two modes of public action: on the one hand, the old style intercessionary activity of self-appointed notables on behalf of their own communities or on behalf of its individual members and, on the other hand, a new style of action by supracommunal groups on behalf of particular communities or of some publicly proclaimed, supracommunal (and therefore, by still clearer implication, *national*) interest. In the former case, associated classicly with the eighteenth-century *Hofjuden*, the interest or cause would tend to be specific and limited in scope and relevance. In the latter case—and here it is the Alliance Israélite Universelle, the Anglo-Jewish Association, the Hilfsverein, and the Vienna Allianz that come immediately to mind—scope and relevance would necessarily be wider by reason of the mode of action adopted, but still more in consequence of the supracommunal function assumed by the activists concerned. For such a function would entail the understanding that action by Jews for Jews was legitimate regardless of the formal, legally defined nationality of those involved. This was (and remains) a hugely complicated question; and it arose unfailingly to trouble the minds of the activists and feed the attacks of those who opposed them. In what way, for example, if any at all, should such cross-national action be limited? Were there causes that might not properly be adopted and promoted, or circumstances (as in wartime) in which otherwise legitimate causes might not, in practice, be pursued? What means, methods, and resources might properly and usefully be mobilized in such supracommunal interests?

Such issues as these, together with questions and dilemmas specific to time and place, arose ineluctably with the shift from mere intercession (*shtadlanut*) to something very much like, if not actually amounting to, political action; and the sharper the shift, the sharper the issues. For it confronted the Jews, in ways that they had not known for centuries, with the twin issues of authority and power. Who was to speak for them? What was he to say? How far might he bind them as he treated with other forces in the political arena? Plainly, these were questions to which an entirely invertebrate Jewry was incapable of providing clear answers; nor did it really have to. It was the slow grafting of political structures on the body of Jewry that rendered them urgent.

But note, too, that the immediate *cause* in the interests of which this early political-national action was taken was wholly protective and defensive. It was the hostile environment that had created the need for action, that impelled the actors to seek to meet it, that justified it in their own eyes and in the eyes of others. Equally, if more subtly, it was the hostile environment that to a very great extent dictated those actors' *modus operandi*. All this can be seen very clearly in that still-embryonic form of political action in the Jewish interest: the early ventures in "Jewish diplomacy."

II

"Jewish diplomacy" is a tricky and in some ways misleading term if only because it may be taken to suggest organization and system where in fact there were none or very little. But it has been favored by some students of the subject and has the advantage of drawing attention to what it chiefly and correctly denotes, namely action by groups and individuals whose base is in one country directed at the authorities in another, but, at the same time, subject to two provisos. One is that the object of the action be one of genuine public, not private, importance and that it concern the status, welfare, or safety of Jews defined as such. The second is that those undertaking the action be able and willing to bring some form of pressure or influence to bear on the foreign government in question and that it is this pressure which is at the basis of whatever change of policy or conduct ultimately ensues. It is thus that the action is rendered political in fact even where the spirit and intention behind it may still be essentially benevolent and philanthropic. Of course in practice, the line distinguishing such political or "diplomatic" action from the ancient forms of philanthropic intercession was rarely clear-cut. In some cases it may be seen to have dissolved. In others, on the other hand, the will and ability to exert pressure—to induce one government to act against another, to mobilize economic resources for use as either carrot or stick, to rouse public opinion—these were unprecedented in their frank and overt character and the confidence displayed by those who sought to bring such classic instruments of public policy to bear. Compare Gerson Bleichröder seeking—with maximum discretion—to make the best use of his connection with Otto von Bismarck with the Rothschilds refusing publicly to help float loans to imperial Russia. Note, too, that the purpose of the effort tended increasingly to be broader than a mere remedy for the specific case of persecution or injustice which (as commonly happened) had been its precipitant. With time, as often as not, there was a larger purpose to the fore, namely to induce fundamental and lasting change in the condition of the Jewish community or communities on behalf of whom the activists sought to act.

Like the old forms of intercession, the new political or diplomatic action was action by the fortunate in the interests of the unfortunate. Unlike those forms, it was founded less on intracommunal inequality of condition than on intercommunal inequality, namely on the ever more striking differences between the condition and status of Jews in some countries as opposed to those obtaining in others. The spectacle of endemic squalor and persecution barely mitigated by slow and unwilling reform and scattered islands of well-being was painful to all but the entirely insensitive and unthinking. It was thus not unnatural that it was from the ranks of those who, in their social and economic achievements and their concomitant rise in status in both the public at large and the Jewish communities to which they belonged, had gone furthest (and so, in their persons and careers best epitomized the transformation of Western Jewry) that the leading activists tended to come. Political action in this form was therefore typically action by the *notables* of Jewry: the very wealthy and the very grand, the statesmen and the politicians in the lands of their residence and adoption, the leaders of the new, essentially secular Jewish institutions that were taking shape in all the countries in question, and finally, if more rarely, the men of letters (in the language of their country) and the established academics.

These notables were to all intents and purposes self-selected, at best representative of self-selected, self-perpetuating oligarchies, and the crucial sources of their authority within Jewry and their capacity to lead and speak for it lay in their position and function in the larger non-Jewish world. Some had been formally elected to leading positions in such quasi-representative institutions as the Board of Deputies of British Jews in London and the Consistoire Central in Paris, but such election commonly hinged on their attainments in the economy, or in politics, or in the professions, or in the press—generally, in society at large. Moreover, by a paradox such notables seem rarely to have been aware of, their ability to act in a Jewish interest turned on their status in the non-Jewish world in the further respect that a great deal depended on the willingness of what might be termed the target government to treat with them. That, too, was usually a function of their status in the non-Jewish world. But it depended equally—and in some cases more—on the degree and variety of the hostility of the authorities in question whose treatment of their own subject Jews was, of course, the original precipitant of action. Scope for action and room for maneuver were therefore always limited. Sights were kept low. Prudence was the watchword by which the enterprise was invariably governed. And the more specific the case, the less typical or more striking the injustice, the more blatant the hostility, the more easily (relatively speaking) it could be remedied and the fewer eggs needed breaking in the process. For then the resistance of governments (in the climate of the nineteenth and early twentieth centuries) to such quasi-political action was more easily softened, and, above all, the limits of such power as the notables of Western Jewry did possess needed never to be reached and tested and the true poverty of the political resources at their disposal never exposed.

It is thus that the Damascus Affair was for so long the textbook case of successful international action. No doubt it encouraged the Jews; rightly it was accounted an important precedent for "cross-national" cooperation by Jewish notables from a variety of countries. But equally it exemplified the limits of what such cooperating notables might usefully aim at. For the Affair was never more than a matter of unfortunates caught up in a tangle of local intrigue in a province of an unpopular and declining empire. Something was done for them in their immediate distress. Little could be done by way of radical change.

Similarly, minor alleviation of the condition of Rumanian Jewry was possible from time to time, but not large reform of their status. As for the huge problem of the distress of Russo-Polish Jewry, it was too deep, too extensive, and too bound up with the underlying ethos and structure of government and society in what was, after all, one of the world's great powers for such modes of action (in themselves) to hold out any hope of change in the condition and status of the Jews in question. The Western Jewish notables, even when they had the ear of the Russian statesmen, even when they threatened, or actually exerted, economic pressure, were confronted with a task that was entirely beyond their power to deal with and to which their techniques, in the final analysis, were irrelevant. Indeed it would be (and, in the event, was) argued that caution, discretion, incrementalism, and seeking to operate behind the scenes and wherever possible through the official channels available to other governments only compounded the failure, that such prudential modes inhibited the employment of resources and techniques that could have been more effective, and that weakness of purpose and paucity of results could not but ultimately undermine the authority of the notables within

Jewry itself, thereby gradually clearing the way for more radical tendencies and bolder spirits to move to the fore.

The truth seems to be that the Western notables were caught in a fundamental contradiction. It stemmed from the fact already alluded to, that both the basis of their authority within Jewry, such as it was, and the basis of their power, such as *it* was, to act in the Jewish interest, were in all decisive respects external to Jewry itself. So in real terms—so, too, nominally, which is to say that it was crucial to their position and central to their own private perception of it that they were not only Jews but equally Englishmen, Frenchmen, Germans, Americans, and so forth. The interests of their own governments had therefore certainly to be respected, and that respect had to be demonstrated. Cooperation with parallel Jewish bodies in countries with which their own happened to be in conflict was necessarily inhibited, as, famously, between French and German Jews after 1870. The charge of disloyalty, always feared, had to be avoided—even, as Lucien Wolf found when he spoke against the Anglo-Russian *entente* of 1907, in the comparatively mild and reasonable political climate of Edwardian England. The range of contact and coordination with the Jewish communities and communal leaders in the target countries, none of them free and open societies, could not but be restricted and dealings with local leaders treated as matters of great delicacy. And the repercussions that action taken in a target country might have in their own had always to be taken into account as well, as—to cite another famous instance—in the case of French Jews seeking the amelioration of the condition of the subjects of France's end-of-century ally Russia. Accordingly the arguments for noninterference and inaction were always strong, so strong, indeed, that it is, if anything, the determination of these public-spirited notables—hardly typical of their own class as such in their high conception of where their duty lay—that is remarkable and needs explaining. Many seem to have been burdened by the fear that the failure of Jews in one part of the world to make progress in civil society put the success of those who had achieved formal equality with non-Jews elsewhere at risk. Evidently some were moved by an exceptionally strong sense of *noblesse oblige*. But it remains that the very elements of their situation which made "diplomatic" action on their part possible, and on some occasions very effective, ruled them out as candidates for the true national, political leadership of

Jewry and as managers of thoroughgoing political action on behalf of the Jewish people as such. Of course few, if any, sought such a role. It would have had to be founded on full identification with the Jewish people defined in explicitly national terms and upon the view that it was their interests that were paramount. That would have been thoroughly inconsistent with the position, status, and interests to which most Jewish notables cleaved.

III

The failure of the philanthropically minded notables of Western Jewry truly to come to grips with the Jewish Problem, especially in its acute form in Eastern Europe—where the governments of Russia and Rumania and, to some extent, the Russian, Polish, and Rumanian peoples, too, were waging a kind of war against the Jews—was therefore twofold. Its daunting scale rendered them incapable of coping with the problem in its material aspects; and the ambiguities of their own situation, along with their reluctance to put their own and their fathers' achievements at risk by engendering greater hostility at home, seem to have rendered them incapable of fully grasping it conceptually. The Jewish Problem seen as a *national*, as opposed to a localized, problem, was not one they could cope with or, for that matter, wish to recognize. Nor was the segment of Jewry chiefly in question, in Eastern Europe, a group or class that they were suited to lead: they were too remote, culturally no less than geographically. The field was therefore open to very different and— having regard to the forms of public action that had been customary in Jewry until very modern times—entirely novel types of claimants to leadership, influence, authority, responsibility. These emerged on the basis, broadly, of two distinct and mutually exclusive platforms or approaches.

One approach conceded that ascriptive national characteristics, as commonly understood (historical, cultural, linguistic, etc.), were indeed of the greatest importance, virtually indelible, and in certain carefully defined respects benign, but held that they were nonetheless subordinate both in weight and in value to class characteristics and class differences. It was the latter that were cardinal; it was in socioeconomic terms, before all else, that the problem of the Jews had to be understood and tackled. The Jews of Eastern Europe *in the mass* were seen as sharing the common lot of the other peoples *in the mass;* and they were therefore bound both by condition and, so to speak, duty to make common cause with them. Such a duty entailed joining in the effort to establish a new political and social order everywhere, but first and foremost at the center of Jewish demographic gravity, in Russia. In effect, it was their duty to help promote revolution.

A call such as this, unreservedly to inject the Jews as a distinct category, or class, or caste into the bodies politic of the countries of their domicile was, of course, totally at variance with the ancient, accepted norms of Jewish practice in the Exile. Equally, it ran counter to all that Jewish notables, both within Russia and outside it, had consistently stood for, whether as a matter of political principle or out of regard for their respective private interests. Still, the Russian-Jewish revolutionaries had at least this in common with the notables, that, if not *fully* loyal and obedient children of the emancipation, they were at least believers in its central message. There is a sense in which they were no less faithful than their more fortunate brethren in the West to the propositions that, subject to certain reforms, the Jews could and should stay put; that despite everything they were, and could properly remain, legitimate and acceptable constituents of the states and societies to which they currently belonged; and that, in sum, the operation to be performed on the bodies politic of imperial Russia, Rumania, and Austria-Hungary respectively should be, so far as the Jews were concerned, therapeutic and rehabilitory in character, not surgical. Amputation was not necessary; the thinking of those who prescribed it was, so they believed, perverse.

The other approach was in some respects more radical, in others more conservative. Its conservatism lay in its acceptance of national distinctions and divisions in general, and the national distinctiveness of the Jews in particular, as primary. In this respect it accorded easily with traditional Jewish notions, self-images, and social practice. It was radical in that it both dismissed the prospect of incremental improvement for all Jews which the Western emancipation had been held to offer as illusory and, at the same time, regarded their contemporary condition as, if not intolerable in practice, then certainly insufferable in principle. The Jews might have to remain in their Exile a while longer. Disgracefully, some might—some evidently would—prefer it. Certainly the extraction of the Jews in great numbers from that Exile would be an immense undertaking, and their resettlement elsewhere, under an entirely fresh, purpose-designed social and political regime, would absorb vast resources of energy, money, and time. Yet it was in that direction and to such purposes that the Jews should aim. All other plans and ideas were doomed to collapse and failure.

It may be said of this latter approach that no other was founded on so hardheaded a reading of the map of Jewish history and on so comprehensive a view of the Jewish condition, or sought to take so fully into account, as this one did, the nature and inner logic of the hatred the surrounding peoples bore for the Jews and its eternally erupting and corrupting consequences. Nor did any other approach present as one of its chief claims the offer to gain for the Jews a restored dignity—or even regard their individual and collective dignities as matters of high concern. Nor, finally, did any other seek, however hesitantly at first, to provide the basis for a wholly fresh relationship with other nations, the only one worth having in its view, namely one of equality: equality of status and equality of esteem; and, so they argued, as an ultimate consequence, an end to the endemic hostility that rendered the Jews' environment so deeply and peculiarly intolerable. Here, then, was an approach to the matter of the Jews that was in all important and accepted senses of the term *national.*

Both tendencies held that a change of direction was vital, a fact that stood them in good stead in the continuing fight for the hearts and minds of the impoverished, set-upon Jews of Eastern Europe, ever more skeptical of the old verities and the old style communal leadership. The class-orientated, socialist, revolutionary creed and parties—notably in the explicitly Marxist form and as embodied in the Bund—had the edge for many years. Its business was more obviously and convincingly with the here and now of Jewish life. In contrast, the out-and-out nationalists could be made to appear as mere visionaries: overambitious, overpessimistic, overdemanding, and overcritical in turn. But it was evident at the time, and is clearly so in retrospect, that it was they, that is, the Zionists, who alone of all tendencies in Jewry embodied the national principle in what can properly be termed its modern form—shorn, or virtually so, of religious content, without overt qualification, with little or no mental reservation. They alone were disposed to turn their minds seriously to a re-forming of Jewry in the light of its real circumstances, on the basis of authentic national institutions, and through uninhibited, unashamed national political action.

IV

Hibbat Zion, the early form of Zionism—proto-Zionism, as it can be termed—contained many of the germs of Zionism proper. Central to the proto-Zionist outlook, as later to that of Zionism proper, was the conviction that the needs and interests of the Jews differed in important respects from those of other peoples. This did not mean that the interests and needs of Jews and non-Jews could not be rendered compatible and a *modus vivendi* between them devised. It did mean that there had first to be a thoroughgoing change in the condition and status of the Jews, a change that the Jews themselves must plan and execute. Only then would there occur a change of heart on all sides and a more serene chapter in the history of tormented Jewry ushered in. But again, it was improbable that any but the Jews themselves could or would seek it. The principle to which everything boiled down was *self-help;* and from its adoption all good things would flow: material improvement, a cultural renaissance, dignity, equality, safety.

Taken together, these views and principles of conduct formed the basis for a national policy; and there was *implied* within them a program that was political both in goal and in method. Of course in the event, the founders and leaders of Hibbat Zion never moved very far along the lines of thought and action on which they seemed, at first flush, to have embarked. At its most characteristic, namely as conceived and led by Y. L. Pinsker and his associates in southern Russia in the 1880s and early 1890s, Hibbat Zion had little by way of institutional cement or resources to keep it together and on a firm and purposeful path of any kind. Throughout the some fifteen years in which it occupied the modernist-nationalist stage virtually unchallenged, it remained a loosely bound, imperfectly articulated association of associations. The ideological lead was vague. The resources available were pitifully disproportionate even to the extremely modest concrete targets in view. Above all, the activists' conception of their own role was so timid and so marginal to the crushing material distress and terrifying insecurity of the Jewish masses around them that the plain men and women in the street could not fail to know in their bones that their own lives would be unaffected by anything Hibbat Zion might accomplish in real terms and on the ground. And this essential irrelevance, at best marginality, to the great, hostile forces of "push" beating about the Jews—however remarkable might have been Hibbat Zion's embodiment for the times of the forces of "pull"—doomed it in short order to decline and to a place in the historical record wholly contingent on the achievements of the movement that replaced it. For it is the case that the effect of the rise of Hibbat Zion on the general climate of ideas in Jewish public life (as opposed to the real circumstances of the Jewish people), while never decisive or dramatic, was a marked one. The local associations were weak, but such associations can be seen to have been formed, or to have coalesced more or less spontaneously, in almost all the major Jewish centers, especially in the lands of Jewry's greatest distress. The fact that the movement was preponderantly middle class and moderately secularist (and therefore, by the same token, composed of men and women who tended to have achieved a modest degree of integration into society at large) undoubtedly militated against radical action on their part. But, on the other hand, this social composition helped enormously to propagate the ideas of Hibbat Zion—above all the fundamental idea that there could be a clear yet nonassimilatory alternative approach to the Jewish Question—and propagate them throughout the Jewish world, and with great rapidity. For these were members of the reading and writing public *par excellence*, the Jewish intelligentsia, who, whatever may have been their shortcomings as men of action, were nothing if not habile in the examination and manipulation of ideas. Thus, by the time Zionism proper, under its foremost leader and virtual inventor, burst on the scene in 1896–97, there was in being a class of people who were already attuned to many of its central tenets and willing to listen, at the very least, to arguments for a vastly more ambitious plan of campaign.

V

Theodor Herzl's program was unique in that it was expressly and uncompromisingly political. In its preliminary form it argued for the establishment of a state; and even after a certain amount of watering down of this originally explicit goal had occurred in the early stages of his movement it was clear to all that political autonomy, that is to say, Jewish self-government in some form, was an absolute requirement. But it was political in a related, yet more fundamental, sense. The environment in which the Jewish national movement had necessarily to operate was seen by Herzl and his truest followers not fatalistically, as had been the traditional mode, as a world of *gzerot*, of given brute facts and brute forces, deeply, incurably hostile, but as one of much complexity and many contradictions. They saw it as, among other things, political in character, containing within it conflicting, unequal, and ephemeral forces in a state of constant movement. It was amenable to—and indeed required—political interpretation and politically inspired and motivated conduct. It was a world in which the Jews could and therefore should find a way of participating along with others. If they did so they would find that all was in some measure fluid and conjunctural, that nothing was fixed and inevitable, and that, accordingly, there were neither permanent and ever-reliable amities, nor eternal and hopeless hostilities. Moreover it was a world in which the central forces for good and ill, the Powers, were of a political character before all else. They could therefore be engaged and treated with, not simply petitioned. Certainly to that end there was much to learn and much to do. (And indeed a large part of the history of Herzl's movement is the record of its learning the ways and means of international politics.) The Jewish people, the Jewish "masses," had to be mustered and led. The notables who commanded what Herzl believed to be the most important Jewish resource—money—had to be mobilized. An open, elected, representative assembly in which the major issues before Jewry might be thrashed out and an executive elected by it to function as a sort of provisional Jewish government had to be established. And there was to be a financial arm and in due course newspapers, a publishing house, regular lines of communication between the movement's center and its periphery, a central office to help implement policy, and outlying missions to represent it. All through, the thinking had to be bold, unashamed, *large:* as befitted the immensity of the problem.

Here plainly, taken together, were in form and even in substance, if not always in efficacy, the classic instruments of government and policy. There were no armed or police forces or other instruments of external or internal coercion. But otherwise virtually all the chief institutions of government, along with many of the common practices and routines, were planned and acquired within the first decade or so of the Zionist Organization's history; and there followed upon them the major elements and forms of internal political life (in its parliamentary-democratic mode)—albeit, once again, with the important exception of those hinging, ultimately, on force and coercion. Parties evolved; leadership was fought for; office was sought and contested; policy was debated; votes were canvassed; allies were courted. And all these were in evidence well before the territory to which they were intended ultimately to be applicable was available even in theory and long before the independent state that they would, in some sense, embody was even on the horizon.

The importance of this rapid establishment of political structures, along with their successful articulation, was twofold. In the first place, there was established an arena upon which the attention of all who subscribed to a modern form of Jewish nationalism was naturally concentrated. The effect was enormously to encourage sympathizers in all degrees. In the second place, by virtue of its Congress, its elections, and its other quasi-governmental institutions and procedures, the Zionist movement gained for itself kinds of legitimacy and authority that no other Jewish institution or body could claim or could equal. Zionism in its practice, no less than Zionism in its purposes, began to be seen as better attuned to the needs and standards of the times than other, more traditional if equally indigenous, Jewish tendencies and movements. It was much more clearly part of the modern, forward-looking world in which the "nation" was rapidly replacing the "church" (or God himself) as the source of final authority. Finally, it was a movement and a program that foreign statesmen could, as Herzl had anticipated, readily understand and consider dealing with. In brief, it equipped the Jews with an instrument by means of which, if they so wished, their collective needs might be articulated and policy on their behalf laid down. Indeed, it is crucial to an understanding both of the opposition to Zionism within Jewry, and of the immense change in the Jewish scene which Zionism was to precipitate, that it was at least as much the idea that such collective needs might be defined at all, and that general, *national* remedies might be pursued, that struck the contemporary mind—and struck it with force—as the particular definitions and specific remedies the Zionists actually proposed.

In the final analysis, the success of the Zionist enterprise in these initial stages depended, before all else, on recognition both by Jews and by others, the more so as the two varieties or sources of recognition were interdependent and mutually reinforcing. The Zionists could not gain access to the arena of established international politics in which the decisive responses to their demands would be made, if they were to be made at all, by mere imposition. The forces regularly inhabiting that arena had first to recognize them as in some sense, if only for certain purposes, representative and effective spokesmen for the Jewish interest. And the prior condition on which they depended for this was a degree, a fairly high degree, of acceptance—or at the very least acquiescence—within Jewry itself. At the same time their acceptance in and by Jewry as legitimate and suitable spokesmen depended in turn, certainly in part, on the degree to which the governments and ruling circles inhabiting the larger world outside Jewry were prepared to treat with them. The Zionists, in brief, had somehow to pull themselves up by their own bootstraps. Their position—in effect, their capacity for action—hinged on a delicate structure of influence. This they were able to erect, sustain, and develop only because they alone among the public bodies active in the pre-1914 Jewish world were prepared to make the large, if not—on the face of it—pretentious, claim to speak for the Jewish people as a whole and in terms of its common needs, having established at least the semblance of a national authority and having sought actively to treat the governments of the day on an explicitly political basis.

True, after the first ambitious spurt of energy and action there occurred a series of tactical retreats in matters of detail and a certain narrowing and reduction of aims and options. So it was under Herzl, as already suggested; so it was, and much more plainly so, after Herzl's death. There then ensued a particularly long interval of weak leadership and uncertain tactics, second thoughts even on matters of principle, and a marked tendency to seek relief from the ever-present prospect of failure in the absorbing, but always small-scale, settlement activities in Eretz Israel. By the eve of the Great War the thrust of the original Herzlian Zionism had so weakened that it may fairly be said that the movement was tending strongly toward the patterns of thought and action which had been characteristic of Hibbat Zion a generation earlier and which Herzl and his following had begun by rejecting. Even that famous disparagement of European liberalism and legal emancipation as putative sources of salvation for the Jews which had been common and fundamental to Hibbat Zion and political Zionism alike was failing to gain automatic assent as Zionist activists allowed themselves to be drawn into the internal politics of the lands of their domicile, notably in Russia and Austria. That the origins of these trends may be traced in part to lack of progress toward the goals of Zionism proper in Eretz Israel itself, and in the international political arena where its fate—and perhaps that of the Jews generally—seemed likely to be played out, served only to underline the seriousness of the decline. Yet Herzlian Zionism never faded totally. The banner of the "political Zionism" of which he had been the progenitor assuredly grew tattered in the winds of disbelief that blew upon it in the years immediately subsequent to his death; but it was never quite hauled down.

It may well be asked why this was so. What, after all, at the end of his day, had Herzl accomplished? His negotiations with the Ottomans had been long and tortuous but had led nowhere. The negotiations with the Russian government had provided some short-term relief for Zionists within the empire, but the promise of major political assistance and cooperation in Constantinople dissolved almost as rapidly as it had been given. The ostensibly greater breakthrough achieved by Herzl in his negotiations with the British government had borne nothing but internal dissension. Nothing had come of his old plan of mobilizing Jewish capital in the collective Jewish interest. Above all, the greater part of the people themselves remained trapped in their misery.

Yet when all that has been said, what remained of Herzl's legacy was cardinal. The Zionist institutions continued to function and were in reasonably good working order when new men in new circumstances arose during the First World War to make good use of them. The ideas of political Zionism remained alive and, what is more, gained much in plausibility in those new circumstances. In the crucial years 1914–19 they reemerged as ideas whose time had finally come in the sense that they were beginning to be judged as they had never been before: that arguably they made good social and political sense after all; that demonstrably they pointed to lines of policy and action in the Near East that certain powers in the land (Great Britain in the first place, but to some extent the other Entente Powers as well) were prepared to consider for their own national profit; and that the Zionists, for certain, if admittedly limited purposes, were useful partners. In the new climate of opinion, in which the collapse of old empires and timeworn political systems on the one hand and renascent nations and new states on the other were the rage, it was the public and political (as opposed to the private and intercessionary) approach to the dilemmas, predicaments, and afflictions of the Jews that tended to win the ears of those who mattered most. Even the older, quasi-intercessionary groups and institutions such as the Alliance Israélite and the Conjoint Foreign Committee of the Board of Deputies and the Anglo-Jewish Association recognized this and tended by and large to rely upon it. It may be that Zionism in its basic, which is to say political, form, and in its essential simplicity, seemed to many to possess a measure of grandeur and spirit to which the more cautious, less sweeping approaches did not aspire and could not touch. That it argued for a profound reform of Jewry both internally and in its external relations and that it offered, or more precisely claimed to offer, a real and dramatic alternative to all that had gone and been attempted before—this now stood it in good stead.

For it was the case that, from the first, Zionism had been a program and a creed that was particularly attractive to those Jews who were hardest pressed and who, at the same time, in their social attributes and in their own minds were most clearly members of a Jewish *nation*—untroubled, that is to say, by any separate, parallel national identity, or aspirations thereto, speaking a national language, living in fairly compact groups and in reasonably well-defined areas. These were, of course, the Jews of Eastern Europe. It was to them that these ideas had always had a natural appeal. Of all the categories and classes of Jews, it was they who were most prepared to countenance a radical cure to their predicament—much as it had been they, all along, as private individuals, who had been readiest to take the no less bold, near-irreversible step of migrating overseas—essentially, although not wholly, because their predicament was the most acute. It was also the case that the terms in which the causes and dynamic of their predicament could best be grasped and a cure for them best be advanced were *national*. Equally, these were the terms in which the endemic hostility to them in the lands of their domicile was best understood. This was the language of the times. This was what made most sense to most observers. At this extraordinary moment of national and political rearrangement and redistribution, the Jews of Eastern Europe fell for once into a larger category, that of the submerged, now newly emancipated peoples all around them.

What happened during the Great War and in its immediate aftermath was not that the general hostility to Jewry had diminished. On the contrary, it was precisely at this point that the period of greatest horror was being ushered in. It was rather that the matter of Jewry had been finally entered on the general international agenda—the matter of Jewry as a problem, the matter of Jewry as a political factor—just as the Herzlians had always wanted it to. It came up at last for discussion in an arena where interests were generally perceived without heat and tended to outweigh beliefs and sentiments, even the most passionately held. And there, briefly, the political conjuncture was propitious and even hostility in the form of an exaggerated notion of the power of the Jews and a wholly absurd fear of the danger they might represent to organized society could be turned to good effect. Some may think that the credit for the moderately favorable outcome should go to the Zionist diplomats of the day for seeing their opportunity. Others may think they should be judged essentially as no more than Herzl's belated legatees. There is a fine topic for debate there, if one too intricate to be dealt with here and now. What does seem clear, what does really matter, and what can at least be argued on the basis of the available evidence is that if the movement had not been there to function and respond in those crucial years it is more than likely that the unique moment of opportunity would have passed the Jewish people by.

Shlomo Lambroza

Jewish Responses to Pogroms in Late Imperial Russia

Russian Jews suffered a great deal under the antisemitic policies of the tsars. After the Polish partitions of the eighteenth century, Jews lived as an oppressed minority—*inorodtsy* (alien subjects) of the empire. In their attempt to preserve the community, Jews adapted their lives to the oppressive conditions. They endeavored to live out the social, religious, and intellectual values of the community. Even when forced to live in the confines of the Pale of Settlement, Jews were nonetheless able to adjust and to a certain extent prosper. As Russia entered the twentieth century, attitudes toward Jews changed. Antisemitism, which since the creation of the Pale had taken the form of social and political discrimination, now manifested itself in violent attacks against Jews. Unlike government discrimination, which was inconvenient but which Jews had learned to live with, these attacks threatened the future existence of Russian Jewry and its established way of life. In 1881–84 and again in 1903–1906 Russian Jews were victimized by a wave of antisemitic riots called pogroms.

The Jewish community was unprepared, both physically and psychologically, to deal with the hostilities that erupted in 1881. Since the creation of the Pale by Catherine the Great in 1791, there had been only three anti-Jewish incidents—1821, 1859, and 1871, all in the city of Odessa—and these had little in common with the wide-scale violence of 1881. Although the community struggled to deal

I would like to express my deepest gratitude to Marybeth Burke for her comments, criticisms, and moral support.

with the pogroms as they occurred, the primary response came after pogroms abated. The main concerns were what steps to take to protect the community and to prevent hostilities from recurring. The community was significantly divided over these issues. Some felt that the only solution was for Jews to leave the empire, which they did in the thousands after the pogroms, while others argued for the need to continue the struggle for legal rights and citizenship. Emigration and emancipation, therefore, became the primary concern of Russian Jewry after 1881.

When pogroms recurred in the spring of 1903, the Jews of the Pale were better prepared. Several Jewish workers' groups had organized and trained self-defense units since 1902. Although the controversy over emigration and emancipation continued, the exceedingly violent and more numerous pogroms made the issue of self-defense paramount. The extent of the new hostilities presented a more formidable threat than in 1881, forcing the community to shelve its differences and unite in defense.

Integral to a discussion of Jewish responses is an understanding of the central government's attitude toward and position on the pogroms. Each response, whether it was self-defense, emigration, or emancipation, was a reaction, in part, to the government. This issue is especially relevant given the historical controversy regarding the government's role during pogroms. The traditional school of historians believed, as did many individuals at the time, that the government could have, but chose not to, take the appropriate action to end pogroms. It was also thought that the government undertook a pogrom policy that included a conspiracy with right-wing political groups to stage pogroms.[1] Recently the role of the central government has been reevaluated. Contemporary scholarship suggests that there is no evidence to support a conspiracy theory but acknowl-

---

1. For more on the traditional school, see Grigorii Krasni-Admoni and Simon Dubnov, *Materialy dlia istorii antievreiskikh pogromov v Rossii* (Petrograd, 1923), vols. 1, 2; Dubnov, *The History of the Jews in Russia and Poland*, trans. I. Friedlaender (Philadelphia, 1918, 1920), vols. 2, 3; Dubnov, "Iz istorii vosmidesiatakh godov," *Evreiskaia Starina*, year 7, vol. 8, nos. 3–4 (July-December 1915); Heinrich Ellenberger, *Die Leiden und Verfolgungen der Juden* (Budapest, 1882); Elias Tcherikower, "Naye materyaln vegn di pogromen in rusland onheyb di 80er yorn," *Historishe shriftn* (Vilna) 2 (1937): 446–65; Mark Vishniak, "Di yidn in rusland un di pogromen in di 80er yorn," in *Geshikhte fun der yidisher arbeter bavegung in di fareynikte shtatn*, ed. Elias Tcherikower (New York, 1943); Vishniak, "Anti-Semitism in Russia," in *Essays on Anti-Semitism*, ed. Koppel S. Pinson (New York, 1942), pp. 130–41.

edges that the government's antisemitic attitude encouraged pogroms and concludes that it shares blame and responsibility.[2]

The Pogroms of 1881

The outbreak of pogroms was directly related to the assassination of Alexander II. The tsar was murdered on March 13, 1881, by a member of Narodnya Volya (The People's Will), a populist terrorist organization. Shortly afterward two rumors circulated in the Pale. The first stated that Jews were responsible for the tsar's death. The second, far more dangerous than the first, stated the government's intent to pass a *ukase* (edict) instructing the people to beat and plunder Jews for having murdered the tsar and for exploiting the *narod* (people). There was little truth to either rumor. The government had not singled out Jews as responsible, nor were there any decrees ordering Russians to take revenge upon Jews.

The popular press validated the rumors to a certain degree. Several newspapers, even before 1881, had waged an active antisemitic campaign.[3] Articles in these papers claimed that Jews relentlessly and mercilessly exploited the *narod*. They disapproved of the liberal policies toward Jews advanced during the reign of Alexander II and urged the government to enact new and even more stringent laws to end Jewish economic dominance of the *narod*. After the assassination of Alexander II the antisemitic campaign and Jew-baiting by the popular press intensified. Articles published by these papers alluded that Jews shared responsibility for the tsar's murder.[4] The innuendos

2. For a reassessment of pogroms, see Hans Rogger, "Government, Jews, Peasants and Land in Post-Emancipation Russia," *Cahiers du Monde Russe et sovietique* 17, nos. 1, 2–3 (1976): 5–21, 171–211; Rogger, "The Jewish Policy of Late Tsarism: A Reappraisal," *Wiener Library Bulletin* 25, nos. 1–2 (1971): 42–51; Rogger, "Russian Ministers and the Jewish Question, 1881–1917," *California Slavic Studies* 8 (1975): 39–45; I. M. Aronson, "Geographical and Socioeconomic Factors in the 1881 Anti-Jewish Pogroms in Russia," *Russian Review* 39, no. 1 (January 1980): 18–31; Aronson, "The Origins of the Anti-Jewish Pogroms in Russia in 1881: A Reexamination of the Conspiracy Theory" (photocopy); John D. Klier, "The Russian Press and the Anti-Jewish Pogroms of 1881–82," *Canadian-American Slavic Studies*, vol. 17, no. 1 (Spring 1983): 199–221; Shlomo Lambroza, "Plehve, Kishinev and the Jewish Question: A Reappraisal," *Nationalities Papers* 12, no. 1 (1984): 117–27; Lambroza, "The Pogrom Movement in Tsarist Russia, 1903–06" (Ph.D. diss., Rutgers University, 1981).

3. Most hostile to the Jews were the newspapers *Novoe Vremia, Kievlianin, Vilenskii Vestnik,* and *Novorossiiskii telegraf.*

4. For a detailed discussion of the role of the press during the pogroms, see Klier, "Russian Press."

and near-accusations confirmed the circulating rumors in the minds of the *narod.*

The first pogrom occurred on April 15, 1881, in the southern Russian city of Elisavetgrad. Of the city's forty-three thousand inhabitants, thirteen thousand were Jews. The police chief of the city, known for treating Jews fairly, responded to rumors of an impending pogrom by calling in military reinforcements, closing several taverns, and imposing a curfew. By April 15 it appeared as if tensions between Jews and Gentiles had abated and the city of Elisavetgrad was returning to its normal routine. The reinforcements were sent back to camp, taverns were reopened, and other precautionary measures relaxed. But that night an altercation between a Jewish tavern owner and a Gentile patron escalated into an all-out pogrom. A report on the pogrom described what occurred in Elisavetgrad.

> The city presented an extraordinary sight: streets covered with feathers and obstructed with broken furniture; houses with broken doors and windows; a raging mob . . . continuing its work of destruction. . . . Toward evening the disorders increased in intensity owing to the arrival of a large number of peasants from the adjacent village who were anxious to secure part of the Jewish loot.[5]

One of the worst pogroms of 1881 occurred in the Ukrainian city of Kiev. The authorities in Kiev were less predisposed to Jews than those in Elisavetgrad. The governor general of Kiev, A. P. Drenteln, was a reactionary and an antisemite. Although the date of the pogrom was known in advance, the only precautionary measure taken was to warn Jews not to leave their homes. On April 26 the pogrom began in the Podol, the Jewish section of the city. By the end of the pogrom four Jews had been killed, dozens wounded, and twenty-five women raped.[6] Contemporary accounts said that troops and police were indifferent to the plight of the Jews and acted irresponsibly in suppressing the disorders. A letter from a Kiev resident stated:

> What aggravated the dreadful scene was the fact that police actually witnessed the gross outrages, without making the least attempt to arrest the ruffians. . . . Nor were police alone in their disgraceful attitude. I myself saw a large number of soldiers, who had been sent to various parts to restore peace, applaud and fraternise with the mob.[7]

5. Quoted in Dubnov, *History of the Jews,* 2:250.
6. *Times* (London), January 11, 1882, p. 4, cols. 1–3.
7. Quoted in *Russian Atrocities, 1881,* Published by the Russo-Jewish Committee (London, 1882), p. 31.

The historian Simon Dubnov expressed the thought that had the authorities been "so minded, the excesses might have been suppressed on the first day."[8] Dubnov insinuated that, in Kiev, government inaction allowed the pogrom to continue when it was equally possible to end it. Traditional Jewish history has interpreted the authorities' attitude and unresponsiveness during pogroms as possibly conspiratorial. These scholars believe that the central government and a secret organization called Sviaschennaia Druzhina (Holy Brotherhood) made up of local aristocrats working for the government bore responsibility for pogroms. Evidence indicates that the central government neither organized nor instigated pogroms. The reaction of Alexander III clearly reflected the government's displeasure with pogroms. After hearing of the brutality during pogroms, Alexander demanded a full investigation. He was especially upset over rumors of police and troop participation in pogroms. When he was informed that one of his officers incited a pogrom, he stated, "A fine officer! A shame!"[9]

Alexander's words in no way vindicated the authorities for their actions. Louis Greenberg, a historian of the pogroms, echoed Simon Dubnov's belief that, had the government acted with more resolve and dispatch, the pogroms and the bloodshed could have been averted: "The government cannot be absolved of responsibility of guilt. The government which exhibited so much energy and resourcefulness in dealing with revolutionary activities could have put a quick stop to pogroms had it seriously wished to do so."[10]

While there is no evidence of government conspiracy to stage pogroms, historians agree with Louis Greenberg that the government could have been more responsive. The government of Alexander III did not immediately suppress pogroms. At first pogroms were rationalized as a response to the coming of the Easter holiday; anti-Jewish activities were common during Easter. But, as the number of pogroms steadily increased rather than declined after Easter, the government became more concerned. By the end of April officials posited the idea that the pogroms were the work of populist revolu-

8. Dubnov, *History of the Jews*, 2:255.
9. Quoted in R. M. Kantor, "Aleksandr III o evreiskikh pogromakh 1881–83 gg.," *Evreiskaia letopis* (Leningrad, 1923), pp. 149–58. For a detailed discussion of the conspiracy theory, see Aronson, "Origins of the Anti-Jewish Pogroms."
10. Louis Greenberg, *The Jews in Russia: The Struggle for Emancipation* (New Haven, 1944–51), 2:24.

tionaries, *narodniki*. It was believed that the *narodniki* would exploit the pogroms for their own purpose of spreading revolution. This analysis, too, was abandoned when it became clear that there was no evidence of *narodniki* involvement. Finally the government settled on an explanation compatible with traditional attitudes toward Jews. The autocracy saw the 1881 pogroms as a justifiable outbreak of public wrath against Jews. The violence was explained as a reaction by concerned Russians who felt that Jews were undermining the Russian nation and people. N. P. Ignatiev, minister of the interior under Alexander III, claimed that the pogroms were a product of traditional Jewish clannishness, Jewish religious fanaticism, Jewish prominence in the ranks of the opposition, and a Jewish propensity for exploiting the *narod*. Ignatiev produced a report on the pogroms issued in September 1882 which stated that Jews devoted their attention "to defrauding by their wiles" the Russian *narod*. He went on to implicate Jews for causing pogroms: "The conduct of theirs [Jews] has called forth protests on the part of the people, as manifested in acts of violence and robbery."[11]

The attitude articulated by Ignatiev became the basis for further legal sanctions against Jews. In direct response to the pogroms, a series of temporary regulations called the May Laws were passed in 1882.[12] The laws were a series of provisional statutes regulating the Jewish community. Ignatiev reasoned that regulating the activities of Jews in the Pale would create less opportunity for them to exploit the Gentile population and thereby bring an end to pogroms. He could not have been more wrong. The laws led to a more concentrated Jewish business community within the Pale and exacerbated antagonisms between Jews and non-Jews. Even more tragic, Ignatiev's reasoning reflects the characteristic attitude of "blaming the victim" adopted by the government and the belief that Jews, not *pogromshchiki*, bore responsibility for pogroms. In effect, the victims were treated as the instigators.

What was the Jewish community to do in the face of increasing

11. For N. P. Ignatiev's statement and his attitude toward the Jewish Question, see Iulii Isodorovich Gessen, "Graf N. P. Ignatiev i 'Vremennyia pravila o evreiakh 3 maia 1882 goda,' "*Pravo, Ezhenedelnaia Iuridicheskaia Gazeta*," July 27, 1908, no. 30, pp. 1631–37, and August 3, 1908, no. 31, pp. 1678–86. See also the *Times* (London), January 13, 1882, p. 4, cols. 2–3.

12. A full documentation of the May Laws can be found in Lucien Wolf, ed., *The Legal Sufferings of the Jews in Russia* (London, 1912), pp. 83–97.

hostilities both in the populace and by the government? The response of the community was twofold: first, the more immediate issue of defending itself and assisting the victims; second, the broader issue of how to prevent pogroms from recurring.

It should be made clear that the community was caught off guard by the wave of popular violence. With the exception of the three isolated incidents in Odessa, there had been no extensive, violent anti-semitic activity in nearly one hundred years. By the time the pogroms had subsided, 40 Jews were dead, thousands were injured, and 225 women had been raped. The London *Times* insinuated that in some cases "lust seemed more of a principle motive than plunder."[13] In all there were 259 pogroms, causing an estimated £16 million worth of damage. Nearly 100,000 Jews were reduced to poverty and 20,000 left homeless.[14] The community was unprepared to deal with these excesses. There was virtually no organized defense; the means for the redress of hostilities were limited; and aid for the victims was scant. Initially the Jews, as subjects of the tsar, expected government assistance, but when they realized this was not forthcoming, they appealed to the Jewish community within and outside Russia.

Surprisingly, the support groups within the Jewish community did not act with requisite dispatch in sending aid to pogrom victims. The initial contributions by the established leadership in St. Petersburg were ridiculously small.[15] Possibly the Jews in that city had not understood the magnitude of the pogroms; nor had they ever been faced with such wide-scale need. The pogrom crisis was of unprecedented proportion, and the Jewish leadership did not know how to respond. When it became clear that the pogroms constituted a major disaster, the leadership in and outside the empire responded more appropriately. The wealthy banking families in St. Petersburg, especially the Gintsburg family, contributed large sums of money and dispensed aid to the various *gubernii* (provinces). Outside of Russia committees were set up to raise funds for victims. Most active of the groups were the Mansion House Relief Fund in London and the well-established Alliance Israélite Universelle in Paris. Collected funds

---

13. *Times* (London), January 11, 1882, p. 4, cols. 1–2.

14. Ibid., January 13, 1882, p. 4, cols. 2–3.

15. Jonathan Frankel, *Prophecy and Politics: Socialism, Nationalism and the Russian Jews, 1862–1917* (Cambridge, 1981), p. 52, states that the "railway magnate S. S. Poliakov reportedly gave 1,000 rubles and the banker A. Zak a mere 500."

were usually sent to the St. Petersburg Aid Committee, which distributed aid to committees within each *gubernia*.

Within the Pale local relief and aid committees were organized. These organizations collected funds from abroad and, within the Pale, provided shelter and food for the homeless, supplied assistance to those who were injured or had lost family members, provided for orphans and widows, maintained records, and, most important, attempted to restore order in the lives of pogrom victims.

Attempts were made by various groups and individuals within the community to organize resistance to pogroms. In Odessa, a city with a history of violent antisemitism, Jewish students at the university began organizing defense in response to rumors of an impending pogrom. On May 2, 1881, the students called for a public meeting at the city synagogue. Speaking in Yiddish, they implored the community to join them in their defense efforts. The students described plans to recruit, arm, and train neighborhood defense units. The community was supportive: "Everywhere, absolutely everywhere, the youth met only the most profound gratitude and more important, absolute trust."[16] The intentions of the students were commendable, but they started organizing too late. The pogrom began the following morning, May 3, before defense units could be armed and organized. Although there was no sustained organized resistance, those students at the forefront of the defense effort battled rioters and, as the London *Times* reported, "The Jews have been most energetic in their resistance."[17]

Another attempt at organized defense was made during the Balta pogrom of March 29–30, 1882. Balta, a city with a large Jewish population, endured the most brutal and destructive pogrom. As in Odessa, rumors circulated of an impending pogrom. In preparation a Jewish teacher in the city organized a self-defense unit. When the pogrom started, defenders initially contained the rioters, yet were only marginally successful, as the following eyewitness account reveals.

> At the beginning of the pogrom, the Jews got together and forced a band of rioters to draw back and seek shelter in the building of the fire department. But when police and soldiers appeared on the scene, the rioters decided to leave their place of refuge. Instead of driving off the dis-

16. Quoted in ibid., p. 54.
17. *Times* (London), January 11, 1882, p. 4, cols. 1–3.

orderly band, the police and soldiers began to beat the Jews with their rifle butts and swords.[18]

Conditions in the city worsened the next day when 5,000 peasants from the nearby countryside converged on the city to participate in the pogrom. By the time the pogrom subsided, 15,000 Jews were left homeless, 1,250 homes and shops had been destroyed, and more than 40 Jews had been killed or injured. The authorities' hostile attitude toward defenders made their efforts futile.

Scattered resistance efforts at Odessa and Balta were the exception. Mostly, Jews responded individually or in groups to the immediate crisis. At times, such as at the Berdichev railway station where "a large Jewish guard armed with clubs"[19] averted a pogrom, defense was successful, but, more frequently, isolated or even organized attempts at defense were unsuccessful. Defense efforts were hampered by lack of organization and arms and by hostile attitudes by police and troops toward defenders, all of which thwarted effective retaliation. Above all, the community expected the government to take a more active role in protecting Jews from pogroms.

The extent of the 1881 pogroms demanded a response from the community that went beyond the issues of self-defense or aid to victims. The pogroms exposed the oppressive and now dangerous conditions that existed for Jews in the Pale. Two clear alternatives emerged from the crisis of 1881. Jews could leave Russia and make their way to Western Europe, the United States, or Palestine, or they could stay and resolve to battle discrimination and become equal citizens of the empire. It was a direct result of pogroms that emigration and emancipation became the major issues facing the Jewish community at the turn of the century. The conflict was most acutely articulated by a resident of Kiev: "Either we get civil rights or we emigrate. Our human dignity is being trampled upon, our wives and daughters are being dishonored, we are looted and pillaged; either we get decent human rights or else let us go wherever our eyes may lead us."[20]

Many Jews of the Pale appealed to the established leadership in St. Petersburg for guidance during the crisis of 1881. The leadership, composed primarily of the upper strata of Russian Jewry (*les couches*

18. Quoted in Dubnov, *History of the Jews*, 2:300.
19. Ibid., pp. 256–57.
20. Quoted in Greenberg, *Jews in Russia*, 2:62.

superieur), advocated a conservative policy of working with the government to establish reforms. These leaders opposed radical emigration schemes and strongly urged that if Jews wished to ameliorate their condition and avoid further pogroms, they must work toward emancipation.

In response to the pogroms of 1881 the leadership organized a Conference of Jewish Notables that convened in St. Petersburg in April 1882. Called by Baron Horace Gintsburg, it included nearly forty of the most prominent Jews in Russia. The conference rejected wide-scale emigration as unreasonable and impractical. Where would the Jews go? Where would the funds come from? Most important, what would be the repercussions for those Jews who remained? The leadership pointed out that emigration under the Russian criminal code was illegal and punishable. It was also concerned about the government's appraisal of emigration as disloyal and unpatriotic. The conference resolved to reject "emigration as being subversive to the dignity of the Russian body politic and of the historical rights of the Jews to their present fatherland."[21] The sentiments of the leadership were echoed in the Jewish newspaper *Razsvet* (Dawn): "The Jew will remain in Russia ... because Russia is his fatherland, the soil of Russia his soil, the sky of Russia his sky. The Jewish problem is a Russian problem."[22]

Adherents of emigration questioned the motives of the St. Petersburg leadership. They believed that the leadership did not want to endanger its privileged status by supporting an emigration policy the government opposed. Also, emigration was costly, and the financial burden would fall most heavily on the wealthier Jews. There is some truth to both allegations, but it is necessary to examine the motives of the leadership more critically. The leadership argued that emigration was a slow process and could not satisfy the immediate needs of the Jews in the Pale. In addition, mass migration might significantly weaken attempts to reform the legal and socioeconomic position of Jews. The leadership was optimistic that liberal policies toward Jews adopted by Alexander II might be continued by his successor. Finally, and possibly the leadership's most credible argument, was the tsarist government's anti-emigration policies.[23] Minister of

---

21. Quoted in Dubnov, *History of the Jews*, 2:306–7.
22. Quoted in Greenberg, *Jews in Russia*, 2:64.
23. On government emigration policy, see Hans Rogger, "Tsarist Policy on Jewish Emigration," *Soviet Jewish Affairs* 3 (May 1973): 26–36; I. M. Aronson, "The Attitudes of Russian Officials in the 1880s towards Emigration," *Slavic Review* 34 (1975): 1–18.

the Interior Ignatiev stressed that to encourage emigration was an "incitement to sedition."[24] There is also evidence that Alexander III pressured the leadership by personally asking the bankers Horace Gintsburg and A. I. Zak to do whatever possible to discourage emigration.[25]

Opposing the leadership was the Jewish intelligentsia, a group of forty or so journalists and writers, who until 1881 played a passive role in Jewish politics. The leadership's seemingly inadequate and indifferent attitude disturbed members of the intelligentsia. They asked what the leadership was doing for the masses and whose interests it was serving. They pointed out that the Conference of Jewish Notables merely reaffirmed pre-1881 policies, policies ineffectual in preventing pogroms.[26] The position of the St. Petersburg leadership was seen as complacent and compromising, and it provoked the intelligentsia to action. The conflict produced a split in the leadership of the Jewish community—on one side the traditional leadership and on the other the newly politically active intelligentsia. The core of the intelligentsia's activism was the issue of emigration.

Although united in opposing traditional leadership policies, within its own ranks the intelligentsia disagreed as to where and how emigration should proceed. The primary debate was between the *Amerikanstvo*, those who favored emigration to the United States, and the *Palestinstvo*, those who favored Palestine. The *Amerikanstvo* argued that greater economic opportunity was available in America. The insatiable demand of American industry for cheap labor could provide immediate employment and financial security. Added incentives included low rates for ocean travel by steamship companies and an already burgeoning Jewish community in several U.S. cities. Most important, America offered Jews the opportunity to live as citizens with rights, dignities, political independence, religious freedom, and freedom from the horror of pogroms.

The *Palestinstvo* had taken a fundamentally different approach to emigration. The ideology of the *Palestinstvo* was advanced in several influential articles by the Hebrew novelist and publicist Perez Smo-

---

24. Quoted in Rogger, "Tsarist Policy," p. 28.
25. N. M. Gelber, "Di rusishe pogromen onheyb di 80er yorn in shayn fun estray-khisher diplomatisher korespondents," *Historishe shriftn* (Vilna) 2 (1937): 466–96.
26. For a complete discussion on the intelligentsia, see Frankel, *Prophecy and Politics*, pp. 49–132.

lenskin.[27] Smolenskin opposed assimilationist policies. Instead he envisioned a unified Jewish people instilled with a "national spirit," living in a new Holy Land. He argued that the creation of a Jewish nation in Palestine was the Jew's only escape from ubiquitous persecution. Smolenskin's articles stimulated the development of a national consciousness among the Jewish intelligentsia. They argued that emigration to the United States was only a halfway measure to true liberation and advocated instead the creation of a Jewish homeland in Palestine. Thus from the rubble and violence of pogroms arose the Zionist movement in Russia.

The question of emigration versus emancipation was hotly debated among the competing leadership of the Jewish community. But for the masses, traumatized by pogroms, living in desperately poor conditions and under constant threat of greater, more violent pogroms, emigration seemed most plausible. Emigration offered an escape from the oppressive conditions of the Pale and safety from the violence of pogroms. Prior to 1881, emigration was an abstract ideal, almost mythical, but now the myth became an urgent reality. An emigration fever swept the Pale, and an exodic vision took hold. Throughout the Pale, in almost every town and city, emigration societies were organized. Appeals were made to the Jewish community outside Russia, and societies were organized to facilitate emigration. In November 1881 the Hebrew Emigrant Aid Society was established in New York to manage the mass of Jews who had already left the Pale and were now stranded in Brody, a town on the Russian-Austrian border. The Alliance Israélite Universelle in Paris and the Mansion House in London raised funds and prepared to aid the many Jews who wished to emigrate. The largest and most ambitious emigration project was undertaken by Baron Maurice de Hirsch. Through a series of financial transactions Hirsch acquired extensive tracts of land in Argentina. In 1891 he founded the Jewish Colonization Association in hopes of helping 125,000 Jews a year settle in Argentina. The project settled thousands of Jews, but never the number Hirsch envisioned.

Historians who have studied emigration patterns of Russian Jews point out that it was not necessarily pogroms that started outmigration. They argue that a significant number of Jews, in response

27. The articles were published in the Hebrew periodical edited by Perez Smolenskin called *Hashahar* (Vienna), no. 7 (1882): 329–56.

to depressed economic conditions in the Pale, started emigrating as early as 1870.[28] Although this is true, it is clear that the crisis of 1881 radically increased emigration. In the decade before the pogroms (1870–80), 4,500 Jews left Russia annually. In contrast, in the five-year period following the pogroms (1881–86), the yearly average tripled to 12,586 Jews. The United States was the most popular place to go; 70 percent (135,000 Jews between 1881 and 1890) of all those who left Russia went to the United States. The remaining 30 percent emigrated to Canada, Western Europe, England, and South Africa; a small percentage went to Argentina, and an even smaller percentage to Palestine.[29]

Of the two solutions proposed by the community—emigration or emancipation—neither wholly improved conditions in the Pale. Emigration could not keep pace with the natural increase of Jews in the Pale. There were more Jews being born (40 per 1,000 population) than could possibly hope to emigrate.[30] In addition, government emigration policies and regulations made it difficult for Jews who wished to leave. Most important, emigration, although in the long run the best possible solution, did little for the 4.8 million Jews who for one reason or another remained in the Pale. Policies of emancipation as articulated by the St. Petersburg leadership were also doomed to failure. In the years following the pogroms of 1881 both the legal and socioeconomic condition of Jews steadily deteriorated. Any optimism for the revival of liberal policies was crushed by the reactionary regimes of Alexander III and his successor Nicholas II. In essence, no significant policies were forwarded by the intelligentsia, the St. Petersburg leadership, or the central government to avert pogroms.

The Pogroms of 1903–1906

The Jews of the Pale enjoyed a brief, but peaceful, hiatus between 1884 and 1903. Emigration continued to grow at a steady pace, with an average of forty thousand Jews leaving Russia annually. Zionism

28. Jacob Lestchinsky, "Di yidishe imigratsye in di fareynikte shtatn," in *Geshihkte fun der yidisher arbeter*, 1:27–40.
29. For emigration statistics, see Report of the U.S. Immigration Commission, *Emigration Condition in Europe* (Washington, D.C., 1911), pp. 251–64; Zosa Szajkowski, "How the Mass Migration to America Began," *Jewish Social Studies* 4 (1942): 300–309.
30. Salo Baron, *The Russian Jew under Tsars and Soviets* (New York, 1964), p. 78.

acquired more adherents, especially under the leadership of Theodor Herzl and the World Zionist Organization. Russian Zionism was a central issue at the First Zionist Congress in Basel in 1897. The St. Petersburg leadership continued to advocate reform, but with minimal success. Nicholas II, who ascended the throne in 1894, showed little interest in Jewish emancipation or civil rights. A stronger voice for emancipation and reform came from the Bund, a radical Jewish workers' organization. The Bund basically agreed with the goals of emancipation and assimilation put forward by the traditional leadership of the Jewish community, but it advocated radically different tactics to achieve these goals. The Bund's programs stressed a break with the passive, nonviolent, and accommodating methods of the St. Petersburg leadership. The Bundists extolled the virtues of physical resistance and self-defense and exhorted the Jewish workers to struggle actively for civil rights.

Amid the changes occurring in the Jewish community a new wave of pogroms began. They started in April 1903 in the Bessarabian city of Kishinev and ended with the Bialystok pogrom of June 1906. Unlike the 1881 pogroms, these were markedly greater in number and significantly more violent and destructive. The pogroms occurred in three phases: first, the early pogroms of 1903–1904 that were isolated, localized incidents; second, pogroms that occurred as a consequence of the Russo-Japanese War; finally, those that occurred during the 1905 Revolution.

The first pogrom of the twentieth century took place in Kishinev on April 19–21, 1903.[31] It was devastating; forty-seven Jews were killed (more than the total number killed in 1881); four hundred others were wounded; and property damage exceeded three million rubles. The pogrom had been instigated by a local antisemitic newspaper, the *Bessarabets*. Local officials did little to discourage the pogroms, and police stood idle as Jews were murdered and beaten and their homes set on fire. At first the central government denied the massacre at Kishinev.[32] In the face of overwhelming evidence, however, the government changed tactics. It acknowledged that the

31. On Kishinev, see Krasni-Admoni, "Dubbossarskoe i Kishinevskoe dela 1903 Goda," *Materialy dlia istorii antievreiskikh pogromov*, vol. 1; *Bulletin de l'Alliance Israélite Universelle* (Paris), special ed., 1903; Michael Davitt, *Within the Pale* (London, 1903); Cyrus Adler, *The Voice of America in Kishinev* (Philadelphia, 1904).
32. The U.S. ambassador to Russia in 1903 cabled the State Department that the Russian government had denied that a massacre occurred in Kishinev. See the *Papers Relating to the Foreign Affairs of the United States* (Washington, D.C., 1903), p. 712.

events had occurred but, as in 1881, blamed the pogroms on the victims. Count Arthur Cassini, Russian ambassador to the United States, stated: "The Jews ruin the peasants with the result that conflicts occur. . . . But notwithstanding the conflicts the Jews continue to do the very things which have been responsible for the troubles that involve them."[33]

The Kishinev pogrom set certain patterns for the remaining pogroms of 1903–1906. Most important it showed that: (1) the antisemitic press was effective in agitating the public against Jews; (2) some local officials were willing to allow pogroms to occur; (3) Jews of the Pale could not depend on the local police for protection; (4) the central government was unwilling to discourage pogroms; (5) little if any legal action would be taken against *pogromshchiki;* and (6), finally, the government's position that Jews bore the responsibility for the violence committed against them was reemphasized.

Apart from Kishinev, localized pogroms occurred in the town of Smela, Rovno, Sosnowiec, and Gomel. In all, twenty-five localized pogroms followed the Kishinev pattern. In Gomel the pogrom raged for three days, destroying hundreds of shops and taking the lives of eight Jews. As was the case in Kishinev, the authorities did little to stop it.[34]

A sustained outbreak of pogroms began in September 1904. While awaiting departure to Manchuria to fight in an increasingly ineffective and unpopular war, groups of men from both urban and rural areas instigated a wave of twenty-four pogroms. Fanned by the antisemitic press, which tried to shift the blame for the failing war from the autocracy to the Jews, the attacks persisted until December of that year.

As in the earlier pogroms of 1903, there is little evidence that local authorities did anything to discourage or suppress mobilization pogroms. It appears that local officials sympathized with pogroms or felt it would be dangerous to use coercive measures against armed troops. Their unwillingness to discourage reservists stemmed from a reluctance to antagonize an already disgruntled army. There were

33. For a complete text of Count Arthur Cassini's remarks, see the *New York Times*, May, 19, 1903, p. 5, col. 5.

34. USSR dossier "Mogilev," Archives, Alliance Israélite Universelle Paris (hereafter AIU Archives); B. A. Kreverom, ed., *Gomeleskii pro. ss* (St. Petersburg, 1907); "Der protess fun der bundisher zelbstshuts in Homel in 1904," *Naye Folktsaytung*, September 19, 1937; "Pogrom v Gomele," September 1903, Bund Archives, New York.

forty-nine pogroms during 1903–1904, almost half related to mobilization.

The frequency of pogroms increased with the beginning of the 1905 Revolution. From January to September 1905 there were twenty-two pogroms, the most serious in Kiev, Lodz, and Zhitomir. After the issuing of the October Manifesto, the number of pogroms rose dramatically—to 657.

As in the past, the central government was lax in stopping pogroms. Given the political situation in which Nicholas II found himself after October 1905, it is not surprising that the authorities believed it in their best interest to encourage the activities of counterrevolutionary right-wing organizations. The authorities' position was the Jews were responsible for pogroms and for the revolution. Nicholas II wrote to his mother the empress: "Nine-tenths of the troublemakers are Jews, the People's whole anger turned against them. That's how the pogroms happened."[35]

The radical Right strongly supported the autocracy's position. Having lost faith in the government's ability to maintain power, the Right took it upon itself to oppose the revolution. To this end reactionary groups sponsored popular demonstrations supporting Nicholas II and return of power to the autocracy. Included in such activities was the initiation of pogroms by the Soiuz Russkogo Naroda (Union of Russian People) and its terrorist arm the Chernosotenstvo (Black Hundreds).

Estimates of the number of pogroms occurring after the October Manifesto vary, but it is safe to speculate that there were at least 657.[36] During these pogroms almost 3,000 out of 4.89 million Jews died. At least one-fourth of all those killed were women. The number of children orphaned is estimated at 1,500; about 800 children lost one parent. In all, 2,000 people were seriously wounded, a figure that reflects only those who sought medical attention from a hospital or physician and does not include those treated at home or by friends or relatives.

Total destruction of property due to pogroms in 1903–1906 is esti-

35. Quoted in Edward J. Bing, *The Secret Letters of the Last Tsar* (New York, 1938), pp. 187–88.
36. Leo Motzkin, *Die Judenpogrome in Russland* (London, 1910), counted 690 pogroms, 666 occurring within the Pale. A study conducted by the St. Petersburg Aid Committee counted 638 pogroms. Its findings were published in *Die Welt* (Vienna) 9, no. 43 (October 27, 1905): 17. My own study of pogroms, "Pogrom Movement," counted 657.

mated to be 57.84 million rubles within the Pale and an additional 8.2 million outside it. Fire caused the greatest property destruction. Many reports and letters described entire towns being destroyed by fire. Although synagogues were usually the first to be burned, when this was not the case they were ransacked and pillaged.

One aspect of pogroms not reflected by quantitative analysis is the extent of the violence. Newspapers and personal accounts detail rape, torture, and mutilation. Jews were burned alive; they had had tongues, ears, and hands severed; their eyes were gouged out; nails were driven into the heads of living individuals. The incalculable atrocities are ample evidence of the excessive violence that permeated Russian society during the year 1905.

The violence of pogroms demanded a response from the Jews of the Pale. The Jewish community had three alternatives: submission, emigration, or resistance. The more religiously Orthodox argued for submission and cooperation with the authorities, while Zionists championed emigration. The Bund supported active, armed resistance against pogroms, arguing that effective resistance required an armed group which would discourage pogroms.

The religiously Orthodox believed that survival depended on cooperation with the authorities. They argued that pogroms manifested God's will and that the only solution to pogroms was to suffer the consequences. As one rabbi implied, Jews should submit; the community should be "as quiet as the water and lower than the grass."[37] Given the violence that raged through the Pale, this approach was questionable.

Another alternative was emigration. Zionist groups had actively supported wide-scale emigration since the pogroms of 1881. Emigration, as discussed earlier, was a complex issue. The government did not support those who wished to emigrate. Policy vacillated between unrestricted emigration and legislation making purchasing passports financially prohibitive. The government's policy, characterized by indecisiveness, inconsistency, and uncertainty, prevented emigration from being a viable solution to pogroms. Although emigration was the most plausible long-term solution for Russian Jews, it did not address the more immediate threat of pogroms. More realistic was the Bund's proposal for organized resistance.

37. Rafail A. Abramovitch, *In tsvey revolutsyes, di geshikhte fun a dor* (New York, 1944), p. 95.

The Bund's armed resistance program was not universally approved by the Jewish community. The community was less averse, however, to armed resistance than it was to the revolutionary aims of the Bund. It was not anxious to play into the hands of the anti-semitic press and the Union of Russian People, which branded Jews as revolutionaries. The community was trying to dispel, not feed, the notion that all Jews were revolutionaries, and it found itself in a precarious position. On one hand, support for the Bund would lend support to antisemitic rhetoric; on the other, the Bund seemed to offer the best solution to the violence of pogroms.

The Bund asserted that the community could no longer remain passive victims of brutality. Its members preached a new sense of pride and dignity, a self-awareness among Jews heretofore absent in the community. This position was expressed in the Bund publication *Di Arbeter Shtime:* "In such instances [pogroms] we must come out with arms in hand, organize ourselves and fight to our last drop of blood. Only when we show our strength will we force everyone to respect our honor."[38] Also supporting this position were the Poalei Zion (a Zionist workers' group) and the socialist Zionists. All agreed that active resistance was the only viable solution to pogroms.

The Jewish community remained skeptical of the Bund's program. A century-old tradition of nonviolence was not readily overturned by young revolutionaries. Community members feared that an aggressive policy of self-defense would only exacerbate the situation. The Bund therefore redoubled its efforts to convince Jews generally of the validity of its argument.

The community's attitude changed as the number and severity of pogroms increased. More and more the Jews realized the desperateness of their situation. The Bund's position on active resistance received important recognition after the 1905 pogrom in Zhitomir. The successful resistance at Zhitomir elevated the struggle to a legend. Details of the Zhitomir pogrom were recorded by a participant who published his story in *Posledniia Izvestiia.* The story relates how the community prepared for the pogrom. The *kamf-grupe* (fighting group) was divided into two units of twenty-five men, and an additional reserve of four hundred stood in readiness. Local students and the Poalei Zion cooperated, and arms, daggers, whips, and home-made bombs were distributed. When the fighting broke out, the de-

38. *Di Arbeter Shtime,* October 30, 1902, no. 19.

fense behaved valiantly and defeated the *pogromshchiki*.[39] One of the inhabitants commented, "If not for the self-defense, Zhitomir would have been another Kishinev."[40] Reports indicated that during the struggle heavy casualties were suffered by the defenders and the *po-gromshchiki*.

By the end of October 1905 the joint activities of the Bund, Poalei Zion, the socialist Zionists, and other self-defense groups had won over many segments of the Jewish community that had initially withheld support. When asked for a donation for self-defense, Maxim Vinaver, lawyer and member of the 1905 Duma as well as proponent of Jewish rights, handed over a blank check with the comment, "After all, we are all Bundists."[41]

The efforts of the Bund and the spirit of self-defense made the *yidishe gas* (Jewish streets) alive with political activism. Even where the Bund had no active, organized defense the spirit of resistance flourished in the small towns and *shtetlekh* of the Pale. Reports from these towns, especially in the south where the Bund was not so active, reflect this spirit. In these areas shopkeepers, students, and other community members banded together to protect their homes and families. The spirit was a product of the Bund's aggressive attitude. Simon Dubnov stressed this point in a letter to the Jewish people, first published in *Voskhod*.

> The past decade has taught us that our fate depends not on our environment but on ourselves, on our will and on our national effort. The new pogroms have engraved the watchword "self-help" in flaming letters on the Jewish nation. It is as if a powerful electric shock has passed through the body of our humiliated people. ... The principles of self-help and self-defense have never been as clear to all the classes of our people, from the highest to the lowest strata, as at the present time.[42]

Through November and December 1905 the Jewish community waged strong self-defense efforts against attacks. Even the most ardent Zionists temporarily relegated their mission to establish a Jewish state in order to help with the urgent needs of the Pale. The defenders were not always successful. In Odessa, for example, the well-armed, well-organized squads were effective only in containing

39. *Posledniia Izvestiia*, June 1905.
40. *Pogromen Blat*, July 16, 1905. See also, USSR dossier "Zhitomir," AIU Archives.
41. Quoted in Abramovitch, *In tsvey revolutsyes*, pp. 189–90.
42. Simon Dubnov, "A Historic Moment (The Question of Emigration)" (1905), in *Nationalism and History: Essays on Old and New Judaism*, ed. Koppel S. Pinson (New York, 1970), p. 193.

the pogrom; and the same was true of Bialystok, which suffered the last of the large-scale pogroms to occur in the Pale. It became increasingly evident that resistance was least successful against police or military involvement in pogroms. As troops and police played a more active role in pogroms, the Bund adopted a new strategy—to take aggressive action in case of a pogrom. The Bund issued a general call to arms in May 1905.

> It must become a general rule that each worker who considers himself part of the struggle should carry a revolver in his pocket. . . . And as tens of thousands of workers will go into the streets and each feel he is prepared for the struggle then the uprising will take on a different appearance. Arm yourself. Learn how to handle a weapon.[43]

The Bund argued that new tactics were critical to combat successfully the military's manpower and arms. Some Bund members even advocated retaliation by bombing town areas or assassinating local officials, but terrorism had never been the Bund's policy, and these suggestions were rejected. However, a change of tactics and a bolder strategy were recommended: "To fight a hooligan a revolver was enough. But to fight the military one needs dynamite. With a hooligan you can fight in the open spaces, but against the military you must fight from behind barricades."[44]

It was also decided to establish a highly organized group to gather intelligence and act as a coordinating unit. The group was named Mayim (Hebrew for "water"), and it carefully planned defense and emergency procedures for many cities of the Pale, preparing street maps and shelter areas for women and children and smuggling arms and munitions to local self-defense groups with the aim of aborting impending pogroms. Mayim was the elite fighting unit of the Bund, a militant cadre of defenders who saw themselves as the vanguard of the revolution. The group lauded the merits of armed revolution rather than the ideals of self-defense.[45] Leonard Rowe has commented: "The force organized to resist violence against Jews was considered more than a defense organization. In the eyes of the Bund, it was the nucleus and the vanguard of the revolution that was bound to come."[46]

Armed revolution was not what the Jewish community had in

---

43. *Der Bund* 2, no. 7 (May 1905): 3–4.
44. *Der Glok*, October 3, 1906, no. 3, pp. 6–7.
45. Leyb Berman, *In loyf fun di yorn* (Warsaw, 1936), p. 361.
46. Leonard Rowe, "Jewish Self-Defense: A Response to Violence," in *Studies on Polish Jewry, 1919–1939*, ed. Joshua A. Fishman (New York, 1974), p. 108.

mind when it lent its support to the defense units of the Bund. The radical posture taken by Mayim, combined with its limited success against troops and police, diminished the community's initial enthusiasm. By early 1906 the community gradually began to withdraw support; the attitude of the Jews of the Pale had come full circle. They were intimidated by the Black Hundreds and by police participation in pogroms. Meetings were poorly attended, contributions fell off, and membership of reserve units was curtailed. Guns were returned to group leaders by those who no longer wanted any part of armed resistance. One leader had to dispose of several dozen returned revolvers; he hired a rowboat and dropped the guns into the middle of a river.[47] The Jewish community had been willing to provide financial, physical, and spiritual support for defense, but it was not equally prepared to do so for revolution. When the Bund attempted to use its self-defense units as a proto-revolutionary militia, it lost many of its supporters.

The reaction of some segments of the community to the revolutionary activities of the Bund were understandable. The reality of attempting to drown the revolution in Jewish blood had made itself felt in the years 1903–1906. While the Bund was able to maintain some support in the Pale, its revolutionary stand had alienated large segments within the Jewish community.

In what light should we view the reaction of the Jewish community to the pogroms of 1903–1906? Most important, the community acted to serve the needs of the greatest number. Its initial caution and skepticism of the Bund represented a genuine concern that a strong affiliation with that organization might intensify the persecution. Yet the community also recognized and supported the Bund's philosophy of establishing dignity through resistance. The new self-confidence celebrated throughout the Pale rallied the divergent groups within the Jewish community, forcing them to overlook political and religious differences in order to nurture united community action.[48]

Fortunately for the Jews of the Pale, in the aftermath of the 1905 Revolution the central government moved to reestablish the *status*

---

47. Leyb Blekhman, *Bleter fun mayn yugnt* (New York, 1959), pp. 279–80.

48. For a more detailed discussion on self-defense, see Shlomo Lambroza, "Jewish Self-Defense during the Russian Pogroms of 1903–06," *Jewish Journal of Sociology* 23 (1981): 123–34.

quo ante. Government policies after 1906 discouraged mass demonstrations including pogroms. Although reactionary and antisemitic sentiments continued to grow, there were no pogroms between June 1906 and 1917. The government of Nicholas II refused to encourage or tolerate pogroms during these years. It became clear that popular demonstrations, whether reactionary or revolutionary, were as dangerous for the government as they were useful.

The reestablishment of order was short lived. As Vladimir Ilyich Lenin stated, 1905 was merely a "dress rehearsal" for 1917. With the outbreak of the 1917 Revolution and the Civil War that followed, pogroms reappeared. The pogroms of 1917–21 far surpassed earlier pogroms in their brutality; nearly sixty thousand Jews were killed. Again the Jewish community united to defend itself, but was no match for the Red and White armies that descended upon the Jews.

This essay has described the various alternatives and strategies employed by the Jews of the Pale to maintain and protect the community. After 1881 issues of emancipation and emigration were paramount, while in 1903–1906, during significantly more brutal pogroms, self-defense took precedence. With each alternative the community had to consider a government whose policies toward Jews were discriminatory and antisemitic. The laws of the empire toward Jews were retrogressive; they worsened the Jews' material existence and intensified the animosity between Jews and Gentiles.

In the wake of pogroms, thousands of Jews left the Pale searching for an environment that was accepting and nurturing instead of denying and violent. Although many chose to stay and continue the struggle for emancipation, clearly the best solution and the path to true liberation was to leave Russia. The path out of Russia taken by Jews after the pogroms is the same path sought by thousands more now waiting to leave.

Chone Shmeruk

Responses to Antisemitism in Poland, 1912–36

A Case Study of the Novels of Michal Bursztyn

The Yiddish novels written in Poland during the interwar period are by and large mimetic. In the literary terminology of the period, they exhibit markedly "realistic" tendencies, bordering at times on naturalism, in their treatment of real events and circumstances. This fiction seldom journeys into the distant past, or even back into the nineteenth century; rather, it focuses on the Jews of Poland in the twentieth century.

The Yiddish novel of this period may be defined as Judeocentric and, like the bulk of modern Yiddish literature, essentially "secular." It reflects the modern transformations that took place in Jewish society within the experience of the writers, almost all of whom grew up within traditional Jewish society only to leave it behind. This secular stance is evident in these novels even when, in retrospect, the writers succumb to feelings of nostalgia for a way of life they had grown to despise. This fiction tends to be concerned with social, political, and ideological issues from a perspective of intimate familiarity, an eyewitness view of events as they unfold.

These noted characteristics of the Yiddish novel in interwar Poland seem to suggest a considerable interest on the part of the writers in their own times and events. This interest was not their sole reserve, however. There are clear indications to suggest that foremost among the preferences of the Yiddish reader, at all levels, was the depiction of recent and familiar events in a literary form essentially fictional in nature.[1] For this reason, the Yiddish novel may be

1. The tendency toward depiction of nearby surroundings familiar to the reader likewise dominated the noncanonical literature that appeared in installments in the

expected to provide a trustworthy, albeit at times simplistic, reflection of the world familiar to its loyal readership. Indeed, this very authenticity served to guarantee the novel's success among the reading public.

These general opening remarks, which require more detailed historical and literary examination, serve to focus attention on the considerable documentary value of Yiddish literature that has been sorely neglected in historical research into Polish Jewry of recent times.[2] A discussion of the responses to antisemitism in Poland depicted in the three novels of Michal Bursztyn will serve to illustrate this genre of literature as a historical source as well as guide the reader through the complex web of problems that these novels attempt to confront.

The literary legacy of Michal Bursztyn (1897–1945) includes three novels: *Iber di khurves fun Ployne* (Over the Ruins of Ployne) (1931), *Goyrl* (Fate) (1935), and *Bay di taykhn fun Mazovye* (By the Rivers of Masovia) (1937).[3] Together they deal with Jewish life in Poland over a period of some twenty-five years, from approximately 1912 to 1936. It should be noted at the outset that the time frame of Bursztyn's novels is consistent with the bounds of his own personal experience.

Yiddish press. It is most strikingly revealed in subtitles of the novels that announce the story's Polish-Jewish background. Three novels by Israel Rabon, published in installments in the newspaper *Haynt* between 1929 and 1936, have an identical subtitle: "A Novel about Jewish Life in Poland." See my "Sifrut ha-shund be-yidish," *Tarbiz* 23 (1983): 347. A significant number of the novels published in installments in newspapers were merely Jewish adaptations of novels in other languages that had no bearing on Jews. An integral element of the Judaization of these novels was their transplantation from foreign surroundings to places of large concentrations of Jewish population, such as Warsaw. The same is true for Isaac Bashevis's treatment of a German novel (ibid., pp. 339–40) and the adaptation of a Danish novel for *Haynt* in 1909. See my article on the novel *In nets fun zind*, "Teudah nedirah le-toldoteha shel ha-sifrut ha-lo-kanonit be-yidish," *Ha-sifrut* 32 (1982): 15–18. As these novels focus on actual events, they often contain considerable information of a documentary nature.

2. See William M. Glicksman, *In the Mirror of Literature: The Economic Life of the Jews in Poland as Reflected in Yiddish Literature (1914–1938)* (New York, 1966). As far as I know, Glicksman and only a few other historians make reference to Yiddish literature of the period in a historical discussion.

3. On Bursztyn, see the article in *Leksikon fun der nayer yidisher literatur*, vol. 1 (New York, 1956), pp. 273–75. *Iber di khurves fun Ployne* (Vilna: B. Kletskin, 1931), was reprinted in the series "Dos poylishe yidntum" (Buenos Aires, 1949). *Goyrl* was published by Kh. Bzshoze in Warsaw in 1935. Bursztyn's last novel, *Bay di taykhn fun Mazovye* (Warsaw: n.p., 1937), had three additional editions: "Der emes" (Moscow, 1941); "Yidish-bukh" (Warsaw, 1951); and in a volume entitled *Erev khurbn*, "Musterverk fun der yidisher literatur" (Buenos Aires, 1970), pp. 21–210. References in this article will be to the first edition; where possible, subsequent references to Bursztyn's novels will appear in the text. On the censored Soviet edition, see n. 24 below.

The order of appearance of Bursztyn's novels does not correspond with the chronology of historical events they describe. *Goyrl*, his second novel, depicts the years preceding World War I and ends with the outbreak of the war. The novel about Ployne is set in the mid-1920s in independent Poland. The last novel spans the mid-1930s, following Adolf Hitler's rise to power until just after the death of Józef Piłsudski, the leader of independent Poland, in 1935.

Those familiar with the history of Poland and its Jews will easily discern that Bursztyn has set each of the three novels in periods of intense antisemitism. *Goyrl* focuses on the election of the Polish socialist Eugeniusz Jagiełło to the Russian Duma with the help of Jewish votes. This affair exacerbated the political enmity toward Jews in Congress Poland and produced the notorious Polish economic boycott of Jewish trade.[4] The era of Władysław Grabski (1874–1938), Poland's prime minister and minister of the treasury in 1923–25, provides the background for the novel about Ployne. These years were best remembered by the Jews of Poland for the oppressive economic measures that hit hardest at the Jews and were indeed perceived as directed against them. At the end of his last novel, Bursztyn depicts the violent antisemitism during 1935–36 in his treatment of a pogrom in a Jewish town.[5]

Did Bursztyn choose as realistic settings for his novels these three periods in the history of Polish Jewry because of the antisemitic tension by which they are marked? It would seem that this was a consideration, though we lack direct evidence to substantiate it.[6] What

4. On this affair, see Frank Golczewski, *Polnisch-Jüdische Beziehungen, 1881–1922* (Wiesbaden, 1981), pp. 90–120.
5. On the Jews of independent Poland between the world wars, see the general survey in Ezra Mendelsohn, *The Jews of East Central Europe between the World Wars* (Bloomington, Ind., 1983), pp. 11–83. On economic antisemitism, see also Isaiah Trunk, "Economic Antisemitism in Poland between the Two World Wars," in *Studies on Polish Jewry, 1919–1939*, ed. Joshua A. Fishman (New York, 1974), pp. 3–98, also in Trunk, *Geshtaltn un gesheenishn* (Tel Aviv, 1983), pp. 170–273; Joseph Marcus, *Social and Political History of the Jews in Poland, 1919–1939* (Berlin, 1983). On the period after Józef Piłsudski's death, see Emanuel Melzer, *Maavak medini be-malkodet: Yehudei Polin, 1935–1939* (Tel Aviv, 1982). See also nn. 22, 25 below. All the works here and in n.4 above include bibliographical references to earlier works. I found no references anywhere to Yiddish literature.
6. It may be noted that, beyond the novels discussed here, Bursztyn was preoccupied with antisemitism and attacks on Jews. Bursztyn's last publication, a collection of stories entitled *Broyt un zalts*, published in 1939 with the assistance of PEN Club in Warsaw, includes a number of stories that deal with antisemitism: In "Studentn" (Students), reference is made to the special benches designated for Jews at Warsaw Univer-

is clear, however, is that Bursztyn's novels reveal an acute historical sense of both the obscure and the apparent connections among the three periods depicted in his novels. His writing focuses on the considerable tensions that existed between Poles and Jews during periods of time that may be regarded as crucial in the history of their relations prior to the Holocaust.

These novels were not originally intended as a trilogy; nor do the same characters appear in them. Nevertheless, they share a number of elements. All three "take place" in small towns (*shtetlekh*) with sizable Jewish communities that constitute the vast majority of the total population.[7] Situated in close proximity to Warsaw, which appears in the background, all three towns bear fictitious names: the town in *Goyrl* is named Tshubin; the town in the last novel is called Smolin; the town in the first novel is named Ployne. Bursztyn himself was born in a town that bore the Polish name Błonie and was known to the Jews as Bloyne, situated some twenty kilometers west of Warsaw. Not only does Bloyne, thinly disguised as Ployne, appear in Bursztyn's first novel, but the life of its Jews seems to be depicted directly in his writing. Indeed, his native town appears to have served as a model for all three fictional towns.

Moreover, each of the novels features similar young, educated, secular Jews from whose perspective the story is told. *Goyrl* focuses on a young man who manages the development projects of a wealthy Jewish landowner. The novel about Ployne portrays a law student and native of Ployne studying in Warsaw. The protagonist of the last novel is a doctor who returns to the town of his birth after completing his training, disenchanted with the big city and feeling nostalgic for his hometown. While each of these protagonists is distinctive, they all bear a certain resemblance to the author himself, who, for example, also left his native town only to return later. In addition,

---

sity and the student protest against this decree (pp. 15–35). In "A geredter shidukh" (An Arranged Marriage), there is mention of the Polish boycott (p. 99). "Rut fun Bozshe Volye" (Ruth from Bozshe Volye) refers to the trial of Mendel Beilis and accusations against Jews of spying for the Germans during World War I (pp. 133–40). The theme of "A farshterter Tisha be-Av" (A Disrupted *Tisha be-Av*) is the pogrom in the *shtetl* (pp. 170–75). During the German occupation, while in the Kovno ghetto, Bursztyn wrote another novel, *Di gele late* (The Yellow Patch), describing the years immediately preceding the war up to the Jews' incarceration in the ghetto. The novel was never recovered. See the memoir by his widow, Rokhl Bursztyn, "Michal Bursztyn in Kovner geto," *Dos naye lebn* (Warsaw), April 18, 1948. See the abridged version in *Di goldene keyt* 2 (1949): 207.

7. The Jews of Tshubin, the fictional setting of *Goyrl*, constitute 75 percent of the total population. *Goyrl*, p. 142.

the characters share a number of traits that conform to the particular Polish literary model which guided their creator.[8]

I

In *Goyrl*, Bursztyn goes to great lengths to provide the reader with as comprehensive a picture as possible of Jewish society in a Jewish town on the eve of World War I. The Jews of Tshubin who appear in the book are supposed to represent a cross-section of the town's society that, even in those days, was sharply defined by social differentiation. "Progressive" youths rebel against their traditional parents; workers rise up against the local bourgeoisie and government; the native, traditional Jews virulently oppose the ideas and activism of the foreigner—the *Litvak*. The central protagonists of this novel are a group of assimilated Jews, converts to Christianity and their Polish friends.

Naturally, in a novel of only 258 pages, the "representatives" of the diverse camps, positions, and ideas cannot each receive extensive attention. The characters that stand out are those whose views Bursztyn presents in detail. Meshullam Alter is one of them. An affluent merchant and traditional Jew, Alter serves as the head of the *kahal*. As his name intimates, his roots in the town go far back. In direct counterpoint to him is Aharon Zhitomirski, whose very name indicates his foreignness to Congress Poland. A victim of the Gomel pogrom of 1903, where he lost all of his possessions, Zhitomirski and his daughter have only recently settled in Tshubin. The contrasting responses of Alter and Zhitomirski to manifestations of antisemitism are central factors in the shaping of these two prominent Tshubin characters.

Meshullam Alter professes two principles: Jews should behave humbly and should not flaunt their wealth since it evokes jealousy and hatred of Jews; and Jews should not interfere in the affairs of others.[9] These principles reflect a conservative outlook, fatalistic in nature, which sees neither the possibility nor the wisdom of change

---

8. The reference here is to a very famous model in Polish literature, the character of the doctor Judym in the novel *Ludzie Bezdomni* (1923) by Stefan Żeromski. See my essay, "Jews and Poles in Yiddish Literature in Poland between the Two World Wars," *Polin: A Journal of Polish-Jewish Studies* 1 (1986): 176–95.

9. Relevant passages in the text include: "When I build a stone house, it will be luxurious, and those others will view the Jews with a jaundiced eye." "Jews should be modest and not celebrate balls." "Jews shouldn't interfere." *Goyrl*, pp. 58, 142.

and prefers to maintain the status quo. This attitude dictates Meshullam Alter's vociferous opposition to the establishment of a "reformed" *heder* in the town. At the same time Alter opposes plans that call for the resettlement of Jews on the land as a socioeconomic solution to the eviction of Jews from commerce during the Polish boycott, itself a consequence of Jewish activism in the election of Jagiełło to the Russian Duma. Alter's outward response to virulent manifestations of antisemitism in the wake of the Jagiełło Affair is to blame the foreign Jews: The *Litvaks* are to blame, while the traditional Jews had no hand in the matter! These thoughts are presented in response to the direct accusations of the Polish mayor, who is sympathetic toward the Jews and with whom Meshullam Alter maintains a relationship of mutual understanding that smacks of traditional *shtadlanut*. The conversation between the two illustrates Meshullam Alter's arguments as they appear against the background of the events depicted in the novel.

> The mayor spoke candidly: "The Jews of Warsaw have sinned and the Jews of Old Tshubin are to suffer the punishment. Why did the Jews elect that socialist Jagiełło? Aren't the socialists waging war against the Jewish shopkeepers? Now the liberals of Great Poland in Old Tshubin want to change the market day to Saturday to prevent Jews from doing business. As long as I am mayor, I will not allow it. But we are all under the enemy's whip, and the Jews must lend us their support. They must side with the townspeople, not with the socialists."
>
> "My very thought," Meshullam Alter agreed. "You're absolutely right. This is the work of the *Litvaks*. They are responsible. They come here from Russia and lead the simple folk astray. They barge in uninvited and spread heresy among the pious Polish Jews." (p. 204)

It quickly becomes apparent to the reader that Meshullam Alter's words do not correspond with the facts as presented in the novel. The leader of a group of local youths who share Zionist and populist inclinations and call for autonomous rights for the local Jewish population is none other than Meshullam Alter's son. Likewise, the proponent of plans to transform impoverished Jewish merchants into farmers is the son of an established and respected Tshubin family. To present them as *Litvaks* is to distort the truth. The reader is bound to wonder whether Alter's arguments are merely expedient in the context of the discussion with the Polish mayor or indeed reflect Alter's views that all the catastrophes that have befallen the Jews of Poland, including the wave of antisemitism that followed in the wake of the Jagiełło Affair, are the responsibility of the Russian Jews who have "overrun" Congress Poland and spread the disease of social and political activism among the local Jews. Meshullam Alter reiterates this belief to Aharon Zhitomirski, the "representative" of foreigners in Tshubin, in a heated discussion regarding the proportionate representation of Jews in the elections. Meshullam Alter voices his opposition to Zhitomirski's demands.

> "It's not a matter of life and death. What difference does it make how many Jewish electors there are? It isn't worthwhile antagonizing the Christians."
>
> "But it does make a difference. The greater the number of Jewish electors in the province, the greater the say Jews will have in choosing the regional representative. The fourth Duma will decide over the issue of self-determination for Poland. Do you understand? Self-determination."
>
> "Yes, yes, Aharon, I understand. Jews are living in exile. We must live peaceably with the world. We Polish Jews feel this responsibility. You're not a Polish Jew. Where you come from in Gomel . . ."
>
> "Well, and what if I've come from Gomel? I didn't choose to come here. Does that mean I mustn't breathe? I mustn't enlighten the people?"
>
> "No!" Meshullam Alter retorted. "You're a stranger here and strangers sit still. Give thanks to the Creator of the Universe that you have a loaf of bread and a knife to cut it with and don't play politics. We'll take care of our own town."
>
> "Imagine that! 'This one fellow came in to sojourn, and he will needs be a judge.'[10] A stranger has come among us to judge us." (p. 143)

Presented here is the conflict between political activism, as regards antisemitism as well, and a conservative stance of noninvolvement that attempts to cast activism as a foreign import and the cause of antisemitism. Forcing the submission and silence of the foreigners, the *Litvaks*, is perceived as the means of averting antisemitism.

Zhitomirski's activist position on the specific issue of the elections should be understood in the context of his views on other matters. The character is not, by any stretch of the imagination, a revolutionary. Indeed, quite the opposite:

> "Revolution! [Zhitomirski yelled in response to the revolutionaries] Revolution means pogroms against Jews, a repeat of Kishinev, Bialystok, and Gomel. Believe me, youngsters, I no longer have the strength to endure all that. I lived through one pogrom, and that's enough for me." (pp. 146–47)

Zhitomirski has associated himself with the traditional, simple folk in whose midst he promotes Zionism, political activism on the local level, and the establishment of a "reformed" *heder*. He opposes the proponents of plans to resettle Jews in agricultural settlements

10. Gen. 19:9.

in Poland as well as the revolutionaries. Alternatively, he proposes Zionism as the only effective response to antisemitism and the solution to the Jewish Problem.

> "We're beginning to get smart when they attack us, when they instigate a pogrom or blood libel against us. The Beilis trial has stirred up Jews in all corners of the world. Even more so than in the Tisza-Eszlar trial, people are yelling, defending themselves, and appealing to the civilized world. The Jews of St. Petersburg have engaged the finest attorneys, and great people have rallied to our defense. Nothing will change as long as Jews live in exile. There is only one solution: a land of our own, the land of our forefathers, Eretz Israel." (p. 70)

The uniqueness of Bursztyn's novel does not lie, however, in the depiction of traditional Jewish society or those active in its midst. Both in this novel and in a number of short stories,[11] Bursztyn set out to portray a particular social group that heretofore had escaped the attention of Yiddish writers.[12] At the focus of Bursztyn's novel is the character of Herman Lubliner and his family. An extremely wealthy man and faithful Polish patriot, Lubliner is immersed in extensive development projects such as the draining of swamplands, the establishment of a health spa, and the construction of trolley cars, all in keeping with the ideology of "organic labor," one of the slogans of Polish Positivism following the failure of the 1863 rebellion. Formally he and his wife and family have remained Jews, although a part of his wife's family has already converted to Christianity. Mrs. Lubliner's sister is a convert and, in exchange for a sizable dowry, her father arranged for her marriage to a member of the respected Polish nobility.[13] Lubliner's wife was assured of a similar match upon conversion, and it was a mere coincidence that she married a Jew. Actually, the fact of conversion is insignificant, insofar as those who have already converted and those who have formally re-

11. See the following stories in *Broyt un zalts:* "Tsurikgang" (Return), pp. 117–25; "Di eyntsike trern" (The Only Tears), pp. 176–81; "Der fremder" (The Stranger), pp. 204–9; and "Antoyshung" (Disappointment), pp. 257–60.

12. The lack of attention is noted by Isaac Bashevis in a review of *Goyrl* in *Forverts,* May 10, 1936, entitled "A roman fun yidishn lebn in Poyln"; see also n. 35 below. Bashevis himself depicted this society of assimilated Jews and converts in his novel *Der hoyf,* which appeared in installments in *Forverts,* January 10, 1953–February 12, 1955. The novel was adapted in English and appeared in two volumes as *The Manor* (New York, 1967), and *The Estate* (New York, 1968). It was also translated from English to Hebrew as *Ha-ahuzah* (Tel Aviv, 1972), and *Ha-nahalah* (Tel Aviv, 1976). See also my "Hayahasim ben yehudim le-polanim ba-romanim ha-historiyim shel Itshak Bashevis Singer," *Yahadut zmanenu* 2 (1985): 61–71.

13. These marriages were a most popular subject of Polish antisemitic literature, which generally portrayed the phenomenon derisively. See, for example, *Mechesi* by Marjan Gawalewicz (1852–1910), which first appeared in book form in 1893–94.

tained their religious affiliation live side by side and together suffer from Jewish self-hatred as well as disgust and disdain for Jewish society, which serves as an unpleasant reminder of their not-too-distant past.

In this society antisemitism is perceived as directed exclusively at traditional and nationalistic Jews who refuse to discard their particularity and assimilate. It is this particularism that antagonizes the Poles and turns them into antisemites. Members of this society are prepared to assist the Jews of Tshubin through philanthropy and to enhance their usefulness by establishing trade schools to draw them away from their traditional occupations in business and commerce, which arouse revulsion among their Polish neighbors. Lubliner is unwilling to accept the proposal of his Jewish manager to settle five hundred impoverished Jewish families on his drained lands. His apparently good relations with the Poles in his midst have dulled his sensitivities and feelings in the wake of attacks against Jews. He is not disturbed by the refusal of his Polish employees to work alongside Jews; nor does he react directly to their attack on his Jewish manager.

Norbert Yanash, Lubliner's brother-in-law, a doctor and educated man, is active in the dissemination of education among the Jews. The sole objective of this education is to turn them into Poles in accordance with the philosemitic goals of the Polish Positivists. And just as the Positivists turned antisemitic in the face of Jewish nationalist aspirations,[14] so, too, Norbert Yanash is gripped by despair when, at a ceremony at the trade school established by his own family, the youth of Tshubin demand that Jewish history be included in the curriculum—one group calling for Yiddish, another for Hebrew, as the language of instruction (pp. 210–16). The Tshubin Jews' rejection of Polish prompts a despairing Norbert Yanash to take the ultimate step of formal conversion.

The conversion takes place at the beginning of World War I. Yet even after his conversion, Yanash holds fast to his conviction that total assimilation of the Jews into Polish society is the sole solution to the Jewish Problem. With assimilation, antisemitism will disappear.

"In a free Poland," Yanash said decisively, "there will be no Jewish Question. Separatism will disappear. Just as in America, Germany, and other countries, Jews will adapt themselves to the culture of the land.

14. See my *Sifrut yidish be-Polin* (Jerusalem, 1981), pp. 247–48.

They will adopt the Polish language and way of life and every form of antisemitism will vanish." (p. 245)

Of course, in accordance with his own naïve perception and personal example, the ultimate end of assimilation is conversion.

Bursztyn's presentation of the various solutions offered in response to Polish antisemitism on the eve of World War I is deliberate. His intent was relentlessly to put the ideas of the various spokesmen to the test of the fateful reality and times in which they existed. The very title of the novel—*Goyrl* (Fate)—signifies a common fate for all Jews, with no distinction among them on account of their particular views. At the start of World War I, the Jews' sense of alienation intensified. Accusations of their spying for the Germans was a contributing factor, as was Russian discrimination against the Jews in favor of the Poles, an element in the Russian army's strategy to win the hearts of the Poles by ensuring their safety.

Politically and socially alienated in troubled times, the Jews attempt to appease and placate their Polish neighbors.

> Without prior consultation, each and every [Jew] resolved not to antagonize his neighbors, not to demand repayment of outstanding loans and to maintain friendly relations with the Christians. However, the latter quickly realized that the Jews were ingratiating themselves, and Jewish eyes were casting obsequious glances. Their instincts told them that the Jews had fallen out of favor and were to be avoided. (p. 236)

Jews *per se*, regardless of their differing views, share a common fate. Zhitormirski is executed after being convicted on the trumped-up charge of spying for the Germans. Meshullam Alter, the traditional Jew, is taken hostage by the retreating Russians, along with Herman Lubliner, the assimilated Polish Jew. In these troubled times a sense of belonging to the Jewish people is awakened in Lubliner, and he is drawn into the fold. In this fateful hour the diverse responses to antisemitism lose their significance. Fatalistic helplessness and total despair take the place of doctrines and ideologies.

II

Iber di khurves fun Ployne, Bursztyn's novel about a Jewish town in Poland in the mid-1920s, focuses on economic antisemitism and its consequences. The atmosphere of the town in this period is aptly conveyed to the reader through such traditional phrases as, "It is a time of trouble unto Jacob" or "For the waters are come even unto the soul."[15] These phrases, conveying a feeling of distress, are even more evocative when they appear in their Hebrew original within the Yiddish context. In characterizing the drastic economic measures taken by the Polish government, Bursztyn likewise borrows a traditional term, referring to them as "Grabski's Evil Decrees" (p. 131). The term *gzerah* (evil decree), recalls the severe persecution of Jews in the distant past. Thus the phraseology Bursztyn selects for his novel gives the reader a sense of the great calamity and confusion that engulf the Jews of the town.

The book is replete with references to unbearably heavy taxes, which indeed prove too burdensome for the small shopkeepers and established entrepreneurs alike. In debt to the Christian tax authorities, Jewish shopkeepers find their merchandise confiscated along with their private household belongings and sold at public auctions.[16] Tax collection and the confiscation of property are carried out methodically and with vehement efficiency.

Concurrently, the *spółka* figures prominently throughout the book. It is a Polish cooperative general store established in order to undermine the Jews' monopoly over local retail trade. There is no need to go into detail on the various taxes and modes of collection or the war waged against Jewish trade in the town. Suffice it to say the Jews are left helpless, and, toward the end of the novel, Bursztyn describes the near-pauperization of small shopkeepers as well as affluent merchants. To the reader who recalls the Polish boycott after Jagiełło's election, depicted in another Bursztyn novel, the events in Ployne in the mid-1920s can only appear as a sequel and postscript to that prewar boycott.

Shopkeepers, large and small, are forced to close their businesses and become peddlers who travel daily to Warsaw to hawk their wares, at reduced prices, at the homes of Jewish wholesalers who used to be their suppliers. The wheel of fortune has turned. Bursztyn's description is biting and convincing.

> Fayvish, the rabbi's son, stood outside the wholesale grocery store on Przechodnia Street[17] holding a basket of meat. The merchant, admiring his own manicured nails, smiled pleasantly:
> "Well, well, Reb Fayvish, times change: You used to be my customer

---

15. "Ve-eyt tsarah hi le-Yaakov," echoing Jer. 30:7; Ps. 69:2. See *Iber di khurves fun Ployne*, pp. 25, 27.

16. See *Iber di khurves fun Ployne*, pp. 11, 26, 29, 31–32, 45–49, 74–76, 89, 105, 107, 111, 131, 136, 163, 173, 179, and 185–86.

17. Przechodnia Street is in the vicinity of Warsaw's central marketplace.

and now I'm yours! Meat? Mm ... and butter in the other basket? Ployne's butter is famous! Well, since you want me to become your customer, let's try it out! Hey, Leon! Take this Jew upstairs to the missus[18] and tell her I said to buy."

Two Polish mademoiselles [19] came into the store to buy merchandise for the Ployne *spółka*. The merchant sighed deeply so that Fayvish might hear, bowed politely to the young mademoiselles, and took his place behind the counter.

Fayvish followed dutifully behind the servant. Just last year he used to tip this lad with the shiny visor beer money for hailing a *droshky* to take him to the Ployne train, and now ... Oh, how quickly the wheel of fortune turns over! Now he, Fayvish, is beholden to him.

Leon led the way to the gate. The lad no longer had the time or the patience, so Fayvish continued upstairs alone. After each flight of stairs, he stopped and remembered something. And at each landing the baskets tugged at him, drawing him lower and lower. (p. 200)

This meeting in Warsaw of the Jewish wholesaler and the former Jewish merchant impoverished by the new Polish trade—represented here by the young Polish women—sharply outlines the actual effects of Grabski's Evil Decrees on Jewish trade in the town. Under the guise of pure Polish trade, the *spółka*—heir to Jewish trade in the town—depends on the same Jewish wholesaler in Warsaw, while the Jewish merchant in Ployne sinks into mendicancy.

It is customary, from an economic perspective, to justify the draconian measures introduced by the Polish government as a means of stabilizing Poland's currency and economy.[20] While these measures may perhaps be justified as a rational policy formally directed at the population as a whole, and not exclusively at the Jews, there is little doubt as to their very real and ruinous effect on broad sections of the Jewish population in the *shtetl*.[21] The full weight of the tax measures was mercilessly brought to bear against the Jews; their implementation was not perceived as merely a means of reviving the Polish economy. The Jews felt they were the victims of a policy designed to force them out of *shtetl* commerce for the benefit of Polish merchants and trade cooperatives. Bursztyn's novel provides crucial evidence of the unbearable conditions of the Jews in the Polish towns of this period.

18. In Polish, *pani*.
19. In Polish, *panny*.
20. See A. Landau i J. Tomaszewski, *Gospodarka Polski Miedzywojennej*, vol. 2, *1924–1929 Książka i Wiedza* (Warsaw, 1971), pp. 185–200, 255–68.
21. See Trunk, "Economic Antisemitism in Poland." For critical comments on the latter, see Jerzy Tomaszewski, *Biuletyn żydowskiego Instytutu Historycznego w Polsce*, no. 109 (1979):111–12.

Feelings of animosity between Jews and Poles intensified and deepened during this period against a background of economic persecution and unfair competition of Polish merchants supported by the government. Bursztyn's novel portrays this animosity in a most revealing episode. The town *spółka* is burglarized at night. The Jews are accused without cause; their guilt is simply assumed, since they are believed to have the only motive to perpetrate an act that would harm the *spółka*. Induced by the *spółka* owners and aided by the town's Polish residents, local authorities decide to conduct a massive search for the stolen goods in Jewish shops. The search arouses great fear and antagonism among the Jews and a fervent desire to retaliate by force.

> The butchers stood on the thresholds of their shops, gritting their teeth. Across the way Jewish stores were being ransacked. The Polish residents of the town lent a hand. A fire raged in their hearts and their fists grew tight. Were it not for their being in exile, the Ployne butchers would have taught these *spółka* folk a lesson. (p. 128)

The thieves—non-Jewish workers living in the vicinity—are eventually apprehended. The affair serves to underscore the Jews' vulnerability and their inferior status *vis-à-vis* the other residents of the town. Their hands are tied. Their condition is again described in traditional phraseology as *galut* (exile), a term charged with considerable emotion and carrying, at the same time, the possibility of redemption. It is natural therefore, that, as a sole remedy to their condition, the townfolk propose emigration from Poland, the bitter exile, to Eretz Israel. As government fiscal pressures mount, so, too, does the number of those considering emigration to Eretz Israel as a direct and natural response to economic antisemitism.

The following conversation, which appears at the beginning of the book, is instructive.

> "Are you really thinking about Eretz Israel, Uncle?"
> "Who isn't thinking about Eretz Israel these days?" (p. 23)

The direct link between the tax burden and its consequences and ideas of *aliyah* to Eretz Israel is illustrated in the thoughts of a former merchant and part owner of a flour mill. The mill is eventually confiscated for back taxes and sold to the highest bidder at a public auction.

> Pinkhesl wanted to drive away sad thoughts, so he began to think of Eretz Israel, and his eyes grew bright. Upon my word, it wouldn't be

such a bad idea to pack up kit and caboodle, the entire family, and take to the road. And good riddance to the taxes and the auctions and the headaches! (p. 89)

Sooner or later all the Jews in Ployne think about *aliyah* and evaluate their remaining assets, followed by actual consultations regarding the viability of *aliyah*. The movement toward *aliyah* becomes increasingly widespread and constitutes a predominant plot line of the novel. The traditional yearning for Eretz Israel and redemption from the bitter exile takes on realistic dimensions in the aspirations toward *aliyah*, aspirations that arise in direct response to unbearable conditions and antisemitism, in accordance with the classic Zionist model. These traditional feelings and the actual circumstances in Poland are beautifully interwoven in the description of a Zionist sermon in the synagogue and the reactions of the congregants (pp. 97–99).

This melancholy book about a Jewish town in Poland during the time of Grabski's Evil Decrees closes with a pathetic chapter entitled "Levi's Aliyah," which portrays the leave-taking of the town's first emigrant to Eretz Israel. This was the beginning of the Fourth Aliyah, which, in Zionist historiography, has earned the name Grabski's Aliyah.[22]

III

Bursztyn's last novel, *Bay di taykhn fun Mazovye*, depicts the 1930s in a town named Smolin. We learn from it that the condition of the Jews in Poland's towns has not effectively improved in the years that have elapsed since the days of Grabski. The tax burden is a constant source of concern and anxiety (pp. 21, 23, 107, 124), compounded by the moratorium on outstanding debts that results in the pauperization of affluent individuals. The novel depicts the suicide of someone who was considered the wealthiest Jew in town and whose entire fortune was tied up in outstanding loans (pp. 129, 137–39). This period in the lives of Polish Jews is noteworthy for other reasons, however, as it is marked by violent antisemitism that threatens the very physical existence of the Jews and already begins to count its victims.

It must be recalled that in Poland of those days, censorship pre-

---

22. For a concise treatment of the subject, see Ezra Mendelsohn, *Zionism in Poland: The Formative Years, 1915–1926* (New Haven, 1981), p. 257.

cluded frank and detailed reports of the attacks on Jews that grew ever more widespread during the latter half of the 1930s.[23] The facts are known: after 1936 place-names such as Pshitik (in Polish, Przytyk), Mińsk Mazowiecki, and Brest-Litovsk became terrifying milestones in the evolution of violent antisemitism. Due to censorship, these events did not receive much coverage in Poland itself. For this reason, it appears, Bursztyn refrained from mentioning the real names of places where violent acts had been perpetrated. This would also explain the novel's description of a pogrom in a town bearing a Chinese name Sa-Ma-Lin. Moreover, not only do events occur in places bearing fictitious names, but the events themselves are only indirectly depicted. The book hints broadly at events in neighboring towns—"Tsintsimin" (pp. 6, 8) and "Bozshe Volye" (pp. 9, 98)—that terrify the Jews of Smolin. There is little doubt that, when the book appeared in 1937, readers were able to decipher these vague allusions.

Two factors of striking political significance form a background to the worsening condition of Polish Jews in the latter half of the 1930s. The first is Hitler's rise to power in Germany. His influence is not limited to the German "colonists" in Smolin and vicinity, who maintain close ties with their Nazi homeland, whence they receive their inspiration (pp. 14, 31–32, 64, 89–91). Bursztyn stressed in his novel the friendly ties that began to develop between Poland and Germany, expressed, for example, in the invitation to Hermann Goering to hunt in Poland.[24]

The second factor relates to internal Polish affairs, specifically to the political turmoil in Poland following Józef Piłsudski's death in 1935. One of the definitive signs of the times was the political use Piłsudski's successors made of antisemitism to win the support of extremist nationalists.[25] The Jews had viewed Piłsudski as their pro-

23. On the violent attacks, see Melzer, *Maavak medini be-malkodet*, pp. 78–96. On restrictions imposed by the Polish censor, see ibid., p. 79.

24. The Soviet edition of *Bay di taykhn fun Mazovye* appeared in Moscow in 1941 while the Ribbentrop-Molotov Pact was in effect, which forbade derogatory references to Hitler and the Germans. The Soviet censor eliminated all references in Bursztyn's book to Hitler and replaced them, in some instances, with references to Haman. Compare, for example, the title of chapter 19 in the first edition—"Hitler Isn't Beating the Pious Jews" (p. 89)—and in the Moscow edition, "He Says They Aren't Beating the Pious Jews" (p. 78). The second Warsaw edition was copied from the Soviet edition.

25. For a treatment of the attitude toward the Jews of Piłsudski's successors in the Polish regime, see Edward D. Wynot, Jr., "'A Necessary Cruelty': The Emergence of Official Anti-Semitism in Poland, 1936–1939," *American Historical Review* 76 (1971): 1035–58.

tector in the face of their antisemitic enemies. This is not the place to examine the veracity of that feeling. Its sheer intensity in the wake of developments following Piłsudski's death, however, is forcefully expressed in the title of chapter 34, "And Joseph Died," which is taken from Exodus 1:6. The text continues in the same vein, quoting verse 8 with all its implications for the situation in Poland: "Now there arose a new king over Egypt who knew not Joseph" (p. 163). Here again the biblical quotations enable Bursztyn to make the traditional associations that amplify the sense of oncoming catastrophe for Smolin and its Jews.

The book merely hints at attempts by simple Jews to respond with force to violent attacks. Here, too, Bursztyn's avoidance of detailed and frank description may be attributed to the fear of the censor. Nevertheless, careful reading of the novel reveals that direct physical response is a recurrent theme. Through the character of Bertshik Shmate, a strong young man who peddles rags and bones in Smolin's neighboring Polish villages, Bursztyn illustrates the existence of this particular response to antisemitism and outlines its limitations as well.

At the very beginning of the novel Bertshik declares his willingness to respond to antisemitism with force (p. 7). What Bertshik actually did at the Vishegrod fair is unclear. The writer only hints at the events, concealing more than he reveals.

> Bertshik spent half a year in the Plotsk jail for having allegedly said "such and such" at the Vishegrod fair. Grown lean and genteel, he stood in the synagogue now, proud of himself for having suffered on account of the Jews (p. 130).

The text clearly suggests that Bertshik did more than merely say something. But the ultimate outcome of Bertshik's response is a dramatic transformation. He is afraid to react; he is quiet and apathetic even when directly provoked.

> Bertshik sits atop the wagon like a philosopher. He learned how to keep silent. The six months he spent in the Plotsk jail added dark rings under his eyes. He grew accustomed to keeping his hands to himself when he felt the urge to hit someone. Bertshik Shmate is gone, no longer the fighter he used to be. That's to say, he was no longer Bertshik. He keeps quiet when the town dogcatcher runs onto the road in front of his wagon and begins to curse him: Jewish snout, rotten seed. Bertshik bites his lips and says nothing, because he knows only too well that if he lets off steam he'll go right back to Plotsk. He learned not to respond, although it went against his nature. People wondered: this isn't the same Ber-

tshik. He's grown humble and become one of the thirty-six Righteous Men. (pp. 144–45)

The irony at the end of this description underscores the dramatic change in Bertshik's personality, formerly very self-assured and capable of brute force. The transformation is, however, merely superficial. During the Smolin pogrom, Bertshik is a victim of a struggle with the pogromists (p. 180).

The character and fate of Bertshik provide Bursztyn with a vehicle for depicting a reaction of force to violent antisemitism as well as an examination of its limitations. Bertshik's arrest, and what happens to him during his incarceration, as well as his death during the pogrom, would seem to question the effectiveness and practicality of active resistance in general.

Conflicting issues abound in Bursztyn's third novel about the Jews of Smolin during the 1930s. The title of the book "By the Rivers of Masovia," which echoes the opening line of Psalm 137, "By the rivers of Babylon,"[26] alludes to the condition of exile and longing for Zion, a theme central to that particular Psalm. Despite the apparent message of the title, however, *aliyah* to Eretz Israel was no longer considered a productive response to Jew-hatred. The viability of this solution was undermined by a number of factors, including restrictions on immigration to Eretz Israel and memories of the limited effectiveness of Grabski's Aliyah.[27] The possibility of emigration to other destinations was likewise limited. All these factors combined to produce an ideology of *doikeyt* (literally, "hereness"), which promoted the belief in a Jewish future on Polish soil and rejected emigration as a solution to the Jewish Problem, a solution now promoted by Polish antisemites belonging to a variety of political camps.[28] Such is the enigmatic message of Bursztyn's novel, which appeared in 1937 and was written no doubt in response to contemporary events.[29]

26. Naftale Veynig noted the echo of the Psalms in a review in *Literarishe bleter*, no. 19 (1938):325, 327.

27. See Isaac Bashevis's story about a man who made *aliyah* during Grabski's Aliyah and returned to Poland. "Tsurikvegns" (On the Road Back), *Literarishe bleter*, nos. 47–50 (1928):927–29, 946–48, 966–68, 987–89.

28. On opportunities for emigration, see Melzer, *Maavak medini be-malkodet*, pp. 140–63. On the successes of the Bund in elections held in Poland during the latter half of the 1930s, see ibid., pp. 280–88. Support of the Bund in those years may be understood in light of the ideology of *doikeyt* as opposed to other solutions.

29. Veynig noted, with some degree of justification: "One often gets the impression that Bursztyn is an avid reader of the press and immediately incorporates all the news,

Three victims lose their lives in the Smolin pogrom: Golda, the wife of Dr. Gabriel Priver, who left Warsaw to return to his Jewish roots in Smolin; Golda's grandfather, an old and distinguished resident of the town; and Bertshik. The Jews of Smolin hold a joint funeral. Following the recitation of the Kaddish at the grave of the eldest victim, the spokesman for the poor folk of the community announces:

> "I hereby inform you, Reb Isroeltshe, that the town will be rebuilt. I, Hersh Lustik, give you my word."
> His face was ablaze with courage in the red sunset.

These strikingly dramatic words close the book with a message of significant emotional and political impact. Lustik's assertion is reinforced by the title of the closing chapter, "Gabriel Stays in Sa-Ma-Lin," which announces the doctor's decision to remain in the town despite the tragedy that has touched him personally.

Notwithstanding this message, which Bursztyn stressed in every possible way at the book's conclusion, the reader cannot shake off a sense of impending catastrophe. The words of the omniscient narrator in the second chapter of the novel, which describe the town marketplace, are particularly compelling.

> Wooden houses and chimneys stand in formation around the magistrate building like stubborn goats, engulfed by its shadows. At any moment the magistrate building could run rampant and trample the houses. The walls will collapse, and the roofs will cave in, burying the living. (p. 14)

To the contemporary reader after the Holocaust, these words sound an ominous prophecy that he knows came true. After World War I the peasants in the Ployne-Tshubin-Smolin vicinity used to collect human bones that had surfaced from shallow graves and lay scattered over the fields: "In the autumn, when the harsh winds blow, parched human bones roll around the harvested fields. Peasants gather them up in sacks, grind them up on handmills[30] and use them to fertilize their fields (p. 3)." History repeats itself. Now the bodies and bones of Jews enrich the fields across Poland, whose towns are bereft of Jews.

---

including the editorials into his belletristic material." Review of *Bay di taykhn fun Mazovye*, p. 325.

30. The original mistakenly printed *shteyner* (stones); it has been corrected here according to the Moscow edition.

IV

Close study of Michal Bursztyn's novels inevitably raises the question of the reliability of essentially fictional writing as a historical source. It is not always possible to verify the authenticity of a novel's contents. Yet there is an authenticity about Bursztyn's first novels that enables us to draw inferences about his writings as a whole as well as about most of the "realistic" novels in Yiddish that deal with Jewish life in Poland between the wars.

Speaking at a literary soiree held in Warsaw to mark the publication of *Goyrl*, the author acknowledged the personal background of his first two novels.[31] He related details of his own experience that motivated him to write and eventually found expression in his novels. Early on in his youth, Bursztyn was taken from his native *shtetl* environment. He grew up among assimilated Jews who had consciously become estranged from their Jewishness; many had even converted to Christianity. While grateful to his benefactors in this society, Bursztyn felt that "his ties to his home and to the Jews were being torn asunder." His closest relatives had emigrated from Poland to a distant land, and he himself "did not want to and could not leave Poland."[32] Although no close family remained in his hometown, he experienced strong feelings of nostalgia.

> Even as I grew accustomed to the strange environment, my yearnings for home grew stronger. I felt the need to do something for myself so that my life might have some meaning. And then, it was during the so-called Grabski era, a muffled cry of pain from the *shtetl* reached my ears.

Bursztyn responded to the call of pain and came home. He did not find what he had left behind in his childhood. Instead, "Degradation, submission, and collapse permeated Jewish life. And above all loomed the terrible fear of an uncertain tomorrow."[33]

It seems, therefore, that the novel about Ployne was the record of the response of one intimately familiar with the events. The author himself viewed the novel as the repayment of a debt to his town at a

---

31. Michal Bursztyn, "How I Began to Write," *Literarishe bleter*, no. 10 (1936):151.

32. Ibid. Compare the family of Yakov Psheborski, the protagonist in *Goyrl*: "His parents lived somewhere off in London's Whitechapel, immigrants uprooted from their homes" (p. 152). This is only one of many autobiographical details Bursztyn incorporated into the lives of his fictional characters.

33. Bursztyn, "How I Began to Write," p. 151.

time of degradation during the Grabski era. At the end of his talk in Warsaw, Bursztyn drew the connection between his first two novels.

> *Ployne* and *Goyrl* constitute two sides of the same coin. When I wrote *Goyrl*, echoes of Ployne intruded. The assimilated Jewish intelligentsia and the folk are now equals, rendered so by the tragic Jewish reality. All Jews share a common fate.[34]

With respect to *Goyrl*, Bursztyn's statement explains his interest in the recent past. In the period before World War I he discovered early evidence of the failure of Polish assimilationist ideology, the futility of which he appears to have experienced personally.

The writer and literary critic Y. I. Trunk is skeptical about the authenticity of Bursztyn's portrayal of the lives of the assimilated Jews and their salons in *Goyrl*.

> In *Goyrl* we have for the first time in Yiddish literature in Poland a depiction of the salons of the assimilated. M. Bursztyn never stepped inside these salons. From without, he peered through brightly lit windows. As a result he often appears somewhat naïve.[35]

Trunk may well be justified in his evaluation of the love affairs, infidelities, and adventures of high society, which are depicted excessively and often unconvincingly and shallowly.[36] Notwithstanding, there is no doubt as to the authenticity of Bursztyn's writing in all that pertains to the problematic nature of the assimilationists' Jewishness, their reaction to events in nearby Jewish society, and their contacts and anxieties outside the Jewish environment. Bursztyn was raised by members of this society and had an intimate knowledge of it.

The authenticity of Bursztyn's writing is also confirmed by the fact that a well-known contemporary inspired the character of Norbert Yanash, the leader of the assimilationists in *Goyrl*. The model for this fictional character, who ultimately converts to Christianity, is easily identified Dr. Henryk Nusbaum (1849–1937). Upon Nusbaum's death, Bursztyn published in a Yiddish periodical a sympathetic

34. Ibid.
35. Y. I. Trunk, *Di yidishe proze in Poyln in der tkufe tsvishn beyde velt-milkhomes* (Buenos Aires, 1949), p. 90. Compare Bashevis on this novel: "In this novel Bursztyn displayed adeptness in an area where Yiddish writers are generally deficient. When he describes a salon, a castle, or an art gallery, one gets the impression that he is at home there." "A roman fun yidishn lebn in Poyln."
36. Critics generally appreciated Bursztyn's novels although they did not refrain from pointing out conspicuous artistic flaws. Bashevis writes: "It is elegantly written and displays a sense of good measure. Notwithstanding, it lacks a certain artistic ripeness." Ibid. See also his comments on *Bay di taykhn fun Mazovye* quoted in n. 38 below.

obituary that bore the title "The Knight of Assimilation." Many essential details of the novel correspond with the facts of Nusbaum's life as related in the obituary, which in turn are corroborated in an article about Nusbaum that appeared recently in a Polish biographical lexicon.[37]

It is not always possible to authenticate the contents of fictional writings through outside sources. In Bursztyn's case, however, that authentication is to some extent possible and it serves to validate his depictions in general, with the possible exception of his clearly fictional stories that were never intended to be documentary. In the three novels discussed here, Bursztyn presented an expressive picture of Jewish society in the *shtetl* during the very periods that have absorbed the historians of Polish Jewry. Bursztyn's novels do not yield the sort of dramatic revelations about these historical periods to be found in the research literature. Yet even the experienced historian will discover in them the vibrant human element so often lacking in documents as well as the perceptions of a sensitive contemporary eyewitness.[38] From this perspective, there is no doubt that Bursztyn's novels and those of other Yiddish writers in Poland between the wars constitute a most significant legacy.

37. Michal Bursztyn, "Der riter fun der asimilatsye (Tsum toyt fun Dr. Henryk Nusboym)," *Literarishe bleter*, no. 11 (1937):173. See also the article on Nusbaum by Tereza Ostrowska in *Polski słownik biograficzny*, vol. 23 (Wrocław, 1978), pp. 412–14. The bibliography in Ostrowska's article does not include Bursztyn's obituary, nor does she seem to be aware that Nusbaum served as a model for a foremost protagonist in a Yiddish novel.

38. Pursuant to Veynig's comments on the documentary nature of *Bay di taykhn fun Mazovye*, Bashevis's critique of the same is noteworthy: "The raw material which the author uses is too actual, too close. Distance and perspective are lacking. The events are captured in the process of becoming, to use Bergsonian terminology. *Bay di taykhn fun Mazovye* is more of a *scattered chronicle, a document of the times, than a novel.*" *Di tsukunft*, April 1939, p. 244, my italics. This kind of criticism underscores the value of these novels as a historical source.

Ezra Mendelsohn

Jewish Reactions to Antisemitism in Interwar East Central Europe

An article on Jewish reactions to antisemitism in post–World War I East Central Europe[1] should start off by saying something about the nature and degree of antisemitism in that region. It would be difficult, though not impossible, to argue with the general proposition that East Central Europe in the 1920s and 1930s was an unfriendly environment so far as the Jews were concerned. The reasons are evident. The region was dominated by newly established and highly nationalistic states, most of which possessed little in the way of a liberal political tradition. Nearly all were poor and faced intractable social and economic problems that grew much worse with the economic depression of the second decade of the interwar years. The stability of these states was further undermined by the activity of their neighbors, Germany and the Soviet Union, which refused to recognize the frontiers established at Versailles and played a significant role in making the already insoluble problem of national minorities even worse. All this paved the way for the rise of right-wing extremism and the establishment, in most cases, of fascistlike regimes.[2]

The combination of backwardness, chauvinism, and right-wing as-

1. This region can be defined geographically in various ways. See the comments in the best guide to the subject, Joseph Rothschild, *East Central Europe between the Two World Wars* (Seattle, 1974), pp. xi–xii. In my book, *The Jews of East Central Europe between the World Wars* (Bloomington, Ind., 1983), I concentrate on Poland, Hungary, Rumania, Czechoslovakia, Lithuania, Latvia, and Estonia.

2. Along with Rothschild, see, for example, Antony Polonsky, *Politics in Independent Poland, 1921–1939* (Oxford, 1972); and C. A. Macartney, *October Fifteenth: A History of Modern Hungary, 1929–1945* (Edinburgh, 1956–57). Czechoslovakia was something of an exception in this regard. See Victor Mamatey and Radomír Luža, eds., *A History of the Czechoslovak Republic, 1918–1948* (Princeton, 1973).

saults on the established order boded ill for many elements within Eastern European society—among others, the working classes, the political Left, and religious and ethnic minorities, including, of course, the Jews. The Jewish Question was clearly part and parcel of the larger Minorities Question, but it possessed its own special characteristics. In most Eastern European states the Jews constituted a significant, sometimes even dominant, proportion of the urban population and were overrepresented in commerce, the professions, and cultural life. As such, they were obvious targets for those nationalists who believed that "Poland belongs to the Poles," "Rumania belongs to the Rumanians," and so forth. The popular slogans of "Polonization," "Romanization," and others were usually anti-Jewish, calling for the ousting of Jews from positions of influence in the economy and national life. Moreover, Jews were often identified, sometimes with a certain degree of accuracy, as enemies of the new ruling nationalities and their newly awakened national cultures. In Poland the Jews of the western regions were regarded as pro-German in politics and culture, while in Eastern Galicia and in the Lithuanian lands they were accused of being either pro-Ukrainian or pro-Lithuanian, as some undoubtedly were. In Transylvania and Slovakia, Rumanians and Slovaks looked upon Jews as wicked Magyarizers, guilty of having played a significant role in the subjugation of their native cultures, while the Czechs regarded the Jews as traditionally pro-German and pro-Habsburg. Nor should we forget that in this fervently anticommunist part of the world, where the Soviet Union was seen, with some justification, as a major threat to political and social stability, Jews were often closely identified with the Left. Thus in both Poland and Hungary short-lived communist successes were followed by anti-Jewish campaigns.

Finally, above and beyond these aspects of the Jewish Question was the fact that traditional antisemitism was deeply rooted in the entire region. The Jews of Russia and Rumania achieved formal emancipation only in 1917 and 1919, respectively. The church was a powerful force everywhere, and its role in the antisemitic movement was often undisguised. Thus, while there was much hostility directed toward all minorities—the Germans, for example, were far from popular in Poland, Hungary, and the Baltic states, and the Poles were much disliked in Lithuania—hostility toward the Jews was unique. It called forth passions and even brought about a degree of consensus that dislike of other groups did not. As such, it was an

extremely useful tool in the hands of the various political elites jock-
eying for power in the successor states.[3]

The precise extent of antisemitism in the region, however, is extremely difficult to measure. Let us take, for example, the case of
Poland, home of by far the most important Jewish community in
East Central Europe. Jewish scholars have tended to portray the Polish Republic as ferociously antisemitic. They have described the
Jews of the 1918–39 period as standing "on the edge of destruction."[4]
But Polish scholars, and even a few Jews, have rejected this approach, claiming that Poland's poverty and social backwardness,
rather than a systematic anti-Jewish policy, were responsible for the
admittedly sorry state of Polish Jewry, especially in the 1930s.[5] A
distinguished British historian of Poland has noted, correctly, that
the Jewish community was extremely creative and achieved a great
deal during this period; if things were so bad, he asks, how could
they have been so good?[6]

The fact is that antisemitism is often in the eyes of the beholder.
And, to complicate the matter even further, even Jews sometimes
accused each other of antisemitism. Thus, when Yitzhak Gruenbaum
and Vladimir Jabotinsky made it known in 1936 that, in their view,
there were far too many Jews in Poland, they were attacked by many
Polish Jews—not all of whom belonged to opposed political camps—
as being no better than the Polish National Democrats, who called

3. For details, see my *Jews of East Central Europe*. An impressive study of anti-
semitism in Poland is Frank Golczewski, *Polnisch-Jüdische Beziehungen, 1881–1922*
(Wiesbaden, 1981). I have not come across any detailed comparative studies of atti-
tudes toward Jews and other minorities in the region. For a relevant study on the
Soviet Union, see Binyamin Pinkus, "The Extra-Territorial Minorities in the Soviet
Union, 1917–1939," *Studies in Contemporary Jewry* 3 (1987).

4. This is the title of an influential book on the subject: Celia Heller, *On the Edge of
Destruction: Jews of Poland between the Two World Wars* (New York, 1977). See also
Pawel Korzec, *Juifs en Pologne: La question juive pendant l'entre-deux-guerres* (Paris,
1980); Isaiah Trunk, "Economic Antisemitism in Poland between the Two World Wars,"
in *Studies on Polish Jewry, 1919–1939*, ed. Joshua A. Fishman (New York, 1974), pp. 3–
98; Korzec, "Antisemitism in Poland as an Intellectual, Social, and Political Movement," ibid., pp. 12–104.

5. See, for example, Jerzy Tomaszewski, "Zarys dziejów Żydów polskich w XIX i XX
w.," in *Żydzi polscy: Dzieja i kultura*, ed. Marion Fuks (Warsaw, 1982), pp. 32–42; also
his "Stosunki narodowościowe w Drugiej Rzeczypospolitej," in *Polska niepodległa*,
1984, p. 161; and his paper delivered at the 1985 World Congress of Jewish Studies at
Jerusalem: "Some Methodological Problems in the Study of Jewish History in Poland
between the Two World Wars." A Jewish scholar who also takes this "revisionist" point
of view is Joseph Marcus, *Social and Political History of the Jews in Poland, 1919–1939*
(Berlin, 1983); see, for example, his remarks on p. 231.

6. Norman Davies, *God's Playground: A History of Poland*, vol. 2 (Oxford, 1981), p
409.

for mass Jewish emigration from Poland.[7] Was Władysław Grabski's economic program of the mid-1920s, which resulted in heavy taxation of the merchant class, a positive step toward the stabilization of the Polish economy or a measure intended to ruin the Jewish community? Was the obligatory Sunday rest law an act of progressive legislation or another example of Polish antisemitism? It all depends on how one looks at it.[8]

Nevertheless, to sum up this introduction, one can hardly escape the conclusion that in the Eastern European environment of the 1920s and 1930s the Jews were usually regarded, in fact if not in the legal sense, as second-class citizens and as obstacles to the achievement of the just national aims of the ruling nations.[9] This does not mean that they were continuously subjected to violent harassment. Nor does it mean that they were prevented from developing their own cultural life, as they were in the Soviet Union, especially in the 1930s. It does mean that they faced discrimination and, above all, that by the 1930s the situation had so deteriorated that large numbers of Jews, in particular young people, had come to the conclusion that there was little or no future for them in Eastern Europe.[10]

As for the question of Jewish reactions to antisemitism, here, too, there is an initial difficulty, which should at least be mentioned. It can be argued that virtually everything the Jews do is in one way or another related to antisemitism. Thus emigration, religious practices, economic activities, the establishment of political parties, rates of intermarriage, and so forth are all related to this phenomenon—or to its relative absence. If this is the case, then a complete answer to the question posed in this essay would have to deal with virtually all aspects of Jewish life in the region. This is obviously impossible. I will therefore limit myself to an examination of certain

7. For the storm that emerged after Yitzhak Gruenbaum's remarks, see *Haynt*, August 5, 1936, p. 3, and August 6, 1936, p. 5. On Vladimir Jabotinsky's "evacuation" scheme and the controversy it aroused, see Emanuel Melzer, *Maavak medini bemalkodet: Yehudei Polin, 1935–1939* (Tel Aviv, 1982), pp. 149–57.

8. I have tried to deal with this issue in my article "Interwar Poland: 'Good for the Jews or Bad for the Jews?'" based on a lecture given at the conference on Polish-Jewish relations at Oxford in 1984. It is published in *The Jews in Poland*, ed. Antony Polonsky, Chimen Abramsky, and Maciej Jachimczyk (Oxford, 1986), pp. 130–36.

9. There were, of course, important differences among the attitudes of the political elites in the various countries. I would say that the Czechs (but not the Slovaks) were the least prone to antisemitism and that on the whole the Jews fared better in the Baltic states than in Poland, Hungary, and Rumania.

10. See the study by Max Weinreich, *Der veg tsu unzer yugnt* (Vilna, 1935), pp. 207–10. See also the comments of Fishel Rotenstreich in *Opinja*, July 26, 1936.

Jewish reactions relevant to Jewish political—and, by extension, cultural—behavior.

Justification for concentrating on political responses may be derived from the fact that in this period other, more traditional, Jewish responses to the enmity of the majority were virtually ruled out. Mass emigration to the West, for example, was no longer a viable option after 1914. Integration—the aspiration of many Jews since the days of the Enlightenment—was also not a viable option for the Jewish masses of Poland, the Baltic states, and most parts of Rumania and Czechoslovakia, although it had its adherents everywhere and remained the ideology of organized Hungarian Jewry throughout this period. If emigration and integration were largely ruled out, the one by the anti-immigration laws of the United States and other countries, the other by the very nature of the host societies in Eastern Europe, then the strengthening of a third response—namely "nationalization"—is not surprising. In fact, the interwar years witnessed, in most regions, the speeding up of a process by which many Jews were coming to regard themselves as a modern ethnic or national minority. By this I mean that many of them now identified themselves as "Jews by nationality" as well as "Jews by religion."[11] The Central and West European model expressed by the formula "Germans of the Mosaic persuasion" was not unknown in Eastern Europe, but the nationalistic and antisemitic environment certainly encouraged many Jews to embrace a modern Jewish national identity, which had obvious implications for Jewish politics. These implications were well understood by the Polish socialist leader Ignacy Daszyński, who complained in 1928 that before the war Jews had voted for him as their representative to the Austrian parliament, but now, having become "nationalists," they voted for Zionists.[12] It may be pointed out in passing that the process of "nationalization" had parallels among certain non-Jewish minorities, such as the Germans

11. This can be seen in the census reports of the various countries of the region, data on which are collected in my *Jews of East Central Europe*. Only in Hungary did the vast majority of Jews reject the Jewish national identity in favor of a Hungarian national identity. In the Soviet Union, too, numerous Jews sought to integrate into Russian communist society—how successful they were is a matter of some controversy. See Mordecai Altshuler and Ezra Mendelsohn, "Yahadut brit-ha-moatzot u-folin beyn milhamot ha-olam: Nituah hashvaati," in *Contemporary Jewry: Studies in Honor of Moshe Davis*, ed. Geoffrey Wigoder (Jerusalem, 1984), pp. 53–64.

12. See Leib Jaffe's report of his meeting with Ignacy Daszyński in the Central Zionist Archives, Jerusalem (hereafter CZA), KH4/B/2154.

(the *Volksdeutsche*), whose situation in many ways closely resembled that of the Jews, and the Ukrainians.[13]

The general chauvinistic environment was not the only factor at work in the nationalization process, however. Nationalization was also the result of the dramatic and unexpected establishment of new national-cultural regimes that, in many cases, halted previous tendencies toward acculturation and integration. Thus the Jews of the Baltic region (Latvia and Lithuania), whose secularizing elites spoke Russian before the war, now found themselves in new states whose dominant culture was completely foreign to them. Obviously it would have been absurd for them to identify themselves as Lithuanians or Latvians, just as it was absurd for the Jews of Transylvania, Bessarabia, and Bukovina to attempt to transform themselves overnight into Rumanians. Since identification with the prewar dominant nationality (Russian, Hungarian, or German) was clearly unwise in the 1920s and 1930s, the obvious alternative was to turn to a national Jewish identification.[14] External factors were also important, for Jews as well as for non-Jewish minorities. The German occupation of parts of Eastern Europe during 1915–18 emancipated Jews from the tsarist yoke and made possible an explosion of Jewish national political activities.[15] The Balfour Declaration and the establishment of British rule in Palestine were also very important in strengthening Jewish national sentiments of a Zionist nature in Eastern Europe.

Moreover, while it cannot be denied that the Eastern European environment encouraged Jewish nationalism, it must be emphasized that this was not true everywhere in the region. Consider the case of Hungary. The atmosphere in that country, quite friendly to Jews in the days of the Habsburg Empire, turned decisively against them after the disasters of war, revolution, and loss of national territory. Antisemitism, however one defines it, was indisputably on the rise in interwar Hungary, and the Jews could only look back nostalgically

13. See my essay "A Few Remarks on Germans and Jews in Interwar East Central Europe," to be published in a volume of essays in memory of Paul Glikson, Jerusalem, edited by Chone Shmeruk and Ezra Mendelsohn, forthcoming.

14. For a Ukrainian parallel from Subcarpathian Rus, see Paul Robert Magocsi, *The Shaping of a National Identity: Subcarpathian Rus, 1848–1948* (Cambridge, Mass., 1978), p. 273.

15. On Poland, see my *Zionism in Poland: The Formative Years, 1915–1926* (New Haven, 1981), pp. 37–41. The national consciousness of the German minorities in Poland and Lithuania was also much affected by the German occupation.

to what they believed to be the good old days of old-regime Hungarian liberalism and pluralism. Nonetheless, the vast majority of Hungarian Jews did not react to the new, hostile environment by taking part in the general nationalization process described above. On the contrary, they clung to their belief in the necessity and efficacy of identification with the leading nationality, whose language and culture they had adopted with great enthusiasm during the nineteenth century.[16] This suggests that antisemitism does not inevitably lead to a Jewish national identity but does so only among certain types of Jewish communities, like those of Poland, Lithuania, Latvia, Bessarabia, and Bukovina, which were Yiddish-speaking, basically unacculturated (though acculturating), lower middle class and proletarian, Orthodox but in part secularizing. Jewish communities of the Trianon Hungarian type remained largely immune to the message of modern Jewish nationalism.[17]

Finally, the process of nationalization in Eastern Europe, paradoxically enough, did not preclude a parallel process of acculturation— but not integration or assimilation. In Poland, for example, despite the unfriendly environment and the impossibility of Jews converting themselves *en masse* into Poles, linguistic Polonization made such inroads into the Jewish community that some observers despaired of Yiddish and predicted its rapid demise.[18] Even the Zionists, partisans of Hebrew, and to a lesser extent Yiddish, were obliged to use Polish as their main language of communication.[19] The combination of nationalization and linguistic acculturation was also found in Rumania and even in the Baltic states.[20] It was a factor in lending to Jewish politics at least one peculiar characteristic that I shall mention below.

16. Two relatively new studies of interwar Hungarian Jewry are Randolph Braham, *The Politics of Genocide: The Holocaust in Hungary*, vol. 1 (New York, 1981); and Natanel Katzburg, *Hungary and the Jews: Policy and Legislation, 1920–1943* (Ramat Gan, 1981).

17. Other examples are the Jewries of Bohemia and the Rumanian Regat, especially Wallachia, though Zionism in both these regions was stronger than in Hungary.

18. See, for example, the remarks of Shmuel Czernowitz in his "Ha-ziyonut be-Polanyah, Tazkir," July 28, 1927, CZA, KH4/B/2143. See also a letter from Vilna published in *Opinja*, January 26, 1936, which documents the decline of Yiddish even in that center of autonomous Jewish culture.

19. Thus the major Zionist newspapers in Lvov and Cracow were in Polish. In 1933 an important new Zionist newspaper, *Opinja*, was founded, also in Polish. *Hatzfirah*, the veteran Hebrew Zionist journal, suffered from a chronic lack of readers and shut down for long periods of time.

20. For evidence of this trend in Lithuania, where the dominant language was quite unknown to Jews in the prewar period, see my *Jews of East Central Europe*, pp. 234–35.

Let me now point to a few specific political reactions to anti-semitism subsumed in the general process of nationalization. Most important was the remarkable attraction of Jewish national political parties and youth movements in the Polish-Lithuanian-Latvian-Bessarabian-Bukovinian core, and even beyond it. The interwar period was one of dramatic political mobilization on the "Jewish street," as tens of thousands of Jews came to associate themselves with the many political organizations that together held up the banner of Jewish nationalism, no matter how much they disagreed on the content of that nationalism. One might include here, perhaps, even the Orthodox party Agudat Israel, which though antinationalist in the modern sense and strongly anti-Zionist, nonetheless had a good deal in common with the nationalist parties.[21] In certain regions of East Central Europe, Jewish national politics achieved an unprecedentedly large following and its leaders became the political leaders of the entire Jewish community. The emergence and electoral successes of Jewish national parties even in Rumania and Czechoslovakia, not to mention Poland and the Baltic states, demonstrate the appeal of Jewish national politics and a natural Jewish preference to vote for specifically Jewish parties that sought, among other things, to protect the Jewish minority from antisemitism. Indeed, the interwar years in East Central Europe represented the heyday of Jewish national politics in the Diaspora, a period in which Jewish national politicians, like Yitzhak Gruenbaum of Poland, achieved tremendous popularity among the "masses." There had been nothing like this before in modern Jewish history, and there has been nothing like it since.[22]

Of all the Jewish political movements in this period, Zionism was the most powerful, although it had its ups and downs and, by the late 1930s, was in a state of serious decline. The rise of Zionism is obviously connected with antisemitism and the fact that hundreds of thousands of Jews in the Zionist heartland of Poland-Lithuania-Latvia-Bessarabia-Bukovina were committed to a Zionist solution to the Jewish Question demonstrates that they held out little hope of

---

21. See my remarks in *Jewish Politics in East Central Europe between the World Wars,* Beiner-Citrin Memorial Lecture (Cambridge, Mass., 1984).

22. It would, for example, be difficult to compare Gruenbaum's status among the Polish Jews with that of any of the Russian Zionist or Bundist leaders before the Russian Revolution, when conditions were much less favorable for leaders who depended upon the existence of democracy in order to build their power base.

successful integration in their countries of residence. To be sure, not all Zionists, even in Eastern Europe, thought in terms of *aliyah*. But on the whole, Eastern European Zionists took much more seriously the idea of Zionism as a personal solution to their problems in the Diaspora than did the Zionists of the West. Wyndham Deedes, the well-known Gentile Zionist, commented in 1928 that "the Jews of Poland . . . are for the greater part ardent Zionists. No 'lip-service' Zionists, but men and women who have already done great things for and in Palestine."[23] This was particularly true among the youth, and one of the most striking political reactions to antisemitism in Eastern Europe was the emergence of Jewish youth movements, mostly Zionist, which won the allegiance of large numbers of young people. Jewish young people were particularly vulnerable to the campaigns of Polonization, Romanization, and the like, which characterized the region. Desirable places in the economy and in the educational system were denied to them, and the result was the emergence of what was sometimes termed "a youth without a future" (*a yugnt on a morgn*). One reaction to this state of affairs was the readiness to join youth movements that offered, or appeared to offer, what the state, and even one's own family, could not—solutions to a tragic situation. For this reason certain regions in interwar East Central Europe were uniquely favorable environments for the flourishing of such Jewish youth movements as Hashomer Hazair, Gordonia, Betar, Yugnt, Zukunft, and so forth, as well as for the emergence and success of the Halutz movement.[24] For many youngsters these organizations were literally islands of hope in a barren and hopeless world.

Again, we must be careful. Nationalist youth movements and the *halutzim* did not arise only because of antisemitism, and in some antisemitic environments, most notably Hungary, they totally failed to capture the allegiance of significant numbers of young people. In Hungary a more typical political reaction on the part of many young Jews was to adhere to one of the parties of the Left, in particular to the Communist party. To what extent this phenomenon—familiar in other countries of the region as well—was a direct result of

23. See Wyndham Deedes to Leib Jaffe, July 17, 1928, CZA, KH4/B/2153.
24. Studies on these youth movements are few and far between. For a detailed account of the Halutz movement in Poland, see Yisrael Openheim, *Tnuat he-Halutz be-Polin (1917–1929)* (Jerusalem, 1982).

antisemitism is very difficult to say, but surely antisemitism was a factor.[25]

Certain peculiar characteristics of Jewish nationalist politics, I believe, may also be attributed to the impact of the antisemitic environment. For example, Jewish political parties often dispensed to their followers a remarkably wide range of services—summer camps, teahouses, cultural institutions, and, above all, youth movements and schools. In this case a fervent attachment to ideology, to the specific Jewish political-cultural future advocated by the political party in question, led to the creation of well-defined subcultures made all the more necessary by virtue of the fact that the hostile environment failed to attend adequately to Jewish needs. The result was a "Bundist world," a "Mizrahi world," a "Poalei Zion world," and so forth. All students of Eastern European Jewish politics know how important this phenomenon was in the forging of a specific Jewish political culture.

Another characteristic, and here I am on more contentious ground, has to do with the adoption of certain antisemitic attitudes absorbed from the outside world by nationalist Jewish political leaders and organizations. The adoption of these attitudes, which had begun in the prewar years, was clearly speeded up by the acculturation process I have already mentioned. This phenomenon is most clearly seen in the Zionist movement, for obvious reasons. Some Zionist organizations, in particular the youth movements, aimed at establishing a "new Jewish man" to replace the unpleasant Diaspora type whose characteristics and environment are often described in terms identical to those used by the antisemites. This does not necessarily mean direct borrowing, but it would be difficult to deny all outside influence.[26] When, in the mid-1920s, middle-class Polish Jews adversely affected by the economic crisis went off to Palestine, the Jew-

25. This subject, too, has been little studied, though it is obviously of great interest and importance. On Hungary, see the interesting data for the years 1900–1919 in Andrew C. Janos, *The Politics of Backwardness in Hungary, 1825–1945* (Princeton, 1982), p. 177; and the stimulating study by William McCagg, "Jews in Revolutions: The Hungarian Experience," *Journal of Social History* 6 (1972): 78–105.

26. Thus, for example, the statement in an early Hashomer Hazair publication that the Jew of today (1917) is a "caricature," and Betar's emphasis on the need for *hadar* (splendor, dignity) in Jewish life, which has been ruined by the unhealthy Diaspora. See Hashomer Hazair's "Our World-View," in *The Jew in the Modern World: A Documentary History*, ed. Paul R. Mendes-Flohr and Jehuda Reinharz (New York, 1980), p. 454; and Vladimir Jabotinsky, *Ideologja Bejtaru* (Lvov, 1934), p. 24.

ish Left denounced their "parasitical" behavior in classic antisemitic terms. Indeed, some of the critics of the Fourth Aliyah were explicitly denounced as "antisemites" by defenders of the hapless "bourgeois" immigrants who did not agree with the Left's insistence on the need to transform Jewish traditional life and rid it of all "ghetto" characteristics.[27] Selective absorption of external attitudes may be observed most clearly on the Jewish secular Right. Betar, for example, openly admired and even imitated the statism, anticommunism, and militarism of the Polish nationalist camp and aimed at transforming the cowardly Jew of the Diaspora into a disciplined and heroic defender of the Jewish people.[28] For Betar, as for Hashomer Hazair, the "new Jew" was a Jew who eschewed most of the characteristics associated with the negative Jewish stereotype so emphasized in antisemitic propaganda. Indeed, a Jew of this type, and only he, could live on equal terms with the Gentile world. This view was well expressed in 1919 by Szymon Wolf of Hashomer Hazair, who in a rather pathetic appeal to Polish youth noted that the Jews honor the Poles' struggle for freedom and called on the Polish youth to support the Jews' parallel struggle.[29]

Let me now briefly mention one particular Jewish political strategy adopted in interwar East Central Europe to deal with, among other things, the challenge of the antisemitic environment. The program of Jewish national autonomy in the Eastern European Diaspora was proposed before the war, and its implementation was attempted, with varying degrees of success, in the immediate postwar period. This program had many aims, the best known among them the preservation and development of Jewish national life. Another aim, perhaps somewhat neglected in accounts of the subject, had to do directly with the Jewish struggle against antisemitism. Some advocates of Jewish autonomy felt that it might resolve some of the

27. See the speech of Yehoshua Gottlieb at the Zionist Congress of 1925: "Wenn man diese Schriften [i.e., of those who attacked the Jews who went to Palestine during the Fourth Aliyah] las, hatte man das Gefühl, dass sie von antisemitischen Schriften abgeschrieben worden sind." *Protokoll der Verhandlungen des XIV Zionisten-Kongresses* (London, 1926), p. 148.

28. For the warm feelings held by members of Betar for the Polish military and nationalist tradition, which was often, though not invariably, antisemitic, see the description of their march to the tomb of the Polish unknown soldier in *Haynt*, October 30, 1933, p. 2.

29. *Nowa młodzież*, no. 1 (February 1, 1919):7–8. For a further discussion, see my "A Note on Jewish Assimilation in the Polish Lands," in *Jewish Assimilation in Modern Times*, ed. Bela Vago (Boulder, Colo., 1981), pp. 141–50.

tension between Jews and Gentiles and therefore serve to lessen the antisemitic onslaught. In 1912, for example, Jews in Warsaw had lent their support to a Polish socialist in elections to the Fourth Russian Duma, thereby incurring the wrath of the Polish nationalist camp and calling forth an organized boycott of Jewish shops.[30] In order to prevent this, Jews would create their own special political "sector" and would vote for Jewish political parties. Perhaps they would have a guaranteed number of seats in parliament, thus obviating any interference in Gentile politics.[31] In this way, too, Jews would avoid accusations of being pro-German (in Posen), pro-Lithuanian (in the Vilna region), or even pro-Polish, as they were accused of being by the Ukrainians of Eastern Galicia. Similarly, Jews in certain parts of this region attempted to establish special educational networks that would serve both to preserve and develop Jewish autonomous culture and to shield Jewish youth from the antisemitic state school. Thus, for example, Tarbut schools were set up by the general Zionists in order to create a new Hebrew-speaking, nationalist Jewish generation that would be called upon to build Palestine. They also functioned as Jewish educational islands in a Polish sea, an attractive alternative to Polish schools, where the atmosphere was often highly nationalistic and therefore antisemitic.[32] In culture, as in politics, the idea was to foster a separate Jewish "realm" that would, among other things, refute antisemitic claims that the Jews were far too influential in the political and cultural life of the host nationality. Jews would vote for Jewish parties and send their children to Jewish schools. Antisemitism would decline.

I shall conclude this brief survey by asking how effective these Jewish reactions to antisemitism in interwar Eastern Europe were. I have already pointed out that the process of nationalization and mass mobilization for national Jewish political purposes affected only a section of Eastern European Jewry. The same should be said of efforts to promote Jewish national autonomy and a Jewish national school system. But even within the Polish-Lithuanian-Latvian-Bessarabian-Bukovinian core the "national performance" was not very impressive. I have, in a separate article, tried to make the case that Jewish national politics in the interwar period was

30. See Golczewski, *Polnisch-Jüdische Beziehungen*, pp. 101–20.
31. See, for example, the memorandum of the Zionist Organization in Poland of 1919 on the Jewish Question in Poland, CZA, A127/128.
32. On these and other Jewish schools, see my *Zionism in Poland*, pp. 186–206.

hardly crowned with success, as neither the Zionists nor their various national adversaries were able to alter or even affect in any serious way the antisemitic tendencies and policies of the successor states.[33] Zionism was certainly a powerful movement in Eastern Europe, undoubtedly the backbone of European Zionism and the unchallenged main source of *aliyah*, especially of pioneering *aliyah*. Yet the number of emigrants to Palestine was insignificant so far as the masses of Eastern European Jews were concerned, proving that Zionism's enemies were right when they voiced their traditional belief that Zionism could never solve the Jewish Problem in countries like Poland.[34] Paradoxically, the antisemitic environment was one reason why many Zionist leaders spent so much time on *Gegenwartsarbeit* (work in the Diaspora) and sometimes neglected the Palestinian aspects of their movements, thereby bringing down upon themselves the scorn of leaders of the Yishuv, who believed that by so acting they were reducing the potential for Eastern European *aliyah*.[35] Jewish nationalist deputies in the various parliaments, often accused of advocating *Sejm Zionismus*, fought the good fight for Jewish rights, but by the 1930s they were relatively few in number and operating in an increasingly antidemocratic atmosphere. Whatever tactics were used—ranging from Agudat Israel's *shtadlanut* via the Galician Zionists' accommodationism to Yitzhak Gruenbaum's confrontationist policies—had little effect.[36] National autonomy schemes aiming at the establishment of separate Jewish "sectors" failed, both because the host societies refused to cooperate and because of chronic

33. Ezra Mendelsohn, "Zionist Success and Zionist Failure: The Case of Interwar East Central Europe," *Herzl Yearbook*, forthcoming.

34. During the years 1919–42 approximately 140,000 Jews went on legal *aliyah* from Poland to Palestine. See David Gurevich and Aharon Gerts, *Ha-aliyah, ha-yishuv ve-ha-tnuah ha-tivit shel ha-ukhlusya be-Eretz Israel* (Jerusalem, 1944), p. 59. Many Polish-Gentile friends of Zionism also pointed out that Zionism could never solve the Jewish Question. See the remarks of Ignacy Daszyński referred to in n. 12 above. The Polish socialist points out, unhappily, that the Jewish birthrate in Poland is too high and the number of Jews going to Palestine too low.

35. See, for example, Leib Jaffe's comments in 1929: "I admire very much the political work of our friend Gruenbaum, but Eretz Israel is more important than all other countries and all politics." In "Protokol shel ha-moshav ha-rishon shel moetzet Keren ha-Yesod be-Polanyah," March 3, 1929, CZA, KH4/B/2157. This was a rather mild reproach by Zionist standards. Others accused Polish Zionists of being concerned exclusively with political careers in Poland and not with building Palestine.

36. See Ezra Mendelsohn, "The Dilemma of Jewish Politics in Poland: Four Responses," in *Jews and Non-Jews in Eastern Europe*, ed. Bela Vago and George Mosse (New York, 1974), pp. 203–20; Joseph Rothschild, "Ethnic Peripheries Versus Ethnic Cores: Jewish Political Strategies in Interwar Poland," *Political Science Quarterly* 96 (1981–82): 591–606.

Jewish disunity.[37] Jewish modern national educational networks were set up but, with a few notable exceptions, failed to attract a majority of Jewish children.[38] There were many reasons for this failure, among them the central fact that in most cases the state refused to subsidize Jewish education. Jews continued to be involved in the political and cultural clashes that characterized Eastern Europe, sometimes, as in the case of the famous minorities' bloc of 1922 in Poland, with unpleasant results. In that year Jews joined together with other national minorities and won a large number of seats in the Sejm (parliament), thereby "proving" to Polish antisemites that they constituted an antistate element linked to forces that wanted to dismember Poland.[39]

The most striking example of the failure of the Jewish political reaction to antisemitism involves the utter inability to overcome Jewish fragmentation. There were good reasons for this fragmentation, which in countries like Poland became one of the most outstanding features of Jewish political life.[40] It is notable that even in the 1930s, when antisemitism grew apace, Jewish unity remained a slogan on the lips of politicians rather than a fact of life.[41] Indeed, the dramatic growth of antisemitism served to accentuate the traditional divides in Jewish politics, as seen in the storm that arose in Poland and elsewhere over Jabotinsky's "evacuation" scheme and, to cite another example, the transfer agreement. Thus, not only did the various solutions put forth in the struggle against antisemitism fail, but also all attempts to unite the proponents of these solutions.

This brief essay has described how the general antisemitic environment of interwar East Central Europe gave rise to the nationalization and politicization of the Jewish population in at least some of the countries of the region. It has also claimed that this reaction was not very efficacious. But I would not want to end on a purely nega-

37. In Poland, for example, the state refused to subsidize Jewish schools. In Lithuania the state dismantled the rather elaborate national autonomy institutions, and by the mid-1920s little was left of them.

38. This was the case in Poland and Rumania. In Lithuania, Jewish schools succeeded more than anywhere else, thanks to the Jews' general reluctance to study in Lithuanian schools (Lithuanian culture not being very attractive to them) and to the state's readiness to help finance these schools.

39. See Golczewski, *Polnisch-Jüdische Beziehungen*, pp. 334–51.

40. Among these reasons were the unique or nearly unique problems that Jews confronted—such as whether to seek a solution to the Jewish Question in the Eastern European Diaspora or in Palestine and whether to maintain religion as the primary force in Jewish life or to strive for a secular Jewish society.

41. See especially the important study by Melzer, *Maavak medini be-malkodet.*

tive note. If the Jewish political reaction to Eastern European anti-semitism failed to solve the Jewish Question, it was nonetheless of considerable psychological import, since it offered hope and even inspiration to the Jewish population. Moreover, we should place the Jewish failure in a broader context. How successful were the Ukrainians, who had more powerful patrons than the Jews, in protecting their rights in Poland? Or even the Germans? Not very. The fact is that the Jews' failure to mitigate in any significant way the anti-semitic onslaught derived not so much from their lack of unity, or from their lack of inventiveness, or even from their lack of realism (though there was, as we can see with hindsight, a good deal of wishful thinking) but from the essential helplessness of the Jewish minority in the face of local antisemitism and American and British immigration laws. (It might be said that this is a Zionist analysis of the failure of interwar Zionism.) The triumph of the national principle in post–World War I Eastern Europe, which implied, among other things, the rise of anti-Jewish feelings, also led, in some cases, to the triumph of Jewish nationalism in various forms. Thus the Eastern European context provided, paradoxically, both great possibilities and grave dangers for the Jewish minority. In the last analysis the dangers proved all too real and the possibilities—in the form of establishing powerful national movements—all too limited.

THE WESTERN
HEMISPHERE
AND ARAB WORLD

Naomi W. Cohen

Friends in Court

An American-Jewish Response to Antisemitism

If antisemitism is defined loosely as discrimination against Jews, American history provides a wide assortment of examples. Private institutions have been the worst culprits, but no level of government—federal, state, or municipal—can boast a completely unsullied record. To be sure, American antisemitism, both overt and ideological, never reached the extremes of other countries, nor did it seriously impede the overall, rapid socioeconomic mobility of American Jews. However, a history of anti-Jewish persecution over two millennia and a keen sensitivity to the vibrations emanating from the American majority have kept American Jews ever on the alert.

In nineteenth- and twentieth-century America, Jews employed various tools for combatting antisemitism. Singly or through defense organizations that reached back to the Board of Delegates of American Israelites of 1859,[1] they have labored to fight bigots and to build up Jewish security. The phrase "friends in court" in the title of this essay applies to two distinct approaches. The first is the activity of the communal steward, the person with entrée into the circle or "court" of the power brokers, who intercedes for his fellow Jews. The second is the use of the "friend of the court" (or *amicus curiae*) brief, an impersonal way of advancing Jewish interests through general litigation. The first is older, a derivative of the *shtadlan* (or intercessor) of medieval times and the *Hofjude* (or court Jew) of Central Europe in the seventeenth and eighteenth centuries. The second is a twentieth-century phenomenon drawn from the American experience. Although otherwise unrelated, the two shared the aim of win-

1. Allan Tarshish, "The Board of Delegates of American Israelites (1859–1878)," in *The Jewish Experience in America*, ed. Abraham J. Karp (Waltham, Mass., 1969), 3:123–39.

ning Jewish ends by enlisting government support. Each in its own way has reflected both the priorities and the degree of self-confidence of an accommodationist minority.

I

The activities of the European court Jew have been analyzed by Selma Stern, who interprets his evolution as a product of the age of absolutism. She presents him as a man chosen to render special administrative services, usually of an economic nature—supplier for the army, banker and moneylender, developer of commerce and industry—for a king or prince struggling to maintain centralized authority. Rewarded financially or socially for his labors, the court Jew was also frequently appointed by his ruler to head the Jewish community. Since he enjoyed a special relationship with the court, he was in a position to mediate the interests of the Jews and to intercede for favors.[2]

The court Jew's counterparts in America—men like Jacob Schiff, Oscar Straus, and Louis Marshall—operated without government appointment, but they shared certain characteristics with their forebears. By virtue of economic or political position achieved on the larger American scene, they, too, had access to government officials. They, too, were solidly entrenched within the Jewish community and, steeped in a heritage that emphasized communal responsibility, were prepared to use their personal influence on behalf of fellow Jews. Administrators and lawmakers to whom they turned usually listened graciously to their requests. The Jewish stewards had made it in American society, and their basic conservatism, precluding any desire for radical change, was above question. No more than the power wielders whom they approached did the Jews desire to "make waves." Besides, they knew the pulse of the Jewish community and could aid politicians who sought ways of cultivating Jewish support. Admired and respected by their co-religionists for their Jewish loyalty and because they had the ear of people in high places, they could help mold Jewish opinion and sway Jewish votes.

How strongly identified a Jew was with his community played an important part in determining any show of favor he was granted. For example, after he received the Republican nomination in 1904,

2. Selma Stern, *The Court Jew* (Philadelphia, 1950).

Theodore Roosevelt asked Oscar Straus, Jacob Schiff, and Nathan Bijur—familiar names among the Jewish rank and file—to read the portion of his acceptance speech dealing with Russian discrimination against Jewish passport holders. When Woodrow Wilson was considering Louis Brandeis for the cabinet, he solicited the opinions of Schiff and Louis Marshall. In that instance Brandeis was rejected because both they and the president preferred a "representative Jew," or one whose credentials were more solidly Jewish.[3]

The heyday of the American court Jew on the national level was reached between the 1880s and World War I. By that time the heavy volume of Jewish immigration from Eastern Europe was dramatically altering the face of American Jewry. Leadership rested, however, in the hands of the now fully acculturated German stratum of the community. Not surprisingly, the spokesmen from that element chose a tool familiar to them from their European heritage. Schiff, Straus, Marshall, and a few of their intimate circle stand out as the most prominent of the stewards, and from their numerous encounters with presidents, members of Congress, cabinet members, and diplomats we can extrapolate the general techniques of the court Jew approach.[4]

The Jewish leaders usually operated without organizational or communal mandate. Self-appointed, they co-opted men of similar stature and outlook to whom they were tied socially or by business. They charted strategy in informal meetings or through letters, and then singly or in small committees they presented their request to the proper official. The basic rule was secrecy. None but the handful concerned knew of the negotiations, and the backstairs interchange was direct and candid. Without publicity and worries of public image, a swift and decisive response, so important in crisis situations, was more readily forthcoming. Petitioners were well aware of the possibility of losing favor by excessive or unviable requests; on occasion they displayed timidity or even obsequiousness. At the same

3. Naomi W. Cohen, *A Dual Heritage: The Public Career of Oscar S. Straus* (Philadelphia, 1969), pp. 131–32; Yonathan Shapiro, *Leadership of the American Zionist Organization* (Urbana, Ill., 1971), pp. 63–65.

4. Activities of some stewards were recounted in biographical or autobiographical form. On Schiff, see Cyrus Adler, *Jacob H. Schiff* (Garden City, N.Y., 1929); on Straus, see Oscar S. Straus, *Under Four Administrations* (Boston, 1922), and Cohen, *Dual Heritage*; on Marshall, see Morton Rosenstock, *Louis Marshall: Defender of Jewish Rights* (Detroit, 1965), and Charles Reznikoff, ed., *Louis Marshall: Champion of Liberty* (Philadelphia, 1957).

time, however, they tenaciously held to their purpose when no other option was available even in the face of rebuffs.

The *Hofjude* approach can be utilized on any level of government, and the level of government in turn was determined by the court Jew's agenda. Before World War I the garden variety of antisemitism—discrimination in employment and social institutions, burdens imposed by Sunday laws or Christian teachings in the public schools—were matters exclusively within the domain of states, municipalities, and the private sector. Since the men alluded to were "friends in the *federal* court," they fought other dimensions of antisemitism, primarily the persecution of Jews in Eastern Europe. To them the problem was of highest priority, for it bore very much on American-Jewish security. Experience had taught them that antisemitism was indivisible. When Switzerland did not want the immigration of Alsatian Jews, it also prohibited the entry of American Jews; when Russia discriminated against its own Jews, it also discriminated against American-Jewish passport holders.[5] Furthermore, aided by the growing popularity of racist thought, bigots now questioned the ability of *any* state, Western or Eastern, to absorb the "peculiar" Hebrews and, by implication as well, the very emancipation and equality of Jews in any land. Since a gain for Russian Jewry would also redound to the benefit of Jews generally, the reasoning went, a prime objective of the American stewards was to secure American condemnation of Russian persecution.

Like the conduct of foreign relations, the regulation of immigration was a federal power, and that matter dovetailed with Jewish priorities. Since Jewish victims of persecution increasingly sought refuge in the United States, their impoverished condition could provide the government with another reason for protesting oppression. Besides, if the situation in Eastern Europe did not improve, American Jews would be saddled with a flood of new immigrants and their attendant problems. Far from sanguine over that prospect, the Jewish stewards feared that the Eastern Europeans could tarnish the image of the established American Jews. Nevertheless, out of a sense of Jewish responsibility, they fought to keep the American doors open to their co-religionists.

On issues of diplomatic pressure and immigration, the "friends in

5. Naomi W. Cohen, "The Abrogation of the Russo-American Treaty of 1832," *Jewish Social Studies* 25 (1963): 3–41; Cohen, "American Jews and the Swiss Treaty," in *The Solomon Goldman Lectures*, ed. Nathaniel Stampfer, vol. 3 (Chicago, 1982), pp. 83–100.

court" scored some significant victories during the administrations of Benjamin Harrison, Grover Cleveland, Theodore Roosevelt, and William Howard Taft.[6] Quietly or publicly, the government spoke out at various times against Russian oppression, and Congress, subject to strong pressure on behalf of immigrants, held off on the passage of restrictionist laws. To be sure, no dramatic changes occurred in Eastern Europe, but the "friends in court" could rightly claim that they had heightened America's sensitivity to human rights in other lands.

Reliance on the *Hofjude* approach waned considerably in the decades after World War I. The maturation of the American-Jewish community, where native-born outnumbered immigrant by 1940, aggravated dissatisfaction with self-appointed leaders who ignored or dictated to their constituency. The priorities of the stewards may have been correct, but their methods were unacceptable to a group increasingly knowledgeable about representative democracy. A growing assertiveness crested around 1960 in tandem with a general interest in ethnicity and group identity.[7] Ethnic groups, and Jews among them, were less timid about voicing what they considered to be legitimate demands. In that setting both the figure of the "friend in court," a supplicant with hat in hand, and that of the benevolent official who dispensed favors were utterly out of place.

In addition, by the 1930s the entrenchment and professionalization of the major Jewish defense agencies had eclipsed the individual. More and more, paid professionals made decisions and lobbied with public figures. Prominent individual Jews still met with officials, but frequently the encounters were orchestrated by the agencies and their staffs.

Over time the other variable in the court Jew equation changed, too. Since the days of Franklin D. Roosevelt, presidents have had special advisers on Jewish affairs. That office serves not only as a conduit between the administration and the Jewish minority, but it can be used as well to shield the president from individual pleas adjudged to be inopportune or impolitic.

From both sides, then, the *Hofjude* approach has been undercut. Quiet, behind-the-scenes diplomacy will doubtless continue, but the day of the independent "friend in court" is over.

6. Cohen, *Dual Heritage*, chaps. 4, 7; Naomi W. Cohen, *Not Free to Desist: A History of the American Jewish Committee, 1906–1966* (Philadelphia, 1972), chaps. 3, 4.
7. Stephen D. Isaacs, *Jews and American Politics* (Garden City, N.Y., 1974), chap. 13.

II

In present-day America it is a widely accepted phenomenon for Jewish religious and secular organizations to become involved in all sorts of issues crowding the nation's political agenda. From abortion to arms control, from public schools to PLO, the Jewish voice (or, in many cases, voices) is heard on domestic and foreign policy matters. Like other interest groups—religious, ethnic, legal, economic, or patriotic—Jewish organizations publicize their position papers and resolutions, present testimony to legislative committees, and file briefs in court cases where principles of concern are at stake. Although that last avenue of activity, the *amicus curiae*, or "friend of the court," brief, has received far less attention than the older court Jew, it has become the American-Jewish weapon against antisemitism.

While "friend of the court" is a device applicable to all sorts of issues, Jews have used it principally in the areas of civil liberties and civil rights. To be sure, in many instances the connection between Jewish interests and the specific case before the court may be less than self-evident. Why, for example, did the American Jewish Congress in 1967 join the American Civil Liberties Union in contesting an antievolution law in the state of Arkansas?[8] But no matter how far afield an individual case may seem, a common proposition has motivated the Jewish approach: by broadening the definition of freedom and by extending the area of freedom for all Americans—be they Jews, Christians, atheists, white, or black—Jewish security is strengthened.[9]

Several derivatives, especially significant for the historian, emerge almost automatically from that proposition. First, just as traditional Jews of premodern times sought to construct fences around Jewish law to lessen the chances of violation, so did American Jews labor to secure individual rights and liberties recognized by American law beyond the reach of potential violators. Ever an accommodationist minority, American Jews have consistently equated their interests with good and proper Americanism. What they sought for themselves or for other minorities was interpreted by them to be no more

8. Naomi W. Cohen, "Schools, Religion, and Government: Recent American Jewish Opinions," *Michael* 3 (Tel Aviv, 1973): 365–66.

9. For a recent interpretation of the universalist thrust of Jewish activity, see Steven M. Cohen, *American Modernity and Jewish Identity* (New York, 1983), pp. 46–48.

than what the tenets of Americanism, originally propagated by the founding fathers, promised. Second, unlike the Jewish experiences of other eras and other lands, American Jews have enjoyed a singular luxury—the opportunity to shore up Jewish strength by contesting bigotry in its multiple forms even before Jews became the principal victims. Since they never confronted critical eruptions of native antisemitism, when responses are perforce reactive rather than active, Jews in the second half of the twentieth century have had the chance to invest in the future and not merely fight for survival in the present. We may, therefore, call their approach anticipatory anti-antisemitism.

Resort to the *amicus curiae* briefs became noteworthy only after World War II, but American Jews singly had looked to the courts as the ultimate guardians of their rights since the earliest days of the Republic. In the first half of the nineteenth century there were numerous cases involving Jewish litigants who contested the validity of municipal and state Sunday laws. (When non-Jewish groups fought for the same principle, Jewish leaders and the Anglo-Jewish press registered their sympathetic concern.) Sunday laws posed a severe challenge. Not impinging on the right of Jews to worship as they pleased, the laws (frequently upheld on Christian religious grounds) negated the Jewish claim to *equality* of religion. Given their small numbers, Jews believed that as long as American law bowed in any way to Christian usage or belief, they, the Jews, bore the stigma of less than equal citizens. And only the court could erase that invidious distinction.[10]

Two factors contributed to Jewish reliance upon the judicial arm of government. Their own cultural heritage and training, wherein law was a key component, assured their respect for the system of American constitutionalism and its teaching that man-made law could be measured against state and federal constitutions by independent judges. Rabbi Isaac Mayer Wise wrote in 1865 that the judge was "the mouthpiece of the law," the supreme authority for expounding fundamental law.[11] Furthermore, American Jews early on adopted the posture of political neutrality. They argued that if Jews desired easy acceptance into the body politic, they were constrained to repudiate any Jewish or group political interests. As long

10. Naomi W. Cohen, *Encounter with Emancipation: The German Jews in the United States, 1830–1914* (Philadelphia, 1984), pp. 79–87.
11. Isaac Mayer Wise, "Church and State," *Israelite*, April 14, 1865, p. 332.

as Jews conformed to that code—and for the most part they did during the nineteenth century—they gave up the ballot as a potential defensive or corrective tool.[12] Deliberately forgoing a clear input into legislation and the choice of legislators, they were left perforce with the courts.

Unlike their twentieth-century successors, even where nineteenth-century Jews could have made common cause in the struggle to secure their rights with similarly concerned Christian minorities—say, Seventh Day Adventists, Baptists, or atheists—Jewish action was solitary. Insecurity and suspicion bred of the long history of suffering at the hands of Christians underlay this stand. Nineteenth-century American Jews, like their premodern ancestors, believed that antisemitism was at bottom spawned by Christian religious teachings. Moreover a popular and active Christian interest—an interest that transcended sectarian differences—in the conversion of the Jews made the latter wary of forging alliances with non-Jews.

Present-day Jewish organizations employing the "friend of the court" brief to state their case are resorting to a legal device whose antecedents date back to Roman and common law. Originally the *amicus curiae* was literally the "friend of the court," one who without any interest in the case protected the court by informing the presiding judge of points of fact or of law. In time the role of "the friend" changed from that of a neutral to an advocate or representative of one side of the issue at stake. Among the first private interest groups to avail themselves of the use of a partisan *amicus curiae* brief were racial minorities. Through the better part of the nineteenth century and well into the first half of the twentieth, the American "friend of the court" was a lawyer. By the 1930s, however, it was commonly accepted for an organization rather than an individual attorney to sponsor and file an *amicus curiae* brief. A form of lobbying, in this case judicial lobbying, an organizational brief offered the sponsoring group more than the opportunity to raise issues for both aggressive or defensive purposes. On a more mundane level, it became a way of achieving publicity or enhancing the group's image—devices for attracting new members and delighting old. Indeed those benefits accrued irrespective of how significant the brief itself was in shaping the court's final decision. Meantime the litigant received the benefit of the organization's prestige and, at times, the willingness of "the

12. Naomi W. Cohen, *Encounter with Emancipation*, pp. 129–58.

friend" to introduce supplementary, "riskier," points of law from which the litigant himself might shy away.[13]

For Jewish leaders and organizations the *amicus curiae* brief provided distinct advantages over the *Hofjude* approach. First of all, judicial lobbying was free of the vagaries of personality and partisan politics that enveloped the *Hofjude's* encounter with a power broker. In addition, a faceless organization turning to a faceless court had no qualms about using up favors or jumping into similar cases and repeating arguments time and again. Moreover, the *amicus curiae* brief permitted the pursuit of long-range goals chartered by the organization as opposed to *ad hoc,* immediate responses to crisis situations. Whereas the *Hofjude* argued for the specific, the organizational brief used the specific to argue the principle. And, if it emerged on the winning side, it helped forge precedent that could easily be invoked in future situations.

The three present-day major American-Jewish defense agencies— the American Jewish Committee, the American Jewish Congress, the Anti-Defamation League—used the *amicus curiae* brief infrequently before World War II. By 1958, however, an authoritative survey disclosed that the American Jewish Congress ranked with the ACLU, the National Association for the Advancement of Colored People, and the AFL-CIO among the most active brief filers.[14] A short survey cannot do justice to the litigation work of the American Jewish Congress, or for that matter to that of other Jewish organizations. Rather, I propose to examine some premises underlying American-Jewish participation in court cases and to see how that activity contributed to the Jewish struggle against antisemitism. I am limiting myself to the American Jewish Committee, the oldest and the most conservative and restrained of the three agencies. A few of its *amicus curiae* briefs will elucidate some priorities of the modern American-Jewish defense agenda.

In 1909 attorneys Max J. Kohler and Abram Elkus filed the committee's first *amicus curiae* brief in defense of a recent Jewish immigrant from Russia, Hersch Skuratowski. Skuratowski, who had arrived in the United States with less than three dollars in his pocket, was ordered deported by the Board of Special Inquiry at Ellis Island.

---

13. Samuel Krislov, "The Amicus Curiae Brief: From Friendship to Advocacy," *Yale Law Journal* 72 (1963): 694–721. I am grateful to Lawrence Newman for calling this article to my attention.

14. Henry J. Abraham, *The Judicial Process,* 3d ed. (New York, 1975), p. 235.

Kohler and Elkus challenged the decision, arguing that Immigration Commissioner William Williams had exceeded his authority by fixing as law certain economic requirements not mandated by congressional legislation. Besides, since Skuratowski had not enjoyed the aid of counsel at the board's hearing, his rights to due process had been denied. Finally, Skuratowski's classification as a "Russian Hebrew" by the immigration officials was illegal, both in the religious and racial sense, and in violation of the Constitution.

When the arguments are viewed in the social context of that day, the motives of the committee become abundantly clear. It was primarily concerned about the chance of Russian Jews, victims of pogroms and other forms of oppression, to find a haven in the United States. Skuratowski's predicament provided the platform for challenging the champions of immigration restriction, the influence of which was then significantly on the rise. More specifically, the case afforded the opportunity of exposing the antisemitism of Commissioner Williams and his subordinates on Ellis Island. Perhaps more important, it permitted the committee to contest the popularity of racist thought and jargon, which were then sweeping the entire Western world. Kohler and Elkus mustered authoritative sources for their brief to show that the word "Hebrew" was not a racial classification and that the very ideas of racial traits or racial superiority or inferiority were ungrounded. Not surprisingly, a substantial part of the brief was devoted to the race issue, for the committee knew that on *that* point American Jewry stood in the dock with Skuratowski.[15]

The committee's efforts in the Skuratowski matter were thwarted, since the scheduled judicial hearing never took place. Fifteen years later, however, the agency did better. In the case of *Pierce* v. *The Society of Sisters*, Louis Marshall, president of the committee, supported the claims of a parochial and a private school that challenged a Ku Klux Klan–inspired Oregon law compelling attendance of all children at public schools. The committee's participation in the case was in response primarily to a request from William Guthrie, a Catholic friend of Marshall's and counselor for the parochial school. Guthrie had called for Marshall's help, stating that the principle in-

15. Brief for Petitioner, In the Matter of Hersch Skuratowski, U.S. District Court, Southern District of New York, 1909, American Jewish Committee (hereafter AJC) Files, New York; Esther Panitz, "In Defense of the Jewish Immigrant (1891–1924)," in *Jewish Experience in America*, 5:27–32.

volved concerned all religions. Participation also permitted a public swipe at the Klan, whose hatemongering campaigns were directed at Jews as well as Catholics. To be sure, Marshall and his circle traditionally gave their unqualified support to public schools, but the compulsory element in Oregon's law emitted certain danger signals.

In his brief Marshall wrote that he was representing Jewish parents who desired day schools for their children. He went on to argue eloquently against state suppression of free thought and free expression of religious convictions. A unanimous Supreme Court held the Oregon law unconstitutional, and Justice James Clark McReynolds, who wrote the decision, echoed some of Marshall's points.[16] In the balance of communal priorities, Jews stood only to gain. Noninvolvement would not have endeared them to the Klan, whereas Marshall's *amicus curiae* brief bolstered relations with the Catholics while it defended Jewish day schools. As in the Skuratowski matter, the specific legal issue offered the channel through which to fight for a larger principle—in this case, a pluralistic society in which minority opinions could thrive. During those years, when the public temper emphasized Anglo-Saxon conformity,[17] such efforts on behalf of American-Jewish security were particularly significant.

In a third early brief of 1938, the committee took a seemingly unexpected stand. Allied with the American Committee on Religious Rights and Minorities, the American Jewish Congress, and the National Council of Women, it sided *with* a notorious Jew-baiter, Robert Edmondson. Edmondson, whose organization circulated millions of antisemitic releases, had been indicted on one of three counts for criminally libeling Jews. The "friends of the court" agreed that he had perverted the right of free speech, but in their brief they questioned whether libel laws constituted the best means for defending religious tolerance. Were the bigot acquitted, his propaganda would appear legally vindicated; were he convicted, he might be made into a martyr. Either way his writings stood to gain added attention. Equally important, Jews might be portrayed as inquisitors out to curb freedom of speech, and public reaction against them could mount. The brief rather lamely concluded that the proper reply to

16. Marshall's brief is printed in Reznikoff, *Marshall*, 2:957–67, see also p. 887; and Rosenstock, *Louis Marshall*, pp. 212–13.

17. See, for example, John Higham, *Strangers in the Land* (New York, 1973), chap. 7.

Edmondson lay in a campaign of education undertaken by enlightened groups.[18]

What may appear now to be an excessively timid posture and one that held on to a misplaced faith in man's rationality can only be understood by an examination of its setting. In Europe, time was running out for the Jews, and neither lobbying nor public relations campaigns swayed the United States to fight for the victims of the Nazi fury or even to loosen American immigration laws. Meantime, making full use of Hitler's teachings, American antisemitic organizations were flourishing—some 120 during the decade of the 1930s according to a conservative estimate.[19] Despite these realities, good people still retained a faith in the defeat of the lunatic fringe and the ultimate triumph of enlightened public opinion. In short-range terms, to act the role of censors of Edmondson and free speech, when even neutral non-Jews like the editors of the *New York Herald Tribune* and *Christian Century* warned against it, seemed impolitic. The line between freedom of speech and a minority's defense of its good name was always difficult to draw. Of all times, the 1930s were the least propitious for risking public disapproval. Even those in the Jewish community who had applauded Mayor Fiorello LaGuardia for issuing the summons against Edmondson in 1936 slowly lost interest as the case dragged on. Thus, the committee decided, "It [is] better to suffer the activities of a bigot than to deprive him of the right of freedom of speech and of the press."[20]

True, the committee could have remained silent. But by actively joining in the defense of an antisemite—and indeed the arguments of the *amici* were cited by the judge who dismissed the charges—it was showing mainstream liberals that Jewish priorities were primarily to secure American values. That stand, the committee believed, did more for American-Jewish security than the suppression of one bigot.

In 1947 the committee did a complete about-face with respect to its traditional interpretation of the needs of Jewish defense. On the

18. Memorandum Submitted as *Amici Curiae* . . . , *New York* v. *Robert Edward Edmondson*, Court of General Sessions of the County of New York, April 1938, AJC Files; Dov Fisch, "The Libel Trial of Robert Edward Edmondson: 1936–1938," *American Jewish History* 71 (1981): 79–102.

19. Donald S. Strong, *Organized Anti-Semitism in America* (Washington, D.C., 1941), p. 14.

20. Memorandum Submitted as *Amici Curiae* . . . , *New York* v. *Robert Edward Edmondson*, pp. 2–3; Fisch, "Libel Trial of Edmondson," pp. 94, 97–98; Naomi W. Cohen, *Not Free to Desist*, p. 210.

grounds that the rights of all could not be separated from the rights of any particular group, that defense against antisemitism meant the extension of freedom in universalist terms, it resolved to embark on a broad social action program.[21]

The committee's decision drew from various sources. It fit with the political momentum generated by the New Deal and the Fair Deal, the legislative programs of which took cognizance of the non-WASP and have-not groups. While Congress widened its horizons, the Supreme Court in the aftermath of Franklin D. Roosevelt's court "reform" plan of 1937 turned increasingly to its function as guardian of individual rights. The decision also drew from the Jewish situation. The confidence of American Jews mounted as the community became increasingly native-born. The Holocaust and the birth of the State of Israel contributed as well to the heightened resolve of a scarred minority. At the same time, organized antisemitism in the United States was declining, and the phenomenon of antisemitism was explained by some as a threat to democracy, an aberration from social normality, rather than as a Jewish problem. Meantime Americans increasingly endorsed, at least by lip service, the concepts of pluralism. Since Christian and secular organizations were already very much involved in social action crusades, the moment had come to forge alliances and cement friendships with non-Jewish groups.[22]

To be sure, crasser motives played a part, too. The committee stood to lose prestige if it yielded the field to other agencies like the American Jewish Congress. Struggles for legislation and litigation also enabled laity and professionals within the agency to channel personal secularist and politically activist leanings through a Jewish conduit and even to carve out niches of personal power.[23]

Whatever the causes, social action merged defense against antisemitism with the broader current of American liberalism. The cloaking of the particular within the universal through charted, on-

21. Naomi W. Cohen, *Not Free to Desist*, pp. 384–87. The committee repeatedly invoked that reasoning to explain its involvement in the area of civil rights. See, for example, the brief filed in *Barrows* v. *Jackson*, 1952, a case dealing with restrictive housing covenants aimed against blacks: Brief on Behalf of American Jewish Committee and Anti-Defamation League of B'nai B'rith, pp. 2–5, AJC Files.

22. Civic Action [1947], Statement of Principles Affecting AJC Program in the Area of Civic Action, August 29, 1949, and Maurice Goldbloom, "Outline of Factual Highlights on Civil Rights and Civil Liberties," December 1955, AJC Files.

23. An Examination of the Action Program of the Legal and Civil Affairs Committee, January 20, 1948, ibid.; Murray Friedman, "A New Direction for American Jews," *Commentary*, December 1981, p. 39; Charles S. Liebman, "Leadership and Decision-making in a Jewish Federation," *American Jewish Year Book* 79 (1979): 26.

going programs that involved the lawmakers, courts, and communal education became the hallmark of mid-century American-Jewish defense.

Litigation was an important component of the committee's new posture, and the number of its *amicus curiae* briefs, devoted primarily to civil rights and church-state issues, multiplied rapidly. Various considerations, however, tempered any headlong, indiscriminate plunge into social or libertarian causes.[24] As a Jewish defense agency, the committee could not evolve merely into a branch of the ACLU. It had to reckon as well with the question of allies. For example, would a partnership with Jehovah's Witnesses, known as bitter anti-Catholics and yet in the forefront of battle for broadening the First Amendment, damage the agency's interreligious work with Catholic elements? Would involvement on behalf of atheists evoke a public outcry against so-called secularist and godless Judaism? The committee had to think also of the local problems of its far-flung constituency situated so differently from its New York City base. Would daring action in the cause of civil rights or separation of church and state endanger the well-being of certain of its chapters? Would it rupture overall American-Jewish communal unity? And, finally, if social action raised anti-Jewish feelings in some quarters, would the committee be risking American help to the State of Israel? The degree of involvement depended, therefore, on balancing the risks and advantages of each separate action. Similarly, success had to be measured not only by a particular court decision that may have vindicated the organization's brief but rather by the effect the decision had on public opinion about Jews and their communal priorities.

The 1962 case of *Engel* v. *Vitale* merits our attention. There the Supreme Court ruled that the prayer composed and endorsed by the New York Board of Regents for use in the public schools violated the establishment clause of the First Amendment—namely, Congress shall make no law respecting an establishment of religion.[25] A landmark in the story of church-state separation and a victory for all separationists, it was especially gratifying to American Jews whose struggle for that goal was almost as old as Jewish settlement in this country. Unlike nineteenth-century Jews, they were not content

24. Naomi W. Cohen, *Not Free to Desist*, pp. 386–87, 391–92, 438; Newman Levy, "Memorandum on the Proposal to Extend the Activities of the Civil Rights Division," November 7, 1949, AJC Files.
25. *Engel* v. *Vitale*, 370 U.S. 421.

merely with exemption from Christian-inspired laws,[26] and in the *Engel* case the principle they championed—that any form of prayer in the public schools violated the meaning of church-state separation—had triumphed.

For the historian examining the struggle against antisemitism, the *Engel* case had deeper meaning. What prompted the committee to file an *amicus curiae* brief? Did the separationist stance adopted by most Jewish organizations redound to the benefit of the Jews? An analysis of the case, the committee's involvement, and the backlash that ensued illuminates some of the general points about Jewish use of the tool of "friend of the court."

The facts of *Engel* v. *Vitale* went back to 1951, when the New York Board of Regents recommended that public schools begin each day with a nonsectarian prayer. The board suggested a twenty-two word prayer: "Almighty God we acknowledge our dependence upon Thee, and we beg Thy blessings upon us, our parents, our teachers and our country." Reflecting the increased tensions spawned by the cold war and McCarthyism, when secularism was equated with communism and agnosticism and when schools were denounced as ungodly, the prayer was defended by many as a means of shaping God-fearing children and protecting American freedom. Opponents, and Jews stood out conspicuously on that side, charged that the prayer violated separation of church and state and that it imposed majority rule without regard for minority rights. Even nonsectarian prayers could lead to religious interpretation by teachers and perhaps to religious indoctrination. Most important, the prayer could become a significant entering wedge to fix sectarian teachings into the classroom curriculum.[27]

In 1952 the committee issued a statement opposing the Board of Regents' recommendation. In light of the contemporary scene and to avoid the charge of secularist or communistic, it couched its opposition in prudent words. It affirmed the centrality of religion to Jewish and American life, and it endorsed the board's commitment to inculcate moral and spiritual values in the schools. But, in order to avoid sectarian interpretations and to protect children from non-

26. Naomi W. Cohen, *Encounter with Emancipation*, p. 86.
27. New York State Board of Regents Statement on Prayer and Pledge of Allegiance, January 14, 1952, and Arguments for and against the Regents' Recommendation for Public School Prayer, February 1952, AJC Files; Naomi W. Cohen, *Not Free to Desist*, pp. 437–38, 440–42.

believing homes as well as those from traditional Jewish homes accustomed to other settings for prayer, it advised that the board explore other avenues for achieving its purpose.[28]

Six years later, in 1958, when a school board in New Hyde Park, Long Island, instituted the Board of Regents' prayer, suit was brought by five parents—two Jewish, one Unitarian, one Ethical Culture, and one agnostic. Their challenge of unconstitutionality was dismissed by three New York courts before the case went to the Supreme Court. Along with other organizations, the American Jewish Committee and Anti-Defamation League filed a joint *amicus curiae* brief in 1961 on behalf of the petitioners. The brief was less conciliatory than the committee's 1952 statement. It said in part:

> The constituency of the *amici* believe . . . that prayer, in our democratic society, is a matter for the home, synagogue and church, and not for the public schools. . . . Freedom of religious belief, observance and worship can remain inviolate only so long as there is no intrusion of religious authority in secular affairs or secular authority in religious affairs. Each breach in this separation of role and function tends to beget additional breaches.

It went on to invoke the famous words of the *Everson* decision of 1947.

> The "establishment of religion" clause of the First Amendment means at least this: Neither a state nor the Federal Government can set up a church. Neither can pass laws which aid one religion, aid all religions, or prefer one religion over another. Neither can force or influence a person to go to or to remain away from church against his will or force him to profess a belief or disbelief in any religion. No person can be punished for entertaining or professing religious beliefs or disbeliefs, for church attendance or non-attendance.

On the basis of *Everson* v. *Board of Education* as well as other cases, the brief argued that the Board of Regents' prayer was unconstitutional. It "blends religious and secular concerns and commingles God and Caesar." The fact that children objecting to the prayer could be excused did not lessen its unconstitutionality.[29]

The more resolute stand of separationism reflected, again, a reading of public opinion and an evaluation of Jewish communal priori-

28. Statement Opposing the New York Board of Regents' Recommendation on Daily Prayer in the Public School, January 4, 1952, AJC Files.

29. Brief of American Jewish Committee and Anti-Defamation League of B'nai B'rith, *amici curiae*, *Engel* v. *Vitale*, Supreme Court of the United States, October Term, 1961; and Theodore Leskes, "The Supreme Court Decision in the New York Regents' Prayer Case," July 2, 1962, ibid.

ties. The cold war simmered on, but it had become a fact of life for most Americans; McCarthy's witch-hunt, from which Jews as a group had emerged unscathed, was over; and, testimony to greater acceptance on the part of Americans to the values of tolerance and pluralism, a Catholic was in the White House. Furthermore, in light of the long history of American-Jewish devotion to separation of church and state, it would have been sheer cowardice for the committee to have abstained at a moment when school prayer might have been sanctioned by the court and legitimized as part of the law of the land. On the other hand, were the Supreme Court to strike down the Board of Regents' nonsectarian prayer, it would be infinitely easier to contest sectarian school practices like the recitation of the Lord's Prayer or Bible reading in the classroom.[30] Increasingly the issue of federal aid to public schools was demanding congressional attention, and a separationist decision in *Engel* could serve as ammunition with which to fight the upcoming battle against aid to parochial schools.

Nor did the committee see any serious risks by its involvement. The Jewish community was still united on the issue of separation, and similar stands by important non-Jewish secular and religious organizations seemed likely to offset the anticipated opposition from certain Christian groups. To be sure, the Second Vatican Council loomed in the background, and the committee was simultaneously involved in efforts to secure an amendment of the church's official teachings about the Jews.[31] But since prayer in public schools was not as touchy an issue to Catholics, say, as government aid to schools, the committee's participation in *Engel* did not appear to jeopardize its moves with Vatican Council II.

The majority opinion in *Engel* v. *Vitale*, handed down in June 1962, gladdened the hearts of all separationists. Written by Justice Hugo Black, the decision held that the Board of Regents' prayer violated the establishment clause of the First Amendment, which the due process clause of the Fourteenth Amendment made binding upon the states. Neither its neutral quality nor the fact that student participation was voluntary freed the prayer from the limitations of that

30. Edwin Lukas to Marcus Cohn, March 14, 1963, ibid. The antiseparationists also realized that the *Engel* case could be a turning point, for eighteen state attorneys general, believing that religious practices in their states' schools might be affected by the outcome, filed as friends of the New Hyde Park school board. Leskes, "Supreme Court Decision," ibid.
31. Naomi W. Cohen, *Not Free to Desist*, pp. 462–79.

clause. Citing James Madison, the Court agreed that allowing even that innocuous prayer constituted an entering and alarming wedge in the domain of individual liberties. The decision drew heavily on English and early American history, sketching a picture of the evils of government's involvement in religion and upholding the idea that "a union of government and religion tends to destroy government and to degrade religion." According to the Court, it was "neither sacrilegious nor anti-religious to say that each separate government in this country should stay out of the business of writing or sanctioning official prayers and leave that purely religious function to the people themselves."[32] In 1963 the Court followed the same reasoning when in a Pennsylvania and a Maryland case it outlawed the reading of verses from the Bible at the beginning of each school day. In those cases, too, the plaintiffs were buttressed by Jewish *amicus curiae* briefs.[33]

On the surface, at least, these decisions constituted impressive victories for American Jews. Not only did they prove that American Jews had mastered the art of judicial lobbying, but their initiative in constructing a more solid wall between church and state was noteworthy. They had finally achieved the law's acknowledgment of separation in an extreme sense, and if the age-old American-Jewish logic held true, the more complete the separation the more secure the Jewish community.

The aftermath of the *Engel* decision, however, shrank the dimensions of the Jewish achievement. The outcry against the Court's ruling, well-nigh hysterical at first, was greater than anticipated. Outraged Americans called it tragic, infamous, and communistic. Condemnatory statements came from Catholic and Protestant religious leaders, from members of Congress and state legislatures, and from governors. The volume of letters attacking the decision was the largest in the Supreme Court's history, and bills were hurriedly introduced in Congress for a constitutional amendment. The Court itself was subjected to a public barrage; as Chief Justice Earl Warren recalled, one newspaper headlined the story "Court Outlaws God." Notable critics included not only conservative religious authorities

---

32. 370 U.S. 422–36.

33. Henry J. Abraham, *Freedom and the Court* (New York, 1967), pp. 217–18; Brief of American Jewish Committee and Anti-Defamation League of B'nai B'rith, *amici curiae*, *Murray* v. *Curlett*, *Abington* v. *Schempp*, Supreme Court of the United States, October Term, 1962, AJC Files.

but liberal theologians like Reinhold Niebuhr and John Bennett. Since opponents to the decision were clearly in the majority, the community relations department of the American Jewish Committee labored energetically to produce numerous fliers that attempted to answer the basic objections.

The backlash evoked by the decision underscored some grim realities. Perhaps most important, as the committee soon learned, expected support from liberal groups did not materialize. A confidential report disclosed: "For the most part, the liberals, with whom many Jews have tended to identify, have either been critical of the Court or remarkably reticent." To make matters worse, some critics, mostly Catholic, singled out Jews for their antireligious posture and for their agitation. The influential Jesuit weekly, *America*, advised Jews to control their "militant colleagues." "What will have been accomplished," the journal asked, "if our Jewish friends win all the legal immunity they seek, but thereby paint themselves into a corner of social and cultural alienation?" Not only did the decision polarize organized religious groups, but it fueled the drive of certain religious extremists. In Congress the backlash also threatened the civil rights program to which agencies like the American Jewish Committee were committed. A representative from Alabama said it this way: "They put Negroes in the schools, and now they've kicked God out." Finally the unity of the Jewish camp on separation began to crack, and more Jews began to question whether a doctrinaire principle was worth interreligious friction and heightened anti-Jewish feeling. For all of these reasons the committee realized it had to bend and to seek accommodation with Christian groups on church-state matters.[34]

On balance then, the *Engel* case showed a polished use of the *amicus curiae* weapon but a miscalculation of the risks involved. The decision raised new problems for the American-Jewish establishment and challenged its traditional reliance on separation as the key

34. Sources for this and the previous paragraph include Public Reaction to the *Engel v. Vitale* Decision, September 11, 1962; Notes on Program re Church-State Separation, November 9, 1962; memorandum of October 9, 1962, Federal Aid to Education" folder; Religion and the Public Schools/Prayers/AJC folder, all AJC Files; *America*, September 1, 1962, pp. 665–66; Bernard Schwartz, *Super Chief: Earl Warren and His Supreme Court* (New York, 1983), pp. 441–42; Philip Jacobson, "Church-State Issues," *American Jewish Year Book* 64 (1963): 107–15; John H. Laubach, *School Prayers* (Washington, D.C., 1969), pp. 1–5; *Dialogue*, October 1962, pp. 6–12; Philip Jacobson, "The School Prayer Controversy: Why Jews Take Sides," *Council Woman*, April 1963; Will Herberg, "Religion and Public Life," *National Review*, July 30, 1963, p. 61.

to Jewish security. It also hinted that perhaps the Jewish-liberal alliance was less than perfect or permanent. The Bible reading cases of 1963 generated less furor, but the tip of the iceberg had been exposed. By the end of the 1960s the committee and other Jewish organizations could no longer ignore Americans' mounting concern about the public schools and the counterculture's impact on traditional religion and morality. During the twenty-odd years from *Engel* until today, the Jewish leadership has received new signals: Jews as well as Catholics have supported aid to parochial schools; the New Left has taken an anti-Israel stand; the Moral Majority has supported Israel.[35] An effective American-Jewish defense network will need to rank its priorities and choose its allies within that setting.

Perhaps more than any other single factor, the insecurity bred of past and ongoing prejudice has shaped the character and activities of American-Jewish institutions. As long as that insecurity persists, American Jews will continue to search for responses to antisemitism that belie neither their desire to integrate fully into American society nor their desire to act out a Jewish identity.

35. Friedman, "New Direction for American Jews," pp. 37–44; Irving Kristol, "The Political Dilemma of American Jews," *Commentary*, July 1984, pp. 23–29.

Judith Laikin Elkin

Antisemitism in Argentina

The Jewish Response

The nature of Argentine antisemitism presents as tortured a question as the nature of the Argentine polity. In order to understand the former, it is necessary to understand the latter. And both must be taken into account before one can assess the response to antisemitism by the Argentine Jewish community.[1]

Contemporary Argentine society is the product of two divergent and conflicting traditions: Spanish Catholicism and Enlightenment thought. These act through entirely distinct institutions that coexist uneasily and have not ceased to struggle for supremacy. As a result, Argentine history has not been an uninterrupted march toward modernity but rather a baffling pattern of shifts between authoritarianism and democracy.

The authoritarian institutions inherited from the Spanish past—the church, the army, and the landed gentry—are older than the state. Each is extremely strong—during certain periods, stronger than the government—and each is structured in such a way as categorically to repel participation by Jews. They function, however, in an intellectual milieu whose origin lies in the Rights of Man and the United States Constitution. This parachronistic juxtaposition of antithetical elements offers toleration both to Jews and to antisemites. A brief description of these institutions and of the society

---

1. There is a small but insightful literature on Argentine antisemitism that includes Juan Jose Sebreli, ed., *La cuestion judía en la Argentina* (Buenos Aires, 1968), particularly the essay by Gino Germani, "Antisemitismo ideológico y antisemitismo tradiciónal," pp. 177–90; Robert Weisbrot, *The Jews of Argentina from the Inquisition to Perón* (Philadelphia, 1979), pp. 209–75; Comité Central Israelita del Uruguay, Circulo de Reflexion Judía, "Antisionismo y antisemitismo hoy en America latina," 1983, no. 2; Pablo Lopez, "El antisemitismo en Argentina," *Areito* 5, no. 18 (1979): 24–27; Egon Friedler, "Is There Anti-Semitism in Argentina?" *Midstream*, February 1983, pp. 56–58.

within which they function will lay bare the structural supports of antisemitism in Argentina and provide context for analysis of the Jewish response.

The church antedates the government, having been exported to the territory by Spain three centuries before there was an Argentina at all. This was the Counter-Reformation church, shielded from reform by a monarchy that never accepted the necessity of reconceptualiz- ing theology inherited from the Middle Ages. During the turbulent half century of civil war that followed Argentine independence in 1810, the church became the sole stabilizing element in a chaotic political and military scene. Afterward, hard-pressed governments relied on the church to reinforce authority over the restless land. The church provided tradition and continuity in periods when govern- ment was ineffectual and violence threatened to strangle the Argen- tine nation.

Today, although Argentines are arguably less religious than they were in the nineteenth century, Catholicism remains at the core of what it means to be Argentine. The church, from its privileged posi- tion in the Constitution, continues to hover as a guardian presence over the sense of Argentine nationality.[2] Unchallenged by counter- vailing forces within society, the church hierarchy remains precon- ciliar in its orientation. This is the church that has, over the past quarter century, become more, not less, closely identified with Ar- gentine nationalism. The very word *nacionalista*, which translates benignly as "nationalist," has nativist and Catholic undertones and excludes Jews by definition.[3]

This church is nurse to the Argentine officer corps. The National War College and the preparatory schools that feed into it are suffused by an ultramontanism that disallows the acceptance of Jews on a basis equal with Catholics. Jewish young men are drafted into the army along with their peers, but entry into the officer corps is guarded by military fraternities that partake of the nature of sodali- ties. The pedigree of each applicant is scrutinized for Old Christian ancestry, and no Jew has been allowed to become a commissioned

2. The Argentine Constitution, while guaranteeing religious freedom to the individ- ual (preamble, art. 19), states that "The Federal Government supports the Roman Catholic Apostolic Faith" (sec. I, chap. 1, art. 2) and reserves the office of the presidency to men who belong to the Roman Catholic Apostolic church (sec. II, chap. 1, art. 76).

3. Rolando Costa Picazo, Argentine translator, interview with author, Buenos Aires, July 5, 1984.

officer since the 1930s.[4] Exclusion from military command would be a serious matter in any country; it is much more so in Argentina, where the army holds itself superior to civilian authority and either rules by itself or determines who shall rule in its place.

Cattlemen were the traditional elite of Argentine society, but their status was badly eroded by the onward course of industrialization as well as by the depredations of the Peróns (1945–55). Based on enormous landed estates that were parceled out long before any Jews had entered the country and cemented by the sort of social snobbism that generally prevails against Jews in such circles, the Jockey Club and the Sociedad Rural provide no entry point for Jews into general society. By extension from these institutions, Jews are also excluded from the diplomatic corps and the magistracy. Although it may be possible to identify individual appointees from time to time, these are exceptions who confirm the rule.[5]

Labor unions are far more recent power contenders and might have offered Jews a point of entry into general society, as they did in the United States. In fact, arriving Jewish immigrants were largely proletarian, and many of them took part in the formation of labor unions as well as in the founding of the Partido Socialista Argentino (Argentine Socialist party).[6] But certain historical forces combined to limit the participation of Jewish workers in the Argentine work force. Chief among these were attacks by pogromist forces in 1909 and again in 1919 that marked the limits of the permeability of Argentine institutions and signaled the definitive marginalization of the Jews. In the 1940s the capture and domestication of the union movement by Juan Perón resulted in the infusion of *nacionalista* values into the working class and corresponding pressure on Jewish workers to assimilate. Meanwhile economic success had propelled the majority of Argentine Jews utterly out of the working class and into the bourgeoisie. Today, though there are Jews in labor unions and among *peronistas*, they act and react as Argentines, not as Jews.

4. Robert A. Potash, author of *The Army and Politics in Argentina, 1928–1945* (Stanford, 1969), interview with author, Buenos Aires, June 23, 1984.
5. Dr. Sion Cohen Imach, president of Delegación de Asociaciónes Israelitas Argentinas (DAIA), address to the organization's territorial convention, October 11, 1983, published in *Convención Territorial de la D.A.I.A., Buenos Aires, 11 al 13 de Octubre de 1983* (n.p., n.d.), pp. 9–11.
6. The Argentine Jewish labor movement has not been adequately studied. A prime source is Pinie Wald, "Di yidishe arbeterbavegung in Argentina," in *Pinkus fun der kehilla*, ed. Asociación Mutual Israelita Argentina (Buenos Aires, 1954–55), pp. 109–43.

These, then, are the institutions that structure Argentine society. Each has shown itself, alone or in combination, to be tougher, and to attract more intense loyalty, than the government (which is often seen as the playground of incompetent civilians) and to be capable of bringing about the latter's downfall. In Argentina, the "fall" of a government does not imply a mere change in administration but the collapse of civil authority and the intervention of the military.

The antisemitism built into society by these institutions forms the context in which antisemitic acts can be carried out with impunity, since they are acceptable to large sectors of the Argentine public. It is often proposed that an émigré Nazi community is responsible for the persistence of antisemitism. But Nazis were also admitted to the United States and Canada, and those societies did not develop the stigmata of organized antisemitism. In those countries religious toleration and respect for cultural differences confine Nazis to the fringes of society; in Argentina, Nazis share common ground with major social institutions.

But alongside the traditional Argentina, another Argentina developed that drew its inspiration from the Enlightenment, welcoming immigration by diverse peoples and celebrating their assimilation to the national norm. This Argentina minimizes the influence of the church, rejects the guardianship of the military, and envisions a nation that is both secular and liberal. During democratic interludes, Argentina imposes few or no bars to civic participation by Jews. Elections, when they have been held, have always brought individuals who are Jewish into the state and national legislatures, demonstrating widespread acceptance of Jews among the Argentine electorate.[7]

During liberal interludes there is freedom of expression for Jews as for non-Jews. The writer Alberto Gerchunoff, the dramatist Samuel Eichelbaum, the Egyptologist Abraham Rosenvasser, and many other acknowledged Jews are honored members of the Argentine pantheon. In democratic periods such as that which followed the elections of October 1983, Jewish names and Jewish themes surge to the surface. The impression at such times is of a society entirely open to Jews.

7. In Argentina, however, it is the president, not the Congress, who governs. There is little doubt, writes Peter Smith, "that ultimate power has, for the most part, resided in the Executive branch." *Argentina and the Failure of Democracy* (Madison, Wis., 1974), p. xviii.

Yet awareness of the Jewishness of the artist is never lost. An effusive encomium to Alberto Gerchunoff published in a major national newspaper in 1984 reads in part:

> Gestated in the adolescence of Gerchunoff, this book [*Los gauchos judíos*] came to birth as the fruit of ancestral sentiments that live on as biological facts in his race, whose blood is curdled by unjust and archaic curses and persecutions. The book also represents the healthy explosion of a spirit charged with nobility from the time he espied, while still in his native Entre Ríos, hopes of winning that spiritual and ethical golden fleece that for his brothers in race signifies peace, productive labor, and liberty, all desired but unobtainable in the millennia that had until then transpired.[8]

It is apparent, from this and thousands of similar effusions, that Argentine philosemitism and antisemitism share a common racist core.

It was on the basis of their alleged peculiar racial heritage that the admission or exclusion of Jews from Argentina was debated in the nineteenth century.[9] The liberals won this debate, and the gates of Argentina swung open for a while. But it has often been pointed out that the price of admission was set at total assimilation. The crucible, not the melting pot, became the metaphor for immigrant absorption; cultural pluralism was abjured as alien. All that is different about the immigrant, all that fails to conform to the national paradigm, must be refined out of the person who wishes to be accepted as Argentine.[10] While nativists reject Jews entirely, liberals welcome those who pass through the crucible and emerge totally Argentine; they accept the Jew, not his Jewishness.

How have Jews reacted to the pressure to assimilate? Argentina had been proposed as a haven for Jews during the repressions in Russia following promulgation of the May Laws in 1882. Word of its vast open spaces and hospitable immigration laws prompted a mass migration of Jews, including but not restricted to those recruited for the agricultural resettlement movement sponsored by Baron Maurice de Hirsch. Within a generation, however, this hospitable climate changed radically, as evidenced by passage of antiforeign legislation,

8. Narciso Marquez, "Alberto Gerchunoff y 'Los gauchos judíos,'" *La Nación*, December 2, 1984, sec. 4, p. 2.

9. For a discussion of Argentine immigration policy as it affected Jews, see Judith Laikin Elkin, *Jews of the Latin American Republics* (Chapel Hill, N.C., 1980), pp. 29–36.

10. A perceptive discussion of this phenomenon is to be found in Leonardo Senkman, "La inmigración judía en America latina, integración e identidad," in *Segundo coloquio latinoamericano sobre pluralismo cultural* (Buenos Aires, 1980), pp. 159–79.

press attacks against "foreign agitators," and violent actions by the Buenos Aires police. Events were crystallized by an assassination. On November 14, 1909, a young Russian-Jewish anarchist, Simon Radowitzky, assassinated Chief of Police Ramon L. Falcon in revenge for the slaying of workers in a May Day parade. There followed assaults by the city's gilded youth against workers' institutions, including the Jewish socialist cultural center, Biblioteca Rusa, as well as against Jewish businesses in the Once District of the city. The press repeated unfounded accusations that schools in the Jewish agricultural colonies were teaching anti-Argentine beliefs and some immigrants, including Jews, were deported as agitators. The Buenos Aires correspondent of the Vilna paper *Haolam* reported that antisemitism was developing at a fast pace.[11]

In this period of reaction against immigration in general and Jewish immigration in particular, the Jews of Buenos Aires had not yet organized a communal structure. Responses to these attacks were therefore free to divide along class lines. The most forthright reaction came from the Jewish proletariat and Zionist movements, which urged Argentine Jews to protest against injustice and defend the community against attacks, some of which were known to have the backing of the government. The Federación Israelita Argentina, representing the established Ashkenazi community of the city, took a different tack. Siding with government repression of workers' strikes, it sent flowers to Falcon's funeral and refrained from taking any action on behalf of Jews who had been imprisoned.[12]

Ten years later, in the aftermath of a week of pogroms and anti-union riots (La Semana Trágica of January 1919), the tone of Jewish responses was weak and apologetic. The Zionist Federation repudiated "hot-headed elements" *within the Jewish community*, who were not to be confused with "the great and pacific Jewish community." Poalei Zion denounced aggressions against Jews but also distanced itself from "internationalism" and "cosmopolitanism." The Congregación Israelita de la República Argentina, speaking for a large number of other Jewish organizations, repudiated the (Jewish)

11. Victor Mirelman, "The Jews in Argentina (1890–1930): Assimilation and Particularism" (Ph.D. diss., Columbia University, 1973), pp. 74–82.

12. Ibid., p. 84. The martyred Falcon's tomb bears a memorial plaque placed by the Federación Israelita Argentina that reads: "Sar gadol nafal hayom" (A great lord fell that day).

malefactors whom society was justified in punishing.[13] As Sandra McGee Deutsch has shown, during this same period middle-class Jewish businessmen and small farmers were joining the strikebreaking brigades of the Liga Patriotica Argentina, which formed in the aftermath of La Semana Trágica to defend "Fatherland and Order." These brigades were directing strikebreaking activities against unions that included numbers of Jews.[14] In the atmosphere of a liberal Argentina that was just beginning to turn back to its Spanish and Catholic roots, the evidence is that Argentine Jews interpreted their interests along class lines, not along a line of maintaining Jewish communal unity.

The trajectory of Jewish history in Argentina has been chronicled elsewhere.[15] Despite episodic concern for the continuity of Jewish life in the country, the economic and social conditions for survival continued to exist. But the years 1959–65 saw an upswing of antisemitism in Argentina that alarmed and astonished the community by its virulence and its open adherence to Nazism. The kidnapping of Adolf Eichmann from the streets of Buenos Aires increased the hysteria of anti-Jewish sloganeering; attacks on synagogues and cemeteries were followed by an assault on a young Jewish woman and the carving of a swastika on her breast. The response of the Delegación de Asociaciónes Israelitas Argentinas (DAIA) to this outrage was to call for a shutdown of all Jewish commerce in the city, an act to which the DAIA urged the "adhesion of all democratic forces." According to Leonardo Senkman's analysis, the strategy of the DAIA at this time was threefold: to denounce *nacionalista* attacks; to alert the Jewish community to the danger they posed; and to solicit the support of democratic public opinion by pointing out that attacks on Jews were in fact assaults on the entire democratic order.[16] (A military coup did take place in 1966.)

13. Quotations and references in Victor Mirelman, "The Semana Trágica of 1919 and the Jews in Argentina," *Jewish Social Studies* 37 (1975): 61–73.

14. Sandra McGee Deutsch, "The Argentine Right and the Jews, 1919–1933," *Journal of Latin American Studies* 18 (1986):113–34.

15. See, for example, Bernard D. Ansel, "The Beginnings of the Modern Jewish Community in Argentina, 1852–1891" (Ph.D. diss., University of Kansas, 1969); Eugene F. Sofer, *From Pale to Pampa: A Social History of the Jews of Buenos Aires* (New York, 1982); Weisbrot, *Jews of Argentina;* Elkin, *Jews of the Latin American Republics;* and Judith Laikin Elkin, "Latin American Jewry Today," *American Jewish Year Book* 85 (1985): 3–49.

16. Leonardo Senkman, "El anti-semitismo y las crisis Argentina, 1959–65," in *Controversia de ideas sionistas*, ed. Eliahu Toker (Buenos Aires, 1983), p. 13.

Notably lacking from this strategy was any approach to the central structures of society: the church, the armed forces, the landowning elite, or the unions. The fact is that the Jewish community had no leverage with these institutions at all. It had to rely, therefore, upon an undifferentiated enlightened opinion, but it could neither predict nor mobilize the extent of that support. In the event, sympathetic non-Jews centered in the universities and some union locals participated in the shutdown, but the Jewish community lacked the capacity to consolidate this support and mobilize it on a continuing basis in defense of Jewish interests.

The *nacionalistas* now resurrected the accusation that the Jewish community was involved in a communist plot to take over Argentina. In December 1962, in the midst of a press campaign against alleged Jewish economic crimes, the government closed eleven institutions affiliated with the Idishe Cultur Farband (ICUF). As these were the only leftist organizations the government acted against, the implication was clear: Jews and communists were the same people. The accusation was repeated over the next two years, culminating in the assassination of Raul Alterman. The assassins left a note for Alterman's parents informing them that their son had been killed as "a dog of a Jew and a communist." In combination with other outrages, the Jewish community began to fear that, in the minds of the uninformed, Jews were becoming inextricably linked with communists. By February 1964 the reaction of the DAIA to continuing outrages had become very attenuated indeed, as evidenced by its announcement that, "Faced by increasing terrorist activity that is destroying public tranquillity and social peace, ... the authorities of the DAIA have constituted themselves in permanent session."[17] There was no longer anyone to whom the DAIA could appeal.

At that point, *Horizonte,* organ of Ajdut Avoda, the socialist Zionist party in Argentina, interviewed a range of Argentine politicians concerning their attitudes toward the existence of antisemitism in the country. Perhaps the most interesting response came from Arturo Juaretche, a *peronista* leader. Juaretche rejected antisemites who opposed the integration of Jews into the Argentine nation. Peronismo, as a Christian and humanistic movement, favored the Jews' total assimilation. Owing to this policy, there had been no attacks on Jews

17. Cited in ibid., p. 35.

during the Perón administration. Agreeing with the reporter that Zionism is a movement for the liberation of the Jewish people, Juaretche went on to state categorically that he believed Zionism to be incompatible with Argentine nationalism. "My opposition to Zionism grows out of my constructive Argentine *nacionalismo*," he said. "I want to make Argentines of the Jews who were born here, while you [the reporter] want to make them Israelis—or both, which to me seems incompatible."[18]

Attacks on Jews and denial of the legitimacy of Argentine-Jewish culture inevitably conditioned Jewish attitudes. It was apparent that political activity on their part would be punished twice over: the Jewish political activitist would be punished both as an activist and as a Jew. It followed that, as one could not be both, a choice had to be made. This was likewise the perception of Argentine liberals. As Juan B. Justo, founder of the Argentine Socialist party and himself married to a Jew, wrote in an article entitled "Why I Do Not Care to Write for a Paper That Calls Itself Jewish":

> It is not that I find it difficult or disagreeable to deal with persons who call themselves Jews, or of whom it is said that they are Jews. Quite the contrary. I accept gladly the task of translating Marx, half of whose blood was Jewish. . . . The grace of the Jewish woman enthralled me as though I had never passed through the rite of baptism. But at the same time, [Jews] leave me puzzled and suspicious. Because they wound my national sentiments.[19]

The lesson continues to reverberate through Argentine-Jewish history. A Socialist party deputy stated on the floor of the Chamber in 1984, "I don't practice Judaism; I merely acknowledge my name." A Radical party deputy stated on the same occasion, "I know that I was born Jewish because they told me afterward, but I feel Argentine and for that reason I have never practiced Judaism."[20]

The exceptionally high rate of intermarriage with Jews in a society that is structured for their rejection is a major point of contact between the Catholic and Enlightenment cultures. While nativists reject Jews entirely, "liberals" (including Jews) accept them as individuals but deny the validity of the culture that formed them. Individuals may be married to Jewish mates *and* totally integrated into Argentine society. Such people tend to deny the existence of anti-

18. *Horizonte,* November 25, 1964, p. 13, cited in ibid., p. 48.
19. Juan B. Justo, "Porque no me gusta escribir para una hoja que se dice judía," *Vida Nuestra,* November 6, 1923, reprinted in Sebreli, *La cuestion judía,* pp. 86–90.
20. Quoted in *Convención Territorial de la D.A.I.A.,* p. 11.

semitism without recognizing that Jews and Judaism are defined out of the institutions that structure their daily lives.

Jews are thus faced by a choice between "either total assimilation to dominant cultural patterns or existence as a cultural enclave at the margin of national society and rejected by it."[21] Those who wish to retain their self-conscious Jewish identity have organized their own tight social structures that mimic those of the greater society. In response to societal rebuff, which is not in the least affected by good interpersonal relations, these Jews retreat into an enclosed space that is distinctively Jewish and to that degree alien to the Argentine culture. Accepting the commandment, "Al tifrosh min hazibur" (Do not separate yourself from the community), these Jews make themselves at home within the *kehillah*, creating an all-embracing Jewish ambience. They reject participation in the larger society as chimerical and undesirable, a letter of credit that is valid only so long as the current government is in power.

It is not novel to observe that Jews take on the coloration of their host societies. Jews organized institutions that were the mirror image of those other, closed institutions that bar their entry into Argentine society. Like the institutions of the larger society, they likewise bar aliens, as defined by the Orthodox rabbinate. For a community that has been throughout its history utterly nonreligious, this exclusionary rule is curious. But the *kehillah*'s total exclusion of the intermarried, combined with its refusal to recognize conversions to Judaism, is functional in that it serves to maintain the structures without which Argentine Jews cannot conceive of their survival. In Argentina, one is either inside or outside the *kehillah*; one cannot have it both ways.

The organized *kehillot* subsist in the interstices of society, in territory not preempted by institutions regulated by Catholic norms. The structures of the Jewish community are recognized by government; their leaders are recognized as spokesmen for the Jewish community. The *kehillot* tend to get along with the government in power, be that democratic or authoritarian. They are viewed as legitimate, but they are not liked and are widely regarded as foreign. Non-Jewish Argentines perceive the *kehillah* as a closed, mysterious entity that confirms the myth of the international Jew up to no good behind closed doors.

21. Senkman, "La inmigración," p. 175.

Intellectuals in the free professions, the arts, and politics, eager for acceptance by the majority society and perhaps not attracted to the smaller universe of the Jewish community, experience the all-embracing Jewish ambience of the *kehillah* as claustrophobic. Jewish blue-collar workers whose identity is forged by their proletarian condition are inclined to see the *kehillah* as the bastion of the middle class. Both tend to conform to societal expectations by moving away from Jewish identification and into a nondifferentiated Argentine identification. During democratic interludes, while Enlightenment principles are in the ascendant, Jews such as they function quite well. The return of Spanish-Catholic morality, however, leaves them unshielded, in the street, vulnerable to reprisal as nonconformists and Jews.

The test of the survival capacities of the Jewish community as presently organized took place during the "process of national reorganization"—the period of military dictatorship, 1976–83. The so-called Proceso bore neo-Nazi hallmarks without having had to abandon a well-established Argentine tradition of authoritarianism, corporativism, and racial exclusivism.

It was a seeming anomaly of the repression that Jewish institutions flourished while Jews out on the street or in the universities were being persecuted. Within these institutions, moreover, relative freedom of speech prevailed, while it was being violently suppressed on the outside. But the anomaly can be resolved through our analysis: the structures of the Jewish community, which are accepted by Argentines as legitimate, were permitted to remain intact; outside them, Jews took their chances along with everybody else.

Investigation of atrocities by a commission appointed by President Raul Alfonsín in 1983 confirmed what was already suspected; about 15 percent of *desaparecidos* (the Disappeared, those who were secretly murdered by the government), were Jews. This seems to have come about not because of a dedicated anti-Jewish policy on the part of the Proceso but because of the disproportionately large number of Jews in the social sectors that were being repressed: university faculty and students, the psychoanalytic profession, social workers, potential political activists.[22]

22. Rabbi Marshall Meyer and Dean Gregorio Klimovsky, the two Jewish members of the Comisión para los desaparecidos (Commission for the Disappeared), interviews with author, Buenos Aires, May 17 and June 1, 1984. It is important to keep in mind that, among those killed, there were many persons who were not guilty of anything,

Jewish families that were untouched by the repression believe that membership in Jewish institutions protected them from government savagery. The junta's reasoning appears to have been that Jews who were praying or learning Israeli dances were not simultaneously involved in guerrilla activities. The single exception to this rule—the extermination of a Hashomer Hazair *garin* in Córdoba—seems to prove the case. This group had either joined the leftist guerrillas (ERP) or been infiltrated by them; in either interpretation, it was attempting to apply ideology learned in a Zionist context to the social realities of Argentina. Some two dozen youths were killed by the Proceso or forced into exile. Although the details—as in so many other undocumentable atrocities—are shadowy, the case appears to substantiate the argument made here. Argentine Jews were permitted to continue almost unhindered with their communal life, but action on the larger Argentine scene was punishable by the same sanctions imposed on everybody else.

Hashomer Hazair closed down for the duration, and this incident was not repeated. Community leaders became more circumspect. Jewish parents flocked to enroll their children in mainstream Jewish institutions: synagogues, libraries, and sports clubs. The expectation was that Jewish prayer, Jewish soccer, *the Jewish community,* would identify them in the eyes of the security forces as not the type to associate with radicals.

Within the limits demarcated by the government, Jewish institutions took their responsibility seriously. The DAIA made periodic appeals to the generals to silence particular antisemitic publications and broadcasts—and met with some success.[23] It then found itself being asked to reciprocate the "favor" when Minister of the Interior Gen. Albano E. Harguindeguy politely requested the organization to persuade Jewish newspapers not to criticize the regime.[24] The DAIA

---

even by the broadest of the government's definitions of subversion; they simply happened to be in the wrong place at the wrong time. Since the *desaparecidos* were never brought to trial, it is impossible to establish the "guilt" or "innocence" of any of them.

23. *Nueva Presencia*, March 13, 1981.

24. "Just as your institution comes with its qualms or requests in the case of any antisemitic activity in the Argentine Republic, I assume that, to be consistent, you ought to make your voices heard as Argentines of Jewish descent when any action or false and distorting information [concerning Argentina] has its origin in or is published in the State of Israel." Albano E. Harguindeguy, Minister of the Interior, to Nehemias Resnizky, President of the DAIA, June 5, 1978, protesting the publication in Tel Aviv of an article headlined "The Tragedy of Jews in Argentina and the Soviet Union" that had originally been published in *Le Monde*, March 4, 1978. Harguindeguy's letter

complied—by threatening to cut off the supply of newsprint to a Jewish newspaper that was publishing articles on human rights violations.[25] The DAIA's claim that it submitted lists of names of *desaparecidos* to the Ministry of the Interior can be established by reliable witnesses, as well as by documents that the DAIA itself published in 1984.[26] Apparently no positive reply on the whereabouts of any of *desaparecidos* was ever received.

The private shame of many Argentine intellectuals is that, during the height of the repression, they burned books that might have incriminated them with the police. Jewish libraries did not escape the same humiliation. Government repression and *kehillah* response had the effect of further alienating Jewish radicals and pushing the *kehillah* farther to the political Right. By 1982 the *kehillah* had abjured Jewish leftists, radicals, and anyone who was not involved in Jewish life. From there it was but a small step to abjure all those who had been arrested, attributing to them a hypothetical guilt that was never proven, or even charged, in court. According to the testimony of numerous relatives of *desaparecidos* the DAIA was at first sympathetic to their plight. But as the war of extermination ground on, bereaved relatives became the object of hostility. Early efforts to help were replaced by attempts to shift the blame onto the parents: if they had raised their children properly (read: in the bosom of the Jewish community), they would not have gotten themselves into such a mess. Nor was this attitude unknown to the unaffiliated, many of whom did not apply to DAIA for help or who went there only when all other resources had been exhausted.[27]

The effect of the Proceso on the Jewish community was to split it, probably irrevocably. The majority found its conservativism reinforced by the terrible penalties exacted from Jewish radicals. For many self-aware Jews, the experience of repression fortified the conviction that children must be insulated from Argentine society if they are to survive and that survival can only be assured through

is reprinted in *Informe especial sobre detenidos y desaparecidos judíos, 1976–1983* (Buenos Aires, 1984).

25. Herman Schiller, editor of *Nueva Presencia*, interview with author, Buenos Aires, June 29, 1984.

26. *Informe especial sobre detenidos y desaparecidos judíos.*

27. In summer 1984 I interviewed some fifty surviving members of families of *desaparecidos*. Some findings are reported in my "The Good Germans of Buenos Aires," *Jewish Frontier* 52, no. 2 (February 1985): 7–11; and "The Jewish Community of Buenos Aires: Dilemmas of Democratization" (Paper presented at the Ninth World Congress of Jewish Studies, Jerusalem, August 8, 1985).

the maintenance of a closed *kehillah*. The Enlightenment's promise of free access to public life appears to them to be chimerical. With the opening up of society that democracy entails, they fear that their children will get sucked into the political currents around the universities and fall victim in the next round of repression. For this sector of opinion, the response to democracy has been to turn away from false promises and toward religion. Synagogues and schools, both Orthodox and Conservative, are experiencing unexpected growth. Adult education efforts have intensified. There is an almost palpable resurgence of the desire for a positive Jewish identity. With assimilation or resegregation the only options offered by Argentine society, these Jews are headed in the direction of intensifying their isolation. Heightened Jewish awareness is inseparable from the conviction that Argentines will never accept Jews as equal citizens. It is the end of the liberal dream.

Meanwhile, beyond the perimeters of the *kehillah*, a substantial cohort of individuals who happen to be Jewish are taking active part in Argentine politics and the arts. They are making their contribution in the enlightened spirit that pervades this democratic period, and they experience success and acceptance in their respective endeavors. Few are affiliated with the *kehillah*. They are characterized by indifference to Jewish custom or law and lack of interest in a specifically Jewish future. They are doing very well in the Argentina of the mid-1980s, which, to all intents and purposes, is completely open to them.

While unaffiliated Jews make their own way as Argentines, the organized Jewish community follows a set agenda in relation to the larger society. *Kehillah* leaders accept as given the discriminatory structure of Argentine society and do not challenge it. Naturally they make no claim on entry into the church. Until 1984, however, they made no concerted effort to enter into dialogue with the church hierarchy. As far as can be determined, the *kehillah* had no liaison with this all-important institution during the repression, a time when church officials were among the few who had any credence with the military. Nor has the *kehillah* publicly challenged the exclusivity of the armed forces. The appointment of four Jewish army chaplains during the Falklands/Malvinas War was hailed as a victory by the Jewish community, though this privilege was gained not by any action of its own but in reciprocity for Israel's sale of weapons to the regime.

Admission to the cattlemen's clubs is not worth discussing; the clubs are for the social elite only and in any event have been almost eclipsed in importance. Likewise Jewish leadership of labor unions is unrealistic at a time when most Jews have moved into the middle class. Thus the main institutions of Argentine society are likely to remain *judenrein*. The administration of Raul Alfonsín has appointed numerous Jews to positions in government and the universities. But as in the case of the legislature, these gains can be retained only in the absence of military intervention.

In order for Jews to challenge these powerful excluding institutions, two preconditions would be necessary: there would have to be some overarching ideal to which they could appeal; and Jews would have to find allies in other sectors of society. As we have seen, there is no ideal of cultural pluralism in Argentina; to the contrary, Catholicism remains at the heart of Argentine nationalism.

Being few in number and without a political base, Jews cannot challenge fundamental institutions on their own. Racial exclusivism severely limits their options on the right; there are equally profound obstacles to their left. As we have seen, the best of Argentine liberalism extends total acceptance to Jews, but at the cost of assimilation. This is a price the organized community will not pay.

Furthermore, liberalism in Argentina, as in the United States, implies belief in the rights of free speech and free press. But antisemitism is at its worst in Argentina when the right of free speech exists. It is then that printed incitements to antisemitic violence pour out of the street-corner kiosks and magazine racks. Dictators, on the other hand, control antisemitic expressions because they control everything. It is possible to make a deal with dictators, while a free press is not controllable by either law or social disapproval.

The dilemma of Jews in Argentina is that they lack natural allies. They do not regularly align with any other interest group, nor is their support sought by others. The DAIA is not involved in lobbying for fair-housing practices, minimum wage legislation, civil rights of Indians, or other causes that elsewhere unite broad coalitions of interest groups. The organization, according to its official spokesperson, concentrates its efforts on two goals: combatting antisemitism and supporting Israel.[28]

28. N. Barbaras, public relations officer for the DAIA, interview with author, Buenos Aires, May 10, 1984.

The community's intense engagement with Zionism adds to its foreign appearance and contributes to its political isolation. Argentine Jews are more susceptible than most to the accusation of double loyalty, since they became ardent Zionists before they had succeeded in rooting themselves in Argentine soil. Of course the accusation of dual loyalty was always an antisemitic canard and not reason to abandon one's loyalty to the Jewish people. But a Jewish community whose two main goals are to combat hatred of itself and to support a foreign country presents an alien picture to many Argentines who do not know or care what a Jew is, but know what they want Argentina to be.

Norman A. Stillman

The Response of the Jews of the Arab World to Antisemitism in the Modern Era

Antisemitism is but one of many ideological and intellectual currents that have been imported into the Arab world from Europe in modern times, along with Western goods, technology, and fashions. As with many of the European cultural imports, its adoption over the past century or two has been irregular, even haphazard, and it has not infrequently been syncretized with genuine, native intellectual traditions.

The appearance and indeed apparent flowering of antisemitism in the modern Arab world is a rather remarkable historical development. As is well known, Judeophobia is simply not a *leitmotif* of Islamic social and cultural history as it is in the annals of Christian Europe. Islam did not begin as a sect within Judaism, as did Christianity. It did not depend upon Jewish Scriptures for its fundamental legitimacy; nor did it ever claim to be *versus Israël*. This is not to say that the premodern Arab world did not possess its own indigenous store of negative attitudes toward the Jews or that there was not periodic anti-Jewish agitation and in some cases persecution. These were on the whole mitigated, however, by a variety of legal, social, and historical factors specific to Islamic society that have been treated in depth elsewhere and require no discussion here.[1]

Much of the archival research upon which this essay is based was carried out under grants from the Anti-Defamation League of B'nai B'rith, the Bronfman Foundation, the International Sephardic Education Foundation, and the Research Foundation of the State University of New York at Binghamton. It is also my pleasant duty to acknowledge the kind assistance afforded me by the staffs of the Archives et Bibliothèque de l'Alliance Israélite Universelle, Paris; the Ben-Zvi Institute Library, Jerusalem; and the Central Zionist Archives, Jerusalem.

1. The best general treatments of the Jew in Islamic society are S. D. Goitein, *Jews and Arabs: Their Contacts through the Ages*, 3d ed. (New York, 1974); Norman A. Still-

The earliest principal agents of European-style Jew-hatred were French ecclesiastical and secular antisemites in the eighteenth, nineteenth, and early twentieth centuries. They found an audience mainly among their Levantine Christian protégés. These native Christians not only shared the traditional Arab social contempt for the Jews but also viewed them as economic rivals, especially as both groups began to enjoy the benefits of increased civil emancipation during the course of the nineteenth century. New vectors of antisemitism made their appearance in the present century. During the 1930s and 1940s, it was the Germans and to a lesser extent their Italian allies who propagated the ideology of Jew-hatred among Arab nationalists already chafing under colonial domination and becoming progressively hardened over the Palestine Question.[2]

The responses of Middle Eastern and North African Jewry to antisemitism have varied over time from country to country. The nature of Jewish existence in traditional Islamic Arab society at first limited the options that were open to Jews for responding to antisemitism. As a tolerated non-Muslim minority, the Jews were *ahl al-dhimma* or *dhimmīs* (People of the Pact)—protected subjects of the Islamic state. They could appeal to the often corrupt authorities for justice in cases of abuse, persecution, or false accusations, but they could do little more. In general, they seem to have accepted their lot in good times and bad with a high degree of resignation and quietism.[3] They considered their overall condition to be part of the burden of a people in exile. As a Yemenite Jew early in this century observed when asked by a representative of the Alliance Israélite Universelle how he and his co-religionists bore their onerous existence in Yemen, "We are in *jaluth* [Yemenite pronunciation of Hebrew *galut*, or exile]; we are made for suffering."[4]

man, *The Jews of Arab Lands: A History and Source Book* (Philadelphia, 1979); and Bernard Lewis, *The Jews of Islam* (Princeton, 1984).

2. For the role of the French as early propagators of antisemitism in the Middle East, see Norman A. Stillman, "Middle Eastern Jewry and the Beginnings of European Penetration," in *World History of the Jewish People*, ed. Michel Abitbol (Jerusalem), forthcoming; and Stillman, "Antisemitism in the Contemporary Arab World," in *Antisemitism in the Contemporary World*, ed. Michael Curtis (Boulder, Colo., 1986), pp. 70–86. For German and Italian antisemitic propaganda, see Lukasz Hirszowicz, *The Third Reich and the Arab East* (London, 1966); and Michel Abitbol, *Les Juifs d'Afrique du Nord sous Vichy* (Paris, 1983), pp. 34–38.

3. For the status of the Jews both in Islamic law and in actual practice, see Stillman, *Jews of Arab Lands*, pp. 24–39, 157–62, and passim; Goitein, *Jews and Arabs*, pp. 62–88; and Lewis, *Jews of Islam*, pp. 3–66.

4. Quoted in Y.-D. Sémach, *Une mission d'Alliance au Yémen* (Paris, 1910), p. 13. See also a similar remark made by a Jew in Tripoli, Libya, to an Alliance Israélite Univer-

During the nineteenth century the great mercantile and colonial powers of Europe began a process of economic penetration, political influence, and ultimately political domination in the Middle East and North Africa. Out of a combination of sincere moral sentiments and imperialistic designs, the European nations openly espoused the cause of the non-Muslims in the Islamic world. From the European point of view, religious tolerance in the Muslim countries was one of the necessary first steps toward progress in the region.[5]

Ironically, it was just as the European powers were exerting pressure upon the Ottoman sultan and the petty rulers of North Africa to ameliorate the civil status of the non-Muslims in their territories that Western-style antisemitism began to make itself felt in the Arab world. Because of the rise of European influence in the region, however, Oriental Jewry found a new avenue of response in cases of anti-Jewish agitation; it turned to the foreign powers.

The first significant instance in which antisemitic calumnies stirred Middle Eastern Jews to seek foreign intervention was the infamous Damascus Affair of 1840. This affair was touched off by the disappearance of an Italian Capuchin friar and his native assistant on February 5 of that year. The native Christians, egged on by the French consul in Damascus, Ratti-Menton, himself a rabid antisemite, accused the local Jews of having murdered the two men in order to obtain their blood for the coming Passover. A Jewish barber was taken into custody and tortured into a confession in which he implicated seven leading members of the community, who were also arrested and put to torture. Two of the detainees died, one saved himself by embracing Islam, while the others also "confessed." Jewish children were held hostage by the pasha of the city in order to force the community to reveal the whereabouts of the martyrs' blood.[6]

One Damascene Jew who had obtained Austrian citizenship sought the protection of his consul. The reaction of most Syrian Jews to these events was to turn to their brethren in the Ottoman capital

selle representative, quoted in Renzo De Felice, *Jews in an Arab Land: Libya, 1835–1970*, trans. Judith Roumani (Austin, Tex., 1985), p. 10.

5. For a succinct analysis of European thinking on this subject, see Norman Daniel, *Islam Europe and Empire* (Edinburgh, 1966), pp. 338–47.

6. See Stillman, *Jews of Arab Lands*, pp. 105–6, 393–402; A. J. Brawer, "Damascus Affair," *Encyclopaedia Judaica* (Jerusalem, 1971), vol. 5, cols. 1249–52; and Albert M. Hyamson, "The Damascus Affair, 1840," *Transactions of the Jewish Historical Society of England* 16 (1952): 47–71, where an extensive bibliography is provided.

to get the court Jews there to intercede on their behalf.[7] This was the primary, traditional response of a Middle Eastern Jewish community to persecution. The leaders of the Istanbul Jewish community did not turn to the Sublime Porte, which in any case had only nominal control over Syria at that time, but rather to the British ambassador in Constantinople, to the English-Jewish philanthropist Sir Moses Montefiore, and to various members of the Rothschild family.

England's and France's other rivals in the competition for influence in the Middle East did, in fact, intervene on behalf of the Jews of Damascus. A delegation of British and French Jews headed by Sir Moses Montefiore and Adolphe Crémieux was sent to Mehemet Ali (who actually controlled Syria at that time) in Egypt and to Abdül-mecid in Constantinople to take the part of the accused. They succeeded in getting the Jewish prisoners released and obtained from the sultan a firman denouncing the blood libel.[8]

The success of the mission encouraged Levantine Jewry to turn more and more to the foreign powers and to their brethren abroad in future instances of antisemitic agitation. In the decades following the Damascus Affair, Middle Eastern Jews turned directly to the local British consuls who were viewed as defenders of Jewish interests. When the Greek Orthodox in Jerusalem, for example, accused the local Jews of attempting to murder a Christian boy for ritual purposes, it was to the British consul, James Finn, that the Jews turned for help.[9]

Jews turned to the consuls not only for aid in incidents sparked by the newly imported antisemitism (which usually involved Middle Eastern Christians), but also in cases of more traditional Middle Eastern and Islamic Jew-baiting, as for example, when Jews were accused of having blasphemed against Islam or been disrespectful toward its prophet.[10] In one such instance in Aleppo in 1889, the Jewish community was able to secure the release of a peddler ac-

7. For an example of one such letter, see Stillman, Jews of Arab Lands, pp. 393–95.

8. The text of the sultan's firman is given in translation in Stillman, Jews of Arab Lands, pp. 401–2.

9. James Finn, Stirring Times; or, Records from Jerusalem Consular Chronicles of 1853 to 1856, vol. 1 (London, 1878), pp. 107–10.

10. For a non-Muslim to insult Islam was considered a major breach of the pact of protection and a capital offense. See A. M. Turki, "Situation du 'Tributaire' qui insulte l'Islam, au regard de la doctrine et de la jurisprudence musulmanes," Studia Islamica 30 (1969): 39–72. Since the word of a dhimmī would not be accepted over that of a Muslim in an Islamic court, this accusation was invariably disastrous for the accused. Jews everywhere in the Muslim world were in danger of such accusations whenever they had a falling out with a Muslim or tried to collect a bad debt.

cused of insulting the Islamic faith through the good offices of the French consul in that city.[11] In a case thirty-six years earlier in Mosul, the British consul and later his superiors in Constantinople took the part of a rabbi accused of disrespect to the Prophet Muhammad.[12] Although turning to the foreign consuls for help was frequently efficacious in such situations, it was not invariably so. In the famous case of Batto Sfez, a Tunisian Jew accused of blasphemy in 1857, the intervention of the European consular corps in Tunis proved of no avail, and the hapless Jew was executed.[13]

The founding of the Alliance Israélite Universelle (AIU) in Paris in 1860 opened another avenue of redress for Middle Eastern and North African Jewry in cases of injustice and antisemitic agitation. The Alliance was the first modern, international Jewish organization of its kind, dedicated to Jewish emancipation and progress throughout the world, the alleviation of Jewish suffering, and the combatting of antisemitism. From its earliest days many of the Alliance's efforts and activities were on behalf of the Jews in the Muslim world. In addition to setting up a network of modern, Western-style Jewish elementary and secondary schools that by the end of the nineteenth century stretched across the Islamic world, the Alliance engaged in diplomatic activities on behalf of its oppressed brethren.[14]

The Jews of the Islamic world quickly came to see the Alliance's Central Committee in Paris as the primary address for their complaints and petitions for assistance. Letters detailing injustices or abuses either against individual Jews or against Jews as a group began to flow into AIU headquarters from all over the Middle East and North Africa.[15] In more than a few instances the "pogroms" de-

11. Letter from Nissim Raffoul, September 26, 1889, Alliance Israélite Universelle Archives, Paris (hereafter AIU Archives), Syrie I.C.3.

12. See Stillman, *Jews of Arab Lands*, pp. 385–87. Numerous charges of blasphemy were leveled against Jews in Iraq during the nineteenth century. See Abraham Ben-Jacob, *Yehudei Bavel: Mi-sof tkufat ha-geonim ad yamenu*, 2d rev. ed. (Jerusalem, 1979), p. 143, esp. n. 9. As late as 1909 such accusations were still a frequent problem in Basra. See the correspondence from the Jewish community of Basra to Haham Bashi Hayyim Nahum, Constantinople, June 2–October 22, 1909, AIU Archives, Irak, I.C.5.

13. See Stillman, *Jews of Arab Lands*, p. 104, and the sources cited there in n. 23.

14. For general historical surveys of the AIU's activities, see André N. Chouraqui, *Cent ans d'histoire: L'Alliance Israélite Universelle et la renaissance juive contemporaine (1860–1960)* (Paris, 1965); and Narcisse Leven, *Cinquante ans d'histoire: L'Alliance Israélite Universelle (1860–1910)* (Paris, 1911–20). For an in-depth survey of the AIU's activities in one country of the Muslim world, see Michael M. Laskier, *The Alliance Israélite Universelle and the Jewish Communities of Morocco: 1862–1962* (Albany, 1983).

15. For some examples of such pleas, see the letters of October 28, 1864, and February 14, 1869, AIU Archives, Tunisie, I.C.3, translated in Stillman, *Jews of Arab Lands*, pp. 410–12. Many still unpublished petitions can be found in the AIU Archives. See,

scribed in the letters by members of the local Jewish communities or by Alliance teachers in the field were not strictly of an antisemitic character but part of the general lawlessness of the period in which weak groups—and in particular non-Muslims—were especially vulnerable targets.[16] Some of the requests for assistance were, however, definitely in instances of antisemitic agitation, as in the case of a blood libel that occurred in Damanhur, Egypt, in 1879.[17]

Even Jews in some of the most isolated regions of the Muslim world, such as Yemen, which was almost entirely cut off from direct contact with Europeans, turned to the Alliance for help. A letter from the leaders of the Jewish community of Sana, dated 1874, described a variety of persecutions and injustices to which they and their co-religionists were subjected and sought the assistance of the Alliance.[18]

The frequent intervention of the European consuls and their governments on behalf of non-Muslims in the Islamic world, the growth of the Alliance Israélite Universelle, and the development of its widespread educational network, which produced cadres of Westernized Middle Eastern Jews who possessed a distinct advantage of opportunity over the largely illiterate Muslim masses as the region was being drawn ineluctably into the modern world economic system, all fostered in Oriental Jewry a new sense of confidence. This confidence may be seen in the Jews' new unwillingness to accept in silence their traditional second-class status, much less persecution or new, imported forms of antisemitism. Indeed, some Jews came to overestimate the power of their brethren abroad and had to be warned by the Alliance leadership to "refrain from boasting about the help from [foreign] governments and of deliverance from afar."[19]

In addition to increased self-confidence, the urban Jewish elite in

---

for example, the files Algérie, II.C.10; Irak, I.C.1, 2, 3, 5, 7; Liban, I.C.1, 3; Lybie, I.C.1, 14, 16, 20; Maroc, II.C.9, III.C.10, IV.C.11; and Syrie, I.B.1–8.

16. For a critical discussion of this point, see Stillman, *Jews of Arab Lands*, pp. 101–2, and the sources cited there, p. 102 n. 14.

17. Letter of September 15, 1879, AIU Archives, Egypte, I.C.1, translated in Stillman, *Jews of Arab Lands*, pp. 426–27.

18. Hebrew letter dated 12 Kislev 5634, AIU Archives, Pays Isolés—Yémen. The Yemenites also appealed to the Alliance for monetary assistance in times of famine. See ibid. and the file Pays Isolés—Aden.

19. Adolphe Crémieux and Isadore Loeb to the Jews of Morocco, November 21, 1873 [1 Kislev 5634], published by David Ovadia, *Qehillat Ṣefrū*, vol. 1 (Jerusalem, 1974), p. 281, abridged translation in Laskier, *Alliance Israélite Universelle and the Jewish Communities of Morocco*, p. 47. See also the words of warning by the director of the AIU school in Tetuán, in ibid., p. 46.

the Middle East and North Africa began to exhibit a heightened sense of international Jewish solidarity as the twentieth century was dawning. Hebrew newspapers such as *Hamelitz, Hayehudi,* and *Hatzefirah,* as well as European-language journals, were available in the major towns of the region with reports on the new Zionist movement and other Jewish news, including reports on the pogroms in Russia.[20] For the first time in the modern period, we can see Levantine Jews responding to antisemitism directed not against them but against their co-religionists abroad. In Cairo in 1905, for example, the teachers and students in four Jewish schools took up collections for victims of the pogroms.[21] Similar collections were taken up in other cities of the Middle East at the initiative of Alliance teachers and alumni.

Local Jewish newspapers had begun to appear in the Islamic world during the last decades of the nineteenth century. Even in the earliest such papers one can find occasional exposés of contemporary antisemitism, as for example in the first North African Judeo-Arabic journal *Adzīrī* (*L'Israélite Algérien*), published in Algiers in 1870.[22] With the rise and growth of Jewish self-confidence, these journals became organs of response to antisemitism, particularly the antisemitism of the general Arab press in which a leading role was played by Levantine Christians, who, as has already been noted, were the first native group to be receptive to European antisemitic notions. One of the pioneer Jewish papers in Egypt was the Judeo-Arabic journal *Misraim,* founded in 1904 by Isaac Karmona specifically in response to what the Jewish community of Cairo perceived to be "an antisemitic campaign which from day to day takes on very disturbing proportions." "For it is only with weapons of this sort," Karmona wrote, "that we can combat our adversaries and safeguard the interests of Judaism in this country."[23] Similar reasoning lay in

20. A letter of March 17, 1903, from the newly formed Ahavat Zion Society in Safi, Morocco, to Theodor Herzl, mentions that the founders had first learned of the Zionist movement through the Hebrew press. See Central Zionist Archives, Jerusalem (hereafter CZA), Z1/343. Religious as well as secular leaders read the Hebrew press. The chief rabbis of both Alexandria and Cairo at the turn of the century are two well-known examples. See Zvi Zohar, *Halakhah u-modernizazyah: Darkhei heanut hakhemei Mizrayim le-etgarei ha-modernizazyah, 1822–1882* (Jerusalem, 1982), pp. 178, 183.

21. AIU Archives, Egypte, I.D.3.

22. See Robert Attal, "Ha-iton ha-yehudi ha-rishon ba-Magreb: *L'Israélite Algérien,* 1870," *Peamim,* no. 17 (1983): 92–93.

23. Isaac Karmona to Narcisse Leven, AIU President, November 27, 1904, AIU Archives, Egypte, I.C.19, abridged French text published in Jacob M. Landau, *Jews in Nineteenth Century Egypt* (New York, 1969), p. 315, also in Maurice Mizrahi, *L'Egypte et*

part behind the establishment of the Iraqi-Jewish magazine *al-Miṣbāḥ* in Baghdad in 1927. According to its founder and editor Salman Shina, one of the paper's aims was to defend Jewish "sacred rights" against "local Arab papers [that] were ransoming the Community whenever the opportunity presented itself."[24]

The Jewish community in early twentieth-century Egypt was perhaps the most outspoken in responding to antisemitic currents in the Arab press. A stream of antisemitic articles that appeared in the journal *al-Nīl*, for example, prompted a Jewish boycott of the paper that apparently caused the editor to change his line and offer apologies.[25] Some Egyptian Jews, such as Robert Gazi (Ghazi), a Cairo businessman, also took to writing articles and letters to the editor in the general press, defending Jewish positions or answering antisemitic propaganda and the increasing attacks on Zionism.[26]

Not all communities had the courage to stand up to the antisemitic propaganda of the Arab press either through their own publications or through replies in the non-Jewish papers. Syrian Jewry, which had no organ of its own,[27] showed itself to be generally timorous in response to the highly charged and often violent political atmosphere of modern Syria even under the French Mandate. The primary response of Syria's Jewish community to the virulent wave of anti-Jewish and anti-Zionist agitation in the Christian and Arab nationalist press in 1929 was to assert its total loyalty to the Arab cause with anti-Zionist demonstrations and public statements. In a public declaration disassociating itself from Zionism, the Jewish Youth Association in Damascus pointed out on August 27, 1929, that "certain newspapers do not distinguish between Arab Jews and Zionists." The statement went on to request that such a differentiation be made and concluded with the plea, "We, therefore, beg the population and the press to consider the Jews of Damascus to be Arabs

---

ses Juifs: Le temps revolu (XIXᵉ et XXᵉ siècles) (Geneva, 1977), p. 98, where the passage is attributed to the first issue of the paper.

24. Salman Shina to the Zionist Executive, July 30, 1924, CZA, Z4/2470. This defensive purpose is, however, not mentioned by Shina in his introductory editorial statement of the journal's goals in the maiden issue. See "Kalimatunā al-Ūlā: Khiṭṭatunā," *al-Miṣbāḥ*, April 1, 1924, no. 1, pp. 1ff.

25. Report from Samuel Hassamsony, Cairo, to the Zionist Organization in Berlin, December 12, 1912, CZA, Z3/752.

26. There are numerous letters between Robert Gazi (Ghazi) and the World Zionist Organization, 1912–13, in ibid. See *inter alia*, Gazi's articles in *al-Muqattam*, July 18 and 31, 1912, the first under the pseudonym "M. Mizraim."

27. The only Jewish paper that was put out in Greater Syria was the Lebanese bimonthly *al-ʿĀlam al-Isrāʾīlī*, published in Beirut from 1921 to 1946.

who share entirely all the feelings of their fellow citizens both in good times and in adversity."[28] However, even extreme protestations of loyalty to the Arab cause such as this and others made by delegations of Jewish leaders before Muslim notables failed to stem the anti-Jewish campaign either in the Syrian press or in daily life.[29]

European antisemitism began to have a perceptively wider impact in the Arab world during the 1920s and 1930s. The single most important catalyst for precipitating the new antisemitism within the majority Muslim community, which heretofore had not been much affected by it, was undoubtedly the increasingly sensitive issue of Palestine. The fierce anti-Jewish agitation in Syria in 1929, which had such a demoralizing effect upon the Jewish community of Damascus, had been set off as a direct result of events in Palestine.[30]

As early as the 1920s, Palestinian nationalists began citing the infamous *Protocols of the Elders of Zion* in their propaganda.[31] Anti-Jewish and anti-Zionist agitators in other Arab countries, like Ṣādiq Pasha al-Qadrī, who appeared in Iraq in 1924, also took up the libels of the *Protocols* and were given considerable assistance in the Iraqi-Arab press. Jewish requests for government intervention went unheeded, and when some Baghdadi Jews wrote counterarticles in their own newspapers, the editor was warned by officials that if he continued to print them the paper would be shut down. Communal leaders were sufficiently alarmed to request secretly that the Zionist Executive in London intervene with the British Colonial Office.[32]

Relatively few Jews in the Arab world responded to antisemitism during the 1920s through the open espousal of Zionism, although the Jewish national movement did enjoy considerable popular sympathy and Jewish supporters had been active in the Maghreb and Egypt

28. Quoted by A. Silberstein, director of the AIU school in Damascus, in a letter to Paris headquarters, August 31, 1929, AIU Archives, Syrie, I.G.2.

29. Letter from Silberstein, December 7, 1929, ibid. Silberstein's many detailed letters reporting on the situation in Syria at the time indicate the need for revision of Hayyim Cohen's view that it was only in 1935 that the Jews of Syria began to experience problems of this sort. See Hayyim J. Cohen, *The Jews of the Middle East, 1860–1972* (New York, 1973), p. 45.

30. Letters from Silberstein, September 9, November 7, and December 4, 1929, AIU Archives, Syrie, I.G.2.

31. See Elyakim Rubinstein, "Ha-protokolim shel ziknei zion ba-sikhsukh ha-aravi-yehudi be-Eretz Israel bi-shnot ha-esrim," *Ha-mizrah he-hadash* 26, nos. 1–2 (1976): 38. On the *Protocols of the Elders of Zion* in modern Arab polemics, see Stillman, "Antisemitism in the Contemporary Arab World," pp. 75–76.

32. Confidential letter from the Secretary of the Zionist Organization in Baghdad to the Zionist Executive, London, October 30, 1924, CZA, Z4/2470. The writer mentions that the community believed Ṣādiq Pasha also to be a British agent.

from the time of the first Basel Congress in 1897 and in the years immediately following.[33] Early Zionist associations began to appear in Iraq just prior to World War I, in Libya during the war itself, and in Syria shortly thereafter.[34] However, much of the sympathy in the Oriental Jewish communities was of a traditional religious and philanthropic character and, on the whole, not as an ideological response to antisemitism *per se* or as a solution to the existential problem of the Jewish people.[35] The rising tide of Arab-Jewish violence in Palestine during the 1920s and the concomitant inflammation of passions among the Muslim masses throughout the Arab world acted as a serious damper to the open espousal of Zionism by Jewish communal leaders. The Zionist option was to be widely adopted as a response to antisemitism by Arabic-speaking Jewry only with the Second World War and the tide of events that engulfed world Jewry in its aftermath.

The recrudescence of antisemitism on the European Right and especially the rise of National Socialism in Germany during the 1930s also had a significant effect upon the Jews of the Middle East and North Africa. The manner and degree to which they were affected, however, and the nature of their response differed from country to country. The Jews of Syria, for example, who were already in a state of semipanic on account of the threats of their nationalist Arab neighbors, were too cowed to show much in the way of an outward response beyond modest collections for the benefit of the Jews in Germany and Eastern Europe.[36] Even in Lebanon, where the overall situation of the Jewish community was considerably better than in

33. See Michel Abitbol, "Zionist Activity in the Maghreb," *Jerusalem Quarterly* 21 (Fall 1981): 61–84; and Zvi Yehuda, "Reshitah shel ha-peilut ha-ziyonit be-Mizrayim— agudat 'Bar Kokhva' (1897–1904)," *Sefunot*, n.s., 1 (1980): 311–52.

34. For some of the earliest correspondence between Iraqi Jews and the Zionist Organization in Berlin, see the file Türkei, 1911–13, CZA, Z3/981. Concerning the emergence of the Circolo Sion in Tripoli, see De Felice, *Jews in an Arab Land*, pp. 95, 326 n. 42. At the end of the First World War, modern, national-oriented Hebrew schools run by teachers from Palestine were opened in Damascus, Beirut, and Saida. See CZA, S2/ 628, S2/657, S2/691, S2/692, and S2/777. The only general sketch of Zionism in Syria is Avidan Mashiah, "Zionism in Syria and Lebanon," in *Encyclopedia of Zionism and Israel*, ed. Raphael Patai (New York, 1971), pp. 1086–88.

35. For the various perceptions of the Zionist movement and their evolution in one Oriental Jewish community, see Zvi Yehuda, "Ha-irgun ha-ziyoni be-Morocco bashanim, 1900–1948" (Ph.D. diss., Hebrew University, Jerusalem, 1981), pp. 38–49.

36. For example, the Union de la Jeunesse Juive in Aleppo collected 1,020 francs for their co-religionists in Europe on May 22, 1933; see AIU Archives, Syrie, I.B.2. Compare this with 12,245 and 16,551 francs collected by the much more comfortable (politically and economically) Beirut Jewish community on May 11 and June 11 of that same year. Ibid., Liban, I.C.1.

Syria, the consensus during this period was that any sort of overt communal demonstrations would be disastrous.[37]

As in the case of Syrian Jewry, the much larger and wealthier Jewish community of Iraq found its options for responding to antisemitism extremely limited during the 1930s by the rising tides of both anti-Zionism and pro-Nazism. There was little Iraqi Jews could do to counter the activities of Arab nationalist and profascist groups such as the paramilitary Futuwwa, the Katā'ib al-Shabāb, and the unabashedly Nazi al-Muthannā. Frustrated by the rebuff of their appeals for government intervention and by the anti-Jewish violence that followed in the wake of the Palestinian disturbances of 1936, the Jews of Baghdad finally went on a three-day protest strike that had a serious impact on commerce. The strike moved the Iraqi government at least to threaten to punish anti-Jewish agitators.[38] The Iraqi-Jewish leadership then adopted a strategy of disassociation from Zionism (not as vehement at first as their co-religionists in Syria) and of a demonstrative public patriotism that was marked by volunteerism and generous monetary contributions to Iraqi national causes.[39]

Initially the reaction of Egyptian Jews to the antisemitism of the 1930s was very different from that of their brethren in Syria and Iraq. The generally activist, even aggressive response of the Egyptian-Jewish community was due in no small measure to the fact that throughout the first half of the decade neither Egypt's political leaders nor its Muslim masses had been sufficiently galvanized by the Palestine issue for a variety of internal political and social reasons.[40] During the years 1933–35, antisemitism in Egypt made little headway and was of a distinctly exogenous character. Its principal agents were the local representatives of the Nazi party among the members of Egypt's German colony.[41]

37. See the letter (in Hebrew) from Joseph D. Farhi, president of the Beirut Jewish Community, to the Zionist Executive, Histadrut Department, January 22, 1937, CZA, S5/2204. Both the Lebanese and Syrian Jews were apparently willing to send telegrams of protest to the German consul in Beirut. See Dan Eldar, "Teguvat ha-yehudim be-arzot ha-mizrah al ha-mediniyut ha-antishemit be-Germanyah, February 1933–April 1934," *Peamim*, no. 5 (1980): 63.

38. Ben-Jacob, *Yehudei Bavel*, pp. 248–49; Cohen, *Jews of the Middle East*, pp. 27–28.

39. In addition to the two sources cited in the previous note, see Sylvia G. Haim, "Aspects of Jewish Life in Baghdad under the Monarchy," *Middle Eastern Studies* 12 (1976): 192–93.

40. See Barry Rubin, *The Arab States and the Palestine Conflict* (Syracuse, 1981), pp. 61 and passim; and Lois Gottesman, "Israel in Egypt: The Jewish Community of Egypt, 1922–1957" (M.A. thesis, Princeton University, 1982), pp. 43–44.

41. For a detailed and well-documented survey of Nazi activity in Egypt at this time and of the Jewish response, see Gudrun Krämer, *Minderheit, Millet, Nation? Die Juden*

The Egyptian-Jewish community, which was sophisticated, well-organized, and well-informed of events in Europe, reacted swiftly and with vigor. A number of mass public protests were organized at the initiative of the influential B'nai B'rith lodges in March and April 1933 in Cairo, Alexandria, Port Said, Mansura, and Tanta. Thousands of Jews, including the chief rabbis and representatives of the community councils, took part. A defense organization called La Ligue contre l'Antisémitisme Allemand, Association formée par toute les oeuvres juives en Egypte, was formed to counter Nazi activities and propaganda in Egypt. The league was headed by a committee of leading Jewish public figures from Alexandria and Cairo and soon merged with the Ligue Internationale contre Antisémitisme (LICA, the International League against Racism and Antisemitism), becoming its Egyptian branch. By 1935 it counted fifteen hundred members. In addition to LICA, Jewish students formed a youth association called Ligue Internationale Scolaire contre l'Antisémitisme (LISCA), which in theory included all of the students in Egypt's Jewish schools. LICA's principal activities were in countering German propaganda and organizing the boycott of German goods. Its publicity efforts were facilitated by the significant number of Jewish journalists in Egypt who wrote not only for the Jewish newspapers, such as *L'Aurore, Israël, La Tribune Juive*, and *al-Shams*, but for the major English- and French-language papers of the country such as the *Egyptian Gazette, Egyptian Mail, La Bourse Egyptienne*, and *Le Journal du Caire*.[42]

The boycott of German imports, films, and local businesses were ushered in by an appeal published by Leon Castro, one of the leaders of LICA, in various Jewish newspapers calling upon the Jews of Egypt to "break every material, intellectual, social and worldly relation with them [the Germans]."[43] Egyptian Jewry met the call, and the boycott was successful enough to hurt some German business interests, to drive German films completely out of the Egyptian movie houses, and to alarm some German officials.[44] Fearing a serious breakdown of public order and possible financial dislocations,

---

in *Ägypten, 1914–1952*, Studien zum Minderheiten Problem im Islam 7 (Wiesbaden, 1982), pp. 259–79; and Mizrahi, *L'Egypte et ses Juifs*, pp. 103–15.

42. Krämer, *Minderheit, Millet, Nation?*, pp. 261–64.

43. Quoted in ibid., p. 267.

44. Ibid., pp. 268–270; Eldar, "Teguvat ha-yehudim be-arzot ha-mizrah al ha-mediniyut ha-antishemit be-Germanyah," pp. 66–71; Mizrahi, *L'Egypte et ses Juifs*, pp. 105–6.

Egyptian and British authorities finally stepped in during the summer of 1933 to halt the most vocal public aspects of the campaigns of both sides.[45] The boycott thereafter had to be carried out unofficially on the individual level. Although other actions taken by members of the Jewish community, such as a highly publicized libel trial in 1933–34 against the head of Cairo's German Club,[46] failed, the Jewish leaders of Egypt continued to protest antisemitism and the persecution of Jews in Europe and in the neighboring Italian colony of Libya.[47]

The rise of anti-Zionist sentiment and activities of pan-Islamic and paramilitary groups such as the Muslim Brotherhood, the Miṣr al-Fatāt, and the Young Men's Muslim Association, although highly disquieting, did not cow the Jewish community into silence or making abject statements condemning Zionism. Jewish leaders, however, increased their efforts with government officials and Muslim religious leaders behind the scenes.[48] In addition to asserting Egyptian-Jewish patriotism, the main strategy seems to have been in calling for moderation and conciliation *vis-à-vis* the Palestine issue and for Egypt to play an important intermediary role.[49]

The Jews of Algeria, who were the most Europeanized of the Jewry in the Arab world, faced bitter antisemitic campaigns during the 1930s, as they had during the latter part of the nineteenth century. The anti-Jewish agitation did not emanate from the native Muslim population but from the European settlers, the *pied-noirs*. The Algerian-Jewish response in both periods was twofold: by acting through the French political process and by asserting their own complete identification with France and its ideals.[50]

Because the governing bodies of Algerian Jewry, the local consis-

---

45. Krämer, *Minderheit, Millet, Nation?*, pp. 272–74; Eldar, "Teguvat ha-yehudim be-arzot ha-mizrah al ha-mediniyut ha-antishemit be-Germanyah," pp. 69–70.
46. For details of the *Jabes* v. *van Meeteren* trial and appeal, see the Egyptian-Jewish press between January 1934 and May 1935; and Krämer, *Minderheit, Millet, Nation?*, pp. 265–67.
47. See, for example, the lead articles "Les Juifs et la provocation allemande" and "Protestations des organisations juives d'Egypte contre les excitations nazis au meutre des Juifs," *Israël*, May 18, 1934, p. 1; and "Antisémitisme en Lybie," ibid., January 4, 1937, p. 3.
48. See Krämer, *Minderheit, Millet, Nation?*, pp. 279–303; and Gottesman, "Israel in Egypt," p. 55.
49. Krämer, *Minderheit, Millet, Nation?*, pp. 295–303.
50. Concerning the antisemitic campaigns of 1871–1900, see Michel Ansky, *Les Juifs d'Algérie du Décret Crémieux à la Libération* (Paris, 1950), pp. 45–62. For the 1930s, see ibid., pp. 63–83; and, now especially, Abitbol, *Les Juifs d'Afrique du Nord*, pp. 17–32.

tories, were forbidden by law from dealing with political matters, the initiative for responding to the growing antisemitism of the 1930s fell upon local organizations like professional associations and unions. Jewish communal leaders also formed new organizations outside the community structure. The most important of these was the Comité d'Etudes Sociales d'Alger (CESA), which came to be regarded as the spokesman for Algerian Jewry as a whole.[51] The basic line of the CESA, and indeed of most Algerian-Jewish leaders, was that "truth must rise up against falsehood and reveal the unavowed motives of the agitators and their mercenary connections."[52] However, as Michel Abitbol has observed, the leaders of Algerian Jewry "were more at ease denouncing the 'anti-republican' and 'anti-French' message of the antisemitic line than in condemning its particularist character, openly directed against a definite group in society."[53] Their faith in the ultimate triumph of the French ideals of Liberty, Equality, Fraternity was maintained even during the years of Vichy persecution. Nevertheless, in the face of Vichy antisemitism and the indifference of the general public to their plight, the Jews of Algeria—and their co-religionists in neighboring Morocco and Tunisia—underwent a powerful reaffirmation of their Jewish identity, a "return to self" (retour sur soi), as they called it.[54] Even the most assimilated members of the Jewish elite were affected by this return to selfhood.

Throughout the Maghreb, Jewish communal institutions were strengthened in the face of Vichy's discriminatory laws. In Algeria, in particular, the Jews had to create virtually ex nihilo an entire infrastructure of communal organizations and services.[55] A similar phenomenon may be observed among Libyan Jewry under fascist control. The antisemitic legislation and subsequent persecutions of 1938–43 resulted in restoring a communal esprit de corps, which had weakened in the preceding decade, and in strengthening the Libyan Jews' sense of identity.[56]

51. Abitbol, Les Juifs d'Afrique du Nord, p. 31.
52. Quoted in Ansky, Les Juifs d'Algérie, p. 78.
53. Abitbol, Les Juifs d'Afrique du Nord, p. 31.
54. Ibid., p. 90.
55. Ibid., pp. 59–96. See also the memoir of the chief rabbi of Algiers for this period, Maurice Eisenbeth, Pages vécues, 1940–43 (Algiers, 1945), passim. Concerning the creation of an entire Jewish school system in Algeria, see Robert Brunschvig, "Les mesures antijuives dans l'enseignement en Algérie, sous le régime de Vichy," Revue d'Alger 2 (1944): 57–79.
56. De Felice, Jews in an Arab Land, p. 117.

The Second World War was traumatic for Oriental Jewry—as for all Jews. Many of the Arab countries and, indeed, many Arab nationalists were openly sympathetic to the Axis—the enemy of their colonialist overlords Great Britain and France. One Arab country—Iraq—was actually taken over during the month of May 1941 by the pro-Nazi regime of Rāshid ʿAlī al-Gaylānī, who was associated with the Jew-baiting ex-mufti of Jerusalem, Ḥājj Amīn al-Ḥusaynī. Just before Rāshid ʿAlī's short-lived government fell to the invading British forces, the Iraqi soldiers returning from the front went on an anti-Jewish rampage in Baghdad on June 1 and 2. As a direct result of this pogrom, known as the Farhūd, Iraqi Jews began turning in greater numbers to the Zionist response, and throughout Iraq underground defense movements and Zionist cells were organized.[57]

So, too, in North Africa—from Libya across to Morocco—the war years engendered among the Jewish population, and especially among the younger generation, a heightened receptivity to Zionism as the ultimate answer to the antisemitism of the European colonialists and the Arab nationalists. These sentiments were fostered and strengthened by encounters with Jewish soldiers serving in various Allied armies and by renewed contacts with representatives of organized Zionism.[58]

At the war's end, the lesson of the destruction of much of European Jewry was not lost upon the Jews in most of the Arab world. As Arab anti-Zionism and antisemitism rose to a violent pitch with the partition of Palestine, most of Arabic-speaking Jewry responded—so to speak—with their feet and, during the first few years of Israel's statehood, emigrated *en masse*.

57. Concerning the Farhūd, see Hayyim J. Cohen, "The Anti-Jewish Farhūd in Baghdad, *Middle Eastern Studies* 3 (1966): 2–17; and the symposium of articles in *Peamim*, no. 8 (1981): 20–91. For the emergence of the Zionist underground, see Yosef Meir, *Meever la-midbar: ha-mahteret ha-haluzit be-Iraq* (Tel Aviv, 1973); and Mordecai Bibi, "Ha-mahteret ha-haluzit be-Iraq," *Peamim*, no. 8 (1981): 92–106. See also the important articles and documents in Zvi Yehuda, ed., *Mi-Bavel li-Yerushalayim: Kovetz mehkarim ve-teudot al ha-ziyonut ve-ha-aliyah me-Iraq* (Tel Aviv, 1980).

58. For the role played by Palestinian-Jewish soldiers serving in the British army in various Middle Eastern and North African countries, see Yoav Gelber, *Toldot ha-hitnadvut*, vol. 3, *Nosei ha-degel* (Jerusalem, 1983), pp. 1–132. For the activities of Zionist representatives in Morocco at this time, see Yehuda, "Ha-irgun ha-ziyoni be-Morocco," pp. 155–225.

THE HOLOCAUST

Otto Dov Kulka

The Reactions of German Jewry to the National Socialist Regime

New Light on the Attitudes and Activities of the
Reichsvereinigung der Juden in Deutschland
from 1938–39 to 1943

If the striking of the old tower clock is so audible
as if it had never struck before, then it is time to
interpret the ringing and the clock itself. The interpretation does not have to be invented, should
not be invented; one must simply recognize that
which has existed since time immemorial, as the
truth after all has, and pronounce it. Why pronounce it? In order that the bond, which has perceived its fate in that hour and its recognition,
stays together although it is torn apart in space.
Whether it stays together as a community, nay
whether it becomes one, whether it becomes one
again, this will mysteriously determine the next
ringing of the chimes. If it breaks up into indefi-
nite individuals then it, and perhaps more than it,
is lost.

—Martin Buber,
preface to *Die Stunde und die Erkenntnis*, 1936

The Reichsvertretung der Juden in Deutschland (National Representation of the Jews in Germany) was established in September
1933 as an umbrella organization of the various unions of Jewish
communities in the German states and of nationwide Jewish politi-

cal and religious organizations. In July 1938 the council of the Reichsvertretung decided to transform the organization into a more centralized confederation and change its name to the Reichsverband der Juden in Deutschland. These changes were not immediately implemented, however, because of political developments related to the Munich Crisis and the *Kristallnacht* pogroms. It was only in February 1939 that the Reichsvertretung proclaimed the formation of the "new" organization under yet another name—the Reichsvereinigung der Juden in Deutschland (National Union of the Jews in Germany)—whose legal status was determined by a special law of July 1939. Following this development I chose to view 1938–39 as a transitional stage between two periods in the history of German Jewry during the Third Reich.[1]

The historiography of the first period, under the leadership of the Reichsvertretung, has offered a variety of controversial appraisals. These five years between 1933 and 1938–39 have been described as, *inter alia*, "one of the strangest episodes in the history of the Jewish people"; "an internal renaissance of German Jewry"; "revival and defiance under ignominious conditions"; "euphoria before the end"; and "a fools' paradise between Weimar and Auschwitz."[2]

1. The question of two distinct periods will be discussed at greater length later in this essay. The problems connected with the transition from the Reichsvertretung to the Reichsvereinigung are surveyed in my *Ha-Sheelah ha-Yehudit ba-Reich ha-Shlishi* (Jerusalem, 1975). They are further developed and systematically examined in Esriel Hildesheimer, *The Central Organisation of the German Jews in the Years, 1933–1945* [in Hebrew with English summary] (Jerusalem, 1982); this book will soon be published in English by the Leo Baeck Institute.

2. Viewpoints such as these can be found, for example, in Robert Weltsch's introduction to the *Leo Baeck Institute Year Book* (hereafter *LBIYB*) 1 (1956): xxx–xxxi, as well as in Max Gruenewald, "Education and Culture of the German Jews under Nazi Rule," *Jewish Review* 5 (1948): 56–83; and Ernst Simon, *Aufbau im Untergang; Jüdische Erwachsenenbildung im nationalsozialistischen Deutschland als geistiger Widerstand* (Tübingen, 1959). For more detailed studies on the Jewish organizations of this period, see the various works of Avraham Margaliot and the somewhat problematic studies of Jacob Boas, "The Jews of Germany: Self-Perceptions in the Nazi Era as Reflected in the German Jewish Press, 1933–1938 (Ph.D. diss., University of California, Riverside, 1977), and Boas, "German-Jewish Internal Politics under Hitler, 1933–1938," *LBIYB* 29 (1984): 3–25. Boas's most recent assessments of the Reichsvertretung ("German-Jewish Internal Politics," p. 12) as "the self-appointed political representative of Germany's Jews . . . , the creation of roughly two dozen prominent German Jews" an organization for which "no popular elections preceded its formation" and in which "the traditional centres of active Jewish life, the Jewish communities, received only token representation," obviously ignore the present stage of research. The establishment of the Reichsvertretung der jüdischen Landesverbände in January 1932 by democratically elected representatives of the Jewish communities and the major Jewish political organizations must be seen as the culmination of continuous efforts to set up a central organization of German Jews that go back to the second half of the nineteenth century. It is

On the other hand, the second five years of the period, between
1938–39 and 1943, have been portrayed consistently and unequivocally as the era presided over by the "Gestapo-appointed" Reichsvereinigung, which acted as the "executive organ of the Gestapo" in the
final liquidation of German Jewry.[3] The principal grounds for this
assessment—which I shall refute in this essay—are derived in part
from the basic conceptions of the polemic and research literature
dealing with the entire subject of Jewish leadership under Nazi rule[4]

---

more than evident that the Reichsvertretung der Juden in Deutschland set up in September 1933 was a direct continuation of this so-called *alte* Reichsvertretung in terms
of its leadership—representing a balance among the communal and political structures of German Jewry—its constitution, its administrative organs, and its activities
as they developed between 1933 and 1938–39. In addition to Hildesheimer, *Central
Organisation of the German Jews*, see also Hildesheimer "Die Versuche zur Schaffung
einer jüdischen Gesamtorganisation während der Weimarer Republik, 1919–1933,"
Jahrbuch des Instituts für Deutsche Geschichte 8 (Tel Aviv, 1979): 335–64, and the current project, described in n. 10 below. Boas's observations derive from his almost exclusive reliance on personal accounts and memoirs; primary archival material demands a different assessment.
   3. The latest assessment of this kind by Ino Arndt, "Antisemitismus und Judenver-
folgung," in *Das Dritte Reich: Herrschaftsstruktur und Geschichte*, ed. Martin Broszat
and Horst Möller (Munich, 1983), pp. 216, 223, merely paraphrases similar comments
that have appeared in various studies and testimonies since this subject first came
under consideration in the early 1950s in the comprehensive works of Hans Lamm,
"Über die innere und äussere Entwicklung des deutschen Judentums im Dritten Reich"
(Ph.D. diss., University of Erlangen, 1951); Raul Hilberg, *The Destruction of the Euro-
pean Jews* (Chicago, 1961); and Lucy Dawidowicz, *The War against the Jews, 1933–1945*
(New York, 1975). Concerning Arndt's article and the German historiography, see O. D.
Kulka, "Die deutsche Geschichtsschreibung über den Nationalsozialismus und die
Endlösung," *Historische Zeitschrift* 240, no. 3 (1985): 639. See further the particular
studies by Shaul Esh, "The Establishment of the *Reichsvereinigung der Juden in
Deutschland* and Its Main Activites," *Yad Vashem Studies* 7 (1968): 19–38; K. J. Ball-
Kadouri, "Berlin wird Judenfrei: Die Juden in Berlin in den Jahren 1942–43," *Jahrbuch
für Geschichte Mittel- und Ostdeutschlands* 22 (1973): 196–241; and Ball-Kadouri, "Aus
der Arbeit der jüdischen Gemeinde Berlin während der Jahre 1941–43: Gemeindear-
beit und Evakuierung von Berlin, 16. Okt. 1941–16. Juni 1943," *Zeitschrift für die Geschichte der Juden* 9 (1972): 32–52, which is based on Hildegard Henschel's testimony.
For further testimonies, see Ball-Kadouri, comp., "Testimonies and Recollections
about Activities Organised by German Jewry during the Years 1933–1945 (Catalogue
of Manuscripts in the Yad Vashem Archives)," *Yad Vashem Studies* 4 (1960): 317–40, and
similar sources in the archives of the Wiener Library, Tel Aviv, and the Leo Baeck
Institute, New York.
   4. For the controversy on this subject centering on Hannah Arendt's *Eichmann in
Jerusalem: A Report on the Banality of Evil* (New York, 1963), see F. A. Krummacher, ed.,
Die Kontroverse: Hannah Arendt, Eichmann und die Juden (Munich, 1964); Jacob Rob-
inson, *And the Crooked Shall Be Made Straight: The Eichmann Trial, the Jewish Catastrophe, and Hannah Arendt's Narrative* (New York, 1965); and R. Y. Cohen, "On the Respon-
sibility of the Jews in Their Destruction by the Nazis as Seen in the Works of Bruno
Bettelheim, Raul Hilberg, Hannah Arendt and in the Public Polemics on Their Works"
(M.A. thesis, Hebrew University, Jerusalem, 1972). Among the works on German Jewry
that deal with the activities of the Reichsvereinigung, attention should be paid to H. G.
Adler, *Theresienstadt, 1941–1945: Das Antlitz einer Zwangsgemeinschaft* (Tübingen,

and in part from the nature of sources that have been available to scholars.[5]

Publications dealing with this subject first appeared at the close of the Second World War and the years immediately following. In examining the problems of historiography on the Jews during the Nazi era and its distinct phases, I defined the writings dominating this period as "literature assessing guilt and rendering judgment."[6] It seems that under the immediate impact of the harrowing and unprecedented act of systematically annihilating millions, it deliberately avoided examining historical processes and ongoing developments in various spheres of life that it held to be irrelevant. The sole relevant standard in this historical literature was a moral—or, to be more precise, moralistic—yardstick that preceded, or even replaced, historical criteria. Thus the description of Jewish society and leadership through the entire period of Nazi domination is limited exclusively to judging the positions assumed in situations in which decisions were categorically irreversible and final, those during the phase of the mass deportations and exterminations. The only categories are "collaboration" versus "resistance" or "participation in the extermination process" versus "attempts at rebellion and rescue." This approach, which was probably the only one understandable and relevant at the end of the war and in the period immediately thereafter, has for various reasons continued to shape publications on this subject to the present day.

As pertains to German Jewry, these remarks are particularly valid for the so-called Holocaust period proper, which in other countries runs parallel to the period beginning with the expansion of the Third

1958); Adler, *Der verwaltete Mensch: Studien zur Deportation der Juden aus Deutschland* (Tübingen, 1974); H. E. Fabian, "Zur Entstehung der 'Reichsvereinigung der Juden in Deutschland,'" in *Gegenwart im Rückblick: Festgabe der Jüdischen Gemeinde zu Berlin, 25 Jahre nach der Neugründung*, ed. H. A. Strauss and K. R. Grossmann (Heidelberg, 1970), pp. 165–79; and esp. Hildesheimer, *Central Organisation of the German Jews*, pt. 2; and the proceedings of the 1977 Yad Vashem Conference, *Patterns of Jewish Leadership in Nazi Europe, 1933–1945*, ed. Yisrael Gutman (Jerusalem, 1979).

5. See Kulka, *Ha-Sheelah Ha-Yehudit*, vol. 1, pt. 1, chap. 2, dealing with sources for research into the Jewish community in the Third Reich.

6. Ibid., pt. 2, chap. 2. Literature of this kind first began to appear at the end of World War II and during the period of the major war crimes trials, and it experienced a revival primarily in the wake of the Kastner trial in the 1950s and the Eichmann trial in the 1960s. Examples of periods of historiography marked by assessments of guilt can be found throughout modern history in the wake of specific historic upheavals or major tragedies, such as the French Revolution and Reign of Terror, the defeat of France by Prussia in 1870–71, and especially World War I. Concerning this stage in German historiography, see my "Die deutsche Geschichtsschreibung," pp. 609–14.

Reich in 1938–39. The general evaluation of the period between 1933 and 1938–39 and the distinction between that period and the following years are based primarily on the viewpoint propounded in the testimonies of prominent German-Jewish leaders who, as a rule, left Germany in 1938–39. Moreover, the abundance of published and unpublished sources that have survived from the period ending in 1938–39[7] has led some studies to stress—and rightly so—the historical continuity, and even intensification, of Jewish communal life that marked this early phase. At the same time, however, they seek to emphasize the sharp distinction between the prewar era and the following period, which purportedly was epitomized exclusively by the extermination process. This impression has been accepted primarily because of the total absence of contemporary primary source material on the activities of the Jewish leadership after 1938–39, as well as the death of almost all Jewish leaders who remained in Germany. Even in the retrospective testimonies of the few prominent figures who survived the Holocaust (for example, Rabbi Leo Baeck),[8] the activities of the Jewish leadership throughout the period are overshadowed by the terrible end.

This picture changed radically with the discovery of primary sources from the Reichsvereinigung archives that cover the entire span of its existence (1939–43), plus important documents from other archives relating in part to the transition from the Reichsvertretung through the Reichsverband to the Reichsvereinigung in 1938–39. The material from the Reichsvereinigung archives was first discovered in the 1960s in East Berlin, where it had been lying for years in the cellar of the half-destroyed synagogue in the Oranienburgerstrasse that had served as the last headquarters of the Berlin Jewish community. Its tens of thousands of pages include minutes of executive board meetings, notes on discussions held with German officials, material on the organization's routine activities, and statistical summaries of its programs relating to the material, social, and spiritual affairs of the entire German-Jewish community.[9] Unfortu-

7. See Kulka, *Ha-Sheelah ha-Yehudit*, vol. 1, pt. 1, chap. 2.
8. See E. H. Boehm, ed., *We Survived: The Stories of Fourteen of the Hidden and Hunted of Nazi Germany as Told to Eric Boehm* (New Haven, 1949); K. J. Ball-Kadouri, "Leo Baeck and Contemporary History: A Riddle in Leo Baeck's Life," *Yad Vashem Studies* 6 (1967): 121–29; and Leonard Baker, *Days of Sorrow and Pain: Leo Baeck and the Berlin Jews* (New York, 1978).
9. For a detailed description of the Reichsvereinigung archives, their structure and content, as far as I could determine them while examining part of the classified material deposited in the Zentrales Staatsarchiv of the German Democratic Republic at

nately the material of the Reichsvereinigung deposited at the Zentrales Staatsarchiv (Central State Archives) of the German Democratic Republic at Potsdam has since become inaccessible to researchers. In order to cope with this situation, a project for reconstructing the Reichsvereinigung's archives has been initiated. Relevant documents are being collected from the archives of numerous German-Jewish communities and organizations, as well as from several departments of the Third Reich that were in contact with the Reichsvereinigung.[10]

In the light of this material, it appears that intensive activity in all spheres of German-Jewish life did not cease in the 1940s. On the contrary it continued, and actually increased in importance, until the liquidation of the entire Jewish community of Germany in 1942–43 and even during that very process. Likewise the sources testify to the resolute stand of the Jewish leadership in its struggle against the Nazi persecutions—including the mass deportations—until the final stage, concurrent with its primary effort to secure the physical and spiritual existence of the remnant Jewish communities of Germany.

This new material also reveals that German Jews maintained contact with other Jewish communities in Nazi-occupied Europe and, until the autumn of 1941, even with Jews in countries outside the area of German occupation. Moreover the archival material from the transitional period of 1938–39, which includes minutes of the Reichsvertretung executive board meetings, clearly indicates that the transformation from the voluntary federative organization of unions of communities and major organizations (the Reichsvertretung) to the official centralist organization of a nationwide community (the Reichsvereinigung) was basically the expression of an intracommunity trend whose motivating factors had been reinforced by the change effected by the March 1938 law abrogating the legal status of the Jewish communities.[11] Definite evidence to this effect is

Potsdam, see Kulka, *Ha-Sheelah ha-Yehudit*, vol. 1, pt. 1, pp. 77–89. I am very grateful to the directors of the Potsdam archives for allowing me to photocopy the greater part of the historically most important documents.

10. I have undertaken this project at the Institute for Jewish Studies at the Hebrew University in Jerusalem together with my colleague Esriel Hildesheimer. We are also reconstructing the archives of the Reichsvertretung from 1933 to 1938, which have most probably been lost. A critical edition of selected documents, O. D. Kulka and Esriel Hildesheimer, eds., "Dokumente zur Geschichte der Zentralorganisation der deutschen Juden im Dritten Reich, 1933–1945," is being prepared for publication.

11. Kulka, *Ha-Sheelah ha-Yehudit*, vol. 2, docs. 33–34a, 40–43, and the introduction to these documents, pp. xxii–xxv, xxx–xxxiv. For an extensive study on this development, see Hildesheimer, *Central Organisation of the German Jews*, pp. 89–108.

contained in a document from the Gestapo—the body that allegedly created the Reichsvereinigung as an instrument of its own designs—or, to be more precise, the Security Service (Sicherheitsdienst, the SD) of the SS, with its Department for Jewish Affairs, which was headed, after its amalgamation with the Gestapo in 1939, by Adolf Eichmann. An internal SD memorandum dated early September 1938 describes the transition that extended over that year and ultimately led to the establishment of the Reichsvereinigung as follows:

> The Reichsvertretung ... is the sole representative body of the Jews in Germany *vis-à-vis* the Reich government. ... At this moment discussions and consultations are still being held on the basis of the March 28, 1938, law with the aim of creating a unified framework for the regional unions of communities and the communities. ... The differences of opinion that arise in the course of these discussions, and that have been unresolved since April, constitute marked proof of sluggishness of the *system of democratic rule* and the stark failure of the Jews in the administrative field, even when questions pertaining to their very existence are at stake.[12]

This instructive memorandum and many other external and internal documents that have been preserved from 1938–39 indicate that the transformation from the federative framework of the Reichsvertretung to the centralized organization of the Reichsvereinigung was the product of extended negotiations with the Nazi authorities and internal, democratic deliberations among the component bodies—primarily the Jewish communities and unions of communities—during which it was finally agreed that the latter would disband as an autonomous framework and merge into a unified national body. According to the detailed regulations adopted at a meeting of the Reichsvertretung council on July 27, 1938, the new organization was conceived as a centralized, national organization embracing all the Jews of Germany on the basis of individual membership, while preserving a measure of the autonomous structure of the large communities and regional concentrations of small communities. It also perpetuated the existing proportional representation allocated to major Jewish political and religious organizations.

It was in this organizational structure that the leadership emerged a year later, with the publication of the state law of July 4, 1939,[13] by which the Reichsvereinigung der Juden in Deutschland was officially

---

12. Kulka, *Ha-Sheelah ha-Yehudit*, vol. 2, doc. 35, my italics.
13. *Reichsgesetzblatt*, 1939, p. 1079; *Jüdisches Nachrichtenblatt* (Berlin), February 17, July 11, 1939; "Arbeitsbericht der Reichsvereinigung der Juden für das Jahr 1939" [Berlin, early 1940s], mimeographed.

constituted. As before, it was headed by Rabbi Leo Baeck and Otto Hirsch and included almost all the other members of the Reichvertretung's representative leadership. The law itself was essentially the realization of the declared intent of the Reichsvertretung to regain recognized legal status as a supracommunity organization (and, I might add, as a centralized and united one).

The final version of the law published on July 4, 1939, long served as the sole basis for the historiographical discussion of the origin of the Reichsvereinigung. This treatment totally divorces the Reichsvereingung from the prior developments that the law essentially served to summarize and climax. But even the declaration of the Reichsvereinigung executive that accompanied the publication of the law states emphatically that, with the exception of the clause on obligatory membership according to racial definition, the organization's legally recognized statutes are based on the charter accepted at the meeting of the Reichsvertretung council of July 27, 1938.[14]

The documents from the archives of the Reichsvereinigung from the war years testify to the continuity of both the leadership that served in 1938 and the basic direction and objectives of the organization's activities: in external affairs, resolute representation of the Jewish community in the efforts to safeguard its status, including opposition to local and regional deportations in the years 1939 to 1941; in internal affairs, a struggle to secure the material, social, and cultural existence of the Jewish community and to organize and finance emigration—albeit limited by objective circumstances—until exit from Germany was unconditionally prohibited in the autumn of 1941. Thus in contrast to the impressions conveyed by descriptions and assessments contained in the testimonies on the period from 1933 to 1938–39, various intensive communal activities did continue throughout this last phase as well.

These remarks relate primarily to the continued activities of the Kulturbund; the perpetuation and even expansion of Jewish educational programs, including adult education, vocational training (particularly in agricultural collective groups like the *hachsharah* and even the Hochschule für die Wissenschaft des Judentums in Berlin; the continued activities of health and welfare institutions; ongoing material and organizational aid and the allocation of funds for

14. The minutes of this meeting, which are appended to the detailed regulations, have been preserved in a private archive. See Kulka, *Ha-Sheelah ha-Yehudit*, vol. 2, doc. 35.

emigration; the continuous efforts to ensure funds for the Reichsvereinigung and the individual communities by means of taxation, the selling of Jewish communal property (among others, the plots of synagogues that had been destroyed in 1938), internal fund-raising campaigns, and until 1941, the soliciting of aid from Jewish organizations abroad (out of which funds were even transferred to the Polish-Jewish community). Data on the Reichsvereinigung's budget structure allow us to discern its priorities in various spheres and during the various periods of its tenure.

The minutes of the executive's sessions also indicate the persistence of internal ideological and religious friction over the character of the Kulturbund's activities, the quality of Jewish education in its various programs, and the aim of the social welfare policy. These activities continued, for the most part, until the mass deportations and the liquidation of German Jewry.

Two examples from the documents of the Reichsvereinigung archives will serve to illustrate the stand and conduct of the Jewish leadership in its relations with the Nazi regime, meaning, in practice, Eichmann's department in the Reichssicherheitshauptamt (RSHA, the Reich Security Main Office). The first relates to one of the initial mass deportations executed on a regional scale, in which the entire Jewish population of three provinces in Southwest Germany was deported to France in a lightning action in October 1940. This affair and the related exchange of views between the Vichy government and the German Foreign Ministry are mentioned in several studies,[15] but nowhere had the German-Jewish leadership's active role in campaigning to stop the deportations and its subsequent efforts to return the deportees been noted. Only the archival sources now in our possession indicate that the immediate response of the Reichsvereinigung executive was bold to the point of threatening to tender its collective resignation.[16] Its actions, which were of both a practical and a symbolic nature, were expressed on three different levels.

---

15. This matter is discussed in, among others, Hilberg, *Destruction of the European Jews,* esp. pp. 392–93; Adler, *Theresienstadt,* pp. 17, 172; Adler, *Der verwaltete Mensch,* pp. 156–167; Helmut Krausnick, "Persecutions of Jews," in *Anatomy of the SS State,* ed. Hans Buchheim et al. (London, 1968), pp. 57–58; Gerald Reitlinger, *The Final Solution* (London, 1968), pp. 77–78; and U. D. Adam, *Judenpolitik im Dritten Reich* (Düsseldorf, 1972), pp. 257–58.

16. See Kulka, *Ha-Sheelah ha-Yehudit,* vol. 1, pt. 3, chap. 5, esp. pp. 239–91; and Hildesheimer, *Central Organisation of the German Jews,* pp. 250–62.

First, on the official level, the executive director, Otto Hirsch, attempted to intervene with Eichmann and halt the deportations already in progress by citing assurances that had been given to the Reichsvereinigung during previous deportations. Among the examples Hirsch cited were the cancellation of the expulsion of the Breisach community, the cessation of the deportation from Schneidemühl and Stettin in February 1940, and efforts to bring about the return of deportees from Poland. He also made a demand (which can be construed as an ultimatum) that the Reichsvereinigung be told of the destination of the deportations and instructed as to how it might act to ensure the return of the deportees.

Second, on the practical level, the staff of the Reichsvereinigung and its local offices warned Jews who resided in the three provinces, but were outside of these areas at the time, not to return to their homes. This widespread, semiclandestine action was discovered in the course of a subsequent investigation by the RSHA. In addition, the Reichsvereinigung provided aid and shelter to Jews who had taken heed of the warning and gone into hiding.

Third, on the public level, the Reichsvereinigung proclaimed a day of fasting, binding for its entire staff throughout Germany, as an act of protest and identification with the fate of the deportees. In addition it introduced special synagogal services devoted to this subject on the following Sabbath. As further expression of public protest, it was decided to cancel all cultural and entertainment activities sponsored by the Kulturbund for the following week. These steps, most of which were immediately prohibited by the RSHA, cost the life of a member of the executive, Julius S. Seligsohn, who was identified as the author of the circular to the communities on these measures, even though the members of the executive insisted on their collective responsibility.

It should be noted here that this response to the deportations of October 1940 was one in a series of similar activities and struggles. Among other goals, it served as an effective means of directing attention to events in Germany by relaying information to the foreign press, mainly of neutral countries; the punitive actions of the RSHA related in part to this aspect of the Reichsvereinigung's response. Its attempts to have deportees repatriated from France were in the same category as efforts to repatriate deportees from Poland and to secure the release of inmates of concentration camps, efforts that continued until the beginning of systematic mass deportations to the death camps, and even during that stage.

A second, different example of the response of the Reichsvereinigung to the deportation edicts had occurred in June 1940 in the wake of the RSHA's disclosure of a "plan for the comprehensive solution of the Jewish problem in Europe by the deportation of Jews from their countries of residence and concentrating them in a reservation [*Reservatgebiet*] in a colonial area." This was the plan to create a detention area for the Jews of Europe on the island of Madagascar. The Reichsvereinigung was ordered to consider measures to prepare the groundwork for implementing the plan and eventually presenting a plan of its own.[17] The only concrete response that has been found among the documents of the archives of the Reichsvereinigung in our possession is an outline charting the course of Jewish education, including adult education and vocational training, in the land to which the Jews would be deported.

A circular on this subject was preserved as an appendix to the minutes of an executive board meeting held at the end of 1940. The version that was approved suggests that intricate negotiations on ideological, religious, and practical aspects of the program preceded its acceptance. The document reads as follows:

> [The executive chairman] Dr. Otto Hirsch . . . stresses the necessity to decide on the principles governing the educational preparations for group and mass settlement [*Gruppen- und Massensiedlung*]. He proposes the following draft for a circular to be addressed mainly to the educators:
>
> The decrease in individual emigration obliged the Reichsvereinigung to prepare group and mass settlement. A reconsideration of the essence of the Jewish community is necessary as a basis for the educational work in the schools, vocational retraining, and adult education. This educational work must be guided by the following principles:
> 1. The Jewish people is the bearer of Jewish communal existence [*Träger der jüdischen Gemeinschaft*]. It is therefore necessary to awaken and strengthen the consciousness of the bonds on nationhood [*volksmässige Verbundenheit*] in every possible way, especially by stressing the continuity of Jewish history.
> 2. The Jewish community was endowed with its spirit and character by the Jewish religion. Therefore, access to it must be granted to every individual and every group.
> 3. Hebrew as the language of the Jewish people and its religion is an essential component of all Jewish education.

17. Kulka, *Ha-Sheelah ha-Yehudit*, vol. 2, doc. 51; Eichmann Trial, doc. T 1143; see also Hildesheimer, *Central Organisation of the German Jews*, pp. 243–50.

4. The demands of mass settlement call for education toward a social community within the community [*zur sozialen Gemeinschaft in der Gemeinschaft*].
5. The aim of this education is to prepare for life in the Jewish settlement. It is our wish that [this settlement] be realized in the Jewish land of Palestine. However, these principles are valid for educational preparation toward life in any Jewish settlement, wherever it may be.[18]

This document clearly demonstrates that the course adopted to cope with the new situation created in the early 1940s was essentially a continuation of, or analogous to, the trends that had forged the character of Jewish education in Germany in the 1930s, when the Jewish community was faced with the rise of the Nazi regime.[19] Although the majority of the members of the executive were not Zionists, we can see the growing influence of Jewish nationalism on its outlook in the emphasis on the Hebrew language and Jewish historical consciousness. At the same time the document foresees a central role for the Jewish religion, even for those who had become alienated from it, and notes the importance of constituting a society based on the principles of social justice in the land to which the Jews would be deported. In a way the idea of a land of exile in which all the Jewish communities of Europe would be concentrated appears in the document as a frightening antithesis of the vision of ingathering of the exiles in the Land of Israel. Yet the educational objectives of the program are to prepare and educate for a life within a comprehensive Jewish community, wherever it may be.

On the surface this document might suggest that the Jewish leadership was oblivious to both the cruel reality of its situation and the gruesome prospect of the Final Solution of the Jewish Question in the near future. But it also indicates that spiritual and social values still assumed an important role in dictating the direction and priorities of the practical work of the Reichsvereinigung. Further surviving documents make it clear that during 1941 these educational objectives were actually implemented in all the educational programs and were pursued even during the time of the mass deportations.

In conclusion, an examination of the documents in the Reichsver-

18. For a photocopy of the document, see Kulka, *Ha-Sheelah ha-Yehudit*, vol. 2, doc. 55.
19. Compare, for example, this document with the educational program presented in Martin Buber's: "Unser Bildungsziel," in *Die Stunde und die Erkenntnis: Reden und Aufsätze 1933–1935* (Berlin, 1936), pp. 89–94; and Ernst Simon, "Jewish Adult Education in Nazi Germany as Spiritual Resistance," in *LBIYB* 1 (1956): 8–69.

einigung archives reveals the basic continuity in the status and nature of the work of the Jewish leadership in Germany during the Third Reich. Consequently, some of the premises that have become established and are mechanically repeated in many publications on this subject must now be rejected.

One additional observation is in order. The materials in the Reichsvereinigung archives permit historians to discern the course taken by the leadership of German Jewry over the relatively long period—ten years—of Nazi rule. We can now see how the patterns of attitudes and activities that emerged during the 1930s influenced the course adopted in the following decade. But it appears that analogous examples can be found in the attitudes and activities of the Jewish leadership in other Nazi-occupied European countries during the relatively short period of the war itself. They, too, may be understood as the continuation of trends characterizing each Jewish community, not simply as attempts to cope with the extreme situation during the ultimate stage of annihilation.[20] It is possible that this approach may bring to light additional dimensions of the unity of Jewish history even during this unique era, beyond the common fate of destruction that befell the Jews of Europe.

20. See O. D. Kulka, "Ghetto in an Annihilation Camp: Jewish Social History in the Holocaust Period and Its Ultimate Limits," in *The Nazi Concentration Camps: Proceedings of the Fourth Yad Vashem International Historical Conference*, ed. Yisrael Gutman and Avital Saf (Jerusalem, 1984), pp. 315–30 passim, esp. pp. 315, 319–22.

Michael R. Marrus

Jewish Leadership and the Holocaust

The Case of France

"The lasting victory of the Nazis is that they brutalized the imagination of mankind."[1] In this somber observation, Marie Syrkin recently called attention to the debased coin of discourse associated with injustice and persecution, especially evident in the popular understanding of the Nazi Holocaust. We are all aware of how familiar and how matter-of-fact has become the terminology of mass atrocities. We live surrounded by news of mass expulsions, starvation, and murder; and as our consciousness strains to grasp the horror, we tend to lose sight of the desperate human encounters that so often accompany massacre. In the consequent dulling of sensibility we are left with caricatures—abstract models with which we attempt to understand the actors in the ghastly drama. But neither the naked victims on their way to the gas chambers, nor the bystanders who so cruelly ignored their fate, nor even the perpetrators themselves, were able to escape their human condition. None of them were species from another planet. It is incumbent upon historians, and those who value their insights, to try to penetrate the veil that we have placed around such monstrous evil as that created by Nazism. Attempting to do so is not only a traditional part of the historian's craft; it is also a struggle against the legacy of Nazism itself.

Let me be more specific. One part of the tendency to ignore the human dimension of the Holocaust has been a recent trend to distort the role of wartime Jewish leadership, to shrug off the excruciating dilemmas they sometimes faced, and to make sweeping accusations about their shortcomings. In the course of these assessments such leaders, often victims themselves, are wrenched from their culture,

1. Marie Syrkin, "The Teaching of the Holocaust," *Midstream*, February 1985, p. 49.

place, and circumstance, to be hauled before a courtroom conditioned by forty years of debate and study about the Holocaust. The idea seems to be to cast at least some of the blame for the destruction of European Jewry upon the Jews themselves and notably on one aspect of Jewish existence—the close identification of Jews, especially their leaders, with the Western nations in which they have lived. These Jews, the argument seems to run, turned their backs on their own people in order to ingratiate themselves with their host societies. They deceived and withheld warnings from the victims, missed opportunities for rescue, and failed to press the great powers to act against Hitler's genocide. (A related, though usually separate case is made about Zionist leaders, whose crime is held to be their excessive identification with their state-building project, to the detriment of immediate rescue possibilities.) If I read these criticisms correctly, they also imply the obverse: if Jewish leaders had behaved otherwise, large numbers could have been saved and Jewish honor enhanced.

France offers particularly fertile ground to test the hypothesis, and several recent studies enable us to do so. Controversy began in 1980, when Maurice Rajfus, a left-wing journalist whose immigrant parents were murdered in the Holocaust, published *Des Juifs dans la collaboration*, a sharp indictment of established Jewry, whom he accused of sacrificing foreign Jews while pursuing their own, class-based interests. Since then we have learned considerably more. Jacques Adler, who survived the war and participated as a young man in a Jewish unit of the Communist resistance, has published a much more careful study, an abridgment of his doctoral thesis at the University of Melbourne. A historian at the Hebrew University of Jerusalem, Richard (Yerachmiel) Cohen, has edited the remarkable wartime diary of Raymond-Raoul Lambert, arguably the most important French-Jewish official in contact with the Vichy government and the Germans during the war. In addition, Cohen has just completed an extensive analysis of the Vichy-imposed Jewish council, a book that should appear soon. Several other investigations, including some studies of the Jewish resistance movements, have put the issue in wider perspective.[2]

2. Maurice Rajfus, *Des Juifs dans la collaboration: l'UGIF (1941–1944)* (Paris, 1980); Cynthia J. Haft, *The Bargain and the Bridle: The General Union of the Israelites of France* (Chicago, 1983); Jacques Adler, *Face à la persécution: Les organisations juives à Paris de 1940 à 1944*, trans. Andre Charpentier (Paris, 1985); Raymond-Raoul Lambert, *Carnet*

Concern with French Jewry during the Holocaust inevitably raises the issues referred to early in my discussion. For in no other country was the Jewish elite more thoroughly integrated into the life of the host society and more deeply identified with its fortunes. Assimilation had been under way for a century and a half when Hitler's armies struck in the West in 1940, and at the head of a Jewish community of about 300,000, half of whom were newcomers, stood a Jewish patriciate little different in manners, beliefs, and political views from its non-Jewish counterparts. As in Eastern Europe, the Jews had forced upon them a Jewish council, known as the Union Générale des Israélites de France (UGIF), which immediately became a tool of Nazi and Vichy persecution. And as elsewhere in Europe, French Jews fed the Final Solution: some 75,000 were deported from Drancy, a collecting camp in the northeast of Paris, the overwhelming majority to be murdered in Auschwitz.

France therefore offers a historical arena in which the theories about the Jewish leadership's response to the Holocaust can be examined and subjected to close scrutiny. My own view is that the evidence runs strongly against the accusers. It is entirely proper, of course, to air the weaknesses of Jewish leaders, to note where their judgment was flawed and where they went wrong. But more than twenty years after Hannah Arendt made her sweeping and ill-considered charges against Jewish officials who cooperated with the Nazis, we can afford to be more judicious and more painstaking in particular cases.

That there were Jewish notables ready and eager to cooperate with the anti-Jewish government at Vichy, fully prepared to participate at the end of 1941 in the newly established UGIF, there can be no doubt. But the background to the formation of this body permits us to see how Jewish leaders perceived their involvement in terms that are not so familiar to us today. Established Jews who became part of this organization knew little of the complex negotiations and strategies that lay behind it. They knew even less about ultimate Nazi plans for the Jews, schemes still being hatched in the inner recesses of the Third Reich.

In Paris since August 1940, SS Hauptsturmführer Theodor Dan-

d'un témoin, 1940–1943, ed. Richard Cohen (Paris, 1985); Richard Cohen, "Hahanhagah ha-yehudit be-Zarfat be-milhemet ha-olam ha-shniyah" (Ph.D. diss., Hebrew University, Jerusalem, 1981); Renée Poznanski, "La résistance juive en France," Revue d'histoire de la deuxième guerre mondiale, no. 137 (1985): 3–32.

necker was Adolf Eichmann's representative and head of the Juden-referat, the police branch for Jewish matters that reported directly to Berlin. Dannecker wanted a *Judenrat* for France, similar to the Jewish councils his SS colleagues had established in Germany and were imposing throughout the Jewish communities of Nazi-occupied Poland. Working with virtually no manpower and little support from other Nazi agencies on the spot, Dannecker bullied and cajoled the French government into sponsoring the Jewish body. Respond-ing to these pressures, the French convinced the Jewish notables with whom they met that Vichy was acting to forestall Nazi moves to set up the council under Nazi auspices. Jewish leaders believed their choice was between a German and a French agency. They ap-proached the new organization with great trepidation and consider-able internal dispute. But they believed the UGIF to be under French authority, rather than that of the SS, and in this they were largely correct.[3]

To understand how Jewish notables related to this new body, we need to recognize the supreme demoralization of French Jewry, stunned by two crushing blows in the previous year. Like all French-men, French Jews agonized over their country's defeat—it was so sudden, so overwhelming, and so unexpected. But in addition, the flurry of anti-Jewish legislation passed by the Vichy government be-ginning that summer of 1940 profoundly disturbed French Jews by striking at the core of their beliefs and expectations. That France, celebrated in their education as the very embodiment of progress and emancipation, could take these steps was inconceivable. Writing in his diary in October 1940, Lambert recorded his pain and incre-dulity: "What shame! I cannot even grasp this denial of justice and scientific truth. . . . This cannot last, this isn't possible. . . . I cried yesterday evening like a man who, suddenly, is abandoned by a woman who is the only love of his life, the only guide of his thoughts, the only director of his acts."[4] As with most Frenchmen, Jews were on the verge of despair in 1940. Nazism seemed securely triumphant. In the East, the Soviet alliance with Germany appeared unshakable. Only Britain remained in the war—the ally who (it seemed) had

3. On German and French strategy and the origins of the Union Générale des Isra-élites de France (UGIF), see Michael R. Marrus and Robert O. Paxton, *Vichy France and the Jews* (New York, 1981), pp. 108–10. Because her analysis of the background to the establishment of the UGIF is seriously flawed, Haft misses this important dimen-sion to Jewish involvement in the organization. See *Bargain and the Bridle*, chaps. 1, 2.
4. Lambert, diary, October 19, 1940, *Carnet*, p. 85.

abandoned France so precipitately at Dunkirk. Britain's ability to continue, and even her survival, appeared very much in doubt. For almost a year Lambert, a man who was temperamentally optimistic, dared not hope that the verdict of 1940 could be reversed. For the overwhelming majority of Frenchmen, Jews and non-Jews, the war was over.

How then to survive? The sharp debates that tore the Jewish leadership over the question of the UGIF reflect little of the "naïveté, resignation, or adherence to the New Order installed by Vichy" that Rajfus sneeringly attributes to this establishment.[5] It is true that most of these notables believed that Vichy antisemitism was Nazi directed and its principal victims foreign Jews, not established French Jews like themselves. (Indeed, this view was common enough even among professional historians in France until the 1980s.) It is also evident that by social preference, friendship, or professional association, some of those leaders had close links to the collaborationist structure now in place. Most notably, Jacques Helbronner, the elderly *conseilleur d'état* who was head of the Consistoire Central, had been a close associate of Marshal Philippe Pétain since the First World War and a classmate of the originally Pétainist Cardinal Pierre Gerlier of Lyon.[6] But the real reason these leaders agreed finally, after much hesitation and agonizing discussion, to work under Vichy control was the feeling that there was no alternative. It is suggested now that these Jews should have had nothing to do with the proposal. Perhaps. At the time, however, working with the French government, which had just violated the rights of Jews, seemed preferable to giving the Nazis a free hand.

Much has been made of the opposition to plans for the UGIF that emanated from the Jewish Consistoire Central, the preexisting, officially recognized structure of the Jewish religious community. Only by distorting consistorial views through hindsight, however, can the

5. Rajfus, *Juifs dans la collaboration*, p. 121. See also Leni Yahil, "The Jewish Leadership of France," in *Patterns of Jewish Leadership in Nazi Europe, 1933–1945: Proceedings of the Third Yad Vashem International Historical Conference, 1977*, ed. Yisrael Gutman and Cynthia J. Haft (Jerusalem, 1979); and Yerachmiel (Richard) Cohen, "The Jewish Community of France in the Face of Vichy-German Persecution, 1940–1944," in *The Jews in Modern France*, ed. Frances Malino and Bernard Wasserstein (Hanover, N.H., 1985), pp. 180–203.

6. On the Consistoire Central, see Zosa Szajkowski, "The 'Central Jewish Consistory' in France during the Second World War," *Yad Vashem Studies* 3 (1959): 173–86. See also Szajkowski, *Analytical Franco-Jewish Gazetteer, 1939–1945* (New York, 1966), passim.

Consistoire be seen as objecting to "collaborating in any way with the enemy."[7] Consistorial leaders certainly protested the imposition of a racial definition of Jews and strenuously objected to the discriminatory laws that followed. Yet when it came to the UGIF, they had great difficulty making up their minds. They were unhappy that negotiations were to a large degree out of their own hands, carried on with representatives of Jewish communal service agencies outside the consistorial fold. Helbronner and his associates simply believed they could get a better deal. In addition, the Consistoire jealously defended its own constitutional standing as a religious association and feared any interference that would further erode the Jewish legal standing in France. For Lambert, heavily involved in discussions with Vichy's anti-Jewish policy coordinator Xavier Vallat and increasingly convinced of his own rectitude, the consistorial protesters were "Jewish princes" attempting to protect their own plutocracy. In a revealing passage in his diary Lambert compared himself to Léon Blum in 1936, fending off the hatred of the far Right. "I am feared somewhat the way the Popular Front was feared. The very rich Jews, the majority in the Consistoire, are afraid that [the UGIF] will make them pay too much for the poor."[8]

Later, in the dark days of 1943, when Jews were being deported to the East and there were no longer real doubts about Vichy's cooperation with murderous Nazi operations, the Consistoire became reconciled to the UGIF and its leadership, and this despite the personal quarrels and clash of personalities that had characterized relations between the two. The UGIF seems to have made no claim before Vichy to represent French Jews in any other but a purely "technical" sense—related to the management of Jewish social services. The UGIF never assumed the position of political preeminence among the Jews that Vichy and the Germans had originally intended. In this sense the identification of the UGIF as a *Judenrat* is inaccurate. The Consistoire, in turn, acknowledged the value of the UGIF's work to relieve the hardship of Jews who had lost practically everything. When the UGIF seemed on the verge of collapse in 1943, Helbronner

7. Haft, *Bargain and the Bridle*, p. 9.
8. Lambert, diary, November 30, 1941, March 29, 1942, August 20, 1943, *Carnet*, pp. 133, 163, 238. See Richard Cohen's portrait of Lambert in his introduction to ibid., and his "A Jewish Leader in Vichy France, 1940–1943: The Diary of Raymond-Raoul Lambert," *Jewish Social Studies* 43 (1981): 291–310.

himself urged its remnant: "You have to remain, to defend the unfortunate people who must be helped."[9]

It is worth adding that involvement with Vichy and the UGIF took considerable personal courage on the part of the Jewish leaders who undertook to do so. Although this may not have been fully evident immediately, when the organization was first established, it soon became clear. By early 1942 the SS was threatening to shoot Jewish hostages in reprisal for attacks on German troops. Jewish Communists had been executed in large numbers in the second half of 1941, and as the pool of these diminished, UGIF members were eminent candidates for such actions. André Baur, a prominent young banker who headed the UGIF in the Occupied Zone, came from a wealthy Jewish family with links both to the rabbinate and to Zionism; he would have had no trouble crossing the demarcation line to relative safety in the south, as Richard Cohen points out, but elected instead to take up his UGIF post in Paris.[10] In part, leaders drawn into UGIF service may have been flattered by high office and moved by a paternalistic sense of obligation to foreign Jews. But it would be wrong to depreciate their sense of responsibility. Lambert repeatedly stressed in his private diary the need to maintain the philanthropic services of the community, now possible only, he felt, under the UGIF. In his conception, UGIF work had to be limited strictly to such activity. On a personal level Lambert seems to have found relief from his own despair in his desperate efforts to provide services in camps, to shelter and feed the homeless. He reflected on how much better this was than to leave for New York—an escape he briefly contemplated. "Hold on and hold out" (*tenir et durer*), he wrote in December 1941, "remains my motto and my rule of action." "I act, and that's the important thing. Action fortifies me, fulfills me, consumes me, and I must take heavy responsibilities. . . . Long live life, and long live human activity!"[11] Albert Lévy, the titular head of the UGIF, finally broke ranks and fled to Switzerland at the end of 1942. During the next year both Lambert and Baur were arrested, taken to Drancy, and deported to Auschwitz. Jacques Helbronner, despite his links

9. Quoted in Yerachmiel (Richard) Cohen, "French Jewry's Dilemma on the Orientation of Its Leadership: From Polemics to Conciliation, 1942–1944," *Yad Vashem Studies* 14 (1981): 199.

10. Cohen, "Jewish Community," p. 187.

11. Lambert, diary, December 11, 1941, January 18, 1942, *Carnet*, pp. 135, 137, 147.

with Pétain, followed them to Poland within a short time. None survived.

The policy of "holding on and holding out" involved inevitable compromises and heartbreaking choices, unfortunately seen by some in retrospect as foolish or even criminal lapses of judgment. Despite ample ground for pessimism, the UGIF view was not entirely black. Behind this strategy lay a glimmer of light, kindled after the Wehrmacht's invasion of the Soviet Union began to stall. This was the hope that the Allies would soon turn the tide and that the liberation of France might find the bulk of the Jews still alive. Lambert hoped against hope that the end was not far off. "Victory is certain," he wrote when the UGIF was first established, "it is even possible in 1942." A year later, when the Americans went ashore in North Africa, he took heart once again. "This is truly the second front expected for the beginning of the winter. The Russian offensive at Stalingrad is going well. I truly believe it will all be over in the autumn of 1943." Six months later, following the Allied invasion of Sicily and the fall of Mussolini: "The Russian offensive is gigantic. . . . I believe that at Christmas we shall be in Paris."[12] This was August 1943. Bombs were by now raining on German cities—a new source of hope. Of course it was not to be. Two more entries, and Lambert's diary terminates abruptly with his arrest.

Were these assessments wishful thinking? Of course. But remember the conditions under which they were conceived. For a time Swiss newspapers were available in unoccupied France, and deductions from the reports they carried had at least an independent factual base. Thereafter, news had to be scraped together from the Nazi- or the Vichy-controlled media, from rumor, and from clandestine radio broadcasts from London. The latter certainly accented the positive; so also did the successes of Allied troops fighting in what was, after all, French territory in North Africa. Reinforcing the hopeful analysis was also the incorrigible patriotism of these French Jews, whose objectives were far indeed, needless to say, from the *attentists* or the men of Vichy. My own conclusion about their prognoses is cautious: they were wrong, but they had good reason for hoping they were right.

Fortified by whatever optimism they could muster, UGIF offi-

12. Ibid., December 28, 1941, March 29 and August 17, 1943, pp. 138, 196, 236.

cials—like their *Judenrat* counterparts in Eastern Europe—conducted desperate negotiations with their persecutors. Adler argues that the basic strategy of "official Judaism" was to protect native French Jews. Certainly occasional statements coming from consistorial circles or even representatives of the UGIF reflect a view that Jewish immigrants had compromised the future of French-born citizens of France. Writing to André Baur in early 1942, Grand Rabbi Paul Haguenauer, later to die in Auschwitz, objected to the Yiddish-language supplement to a UGIF bulletin: "I cannot help but say that all our troubles come from books, newspapers, and periodicals in this jargon, that our foreign co-religionists introduced into France since the armistice [of 1918]."[13] To us the appeals to patriotic service to France on the part of French-Jewish notables appear particularly apologetic in the light of the French police sweeps and the deportations to death camps in Poland. But let us recall that the Final Solution in France did not begin until two years after the French defeat. Apologetics and the occasional disparagement of foreign Jews were rooted in the preceding period and represented the first instincts of a Jewish elite flattened by the collapse of its familiar world.

Massive deportations began in the summer of 1942, from the Unoccupied as well as the Occupied Zone. At the start the victims were almost all foreigners, those whom some established French Jews had considered the real, intended victims and the fundamental cause of Vichy antisemitism. Throughout the deportations the German and French authorities did not oblige the UGIF, as the Nazis did the *Judenräte* of Eastern Europe, to furnish Jews to fill deportation quotas. That task fell to the French, who complied more or less willingly until the summer of 1944—dragging their feet occasionally, near the end, when it came to some native French Jews. UGIF leaders felt trapped and maintained their policy of bargaining for whatever crumbs they could get from Vichy and its bureaucracy. Examples abound. Having been apprised of the great roundup of foreign Jews in Paris intended for mid-July 1942, the northern council of the UGIF hesitated for two weeks without warning the Jewish population. Crucially, it wanted to maintain the confidence of the authorities in charge. Writing to Pétain a month after the Paris roundups, André Baur thanked the marshal for having obtained the exemption of French citizens and asked that French Jews who were in camps

13. Adler, *Face à la persécution*, chap. 4, p. 124.

("most of whom are war veterans and wounded, who were interned without having committed any infraction of the law") be liberated. He made no mention of the cruel fate of foreign Jews.[14] Similarly in the southern zone, Raymond-Raoul Lambert appealed repeatedly to secure exemptions—for the staff of the UGIF, for war veterans, or for those who held foreign entry visas.

One can see this policy as evading a central reality of the Final Solution—that sooner or later all Jews were targeted for murder and that the Nazis made no fundamental distinction between assimilated Western Jews and their co-religionists from Eastern Europe. This approach also reflects a continuing belief that Vichy might treat native Jews more lightly if only the case on their behalf could be sufficiently eloquently and insistently made. On this last point UGIF leaders were not entirely wrong, as their occasional if few successes showed. More important, perhaps, the effort to secure exemptions bespeaks a legalistic frame of mind that was utterly inappropriate during the Nazi Holocaust. After all, a Jew exempted was only temporarily exempted, and in any case another Jew had to be found to take his place. This failure to comprehend the real nature of the Nazis' intentions provides an additional explanation for the priority given to rescuing native French Jews.

But it should not be assumed that the fate of foreign Jews left the established Jewish leadership cold just because these men did not always press their case in their correspondence with Pétain or Pierre Laval. Lambert had been, after all, the head of the Comité d'Assistance aux Réfugiés d'Allemagne (Committee for the Relief of Refugees from Germany) since its establishment in 1936 and a widely recognized champion of Jewish refugees at the time of the Popular Front. Like many in France, he wanted some kind of "statut des étrangers" to relieve tensions caused by waves of refugees in France, but this did not necessarily mean he rejected French liberalism toward persecuted outsiders. His private diary indicates his outrage at the deportation of foreign Jews but suggests also that he felt genuinely powerless to prevent their dispatch to the East. Pleading constantly with police, prefectoral, and ministerial officials, sometimes literally as the trains took their victims away, Lambert grasped what could and could not be achieved in a practical, immediate sense. "Great joy this morning," he wrote in his diary in June

14. Quoted in ibid., p. 117; see also Haft, *Bargain and the Bridle*, p. 34.

1943. "I obtain eight liberations, on the guarantee of the UGIF, among them Henri Abraham, the physician, professor at the Sorbonne." And then he added: "To my credit."[15]

Such notions of success helped inspire what Robert Paxton, in another context, has called "the most corrupting of self-deceptions"— the idea that the leader was indispensable. Across Europe heads of *Judenräte* fell victim to this failing when they refused to crack under the great pressures they all faced. Prying loose favors from an implacable foe, these men riveted upon the bargaining process. Lives indeed hung on their every move. Their "achievements" were few, but all the more valued because they appeared to have been secured against tremendous odds. Meanwhile, of course, the machinery of destruction ground on all around them. To their colleagues, and to the Jews in whose name they claimed to speak, *Judenrat* chiefs increasingly seemed arrogant, single minded, and ruthless. From the leaders' vantage point, however, things looked different. Attacked from many quarters at once, increasingly isolated at the top, facing impossible demands, they felt they were the only hope for a squabbling, bitterly divided Jewish community. For Lambert, who certainly fits this pattern, the chief characteristic of his Jewish critics was their ingratitude. He referred often to these Jewish enemies, the "princes" of Judaism, beside whom Vichy and the Germans were at least predictable and frank. To the last he remained convinced that his few exemptions constituted a significant accomplishment, for which he deserved grateful recognition.[16]

The most cruel test of exemptions policy arose with respect to several hundred Jewish children, cared for under the auspices of the UGIF and thus temporarily sheltered from arrest and deportation. Sometimes parents confided children to the UGIF when they could no longer care for them or on the eve of their own deportations; sometimes the UGIF obtained custody of children liberated from the camps; and sometimes the children were simply taken in hand by the UGIF when their parents were arrested. Between July and November 1942, according to Adler, the UGIF placed more than a thousand Jewish children in private homes or shelters of various sorts.[17]

15. Lambert, diary, June 29, 1943, *Carnet*, p. 232.
16. Ibid., August 18, 1943, p. 237.
17. Adler, *Face à la persécution*, p. 113. On the fate of the children, see also Hillel J. Kieval, "Legality and Resistance in Vichy France: The Rescue of Jewish Children," *Proceedings of the American Philosophical Society* 124 (1980): 339–66; and Michael R. Marrus, "Vichy et les enfants juifs," *L'Histoire* 22 (April 1980): 6–15.

All of this was done with the authorization of Vichy or German officials, who eventually attempted to capture these helpless victims
and deport them to Auschwitz. Adler cites evidence to show how
concerned the official leadership was to preserve the Jewish identity
of the children, many of whom were boarded with non-Jewish families or institutions, and he suggests that this may well have limited
independent rescue work outside the circuits known to the SS or
Vichy police. In any event, the UGIF's scrupulous legalism and insistence on an official structure of placement put the children in grave
jeopardy when the French or the Germans were ready to strike.
Armed with addresses and lists carefully submitted by Jewish social
workers, the Gestapo could swoop down on homes or orphanages at
will. By 1944 some UGIF activists were deeply involved in clandestine activity, and they helped save many of the youngsters by spirit-
ing them away from previous UGIF custody. Georges Edinger, a co-
director of the UGIF in Paris, apparently refused to countenance a
massive escape of five hundred children in UGIF homes in July, with
the result that they were all caught by the SS.[18] By that summer the
official policy of the UGIF, now rejected by many of its operatives,
seems particularly obtuse.

For some, like Maurice Rajfus, this episode provides a fitting and
shameful epitaph for the "Juifs dans la collaboration." While not
seeking to absolve the UGIF of responsibility in every situation, however, we should not ignore the simultaneous existence of other trends
within the organization that finally became more active in the last
year of Nazi occupation. While some doggedly pursued the path of
Vichy legality, which had performed undoubted services for the Jews
in the preceding period, others burned their bridges with the past
and recognized the need for clandestine operations. Tragically, this
realization often came too late.

Richard Cohen alludes to the "dual existence" of this sphere of
Jewish leadership in 1943 and 1944, with some of its work legal,
known to Vichy, and some of it illegal, devoted to resistance or rescue. Here too, appears a phenomenon common to some of the *Judenräte* in Eastern Europe. I am not speaking of simply two different
trends and groups of individuals; some leaders simultaneously
maintained earlier strategies of legality while secretly trying to save
hunted Jews and working with the underground. Lambert himself

18. Adler, *Face à la persécution*, p. 154; Rajfus, *Juifs dans la collaboration*, pp. 256ff.

left some evidence of having done so. During 1943 he had frequent contact with Angelo Donati, an Italian Jew planning a mass evacuation of Jews from the Italian-occupied zone of France; Lambert named two important personalities in the Jewish resistance to UGIF posts, greatly enhancing their ability to move throughout France and coordinate underground activities.[19] One of them, Maurice Brener, was Lambert's cousin and confidant, to whom he wrote several coded letters on the eve of his deportation from Drancy. Richard Cohen found Lambert's wartime diary in Brener's possession, almost thirty years after the end of the war.

Jacques Adler contends that the posture of "official Judaism" prevented the emergence of an alternative Jewish leadership that might have achieved a more united Jewish response to Nazi and Vichy persecution.[20] His judgment derives from an acute sense of how established French Jews failed to provide wholehearted support for the foreign Jews in their hour of need. It is also based on an admiration for the work of the immigrant Jewish community, notably the array of welfare societies coordinated by the Comité Amelot in the Occupied Zone, which met during the occupation on the Paris street by that name. Clearly, in the world of immigrant Jews one breathes a different air than that of "les Juifs français de vieille souche." As outsiders, immigrant Jews were less entranced by the liberal heritage of France and less subject to illusions about French beneficence. Psychologically better prepared for their ordeal, they strove to unify Jewish responses. Many became involved in the Jewish resistance movement. Yet it also seems to me that such activity was made possible partly by the cover and indirect help provided by the established organs of French Jewry. I want to suggest that the much-maligned official Judaism performed important services for the Jewish opposition that emerged during the war.

In financial matters, the UGIF provided a funnel through which several hundred million francs reached Jewish groups from the Joint Distribution Committee, based in New York. UGIF officials managed to transfer funds to the northern zone, despite the Gestapo's and Vichy's knowledge of this illicit action. While none of this aid reached Jewish Communist groups—held at arm's length by estab-

19. Cohen, introd. to Lambert, *Carnet*, pp. 51–52.
20. Adler, *Face à la persécution*, p. 156.

lished Jewry because of their revolutionary politics—it certainly fueled other clandestine operations and rescue activity by immigrant organizations.[21] More generally, it may be argued that various kinds of Jewish assistance agencies could exist openly only because the UGIF structures satisfied the Nazis and Vichy that they had the Jews in hand. An interesting case was the Jewish Boy Scout movement, the Eclaireurs Israélites de France, which Vichy permitted to operate within the framework of the UGIF until the beginning of 1943. Robert Gamzon, founder of the movement and its leading figure throughout the war, was a member of the UGIF council from the beginning.[22] In another example, the southern zone UGIF provided cover for the Oeuvre de Secours aux Enfants (OSE), a child-rescue organization increasingly involved in underground operations during the latter part of 1942.

The Jewish Communists followed their own path, providing an important qualification to what has just been said. As in the general sphere of resistance, the Communists were the earliest in the field, mounted the most extensive attacks on the Nazi-Vichy system, and suffered the most for their efforts. In the Jewish and in the non-Jewish sphere, they were the "parti des fusillés." Drawing upon an immigrant, working-class community, Jewish Communists were the only ones in the immediate postdefeat period, according to Adler, to grasp the predicament of the Jews under Vichy, though couched in their own, Moscow-produced terminology—"that fascism was the enemy of the Jewish people; that Nazism was the worst form of fascism; that Vichy, an antidemocratic regime, would inevitably persist in its hostility toward the Jews."[23] Their Paris-based organization, known as Solidarité, linked the internments of Jews and other anti-Jewish moves in the Occupied Zone with Vichy policy in the south. Following the attack on the Soviet Union in June 1941 the Communists moved into active resistance, while at the same time championing a collective Jewish response to persecution. Specifically Jewish units were formed, Jewish internments became a focal point for agitation and self-help, and wider Jewish political activity was en-

21. Ibid., pp. 134–36, 151.
22. Lambert, diary, December 28, 1941, *Carnet*, pp. 139–40. See also Robert Gamzon's posthumous *Les Eaux claires: Journal, 1940–1944* (Paris, 1980), for another account of his involvement.
23. Adler, *Face à la persécution*, p. 166.

couraged in the shape of the Communist-sponsored Union des Juifs pour la Résistance et l'Entraide (UJRE). From August 1942, according to Adler, the time of massive roundups in unoccupied France, there was an ever-greater accent on specifically Jewish issues and an affirmation of a Jewish national consciousness.[24] Engaged in sabotage, attacks on German personnel, material aid to immigrant Jews, as well as strong denunciations of the UGIF, the Jewish Communist resistance was decimated by the SS and French police during 1943.

Yet despite this heroic struggle, we can question how much the Jewish Communists offered persecuted Jews as a whole in France. The starting point of the movement was Jewish identification with the cause of the Soviet Union, engaged in its titanic struggle against the Hitlerian Reich. For the Communists, Russia was the principal champion of oppressed peoples, and its interests ultimately determined resistance strategy. Therefore Jewish Communists made few direct assaults on the Nazis' anti-Jewish machinery: they blew up no deportation trains, assassinated no SS Jewish affairs specialists, and left it to others to liberate the camp of Drancy, the Parisian antechamber to Auschwitz. Moreover, the party's immigrant organization—the Main-d'Oeuvre Immigré (MOI)—refused to consider Solidarité or the UJRE as specifically Jewish bodies, disowning the line taken by immigrant activists and leaving them even more vulnerable to the Gestapo than they might otherwise have been.[25]

Other Jewish resistance groups drew upon prewar secular Jewish ideologies—mainly Bundism and Zionism—to form networks less powerful than those of the Communists but more closely attuned to Jewish needs in the latter part of the occupation period. Their desperate and dangerous efforts span the full range of underground activity, from independent fighting units, such as the Armée juive, which later became the Organisation Juive de Combat, to rescue activities like those of the Oeuvre de Secours aux Enfants. Renée Poznanski points out that for Jews the antisemitic measures of 1940–41, and then the deportations of the following year, had the same impact as the imposition of forced labor for work in the Reich had in February 1943 for the French community as a whole: they placed Jews before immediate problems, prompting many to go underground

24. Ibid., p. 201; Poznanski, "La résistance juive," p. 19.
25. Adler, *Face à la persécution*, pp. 203–4.

and begin resistance. In general, Jews were drawn into resistance earlier and in significantly greater proportions than the general population.[26]

Tragically, however, even the most clear-sighted resistance leaders had no answers for most Jews caught in the maelstrom of 1940–44. For the young, for those without family responsibilities, armed combat provided a means for Jewish affirmation in the last months of Nazi presence in France; for others, the rescue of Jewish children, the manufacture of false identity papers, and the secret passage of the frontiers into Spain or Switzerland were realistic possibilities. For most Jews, however, little could be done without assistance from the French population, the willingness of Vichy authorities or police to look aside, and extraordinary good luck. The principal political achievement of the Jewish resistance, indeed, looked more toward the postwar period than the last phase of deportations.

From the autumn of 1943 the various Jewish organizations began to move toward a clandestine national Jewish body known as the Conseil Représentatif des Juifs de France (CRIF). The latter brought together representatives from the UGIF as well as immigrant Jews, establishment figures, and Communists. Its first head was Léon Meiss, interim president of the Consistoire Central after the arrest of Jacques Helbronner in October 1943. Feeling against the UGIF ran high within this body, but no decision about it was taken before the end of the war. Until then the UGIF was accepted by this underground agency as a constituent part of French Jewry.

The CRIF was an extraordinary breakthrough, bringing together many divergent communities. It won a Jewish presence in Charles de Gaulle's Conseil National de la Résistance and the provisional government that followed and provided a forum for postwar Jewish claims on the French national scene.

26. Poznanski, "La résistance juive," pp. 7, 9. For additional material on the Jewish resistance, see Annie Latour, *La Résistance juive en France, 1940–1944* (Paris, 1970); David Diamant, *Les Juifs dans la résistance française, 1940–1944* (Paris, 1971); David Knout, *Contribution à l'histoire de la résistance juive en France, 1940–1944* (Paris, 1947); Joseph Ariel (b. Fisher), "Jewish Self-Defense and Resistance in France during World War II," *Yad Vashem Studies* 6 (1967): 221–50; Annie Kriegel, "Résistants communistes et Juifs persecutés," *L'Histoire* 3 (November 1970): 99–123; Lucien Steinberg, *La Révolte des justes: Les Juifs contre Hitler* (Paris, 1970); Abraham Rayski, "La Fondation du Conseil Représentatif des Juifs de France," *Le Monde juif,* n.s., no. 51 (July-September 1968): 32–37; and Asher Cohen, "La presse clandestine face à la 'question juive' de 1940 à 1942: Une etude de l'opinion publique," ibid., n.s., no. 117 (January-March 1985): 1–17.

There may be a masochistic strain in recent Jewish historiography that judges the established Jewish leadership during the Holocaust as particularly manipulative or short sighted. To the general historian of Europe like myself, however, who surveys this period across a wasteland of appeasement and an inability to understand the Nazis, the Jewish actors in this drama of an entire civilization seem no more blind or weak willed than any of the rest. Indeed their record is not unworthy, taken as a whole. The Jews' relative powerlessness before the murderous antisemitism of the Nazi era was a bitter reality to be faced and remains a bitter pill for some to swallow even now. But blaming Jews for this condition, then as now, does not assist understanding, and sometimes serves nefarious political purposes.

Jewish leaders such as I have discussed here faced agonizing choices—to intervene with oppressors or not to intervene, to use resources at hand or not to use them, to attempt temporary relief or to risk all for open, direct resistance. With the help of careful historical work, we are increasingly able to understand why groups and individuals adopted the positions they did. We may choose to admire some and not others. But let us grant them all some benefit of historical doubt: Who knows, in their place, what we might have done?

Anita Shapira

Did the Zionist Leadership
Foresee the Holocaust?

Historical research on the Holocaust is susceptible to more than the ordinary number of pitfalls that lurk in wait for a historian on his tedious route to catch the meaning and feeling of a certain period. Loaded with emotions and arousing deep involvement, it became more often than not a scourge with which Jews tended to chastise one another. The collective sense of guilt, shared by all Ashkenazi Jews who had survived the war, brought about an incessant search for where to place the blame for the pitifully minuscule rescue efforts. During this still ongoing exchange of accusations, words and sentences were taken out of their historical context and endowed with a new meaning, the result of a hindsight acquired in the light of subsequent events.

The Zionist leadership was more vulnerable to these accusations than any other Jewish group. Aspiring to represent the national will and vitality as well as proclaiming itself as the leadership of the whole Jewish people, it had virtually volunteered to carry the burden of the Jewish fate. Thus it was counted on to be capable of doing what other groups and organizations were unable to do, and it became the victim of the very expectations it had aroused. Part of the misconception of Zionist competency stemmed from the Zionist claim to prescience of the impending catastrophe. I propose to look at the sources of this claim and to examine its actual meaning in the light of Zionist policies and plans on the eve of the Second World War.

Zionism was one of the responses to the crisis that emanated from the encounter of the Jews with the threat to their very existence posed by the increasingly violent expressions of Jew-hatred since the pogroms of 1881. This date marks the beginning of the emergency period in Jewish history, which was to continue until after the resettlement of the Holocaust survivors and the establishment of Israel. This feeling of urgency, which to a certain degree had accompanied Jews since the dispersion, became more acute as we draw near to the twentieth century. Though stemming from different origins and using different methods and expressions, the message implied both by the governments in Eastern European states and by the modern political antisemitic movements in Central and Western Europe was essentially the same: the Jews were undesired elements that the antisemites would like to be rid of. More than any persecution and discrimination, it was that nagging feeling of physical insecurity that shaped the Jewish outlook and *Weltanschauung*. Insecurity was the driving force that caused Jews to leave home and hearth and to look for a new haven on the one hand, and to create a Jewish state on the other.

Since the appearance of Theodor Herzl, this vague feeling of personal insecurity was adopted as a basis of the Zionist prediction about the destiny of European Jewry. Some historians tend to minimize Herzl's contribution to Zionist ideology *vis-à-vis* his undisputably singular contribution to the molding of the Zionist movement. I think that they are mistaken, however. Herzl was one of the first thinkers to point out the dynamics of modern antisemitism. He described it as the result of neither church incitement nor Jewish strangeness and isolation but rather as emanating from the modern process of emancipation and assimilation. Modern antisemitism was discerned as the natural offspring of the progress of European society—democratization and the growing involvement of the masses in public life. Jews were hated now not because they kept apart but, on the contrary, because their acculturation was so successful as to turn them into a threat to the emerging non-Jewish lower middle classes, who feared these talented competitors. Thus Herzl outlined a process, built into the mainstream of European modernization, that inevitably linked progress to antisemitism. The conclusions he drew from his analysis were that, irrespective of the good or ill will of rulers, a terrible disaster was inevitable.[1]

This assessment was the first stage in the emergence of Catastro-

---

1. See, for example, Theodor Herzl to the family council of the Rothchilds, June 13, 1896, *The Complete Diaries of Theodor Herzl*, ed. Raphael Patai, trans. Harry Zohn (New York, 1960), pp. 130–32.

phe-Zionism. According to this perception, if the Jews wanted to avoid disaster they had to embark on a completely different path, clearly divorced from age-old Jewish patterns, by establishing their own polity.

The second stage of Catastrophe-Zionism was formulated during the first decade of the twentieth century. While Herzl's vision evolved from the conditions prevalent in Central and Western Europe, the new outlook owed its inception to the social and political climate in Russia at the turn of the century as well as to the specific Jewish malaise there. Heavily influenced by revolutionary currents in Russia, this version of Catastrophe-Zionism tended to emphasize the social and economic trends that would inevitably lead to the destruction of Jewish society. Adapting to the Jewish scene the famous Marxist prognosis about the inevitable polarization of society, young Jewish socialists assumed that unless the Jewish people underwent a revolutionary change they were doomed to be annihilated in the imminent cataclysmic struggle. The Jews belonged mostly to the lower middle classes, which were bound to become extinct as a result of the polarization. The only way in which they could avoid being crushed by the triumphant march of history would be by joining the ranks of the proletariat, that class which by definition was certain to be acclaimed as victor in the ensuing conflict. The polarization, however, which was surely causing even greater pauperization and misery to the Jewish masses than to others, failed to result in the expected proletarization. The reasons this process remained incomplete were complicated, explained the Jewish socialists, but they all seemed to stem from the deep-rooted animosity of the non-Jewish population. Non-Jewish employers preferred to employ non-Jews. Jewish industry was too small and insignificant to provide badly needed jobs for the impoverished Jewish masses. Instead of joining history's march, Jews were being cast to the margins, finding no hope or solace even in the future victory of socialism. Thus, although the socialist analysis was rooted in an outlook and reality completely different from Herzl's a decade earlier, the conclusion was essentially the same. Jewish frameworks and ways of life could no longer sustain the Jewish people. Modern conditions were posing a threat to the survival of the Jews. This was essentially an existential threat.

Life in the Pale of Settlement seemed to supply endless examples to prove the validity of this perception. The combined effects of popular hostility, anti-Jewish riots, and legal discrimination in all the fields that might lead to social mobility were widespread pauperization with no visible hope of change. Thus emerged the well-known Zionist theory of the Negation of Exile. Its first and foremost meaning was that the Jewish people in Europe had no chance of survival. The conclusion was Zionistic: that is, only in a land of their own could the Jewish people experience the necessary processes of regeneration. This stage in Zionist ideology is not part of this discussion, but the vision of Damocles' sword posing an ever-present existential threat actually seems to point to a prescience of the future catastrophe. This vision was to return in the teaching of leading labor leaders, such as Yitzhak Tabenkin, for whom it became not only a tenet of faith but also the inspiration for a widespread educational program, centered on the Halutz movement, intended to hasten as much as possible the rescue of Jewish youth and the upbuilding of Palestine. The imminent catastrophe became, as a matter of fact, a cornerstone in the teaching of all the Zionist youth movements, from Betar on the Right to Hashomer Hazair on the Left. Naturally enough, the more a movement was Palestine oriented, the more it emphasized the impending disaster. The deteriorating state of affairs of Polish Jewry during the 1930s added credibility to this perception and lent force to the demands for increasing the pace of building up Palestine and enlarging the *aliyah* quotas.

The strongest premonitions of doom were, as usual, presented by writers and poets. J. H. Brenner drew a picture of a hopelessly decaying society, and while his heart drove him to Palestine, his logic did not let him enjoy the pleasures of wishful thinking. Like most of the Second Aliyah leaders, he was not certain if the Jewish people could muster the vitality necessary for such an ambitious project. The same sort of insight can be found in the works of U. Z. Greenberg.

Do these manifestations necessarily mean that the Zionists had a foresight of the Holocaust denied to other Jewish theorists? I will try now to examine this point by analyzing their attitudes to a specific issue that caused, at the time, a great controversy. As a part of this controversy, all Zionist leaders made an effort to express their views of the past, the present, and the future of the Jews. The issue was the partition proposal sponsored by the Peel Commission. Formed by the British government in the autumn of 1936 in the wake of the Arab Rebellion that had raged since April of that year, the commission presented the Zionists with the dilemma of accepting half a loaf or gambling on a whole one. It proposed to establish two independent states in Palestine—one Jewish and one Arab. As is well known, the whole question soon became theoretical, as the British eventually retreated from their proposal and instead of establishing the two states, issued the White Paper of 1939, which was disastrous from the Jewish point of view. The ensuing disputes give us, however, an opportunity to observe whether the Zionists, when faced with a momentous decision, were affected by their often-stated fear of the coming catastrophe. In order to decide this point, I propose to review their assessment of the probability of a world war; the spans of time they projected; the place that the fate of European Jewry occupied in their considerations as a whole; and finally, what sort of disaster if any, they envisioned.

As far as I can verify, the first reference by a Zionist to the probability of the outbreak of a new European war was made by Chaim Arlosoroff, then head of the Political Department of the Jewish Agency for Palestine, in his famous letter to Chaim Weizmann of June 30, 1932. The letter, a masterpiece of political acumen, alluded to the rearmament race and the increasing tension in Europe and concluded that one could safely assume a war would break out within the next five or ten years. Arlosoroff went on to analyze the implications of this prediction for the Zionist enterprise. He foresaw the eventuality of a British-Arab alliance, which would be highly detrimental to the Jewish community in Palestine. He worried about the frustratingly slow pace of the upbuilding of the country and pointed out that, if the disastrous economic conditions in Eastern Europe continued and Palestine was unable to offer immediate relief, the Jews might despair of Zionism and seek other alternatives to alleviate their suffering. The time span he referred to in this context was about twenty years. How did he reconcile the incongruity between his vision of an imminent war and his long-range prediction that the Jewish masses would grow tired of waiting for the Zionist dream to materialize? It seems that Arlosoroff did not consider the coming war as a major event, not to mention a watershed, in the history of European Jewry. Taking for granted the continuation of Jewish life in Europe, the next war notwithstanding, he worried only about the Zionist position in Palestine.[2]

2. Chaim Arlosoroff to Chaim Weizmann, June 30, 1932, *Yoman Yerushalayim*, published by Mapai (n.p., n.d.), pp. 338–42.

The following five years saw the Nazis rise to power in Germany and the isolation of the Jews and their exclusion from German society, the outbreak of the war in Manchuria, the occupation of Ethiopia by Italy, and the reentry of the German army into the Rhineland. A civil war was going on in Spain, and the independence of Austria was tottering. In Poland the military junta that had ruled the country since the death of Józef Piłsudski responded to the ugly mood of Polish public opinion and launched an increasingly antisemitic policy. This was the European background against which the Twentieth Zionist Congress convened in Basel to decide whether to adopt or reject partition.

The debate encompassed a great variety of questions, such as: Can a Zionist reconcile his ideology with the partition of Zion? Is partition an *ad hoc* solution, or does the establishment of the state entail an end to Zionist aspirations for the whole country? How is partition going to affect relations with the Arabs? What are Zionist priorities? Should the establishment of a viable Jewish entity precede the establishment of a state, or should the state become the agent of change? Would a state serve as a vehicle for large-scale immigration, or would it be better to decline the offer, continue the slow-but-steady buildup in the country, and wait for better times, assuming that the proposed miniature state would have no chance of survival, to say nothing of absorbing millions of Jews?[3]

The problem that was never discussed, but was implied by many delegates, was the question of time. Was the time factor working in favor of the Zionists or against them? Those who believed that time needed to be gained prepared to postpone the decision on the constitutional change in Palestine. Others believed that time was either running out or had a negative bearing on Zionist interests. They were ready, though mostly with reservations, to accept the partition plan as the lesser of two evils, believing the alternative would be a freeze on the future growth of the national home. The previous years,

3. An abundance of material exists on this subject. The various positions expressed in both open and closed sessions are repeated almost endlessly in newspapers and archival documents. The main sources used in preparing this essay were the relevant minutes of the Mapai Central Committee, the Mapai Council, the Smaller and Greater Actions Committees for 1937–38, and the council meeting of the Labor World Alliance (Ihud), which were published in full in *Al darkei mediniyutenu: Moazah olamit shel ihud Poalei Zion, 29 July–7 August 1937* (Tel Aviv, 1938). Other sources include *Ha-kongres ha-zioni ha-esrim* (n.p., n.d.), the writings and speeches of Vladimir Jabotinsky, and the memoirs of David Ben-Gurion. The primary sources are all in Hebrew; translations throughout the text are mine.

1933–35, had been marked by mass immigration, large-scale investments, and an economic boom. The general feeling was that, given a few more years like 1935, the longed-for Jewish majority in Palestine would materialize and make all sorts of compromises unnecessary. Thus the question of predicting the outline of the next few years became crucial. The pessimistic view, which envisioned a British-initiated freeze on immigration and settlement as the alternative to partition, was motivated primarily by the development of the Arab national movement. The optimistic view tended to minimize its importance. In both cases the context was first and foremost a Palestinian one, and the fact that time was running out in Europe was only marginally mentioned in the whole long and penetrating debate.[4]

Those who browse through the newspapers of 1937 and 1938 might naturally assume that people at the time were aware of the increasing tension and eve-of-war atmosphere in Europe. This we understand in retrospect, however; the Zionist leadership then still perceived war as farfetched. The possibility of a world war does appear among the arguments advanced by both supporters and opponents of partition. Tabenkin presented partition as a British strategy in view of the possibility of war, a strategy that involved discarding its commitments to the Jews and creating two vassal states—one Jewish and one Arab.[5] Among the supporters of partition, David Ben-Gurion, in just one of his many speeches, hinted at the deteriorating international situation, the danger of a new world war, and the international complications that could be expected to follow in its wake.[6] All in all, however, references to the expected world war were few and superficial, and when the prospect of war was mentioned, it was in the context of the fate of Palestine rather than the fate of European Jewry. It seems that Alfred Mond, first Lord Melchett was right when he observed:

> To my astonishment several speeches dealt with the Jewish Problem, as though the question of the Jews exists in a vacuum. . . . We have to study the Jewish Problem in the context of the Spanish Civil War; we should be alert to the undertakings made by England toward Italy and to

4. The pessimistic view in this matter was represented by Ben-Gurion. See the minutes of the Greater Actions Committee, April 22, 1937, Central Zionist Archives, Jerusalem (hereafter CZA), S5/2141. The optimistic view was represented by Yitzhak Tabenkin. See the minutes of the Mapai Council, July 1932, Labor Party Archives, Beit Berl (hereafter BB), 22/12.

5. Tabenkin, in *Al darkei mediniyutenu*, p. 194.

6. Ben-Gurion, in *Ha-kongres ha-zioni ha-esrim*, p. 106.

the dangerous situation in Germany and the defense position of its neighbors.[7]

No comment was made on his remarks.

Reactions were not essentially different outside the World Zionist Organization. Shalom Ash, in an emotional speech before the Jewish Agency Council, spoke of the anxiety shared by many in face of the approaching world war and in the same breath added that, as a result, no plans could be made for more than the next ten to fifteen years.[8] One of the fiercest critics of Zionist policies was Vladimir Jabotinsky, the leader of the Revisionist movement, who in 1935 had quit the World Zionist Organization and had set up the New Zionist Organization. Jabotinsky's political power base was in Poland. However, as late as the summer of 1939, he still would not believe that a world war was about to erupt. Neither, a year earlier, had he foreseen the appeasement policy of the British government. Welcoming the representatives of the Czechoslovakian government to the convention of the New Zionist Organization in 1938, which took place in Prague, he greeted them and the other delegates by declaring, "The great nation that occupies all our thoughts at this time will desert neither you nor us in our hour of need: her word is as firm as a rock and she will keep it."[9]

The only person to mention a time span of less than ten years was Meir Grabovsky, who said, "It might, perhaps, happen that the next five years will be more crucial than the entire generation."[10] In an early session of the Mapai Central Committee he recalled the slaughter that had taken place in the Ukraine during the First World War, and, in the context of the expected war in Europe, he went on to add: "In the light of the spread of antisemitism in Europe, I cannot estimate the future scale of the slaughter which awaits the Jews."[11] These were isolated, chance comments, however, with no follow-up. The threat of war loomed large in newspaper headlines and radio broadcasts. A big rearmament plan debated in Britain was exten-

7. Lord Melchett, in ibid., p. 168.
8. Shalom Ash, in ibid., app. M.
9. Jabotinsky, "Mool tokhnit ha-halukah: Tokhnit ha-asor," speech to the convention of the New Zionist Organization, Prague, February 1938, in his *Neumim: 1927–1940* (Jerusalem, 1948), p. 292.
10. Meir Grabovsky, in *On Our Policy-Making*, p. 130.
11. Grabovsky, in the minutes of the Mapai Central Committee, April 15, 1937, BB, 23/37.

sively reported in the press. Yet there is no evidence to show that the Zionists were really aware that Europe was teetering on the brink of a crisis. On the occasions when they did foresee a crisis, they related it to the Palestinian situation. An extreme example of this focus can be found in the position taken by Yitzhak Gruenbaum, the former leader of Polish Jewry, who was an enthusiastic supporter of partition precisely because he foresaw a world war on the horizon. Even he did not seem to reflect on its implications for his brethren in Poland, however. His only concern was how best to prepare for this eventuality in terms of the Jewish community in Palestine.[12]

Both those for and those against partition made much of the question of *aliyah*. Chaim Weizmann presented the Congress with a plan for the immigration of one hundred thousand Jews per year over the next twenty years. These two million, who were to include the vast majority of the younger generation of European Jewry, would, according to Weizmann, change the face of Palestine.[13] Ben-Gurion referred to similar numbers—the immigration of one hundred thousand Jews per year over a period of fifteen years. This mass immigration, he stated, would open the way for a change in the political situation in Palestine at the end of those fifteen years.[14] Both refer, first and foremost, to the effect of immigration on the political situation in Palestine, and not to its effect on the situation of the Jews in Europe. The figure they mention—one hundred thousand immigrants a year over ten to fifteen years—appear repeatedly in speeches made by both supporters and opponents of partition, and it seems to have been universally accepted. There were those who questioned whether this plan was realistic and argued that the British would not agree to such large-scale immigration to a small and weak state. Others raised the question of what would happen once those fifteen years were up and the small, partitioned state was unable to absorb further immigration, while Jews continued to beat at its gates.[15] The opponents of partition did not disagree with the argument of the supporters that the immediate absorption capacity of a Jewish state would be greater than that of the national home. The

12. Yitzhak Gruenbaum, in the minutes of the Greater Actions Committee, April 22, 1937, CZA, S5/2141.
13. Chaim Weizmann, in *Ha-kongres ha-zioni ha-esrim*, pp. 70–71, 33.
14. Ben-Gurion, in *Al darkei mediniyutenu*, pp. 76, 77.
15. See, for instance, Golda Meirson, in ibid., pp. 122–23.

argument revolved on the question of whether the limited capacity of a tiny state would be sufficient in the long run to absorb millions of Jews, and thus provide a substantial solution to Jewish needs.[16]

Jabotinsky bitterly attacked the partition plan, which he saw as constituting a death sentence for Zionism. He rejected outright the idea that the partitioned state would be a sort of Jewish Piedmont, a bridgehead for expansion over the whole country. He protested against the willingness, expressed at the Zionist Congress, to relinquish most of Palestine. In his opinion this meant "the relinquishment of the territory necessary to save six to eight million Jews without a homeland."[17] At a mass meeting in Warsaw he referred to Weizmann's plan for the immigration of two million young people within twenty years as designed to save only a vestige of the people—only a chosen few—while the remainder would be left to its fate.[18] This passage is often quoted as testimony of both Jabotinsky's prescience and his sensitivity to the fate of the Jews.

As an alternative to Weizmann's plan, Jabotinsky presented his own plan: "Within ten years an additional million Jews should be settled west of the Jordan, thereby ensuring a large Jewish majority in this part of Palestine. At the same time half a million Jews should settle on the other side of the Jordan."[19] Without going into the question of whether Weizmann's plan or Jabotinsky's had the better chance of succeeding, I would like to draw attention to the similarities between them. Both envisioned the scale of immigration at one hundred thousand a year. Both foresaw rapid development rather than revolutionary change. Neither showed a deep concern about the future of the Jewish people in the course of the coming decade. Neither really foresaw the Holocaust.

The partition controversy called attention to the fact that Palestine could not offer an immediate solution for the needs of the millions of distressed Jews in Europe. According to the most optimistic estimates, only two or three million would be absorbed in Palestine in the course of the next two to three decades, whether in a parti-

---

16. See, for example, Dr. Yitzhak Schwartzbart, in *Ha-kongres ha-zioni ha-esrim,* pp. 58–59.

17. Jabotinsky, "Neged tokhnit ha-halukah," a speech to the members of Parliament, July 13, 1937, and "Mool tokhit ha-halukah," *Neumin,* pp. 279, 297, 298, 314.

18. In his speech in Warsaw in 1936, Jabotinsky spoke about giving priority to immigrants aged twenty-three to twenty-seven, a policy similar to that advanced by Weizmann. "Polin taazor ve-teazer ba-tokhnit ha-evakuazyah," ibid., p. 219.

19. Jabotinsky, "Mool tokhnit ha-halukah," pp. 297, 299.

tioned or a whole and undivided Palestine. It is true that the advantages and disadvantages of an independent, though small, state as a vehicle for furthering mass immigration were mentioned. However, mass immigration was presented first and foremost as ensuring the growth and development of the Jewish stronghold in Palestine. Very few involved in the debate presented the needs of European Jewry as grounds for large-scale immediate immigration. Furthermore, in general, even those few who referred to the situation in Europe preferred to do so in relation to its effects on Zionist fortunes. The fear of a wave of territorialism or Bundism, which would follow a loss of faith in Zionism on the part of the Jewish masses, recurred as an argument for partition.[20]

The year was 1937, and although it appeared that the situation of German Jewry had stabilized to the point of continued existence within the well-defined limitations of the Nuremberg Laws, the same year saw a significant deterioration in the condition of Polish Jewry. Pshitik, Brisk, Czestochowa—the names of towns in which pogroms were carried out against Jews—and then reports of the trials of those Jews who had defended themselves against the rioters appeared frequently in the newspapers. The restrictions of Jews to ghetto benches in the universities, their expulsion from campuses, and the murder of Jews in railway cars had become a daily reality that was reported in the Palestine press. Yitzhak Yatziv, a correspondent for the newspaper *Davar*, traveled throughout Poland that summer, and his reports described in detail the acts of brutality and economic dispossession carried out against Polish Jews. In the light of this oppression in Poland, it is surprising how little the situation of the Jews in Europe was mentioned in the partition discussions.

Naturally the representatives of Polish Jewry were more concerned about their desperate situation. They were also aware of the enthusiasm with which the common people in Poland had greeted the partition plan. However, it appears that they, too, like all the others, were divided as to their assessment of the time and impending catastrophe. Moshe Kleinbaum (Sneh) was the most outspoken and unequivocal spokesman of those who raised the problem of Polish Jewry in support of the immediate adoption of the partition plan.

20. See, for example, Eliyahu Golomb, in the minutes of the Mapai Central Committee, August 29, 1937, BB 23/37; Gruenbaum, in the minutes of the Smaller Actions Committee, January 11, 1938, CZA, S5/307; and Eliyahu Dobkin, in *Al darkei medini-yutenu*, p. 161.

The Jews of Poland and of Eastern Europe, he said, now found themselves in an insupportable position: "The question of immigration is a burning matter of life and death [*Noytfrage*] for Polish Jewry, and must be resolved positively."[21] This, in his opinion, was the supreme criterion by which any political proposal should be judged. The uniqueness of Kleinbaum's position lay in the fact that it saw the partition plan from the viewpoint of the immediate interests of Polish Jewry rather than from that of the long- or short-term interests of either Zionism or the Jewish community in Palestine, the perspectives of most of his colleagues. Kleinbaum's stand was bitterly attacked by Yitzhak Schwartzbart, the Polish-Jewish leader of the General Zionist Alliance. Schwartzbart hotly denied the assumption, which could be read into the words of Kleinbaum and others, that Polish Jewry would be prepared to accept any territorial concession in Palestine as long as they received the right to immigrate, and that if immigration should be halted for any period of time they would begin looking for alternative solutions. He even went as far as to term this assumption "a libel against Polish Jewry." Schwartzbart was not the only Polish Zionist leader to hold this position. Heschel Farbstein of the Polish Mizrahi also protested Kleinbaum's demand that the partition plan be adopted in light of the desperation of Polish Jewry: "The Jews of Poland themselves will protest against this forcefully. They will see it as an insult to their feelings, if Zionist policy is based on pity."[22]

The press was filled with reports of the enthusiasm that gripped the masses of Polish Jews upon learning of the proposal for partition. The editor of the newspaper *Haynt* expressed his reservations over partition—according to the tactic dictated by the Zionist executive. He was assaulted by a poor porter, "We've had enough of *Tisha be-Av*," cried the porter. "Give me a bit of *Simhat Torah*."[23]

One Zionist who had quit the Revisionist party declared a march to Palestine, and he was soon joined by a thousand young men. On the other hand, a Revisionist demonstration against the partition plan succeeded in attracting only a few hundred demonstrators.[24]

21. Moshe Kleinbaum, in the minutes of the Greater Actions Committee, April 22, 1937, CZA, S5/2141.

22. Yitzhak Schwartzbart and Heschel Farbstein, in *Ha-kongres ha-zioni ha-esrim*, p. 82.

23. Quoted by Jacob Helmann, in *Al darkei mediniyutenu*, p. 102.

24. Ibid.

The enthusiasm of Polish Jewry for the plan altered the opinion of at least one delegate. Eliahu Dobkin said that his visit to five European countries had persuaded him that "it is impossible to feed the Diaspora with no more than hopes of a great Zionist enterprise in the future."[25] Others, however, exhibiting more than a trace of superiority, declined to take the opinions of the ignorant and suggestible masses into consideration. "For decades we have been fighting with the masses, some of whom were apathetic toward our aspirations and some of whom opposed them outright; so why should we now turn them into our guides?"[26] At their most generous they argued that "what is permissible to a desperate Jew lacking any possibility of fending for himself is absolutely impermissible to a serious political movement such as ours."[27]

Those isolated individuals who brought forward the condition of Polish Jewry as evidence in support of the partition plan painted a grim picture of a world hostile to the Jews. But there were also those who, paradoxically, found hope in that unhappy situation. After all, Jewish misery had always acted as a stimulus to the Zionist enterprise. "I do not maintain that 'the eternity of Israel will not fail,'" exclaimed Meir Kotick, "but rather that 'the troubles of Israel will not fail.' Under the pressure of the afflictions of the Jewish masses, we will overcome any difficulty, including those bound up with the implementation of the mandate."[28]

This fundamentally optimistic outlook, which can be traced back to Herzl's notion that an antisemitic but otherwise enlightened world would adopt a positive solution of the Jewish Problem, was also to be found in Jabotinsky's thinking. His confidence, as late as 1938, that England would eventually make good its vow[29] and his belief in the negotiations he was conducting with the Polish government over a plan for the gradual and orderly evacuation of Polish Jewry from the country were based upon his deep-rooted faith in European culture and humanity. This approach found its expression on the leftist side of the Zionist camp in the words of Mendel Singer:

25. Eliyahu Dobkin, in ibid., p. 161.
26. Mendel Singer, in ibid., p. 143. A protest of attitude toward Polish Jewry was voiced by Kleinbaum and Henryk Rosmarin, in *Ha-kongres ha-zioni ha-esrim*, pp. 144–54.
27. Josef Bankover, in *Al darkei mediniyutenu*, p. 153.
28. Meir Kotick, in ibid.
29. Jabotinsky, "Lamut o likhbosh et ha-har," *Neumin*, p. 325.

"I see serious danger in describing our situation in the world as though everybody and everything are against us."[30] This statement was made after Singer had returned from extensive travels throughout Poland, which he reported in a series of shocking articles in *Davar*.

What characterizes these positions is the lack of urgency. The Zionists foresaw a crisis that had to be acted upon within the next few decades; they described an emergency but not something inescapable and immediate. This feeling that time was running out, and yet not really, that although time was exerting pressure it did not necessitate an immediate reaction at any price, is even to be found in the words of a speaker who began his remarks by saying, "We are faced with the distress of the millions in the countries of exile . . . and they are faced with the danger of extinction in the very near future." At first sight these words seem to express a very real sense of immediate disaster. But Arieh Tartakover continued by raising objections to the idea of partition on the grounds that "we will also not establish a temporary haven that is not viable for an extended period."[31] Only one who feels secure that nothing urgent is bound to happen would reject the idea of "a temporary haven" for the sake of the unforeseeable future. In the debates, arguments, and especially in the newspaper articles of the period, there is a tendency to describe the condition of the Jews of Eastern Europe in the most extreme terms. (German Jewry is scarcely mentioned). Thus, for example, an editorial in *Davar* spoke of "the atrocities of extermination and annihilation in the eastern part of Europe."[32] Zalman Rubashov described the situation in Poland as "the tremendous holocaust that exists there."[33] Chaim Weizmann told the Twentieth Zionist Congress of saving two million young people, calling them "the surviving remnant."[34] The use of terms that for a later period have an unbearably painful significance gives the impression that people at the time were invested with the power of foresight. But an examination of the context in which these words were spoken proves that they were used to describe situations that were difficult, to be sure, but of the

30. Mendel Singer, in *Ha-kongres ha-zioni ha-esrim*, p. 143.

31. Arieh Tartakover, in *Al darkei mediniyutenu*, pp. 130, 131.

32. *Davar*, August 31, 1937.

33. Zalman Rubashov, in the minutes of the Mapai Central Committee, February 2–3, 1938, BB, 23/38.

34. Weizmann, in *Ha-kongres ha-zioni ha-esrim*, p. 33.

same dimensions that the Jews had learned to cope with over generations.

An illustration can be found in Mendel Singer's article, "The Polish Vale of Tears." After describing the desperate state of affairs in Poland, he continued:

> A friend described the situation of the Jews of Poland as being hopeless, with no way out. I tried to console him, and I asked him, "What will the Poles do with three and a half million Jews? If the Poles remove from the Jews the possibility of earning a livelihood, the Jews will become a burden on the government! After all, the government will not let them all die of hunger! The Poles must eventually understand where their policies are leading!" My friend remained silent. We both understood how bitter were these words of consolation.[35]

In summary, the partition debate and its aftermath show the limits of ideology as a guide to the future. Ostensibly the Zionists were best equipped to understand and evaluate the dangerous situation that was evolving. It seems that a wide gap existed, however, between their ideological perception and its eventual application to everyday life. The Zionists tended to project two time tables that somehow did not connect. One timetable related to the prediction of the imminent catastrophe, the other to actual developments. The more the first timetable was used as a propaganda device, the more it became devoid of immediate meaning and assumed the nature of a theoretical concept. The second timetable was applied to the Palestinian sphere. Partition, mass immigration, and the eventuality of a world war were all considered primarily in the light of their implications for the Zionist endeavor in Palestine. When Zionist leaders spoke of an imminent disaster in Europe, they mentioned time spans much longer than those they used in reference to the Palestinian situation. Somehow the two timetables never converged.

It would be wrong to assume, as some imply, that the Zionist leadership was indifferent or not deeply concerned about the fate of European Jewry. One has only to remember that most of them had been born and raised in Eastern Europe, and that their families were still there, to discard such a simplistic notion. The fact remains, however, that in the debates of 1937–38 they attached little importance to the issue of the approaching war and to the fate of European Jewry.

Two false assumptions, so it seems, were at the root of this atti-

35. Singer, *Davar*, June 1, 1937.

tude: one a mistaken assessment of the time until the outbreak of the expected war; the other a mistaken assessment of the possible impact of that war on the Jewish community in Palestine and on European Jewry. The Jewish community in Palestine, the culmination of Zionist hopes, was considered to be in a very vulnerable position, its very existence endangered and precarious. The Jews of Europe, on the other hand, so the Zionists assumed, would somehow manage to survive, just as they had survived war on previous occasions.

Generals tend to prepare for the last war; so did the Jewish leadership, including the Zionists. They expected suffering and disasters in the scale of World War I: battle deaths, famine, plague, rampant pogroms—an ordeal similar to what Jews had already been through. There was nothing in Jewish history to make the Zionists expect a disaster of different dimensions. Deep down in their hearts, Jews still believed in the innate humanity of European culture. But primarily, one simply cannot imagine that which is not supported by historical experience. Even the case of German Jewry did not provide clues pointing toward a holocaust. One might even imagine that Zionist leaders understood Nazi threats about the annihilation of European Jewry as they understood their own prophecies of gloom: partly believing them and partly dismissing them as propaganda.

Thus, in spite of all the theories on the issue of Catastrophe-Zionism, so characteristic of the activist trends in the Zionist movement, on the eve of the Second World War, no one read the writing on the wall.

Leni Yahil

The Warsaw Underground Press

A Case Study in the Reaction to Antisemitism

In almost all the countries that Germany occupied during World
War II, resistance found its first expression in the underground press.
The need for information about the war and its political implications was so pressing that people were ready to take the risk involved
in gathering news, producing papers, distributing them, and—last
but not least—reading them. Nowhere was German vigilance able
to stop the underground flow of information. The clandestine press
thus became one of the most powerful tools of the various resistance
movements in their efforts to promote their points of view and to
stiffen the opposition to the occupation and its collaborators.

The Jews incarcerated in the Warsaw ghetto were in an especially
precarious situation with regard to the gathering and distributing of
reliable information—as they were in everything. The 30 dailies and
130 periodicals in Yiddish, Hebrew, and Polish that they were accustomed to had been abolished in 1939, and they were even forbidden
to read German newspapers. In 1940 the German administration,
the Generalgouvernement, started to publish a weekly paper, *Gazetta
Żydowska* (Jewish Gazette), which contained only the orders and
news the German authorities wanted to communicate to the Jews
and the lies by which they intended to deceive them. The situation
became even more difficult after the ghetto was closed in November
1940. After that, the several hundred newspapers of the Polish underground press were not easy for the Jews to obtain.

However, the Jewish underground press of the Warsaw ghetto continued to provide not only information but a focus for the Jews' determination to hold on despite tribulation. It is no accident that

For Yisrael Gutman.

most of the editors of these publications were leading members of the various prewar organizations, carrying on their activities in the underground. Many of the very young were active in the youth movements and later would be outstanding figures in the ghetto revolts in Warsaw and elsewhere.[1] Thanks to Emanuel Ringelblum's secret archive, Oneg Shabbat, a considerable number of these newspapers have been saved, found after the war in containers buried beneath the ghetto's shambles. Not all containers were discovered, however, and no complete runs of these papers survive. Yad Vashem undertook to publish the 250 issues—comprising 2,933 pages—of fifty-two papers that were preserved. They were put out by eighteen different organizations, ranging from Revisionists to Troskyists. Written in Yiddish, Hebrew, and Polish, they are now being published in Hebrew with an appropriate scholarly apparatus. Three of the projected six volumes are currently in print. They cover the period from May 1940 to October 1941—1,488 pages of seventy-five publications issued by ten different organizations. Some of these papers have only a few pages, while others are the size of a booklet; the largest consists of eighty-nine pages in print.[2] All but one were originally copied by mimeograph, since the Germans had closed down all printing shops. Lack of printing equipment was but one of the many technical handicaps these publications faced; above all was the permanent threat of detection by the Gestapo. The publication of these papers has to be seen as an act of resistance.

According to Joseph Kermish, the editor of the Yad Vashem collection, these papers are being published "in order to perpetuate the memory of the emotional and spiritual world of the underground people, with their various ideological strains representing many different currents, parties, and youth movements, and thereby immortalize their struggle."[3] Some features are common to almost all the papers, however, in spite of their different political outlooks and

1. Among these editors were Yitzhak Zuckerman and Mordechai Anielewicz, leaders of the Warsaw Uprising, and Mordechai Tenenbaum-Tamarof, known for his activities in Vilna and Bialystok.
2. Joseph Kermish, ed., *Itonut ha-mahteret ha-yehudit be-Varshah* vols. 1–3 (Jerusalem, 1979, 1984). For general survey of Oneg Shabbat and the underground, see Yisrael Gutman, *The Jews of Warsaw, 1939–1943: Ghetto, Underground, Revolt* (Bloomington, Ind., 1982), pp. 144–54. Material for the Yad Vashem collection also came from the archives of the Halutz movement and the Bund. Most underground papers ceased with the great deportations from Warsaw to the extermination camps of Treblinka and Sobibór in July through September 1942. See Gutman, *Jews of Warsaw*, passim.
3. Kermish, preface to *Itonut ha-mahteret*, 1:vi.

different languages. They usually start with an editorial or other article indicating the subject the editor wishes to emphasize. Here, of course, the different approaches and convictions of the sponsoring organizations find their specific expression. Yet all the Jews are in the same traumatic situation; they live and act under the same dangerous conditions in confrontation with the deadly enemy. Their interpretation of the present and the future, their reactions to misery, humiliation, and lack of defense in the face of an inexorable fate vary in content but not in character and quality. They all try not only to hold out but are determined to preserve their human dignity and to wrestle, at the same time, with the intellectual clarification of their beliefs. Their beliefs, like their reactions, are not identical, but there is one axiom they all share: in the end, Hitler will be defeated, and afterwards, a better world will rise out of the destruction he perpetrated. They all profess hope against hope. This is their inspiration, the faith that keeps them going. Each one, however, looks at the present and pictures the future according to what was thought and believed in the past, before the catastrophe struck. This is their strength—and their weakness. It is the purpose of this essay to analyze their reasoning as they attempted to reconcile their convictions with the overpowering reality they faced.

Who are these people? To which strata of the prewar Polish-Jewish society did they belong? Half of the political organizations represented in the three published volumes were affiliated with various brands of socialism. The most important among them, and the largest underground organization of the Warsaw ghetto, was the Jewish Socialist party, the Bund. With its youth section, it is represented by the greatest number of papers published in the current Yad Vashem collection—twenty-eight issues, or 37 percent. The two other Jewish-oriented socialist parties represented in the three volumes belonged to the Zionist movement; they are Poalei Zion (ZS)[4] in the right wing of the Zionist labor movement, and Left Poalei Zion. Three small sections of socialists represented were affiliated with Polish parties; they are Jewish communists, Trotskyists, and Polish socialists affiliated with the left-wing Polish Socialist party of the same name (PS).

The other five organizations represented in these three volumes are Zionist youth movements. Three of them were affiliated with the labor movement and belonged to the worldwide pioneer organiza-

---

4. ZS stands for the Zionist Socialists, a party that merged with Poalei Zion.

tion Halutz, each connected with a specific kibbutz movement in Eretz Israel (then still Palestine). They were Dror he-Halutz, Gordonia, and Hashomer Hazair.[5] The nonsocialist Noar Ziyyoni (Zionist Youth) also belonged to the Halutz. Distinct from them was Betar, the youth movement of Vladimir Jabotinsky's Revisionist party.

Thus, with the exception of Noar Ziyyoni and Betar, all these organizations were socialist but represented different currents and held divergent ideologies. The main dissension, however, manifests itself between the radical socialists and the Zionists even though most of the latter combine Zionism with socialism.

War and Ideology

The papers dealing with the general political situation and military developments are accurate in their information but in their interpretation they are very clearly influenced by their respective ideologies. The Bund papers devote the most space to these subjects. Here the information itself is often detailed and surprisingly correct considering the difficulties entailed in listening to the international radio and in obtaining not only copies of local Polish clandestine papers but also news published abroad. The very first item of the collection, the Bund's *Biuletyn* (Bulletin) of May 1940, describes the situation on the Western Front, mentioning specific places and incidents in battles in France, the Netherlands, Belgium, and Norway. British Prime Minister Winston Churchill's new cabinet is reported as including eleven members of the Labour party, with Clement Attlee, Arthur Greenwood, and Herbert Morrison mentioned by name. Yet the report is one-sided, making more of German casualties than of German victories. President Franklin D. Roosevelt is quoted as hinting at the possibility of the United States' entering the war and giving orders for mounting military preparations. To this information the paper adds: "The thought of taking part in the war becomes more and more accepted in America. The anti-German mood

5. Dror (Freedom) was adopted as the name of two youth movements—Fraihait and He-Halutz Hazair—that merged in 1938. Together they comprised 350 branches in all of Poland, including the area occupied by the Soviet Union. See *Itonut ha-mahteret*, 1:112 n. 8. The movement was connected with Hakibbutz Hameuhad in Eretz Israel. Gordonia—after A. D. Gordon, one of the founding fathers of the kibbutz movement—belongs to Hever Hakwuzot. The kibbutz movement of Hashomer Hazair was and is to this day Hakibbutz Haartzi.

is increasing."[6] This exaggeration reflects more wishful thinking than reality.

A month later, in June, the paper allots much space to Italy's entry into the war and analyzes Benito Mussolini's intentions. There is a note of disillusionment in the statement: "America and Roosevelt did not declare war even after Italy joined the war." But there is some consolation: "What does America do? She provides war material to the Allies. The American munitions industry is working unremittingly."[7] In contrast to the hope *Biuletyn* pins on the West and the French people, who will not acquiesce in Philippe Pétain's "Fascist Betrayal,"[8] the paper is very critical of the Soviet Union in general and of Stalin in particular. In this respect the Bund differs widely from all the other radical socialists with whom it shares the conviction that capitalist society is doomed. Viewing the situation in the Balkans in July, the paper reminds its readers of Russia's occupation of the Baltic countries Lithuania, Latvia, and Estonia and of Bessarabia, and North Bukovina, annexed from Rumania. It continues: "The Swiss press relates that these annexations were preconceived in accordance with the pact concluded between Germany and Russia in 1939. . . . The annexation stirred up great tension in the Balkans. Hungary and Bulgaria also claim territorial demands from Rumania."[9]

The Bund's youth movement Zukunft (Future) had its own Yiddish newspaper *Yugnt-Shtime* (Voice of the Youth), which generally promulgated the same thoughts and slogans as *Biuletyn*. Under the headline "We the Young Guard," the editorial of the October 1940 issue proclaims: "We know: Capitalism in the Fascist form is undertaking the last trial. This is the effort of the moribund condemned to die. Out of the birth pangs of suffering mankind new life is born."[10] Under the headline "The Soviet Union and the War," the paper pronounces its harsh verdict on Stalin's policy. Russia is criticized not

6. *Biuletyn*, May 1940, in ibid., p. 9. *Biuletyn* was a Yiddish monthly, one of twelve publications the Bund issued until 1942. The editorial explains Hitler's attack on the West as motivated by the need to show new victories and to secure raw materials. Therefore "Hitler hastes."
7. Ibid., June 1940, in ibid., p. 14.
8. "Fascist Betrayal" is the headline of the editorial in the July 1940 issue of *Biuletyn*. In ibid., p. 21.
9. Ibid., p. 29.
10. *Yugnt-Shtime*, October 1940, in ibid., p. 117. *Yugnt-Shtime* (transcription according to the Yiddish spelling) was a monthly; this is issue number 11.

only for remaining neutral but for strengthening Hitler with huge deliveries of fuel and food. Soviet propaganda is castigated for using every occasion to prove that it was not Germany that started the war, and socialist leaders are denounced as warmongers. Moreover: "It is clear: if Hitler will succeed in the West, he will try to realize his dreams of supremacy in Eastern Europe also." The countries Russia occupies are described as Hitler's gift to Stalin's dictatorship for its attitude in the war. However:

> Hitler is not giving anything free of charge. For the "voluntary" annexation of the said countries [mentioned above] the Soviet Union will be charged a costly price. Hitler likes to give and afterward to take back with interest added. The price which the Soviet Union will have to pay will be enormous.[11]

In September 1940, *Ptomienie* (Flames), the Polish newspaper of the Zionist youth movement Hashomer Hazair, sums up the first year of the war. Its radical socialist conviction makes it unwavering in its justification of the actions of the Soviet Union. "We are witnessing events that will determine the fate of the world." The decisive campaign that is approaching is fought over who will rule the world. Tricky and deceitful Britain, the stronghold of the old order, now appears as the defender of freedom, but her victory will not bring freedom to the millions of subjugated colonial slaves. Like the First World War, this is an imperialistic war about raw materials and markets. Those who suffer are the common people who do not understand what is really going on. Once these common people will revolt, the strong and victorious army of the proletariat (i.e., the Red Army) will move and destroy the tottering strongholds of the reaction.[12] A month later, in a new summary, the paper explains that England is holding out, but her empire is disintegrating; the United States is lying in wait to take over. Russia is in a strong position, for economic advantages, discussed in detail, are offered to her by the Allies and the Germans alike, as each tries to draw her to its side.[13]

The socialist ideology of the Left Poalei Zion, though similar to that of Hashomer Hazair, is even more radical. In January 1941, the Yiddish paper of the party's youth movement, *Yugnt-Ruf* (Call of the Youth), explains that the Hitler regime ascended to power in order

11. Ibid., p. 124.
12. *Ptomienie*, September 1940, in ibid., pp. 89–90. *Ptomienie* was the publication of one of the units of Hashomer Hazair in Warsaw; this is the first issue.
13. Ibid., October 1940, in ibid., p. 134.

to save the declining capitalistic class but will go under together with it. "This is the first historic axiom: Hitlerism—notwithstanding the present jubilation over its victories—is doomed." The war—the paper asserts—is fought between the two "capitalistic-imperialistic blocks: the 'satiated' imperialism with the British Empire at its helm, and the 'hungry' imperialism of fascism." The war, in this view, is a more loathsome and disastrous repetition of the First World War; the "ideological" slogans of both sides are nothing but deceit. "The arch-reactionary Churchill calls for neither more nor less than 'fight for democracy' and 'progress' and 'social reform.'" After both sides have spent their force in the fight, the working class, with the proletarian state at its head, will have the final word.[14] Together with those inclined to fascism, such as Rumania and Poland (sic!), the Western powers are responsible for the attitude of the Soviet Union because, "until the last moment, all these states did not renounce their dreams of anti-Soviet intervention." And therefore:

> The Soviet policy is conducted in the realm of armed neutrality, ready for battle. The proletarian state understood that she should not, even that she is forbidden, to side actively with one of the capitalist blocs. She is obliged to defend her vital interests and not let any of the imperialists impair her boundaries. . . . At the same time, the independent and revolutionary proletarian power has to get ready in every respect to enter the battlefield of the world as soon as the conditions are ripe.[15]

The same pragmatic, Marxist explanations are put forth in Dror (Freedom), the Yiddish paper of the youth movement Dror he-Halutz. Obviously, there is some discussion within the organization about Russia's policy. The author of an article in the October 1940 issue says:

> I have some things to say about the Soviet Union. Several comrades have presented unjustified arguments against the foreign policy of the socialist state. Policy is not connected with morality. Policy works to create the most convenient conditions under given circumstances. It was not difficult to instigate war between the Soviet Union and England or between the Soviet Union and Germany. If this did not happen—and for the time being there seems to be no direct danger to the socialist country [the Soviet Union] and the great socialist upbuilding she has accomplished—it is only because of her policy of "divide and rule."[16]

14. Yugnt-Ruf, January 1941, in ibid., p. 396. The quotation marks, indicating irony, are in the original. This is the first issue of Yugnt-Ruf, which did not appear again until October 1941.
15. Ibid., pp. 397–98.
16. Dror, October 1940, in ibid., pp. 105–6. This is the fourth issue of Dror.

The author is Yitzhak Zuckerman, a leading figure of the movement who survived to become one of the founders of Kibbutz Lohamei ha-Getaot (Ghetto Fighters). The article is, of course, signed with one of his many pseudonyms, as all writers in the underground press guarded their anonymity by using either fictitious names or initials. However, the editors of the Yad Vashem collection have gone to great lengths to establish the identity of even the most obscure writers, an article sometimes being the only memory left of a person.

Confrontation with Reality

Politics is neither the only nor the most important subject of an article in the same issue of *Dror,* whose headline reads, "What We Are Preparing For." Originally this was an address to a meeting of more than one hundred pioneers preparing themselves in groups for *aliyah* to Eretz Israel by doing work in special agricultural-training farms called *hachsharah.* The meeting took place in Warsaw in October 1940. Because of the article's importance, it is related in detail.[17]

The speaker asks himself and his audience if all their dealings with their special problems are not futile in light of what is going on outside in the street.

The street is enmeshed in disaster and agony; the street is full of horror. Does this meeting, with its visions of the future, have any meaning for the gray daily life in the street? May it not be that these visions are nothing but weakness, an escape from this life into the mind? Perhaps someone thinks that we should not have convened today, since our thinking will not in any way determine anything and our talking will not change the order of the world. We are so few. The great socialist family is divided and split. And we—young Jews and young socialists—are a splinter of a people headed for destruction and a tiny splinter of the already split socialist movement. Those who measure our inner strength by our present situation, who do not see anything but our weakness and are not strong enough to see something else, may agree with this perspective. We who know the strength of the *avant-garde,* however, who are aware of the meaning of pioneering, we understand the impact of our discussions. We sit here among ourselves, and we think to ourselves, Toward what shall we educate? What have we to prepare? The shortsighted who maintain that tomorrow will be like today have nothing to prepare for. We, however, know that we have much to lose by apathetic thinking, because then we will not understand the future. The force be-

17. Ibid., pp. 103–7; quotations on pp. 104, 106–7. For information about the meeting, see p. 113 and n. 8.

hind our considerations will show itself and become meaningful as the driving force of ideas pierces the walls that keep tomorrow from our sight.

In the following section "Antek" (Zuckerman's clandestine name) explains the three factors of the future that, in his opinion, "are the most important for the realization of our national and socialist aims." First is "Eretz Israel's political consolidation as a state after the war." On this issue Zuckerman does not want to comment because direct communication with Palestine has been severed by the war. "However, it is possible that after the war we shall be able to claim the right to the country on surer ground than we can today." Second is the belief he shares with all the other socialists that the socialist revolution will take place in Europe after the war. Third is his concern for "the moral and spiritual character of the Jewish communities in the occupied countries that are today exposed to the fire of the war." After the war, when the fate of the nations will be fixed, it will be of paramount importance whether the Jewish people will be able to use the opportunity, or will miss it. Elaborating on this point, he says:

> The present, with all its dangers, is menacing us. It breaks our courage, robs our belief, weakens our resistance, and throws us into the grip of desperation and apathy. Where is the vigor that was inherent in the life of the Jewish community in Poland? The whole life of this community has become dependent on philanthropy.
>
> We have to take upon ourselves the responsibility for the fate of this community. We are responsible for the young generation that is educated under the war conditions, lest without surveillance and without defense, they tumble into the abyss of demoralization.
>
> Our movement comes from the people, and it is meant for the people. The essence of our being and its meaning must not and cannot be determined by mere proclamations of loyalty. We are made for action. Every deed, every positive doing, is a revolutionary act. They want to deprive us of the image of man; they want to break us mentally; they are sowing horror among us; and they are harvesting the destroyed life of Jews. By the force of our belief, by the unshaken force of our will, let us do all we can. Nothing is not important. No deed is too little. We have to educate the young generation and as many strata of the people as possible. We have to get ready in earnest for tomorrow. As much as we can, let us stop the rolling wheel that drags all of us into the abyss. This is our duty today.

The political orientation of Dror was identical with that of Poalei Zion (ZS). The only issue of Poalei Zion's paper *Bafrayung* (Liberation) published so far is that for December 1940. It opens by recalling the ideology and image of the party's founder, Ber Borochov, "the man who created an era in the history of the struggle for the Jewish people's national and social redemption."[18]

Under the headline "WHY," a long article discusses German anti-semitism. Using irony like a fine chisel, the unidentified author says:

> Looking at the huge apparatus Nazi Germany has erected against us, seeing how much time and energy are invested in order to invent ever-new tortures to use against us, one could become filled with a little pride. Common sense could suggest that we are the most important element in this war, that we have infiltrated deep into the enemy's bones. How, otherwise, to explain his zealotry, his burning hate of us?

All this, the author goes on, in these days when the enemy has quite enough other things to worry about. After all, lots of other nations are sworn enemies of the Germans.[19]

Citing the German propaganda's exaggeration of the Jewish influence, the author states that "the entire Jewish people stands today on one side in the war, though we do not have an army of our own. But, it is clear to all that there is no correlation whatsoever between the impact the Jews have and the wicked tortures they are suffering today. . . . *The measuring-rod applied to Jews is completely different from that applied to others.*" This "different measuring-rod"—the author goes on—was not invented by Adolf Hitler; it is as old as the Diaspora. Various explanations have been proposed; today it is said:

> The Hitler regime uses the Jews to fool the German masses. . . . He wants to turn their minds by telling them that they are the best, the crown of the world, and therefore he oppresses and slanders the Jews so that the German masses may measure their fictitious "superiority" by the low stature of the Jews. . . . In any case, it is clear that he needs the Jews' misery, their suffering, and their blood for his own purposes.

But, the author stresses, the main question remains, Why always we Jews? Are we different from all the others? In reply he asserts: "Yes, we are different; *we are not like all the nations.*" We are not better and worse than other people, and we are not different but in one respect: "*We are the only people in God's world that wanders without a home.*" This is the basic cause of all the calamities we have to bear. This root of our difference is not concealed from sight; Zionism disclosed it long ago. The author concludes:

---

18. *Bafrayung*, December 1940, in ibid., p. 178. Under the headline "The Labor Movement at the Crossroads," the paper analyzes the present situation and the future chances of the socialist movement, concluding that the proletariat will decide the future of mankind but until now has failed completely in every historic test. Ibid., pp. 182–85.

19. Ibid., p. 179.

The enemy is sucking the marrow of our bones. No doubt we shall emerge from this bitter experience considerably weakened. However, notwithstanding the weakness, we will have to concentrate what is left of our energy in one direction: to abolish, to erase completely the homeless situation, to be "as all the nations." Perhaps, because of the Hitler catastrophe there will be no repetition of the satanic phenomenon that a multitude of social organizations of Jews oppose [as in the past] the erection of a home for the Jewish people.[20]

Nevertheless, for the people of the Warsaw ghetto, there was no escape from reality. In all the papers the people of the underground are conscious of the disastrous consequences implied in the current situation and are especially worried about their influence on the youth. In the September 1940 issue of *Ptomienie*, Hashomer Hazair reaches conclusions similar to Dror's about the necessity of thought. The war, says *Ptomienie*, has an overpowering influence. "It is infiltrating into the pores of our soul. Who can face this situation and teach [the people] how to resist this influence, if not the young? In all the hard times, the youth have been the faithful and the basis for resistance. But not now."[21]

Among the youth, the struggle for existence has the top priority. One has to get a piece of bread—and nothing more. The prevailing slogan among the young is, "Eat and drink. Today we are alive. Who knows what will happen to us tomorrow? Let's enjoy life as long as we can. Why should we strain our brain with farfetched thoughts? What is to be expected will come anyhow—in spite of us!" The author adds:

At the same time, the head is bowing and the slave-soul is in the making. Our young learn to take off their hats in front of Germans, to smile the smile of obedience and slavery. Inside the heart there whisper envy and deep admiration for brutal fascist haughtiness. And deep down in the heart the dream is hidden: to be as one of them—handsome, elegant, strong, self-possessed. So that we, too, may hit without a trial, strike, loot, despise others as they are now despising me.

Moreover, the young loathe the stripe attached to their right arm that marks them as Jews. "It burns like fire. It is such a great calamity to be born a Jew! If only it would be possible to escape Jewishness."[22]

20. Ibid., pp. 180–82, italics in original.
21. *Ptomienie*, September 1940, in ibid., p. 90.
22. Ibid., p. 91. The "Jewish badge" in Poland was usually a white stripe with a Star of David on it, worn on the right sleeve. Requiring it was a matter of local initiative until the order of November 23, 1939, of Hans Frank, governor of the Generalgouvernement.

The author ponders: The Germans took away the schools, the libraries. Why? Is it not because they are afraid that books might promote thought? Shouldn't the young initiate resistance by *thinking?* It is necessary to think clearly and coldly and to study so that one may analyze historical events accurately. Fascism promotes the low instincts. We have to overcome them in our hearts, to believe, even today, in the good in men, in human solidarity. Reminding readers of Hashomer Hazair's ideology, the author asserts: "We have to understand that the structure of compulsion and oppression will be destroyed according to the inevitable force of history. Our enemies are pitifully deceived people; with their blood they are buying profits for the capitalists." And he concludes:

> We are able to preserve our human and national pride, to walk erect, with our back straight not bowed. We have no reason to escape Judaism. . . . There are pleasures in life that are not vanishing—the pleasure of thinking, of struggle, of revolt.
> *Thinking—this is the slogan and this is the task.*[23]

The Past, the Future, and the Ghetto

The Revisionist youth movement Betar is here represented by only one issue of its fortnightly magazine *Hamedinah* (The State). This is the only Jewish clandestine paper that was actually printed. It came out in August 1940 and is dedicated to the memory of the founder and leader of the Revisionist movement, Vladimir Jabotinsky, who died in New York on August 3, 1940. Jabotinsky's death was a bitter blow for the movement and especially for its young members, who were left incarcerated in Warsaw after most of their elder leaders had fled before the Germans arrived. It must be noted that this loss of leadership was typical for most of the Polish-Jewish organizations, parties, and youth movements, although some of these leaders later returned. By and large, the young had to shoulder new and greater responsibilities in this unforeseen and catastrophic situation, a necessity that had decisive influence on the development of the underground in the ghetto, where young leaders came to the fore.[24]

The young Revisionists' shock at Jabotinsky's death is very much evident in *Hamedinah*, though they try hard to restrain themselves.

23. Ibid., p. 92, italics in original.
24. See Gutman, *Jews of Warsaw*, pp. 120–21.

In accordance with the military form of organization of Betar, the magazine, written Yiddish, opens with "the order of mourning" in Hebrew, fixing the rules the members have to observe during the mourning period of thirty days. There follow words where words seem to be of no avail:

> We have no words to express our sorrow. . . . Nor can we express it in deeds, because our hands are tied up; nor in tears because he has forbidden it. Only keeping silent, grinding our teeth, with tired eyes burning, choking from the knot in our throat—may we somehow express our pain that has no words and our mourning that has no end.[25]

The story of Jabotinsky's life and his dedication to his vision of the Jewish state are recounted, and passages from his speeches and articles of 1935 and 1936 demonstrate how he anticipated great dangers and called for the evacuation of millions of Jews from Eastern Europe to Eretz Israel. (He thought this evacuation would take two generations.) There is some bitterness in the recounting, for the prophecies have come true while Jabotinsky's plea "to evacuate in order to rescue" went unheeded. The reason, the paper maintains, is to be found in Jewry itself.

> As there is no event that came over us similar to the holocaust, there is nothing similar to the inner situation of the [Jewish] people just before the catastrophe. The most terrible period in our history found the masses unprepared, divided, and without a leader. Bewildered peoples were facing an inevitable storm.[26]

The young Revisionists were not the only ones complaining that the elder generation did not understand the omen of their time. A publication of Hashomer Hazair lamented:

> Who would have said that we—children of the twentieth century— would be turned into slaves? Who would have thought that we should be confronted with the walls of the medieval ghetto? Alas, about that our fathers did not dream and our mothers did not sing to us. . . . Why did you not answer the call fifty years ago [when Zionism was proclaimed]? Why, instead of redeeming yourselves and us, did you remain serfs so that we are now thrown back into the Middle Ages? . . . Why, standing on the brink, did you not see the abyss?

This outcry of agony is, however, followed by the vow to end servitude: "The generation to come will not know anymore the dwellings

---

25. *Hamedinah*, August 1940, in *Itonut ha-mahteret*, 1:64. The original has sixteen pages. Ibid., pp. 63–74.
26. Ibid., p. 68.

of the ghetto. We shall build a big Jewish settlement that will know to defend itself; we shall erect a just world that will have no room for the villain."[27]

This is part of the Hebrew opening of *Iton ha-tnuah* (The Paper of the Movement), the most extensive publication of the Hashomer Hazair, 111 mimeographed pages, written alternately in all the three languages. It was published at the end of 1940 and beginning of 1941 and must be understood as a concentrated reaction to the situation after the closing of the ghetto in November, prepared in spite of the tumultuous days of the incarceration. Apparently the intention was not only to summarize the sixteen months of the war but to provide a historical analysis and outline the tasks and possibilities of the movement in the present situation and toward the unknown future, including the circumstances prevailing in the formerly Polish provinces that had now become occupied Russian territory. Thus, the editors implemented their belief that the way to promote resistance to the catastrophic situation was to stimulate thinking connected with learning. They dealt with the following subjects.

First, there is a review of political and military developments since the beginning of the war, starting with a historical analysis of the reasons for the Nazi's ascent to power. This analysis is complemented by a special explanation of the demographic-historic situation in the Balkans, with emphasis put on Yugoslavia's and Russia's strategic interests there.[28]

Second is an extensive discussion of the socialist movement—its history, ideology, policies, auspices, and, of course, the role of the Soviet Union in it.[29] In spite of the intention to justify her internal and foreign policies, the disappointment about her relation to the Jews is evident, especially in connection with the oppression of everything Jewish in the newly occupied territories. In these discussions among the members there are even some remarks critical of the Soviet Union.

Third, much space is allotted to the problems and ideology of the movement itself. The current situation is perceived as not only the

27. *Iton ha-tnuah*, December 1940–January 1941, in ibid.; quotations on p. 261.
28. Ibid., pp. 264–71, 292–97.
29. Socialism is discussed in ibid., pp. 272–83. Included in the discussion on socialism are references to and quotations from socialist leaders like Karl Marx, Friedrich Engels, V. I. Lenin, Georgi Dimitrov, and Otto Bauer. Central events and decisive meetings are also reviewed. The discussion on the Soviet Union is on pp. 289–93.

fate of the Jewish people in the war but of mankind in general. Nothing in the long history of suffering of the Jewish people is similar to the present situation. "This time the effort is made to destroy us completely." Not only their own movement, Hashomer Hazair, in Poland and elsewhere is menaced, but the entire Jewish people is threatened with destruction. The local conditions of Hashomer's branches in the various places affected by the war are surveyed. Yet, in spite of the war, "We must already now make preparations for the peace to come. Our comrades have to be ready for any situation that may evolve." With the coming of the war, a wave of flight erupted, mostly over the Soviet border, which disrupted the movement's organization. Messengers sent from Warsaw to all branches helped to restore communications, and, with great effort, the organization was maintained. With the closing of the Warsaw ghetto, these contacts were interrupted again, but new emissaries were sent to all the branches in order to guide their work on the spot. "This entailed enormous difficulties, but we knew to overcome them." The main thing was not to yield to circumstances, no matter how obstructive they may be.[30]

Fourth, in a section called "Milieu," these circumstances are described in all their harsh reality, starting with the horrors of the war and its tribulations, including the flight over the Soviet border.[31] The precarious situation of Hashomer Hazair's comrades under Soviet rule is openly discussed, and their underground struggle to keep the movement alive is emphasized. In Vilna, where these efforts are centralized, a great accomplishment is detailed: forty-seven members of the Halutz managed to get away from this overcrowded and starving city and to go "on *aliyah*" to Eretz Israel.[32]

There is a major emphasis on education problems: Did the movement's educational method prove adequate to the catastrophic conditions? The answer is in the affirmative: "Our people, starving, in rags, persecuted, harassed, and fearful of the tomorrow, are also troubled by internal ideological debates—Everyone who saw them

30. Special emphasis is put on Ber Borochov's ideology and on the problem and teaching of Jewish national socialism in opposition to the socialist ideology's negation of the Jewish nationality. Ibid., pp. 285–89. The situation of the movement during the war is described on pp. 297–310; quotations on pp. 301, 304.
31. Ibid., pp. 310–49.
32. On Vilna, see ibid., pp. 318–22; on the *aliyah*, p. 347. For a detailed description of events in Vilna, see Yitzhak Arad, *Ghetto in Flames* (New York, 1982), passim.

thus steadfastly adhering to their principles perceived for the first time how powerful the impact of our education has been."[33]

Still, it was inevitable that the revolutionary and shattering experience of the ghetto would provoke emotional reactions of different kinds in young people. In addition to those already mentioned, there are two of special significance. Youngsters whose lives had been focused around the movement, very often in open opposition to their parents, were suddenly physically and emotionally thrown back on their families. In the ghetto they lived together in overcrowded dwellings, starved together, and did not know what would happen next. Thus, a new sense of belonging and responsibility to the family developed in these young people, which was expressed as follows:

> Sadness at home. I know my parents. . . . I revolted against them; my thoughts transgressed their world's circle. However, a deep feeling emanating from the bottom of the soul is never blurred. . . . Our movement, being born out of the young generation's revolt against the grown-ups, overacted more than once in its relation to the family and thus even provided an example of unsocial behavior.

But perhaps the most powerful trauma the young experienced was the confrontation with death, at that time mostly death from hunger. The young people wanted to hold on to life and loathed the defilement and constant degradation of human dignity. Two quotations are characteristic:

> Wherever you look, there is tragic poverty. I wonder why those people do not want to die. . . . Does death ask for greater heroism than the life of extreme poverty and endless humiliation? Perhaps men like their chains? Still, there is a way for people to defend themselves. Even in the most inhuman circumstances there is something that remains to beautify human life, something people are able to fight for. . . . If we renounce our abused right to struggle, we break our only force, the moral impetus, the self-respect.

In another piece a girl writes:

> You know how terrible is the thought that soon the day will arrive when masses of men will die, knowing for sure that redemption is not coming from anywhere, and that this is the end . . .
> What, then, shall be the reaction? True, people with empty stomachs do not ponder about ideals, but this eventuality is bound to provoke a revolt against reality. . . .

33. A special session was held to clarify the educational problems created by the ghetto and to draw practical conclusions. *Iton ha-tnuah*, December 1940–January 1941, in *Itonut ha-mahteret*, 1:337–45. Reviewing the impact of the ghetto situation on their educational system, the participants in the discussion found their education adequate in spite of many obstructions. Ibid., pp. 343–44.

Our reaction, too, will be intensified revolt, for we know the reason and the goal. Aren't we the vanguard? . . .

And this is what I think: when we shall face death by starvation and shall probe our life's meaning, lest we have wasted it, we shall be able to say with full certitude that we did not forfeit life, that we lived as we were obliged to live by our conscience. This is very important.[34]

These are the thoughts of anonymous members of Hashomer Hazair in Warsaw, two years before the Warsaw Uprising.

The ghetto was now their daily reality, and its misery and torment were their way of life. The papers always deal, of course, with this subject, but it does not preponderate. All try to free their readers from those destructive influences, to lift them out of their incessant struggle to keep life going, to demonstrate the truth of the biblical saying that "man doth not live by bread only."[35] Cultural subjects are discussed primarily by the Zionists. The anniversaries of Hebrew and Yiddish writers and poets provide these papers with the opportunity to consider and quote from their work. Poems of living poets like Yitzhak Kaznelson and others are frequently published, and cultural activities, such as the performances of a dramatic circle, are reported. The ghetto itself is reviewed in a historical perspective.[36]

Nevertheless, the piercing realities of ghetto life could not and would not be neglected. Certain subjects stand out, one way or the other, in all the papers. These include hunger and the trials of overcoming it; the unbearable constraint of overcrowded living quarters; the deterioration of public health and the ensuing deaths; the agony of slave labor; and, more than anything else, the deadly torture in the labor camps. Harsh criticism is heaped on the *Judenrat*. In addition to all the suffering of about half a million Jews in Warsaw, there is disastrous news coming in from throughout occupied Poland.[37]

34. Ibid., pp. 327, 328, 334.
35. Deut. 8:3.
36. *Yugnt-Shtime*, November 1940, in *Itonut ha-mahteret*, 1:152–53; ibid., December 1940, in ibid., p. 221; "The Jewish Ghetto: A Historical Summary," *Bafrayung*, December 1940, in ibid. pp. 198–202; "Historical Summary in the Wake of the Erection of the Warsaw Ghetto," *Yugnt-Ruf*, January 1941, in ibid. pp. 404–5.
37. The May 1940 issue of *Biuletyn* brought news about German atrocities in Lublin and information about the ghetto in Łódź, which had just been closed. Ibid., pp. 4–5. Later *Biuletyn* and *Yugnt-Shtime* both included a regular column called "Jewish Chronicle," which reported news from other Jewish communities. Thus, for instance, the March 1941 issue *Biuletyn* describes the expulsion of Jews from the western provinces of Poland into the Generalgouvernement and their being driven from place to place; the deportation of Jews from Vienna to the Generalgouvernement is also reported. Ibid., 2:94–96. See also *Yugnt-Shtime*, ibid., pp. 219–20. In the January-February 1941 issue of *Dror*, Yitzhak Zuckerman reminds his readers of "the hundreds of Jewish town-

Often these themes converge, as in the following article from the May 1941 issue of *Dror*.

As for Jewish existence, the situation is unbearable. The sealed walls have a double impact: From the moral point of view, they depress, break, and degenerate the soul. From the economic point of view, they deprive most everyone of the possibility of sustenance. The consequences are to be seen everywhere. Add to these the demoralization of public life that spread between the walls of the ghetto [as manifested by] the impudent violation of all moral rules by our "tribunes" and "defenders" [the *Judenrat* and the Jewish police], and the trade in human life and health in every respect.[38]

The final accusation here refers to the fact that people could free themselves from coercive labor duty by paying money to the *Judenrat*.

In one of the next issues of *Dror*, there is a detailed description of "The Situation in the Warsaw Ghetto." Included are statistics on the numbers of people coming in and going out of the ghetto; figures on the refugees arriving in Warsaw from near and far, with stories of their desperate situation; figures on the numbers of cases of spotted fever among Jews in the first year of the war; and a comparison between the food rations for the general population and the smaller allotments for the people in the ghetto, an inequality that has necessitated widespread smuggling. The inflated prices for bread and other essentials are listed, together with the taxes that have to be paid for ration cards. The final figure is for the number of funerals each month, which rose from 360 in August 1939 to 1,608 in March 1941, a total three times higher than that for December 1940, immediately after the closing of the ghetto.[39]

The most devastating conditions, however, were in the slave-labor camps, and they also raised the most violent denunciations. Under the headline "Summary of Bloodshed," *Yugnt-Shtime* describes the operation of these camps in 1940. The people slept on bare planks in barns without windows, often without lights, sometimes without a roof. Ten were crowded into a "room" of five by six meters. Water was scarce, and sometimes the inmates were unable to wash or

---

lets that still wait in great fear for what may be at stake. . . . In places where ghettos have not been erected, massive expulsions have taken place." Ibid., 1:353–54.

38. *Dror*, May 1941, in ibid., 2:309.

39. Ibid., May-June 1941, in ibid., pp. 418–23. This double issue is sixty-four pages in the original. Ibid., pp. 380–441. In addition to feature articles, it includes a wealth of literary material. For more on the situation in the Warsaw ghetto, see Gutman, *Jews of Warsaw*, chap. 3.

change their underwear for months. They were plagued by insects, vermin, and diseases. Medicines were unavailable, and sickrooms, if they existed at all, were not much different from the lodgings. "The people," the paper continues, "were literally barefoot and naked. Many sold their clothing for a piece of bread." In addition to living in such conditions, they had to do hard labor in swamps, on highways, and the like. The guards were mostly SS men.[40]

As the labor units were recruited by the *Judenrat*, the people held it responsible for their suffering—and that was exactly what the Germans intended. At the end of the article in *Yugnt-Shtime*, a passage from a letter someone in a labor camp sent to the *Judenrat* of Warsaw is quoted: "Our fate and our life are dependent only on you; you are responsible for everything, and you will not be spared the punishment you have earned. We have made a ceremonial vow that we will take a bloody vengeance at the first opportunity."[41]

In a similar vein, in the May 1941 issue of *Proletarisher Gedank* (Proletarian Thought), Left Poalei Zion reports, under the headline "The Hunting Season for People":

> In the beginning of April the recruitment of people for the infamous labor camps started. The German Labor Office demanded thirty to forty thousand people from the *Judenrat* of Warsaw, mainly to work on the irrigation of rivers. Under what conditions this work is performed the Jews of Warsaw still remember from the camps of last year, which cost the lives of hundreds of young people.[42]

Again the *Judenrat* is held responsible.

In the beginning of 1941 the young Zionists thought that it would be possible to avoid the labor camp by projecting agricultural *hachsharah* on Jewish or Polish farms where members of the Halutz would work during the summer, something they had successfully organized the year before.[43] The Bund attacked the project fiercely. In March 1941 *Biuletyn* reports the German demands, warns of the catastrophic consequences, and threatens the *Judenrat*. The main attack is, however, directed against the Zionists, though without calling them by name: "In connection with this disastrous decree, in con-

---

40. *Yugnt-Shtime*, April 1941, in *Itonut ha-mahteret*, 2:217–18, quotation marks in original. Another detailed description of a labor camp, written by Yitzhak Zuckerman, is in *Dror*, May-June 1941, in ibid., pp. 425–30. Its epigraph is a quotation from Dante. The likening of the Holocaust to Dante's description of Hell is also frequently found in survivor accounts.
41. *Yugnt-Shtime*, April 1941, in ibid., p. 218.
42. *Proletarisher Gedank*, May 1941, in ibid., pp. 295–96.
43. See Yitzhak Zuckerman in *Dror*, January-February 1941, ibid., 1:355–56.

nection with this catastrophe of the 'labor camps,' irresponsible groups have put forth, at this most trying moment, the slogan of 'agricultural *hachsharah.*'" The Jewish "nationalists" are accused of exploiting the "Hitlerist opportunity" and the difficult situation of the Polish farmers, many of whom had been deported as cheap labor to Germany. According to the Bund's way of thinking, it is opportunism to save "several thousand youngsters from being taken to the labor camp. This will not diminish the amount of people languishing in the camps."[44]

This is only one example of the ideological controversies among the different parties in the Jewish public. The Bund defames the Zionists by calling them "strangers to the authentic national interests of the Jewish masses in Poland"[45] and "the young emigrationist organizations."[46] The Bund sees the true interest of the Jewish masses indisputably connected with the future of the Polish proletariat. Only by the alliance with the Polish socialists can the Jews secure their own existence. In the Bund's eyes, the Zionist aspiration at building a Jewish state in Palestine is not only unrealistic but a betrayal of socialism. The Jewish Question will be solved in the classless proletarian society of the future. Therefore, the separate agricultural training of the Halutz is denounced as bourgeois nationalism.

The Zionists attack the Bund as neglecting the true interest of the Jewish masses that lies in the erection of their own national home. Those who believe, however, that the future Jewish commonwealth must be founded on socialist principles attack the Revisionists as "fascists."[47] This internecine struggle among the different parties, inherited from the controversies preceding the war, had tragic conse-

44. *Biuletyn,* March 1941, in ibid., 2:140–42; *Yugnt-Shtime,* March 1941, ibid., pp. 109–10. Actually, only some hundred could avail themselves of the opportunity. See Gutman, *Jews of Warsaw,* pp. 139–40, 442 n. 33.

45. *Yugnt-Shtime,* March 1941, in *Itonut ha-mahteret,* 2:110. A similar wording appears in ibid., July 1941, in ibid., 3:13. Here the Zionist youth movements are classified as "soft bourgeois," disregarding their socialist commitment.

46. Ibid., October 1941, in ibid., 3:464–65. The paper again blames the Zionist youth movements: "They Are Trading in the Youth's Life," the headline says. The reference is to courses in agriculture and gardening, organized in the ghetto with the help of a society called Toporol and with German consent. The vegetables grown were distributed to the needy. In this connection also the *hachsharah* was organized and blamed by the Bund. See also Kermish's explanation, ibid., n. 25, and Gutman, *Jews of Warsaw,* pp. 139–40.

47. Left Poalei Zion, proclaiming radical socialism, attacks the Bund for its criticism of the Soviet Union and the Revisionists because they neglect the revolutionary task of the proletariat. *Yugnt-Ruf,* October 1941, in *Itonut ha-mahteret,* 3:477–79. Hashomer Hazair states that the Bund (without calling it by name) has nothing to offer the

quences at this crucial time, and only after the catastrophe of the major deportation was a way found to cooperate in defense.[48]

From May 1 to June 22, 1941

The various socialist convictions found their most concentrated expression in the different periodicals dedicated to the First of May. All declare their unshaken faith in the final victory of socialism, but the kind of socialism each movement has in mind is determined by its basic philosophy. Most continue to profess their belief in the Soviet Union's righteousness and strength; only the Bund is unshaken in its criticism of communism: "The communist movement is absent from the front. It disappeared from the surface of Europe. Corroded by the tactics of the Comintern, an obedient tool in the hands of the Soviet diplomacy, it did not stand the trial of history."[49] The editorial of *Yugnt-Shtime* addresses itself solely "To the Masses of Workers in Poland," praising them for choosing the right way, which led them "to stubborn resistance . . . in all fields of life." Among Hitler's evildoings, "the massive deportations of people toward famine and destruction and the crime of the ghetto" are singled out, but the Jews as such are not explicitly mentioned.[50]

This time the voice of a communist group in the ghetto, Siep i Młot (Hammer and Sickle), is heard. In the First of May issue of its short weekly *Morgn-Fray* (Tomorrow Free), it calls for unity: "No chosen races, no classes and privileged cliques. People, only people." At this moment, all differences must vanish. The fighters for freedom are all on one side of the barricades; "on the opposite [side] are our enemies and their helpers."[51] Among the enemies they include the community (i.e., the *Judenrat*) because it is sending the people to the labor camps.

On this occasion Hashomer Hazair extensively reviews the move-

---

impoverished masses at this time of great calamities, in spite of its high standard of organization. *Iton ha-tnuah*, December 1940–January 1941, in ibid., 1:262–63. In Hashomer Hazair's Polish periodical, *Neged ha-zerem*, Revisionism is denounced as "the Jewish fascism." *Neged ha-zerem*, February–March 1941, in ibid., 2:57. It must be said, however, that on the whole the Zionist papers did not that much emphasize the discussion with the Bund and did not use the same acid language in these polemics that the Bund's papers used.

48. See Gutman, *Jews of Warsaw*, chap. 10.
49. *Yugnt-Shtime*, May 1941, in *Itonut ha-mahteret*, 2:282.
50. Ibid., p. 278.
51. *Morgn-Fray*, First of May 1941, in ibid., pp. 300–301.

ment's principal conceptions, political views, and actual observations. After describing the mood prevailing in the starving ghetto, the editorial proclaims:

> To this stiffling atmosphere of prison, degradation, and poverty our paper will bring a different blast of wind, alien to it. To the voice of despair and doubt we shall respond with our steadfast belief. To the voice of degradation, with the message about a different kind of life, and to the voices of escape from reality, we shall reply by looking straight into its face.[52]

Dealing with the war situation after the German victories in the Balkans, Hashomer Hazair's Polish periodical *Neged ha-zerem* (Against the Current) emphasizes the danger threatening Palestine: "Victory of Germany implies not only the destruction of European Jewry but to a great extent also a death penalty for the Jewish settlement in Eretz Israel."[53]

Left Poalei Zion is exaggerated in its praise of the Soviet Union and its denunciation of the "Reformist Social Democracy." Moreover, *Proletarisher Gedank* denounces "Bourgeois Zionism and its collaborators, the socialist Zionists." In its perspective, the hope of the Jewish workers for social and national liberation depends exclusively on the world's proletariat. This hope "is not based on empty optimism but on Marxist realistic evaluation of the situation in general."[54]

Dror, too, voices socialist hopes in its editorial: "On the First of May, the workers' file will continue to march, albeit in the underground." The paper assures its readers, "As no force in the world will sever us from the fight for a new social regime in the world, no one will sever us from the country of our hope."[55] The feature article points out that on the First of May, more than on any other day, we have to prove "where, after all, we stand in the world." The author then weighs the pros and cons of the present situation in the socialist movement and concludes that only by force will the people, fighting for their freedom, be able to overcome fascism, but this inevitable clash will be possible only after Hitler has suffered his first defeat.[56]

---

52. *El-Al, Iton ha-zofim* (Upward, Paper of the Scouts), April 1941, in ibid., pp. 226–27. This is the first issue of this Polish periodical.
53. *Neged ha-zerem*, March–April 1941, dedicated to the First of May, in ibid., pp. 163–90; quotation on p. 183.
54. *Proletarisher Gedank*, May 1941, in ibid., pp. 290, 292.
55. *Dror*, First of May 1941, in ibid., pp. 268–69.
56. Ibid., pp. 270, 272.

Although the Bund had anticipated that Hitler would eventually turn against the Soviet Union and massive troop movements had been observed in the Generalgouvernement,[57] the German onslaught on Russia on June 22, 1941, must have come as a shock to the people in the ghetto, especially to the faithful believers in the Soviet Union's political wisdom—all the more so because of the German army's initially quick advance. The Bund, however, claimed not to be surprised and again denounced the German-Soviet pact of 1939: "This was the first stab of the Stalinist dictatorship in the back of the Western countries, in the back of the working class, and also—as we see today—in the back of the Soviet Union itself," writes *Yunge Gwardye* (Young Guard), a new periodical of the Bund, in July 1941. The paper adds that the official announcements of Joseph Stalin and V. M. Molotov give the impression of helplessness and that more than anything else they want to prove that they did not start the war. But "the great failure of the Soviet Union was exactly that she did not attack fascism but waited until it fell upon her."[58]

In a similar vein, the Trotskyite paper *Czerwony Sztandar* (Red Flag) writes in an editorial called "Our War" in July 1941: "Hitler's military action against the Soviet 'ally' was inevitable. We anticipated it at the time, as nothing seemed to trouble 'the friendship' between Stalin and Hitler."[59] The steadfast believers in the Soviet Union, however, try to overcome the shock by reiterating their ideologies and interpreting events accordingly. In August 1941, Left Poalei Zion's *Nadze Hasla* (Our Slogans) defends the "tactical maneuvers and concessions" of the Soviet Union, whose intention was "to avoid the start of the inevitable struggle under unsuitable conditions." Now, however, "the great historical hour arrived, the enormous battle started, that will determine the fate of the human race for generations to come."[60] In September, *Proletarisher Gedank* writes

57. See the communist paper, *Morgn-Fray,* June 15, 1941, in ibid., p. 455.

58. *Yunge Gwardye,* July 1941, in ibid., 3:3, 6. This is the paper's first issue. See also the editorial in *Biuletyn,* August 1941, in ibid., p. 131; and the editorial in the Bund's Polish *Na Nasca i Wasca Wolnose* (For Our and Your Freedom), in ibid., p. 246: "The Soviet-German marriage, doomed to failure, has been a nightmare to us."

59. *Czerwony Sztandar,* July 1941, in ibid., issue p. 45, quotation marks in original. This is number 6 of the Trotskyite periodical, the only one in the Yad Vashem collection. It contains an extensive survey and analysis of political and military affairs. Ibid., pp. 45–64.

60. *Nadze Hasla,* August 1941, in ibid., pp. 202–3. The periodical was published in Polish; this is issue number 3.

in a similar vein and quotes at length the August 22 communiqué of the Soviet information bureau. In its conclusions it says, "The plan to destroy the Red Army in five or six weeks failed—the war will go on for a long time."[61]

In an editorial written in July and published in August, Hashomer Hazair's *Neged ha-zerem* is also sure that the German attack has collapsed. It asserts that the resistance of the Red Army was not broken and the Germans "did not gain a single one of the territorial aims of the onslaught." The paper is adamant in its conviction that "in the end the victory of the Red Army and the deliverance of the world from the Hitlerite nightmare will come."[62]

The three volumes in print so far include a few issues of *Słowo Młodych* (Word of the Young), the Polish periodical of Gordonia. In an editorial in the July 1941 issue, Hitler's war is compared to that of Napoleon. Now, as then, "the way to London goes through Moscow." The paper indicates that the Red Army is much more powerful than most people had the impression after its winter campaign against Finland.[63] In September the headline of the political and military survey reads: "In the East: 'Nothing New.'"[64] Still, the main focus of the paper is its view of Zionism and socialism. Theodor Herzl and the national poet, Hayyim Nahman Bialik, are quoted extensively, especially in connection with the anniversaries of their deaths in the summer.[65]

Shaviv (Spark), the periodical of the Noar Ziyyoni, was not concerned about socialist ideology. The editorial of its June-July issue deals with the spiritual and psychological corruption endangering

61. *Proletarischer Gedank*, September 1941, in ibid., pp. 311–27 passim; quotation on p. 317.
62. *Neged ha-zerem*, August 1941, in ibid., pp. 95, 99. The German-Soviet agreement is justified on p. 98. Some of Hashomer Hazair's factual observations are meant as encouragement. Thus *El-Al* explains in the editorial of its third issue, August 1941, that Germany cannot afford a long war. One feature article envisions how all the troubles will end: The day will come when the revolting armies will point their armor against those who gave it to them and the starving millions will turn toward the Kremlin. Then will come the moment for which it is worthwhile to live and to suffer. The walls of the ghetto will crumble and the Russian soldiers who will enter the sunny streets will address the inhabitants as comrades. Ibid., p. 186.
63. *Słowo Młodych*, July 1941, in ibid., p. 66; this is year 4, issue number 5.
64. Ibid., September 1941, in ibid., p. 331. The headline is a paraphrase of Erich M. Remarque's famous novel about World War I, *Im Westen Nichts Neues* (1929). Because of his sharp criticism, Remarque had been deprived by the Nazis of his German citizenship in 1938. Eventually he became an American citizen.
65. *Słowo Młodych*, July 1941, in ibid., pp. 69–91. Socialism is dealt with in a historical survey. Ibid., pp. 91–94.

the Jews in addition to the threat of physical destruction that they face. To forestall this depravation of Zionist belief, the whole issue is dedicated to Herzl and Bialik.[66] Meanwhile, something occurred that was different from all the Jews in the Warsaw ghetto had experienced until that time. Bit by bit trickled in the hair-raising news of the mass slaughter of Jews in German-occupied territories formerly held by the Russians. In an article entitled "Documents of Fascist Bestiality," the September 1941 issue of *Proletarisher Gedank* describes the brutal deportations of the Jews from several towns in western Poland to the Generalgouvernement, the savage expulsions over the Russian border, and individual acts of sadism, all of which occurred during the last year. To this the paper adds: "However, the tragedy [of the victims of these atrocities] is nothing but child's play compared to the mass murder of the Jewish population in the recently occupied territories of Bialystok, Brisk, Vilna, and Lvov.[67]

This news was first received in July. *Słowo Młodych* reports in the editorial of that month's issue: "Immediately after the crossing of the [river] Bug the blood of thousands of innocent victims stained the streets of Bialystok, Lvov, Brisk, and many other towns."[68] At the time, these acts were still seen as local pogroms, and it was not clear who started them and to what extent the Polish population took part in them. By October it was known that the Germans perpetrated the killings and atrocities together with the newly formed Polish Hilfspolizei (auxiliary police) recruited from members of antisemitic organizations who had been in jail under the Soviet rule.[69]

The most accurate information was received by Hashomer Hazair. One of the movement's members escaped from Vilna and arrived in Warsaw on October 16. His story is told in the September-October issue of *Neged ha-zerem* under the headline "The Days of Blood in Vilna." It includes an accurate description of the massacre in the forest of Ponary and reports on the disastrous situation in the ghetto. The ghetto had been divided into two sectors, one for the skilled

66. *Shaviv*, June-July 1941, in ibid., 2:482–517; this is issue number 5.

67. *Proletarisher Gedank*, September 1941, in ibid., 3:320–23; quotation on pp. 322–23. On deportations and expulsions, see also n. 37 above.

68. *Słowo Młodych*, July 1941, in ibid., pp. 68–69. The original text reads "attained" for "stained"; this printer's error has been corrected here. Left Poalei Zion's *Avangarda Młodiezy* (Young Pioneer) publishes details from a story of a Jewish worker from a factory in Bialystok who escaped. "The facts that this worker tells about what was going on in the regions near the Soviet border are horrifying." *Avangarda Młodiezy*, October 1941, in ibid., pp. 437–39; quotation on p. 437. This is issue number 6–7.

69. In ibid., p. 439.

workers and their families and the other for the people the Germans called "unproductive." The number of people killed after three months of German occupation is given correctly as 35,000 of the 70,000 Jewish inhabitants of Vilna prior to the arrival of the Germans.[70] Yisrael Gutman, examining the same source, concludes: "Neither the article itself, however, nor the rest of the description gleaned from the witness suggests that the events in Vilna are symptomatic of the danger hovering over all the Jews trapped within the Nazi occupation."[71]

Biuletyn, however, arrives in the same month at an overall conclusion. "Hitlerism and the Jewish Problem" analyzes an article published in the official German organ, *Das Reich*, which deals with the solution of the Jewish Question. Its author differentiates between the ghetto of the Middle Ages and the modern one: While in the Middle Ages the Jews performed necessary economic functions, Hitler's state intends to remove the Jews from Europe altogether. The ghetto is only a temporary device. After the victory, the final solution will be implemented. There is also a hint at what this solution entails. No doubt aware of the news from the occupied Russian territory, *Biuletyn* concludes:

> In simple human language, the meaning is: physical extermination of the Jews in the shortest time and the cheapest manner. We can imagine that the Jews themselves will have to finance the penal commandos of German gendarmes who will expel the Jews from Europe, and the Jews themselves will have to dig mass graves for their brethren; everywhere in Europe the mass graves will signify "the new order."[72]

Conclusion

In hindsight, the Bund's relentless analysis of the facts often presents the most penetrating view of the political and military situation. In contrast, the socialist Zionists' orthodox Marxist interpretation of the facts, no matter how true, and the almost unwavering justification of the Soviet Union's politics blur their political insight and refute their claim of "Marxist realistic evaluation."[73] All the so-

---

70. *Neged ha-zerem*, September-October 1941, in ibid., pp. 403–6.
71. Gutman, *Jews of Warsaw*, p. 162.
72. *Biuletyn*, October 1941, in *Itonut ha-mahteret*, 3:420.
73. "The Proletarian Palestineism during the Second World War," *Proletarisher Gedank*, March-April 1941, in ibid., 2:148. "Marxist realistic evaluation" is implemented with: "This sober evaluation bestows on the Jewish worker of Marxist understanding the faith in the general liberation that will come following the present world war, as

cialists, however, have one element in common. While relying on the doctrine and on renowned authorities, they feel the need to recall other revolutionary events; the two outstanding events mentioned are the Paris Commune in 1871 and the uprising of the Schutzbund in Vienna in 1934.[74]

The Paris Commune is mentioned on the occasion of its seventieth anniversary in March 1941 by both the Bund and Left Poalei Zion, despite the vast difference between the Social Democratic approach of the former and the left-wing socialist conviction of the latter. *Yugnt-Shtime* presents a short historical survey opening with the statement that the French workers were the first in history to venture a campaign of liberation and seize power, even if only for a short time. The article concludes: "As the reactionaries could then not uproot the spirit of freedom among the workers of France, the hangmen of today will not uproot the iron will of the working class to overcome the evil and to establish freedom."[75]

Proletarisher Gedank analyzes the reasons for the defeat of the uprising and adds: "The Commune held out for only seventy-two days, but to this day *its memory is precious and holy* to the international proletariat, which is inspired by the heroism and learns the lesson of the errors."[76]

The Bund, Dror, and Hashomer Hazair all mark the anniversary of the revolt of the Schutzbund, which had happened in their time and was aimed against their own enemy—fascism. *Yugnt-Shtime* asserts: "The day after the defeat of the February uprising, the workers' marvelous socialist public in Austria . . . continued their fight for their ideals. *In the underground thousands went on to struggle clandestinely* for socialism and against the fascist slavery."[77]

Dror printed the recollections of the wife of Koloman Wallisch, one of the leaders of the uprising. She explains the failure by the fact that only some of the workers, about 30 percent, were ready to fight

well as in the full social and national liberation of the Jewish workers." The consequence must be "socialist territorialism brought to life as proletarian Palestineism." Ibid.

74. See Karl Marx, *The Civil War in France* (London, 1871); Otto Leichter, *Zwischen Zwei Diktaturen: Österreichs Revolutionäre, 1934–1938* (Vienna, 1968).

75. *Yugnt-Shtime*, March 1941, in *Itonut ha-mahteret*, 2:111–13.

76. *Proletarisher Gedank*, March-April 1941, in ibid., pp. 151–52; quotation on p. 152, my italics.

77. *Yugnt-Shtime*, January-February 1941, in ibid., 1:427, my italics. The article compares the present situation with the underground of the Schutzbund and includes a quotation from Marx's *Civil War in France*.

and quoted her husband as saying to her at the time of the outbreak: *"I am sure that this struggle is organized suicide. . . .* I also know that after the defeat I shall be one of the victims. Better that *my end will come quickly* than to live such a life."[78]

Hashomer Hazair printed the most extensive description and discussion. *Neged ha-zerem* includes the whole story of Austrian Social Democracy, pointing to the successes and criticizing the errors that led to the failure. Still, the paper is full of praise.

> Indeed, the workers of Austria proved their unequaled dedication to socialism and *their readiness to die in its defense.* They proved readiness to pay the price of their errors with their blood. But the sacrifice of their blood will not be in vain if we will learn its lesson so *that we shall know how to prepare for our [finest] hour to come, and come it will!*[79]

An additional feature article discusses the development of the European socialist movement between the two wars and culminates in the oft-expressed belief that the end of the current war will bring the great revolution.[80]

History did not bear out these prophecies, but this "unrealistic" revolutionary vision of the Jewish underground fulfilled a crucial function in the history of the Warsaw ghetto and of many other communities in the occupied territories. Let us recollect the movements' incredible efforts in not only keeping up their organizations but in preserving the fighting spirit of their members, their dedication and their hope for the future, and especially in taking care of the children and the young,[81] all this in declared defiance of the physically weak-

---

78. *Dror,* January-February 1941, in ibid., p. 371, my italics. Wallisch was condemned to death and executed, together with several other leaders of the uprising. See Paula Wallisch's report in ibid., pp. 371–73.

79. *Neged ha-zerem,* February-March 1941, in ibid., 2:29–35; quotation p. 30, my italics. This article was originally published in the movement's Hebrew periodical on March 1, 1934, and now translated into Polish.

80. "Some Problems of Socialism: Thoughts on the Memorial Day of the 'Schutzbund,'" ibid., pp. 35–46.

81. A separate article would be needed to describe the efforts concentrated on saving the young generation from moral and intellectual ruin. The suffering of the children and their tragic situation are apparent. *Neged ha-zerem,* for instance, is worried about the change the young are experiencing: "A leap was done from childhood, from the world of dreams into reality, whose conditions forced upon the children the character of grown-ups—dwindling, despairing [like them]." May 1941, in ibid., p. 353. In the same vein, *Słowo Młodych* describes the child that smuggles food into the ghetto for the family. September 1941, in ibid., 3:347. See also Gutman, *Jews of Warsaw,* pp. 69–70. *Bafrayung* describes the child begging for bread in the street. December 1940, in *Itonut ha-mahteret,* 1:205–6.

ening and morally debauching conditions of the ghetto. To this end comes the conviction of the Zionist movements that they have to fulfill a Jewish national task. The youth movements, in particular, see themselves as the vanguard of "the state under way." Again and again they emphasize: Eretz Israel is our goal and our hope. Moreover, Eretz Israel needs us.

With all their faith in their combined national and social mission, they cannot completely avoid conflicts between their socialist ideologies and their national commitment, which is rejected by Marxism in theory and in practice. There are occasional doubts about the Soviet Union, while, on the other hand, the discord provokes the violent attacks of the Bund. Time and again the socialist Zionists try to overcome the discord by certain intellectual acrobatics. Hashomer Hazair, for instance, proclaims that Eretz Israel has to become a Jewish-Soviet state. Most of the time, however, both points of view are interwoven.[82]

Thus, the fighting spirit of the Jews in the Warsaw ghetto, constantly nourished by *thinking*, was preserved for more than three years of ever-worsening conditions and increasing dangers and fears. The Warsaw Uprising was not born of nothing. Indeed, all the elements admired in the Paris Commune and the revolt of the Schutzbund became alive: "Thousands struggled clandestinely in the underground"; it was "organized suicide" undertaken with the knowledge that "the end will come quickly"; there was "readiness to die in the defense of their conviction"; thus, when the hour came, they were "ready for the sacrifice of life" believing that it would not be in vain.

History bore out their "unrealistic" view. The uprising, which was crushed like the two revolutionary paradigms, left a "precious memory" and the legend of outstanding heroism and dedication. This did not and could not efface the terrible fact of the murder of the defenseless millions. But the Jewish underground's reaction to the

82. *Neged ha-zerem*, August 1941, in *Itonut ha-mahteret*, 3:95. The article calls: "For: The victory of the Red Army! Worldwide socialist revolution! National and social redemption of the Jewish masses in Soviet Eretz Israel!" An earlier discussion within Hashomer Hazair, however, reveals an awareness of the conflict: Eretz Israel cannot develop without immigration; Russia will not concede *aliyah;* so what shall we do at the time of the—hoped for—Soviet victory and Russian rule? *Iton ha-tnuah*, December 1940–January 1941, in ibid., 1:308.

Holocaust helped after the war, like a kernel of grain, to ferment the spirit of renewal in the Jewish people and became thus an agent in the evolution of history. The underground press of the Warsaw ghetto describes the unremitting struggle by which the uprising was prepared for and made possible.

Yisrael Gutman

Jews and Poles in World War II

The relationship between Jews and Poles during World War II and the character of the contacts and links between the two ethnic groups have long been subjects of heated debate. Differences of opinion and an inclination to accept one-sided and stereotypical views in these questions are common not only to laymen among Poles and Jews alike, but they are also sometimes found among scholars and historians as well. One explanation lies in the fact that for both sides the subjects are charged with emotions and prejudice. Another is the difficulty entailed in studying moods and events in societies under occupation, opening the discussion to free interpretation and subjectivity of approach. There do exist, however, rich archival collections that include Polish and Jewish underground newspapers, diaries kept by members of both groups, relevant documents emanating from organizations and individuals in the widespread Polish underground movement, and evidence presented by thousands of survivors. It is reasonable to believe that systematic and objective use of this multifaceted documentary material would enable a highly objective reconstruction of the actual positions, events, and processes. Unfortunately, until the present there has been little serious research conducted in a manner befitting the subject.

An analysis of the pattern of Polish-Jewish relations during the Holocaust must consider, first, the conditions in Nazi-occupied Poland that differed from those in other countries and nations under Nazi rule, and second, the attitude of Poles toward Jews during the last generations prior to World War II.

Nazi-Occupied Poland

Nazi policy in the occupied countries was determined by a number of principles and considerations, including the racial status of the vanquished nation, as defined by Nazi ideology and the quality of that nation's "blood relationship" to the German people, and the importance of the occupied country to both short- and long-term German political strategy. Poland was unfortunate on both counts, as it was considered inferior by the leadership of the Third Reich. In addition, the land was regarded as a natural and traditional sphere for the territorial expansion of the German nation. Furthermore, Hitler thought the Poles ought to be punished for rejecting his proposals concerning Danzig and an extraterritorial highway to link parts of Prussia and for refusing to accept the status of a vassal state. This refusal prompted him to start the war a few years before his original target date, and the battle that began in Poland developed into total war much earlier than he had planned.

Thus the Nazis were not content with a repartition of Poland (the western region was annexed to Germany, the eastern area to the USSR in accordance with secret provisions of the Ribbentrop-Molotov Pact; a Polish ethnic enclave was established in the central regions, called the Generalgouvernement). Even within the Generalgouvernement the Poles were not granted a limited autonomous rule similar to that of the Czech protectorate or the occupied countries of Western Europe. The regime established in Poland, and later in certain areas of the USSR, can be termed "total occupation." All "governmental authority," as the Generalgouvernement governor, Dr. Hans Frank, defined it, except for the very lowest levels, was transferred from Polish to German officials. In March 1940, five months after taking up his position, Frank reported that he received a native of Poland for the first time (Alfred Wysocki) and even this was a special case; Wysocki was received because the Führer personally recommended him, considering him to be the one and only trustworthy Pole.[1]

Thus, not only did the Poles have no say in foreign policy; they had no control over internal affairs. They could neither initiate nor join in planning the anti-Jewish measures enacted by the authorities.

---

1. *Das Diensttagebuch des deutchen Generalgouverneurs in Polen, 1939–1945*, ed. Werner Präg and Wolfgang Jacobmeyer (Stuttgart, 1975), pp. 128, 130.

Moreover, anti-Jewish policy, at least the stage of the Final Solution, was not limited to Poland alone but was implemented throughout Europe. There is also no basis for the charge, made from time to time, that Polish antisemitism led the Germans to choose Polish territory as the most suitable for the death camps (Chełmno, Bełżec, Treblinka, and Sobibór). Though we have no documentary evidence that bears on this question, it is reasonable to assume that the Germans located these camps in Poland because of its Jewish population of several millions and because it was under total occupation and was far enough removed from the major centers of the Western world to permit the atrocities to be committed in secrecy.

Not only were the Poles stripped of their liberties and national independence; they were also the victims of shameful oppression and exploitation. The Nazis were determined to break the national backbone of Poland once and for all. Certain sectors of the population were relocated and exiled; the intelligentsia, underground activists, and all those suspected as possible future sources of renewed Polish nationalism were hunted down, many of them doomed to physical extinction.

But all this notwithstanding, the fate of the Poles was markedly different from that of the Jews. Poles who resigned themselves to the situation were generally allowed to live, work, and earn a living. They were "Aryans," and the Nazis even planned to absorb the "better elements" among them into the German nation. The Jews, on the other hand, were defined as an "antirace." In the first stage, the Germans tried to limit them to reservations and ghettos in complete isolation from other sectors of the population, condemned to slow extinction and degeneration. Later, they planned to exile the Jews from Europe to a faraway and isolated island such as Madagascar, where they would remain forever imprisoned in a sort of concentration camp. Finally, the Germans abandoned all of these temporary solutions in favor of the Final Solution—total physical destruction.

The Poles, then, took no part in formulating overall plans concerning the Jews, and they were not a party to their implementation. They were, of course, a factor that left its mark on what happened to the Jews of Poland under Nazi rule, because of both their numbers and their activities. During the war, Polish solidarity and resistance to the Germans were remarkable. This general resistance prevented the Germans, to a great degree, from penetrating the united populace, and there was, consequently, a great deal of clandestine activity. In time the political underground and the clandestine military organization, the Armia Krajowa (AK, the Home Army), both subordinate to the Polish government-in-exile in London, spread their network throughout the country. Some leading members of this underground called the organization "an underground state" and "an underground army."[2] All political groups active in independent Poland between the two world wars took part in the political and military organization, especially the center parties, which throughout most of the period participated in the government-in-exile. The only groups outside this wide consensus were the extreme right-wing fascists and the Communist Left, which began to rebuild its political power—and later to establish a military organization—from early in 1942. The extensive central bloc that maintained close contact with London, with the aid of the Western anti-Nazi powers, carried much power and widespread authority in the occupied country.

The relevant questions are, therefore, to what extent—if at all—were the Jews accepted into the overall Polish underground movement, and in what manner; to what extent did the Polish underground extend aid to Jews before the implementation of the Final Solution; and to what extent did it defend the Jews and contribute to their survival. Before dealing with these crucial questions in detail, a short survey of Polish attitudes toward Jews in the period preceding World War II is in order, for it is vital to an understanding of what happened during wartime.

Polish-Jewish Relations prior to World War II

In the mid-nineteenth century, both Poles and Jews groups hesitatingly explored the possibility of a closer relationship. The Jews desired political equality, while the Poles wanted to unite all elements of the country's population in a national struggle. Certain segments in Polish society raised the possibility of integrating the Jews and turning them into a third class of Poland's urban population. True, there were segments within the nobility, the weak Polish middle class, and the church who were guided by an anti-Jewish attitude, but the dominant trend one senses is of Jews acquiring important positions in the Polish economy and of Jewish families adopting the

---

2. Stefan Korboński, *Polskie państwo Podziemme* (Paris, 1965); Tadeusz Komorowski-Bor, *The Secret Army* (New York, 1951).

language and culture of Poland. Even though these assimilating Jews were a proportionally small element that had broken away from the mass of the Jewish community, homogeneous in its adherence to religious tradition, many saw in them harbingers of the future. On the eve of the uprising and at the height of the Polish national revolt against the Russian Empire in 1863, Catholic clergymen appeared in a manifestation of solidarity together with rabbis at public nationalist ceremonies, while a proportionally high number of Jews supported the uprising and joined the rebel ranks. It is estimated that several hundred Jews were killed or exiled, more than twenty of them being executed in the Russian punitive expedition that followed the failure of the revolt.[3]

A sense of frustration and powerlessness prevailed after the suppression of the revolt, the punitive action, and the increased efforts at Russification that followed in its wake. When nationalists renewed their activities after an interval of stagnation and waiting, new trends could be discerned. They were deterred by the idea of armed struggle, tried to negotiate with their conquerors, and called for positive "constructive acts now" to strengthen the productive sector of the economy, unite all parts of the population while divesting themselves of the hegemony of the nobility and its value system, and promote a sense of nationalism through education and culture. New political frameworks appeared on the scene: the moderate Left renewed the romantic irredentist tradition, while the radical Left placed revolutionary class cooperation with other nations in the Russian Empire above the ideal of nationalism. In the Center and Right of the political spectrum was the nationalist right-wing party, the Narodowa Demokracja (National Democracy, later known as the Endeks), which dissociated itself from liberal nationalism and affirmed "national egoism," the superiority of the Polish ethnic group, self-regeneration, and readiness for what the future held in store. This movement was markedly antisemitic. Its leader, Roman Dmowski, adopted a consistently anti-Jewish attitude, clearly expressed in his writings. The Jews, he argued, should not be integrated and assimilated into Polish society, for there are insurmountable differences between the mentalities of the two ethnic groups and the Jewish character endangers native Polish characteristics.

3. *Żydzi a Powstanie Styczniowe: Materiały i dokumenty*, ed. Artur Eisenbach, D. Fajnhauz, and A. Wein (Warsaw, 1963), pp. 6–7.

Dmowski pointed to the great increase in the number of Jews and their influence, which had grown because of Poland's weakness and could be shaken off only if they were expelled from controlling positions in the economic and cultural life of the country.

The Jewish community of Poland, too, underwent transformations. Modernization, which meant drawing nearer to the Polish nation and its cultural heritage, was no longer the only path of innovation open to Polish Jews. Social movements arose that professed a separate and unique Jewish national identity, while Hebrew and Yiddish became more prominent in Jewish culture and education. The Poles often complained of this Jewish national consciousness, of their growing involvement in the revolutionary movement and their interest in Russian language and literature—trends resulting from the powerful influence of the *Litvaks*, Russian Jews who settled in central Poland. Jewish historians, on the other hand, generally considered these trends to be signs of innovations in Jewish life that were not specifically limited to Poland, while others claimed that Polish political antisemitism and the increasingly vociferous demand for Jewish disengagement from the Polish economy were catalysts of a Jewish national renaissance that took several forms. Be that as it may, one fact remains clear: in the period preceding World War I, there was a definite retreat from the integration and assimilation of Jews into Polish society. Moreover, on the eve of that war the Endeks mounted a noisy economic boycott of the Jews that was widely supported by the Polish populace.

Between the two world wars, the formal status of Poland's Jews was one of equality in civil rights and unlimited freedom of action in internal public and political affairs. At the same time there was, however, a growing trend in Polish circles, adopted by a wide spectrum of political groups and enjoying widespread popular support, of viewing the removal of Jews from the economic and cultural life of the country as necessary to achieve full nationalist domination and full independence. It would seem that the Minorities Question as a whole and differences of opinion among the major political camps in regard to the national minorities together with domination of the state by the Polish ethnic element did not have direct and main bearing upon the Jewish Question. Furthermore, there is no foundation for the claim, made by some Polish historians, that Polish-Jewish tension was to some extent the outcome of confrontation between two ambitious national movements. True, there was a great increase in the influence of the Zionist movement and its various components upon the Jewish population of Poland between the wars, but there was no real clash of interests between the national aspirations of Jews and Poles.

We shall not discuss here the question of minority rights in Poland, in which the Zionists played an active role. Suffice it to say that Zionism's fundamental objective—emigration of Jews to Palestine and the creation of a Jewish national home—coincided with the inclinations of Polish nationalists. In contrast, it was those Jewish groups such as the Bund, which posited Jewish cultural autonomy in Poland, and the Communists, who opted for complete integration of Jews into Polish society, that openly opposed the regime or status of Poland. Some Polish historians claim that the antisemitism prevalent in the Polish Republic between the wars was the result of the country's general backwardness and the social tensions that plagued Polish society. Jews were especially hard hit by efforts made to change the social structure and reform the economy, but their suffering was a by-product and not the true intention of those who initiated the changes and reforms. Moreover, anti-Jewish sentiment was fed by fierce competition for employment. In other words, Polish antisemitism stemmed from actual needs and the existence of an extensive Polish-Jewish community, larger in absolute and relative terms than any other Jewish population in the world except for those of Palestine and the United States.

These argumentations described indeed a real distress, but the fundamental cause of the anti-Jewish sentiment in Poland between the wars was that Jews were considered a foreign or hostile element which must move aside to make room for the native Poles. In the mid-1930s, after the death of Józef Piłsudski, the situation became even more acute, both because of a further deterioration of the internal situation and growing fascist and Nazi influence from outside the country. At this stage the Jews reached a new level of poverty: almost one-third of them had no permanent occupation. The successors of Marshal Piłsudski adopted an anti-Jewish policy, with accelerated Jewish emigration among the highest priorities of Poland's political objectives. The extreme, fascistlike Right used pogrom tactics and racial legislation to force the Jews to emigrate. The obstacle to mass emigration was, of course, not unwillingness on the part of Jews but the quota limitations imposed by the countries of destination and Palestine, as well as the priority these countries gave to refugees and emigrants from Nazi Third Reich. Though the Polish authorities denounced the use of violence to encourage Jewish emigration, they gave their blessing to an anti-Jewish economic policy. Thus antisemitism spread and became deeply ingrained in the fabric of Polish public and private daily life. Bearing in mind this description of Polish-Jewish relations during the interwar years of Polish independence, and especially the important period immediately preceding the war itself, we can now turn to relations during World War II.

Jews and the Polish Government-in-Exile

The Polish government-in-exile was greatly instrumental in diffusing information about the situation of the Jews in Poland to the British cabinet and to the general public of the free world. It received reports at regular intervals from the underground military command and from the Delegatura, the body responsible for clandestine political and civil action in occupied Poland, which continuously sent reliable information concerning oppression of the Jews.[4] Moreover, emissaries and parachutists who went in and out of Poland were a living link conveying information and clarifications to London. The information, supplied by Polish officials, was sometimes received with disbelief by the British, who thought that it was purposely exaggerated. In June 1942 the British press reported that seven hundred thousand Jews had been murdered in Poland, and Polish Prime Minister Władysław Sikorski referred to mass extermination of Jews in a broadcast over the BBC. These reports, even if they did not specifically state that the murders in Poland were part of an overall plan to exterminate European Jewry, were the first indication of the unprecedented extent of the Nazi crimes. Jan Karski, an emissary who arrived in London from Poland late in 1942, transmitted an appeal that he had committed to memory from the leaders of the Jewish underground in Warsaw. Greatly disturbed by the fate of the Jews, Karski met with political leaders and journalists in Great Britain, and also in the United States, where he was received by President Franklin D. Roosevelt and appeared at many public

---

4. See the relevant chapters in Walter Laqueur, *The Terrible Secret: Suppression of the Truth about Hitler's "Final Solution"* (Boston, 1980). On the whole, Laqueur gives a reliable description of the transmission of information by the Poles, but his analysis of their motives is insufficient.

gatherings. In all his talks and meetings, and in a book that he published, he was preoccupied with the Jewish tragedy in Poland.

On the other hand, we have evidence that Polish authorities withheld information about the mass deportation of about three hundred thousand Jews from Warsaw and the neighboring area in the summer of 1942. One version of the incident claims that the delay resulted from disbelief of the figures reported from occupied Warsaw to Polish government circles in London. Another view holds that the Poles were in no hurry to pass on information to Jewish and other elements concerning the extent and destinations of the deportation, fearing that they would be pressured into taking action on behalf of the victims. Yitzhak Schwartzbart, a leading member of the Zionist movement in Galicia, bitterly confided to his diary in October 1944 that Stanisław Mikołajczyk, then minister of the interior in the Polish government-in-exile and later, after the tragic death of Sikorski, its prime minister, withheld information about the deportation from Warsaw between July and September 1942.[5] In his detailed notations, Schwartzbart often accused Polish officials of not specifying Jews in their appeals for help from outside sources; Polish officials always described the Jewish tragedy as part of the overall reign of terror and murder in occupied Poland, the victims being Poles and Jews alike. Furthermore, the Polish authorities consistently refused to order the underground, or to appeal to the Polish populace, to come to the aid and rescue of the Jews and help them escape. Evidence of Polish reluctance to send a clear directive in this matter from London to Poland is found in the replies representatives of Polish Jews in Palestine received when they appealed to the government-in-exile to intervene on behalf of their brethren. Minister of Information Stanysław Stronski replied, through the Polish consulate in Tel Aviv, that Polish officials "had spread the news about oppression of the Jews throughout the world as early as June [1942]" and added that "an appeal to the Polish populace is superfluous because it itself was the source of information and sharp protests [in this matter]."[6] The argument seemed to run that diffusion of information and protests made action superfluous.

In November 1942, against the background of growing criticism of the Polish government for withholding information about the mass

5. Yitzhak Schwartzbart Papers, Yad Vashem Archives, Jerusalem, M-2/755.
6. Reprezentacja Żydostwa Polskiego, "Sprawozdanie z Działalności w Latach, 1940–1945" (Jerusalem, 1945), mimeographed.

deportation from the Warsaw ghetto, the Polish National Council, the para-legislative body in exile, issued a public statement that read in part:

> The Polish National Council appeals to all Allied nations and to all nations suffering, together with Poland, under the German yoke, to join forces at once against the Germans who trample underfoot and profane principles of human morality, and against the extermination of the Polish nation and other peoples, an extermination most appallingly expressed in the recent mass murder of Jews in Poland and throughout all of subjected Europe. To all those who live in torture and suffering in Poland, to both Poles and Jews who are taking part in the struggle for freedom and are preparing the ground for a just retribution on the German criminals, the Polish National Council sends its message of hope and unshakable faith in the restoration of freedom.[7]

That the government-in-exile did not exercise its authority and influence to initiate aid to Jews in Poland during 1942 merits attention. This lack of action undoubtedly stemmed from general considerations connected with the strategy of armed resistance in Poland and attitudes toward Jews; it also most likely reflected differences of opinion and tensions within the coalition government that included the traditionally antisemitic Endeks. Another factor certainly influenced the government-in-exile and other Polish leaders in London, who were naturally sensitive to the desires and inclinations of the Polish populace in the occupied homeland, where the real battle was being waged: more than a few communications and appeals that reached London from Poland intimated that it would be best to refrain from undue activity and interest on behalf of the Jews, because such appeals were unfavorably received by the population in occupied Poland.

It should be noted that on May 5, 1943, late in the Warsaw Uprising, Sikorski made a vigorous and emotional appeal to his Polish brethren: "I appeal to you to extend all possible aid [to the Jews] and, at the same time, to soften the sting of this terrible brutality."[8] But this unequivocal appeal came only in the spring of 1943, during the final stage of the expulsion and extermination of Warsaw's Jewry, at a time when substantial changes had already occurred both in the overall military situation and in that of Poland, and also in relation to the Jews, with implications I shall discuss further on.

7. Schwartzbart Papers, M-2/5.
8. This appeal was printed in the official Polish daily published in London, *Dziennik Polski*, May 5, 1943.

The Polish Underground and the Jews

Jews had been permanently represented in the Polish National Council from its inception. Yitzhak Schwartzbart was coopted to the first council as a Jewish representative, later joined by Shmuel (Arthur) Zygielbojm of the Bund, who was replaced, following his suicide, by Emanuel Szerer. There were Jews in the government-in-exile, such as Hermann Liberman, but they represented Polish socialists and did not take any special interest in the problems of the Jews *per se.*

But there were no Jews—either in the governing bodies or among the rank and file—in the civil and military underground movements that executed the policies of the government-in-exile and conducted the operations in occupied Poland. A Jewish Department had been established as part of the AK in the beginning of 1942, but it consisted of only one person, Henryk Woliński. Woliński's activities during the fateful year of 1942 were limited to intelligence work—the gathering of information about what was happening in Jewish quarters. This information, the basis for reports sent to London, was of primary importance for a military organization active throughout the occupied territory.

In general, one can sum up Polish underground activity in the Jewish sector during 1942 simply thus: *there was none.* The distress and oppression that were the burden of the Jews did not concern the underground. Whether categorically defined or not, in reality Polish Jewry was considered a foreign element in Poland, not a party integral to the Polish nation and citizenship. The losses, suffering, and struggle of this group were a matter of interest to itself alone and did not obligate the Polish forces to any action.

This generalization should not imply, however, that before the end of 1942 there were no Poles who took an interest in the fate of their Jewish neighbors and even tried to help them as much as they could. There were even a few groups, such as a troop of Catholic scouts, that extended aid to the Jewish underground. But these acts, few and far between, were the result of individual volition and continued relationships that had begun before the war; in no case were they an organized initiative emanating from the official underground command.

How did Polish organizations and officials who ignored the plight of the Jews justify their actions when the war was over? The claims of Gen. Tadeusz ("Bor") Komorowski, for some time commander of the AK and of the Polish uprising in Warsaw in August 1944, are unfounded and cannot be taken seriously. In his memoirs Komorowski asserted that the AK's offer to help the Jews during the great deportation from Warsaw was turned down.[9] The incident is figment of his imagination, however, invented to justify the underground's absolute apathy in those fateful days. Polish historians are to be commended, for not one of them has bought Bor-Komorowski's fabrications. Only Raul Hilberg, a Jewish American, lends credence to this version without even checking it out.[10]

It is sometimes claimed that the smuggling of food into the isolated ghettos, especially the extent of this traffic into the Warsaw ghetto, is an instance of organized Polish aid to the Jews. Even those who make this claim do not go so far as to attribute this aid, or the initiative for it, to the Polish underground. In reality, the traffic in food was a business transaction—albeit a dangerous one—but every act during that period was dangerous and claimed its victims. On the whole, those who engaged in smuggling were adventurous types, Poles and Jews alike, often connected with the underworld, and they earned huge profits. The ghetto paid for the smuggled goods in large sums of money or in property. Within the ghetto, only those who still had funds to pay for food benefited from the smuggled provisions, although small amounts were sometimes slipped under coats, often by children, to feed their immediate families. Very little of this smuggled food reached the tens of thousands of starving Jews in the ghettos.

Official reports are silent about the underground's inactivity among the Jews and why it did not come to their aid. In a secret report sent in May 1944 to the prime minister in exile Mikołajczyk, Witold Bienkowski, a member of the Polish underground who at a later stage was actively involved with the Jews, wrote that during the first phase of the war (until the end of 1941) the Jewish Question did not exist for the Poles, "neither politically nor emotionally."[11] After the war Polish exiles in London published several volumes doc-

9. Komorowski-Bor, *Secret Army*, pp. 99–100.
10. Raul Hilberg, *The Destruction of the European Jews* (Chicago, 1961), pp. 319–20. For a detailed discussion of this matter see my *The Jews of Warsaw, 1939–1943: Ghetto, Underground, Revolt* (Bloomington, Ind., 1982).
11. See Witold Bienkowski's report, in the original Polish, in Yisrael Gutman, "A Report of a Member of the Polish Underground on Polish-Jewish Relations in Occupied Poland," *Michael* 6 (Tel Aviv, 1980): 102–14.

umenting Poland's contribution to the anti-Nazi effort during World War II. The thick third volume, devoted to events in Poland, contains a small chapter on the minority groups. One-half page is devoted to Jews, from which we learn that "at first the Jews adopted a position of wait and see, their reaction to be dictated by the conqueror's attitude toward them. Cut off from the outside world by ghetto walls, the Jews in the Nazi-occupied territory began organized resistance only when Nazi terror assumed most cruel proportions." It is further claimed that the AK established contact with the Zydowska Organizacja Bojowa (ZOB, the Jewish Fighting Force) when the Warsaw Uprising broke out in April 1943, "but the overall situation in the country precluded a premature military campaign to defend them." This description ends: "The Polish public was deeply affected by the Jewish tragedy. Thanks to Polish help, which cost Poles their lives, many Jews were saved from certain death."[12] Nowhere in this short description is it explained why the Polish underground abstained from initiating and encouraging Jewish resistance in the ghetto. Nor are there any details on when the help described above began or of its scope. It is true that many Poles paid with their lives in trying to save Jews, and their activities will be detailed later.

When Bienkowski stated that until the end of 1941 (actually until the end of 1942) the Poles had no political or emotional motive to take any interest in what befell the Jews, he did not explain the cause of this indifference. It is not that during 1941 Jews were in no need of aid or that the situation in the ghettos was not severe enough to arouse in the Polish authorities a willingness and sense of obligation to intervene. The fact is that during 1941 about forty thousand Jews died in the Warsaw ghetto alone, about 10 percent of its inhabitants, mostly from starvation and contagious diseases. Aid in the form of food, medicines, and some encouragement would have been of great importance under these conditions. The Polish authorities did not have unlimited sources at their disposal, but they did control substantial financial and material resources supplied from London; yet they did not lift a finger to ameliorate these terrible conditions. These troubling and depressing facts cannot simply be evaded.

Moreover, until the end of 1942, when the Polish underground finally began to organize rescue operations, almost two million Jews had already been murdered. These tragic events did not happen out-

12. Polskie Siły Zbrojne, *Armia Krajowa* (London, 1951), 3:47.

side the country; the news did not reach Poland as information from abroad, hard to believe. On the contrary, all this happened on Polish territory, and the underground knew exactly where mass murders were perpetrated, how they were carried out, and the number of victims. Again, until the end of 1942, except for a few individual cases, there was no organized aid initiated by the authorities or the underground, no appeals of the church, the farmers, the charitable institutions, or the Polish populace at large to take part in a rescue operation.

Relations between Jewish and Various Polish Underground Movements

In Polish publications, which often emphasize that Jewish armed resistance began at a very late stage, one can sense a condemnation of "too little too late." The publications generally overlook the fact that the Jewish underground, which concentrated on clandestine political activity, underground newspapers, the provision of education (forbidden by the occupation forces), mutual help, and illegal economic activity, was organized and engaged in intensive activity from the outset of the war. Requests made by the Jewish underground to its Polish counterpart to join forces, or at least for cooperation, were turned down on the national level. There was some local cooperation, however, especially by socialist underground groups with their Jewish comrades in the Bund and other Jewish socialists inside the ghettos.

The first Jewish fighting units were organized and activated from the beginning of 1942. It is true that until then the Jews did not envision, and were not prepared for, armed resistance. Actually, except for the Serbs in Yugoslavia, European resistance movements did not immediately engage the enemy in continuous military resistance but only when conditions forced armed resistance upon them or when they believed that long-term political advantages could be gained. The Jews thought that the Germans intended only to isolate them in ghettos, starve them, and bring about their degeneration in body and spirit; it is only natural that they devoted their utmost efforts to counter these measures. On the eve of 1942, in the face of the mass murders committed by the Einsatzgruppen in the occupied areas of the Soviet Union, some Jewish young people in the underground openly voiced their fear that the Nazis were planning the mass extermination of European Jewry and that German tactics were changing from oppression and terror to direct murder, to gradual but total genocide. To their credit, these youth leaders arrived at this conclusion at a very early stage, on the basis of observation and intuition and without possessing authoritative information concerning Nazi plans.[13] At this point Jewish fighting organizations were established in several ghettos. Except for Warsaw, they generally did not receive widespread public support in the ghettos because their claim—that only by armed resistance would the Jewish population be saved—was unconvincing. The Jewish underground fighters were an exception within the European resistance movements. They took up arms not in order to hasten Allied victory over the Nazis, a victory that would ensure the future status of the organization or country for which they fought. They did not even believe, in fact, that by fighting their lives would be saved. Their struggle was a final challenge to superior forces. As one resistance leader put it: "All we wanted was to sell our lives most dearly," or, in the words attributed to a fighter in the Jewish fighting organization in Cracow: "We are fighting to earn three lines on the rolls of history."[14]

We have documentary evidence of desperate appeals for help by Jewish fighting organizations to local commands of the AK in Vilna, Bialystok, Cracow, and elsewhere. They did not request direct intervention by Polish forces to defend their lives and property; they asked for weapons and ammunition, integration of Jewish forces into Polish units fighting in the forests, and the extension of AK protection to Jewish bands of partisans. The replies were polite or evasive but—except in one case—negative. In April 1943 Mordechai Tenenbaum-Tamarof, commander of the Jewish resistance in Bialystok, wrote to the Polish civil underground: "After a few days we received your reply, which read more or less: 'We are very sorry to inform you that we only have a very small quantity of arms at our disposal. On the other hand, we are overwhelmed with volunteers.'"[15] In another letter written that same month, intended to be his last will and testament, Tenenbaum-Tamarof wrote:

13. Proclamation by youth movements in Vilna calling for resistance, January 1, 1942, in *Documents on the Holocaust: Selected Sources on the Destruction of the Jews of Germany and the Soviet Union* (Jerusalem, 1981), p. 433.
14. Quoted in Gusta Dawidshon, *Yoman shel Justina* (Tel Aviv, 1953), p. 131.
15. Mordechai Tenenbaum-Tamarof to the Polish civil underground, April 2, 1943, *Dappim min ha-dlekah* (Lohamei Ha-Getaot, 1949), p. 110.

Officials in the Polish movement led by Sikorski considered their main objective to be propaganda, education and civil war, especially in the economic sphere. They considered any active opposition, any direct act of resistance to the occupation authorities, to be a provocation. "The time is not yet ripe, we must save our strength for the day when the Polish government will give the order to rise up in arms . . . ," but we could not wait.[16]

Paradoxically, then, alongside accusations often made by the Poles—and accepted by Polish historians—that Jews did not resist and lacked the will to fight, we find similar accusations leveled against the Poles in contemporary Jewish documentary sources that the Polish underground "preferred to wait 'with their weapons down.'"[17] This accusation, which reflects contradictory interests or— in truth—completely different situations in which Poles and Jews found themselves and the severe danger to both populations, is supported by the evidence of Henryk Woliński of the AK and Yitzhak Zuckerman, representative of the Jewish fighting organization in Warsaw. Both have reported that on the eve of the Warsaw Uprising in April 1943, Polish underground authorities tried to prevent the revolt and to remove the armed element from the ghetto to the Polish forces hiding in the forests. The logic behind these efforts was that any premature military action that did not fit in with the underground's strategy and might cause uncalled-for unrest should be prevented. Zuckerman states unequivocally that all of these suggestions were firmly refused and the uprising was launched as the Nazis began the final deportation of the Jews of Warsaw.[18]

On the whole, the relationship between the Jewish and Polish military undergrounds in Warsaw was different from that which obtained in other areas of Poland. Here, too, Polish reactions to the first Jewish approaches were apathy and refusal of any ties, but in time an uninterrupted relationship—with its ups and downs—was established before the uprising, during the fighting, and after. The Polish underground supplied the Jews with dozens of pistols and small quantities of grenades and explosives. Gen. Stefan Rowecki ("Grot"), commander in chief of the AK, wrote disparagingly of the Jewish fighting forces then being organized and did not try to hide his reluctance to supply them with arms.[19] In the final tally, the AK recog-

16. Tenenbaum-Tamarof letter, in ibid., pp. 129–30.
17. Quoted in *The Jewish Partisans* (Merhavia, 1959), p. 26.
18. For details, see my *Jews of Warsaw*, pp. 416–17.
19. On January 2, 1943, Stefan Rowecki sent the following message to London: "Jews from all kinds of groups, including Communists, have turned to us lately asking

nized the Jewish units, and there were some members in its ranks, such as Woliński and Aleksander Kamiński, who sympathized with the Jews in their tragic hours and supported the extension of material and moral aid to them. The few weapons supplied by the Poles were not very useful, however. From his experience in the armed resistance, Mordechai Anielewicz, the twenty-three-year-old commander of the Warsaw Uprising, who had never had any formal military training, could observe in the days of the ghetto uprising that pistols were not really efficient weaponry and that there was a serious lack of rifles and machine guns. The Polish professional soldiers of the AK who supplied the Jewish fighters with the pistols knew that they were not what was needed for urban guerrilla warfare.

In the uprising itself, the Jews fought alone. They planned and launched the revolt by themselves, fighting to the end. There were a few Polish attempts to help them, but, being improperly planned, they failed and contributed little to the fighting and rescue attempts. When all is said and done, Polish aid to the Warsaw ghetto was sparse, and Polish relations with the Jewish forces were characterized by a lack of confidence.[20] However, it should be emphasized that there were connections between the two undergrounds in Warsaw, connections that encouraged the spread of the revolt by extending some material and moral support.

A short description and analysis of relations with the Communists is in order. The Communists began to organize their forces in Poland in early 1942. Unlike the larger Polish underground, they aspired to penetrate the ghettos and establish branches. In contrast to the AK, the Communists opted for immediate military resistance, and in this their thinking was in line with the Jewish underground. It is likely that there were many among the veteran Communists in Poland who were sincerely moved by what was happening to the Jewish population.

The Communists did not have the resources necessary to support armed resistance in the ghetto. The member of the Polska Partia Robotnicza (PPR, the Polish Workers' party) who smuggled the first

---

for arms, as if we had depots full of them. As an experiment, I took out a few revolvers. I have no conviction that they will use these weapons at all. I shall not give out any more weapons, for you know that we ourselves have none." Response of the commander of the AK to the Jewish request for arms, *Documents on the Holocaust*, pp. 304–5.

20. See, for example, the question raised by Polish Defense Minister Marian Kukiel on June 12, 1943, and similar documents in Studium Polski Podziemncj, London, 06.3.1.1.

revolver to a Jewish Communist cell in the Warsaw ghetto claimed that it, with another pistol, constituted the total arsenal of the cell in the spring of 1942.[21] PPR members hid people who escaped the ghetto and helped the Jewish Communists secure weapons on the city's "free market." The Jewish fighting force kept its relationship with the Communists a secret from the AK. The Communists, for their part, reconciled themselves to the Jewish organization's contacts with the general Polish underground.

As for the role played by Jews in the Polish partisan movement, in most ghettos groups of youngsters were encouraged to join the guerrillas in the forests. A few groups set out after the Communists promised to lead them to partisan bases, but all these attempts ended in failure and heavy losses. It would seem that in the first half of 1942 the Communists had not yet become firmly established in the forests, so that promises made concerning meeting places, contacts, and guides, as well as units waiting to receive the Jewish reinforcements, had no basis whatsoever. Efforts to join partisan units without the help of Poles were doomed to failure, but the AK's partisan network, too, was not fully developed at the time when the Jews were being massacred. Moreover the AK did not hide its unwillingness and outright refusal to accept Jewish recruits into its units; only a few Jews managed to join them, and often by disguising their ethnic affiliation. During the final stages of the extermination of the ghettos, late in 1942 and during 1943, thousands of Jews who had nothing to lose escaped from the ghettos, transports, and concentration camps, many of them reaching partisan-controlled territory in the forests. In contrast to bands of Polish partisans, who made a planned retreat to the forests, were well supplied, had specific objectives in mind, and could easily merge with the ordinary civilian population if necessary, the Jews arrived in the forests without prior planning, wandering around in the hope that someone would guide and help them to stay alive and join in the armed struggle. They sometimes resorted to violence to secure food, but these were obviously instances in which, lacking the protection of and affiliation with an active underground framework, they had no alternative. In September 1943, General Bor-Komorowski wrote in an order-of-the-day that there were "well-armed bands ceaselessly wandering between cities and villages," carrying out acts of plunder sometimes

21. Bernard Mark, *Walka i Zagłada Warszawskiego Getta* (Warsaw, 1959), pp. 102–3.

accompanied by killings, and that "these attacks are perpetrated by men and women, especially Jewesses, . . . I have ordered regional and area commanders to use arms when necessary to put an end to these robber elements or revolutionary thieves."[22]

Units of the right-wing fascist underground, Narodowe Sity Zbrojne (NSZ), appeared in the partisan concentrations during the last months of 1942. They hunted down Jews with the object of "clearing the forests" of them. Many Jews—we do not have reliable estimates—lost their lives in these operations deliberately directed against them.

Despite these difficulties, groups of Jews were able to organize and form more than twenty regular partisan units. Most of these, in time, came under the aegis of the Armia Ludowa (AL, the People's Army), the Communist military organization, some of them even integrating with AL units. Obviously the tendency toward ties with this organization grew out of the willingness of its leaders and local commanders to extend their protection to Jews and receive them into their ranks. Jews who reached partisan-controlled territory in the forests were often suspected of being Communists, but there is no proof that they had prior inclinations along these lines. Their affiliation with the Communist partisan elements was the result of the AK's policy of refusing to receive or support the Jews on the one hand and the opposite attitude generally evident among commanders of the Communist units on the other.

Polish Rescue Efforts

Organized attempts to rescue Polish Jews began during the summer of 1942, the result of religious, humane, or ideological impulses, a feeling that one cannot simply sit idle and be a silent witness to the raging terror. It seems that the mass deportation from Warsaw was the first impetus that drove the Poles into action. Early in August 1942, when the deportation was at its height, Catholic authoress Zofia Kossak Szczucka issued a dramatic proclamation that included the phrase "whoever remains silent in the face of murder becomes an accomplice of the murderer."[23] A small group of young

22. For the text of order 116, dated September 15, 1943, see Shmuel Krakowski, *The War of the Doomed: Jewish Armed Resistance in Poland* (New York, 1984), p. 14.

23. Unfortunately, in addition to these forthright and unequivocal statements, Zofia Kossak Szczucka's proclamation also included some obnoxious phrases: "Therefore,

Catholics, liberals, and members of the Stronnictwo Demokratyczne (Democratic party) rallied to her call and in September 1942 established the Tymczasowy Komitet Pomocy Żydomim Konrada Żegoty (Conrad Żegota Provisional Council) with the object of helping Jews escape from the ghettos and supplying them with money, lodgings, employment, and false credentials. The Provisional Council joined forces with representatives of the Jewish underground active in the "Aryan" sector of Warsaw and through them made contact with Jews fleeing from the ghetto. They also approached the Delegatura, the representative of the government-in-exile holding authority over the entire underground organization, who agreed to recognize the Provisional Council and extend his patronage.[24]

Before describing the form, extent, and difficulties of the aid extended to the Jews, a few comments as to the background against which it was carried out are in order. The German command in Poland made great efforts to dissuade the local populace from rescuing Jews. Poles who turned in Jews were rewarded, while those who hid Jews were in danger of their lives. Moreover, one must bear in mind that rescue operations had to be carried out in a climate of opinion generally unsympathetic toward Jews and at a time when certain elements among the Poles made a sort of business out of discovering the whereabouts of Jews, blackmailing them or informing on them to the Germans. Obviously the Provisional Council took upon itself a highly dangerous task.

Another point deserving of attention is that the leaders of the Polish underground agreed to the establishment of the Provisional Council and later officially recognized the group as one affiliated with the Delegatura. It stands to reason that underground leaders, too, were deeply shocked by events in 1942, but political interests also played very important—if not overriding—roles in their deci-

we Polish Catholics will raise our voices on their behalf. There has been no change in our attitude toward the Jews. In our eyes they continue to be political, economic, and ideological enemies of Poland. Over and over again we realize that they hate us more than they hate the Germans, and that they blame us for their tragedy. On what grounds—that will remain a secret of the Jewish soul. At any rate, this is a fact that has been corroborated on innumerable occasions. However, even if we are cognizant of these emotions, we are obligated to denounce the crime."

24. This section is based upon the files of the Conrad Żegota Provisional Council and those of the Council for Aid to Jews—Żegota, Yad Vashem Archives, Jerusalem; Władysław Bartoszewski and Zofia Lewin, eds., *Righteous among Nations* (London, 1969); Teresa Prekerowa, *Konspiracyjna Rada Pomocy Żydów w Warszawie, 1942–1945* (Warsaw, 1982); Marek Arczynski and Wiesław Balcerak, *Kryptonim "Żegota,"* 2d ed. (Warsaw, 1983).

sion. London continuously pressured the Polish underground to take practical steps to help Jews, such action being deemed necessary from the point of view of Poland's relations with the Allies.

The Provisional Council made way at the beginning of December 1942 for Rada Pomocy Żydom—Żegota (Council for Aid to the Jews), which became part of the Polish underground. Centrist and leftist elements in the underground were represented in Żegota, together with representatives of the Jewish underground, Abraham-Adolf Berman of the Jewish National Committee and Leon ("Mikolaj") Feiner from the Bund. Chairman of Żegota was the Polish socialist Julian Grobelny, and among its active members were Marek Arczynski of the Democratic party and Tadeusz Rek, a member of the Stronnictwo Ludowe (Polish Peasant's party). The fieldwork was carried out by a loyal band wholly committed to its difficult and dangerous task. Żegota was active mainly in Warsaw, but its emissaries as well as independent cells were also active in other cities, the Cracow branch, led by Stanisław Dobrowolski, achieving appreciable results.

Żegota activity took many forms. First of all, Jews in hiding who approached the council or its members received a monthly cash stipend, not enough for even bare necessities especially in underground conditions but nevertheless a steady source of aid. Żegota also devoted much attention to the welfare of Jewish children hidden by convents and individual families, found hideouts for a small number of Jews closely connected with the underground, supplied medical care in emergencies, and spent large sums of money to release Jews from the clutches of informers and blackmailers. Especially important was the large number of forged credentials supplied by Żegota, papers that enabled their bearers to appear as Poles, working and moving freely about the streets. It is estimated that Żegota aided about four thousand Jews in hiding with money provided by the Delegatura from special funds sent from London, probably donated for the most part by Jewish organizations.

Though a representative of the Delegatura—generally Witold Bienkowski—participated in meetings of the Żegota leadership, relations between the council and leaders of the underground were not always characterized by understanding and harmony. Żegota leaders—or at least several of them—took upon themselves to defend Jewish interests in all their manifestations, often making demands and openly posing harsh questions to underground officials. The underground, for its part, wanted to limit Żegota to rescue and welfare activities, while Żegota claimed to represent other Jewish interests as well. Thus, for example, Żegota demanded arms and equipment for Jewish fighting units, whereas the Polish military underground did not recognize Żegota's right to intervene in this matter. Similarly, Żegota protested against official underground publications that included antisemitic passages. At times it even demanded that rescue operations on an international scale be launched, but the underground leadership, from its own considerations, refused to approve such action.

The harshest confrontations between these two bodies were over the treatment of extortionists. Time and again Żegota demanded that efficient measures be taken to stamp out blackmailers and informers. Extortion became one of the most serious threats to Jews seeking to escape the ghettos, and it limited their numbers. Contemporary Polish historiography tends to play down the role of blackmailers and informers (*szmalcownicy*), claiming they were a small segment of underworld elements, a marginal sector in Polish society that naturally raised its ugly head under the conditions prevailing in occupied Poland, and that this scum of humanity plagued members of the Polish underground as well as Jews. It is reasonable to believe that most of the blackmailers were shady types, but whatever their social composition, the fact remains that extortion and informing reached considerable proportions. Among the hundreds of testimonies or published memoirs of Jews who lived in hiding or passed themselves off as Poles, very few report no incidents with blackmailers. Blackmailed Jews were forced to turn over all or most of their remaining possessions, by which they had hoped to support themselves for some time, in order to flee or, in a few extreme cases, even return to the ghetto to a clear and foredoomed fate. Żegota called for action against extortion, suggested that proclamations be issued warning those who contemplated informing on Jews in hiding, and demanded that death sentences be pronounced and carried out by underground tribunals against the leading extortionists. Żegota itself did distribute such proclamations, but the higher echelons of the underground refrained from active involvement in this matter. At one point Żegota suggested that fictitious death sentences and executions be given publicity as measures of deterrence, but most of these suggestions were rejected on one pretext or another. A few death sentences were, in fact, carried out, but there is a tendency today to exaggerate the measures taken to deter extortionists and informers, the documentary evidence that has survived not always bearing them out.

Outside the framework of Żegota, an organized body, almost institutionalized, active in aiding and rescuing Jews, were hundreds of families and thousands of individuals who held out a helping hand to Jews, many doing so with no thought of remuneration. The nobility and courageousness of their acts are beyond description. More than seven hundred Poles—by far the largest national group—were awarded the Righteous Gentile Medal by Yad Vashem, the Israeli authority for commemoration of the Holocaust. These Poles constitute a category of human beings unique in World War II.

We do not know exactly how many Jews tried to escape, how many actually left the ghettos, how many were caught or killed while hiding among the Poles, and exactly how many were saved by hiding out or assuming Polish identities. The Germans were not experts on Jewish physiognomy, nor did they recognize a Jewish accent in Polish speech. These dangers Jews faced were not limited to Jews alone. At times Poles with features that resembled Jews were apprehended; at other times Poles who hid Jews were informed upon by other Polish citizens, so that those who rescued Jews had to be careful to keep their activities secret from neighbors and relatives. We do not know how many Poles who hid Jews, whether for remuneration or out of noble sentiment, were apprehended by the Germans and executed. Lists of such people continue to be published from time to time in Poland. As their number is still growing, now several decades after the war, it is difficult to know if they include, also, people who were apprehended and executed for other reasons. It is generally estimated, however, that between fifty and sixty thousand Jews fled the ghetto, seeking refuge among the Polish populace. It would seem that about thirty-thousand of them were saved and owe their lives to noble acts of courage of which the Polish nation is justly proud.

Polish Antisemitism during World War II

An examination of Polish antisemitism during the war years should reveal if motifs that developed during this period were added to the traditional hostility. It is sometimes claimed that antisemitism is a permanent characteristic of the Polish nation, a sort of endemic disease. Others claim, however, that the Jews as a rule hate the Poles and in making claims about Polish antisemitism are trying to besmirch the Polish people without due cause.

Władysław Bartoszewski, a well-known Polish author who was among the active members of Żegota and awarded a Righteous Gentile Medal after the war, writes in the introduction to his volume dealing with Polish aid to Jews that, in general, Polish antisemitism waned during World War II. He bases his premise on the humiliation and oppression suffered by both Poles and Jews, it being only natural that common suffering should give birth to a sense of common fate and mutual understanding.[25] It seems, however, that to ascribe to people under subjugation a tendency to see the light and act rationally is an act of enlightened optimism not sustained by actual human experience, especially experience under totalitarian regimes. Viewing the dark reality of life in Nazi concentration camps is sufficient to learn how the Nazis deftly and successfully exploited real or imagined clashes of interest among prisoners. By offering the less weak among them the opportunity to oppress and maltreat those weaker than themselves, or by offering simply an extra slice of bread, the Nazis managed to sow disunity among the suffering and oppressed, building a large part of the camps' regime on this foundation.

The Germans used this same technique of divide and rule in occupied Poland. During January-March 1940, gangs of hooligans attacked Jews in Warsaw, and it is quite likely that their incentive came from the Germans. The Germans, by the way, successfully instigated widespread attacks on the Jews by Lithuanians and Ukrainians immediately after these regions were overrun. Adam Czerniakow, head of the *Judenrat* in the Warsaw ghetto, claims that the attacks by Polish hooligans were at a certain stage "a sort of pogrom."[26] Observers and historians have noted that Polish-language propaganda and newspapers published under direct or indirect German auspices often dealt with the Jews, the recurring theme being that the occupation forces were creating a radical new order in relation to Jews, something that the independent Polish republic had not dared to do. Emanuel Ringelblum notes in his volume on Jewish-

25. See the introd. to Bartoszewski and Lewin, *Righteous among Nations*, pp. ix–xv.
26. Adam Czerniakow, diary, March 24, 1940, published as *The Warsaw Diary of Adam Czerniakow: Prelude to Doom*, ed. Raul Hilberg, Stanislaw Staron, and Joseph Kermish, trans. Stanislaw Staron and the staff of Yad Vashem (New York, 1979), p. 131.

Polish relations that after each appearance of such an item in a Polish-language newspaper published under German control, Jews employed outside the ghetto were in danger of attack.[27] True, there were a few who claimed that relations between Poles and Jews had nothing to do with the German conquerors. Among them was the lawyer Leon Nowodworski, a member of the Endeks, who refused to cooperate in Nazi anti-Jewish action. But the cases of Nowodworski and other solitary individuals, upon whom Nazi techniques had a sobering and even transforming effect, were exceptional, generally occurring only among the politically sophisticated and not characteristic at all of the common people.

At any rate, when Emanuel Ringelblum sums up Polish-Jewish relations, his conclusions are different—and even contrary—to those of Bartoszewski. The journals and memoirs of Jews and non-Jews, such as Chaim A. Kaplan, Zygmunt Klukowski, Ludwik Landau, Abraham Lewin, and Kazimierz Wyka,[28] do not include specific comparisons of the intensity of antisemitism before and during the war, but neither is there any corroboration of Bartoszewski's thesis. Here is how historian Emanuel Ringelblum summed up this question while he was still in hiding in Poland.

> If we take the special conditions in Poland into account, we have to acknowledge that the conduct of those among the Polish educated class, workers and peasants who do hide Jews is exceptionally noble and accords with the tradition of tolerance in Poland's history. These noble individuals face not only the German terror but also the hostility of Polish Fascists, who have not learnt their lesson from the experience of September 1939. . . . Among the Polish families hiding Jews there are doubtless some anti-Semites. It is, however, the anti-Semites as a whole, infected with racialism and Nazism, who created conditions so unfavourable that it has been possible to save only a small percentage of the Polish Jews from the Teuton butchers. Polish Fascism and its ally, anti-Semitism, have conquered the majority of the Polish people.[29]

Among the documentation emanating from this period are two accusations against the Jews that were added to the standard antisemitic slogans of the prewar period. The first deals with the Jews in

27. Emanuel Ringelblum, *Polish-Jewish Relations during the Second World War*, ed. Joseph Kermish and Shmuel Krakowski (Jerusalem, 1974), pp. 195–96.

28. Chaim A. Kaplan, *The Warsaw Diary of Chaim A. Kaplan*, trans. and ed. Abraham I. Katsh, 2d ed. (New York, 1973); Zygmunt Klukowski, *Dziennik z Lat Okupacji Zamojszczyzny, 1939–1944* (Lublin, 1959); Ludwik Landau, *Kronika i Lat Wojny i Okupacji*, vols. 1–3 (Warsaw, 1961–62); Abraham Lewin, *Mi-pinkaso shel ha-moreh mi-yehudiyah* (Lohamei Ha-Getaot, 1969); Kazimierz Wyka, *Życie na Niby: Szkice z Lat 1939–1945*, 2d ed. (Warsaw, 1959).

29. Ringelblum, *Polish-Jewish Relations*, p. 247.

Polish territory occupied by Soviet troops since September 1939. A common accusation was that the Soviet conquerors were received with joy by the Jews and that Jews appointed to administrative positions treated the Polish populace harshly and with disdain.

There is some truth in these accusations. Jews did accept the entry of Soviet troops into Poland's eastern regions with a sense of relief, but it would be a mistake to conclude that they rejoiced in the misery of the Poles or identified generally with Communist rule. From Jewish documents we learn that even those Jews whose social status and philosophy were far from what the USSR represented considered the Soviet occupation a blessing. The reason is quite simple: they knew that the alternative was Nazi occupation, and the Soviets, of course, were the lesser of two evils. What we have, then, is a case of conflicting viewpoints or interests of Jews, on the one hand, and Poles on the other. As far as the Polish populace was concerned, both Nazis and Soviets were hostile conquerors who deprived Poland of her independence. By contrast, the Jews saw as one alternative an enemy that discriminated against Jews and persecuted them with unbridled viciousness—and who knows what that might lead to; the other alternative was a regime that rescinded the Jews' right to independent communal organization and placed limitations upon their religious and cultural expression, but in all other facets of social life treated them as other individuals. The Poles were not always aware of the difference between the two.

It is also true that many younger Communists, including an appreciable number of Jews, were quickly absorbed into the new Soviet administration. They were especially conspicuous because Jews had rarely been allowed to play a role in the government bureaucracy between the two world wars. These new officials and policemen often behaved crudely and arrogantly toward the Poles and, as sources also show, toward Jews who were termed "class enemies." One can only wonder at the lack of understanding exhibited by these youthful Communists who hurried to join the new regime and to behave provocatively, sometimes even as informers, toward Poles who deeply felt the loss of their independence. As usual, many paid the price for the stupidity and fanaticism of the few; the Poles did not identify this behavior as that of individual Jews associated with the new regime but blamed all Jews for treachery and disloyalty. For the record, it should be noted that provocations and accusations were not the sole province of Jewish and Ukrainian officials; the behavior of some Polish Communists was no different. Moreover, both Poles and Jews were exiled to distant regions of the USSR as undesirable elements.

There is another manifestation of Polish anti-Jewish sentiments, generally described in secret documents but sometimes courageously aired in public. Thus, for example, the chairman of the Foreign Relations Committee of the Delegatura wrote a secret memorandum in mid-1943 in which he warned the government-in-exile in London that it should not even contemplate restoring Jewish property to its owners or allowing Jews to return to their former positions and occupations. Any such attempt would arouse bitter opposition and perhaps even lead to outbreaks of violence. On the other hand, Kazimierz Wyka, in his *Życie na Niby* (A So-Called Life), reprimands those elements in Polish society that were quick to take over Jewish commerce and to justify their behavior.[30]

An Israeli historian, Ben Zion Dinur, has intimated that bad conscience was often a cause of intensified hostility toward Jews, and something like this occurred during the war. Jewish presence was a cause of uneasiness, a reminder that much property had changed hands according to criteria established by the occupation regime. Though most of the Jewish property was stolen by the Nazis, part of it—the leftovers—fell into the hands of Polish owners, merchants, industrialists, and craftsmen, who feared the day when the Jews might return to claim it. This apprehension fed hostility and a secret satisfaction with the turn of events that could be phrased thus: "What is being done to the Jews is cruel, but the consequences are positive from Polish point of view, but we Christians and Poles would not have been able to adopt such abominable techniques."

In addition, among various circles, especially observant Catholics, it was claimed that the Jews were permanent sworn enemies of the Polish nation. Even though there is no basis for such a claim, it has become an obsession. This complex question ought not to be dealt with superficially, but it can be pointed out that there are few Jews anywhere in the world who do not have a warm spot in their hearts for the country of their origin, its culture and native population.

Polish political parties did not change their real attitudes toward Jews even in the face of the persecutions and the Final Solution.

30. Wyka, *Życie na Niby*, pp. 97–203. Wyka writes: "The manner in which the Germans liquidated the Jews lies on their conscience. *But the response to this manner lies on our conscience*" (p. 199, italics in original).

They continued to seek solutions to the Jewish Problem, positing that most of the Jews must permanently leave Poland. Only during the final stages of the war, when it became obvious that but a small percentage of Polish Jewry would survive, did the parties somewhat ameliorate this element of their program. Then the various "solutions" posed by leading figures and organizations were no longer needed.

The Polish underground press reflected the whole spectrum of attitudes toward the Jews at the height of World War II. A few examples will suffice. In the midst of the uprising and final destruction of the Warsaw ghetto, an article appeared on April 29, 1943, in *Biuletyn Informacyjny*, the AK paper, entitled: "The Final Act of the Great Tragedy." The concluding sentences read: "We consider the extension of aid to those fleeing the flaming ghetto to be a Christian obligation of the highest degree until such time as the renascent Polish republic will once again bring to this part of Europe full security, true freedom and our old European culture which will once more hold sway."[31] At the other end of the spectrum, *Warszawski Dziennik*, the Endeks' organ, wrote on September 2, 1942, toward the end of the mass deportation from Warsaw:

> History has a strange logic. Today, when the populace of the Jewish quarters is being liquidated in a manner both sadistic and beastly, we must remember that Jews and Germans, Poland's archenemies, acted together in amity and symbiosis to which we must give much thought, making the greatest of efforts to bring destruction upon the Polish people. . . . today fate has turned the tables—the Jews are being persecuted by the Germans. In politics one is not influenced by sentiment and momentary impressions. We must not blind ourselves to the fact that contemporary events—no matter how atrocious—will have historical significance for Poland. The Jews have been, are, and will continue to be Poland's greatest enemies.

A Catholic centrist political organ, *Naród*, thus ended an article dealing with the liquidation of the Jews, published on August 15, 1942:

> We sympathize with the individual Jewish human being and, where possible, will help those who are searching for a haven or are in hiding. We deplore informers. From those who permit themselves to make light of the situation we shall demand a more serious and honorable demeanor in the face of death. But this does not mean that we should express a false sorrow over the fate of this people, a nation we have always dis-

---

31. It is deserving of note that *Biuletyn Informacyjny* over the years supplied its readers with much information concerning Jews and was overtly sympathetic toward them, no doubt owing to the attitude of its editor Aleksander Kamiński.

liked. We must be sincere and true to ourselves at a time when history carries out its sentence.

Polish socialists and Democrats, representing the Left, referred to the Jewish tragedy with sincere anger and anguish, but Polish election results between the wars indicate where the political inclinations of the majority lay.

One aspect of the systematic liquidation of the Jews worried all Poles. They feared that once the Nazis finished with the Jews they would turn against them. The Communist underground press continually emphasized this threat and called for immediate armed resistance. Gen. Stefan Rowecki-Grot, AK commander until he was imprisoned in June 1943, issued an order-of-the-day to the effect that should the Nazis use similar techniques against the Poles, the forces under his command and the whole population were to immediately launch an armed struggle and a general rebellion.[32]

The postwar situation, with its Polish Socialist Republic under Soviet domination, is completely different from that which prevailed during World War II and is deserving of special attention. In the context of the present analysis, however, it should not be overlooked that the antisemitic sentiment that did not wane during the war greatly influenced Polish-Jewish relations in the postwar period. Just as relations during the war can be understood only against the background of what happened between Jews and Poles in the interwar years, so must we take into account the wartime relationship when we try to understand what happened after World War II.

The July 1946 pogrom in Kielce marked the peak of anti-Jewish violence. Some commentators at the time of the pogrom, which made a terrible impression abroad, claimed that it was not initiated by the Polish populace but was provoked by the Soviet secret police. There is no conclusive evidence to support this accusation. Moreover, it should be recognized that such a provocation can succeed only if there are many, perhaps thousands, who are capable of plunder and murder—in the case of Kielce, murder of dozens of people, including some survivors of concentration camps.

Michal Borwicz, a former partisan, coordinated the activities of the Jewish Historical Committee in Cracow immediately after the war. It was his intention at the time to bring to public attention the

32. Ireneusz Caban and Zygmunt Mánkowski, *Zwiazek Walki Zbrojnej: Armia Krajowa w Okregu Lubelskim, 1939–1944* (Warsaw, 1971), 2:60.

names and honorable behavior of Poles who rescued Jews during the Nazi occupation. He relates that he was approached by these courageous people, who requested that he stop giving them publicity because they had been subject to threats and mistreatment at the hands of neighbors and acquaintances.[33]

The comments of Franciszek Ryszka, a prominent Polish scholar who has written on antisemitism, form a fitting conclusion: "Antisemitism, which cannot be erased from our common European cultural heritage, has never killed one person. No idea, even the most fanatical one, has ever caused death. However, the bearers of antisemitism, whether in the past or in the present, cannot have clean consciences."[34]

33. Michal Borwicz, *Ludzie, Ksiazki, Spory* (Paris, 1980), pp. 178–79.
34. Franciszek Ryszka, "Antysemityzm," *Polityka*, April 16, 1983.

Contributors

MICHAEL BURNS is Assistant Professor of Modern European History at Mount Holyoke College, South Hadley, Massachusetts. He is the author of "Qui ça, Dreyfus?" which appeared in *Historical Reflections* in summer 1978, and *Rural Society and French Politics: Boulangism and the Dreyfus Affair, 1886–1900* (1984). Currently he is working on a history of the Dreyfus family from the French Revolution to Vichy.

NAOMI W. COHEN is Professor of History at Hunter College and the Graduate Center, New York. Her publications include *Not Free to Desist: A History of the American Jewish Committee, 1906–1966* (1972) and *Encounter with Emancipation: The German Jews in the United States, 1830–1914* (1984).

STUART A. COHEN is Professor of Political Studies at Bar-Ilan University, Ramat Gan, Israel. He is the author of *English Zionists and British Jews: The Communal Politics of Anglo-Jewry, 1895–1920* (1982) and, with D. J. Elazar, of *The Jewish Polity: Jewish Political Organization from Biblical to Modern Times* (1985).

JUDITH LAIKIN ELKIN is President of the Latin American Jewish Studies Association. She is the author of *Jews of the Latin American Republics* (1980) and editor, with Gilbert W. Merkx, of *The Jewish Presence in Latin America* (1987).

TODD M. ENDELMAN is Professor of History at the University of Michigan, Ann Arbor. He is the author of *The Jews of Georgian England, 1714–1830: Tradition and Change in a Liberal Society* (1979) and the editor of *Jewish Apostasy in the Modern World: Converts and Missionaries in Historical Perspective* (1986).

JONATHAN FRANKEL is Professor of Jewish History at the Institute of Contemporary Jewry and the Department of Russian Studies, Hebrew University, Jerusalem. His publications include *Vladimir Akimov on the Dilemmas of Russian Marxism, 1898–1903* (1969) and *Prophecy and Politics: Socialism, Nationalism and the Russian Jews, 1862–1917* (1981).

YISRAEL GUTMAN is Head of the Institute of Contemporary Jewry, Hebrew University, Jerusalem. Among his publications are *The Jews of Warsaw, 1939–1943: Ghetto, Underground, Revolt* (1982) and *Ba-Alatah uve-Maavak* (1985).

BEN HALPERN is Richard Koret Professor of Near Eastern Studies Emeritus at Brandeis University, Waltham, Massachusetts. Among his publications are *The American Jew: A Zionist Analysis* (1956, 1983) and *The Idea of the Jewish State* (1961, 1969).

HILLEL J. KIEVAL is Assistant Professor of History and International Studies and Chairman of the Jewish Studies Program at the University of Washington, Seattle. He is the author of an essay, "Autonomy and Independence: The Historical Legacy of Czech Jewry," in *The Precious Legacy: Judaic Treasures from the Czechoslovak State Collections* (1983). His current project, *The Making of Czech Jewry: National Conflict and Jewish Society in Bohemia, 1870–1918*, will be published in 1987.

OTTO DOV KULKA is Associate Professor of Modern Jewish History at the Hebrew University, Jerusalem. He is the author of *Ha-Sheelah ha-Yehudit ba-Reich ha-Shlishi* (1975) and *The "Final Solution" and the German People: Secret Reports on the Attitude of the German Population to the "Solution of the Jewish Question" in the Third Reich* (1986).

SHLOMO LAMBROZA is Assistant Professor of History at St. Mary's College, St. Mary's City, Maryland. His publications include "Jewish Self-Defense during the Russian Pogroms of 1903–06," which appeared in the *Jewish Journal of Sociology* in December 1981, and "Plehve, Kishinev and the Jewish Question: A Reappraisal," which appeared in *Nationalities Papers* in the spring of 1984.

MICHAEL R. MARRUS is Professor of History at the University of Toronto. He is the author of *The Unwanted: European Refugees in the Twentieth Century* (1985) and, with Robert O. Paxton, of *Vichy France and the Jews* (1983).

EZRA MENDELSOHN is Professor of Jewish History at the Institute of Contemporary Jewry, Hebrew University, Jerusalem. Among his publications are *Zionism in Poland: The Formative Years, 1915–1926* (1981) and *The Jews of East Central Europe between the World Wars* (1983).

PAUL MENDES-FLOHR is Professor of Modern Jewish Thought at the Hebrew University, Jerusalem. He is the editor of *A Land of Two Peoples: Martin Buber on Jews and Arabs* (1983) and, with Arthur A.

Cohen, of *Contemporary Jewish Religious Thought: Original Essays on Critical Concepts, Movements and Beliefs* (1986).

ARNOLD PAUCKER is Director of the Leo Baeck Institute, London, and Editor of the *Leo Baeck Institute Year Book*. He is the author of *Der jüdische Abwehrkampf gegen Antisemitismus und Nationalsozialismus in den letzten Jahren der Weimarer Republik* (2d ed., 1969) and editor of *Die Juden im Nationalsozialistischen Deutschland/The Jews in Nazi Germany, 1933–1943* (1986).

JEHUDA REINHARZ is Richard Koret Professor of Modern Jewish History and Director of the Tauber Institute for the Study of European Jewry at Brandeis University, Waltham, Massachusetts. His publications include *Fatherland or Promised Land: The Dilemma of the German Jew, 1893–1914* (1975) and *Chaim Weizmann: The Making of a Zionist Leader* (1985).

ANITA SHAPIRA is Professor of Jewish History at the Institute for Zionist Research, Tel Aviv University. Among her publications are *Ha-Maavak Ha-Nikhzav: Avodah Ivrit, 1929–1939* (1977) and *Berl, the Biography of a Socialist Zionist* (1984).

CHONE SHMERUK is Professor of Yiddish Literature at the Hebrew University, Jerusalem. His publications include *Sifrut Yiddish: Prakim le-Toldoteha* (1978) and *Sifrut Yiddish be-Polin: Mehkarim ve-Iyunim Historiim* (1981).

NORMAN A. STILLMAN is Professor of History and Arabic at the State University of New York at Binghamton. He is the author of *The Jews of Arab Lands: A History and Source Book* (1979) and *The Language and Culture of the Jews of Sefrou, Morocco: An Ethnolinguistic Study* (1986).

JACOB TOURY is Professor Emeritus at Tel Aviv University. Among his publications are *Die jüdische Presse im Österreichischen Kaiserreich, Ein Beitrag zur Problematik der Akkulturation, 1802–1918* (1983) and *Jüdische Textilunternehmer in Baden-Württemberg, 1683–1938* (1984).

DAVID VITAL is Professor of Political Science at Tel Aviv University. His publications include *The Origins of Zionism* (1975) and *Zionism: The Formative Years* (1982).

ROBERT S. WISTRICH is Professor of Jewish History at the Hebrew University, Jerusalem. He is the author of *Socialism and the Jews: The Dilemmas of Assimilation in Germany and Austria-Hungary* (1982) and *Hitler's Apocalypse: Jews and the Nazi Legacy* (1985).

LENI YAHIL is Professor Emeritus at the University of Haifa. Her publications include *The Rescue of Danish Jewry: Test of a Democracy* (1969) and *Holocaust: Jewish Chronicle, 1932–1945*, to be published in English in 1987.

Index

Titles of works are indexed under author's name only. Subheadings are divided into topical and geographic references.

476

tion, 319, 322, 328, 329–30, 333; conversions in, 61n, 65, 67–68, 80–81; immigrants in, 66, 80–81, 315, 317, 321–22; immigration to, 33, 46, 48, 58, 261, 263–64, 265, 300, 310, 315, 316–17, 321–22, 324; in Warsaw underground press, 416–17, 418. *See also Amerikanstvo;* New York
Universities, 67–68, 239; antisemitism in, 66, 69–70, 77, 96, 96n, 110, 277n–78n, 407; in Bursztyn's fiction, 277n–78n; in Argentina, 340, 343, 347; in Austria, 206; in Britain, 96, 96n; in Czech lands, 213, 224; in Germany, 66, 69–70, 77, 110; in Poland, 277n–78n, 407. *See also* Students; *universities by name*
Upward mobility, 11, 38, 62, 71, 313, 400. *See also* Integration
Urbanization, 23, 32, 39, 78, 211–12, 297. *See also* Migration, to urban centers
Urjudentum, 143, 144, 148
Usury. *See* Moneylending
Utilitarianism, 88

Vallat, Xavier, 385
Varnhagen, Rahel, 75–76
Vatican Council, Second, 329
Verein zur Abwehr des Antisemitismus (Abwehrverein), 107, 110
Verein der jüdischen Hochschüler (Prague), 230n
Versailles Peace Conference, 96, 296
Veselost, 226. *See also* Rozvoj
Veterans. *See* Military
Veynig, Naftale, 291n–92n, 295n
Vichy France. *See* France, in World War II
Vienna, 54, 55, 75, 168, 170, 177, 179, 181, 183, 184–85, 186, 193–209, 210, 218, 221; conversions in, 63–64, 69, 70n, 71, 77, 78; Court Opera, 69, 79; *Ostjuden* in, 195–96, 200, 203, 208; in Schnitzler's fiction, 72. *See also* Austria
Vigée, Claude, 39
Vilenskii Vestnik, 255n
Village life: in Alsace, 20–41; in Czech lands, 72–73, 214–16; in Russia, 271. *See also villages by name*
Vilna, 183, 302n, 307, 338, 414n, 437–38, 457
Vinaver, Maxim, 271
Violence: in the Arab world, 353–54, 358; in Argentina, 338–39; in Britain, 85, 93; in Czech lands, 176, 177, 216–17, 218–19, 228, 230; in France, 20, 21–22, 25, 28–31, 33, 37, 41; in Galicia, 178–

80; in Hungary, 64; in Poland, 450, 466–67; in Prague, 176, 218–19; in Russia, 253–74, 400. *See also* Exterminations; Massacres; Pogroms
Vital, David, "Nationalism, Political Action, and the Hostile Environment," 234–52
Vocational training, 9, 374, 377. *See* Occupations, retraining
Vogelsang, Karl von, 204
Vohryzek, Viktor, 223, 224–29; "Epištoly k českým židům," 224–26
Volozhin Yeshivah, 48
Voskhod, 271
Vrba, Rudolf, 217–18

"Wacht am Rhein," 218
Wagner, Richard, 12
Wallachia, 302n
Wallisch, Koloman, 439–40, 440n
Warren, Earl, 330
Warsaw, 293–94, 307, 406, 413–42, 457, 458, 459, 460, 462, 463, 466, 470; in Bursztyn's fiction, 276n, 285–86; deportations from, 414n, 451–52, 458, 461, 470; ghetto, 413–42, 457, 458, 459, 460, 462, 463, 466, 470; underground press in, 413–42; University, 277n–78n
Warsaw Uprising, 414, 414n, 441, 452, 455, 458, 459, 470
Warszawski Dziennik, 470
Washington, D.C., 53
Weber, Eugen, 24
Weber, Max, 4n, 135
Wechsberg, Joseph, 72–73, 77
Wehrmacht, 387
Weil, Simone, 75n, 136
Weimar Republic, 119, 122, 124, 131, 132, 138–39
Weininger, Otto, 145–46
Weizmann, Chaim, 137–38, 401, 405, 406, 410
Weltsch, Robert, 105, 137
Western Europe, 17–164, 193, 199, 238–42, 389, 398, 399, 444; immigration to, 261, 265
Westernization, 44
While You Are in England, 89
White, Arnold, 91, 98
White Army, 274
White Paper of 1939, 401
White slavery, 9, 217
White Terror, 64
Wilhelm II, kaiser, 78, 110
Williams, William, 322
Wilson, Woodrow, 315